Travis L. Crosby is Emeritus Professor of History at Wheaton College, Massachusetts. His publications include *Joseph Chamberlain: A Most Radical Imperialist* (I.B.Tauris), *The Two Mr. Gladstones* and *Sir Robert Peel's Administration*.

THE UNKNOWN LLOYD GEORGE

A Statesman in Conflict | *Travis L. Crosby*

I.B. TAURIS

LONDON · NEW YORK

Published in 2014 by I.B.Tauris & Co Ltd
6 Salem Road, London W2 4BU
175 Fifth Avenue, New York, NY 10010
www.ibtauris.com

Distributed the United States of America and Canada Exclusively by Palgrave Macmillan
175 Fifth Avenue, New York, NY 10010

ISBN: 978 1 78076 485 6

A full CIP record for this book is available from the British Library
A full CIP record for this book is available from the Library of Congress

Library of Congress Catalog Number available

Printed and bound in Great Britain by CPI Group (UK) Ltd, Croydon, CRO 4YY.

CONTENTS

LIST OF PLATES

1 Early portrait of an ambitious politician, 1898 (© National Portrait Gallery, London)
2 At his ease as a young parliamentarian in 1905 (photo by Ernest H. Mills/Getty Images)
3 The young family in November 1910
4 A dashing Lloyd George as portrayed by Will Dyson in the *Daily Herald*, October 1912
5 Riding to the rescue as Chancellor of the Exchequer, but soon to be Minister of Munitions of War
6 The Council of Four at the Paris Peace Conference, January 1919
7 In October 1919, a triumphant Prime Minister addresses a crowd from Mansion House in the City of London (photo by Hulton Archive/Getty Images)
8 On the high wire in 1926
9 Lloyd George advocates his land scheme at Kingsway Hall in November 1926 (photo by Fox Photos/Getty Images)
10 Lloyd George uses to advantage new technology to keep his name before the public in 1931 (photo by Jimmy Sime/Central Press/Getty Images)
11 Lloyd George and Churchill in Morocco, 1936 (National Library of Wales)
12 A lesson for an old friend and colleague
13 Lloyd George celebrates his 80th birthday with Frances Stevenson and his daughter Lady Olwen Carey-Evans looking on (photo by Bert Hardy/Picture Post/Hulton Archive/Getty Images)
14 Lloyd George and admirers in late 1944 amid the Kale at Churt, his farm in Surrey (photo by Time Life Pictures/Pix Inc./Getty Images)

ACKNOWLEDGEMENTS

Examining so conflicted and complicated a life as that of David Lloyd George requires considerable research into primary sources such as private diaries, letters, and memoranda. Without the guiding hands of keepers of manuscripts in the United Kingdom, it would have been impossible to give shape and substance to the internal life of one of the most elusive and fascinating of British politicians.

My most significant debt of gratitude is to the National Library of Wales in Aberystwyth. The staff was unfailingly helpful, enabling me to pursue research as efficiently as possible over several years. My special thanks is to J. Graham Jones, Head of the Welsh Political Archive at the NLW, who led me through the rich trove of Lloyd George Papers. He also read the entire manuscript to great advantage. I'm also grateful to Will Troughton, Visual Images Librarian at the NLW, who searched diligently for photo images of Lloyd George.

Other important repositories in the United Kingdom with relevant manuscripts and source materials include the Parliamentary Archives, Houses of Parliament, London, the British Library, London and the National Archives of Scotland, Edinburgh. I happily acknowledge their staffs' exemplary response to my many requests. I am greatly indebted to the pre-publication reviewers whose comments not only prevented errors, but were also encouraging in their comments. Thanks, too, for Pat FitzGerald's heroic labours in fact checking, copyediting, and indexing as she helped prepare the manuscript for publication. A special thanks to Lester Crook, Jo Godfrey and Lisa Goodrum at I.B.Tauris for their continuing support in publishing my efforts at biography. Their patience and good will are a boon to any author.

In the United States, I'm most happy to acknowledge my good friend and colleague of many years, Paul Helmreich, who read the manuscript as a whole. Drawing upon his special expertise in European diplomatic and military history, he caught many a solecism and factual error. Those that remain must be charged to me. Kristen Kiesling spent much of her spare time as an undergraduate at Wheaton College (Massachusetts) discovering and photocopying relevant articles and editorials from *The Times* of London.

Secondary sources at the libraries of Wheaton College, Smith College, Amherst College and the University of Massachusetts at Amherst were crucial to my interpretation of the life of Lloyd George. Special thanks are in order to the Five College Depository Article Request Service for making readily available online articles from scholarly journals. Most of all, thanks to my wife, Susan, whose wizardry with computers was crucial to the completion of this book.

For all the family

INTRODUCTION

It may be thought that the theme of conflict in David Lloyd George's life can also easily be applied to most politicians. In their pursuit of public service and the path to governance, politicians must also engage in power brokering, deal making and often of outright jobbery. Conflicts naturally arise in these circumstances. It can be argued, however, that Lloyd George encountered (and encouraged) conflict to an unusual degree – not only in his political, religious, social, but also in his personal life. Overcoming humble circumstances with few advantages, he fought to make his mark against wealth and privilege. He learned early that what he gained could not be given, but must be earned. English born (Manchester in 1863), Lloyd George was the son of Welsh parents. His schoolteacher father died in Lloyd George's infancy. Returning to Wales when only two years of age, he and his mother found a new home with his uncle Richard Lloyd in the Welsh village of Llanystumdwy.

Lloyd George retained some consciousness of his Welsh roots throughout his life. With his family, on the political platform in Wales and to his closest political comrades he spoke his native tongue. He was known to burst into song, especially Welsh hymns, on any occasion. Wales provided him with two strong influences, which were also to shape and define his early political life – his nonconformist religion and his radical political views. In addition, Lloyd George's early family life and Welsh heritage gave him a sense in his early years of being outside an alien English culture. As a Welshman in English political circles, he was able to stand on the periphery of generally accepted political practices and social conventions. This sense of being removed from the traditional British elite was strengthened by his lack of public school and university education.

Encouraged by his Uncle Lloyd, a surrogate father, Lloyd George was driven to excel in his early years. In schooling, apprenticing to the law and in public life, he was determined to make his mark. In 1890, at the early age of 37, he entered Parliament. Within a short time, he made a reputation as a superlative orator and debater. His initial cause was promoting the interests of his native Wales. In this, he was a gadfly to Liberals and Conservatives alike. By the turn of the twentieth century, he was engaged in his first national cause as a critic of the South African (Boer) War. Lloyd George was among the lonely few to protest the aims, direction and management of that conflict. In the post-war era, he turned his attention to domestic affairs. Now firmly established as a radical Liberal, he was a persistent and effective foe of the Conservative Party then in power. He led the attack against Conservative plans for educational reform, which would have upheld traditional Anglican privileges at the expense of nonconformist practices. In like manner, he became a leading spokesman against another Conservative initiative, tariff reform, which would have levied protectionist import duties on foreign goods, challenging free trade, a Liberal article of faith.

Lloyd George's oratorical power in the countryside and his mastery of Parliamentary technique dominated the House of Commons during the early years of the twentieth century. These years of his earliest national prominence – the Edwardian era, from 1901 to 1914 – have been described as a golden age, a languid summer afternoon which characterized the reign of King Edward VII, who had acceded to the throne upon the death of his mother, Queen Victoria. The dark night of a European war and its tumultuous aftermath seemed in stark contrast. But Edwardian Britain has also been described as a time of severe political and social conflict. Industrial unrest and successive waves of strike action were common. Enmity between workers and management rose significantly. The persistent denial of women's full electoral rights spurred a nationwide women's suffrage movement which turned violent in the face of a stubborn masculine intransigence. In Ireland, the campaign for Home Rule among Irish Nationalists threatened civil war between Protestant Ulster and Catholic Southern Ireland. Internal conflict was matched by insecurity abroad. The British Empire, then at the height of its expansion and influence, faced new competitors. The emergent economic power of the United States had risen steadily, threatening Britain's global supremacy. More menacing was the rise of Germany as the preeminent military power on the continent.[1]

To address these challenges was the primary object of the Liberal government of Sir Henry Campbell-Bannerman, formed in December 1905. Indeed, the government's legislative record made it one of the most significant reformist periods in modern British history. The most persistent voice for change was that of Lloyd George. Rewarded for his service to the cause of Liberalism in his early years in the House of Commons, he first assumed office as President of the Board of Trade. Responsible for initiating legislation that would promote British trade around the globe, Lloyd George was also important in promoting harmonious labour-management relations. Demonstrating unusual skill in resolving conflict between the two sides, he was determined to avoid crippling strikes and a loss of productivity to the nation. His success as a junior member of the Cabinet marked him for early advance. When H.H. Asquith succeeded Campbell-Bannerman as Prime Minister in April 1908, Lloyd-George became Chancellor of the Exchequer. From this position, he launched an extensive programme of social reform.

Perhaps Lloyd George's most significant achievement was winning the battle for national health insurance. In doing so, he confronted entrenched medical interests. To pay for this government-sponsored scheme, he fought for increased taxes among the wealthy. He also successfully legislated old-age pensions and sickness and unemployment benefits for working families. In rallying the country behind his social welfare programmes, he laid the foundations of what was to become the welfare state. His provocative speeches throughout the countryside against the Conservative opposition brought him added fame among his supporters – as well as a greater hatred from his detractors. In Parliament as well, he was fiercely denunciatory of the Conservatives, especially those who sat in the House of Lords. In the midst of his often abrasive and ferocious public statements against various political foes, he nevertheless continued to demonstrate a remarkable ability to work behind the scenes in settling disputes and reaching comprises. As Chancellor of the Exchequer during heated debates on reform and taxation in 1910, for example, he proposed to Conservative leaders a coalition of both parties to carry out the nation's business more effectively and cooperatively. Although this venture failed, he had signalled to all that he had been willing to compromise on important issues. It was a trait that he would often show in the decades that followed.

With the outbreak of World War I in July 1914, the Liberal government was called upon to prepare the nation for the coming conflict. As a wartime minister of state, Lloyd George demonstrated a surprising armoury of talents, quite different from his peacetime duties. He became, as one biographer has noted, the organizer of victory and the great driving power behind the developing British war machine.[2]

Among his actions as Chancellor of the Exchequer in the earliest days of the war was to calm the financial markets by guaranteeing the safety of depositors' banking accounts and restoring confidence in the credit markets. He soon turned his talents for speechmaking, previously honed in the political battles prior to 1914, into a force for mobilizing the country against the enemy. As the war dragged on, his responsibilities grew. He was involved in promoting recruitment, smoothing wartime industrial relations and proposing schemes for a greater productive capacity of the materiel of war. Rising in the estimation of the public at large and in the eyes of his colleagues, he became Minister of Munitions and then Minister of War. In these offices, he continued to demonstrate an energetic and forceful administrative power, determined to harness the nation as a whole towards the common goal of defeating the enemy.

Continued failures on land and sea, however, called into question the military expertise of British generals. The lacklustre leadership of Prime Minister Asquith also hindered a thoroughgoing pursuit of victory. Failures at Gallipoli and the Somme brought matters to a head. In December 1916, Asquith was thrust aside. Lloyd George stepped forward, promising a more energetic approach to winning the war. As the new Head of State, Lloyd George organized a coalition government of Liberals and Conservatives with the intention not only of reducing political party conflict, but also of drawing upon all the talents of the nation necessary to defeat the enemy. Along with an invigorated domestic productive capacity, an increasingly seasoned military leadership and an influx of fresh American troops, he was eventually able to advance on all fronts. Victory was at last achieved in November 1918 with the declaration of an armistice.

At war's end, Lloyd George's energies shifted to making the peace. Rivalry among the victorious and desperate actions of the defeated often brought negotiations to a standstill at the Paris Peace Conference. Here, too, Lloyd George played a dominant role. He was at the centre of every major decision. He was determined to discourage the extreme demands of some Allied powers and to establish a sense of equity and fairness among the vanquished. He argued for leniency, especially with regard to the demands for war reparations among some of the Allies. In the immediate post-war world, too, he sought to create a better climate for maintaining peace through a series of international conferences. He was clearly attempting a return to his pre-war tactical approach of conflict resolution by direct face-to-face intervention.

Continuing conflict on an international scale was not the only contentious post-war legacy. At home, the wounds of war were not easily bound up. Labour unrest during peacetime economic adjustments led to persistent work stoppages. In Ireland, the demand for Home Rule and separation from Britain was increasingly insistent. Domestic politics became strident as the wartime Liberal/Conservative coalition began to fray. Abroad, Lloyd George's attempt to settle post-war problems through a series of international conferences ultimately failed. During the summer of 1922, in a simmering aftermath of World War I, Greek and Turkish hostilities broke out. Under the invigorating leadership of Mustafa Kemal, the Turks (who had fought with Germany and Austria during the war) drove westward, defeating the Greeks and challenging British interests in that part of Europe. Lloyd George, from his position as a guarantor of peace in Europe, in turn threatened war against Turkey. But any renewed military venture was intolerable to a British public whose memory of the recent global conflict was still fresh. Conservative members of the coalition seized their opportunity and withdrew their support on 19 October 1922. Lloyd George promptly resigned.

Once out of power, Lloyd George's influence and political prospects receded. Indeed, his career after 1922 is often presented as a failure, a denouement to his earlier achievements. The primary vehicle of his political power, the Liberal Party, had been weakened and divided by the war. In the post-war era, Liberals at large lost ground to both the triumphant Conservatives on the right and an emergent Labour Party on the left. Internecine struggles with the party prompted further divisions. Many Liberals blamed Lloyd George for their loss of influence. They believed that his wartime coalition government, dominated by Conservatives, had effectively scuttled the Liberal agenda.

Lloyd George was nevertheless determined to reestablish his once paramount position in British politics. The odds against him were undoubtedly high. Forced to operate largely outside the ranks of the ascendant Conservatives, the disillusioned Liberals and the eager Labourites, he sought to establish a centrist position. In his attempt to revive his fortunes, he remained active in pursuing progressive policies. To ease unemployment during the great depression of the 1930s, he advocated increased state aid in sponsoring public works projects. To reduce tensions abroad, he recommended a policy of restraint and accommodation. His countryside speeches could still rally the faithful; and in Parliament, too, he captured the headlines.

By the mid-1930s he stepped up his programmatic approach to politics by organizing a Council of Action. With its slogan, 'Peace and Reconstruction', he hoped to address both the darkening diplomatic skies over Europe and to solve the lingering problems of unemployment at home. In a controversial move, he sought to placate Hitler by travelling to Germany and engaging in direct conversations with the German leader. Upon his return to Britain, Lloyd George publicly declared his support for Hitler's leadership. When war with Germany broke out in September 1939, Lloyd George carefully considered his response. Initially, he raised the possibility of negotiations with Hitler as a means of preventing all out war. Once this option was no longer viable, he supported Winston Churchill government's war effort – though not without some criticisms of detail. Lloyd George's stature remained high enough in the early stages of the war that rumours circulated that he would soon be called into the Cabinet. But Prime Minister Neville Chamberlain was strongly opposed. Moreover, Lloyd George's advanced age – he was 76 in 1939 – prevented this becoming a realistic possibility. As the war went on, his health slowly deteriorated. He was less and less able to attend the House of Commons. In his final days, he left England and returned to Wales. His death on 26 March 1945 came as Britain and its Allies were nearing victory.

At the centre of political conflict all his adult life, Lloyd George also was in continuous personal conflict. Though devoted to his wife, Margaret, Lloyd George's relations with her were never easy. Their separation throughout much of his Parliamentary career – he in London or travelling throughout the country and abroad, and she at home in Wales – doubtless contributed to a gradual alienation between them. More seriously may have been Lloyd George's reputation for engaging in casual affairs with other women. A topic of some private speculation in his own day, these relationships have been more publicly assessed particularly since the 1960s after his own son, Richard, made known his views on what he considered his father's infidelities. Since then, other accounts have examined the evidence in detail. There seems little doubt that Lloyd George was often attracted to women, and they to him. Margaret certainly suspected something and had heard incriminating rumours: it was a topic of considerable tension between them. Although evidence for his sexual philandering remains scanty and unreliable, Lloyd George's posthumous reputation has undoubtedly been adversely affected by continuing allusions to his serial adulteries.

Undeniable and far more significant was his decades' long relationship with Frances Stevenson. Here the evidence is indisputable. Frances was not simply a convenient dalliance: she became in fact his second wife. Indeed, it is not too much to claim that Lloyd George essentially led a bigamous life for more than three decades, including the time of his greatest achievements. How Lloyd George was able to manage his affair with Frances is of more than prurient and passing interest. She was a talented and attractive young woman – younger than Lloyd George by a quarter of a century. A graduate in classics from Royal Holloway College, University of London, she was also a suffragist, fluent in French and keenly interested in politics and public life. Throughout her long association with Lloyd George, she was in continuous contact with those who were in the upper echelons of government. In these exalted circles, she was able to hold her own.

Perhaps most importantly, Frances fulfilled a palpable emotional need in Lloyd George. As we know, he was at the centre of numerous political storms in his life: he was a man who did not shirk conflict. Indeed, he courted it. But this came at some personal cost. Although in public he was often a brash and thrusting political fighter, in private Lloyd George revealed a surprising emotional vulnerability. In letters to his immediate family – to Margaret, to his brother William and to Uncle Lloyd – he continually sought praise and approbation. Letters both published and in the archives at the National Library of Wales reveal in touching terms his frequent demands for unconditional approval of some political action of his, or of some speech in the countryside, or of a Parliamentary success. When absent from home and family, whether he was in London or on holiday abroad, he expected daily letters of support and encouragement. If these were not forthcoming, he would express sadness, or annoyance, and occasionally anger.

In Frances he found not only an attractive younger helpmate, but someone who could also fulfil his need for attention and adulation. She travelled with him extensively as his companion during numerous holidays abroad. She was with him during the many months during the Paris Peace Conference following World War I. She frequently attended his speeches in the House of Commons: afterwards, she sent him notes from the gallery praising his performance. She could be a friendly critic, too, of his political role and of his later work as an author. Officially she was Lloyd George's secretary, an employee on the government payroll. She moved with him in his advance through Cabinet positions from Chancellor of the Exchequer to Secretary for War. When Lloyd George became Prime Minister, she was one of his two official principal private secretaries. Intelligent, industrious and discreet, she not only excelled in her official capacity: she was Lloyd George's indispensable personal companion and vigorous champion during times of distress and misfortune.

As the details of the relationship between Lloyd George and Frances have gradually emerged, the effect upon his posthumous reputation has undoubtedly been damaging. His morals have been deplored and his personal life the subject of considerable criticism. Most importantly, questions about his public life as a politician and a statesman have arisen. How could the Prime Minister give his full attention to affairs of state when so often involved in obvious chicanery and deceptions about his private affairs? Were not these personal matters a distraction from his public responsibilities? How widely known the amorous affiliation between Lloyd George and Frances was in his own time is debatable. Most historians believe that his closest colleagues and many in the highest political circles were aware of the relationship. But it never became a matter of public comment. Those who knew likely enough had their own secrets they wished kept quiet. Privately, he was certainly the object of rumour and innuendo. To his friends and colleagues, it was a venial sin. To his enemies, however, Lloyd George was immoral and a hypocrite.

As Kenneth O. Morgan observed many years ago, Lloyd George has had a unique capacity to inspire or to enrage, both in his own time and since then among historians. Morgan rightly observes that it is difficult to think of any Prime Minister before or since whose character and career have provoked such violent conflict.[3] Little has changed since. John Grigg, in a preface to his unfinished biography of Lloyd George, warns that the complications of Lloyd George's life ensure that 'the last word will never be written on Lloyd George, or on any part of his career'.[4] In assessing Lloyd George, this book does not attempt a last word. But it does attempt an evenhanded approach in examining Lloyd George's life and times. A dispassionate discussion of Lloyd George as reflected in his own words, in the eyes of his contemporaries and in the analysis of historians can lend a depth and perspective to his complex career which may lead to a greater understanding of the tensions and conflicts of his private and public lives. And only then, too, can Lloyd George be fairly evaluated amid the controversy that still surrounds 'the little man who won the Great War'.

1

THE EDUCATION OF A STATESMAN

Born at a time when the traditional British landed elite was at the height of its power and prestige, Lloyd George was representative of a new democracy which would eventually contribute to the eclipse of that privileged class.[1] Although English by birth, Lloyd George grew up in rural mid-Wales. This area is separated from the rest of Wales by the Cambrian Mountains and thus set apart from the eastern counties of the principality, which directly border England. It was a deeper Wales set within Wales; but all were part of the great Celtic arc of Scotland, Ireland, Wales and Cornwall. Proudly Welsh throughout his life, Lloyd George was significantly influenced by Welsh traditions, religion and history. This was both a source of strength to him in later life and a point of differentiation that his political enemies attempted to exploit.

Like much else in the life and career of Lloyd George, the circumstances of his early years in Wales are in contention. One biographer notes 'the handicaps of his humble background', his 'lack of education', 'his early poverty' and his childhood 'deprivation'.[2] Another, however, entitles the first chapter in his biography 'Not-so-humble Origins', while a third describes Lloyd George's family background as 'a relatively secure middle-class one'.[3] Indeed, it is true that Lloyd George's childhood could be viewed as disadvantaged when compared to most English politicians of that era – and some were not slow in holding that against him. But the circumstances of his own life and that of his family of origin suggest a striving upward in status. His mother, Elizabeth Lloyd, was a domestic servant employed as a lady's companion to a Miss Evans who lived at Y Castell (the Castle) in Pwllheli. In 1859 she married William George, whose family was of yeomen farming stock in Pembrokeshire. As a young man, the bookish William had broken from his farming origins to become first a pharmacist's assistant, then an apprentice to a draper. During that time, he was also studying French, German and algebra. In about 1841, he began a peripatetic life, moving first to London to become a student at the Battersea Teachers' Training Institute. Thereafter, he taught at various schools in England before coming to Liverpool where he taught for several years. He also taught in the Hope Street Sunday Schools administered by the Unitarians. Apparently through the school, he made the acquaintance of the Unitarian minister James Martineau. In addition,

William formed a fortuitous friendship with Thomas Goffey, a Liverpool solicitor, who advised him on investments in Liverpool building societies.

William left Liverpool in 1853 and a year later established a school in Haverfordwest in his native Pembrokeshire. Later, William sought another teaching position, this time at a newly opened British school at Pwllheli, where he met his future wife, Elizabeth Lloyd. Following their marriage, they lived for a time with Elizabeth's widowed mother, Rebecca; Elizabeth's young nephew, David Lloyd Jones; and Elizabeth's brother, Richard, in Llanystumdwy, a village not far from Pwllheli. These were cramped quarters in a small three-up and two-down cottage with no indoor plumbing facilities, though this was not unusual for rural Wales. Apparently a baby was born to the young married couple, but died shortly after birth. In 1861 William once again crossed to England, taking his family with him to the small village of Newchurch, not far from Liverpool. Travelling with them was David Lloyd Jones, to be tutored by William.

Perhaps this relocation, not far from Liverpool, where William had once enjoyed a circle of friends, was intended to provide a more congenial atmosphere for a lover of serious books and lively discussions. Shortly after their arrival, their second child, Mary Ellen, was born. Once again, however, the family moved – this time to Manchester, where William took a temporary position in a textile mill school.[4] By then Elizabeth was again pregnant and on 17 January 1863, her first son, David Lloyd, was born, named after her nephew. Within a few months, the restless William returned to Wales, in part it seems because he had decided to give up teaching. He took the tenancy of a small farm of 30 acres in Pembrokeshire. Here he hoped perhaps to find the time to pursue his long-held literary ambitions.[5] But his health, never robust, failed and he died of pneumonia on 7 June 1864 at the age of 43.

The bereft little family, including two small children, had few resources but these were not unimportant. Their immediate need was to find a home which was soon enough provided in Llanystumdwy at the Lloyd cottage ('Highgate') where Elizabeth Lloyd's mother Rebecca and brother Richard still lived. In addition, William's estate, primarily based upon investments in Liverpool building societies, amounted to £768 at his death: this yielded approximately £46 annually. Because their major fixed expense was the £7 annual rent for Highgate, the family's modest income (added to what savings that Richard and Rebecca may have had) was enough to provide for their needs. Their circumstances must have become strained several months later, however, when Elizabeth gave birth to her second son, William, named after his recently deceased father.[6]

In addition to these resources was another, especially important to the early life of David Lloyd George and his brother William – their father's library and literary remains. These books and papers had been packed in tea chests and brought up from Pembrokeshire when Elizabeth and the children moved to Llanystumdwy: they were the largest single item of the young family's luggage.[7] This collection, including William senior's personal diaries and notebooks, allowed his young sons over the years to have a sense of their father's life. It is impossible to know for certain, but one can imagine the youthful Lloyd George perusing his father's diary and hearing tales from his mother about his father's struggles as he sought a professional footing and to improve himself beyond the circumstances of his birth. Certain lessons may have been learned. The young Lloyd George may have thus determined not to follow an indecisive or a feckless path in life and work. He may also have learned to be vigilant about opportunities to advance himself and to be bold in taking advantage of them, which his father sometimes failed to do. Perhaps, too, as the son of a father whose life was cut short, he might have been determined to succeed early in life, and thus be driven to excellence and achievement.

His father's library was also valuable to Lloyd George the student. It was in fact a useful supplement to the village schooling of both David and his brother William. The library included several works on history – including Green's *History of England*, Hallam's *Constitutional History*, the six-volume edition of Burnet's *History of the Reformation* and a *History of the English Revolution* by Guizot in the European Library series. Several serious works on education, including the Commissioner's Reports on education in Wales, published by HMSO in 1848, were also in the collection. *The Journals* of George Fox and Arnold's *Life and Correspondence* were included, as were several anthologies of English poetry and Shakespeare's plays. Essential reference works such as a complete set of the *Penny Encyclopedia* and *Webster's Dictionary* were there. And of course, a Bible.[8] That these works were put to use by both David and his brother William is evidenced by surviving notebooks in which the two boys wrote précis of the books they read. David kept up this habit until he was 16.

By far the greatest influence upon the development of the young David was his Uncle Lloyd, who effectively became his father figure. Richard Lloyd, along with his mother Rebecca, managed the family business, a cobbler's shop. But the shop was not merely a place for repairing footwear: it also made boots for all uses, from working boots for farmers and agricultural labourers to fancier riding boots and boots for the footmen of local gentry.[9] Established by Richard's father (another David), the shop was successful enough to provide for the family for half a century. Indeed, at one time the shop, attached to the cottage, had hired two assistants to handle the increased business. Yet it was also a humble establishment. Richard Lloyd did not own Highgate and, as Price points out, the handmade shoemaking trade was facing stiff competition from increasingly common mechanized shoe production.[10]

Perhaps more important than the financial contributions to the young Lloyd George was the personality and character of his Uncle Lloyd. His love of knowledge, intellectual curiosity and strong sense of responsibility served as models for his nephews. Uncle Lloyd was an omnivorous reader, devouring English classics, Welsh theology and poetry, travel and biography alike. He read one or two newspapers daily. He was particularly interested in politics and religion. His workshop was a centre of village discussion on equally broad topics. Uncle Lloyd had a local reputation for probity and wisdom; and he exerted his considerable influence as an exemplary moral force in his community.[11] His good name was known beyond Llanystumdwy, for he was also a pastor in neighbouring Criccieth. There he was a member of a small splinter group of Baptists, known as the Disciples of Christ. It was said that while at work he would frequently stop for a moment to scribble down an idea, perhaps for

use in a sermon. He constantly sought new meaning in explicating his messages from
the Bible, the main source of his sermons. During his 58 years of ministry, he worked
out of several Bibles, all filled with interleaved pencilled notes.[12] The care that he
took in his sermons, the habit of thoughtful reading and his dynamic style of public
speaking very likely had a strong and lasting impact upon his young nephew. Indeed,
there is some evidence of this in Lloyd George's earliest diary entries. After one of
his uncle's sermons, Lloyd George wrote: 'Uncle Lloyd splendid and all through
his sermon there were the most startling hits, and the peroration swept everything
before him. The audience's feelings drowned in tears. Never heard anything like it.'[13]
Attending his uncle's sermons was no occasional thing: Lloyd George is reported to
have walked the two mile round trip from Llanystumdwy to Criccieth three times
every Sunday and once on Wednesdays to hear his uncle's strenuous exhortations.[14]
    It is not surprising that Lloyd George may have idolized his uncle. Uncle Lloyd's
feeling for his nephew was reciprocal: indeed, it seems that Uncle Lloyd played
favourites. Perhaps he recognized rare promise in the young Lloyd George and
saw him as an apt pupil, worthy of every attention. Decades later, Lloyd George's
younger brother William, admitting some jealousy, remembered with some asperity
that it 'was certainly a bit trying at times to anyone in Uncle Lloyd's entourage who
did not take such an extreme view of Dafydd's perfections'.[15] Historians concur.
Gilbert believes that Richard Lloyd 'spoiled' his nephew 'outrageously'.[16] Pugh
denies that Lloyd George was 'a spoilt child'; but he nevertheless notes not only his
uncle but also his mother, sister and grandmother were 'on hand to pander to his
needs'. Thus Lloyd George was 'cocooned in affection'.[17] Grigg finds fault with the
saintly uncle, claiming that he made no secret of his preference for the older boy,
going so far as to prevent William from adding the surname Lloyd to the patronymic
George as his brother had done.[18] But it is possible that Uncle Lloyd, who was
clearly intelligent and had signs of shrewdness about him, may have not only have
recognized the promise of the young Lloyd George, but also understood his need
for approval and love of approbation.[19] Throughout his life in fact, this was one of
Lloyd George's strongest characteristics, well recognized by his contemporaries and
occasionally noted by historians and biographers since.
    Although evidence is slight and largely anecdotal, Lloyd George's formal
schooling is also a matter of some interest.[20] He had entered the Llanystumdwy
National School before he was four years of age in 1866 and remained there until
1878. Under the patronage of the local landlord, Ellis Nanney, the school was
managed by the Church of England. Basic subjects taught were traditional writing,
arithmetic, reading, geography and history. David Evans, the schoolmaster, was
evidently an exceptional teacher.[21] Apart from the general curriculum, he gave both
Lloyd George and his brother William a solid grounding in Latin. Recognizing their
abilities, Evans provided additional individual tuition in both arithmetic and algebra.
Evans also seems to have inspired a love of books and learning in Lloyd George,
which he retained throughout much of his life when the press of politics did not
intrude. Some idea of the breadth of Lloyd George's early reading may be found in
his diary at a time when he was a struggling lawyer. In January 1886 he records his

pleasure at finishing *The Last Days of Pompeii*: it was a 'splendid novel'. The following day, he was reading Renan's *Jesus*. In early February, he notes that he was perusing Dante ('again') as bedtime reading but that he doesn't enjoy it 'so far half as much as I did Milton'. In March, he brought to bed lighter fare – *Sketches by Boz*. But he also noted in that day's diary entry that he was 'cheaply accumulating a good library'. By August, his evening reading is more serious, Spencer's *Sociology*.[22]

Apart from his thorough schooling in the Liberal arts, Evans also gave, with equal fervour, religious instruction. To all his students, Evans brought to life the stories of the Bible in his classes on Old Testament history. Decades later, William could recall vividly the dramatic narration of Abraham and Isaac. As the two, father and son, advanced up the mountain where Abraham – commanded by God – was to kill his own son, Evans depicted their path on the blackboard. Suspense in the class mounted as Abraham and Isaac neared the mountain top. At the summit, the climax of the parable: the binding of Isaac and placing him on the sacrificial altar, the raising of Abraham's arm with the knife clasped in his hand (represented by Evans with his cane), ready to plunge it into the heart of his son. But then God spoke. A ram is found in a nearby thicket and sacrificed on the altar. Isaac is saved. Abraham has followed, even at the cost of his son's life, the commandment of God. The moral was clear: obedience to God must be absolute.[23]

Such a teacher would likely not only be respected, but also revered. However, honouring the teacher and by implication honouring the subject taught and the religion espoused by Evans set up a tension within the young Lloyd George. Evans, as an Anglican schoolmaster, was responsible each school day for early morning prayers from the Book of Common Prayer. Each day ended with similar prayers. The Anglican Catechism was often repeated. On Church festival days the children were required to march in procession from the school to the village Anglican church. Visits by school governors to hear the students repeat the Creed and Catechism were annual affairs. In none of these periods of instructions and ceremonies would the Welsh language be heard: it was banned from the school. But a vast majority of the students were neither Anglican nor English speakers only. As Davies puts it neatly: 'a great chasm had come into being between life and education in Wales: the life was Welsh and nonconformist, while the education was English and Episcopal'.[24]

Lloyd George was learning at first hand the cultural and religious conflict emerging between England and the great Welsh national revival during the nineteenth century. As Kenneth Morgan has demonstrated in convincing depth, the reawakening of a Welsh national consciousness in the late Victorian era was grounded in its language and nonconformist religion. Independent nonconformist chapels became 'citadels of dissent' against an oppressive English culture. To reclaim an ancient Welsh heritage was also to defend and advance its language. Calvinist Methodists, Congregationalists, Baptists and other sects, if divided theologically, were bound together in their broader vision of a unified Wales. Sponsoring choral festivals, exalting Welsh hymns and espousing greater educational opportunities for Welsh children, fiery Welsh-speaking nonconformist ministers became the cultural leaders of a new Wales.[25] It was a natural progression for Welsh chapels ultimately to provide the locus of a democratic political movement, thus moving beyond religion to an active participation in politics.

The political party of choice for most of Wales during the late nineteenth century was inevitably the reformist-minded Liberal Party, rather than the Conservative Party, which championed the established Church of England.[26] In earlier decades, however, the dominance of landowners who were simultaneously English, Anglican and Conservative went largely unchallenged. Their influence in local politics and upon the social and economic fabric of the principality gave them an unquestioned leadership and made them the natural representatives to the imperial Parliament. This political and religious domination by the landed few over the unenfranchised many, coupled with widespread tales of landlord intimidation of their tenants, was ultimately to shape the ideals and political consciousness of a new generation of Welshmen.[27]

As a local representative of this new sense of Welshness, Uncle Lloyd emphatically protested the Anglican religious doctrines imposed upon his nephews in the local school. Caught between his uncle and his teacher, Lloyd George became briefly rebellious. In a well-known episode, he once led his Welsh schoolmates to remain silent during the affirmation of the Anglican Creed and the Catechism to be said in unison before school visitors. More seriously for Lloyd George was the impact upon his own beliefs of this growing religious controversy. At the age of 12 Lloyd George was baptized in accordance with the beliefs of his sect, which held against infant baptism. Shortly afterwards, however, he entertained doubts about his religious faith. This was a particularly serious matter for the boy, not only because it suggested a rebellion against God, but also against his pious uncle, who had baptized Lloyd George in the brook that ran by the small chapel where he preached his sermons.

Apparently Uncle Lloyd took this irreverent news well, as one might expect given his well-established pattern of favouritism toward his nephew. Perhaps he thought it only a phase in the boy's life. But Lloyd George had turned a corner: he never again believed in the supernatural aspects of Christianity, including the efficacy of prayer, the divinity of Jesus and the doctrine of providence – the belief that God worked in history.[28] Yet he continued outwardly to some degree observing the formal trappings of his former religious faith, in part perhaps to please his uncle and in part because he enjoyed both good sermons and Welsh hymns, as he did all his life afterwards. Additionally, Uncle Lloyd's small chapel, like so many others, was a place where speaking and discussion – not only on religious subjects – were valued.[29] A combination of club, library and seminar, chapels encouraged their members to discuss religious themes to be sure; but in doing so, larger skills were honed which could be applied to any public oration or private discourse, whether sermon or political speech.[30] As his competence and confidence in public speaking grew, we may understand how likely it would be that in his emerging adolescence, Lloyd George enjoyed if not always the content, certainly the form of religious presentation.

By the end of his schooling at age 13, Lloyd George had earned a reputation as a scholar: he was even considered a bit of a bookworm. This suggested teaching, the ministry, or medicine as the most suitable professions for him. But he decided instead upon the law. His decision was apparently based upon several circumstances. The gratitude felt by the family for the services rendered by Thomas Goffey, the Liverpool solicitor who had been the guardian of Elizabeth Lloyd's small annuity bequeathed her by her husband, may have been initially a factor in viewing the law favourably. Perhaps, too, the family was consciously following an emerging trend in Wales whereby the law was beginning to be recognized as a way up for those not of privileged gentry.[31] In addition, Lloyd George's quick, bright and extroverted personality could not be discounted: it would seem to suit the life of a public advocate. Moreover, further schooling would not be necessary. Once a candidate had passed a preliminary examination, he would be articled to a firm of solicitors for a term of legal apprenticeship: a local firm would do. There a candidate might remain for several years, until ready to set up his own practice. This was the path that Lloyd George chose.

In preparing for the preliminary examination, Uncle Lloyd and his nephew continued their remarkable partnership. The requirements for the exam included two languages. Lloyd George already had in hand the rudiments of Latin from headmaster Evans. But French, of which he knew not a word, posed a problem. Uncle Lloyd took charge. Second-hand Latin and French grammars and textbooks were purchased, as the two set about brushing up on Latin and learning French together. After months of study, the two travelled to Liverpool in November 1877 to sit the exam. Lloyd George was not yet 14 when he received notification that he had passed. The next task was to find a firm of solicitors who would accept such a young applicant. Once again, Uncle Lloyd was instrumental in advancing the interest of his nephew. Richard knew a local antiquary and friend of Edward Breese, a partner in the firm of Breese, Jones and Casson of Porthmadog, a small but bustling port town six miles from Llanystumdwy. Breese was a man of some substance, senior partner in the firm, Clerk of the Peace and Clerk of the Lieutenancy of the County of Merioneth. He was also active in Liberal politics. He took in the young solicitor for a six-month trial with the understanding that if he succeeded, he would be articled to Randall Casson, a junior partner. Because of Lloyd George's youth and inexperience, Breese agreed to watch over his welfare personally. During the trial term, Breese invited him to call often at his home, Morfa House, an opportunity Lloyd George seized readily. Work-related contacts also brought the two together: one of Lloyd George's early morning tasks was to bring the office mail to the Breese home. Sometimes he was invited to meals, including at least once a Christmas dinner. On occasion, he played with the Breese children. Clearly the young clerk won the trust and made a favourable impression upon the Breese family. He also won over the firm's principals and was articled to the firm shortly after his sixteenth birthday in January 1879.[32]

Thus the young clerk entered into the work of the law under the benign eye of his patron. He remained in the firm until late 1884, having passed two further official hurdles, the Intermediate and Final examinations. Most of his legal work in the early years was concerned with collecting fire insurance premiums from leaseholders of the Tremadog estate, which the firm represented as solicitors. Other responsibilities included delivering leases, engrossing mortgages and attending court sessions.[33] In his spare time, he was also reading legal texts, as well as Hallam's *Constitutional History*. He also began taking shorthand lessons.

Lloyd George's interests during his late adolescent years were not confined to the law. For example, he maintained some interest – as we have noted above – in theological discussion and disputation. To this end, he made the acquaintance of John Roberts, a junior partner in a local firm of tallow-chandlers whose main customer was the Ffestiniog slate quarries. The candle house was located directly behind the small Disciples of Christ chapel in Porthmadog where Roberts served as deacon. Not unlike Uncle Lloyd in his cobbler's shop, Roberts ran a lively discussion group on political and social topics. But unlike Uncle Lloyd, Roberts was an out and out radical, who denounced Liberal and Tory alike. Espousing republican doctrines, he had little sympathy for the royal family. Whether or not Roberts' influence was critical to developing a radical streak in Lloyd George is unclear. Roberts was important, however, in extending the opportunity first provided by his uncle for Lloyd George to exercise his talents as a public speaker. Soon after Lloyd George became associated with Breese, Jones, and Casson. Roberts introduced him to the Porthmadog Debating Society. There he made his first speech on a looming political and diplomatic issue, the Eastern Question, in which he criticized a growing British jingoist sentiment under the Conservative Disraeli government.[34]

It would seem that Lloyd George took away from John Roberts not his religious bent, but rather more secular lessons. Indeed, it would appear that his religious beliefs, which had been shaken years before at the time of his baptism, continued to shift during his years in training for the law in Porthmadog. This is not to say that he became an atheist, or even that he rejected Christianity. In fact, his diary indicates that he continued to attend chapel, if with less fervour than in his younger days. And he continued to speak the language of religion and of religious belief from time to time. But if the language so well learned in childhood remained, the fundamental belief behind the words continued to fall away. Ultimately, he came to see that the language of nonconformist Wales, especially when used in ways familiar to the faithful, could bring substantial personal and political rewards. Thus his early religious training crucially influenced his later public life in developing his notable debating skills and his public speeches, both of which reflected the Welsh preaching tradition.[35]

By 1880, Lloyd George's growing interest in politics was beginning to overshadow his intended legal profession.[36] He was a declared Liberal, influenced by the Liberal Party's increasing success in the previous dozen years over Welsh Conservatives. At the general election of 1880, the venerable Liberal William Gladstone, a Member of Parliament since 1832, replaced the Conservative Benjamin Disraeli as Prime Minister. In Wales, the Liberals won 29 of 33 Welsh seats. In Britain overall, Liberal gains were less impressive, but substantial nevertheless. The excitement of that election year, complemented by Gladstone's famous Midlothian campaign of 1879, in which he poured forth his transcendent vision of a moral nation united against the evils of an imperialist Conservative Party, appealed mightily to the surging nonconformist majority in Wales. Change was in the air.

Lloyd George, along with members of his law firm, actively participated in the election. His diary for March 1880 shows his activities in detail.[37] He helped check election registers, attended political meetings and spent several days commuting by train to canvass neighbouring villages and towns on behalf of Watkin Williams, the Liberal candidate for Caernarfonshire. The local Liberal campaign was successful as Williams handily defeated George Douglas Pennant, the son of Lord Penrhyn, the wealthiest man in North Wales and a Conservative political force since the 1840s. Lloyd George celebrated this defeat as a 'great blow to landlord terrorism …'.[38] An unexpected second election, however, followed on the heels of the March polling. Watkin Williams accepted a judgeship, forcing a by-election for the now empty Caernarfonshire seat so recently won by the Liberals. As before, Lloyd George pitched into the election battle. William Rathbone, a wealthy Liverpool merchant, stood for the Liberals. Opposing him was the Conservative Ellis Nanney of Gwynfryn Castle, whose estate of 12,000 acres was, as we have noted, very near Llanystumdwy. He was also one of the patrons of the Llanystumdwy national school, which Lloyd George had attended. Perhaps this gave an extra incentive to the young politico. In addition to his canvassing, as he had done in the March election, Lloyd George wrote a pseudonymous letter to the *North Wales Express*, criticizing both Lord Salisbury, the leader of the Conservative Party, and Ellis Nanney. This was the first of his many exercises in political journalism. When published in November 1880, the article omitted a passage that had called Ellis Nanney a 'vampire';[39] but otherwise it was an impressive debut for a 17-year-old boy. Not only was Lloyd George's political precocity thus revealed: in addition, his strong dislike of aristocratic entitlement was once again in evidence. Indeed, he preferred the English Liberal Rathbone over the Welsh Ellis Nanney in part because the former was a merchant and the latter a detested landlord. Rathbone, like his Liberal predecessor Watkin Williams, won the election by a wide margin.

The excitement surrounding Rathbone's success, a second Liberal victory within six months in the same constituency, reaffirmed the lure of the political life for Lloyd George. It may be that even at this early age, he had already set his sights on national office. Reminiscing in his diary on the last day of 1880, he reflected on the past year's events and their impact on his life: 'Ambition itself has had a greater sway in my thoughts than the means of its gratification.'[40] It is certainly true that from about 1881, he determined to make his name known to a variety of potential constituent groups with an eye to winning a parliamentary seat.[41] He continued active in the Porthmadog Debating Society, where some of his addresses caught the attention of the local press. In early 1882, the *North Wales Express* gave a brief account of Lloyd George's 'argumentative and nervous speech' before the society when he spoke against Irish landlords' claims to compensation under the Irish Land Act.[42] At a meeting of the society several months later, he had the temerity to criticize the Gladstone ministry's recent military incursion into Egypt. He defended the Egyptian nationalist leader Arabi 'who had risen up from the people' against the corrupt client government supported by an imperial Britain.[43] Most of his early experiences in public speaking occurred during his membership of the Criccieth Debating Society, which he had joined about this time. It is clear that he had begun to experience the deep satisfaction that public approval gave him. After one of his speeches at the Criccieth Society, on the disestablishment of the Church of England in Wales, he recorded in his diary that his pointed remarks against the Church had 'excited peals of laughter'; and not 'one of the previous or subsequent speeches evoked such a thorough, profound response from the audience'. He recorded further, with emphasis: '*When I sat down I felt I had made my mark in Criccieth*.'[44]

Meanwhile, he broadened his opportunities for debate even further by joining in 1882 the United Kingdom Alliance, under whose auspices he began to speak on temperance and Sunday closing throughout Caernarfon, Merioneth and Denbighshire. In that same year, he joined the Porthmadog Volunteers. To his already busy schedule, he now added regular drilling.[45] It should also be mentioned that – perhaps surprisingly, given what we now know about his religious beliefs – he began to preach to various congregations of Disciples of Christ. In time, he adopted a rather cynical view of this whirlwind activity. After signing the Blue Ribbon Pledge to follow total abstinence, he noted in a single day how the pledge had been broken by two glasses of port and two of beer – 'so that's keeping the Blue Ribbon Pledge grandly'.[46]

About the time that Lloyd George had begun testing the waters of public acclaim, the Lloyd family moved the mile or so to Criccieth, giving up Highgate and its shoe shop. Morvin House, held on lease, was a more pleasant and spacious accommodation than the Llanystumdwy cottage. It was somewhat closer to Porthmadog, and thus Lloyd George no longer took lodgings there. The move may have been brought about because of Uncle Lloyd's declining health ; but also, one may guess, Uncle Lloyd wished to keep an eye on his nephew, fearful perhaps that distractions could intrude upon his nephew's progress in the law. Although the move to Criccieth and Morvin House kept the family under one roof, finances remained tight. By then, Lloyd George's brother was following in his footsteps, becoming articled to the same law firm, and thus without adequate earnings. During the early 1880s Lloyd George had little income. Uncle Lloyd was effectively in retirement. The family managed to survive on small gifts and loans and taking in summer lodgers. William, in his revealing memoir, best recounts their financial burdens. There he quotes at some length the diaries of Uncle Lloyd which reflect the straightened conditions of the family: the plaintive entry of 1 April 1884 is representative: 'May this moneyless period soon come to an end.'[47]

During these same lean years, as we have seen, Lloyd George was laying a foundation for a future political career. He seems largely unaffected by the worries of his struggling family. His own introspections as revealed by his diaries bear this out. This is not to suggest a callous indifference: he likely believed that whatever legal or political success would redound to the family's benefit as well as his own. This may have influenced his decision in 1885 to practice law on his own, rather than remaining with the Porthmadog firm. By then, too, his lengthy service as an articled clerk contributed to his sense of independence: it was time to be his own man. Practicing on his own, he could more easily pursue at will his political agenda without being concerned by the collegial restrictions of legal partners. With reasons enough, Lloyd George established an office in the small back parlour of Morvin House in Criccieth.

During 1885, Lloyd George also worked assiduously to perfect his speaking style. His diary for that year is filled with summaries of various meetings at which he spoke, and his growing confidence in his power to arouse these assembled groups. In a temperance meeting in February 1885, for example, he reported praise from those in attendance. He was told that he 'gave an impression of great earnestness', and that he had 'a kind of tremor' in his voice while describing the evils of intemperance.[48] The following month, after speaking at a political gathering in Criccieth, he recorded: 'When I sat down I felt I had made my mark ... I saw sensible men, of good position, shaking with laughter whilst I was at it. Not one of the previous or subsequent speeches worked such a thorough, profound response from the audience.'[49] Two weeks later, there was another triumph. 'Spoke with much ease', he wrote in his diary, and toward the end of his speech, 'with much fire – getting into the "hwyl" [fun]'.[50] Lloyd George also tracked progress that year in his legal practice. Admitting to overwork in February, he yet believed it to have been productive: he was convinced that in time he would make a 'tolerable advocate'.[51] In fact he had a breakthrough in a case before the Porthmadog court only a few days prior to this diary entry. Previously, he had been discouraged in his inability to be an effective advocate: he could not express himself adequately 'upon the smallest matter'. But on his day of triumph, he had 'commanded quite an interminable torrent of words'.[52]

In early 1886, Lloyd George made his name more widely known at an important political gathering, where he firmly established his reputation as a compelling orator. Michael Davitt, the Irish nationalist and radical reformer, had been invited to speak at Blaenau Ffestiniog on 12 February 1886. Lloyd George had been asked to say a few words at the gathering: the invitation both flattered and alarmed him. He had long followed Davitt's career; but to share a platform with his hero was intimidating.[53] Although he decided to attend the meeting, he seems to have arrived unprepared to speak. At the introductory remarks, however, he was 'astounded' (as he put it) to hear his name read out as a speaker. He stayed to hear Davitt's speech, but then quickly retired to an adjoining room 'to spin out a speech'. He decided to begin with a joke, joining Davitt's first name with the Archangel Michael in suggesting that if the Archangel could not defeat Satan, the two Michaels joining together might dispose of the evil of aristocratic landlordism. Once he told the joke, there was 'a roar of laughter'. The audience was now primed to listen. The substance of his speech was to urge the necessity for working men to unite against privileged power. 'Whilst working men were starving', he declared, the aristocracy 'were squandering the money earned by the sweat of the working man's brow'. As Lloyd George continued extempore to 'rounds of cheering', he found himself drawn on by the crowd: 'I was now on my legs & spoke with great warmth & vigour both of gesture & voice.' Before an important audience of men from all around the surrounding district, Lloyd George wrote in summary of his triumph: 'I have made a good thing of a splendid opportunity.'[54]

Concurrent with the development of his political ideas and oratorical powers, Lloyd George began expanding his legal practice. After he had opened offices in Porthmadog, Pwllheli and Ffestiniog, he visited each in rotation. Such a schedule, even for so energetic a person as Lloyd George, would likely founder without help. Yet in these early days he could not afford to hire an assistant. As so often in the past, Uncle Lloyd filled the breach. Training himself to serve as managing clerk of a solicitor's office, he interviewed clients, collected witnesses, noted their evidence and in general kept order at the head office in Criccieth. His nephew could then run the circuit of the other offices.[55] This not only allowed Lloyd George more time to pursue advocacy, but also to continue his courting of public opinion throughout Caernarfon and beyond.

Lloyd George's coming of age politically and the development of his oratorical skills occurred at a propitious time in Wales. Since 1868, the year of the 'Great Election', Welsh politics was becoming transformed from its earlier domination by 'obscure squireens'[56] into a populist democracy and a stronghold of British Liberalism. The Reform Act of 1884 and the subsequent Redistribution Act of the year following significantly increased the size of the electorate throughout all of Britain, especially among workers and householders in both rural and urban constituencies. In Wales the impact was particularly dramatic. Kenneth Morgan has noted the 'massive effect' of these acts, increasing the county vote, for example, from slightly fewer than 75,000 to slightly more than 200,000. Rural labourers, tenant farmers, industrial miners and tinplate and steelworkers now had the vote.[57] As a result, the general election of November 1885 generated a 'democratic hurricane', removing some of the most entrenched of the old landed families from the House of Commons. Even some backsliding during a second general election a few months later in July 1886 did not materially diminish the enthusiasm of the newly enfranchised.

These developments give point to Grigg's observation that although Lloyd George lacked rank or riches, he was still a privileged child in being born 'to a special historic opportunity'.[58] Lloyd George's developing skill at speechmaking in local venues; his contacts established through his legal practice; his growing acquaintance with the political arts; and his religious connections all combined to endow him with a reputation of a young man with considerable promise. How early in his life Lloyd George saw his ultimate goal as a participant in national politics is a matter of some dispute. Perhaps he always intended to use Wales as a stepping-stone for his greater national ambitions; or perhaps it was a matter of chance and circumstance that he rose quickly from his Welsh origins to national prominence.[59] Whatever his ultimate goal, Lloyd George demonstrated a remarkable perspicacity in bringing together the various elements of Welsh society in crafting a potent political machinery for his own use.

In short, by the early age of 22, Lloyd George was well positioned to take advantage of an increased electorate, most of whom tended to be Liberal, many of whom were nonconformists who urged root and branch religious reform, and others of whom had radical notions of political reform. It was Lloyd George's task to knit together these somewhat disparate factions within the broader framework of the Liberal Party. To that end, Lloyd George raised his sights from lower level campaigning in temperance preaching and local debating societies: the time had come to tap into the more issue-oriented groups which had a broader influence over an emerging and expanding Welsh electorate.

The first of these groups was the Liberation Society, formed to promote the disestablishment of the Church of England for the entire kingdom, not merely in Wales.[60] As we have seen, Welsh dislike of Anglican religious practices and their educational mission was particularly intense at the end of the nineteenth century. Lloyd George began making speeches for the society early in 1885. Related to the aims of the Liberation Society was a broad anti-tithe movement in Wales, whose object was to force the abolition of Welsh landlords' habit of requiring new tenants to pay their tithes directly to the tithe-owners, primarily the Church of England. As secretary of the South Caernarfonshire branch of the Anti-Tithe League, Lloyd George travelled throughout Wales during 1886/87 denouncing tithe owners and landlords.[61] In another example of Lloyd George's cultivation of the rural vote, he paid attention to those aggrieved tenant farmers who were agitating for better terms for their leases and for the rebatement of rent during times of agricultural depression. Thus in 1885, he spoke for the first time before the Farmers' Union in Pwllheli. A third movement that captured Lloyd George's interest was the widespread Welsh temperance campaign. Originating in the mid-nineteenth century as a reaction against perceived heavy drinking among Welsh workers, temperance advocates sprang primarily from Welsh nonconformity, whose chapels – those self-governing ecclesiastical republics – became the centres for drink reform.[62] In his early years, Lloyd George often spoke at temperance meetings and, with the exception of youthful tippling, he abstained from consuming alcohol throughout his life.

The widening circle of Lloyd George's politicking brought him increasingly to the attention of some of the most notable Welshmen of that era. Among them was T.E. Ellis, who represented the new wave of Welsh nationalists replacing the older, more Anglicized Welsh political leaders.[63] His contribution to the Welsh national movement emphasized its indigenous literary and cultural traditions. Born the son of a tenant farmer, Ellis worked his way up the educational ladder before first going to University College at Aberystwyth and then on to New College, Oxford. Four years older than Lloyd George, Ellis had a head start on a parliamentary career, entering the House of Commons at the general election of 1886. Lloyd George sought Ellis's friendship and entered into a cooperative ownership with him in establishing the Welsh language *Udgorn Rhyddid (Trumpet of Freedom)* in January 1888. This was the first example of Lloyd George's use of the newspaper press to mould public opinion to advance a political agenda.

A far more influential Welsh paper was the *Baner ac Amserau Cymru (Banner and Times of Wales)*, edited by the notable Welsh nationalist, Thomas Gee. An ordained Methodist minister, Gee was especially active in the anti-tithe agitation. He was also keenly interested in a broader land reform for Wales, one which would bring to the Welsh tenant farmer fair rents, security of tenure, compensation for improvements and the creation of a land court to adjudicate rents.[64] In the spring of 1888, Lloyd George contacted Gee, inviting him to share a platform for a series of speeches in South Caernarfonshire on the topic of land reform. Lloyd George made it his business to draw together Ellis and Gee, among other leaders of less renown, with the idea of energizing the new spirit of Welsh self-determination under a banner of a coherent and well-organized political force. He was proving unusually adept at political networking. In fact, in a sign that Lloyd George's thoughts were turning increasingly towards a more active political role on a national scale, he tentatively put forward his name as a candidate for Merioneth during the 1886 general election. He withdrew, however, when Tom Ellis decided to stand.

During his intensive cultivation of political contacts from 1885 onward, Lloyd George's law practice had not languished. A larger office than the provisional nook in Morvin House became necessary: one was found on Criccieth High Street. With the addition of his brother to the practice in 1887, the politically ambitious older brother could leave much of the legal work to William – just as he had previously with his uncle. This gave him additional time not only for his political enterprise, but also allowed him to pursue the more political side of legal practice – public advocacy. By the late 1880s, he had gained a reputation as a tenacious defender of the poor and disadvantaged. The climax of his campaign for recognition – and perhaps the most important legal case ever brought before Lloyd George – occurred in 1888.

The facts in the case are somewhat convoluted, but the main issues can be simply stated. In the spring of 1888 an old Methodist quarryman died not long after making a deathbed wish to be buried alongside his daughter in the Anglican churchyard at Llanfrothen near Porthmadog. The practice of allowing nonconformist burials in Church of England graveyards had been allowed since the Burials Act of 1880: the Act also sanctioned nonconformist funeral rites in these cases. But the Anglican rector at Llanfrothen refused to allow it, employing a dubious legal dodge to justify his decision. Incensed, the quarryman's family sought counsel with the firm of Lloyd George and George, who advised that they were entitled to a burial under the parliamentary statute. On the day of the burial, the rector again attempted to deny entry, this time locking the gate to the cemetery. On Lloyd George's advice, the funeral party broke it open with a crowbar and conducted their ceremony. The rector then brought a complaint of trespass against the funeral party: this was heard before Judge John Bishop, County Court Judge for the North Wales Circuit, who had recently been appointed to the bench by the Conservative Marquess of Salisbury's Lord Chancellor. Lloyd George had already had 'some sharp tussles'[65] with the judge prior to the Llanfrothen case. When the jury found for the defendants, Bishop reserved judgement and adjourned for two months. Reconvening the court on 25 July 1888, Bishop unaccountably found for the plaintiffs. This caused a furore among the nonconformist Welsh who once again had clear evidence of English and Anglican prejudice. But Lloyd George discovered that Bishop had wrongly recorded the jury's verdict and immediately appealed. On 14 December, the appeal came before Lord Chief Justice Coleridge in London where Lloyd George, with the jury's original findings in hand, easily secured a reversal of Bishop's verdict.[66]

As William George rightly recalls in his memoir, this case put the firm of Lloyd George and George, 'and particularly Dafydd, well on the Map of Wales'.[67] North Wales was abuzz with the news. Justice for nonconformity; defeat for the English establishment; victory for Welsh nationalism – and all at the hands of a Welsh-speaking, temperance-leaning, forward-thinking solicitor not yet 25 years old. Within a fortnight of the victory, on 3 January 1889, the annual meeting of the Caernarfon District Liberal Association adopted Lloyd George as its candidate for Parliament at the next general election. A few weeks later, Lloyd George was elected an alderman during the first nationwide county council elections under the Local Government Act of 1888. This act had trimmed some of powers of the traditional gentry elite operating through quarter sessions, and provided an opportunity for greater democratic participation in county government. Lloyd George's selection as an alderman gave added lustre to his leadership in the broader Welsh political community. But he did not rest easy: throughout the early months of 1889 he was active in consolidating his political position. He made an appraisal of the Liberal Party organization in his constituency; checked the electoral registers; wrote personal letters to prominent electors; and solicited advice from such national Liberal figures as Francis Schnadhorst, the secretary of the National Liberal Federation and a founding father of the Birmingham Caucus, whose greatest exponent was Joseph Chamberlain.[68]

As Lloyd George's political fortunes advanced, so did his personal life. In January 1888, he had married Margaret Owen. It had been a long courtship and one consistent with his lengthy political campaign. He encountered difficulties, was persistent in the face of them and was ultimately persuasive in winning his objective. He had met Margaret several years earlier in the summer of 1884. Her parents had greater wealth and standing than the Georges and the Lloyds. Richard Owen farmed more than 100 acres, had income from local investments and served occasionally as a land valuer. Their house, a mansion by the standards of Lloyd George's family, lay in farmland on the crest of a hill north of Criccieth. Margaret, as befitted her position, had been educated in a finishing school for young ladies. The Owens were nonconformists, though as Calvinist Methodists they represented a more traditional middle class and somewhat Conservative branch of nonconformity. Margaret's father was also a deacon in his local chapel. For these reasons – matters of status and sectarianism – the Owens were opposed to their daughter's involvement with Lloyd George, refusing at first even to welcome him in their home. Thus Lloyd George and Margaret carried on a furtive courtship for three long years.

Their letters and Lloyd George's diary chronicle the vagaries of their relationship. Although Margaret (or Maggie as she became) was not a great beauty, photographs reveal her as a pleasant, self-assured young woman. Lloyd George by then had attained his physical maturity. He was somewhat below medium height at 5ft 6½in., muscular and already sporting the moustache that he would keep the rest of his life. Perhaps his most striking feature was his lively blue eyes. Most attractive for those who knew him was the nimbleness of his language in both speech and writing. He used these talents to the full in winning over Maggie. His letters to her often contained endearments and regrets when they could not meet. 'I miss you immensely', he wrote to her in September 1886 when they could not work out arrangements for seeing one another.[69] Hoping for a tryst on a December evening, he declared that if she could not come, he would be 'as forlorn & solitary as a stray dog'.[70] By early 1887, he addresses her as 'My little darling' and 'My dearest Maggie'. But he could also be remarkably candid and even brusque in his courtship. When Maggie seemed reluctant to meet with him in July 1886, he chastised her. 'I know you can manufacture excuses by the score – & difficulties by the myriad ... Believe me the best plan always is – first of all to decide upon doing a thing – secondly, to discover the real method of doing it.'[71] In another instance, he criticized her failure to meet him because of a rain shower.[72] For her part, Maggie not only had to deal with her parents' reservations, but also with her own suspicions about rumours concerning her beau's wandering eye. Maggie also often found herself in a dilemma. Writing in late 1887, she complained to Lloyd George: 'My parents are angry with me one day and you another. I am on bad terms with one or the other continually ....'[73] To counter Maggie's jealousy and win her trust required some deft explaining.[74] Furthermore, Lloyd George was – if not demanding – certainly firm about his expectations. He was explicit in his views on career and marriage, and the role that wives must play. As he explained in a lengthy letter early in their courtship: 'I have a purpose in life. And however painful the sacrifice I may have to make to attain this ambition I must not flinch – otherwise success will be remote indeed ....' His 'supreme idea' he continued, was 'to get on. To this idea I shall sacrifice everything ... I am prepared to thrust even love itself under the wheels of my Juggernaut, if it obstructs the way ...'.[75]

Lloyd George's continuous protestations of love, his obvious intelligence and his boundless vitality eventually won Maggie's promise of marriage. Perhaps, too, Lloyd George's tenacity won over Maggie's parents. In any case, the ceremony took place on 24 January 1888 before a few friends in a Methodist chapel not far from Criccieth. Uncle Lloyd was told about the impending marriage only days beforehand, perhaps to forestall any sectarian squabble. Officiating at the wedding doubtless mollified him: he shared the responsibility with a local Methodist minister. The bride and groom spent their ten-day honeymoon in London where they enjoyed both the sacred and the profane, visiting first Spurgeon's Metropolitan Tabernacle, followed by a performance of *Hamlet* at the Globe Theatre. On their return to Wales, they settled in together with Maggie's parents. A year later, a son, Richard, was born to the young couple and the following year a daughter, Mair Eluned (Mary Ellen). To house the growing family, Mr and Mrs Owen sold their interest in the farm and built a pair of adjoining houses in Criccieth in semi-detached style, the Owens living in one house and the Lloyd Georges in the other. From every account both families lived thereafter on amicable terms. With these family concerns now settled, Lloyd George could turn his full attention to politics.

3

TO ENGLAND TO PARLIAMENT

Ten weeks after Lloyd George's selection as a candidate for the Caernarfon Boroughs, the sitting member for that constituency, the Conservative MP Edmund Swetenham, died suddenly in March 1890. A by-election was called for the following month. The young Liberal candidate had little time to prepare for his first parliamentary battle. Luckily for him, the Conservatives were also caught flat-footed, and fell back on Hugh Ellis Nanney, the squire of Gwynfryn Castle. The advantage to the Conservatives was that Ellis Nanney was well known, wealthy and generally regarded as a nice man. Lloyd George brought youth, vigour, an iconoclastic viewpoint, and represented the striving, upwardly mobile middle classes of the new Wales. Moreover Lloyd George, whose life had been geared to debate and speechifying, was a natural on the political stump. Nevertheless, he faced significant opposition, not only from Conservative voters. Some moderate Liberals were suspicious of Lloyd George's radical views. In addition, there were sectarian reservations about his candidacy. Not all nonconformist voters regarded his Baptist faith as righteous.[1] The election, held on 11 April 1890, was very close, with Lloyd George winning by only 18 votes (on two recounts) out of nearly 4,000 votes cast.

Once the election was over, Lloyd George was quickly in harness. Within a week he was in London to be introduced to the House of Commons. Within two weeks, he had participated in Question Time. He was also busily making speeches outside Parliament. On 7 May he addressed the Liberation Society at the London Metropolitan Tabernacle. It was his first important London gathering. Although he spoke to a thinning crowd as the evening wore on, there was no doubt of his enthusiasm. Denouncing the Church of England in Wales as 'the greatest curse which ever afflicted little Wales', he pressed the need for disestablishment.[2] A month later he spoke at Manchester's Free Trade Hall. It may have been on a humdrum topic – the compensation of publicans – but Lloyd George turned the meeting into a rally for temperance causes. Reminding his audience that he was a native son of their city, he drew on his birthright to draw their attention to the evils of drink and its purveyors, the nation's publicans. The sale of liquor, he claimed, must be curbed. The liquor traffic reeked 'with human misery, vice and squalor, destitution, crime and death'. For his share in that infamous trade, the publican deserved nothing less than retribution.[3]

Within a week of his Manchester address Lloyd George had delivered his maiden speech to Parliament.[4] It was a short response during a debate on a customs and excise duties bill during which he once again strongly condemned publicans and public houses. By uniting the cause of temperance with the disestablishment of the Welsh Church Lloyd George hoped to bring together both Welsh and English nonconformists in a pact against the Conservative opposition. Since the late nineteenth century, Conservatives had actively courted 'The Trade', as the alcohol interest was called. In time, a working-class Conservative constituency had been developed through an extensive network of more than 100,000 pubs and beer houses.[5] To counter this influence, Liberal spokesmen had consistently proposed a policy of local option, by which individual communities could decide whether or not to allow the sale of alcoholic beverages. But any remediable legislation for Wales or against the drink trade encountered heavy weather during parliaments of the late nineteenth century. The Anglican Church naturally opposed disestablishment. The dominant Conservative government was strongly supported by the drink trade.

Lloyd George's speeches as a fledgling MP, however, clearly indicated his intention not to be intimidated by any opposition. Determined to support Wales in Parliament whenever possible, he adopted a strategy of capturing Welsh topics as they emerged in the House of Commons in order to turn the debate to a greater Welsh advantage. An early opportunity came in November 1890 when the Conservative government introduced the Tithe Rent-Charge Recovery Bill. It had been brought forward twice before and each time withdrawn – a sign of its contentiousness. At issue was the objection of Welsh nonconformists to mandatory tithes collected by local Anglican vicars. The fact that the amount of tithe was arranged between vicars and landlords (often English and Anglican), and then levied upon tenant farmers (usually Welsh and nonconformist) made tithes doubly burdensome to the great majority of Welsh farmers. The Tithe Bill was in response to the Welsh tithe war of the late 1880s during which some Welsh farmers, after their goods had been distrained for refusing to pay tithes, rioted in protest. As we have seen, Anti-Tithe Leagues mushroomed. Welsh political leaders, Lloyd George not least among them, supported their demands for tithe reduction and security of tenure in speeches throughout the country. This agitation was alarming to the Salisbury government: the prospect of a Welsh agricultural underclass rebelling against an alien landowning and religious elite was only too familiar from the Irish case.[6]

By making landowners responsible for paying tithes, rather than farmers, the proposed Tithe Bill removed Anglican vicars as the targets of nonconformist hostility. Landowners could now incorporate tithes and rents into a single charge to farmers. But this did not satisfy Welsh MPs, most of whom opposed the imposition of tithes on principle. Debates on the bill provided a unique opportunity for the Welsh MPs to set out the historic grievances of their principality. Lloyd George and other members of the Welsh parliamentary party attached amendment after amendment to the bill as a delaying tactic. For nearly three weeks, the House of

Commons was thus taken up by Welsh speakers and Welsh issues.[7] As Lloyd George put it in a speech to the House: 'Our grievance is this: that tithes, which is national property, is at the present moment applied to the purposes of a sect which is the least influential and does the least work of all the religious denominations in Wales.'[8]

The Tithe Bill received the Royal Assent in March 1891 – not a cause lost as far as the Welsh were concerned: they had made their case. A few months later, in July, another opportunity arose for a Welsh demonstration. The government introduced the Church Discipline Bill, designed to facilitate the removal of Anglican clerics for minor criminal activity or immoral acts. S.T. Evans, MP for Mid-Glamorgan, immediately moved an amendment declaring that the state had no business in interfering in the affairs of any religious body. He claimed that the only remedy for clerical misbehaviour was disestablishment. After Evans's amendment failed, Lloyd George followed with one of his own – that the debate be postponed for three months. A brief row followed.[9] When the bill was reintroduced in April 1892, Lloyd George used the occasion not to address the bill itself, but to continue the broader line of attack by Welsh MPs against the Church in Wales. He moved an amendment which stated 'that it is no part of the functions of the State to attend to matters of Spiritual Discipline'.[10] When the bill was referred to the Standing Committee on Law for further discussion and report, Lloyd George and his Welsh cohorts continued their tactics of obstruction and amendment as they had during the debates on the Tithe Bill. Ultimately they failed, as they knew they would: Royal Assent was granted on 27 June 1892. But, as in the case of the Tithe Bill, their greater aim of advertising Welsh grievances was successful.

Lloyd George was intent upon making a name for himself as a spokesman for the cause of Wales not only in Parliament. He was also carefully cultivating the electorate within Wales itself. For this purpose, he relied upon the newspaper press. Even before he became a member of parliament, he understood that speeches alone were insufficient tools for his ambitions. As a young politico, he began to explore the possibility of using the newspaper press to greater advantage. As early as 1888, he was the animating force behind the establishment of a weekly newspaper, *Yr Udgon Rhydid (The Trumpet of Freedom)*. Financed by local supporters, *The Trumpet* often carried editorials and articles by Lloyd George on a variety of topics. The newspaper also served as a vehicle for his personal advancement. For example, when he was elected to the Standing Committee on Law in the House of Commons in 1891, he wrote his brother that it was 'a distinct mark of *substantial* progress made in the esteem of the House'. He then asked William to get the news into *The Trumpet*.[11] This newspaper did not pivot only around the career of Lloyd George. It also advocated radical programmes in general, such as the welfare of the working class and the raising of the Welsh national consciousness. More specifically, it supported an eight hour working day; old age pensions; higher tax rates for the wealthy; fair rents; and disestablishment of the Anglican Church in Wales.

The Trumpet was to prove an ideal vehicle for Lloyd George's candidacy in the general election of 1892, called immediately after the passage of the Church Discipline Bill in June of that year. During the ensuing election campaign, clear differences between the two parties emerged. Liberals had revived somewhat since the election of 1886 and promised – on the basis of their Newcastle Programme of 1891 – a broad reform programme, embracing both Welsh and Scots disestablishment, Irish Home Rule, land reform and local option (the power of local veto over the sale of drink). This platform represented an increasing radicalism within the Liberal Party since the previous election in 1886 and signalled a reinvigorated determination to settle the Irish question. The Conservatives, on the other hand, had been losing by-elections at a steady clip. They lacked a united position and were additionally at a disadvantage because of an economic downturn. The result was a narrow victory for the Liberals with Gladstone forming his fourth and final administration. Liberals won 273 seats and the Conservatives at a near tie with 268. But both sides had also won ancillary seats with 81 Irish Nationalists supporting Gladstone's government on the strength of his Home Rule agenda and 48 Liberal Unionists supporting the Conservative Party. This gave Liberals a margin of only 40, but it was substantial enough to encourage Lloyd George and the band of Welshmen to believe that with Gladstone now in office they had an excellent chance of obtaining disestablishment of the Church in Wales.

Lloyd George himself had won another narrow victory in the Caernarfon Boroughs, this time over Sir John Puleston. It was a notable win. Puleston, unlike Ellis Nanney, was a seasoned politician, a member of an old Welsh family and had substantial parliamentary experience with 20 years in the House of Commons. The greatest advantage for Lloyd George during the election was his performance of the previous two years in supporting wholeheartedly, both in Parliament and out, the legitimacy of Welsh political and religious aspirations. In this he spoke for an overwhelming majority sentiment in Wales. Lloyd George had also improved his chances of re-election by revitalizing the Liberal Party organization within his constituency, removing ineffective Party officials and replacing them with younger and more energetic supporters.[12] The election turnout of slightly more than 4,000 votes resulted in a victory of almost 200 for Lloyd George. In Wales overall, Liberals captured 31 of the 34 Welsh seats.

In the new Liberal government, it would seem that Wales would now find a sympathetic response for its aspirations. As Morgan has pointed out, the election of 1892 was the high tide of a united vision for Welsh nationality. Under Prime Minister Gladstone, who personally favoured in principle disestablishment and some form of Home Rule, the realization of a Liberal Welsh national state seemed imminent. Equally important was the fact that Gladstone's government, with only a 40-vote majority, needed the Welsh band of 31 MPs in any future tight political spot. Bargains could be made. The new Liberal government realized this full well, and the appointment of Tom Ellis as Junior Lord of the Treasury and Deputy Whip acknowledged the importance of the Welsh contribution to the new government.[13] There were other straws in the wind. Arthur Acland was appointed Vice-President of the Council, an office that at that time was responsible for public education.[14] H.H. Asquith, the new Home Secretary, was in favour of Welsh disestablishment. In addition, Stuart Rendel, although English and a wealthy high Anglican, was MP for Montgomeryshire and a supporter of Welsh causes as well as an intimate of Gladstone.[15]

Indeed, Rendel has been seen as the key to Welsh aspirations during the life of the Gladstone ministry.[16] He took it upon himself to bridge any potential difficulties that could develop between a vocal, volatile, and united Welsh body of MPs and the Liberal leadership. For their part the Welsh party, recognizing Rendel's importance, selected him as their chairman. They also simultaneously decided to bring immediate pressure upon the government. Meeting together in conclave, they requested the government to emphasize disestablishment in the Queen's speech that opened Parliament. Clearly, the Welsh were eager for a quick response from the Liberal leadership to their demands. Lloyd George himself had already sent a shot across the bow of the Prime Minister shortly after the election returns were known. In a speech at Conway on 22 July, he warned that the newly-elected Welsh members would not support a Liberal Ministry no matter 'how illustrious the Minister who leads it' unless that Ministry granted Wales the reforms it had long sought.[17]

These admonitions had some effect. On 12 September 1892, Gladstone paid a visit to Wales. Arriving by train at Caernarfon station, he was brought by carriage to Castle Square where Lloyd George met him with a rousing speech. Gladstone was also given a petition from the Caernarfon Liberal Association, praying for religious equality. The Prime Minister spoke in his ineffable style, seeming to promise something while obfuscating much. Addressing specifically the issue of Welsh disestablishment, he declared that 'a reasonable patience' would be necessary for the enactment of that goal. The following day, Gladstone addressed an outdoor meeting gathered on the south slope of Snowdonia. But there, too, Gladstone was not specific in his remarks, striking a cautious note about Welsh aspirations: 'we shall travel towards them as fast and as zealously and earnestly as we can'.[18]

Had Lloyd George or any of the more forward Welsh nationalists been privy to Gladstone's private correspondence in the latter months of 1892, they would have had cause for worry. Tom Ellis, active since the general election in urging Rendel to convey to the Prime Minister the urgency of Welsh concerns, was strongly rebuffed. Only a few days before his trip to Caernarfon, Gladstone expressed to Rendel his reservations about Ellis's inappropriate importunities. 'I had though[t] Mr E. an intelligent man', Gladstone wrote to Rendel of Ellis, 'but this account puzzles me. Does he think Welsh Disestablishment can be carried at the same time with a Home Rule Bill & other claims?'[19] For Gladstone, Irish Home Rule was the premier issue of his administration. As he put it in a communication to his Cabinet in late October 1892, it was 'bad policy' to introduce bills unless there was a reasonable hope of their success. To name them in the Queen's Speech without a fair hope of progress could discredit the government.[20]

Ensuing signs of hesitation from Gladstone were unsettling to the Welsh. Lloyd George in particular took a dim view of the Prime Minister's delaying tactics, as he indicated in a letter to his Uncle Lloyd. 'I fear something of a rumpus with Gladstone', he wrote. 'He is a frightened old fool in some respects.'[21] When the Queen's Speech in January 1893 did not mention Welsh disestablishment, a greater sense of unease stirred among Welsh MPs. Perhaps their dissatisfaction prompted H.H. Asquith, Gladstone's Home Secretary, to introduce early in the session a Welsh Church Suspensory Bill designed to suspend (prohibit) compensation for any new Church livings created thereafter. This was a modest first step in anticipation of a more thoroughgoing measure of disestablishment, and presumably met Gladstone's criteria for a workable bill for the session.[22] But as the session dragged on, more and more time was taken up by the debates on Irish Home Rule, leaving little time remaining for other legislation. Lloyd George was active in various interventions on behalf of Wales during these lengthy debates. He spoke often during the meetings of the Welsh caucus, urging action. He drafted two letters to Gladstone requesting priority for Welsh disestablishment. But it was all of no avail. On 1 September, the Suspensory Bill was withdrawn and there were no further attempts at Welsh disestablishment for the session. On the same day, the Irish Home Rule Bill passed its third reading after 82 parliamentary sittings. It was sent immediately to the House of Lords, where on 8 September 1893, it was overwhelmingly defeated (419:41) after a brief discussion.

The parliamentary recess during the autumn and winter of 1893–94 offered a period of calm and provided another opportunity for the government, after the resounding failure of Home Rule in the Lords, to answer Welsh aspirations. Indeed, the government began to prepare a Welsh Disestablishment and Disendowment Bill, this time skipping the intermediate step of a Suspensory Bill. But on 3 March 1894 a potential bombshell for Wales and for the country as a whole threatened to change drastically the political landscape. On that day, Gladstone resigned, his declining health and growing disagreements within his Cabinet at last striking him down. The Whiggish Liberal imperialist, Lord Rosebery, succeeded him. What this would mean to the Welsh and to Lloyd George in the new parliamentary session was unclear. Lloyd George in fact was not unprepared for this news. Two weeks before the public announcement, he wrote to his brother that he had already received word from an unnamed source that 'the old man is likely to retire soon' and that the Cabinet was 'all at sixes and sevens'. 'I am afraid', he confessed to William, 'that we are going to be thrown over on the Disestablishment question! ... I am going to move at once'.[23] On the very day of Gladstone's resignation, Lloyd George promised William that he will 'try and extract terms out of the incoming Prime Minister on Welsh Disestablishment'.[24]

Matters began well for the Welsh programme. Within a fortnight of Gladstone's resignation, the Queen's Speech opening Parliament announced that disestablishment legislation would be brought forward. The new Leader of the House, W.V. Harcourt, pledged to a delegation of Welsh MPs (including Lloyd George) that Welsh disestablishment would be carried during the forthcoming session. But to the dismay and chagrin of the Welsh, Irish matters once again intruded. Denied a Home Rule Bill by the House of Lords, Irish Nationalists insisted that the new Liberal government enact the Evicted Tenants' Bill, which would facilitate compensation and reinstatement of tenants evicted since 1879. With the pressure of 80 Irish MPs and the security of the government at stake, Rosebery had little choice.[25]

The government announced that Welsh Disestablishment would once again be postponed.

The accumulation of indeterminate responses of the government to Welsh demands for disestablishment was beginning to have an effect beyond the confines of Parliament. At Gladstone's resignation, Stuart Rendel was raised to the peerage as Baron Rendel, elevating him to the House of Lords and causing a by-election in his constituency of Montgomeryshire. During the election campaign, Lloyd George was active in promoting the Liberal candidate, Arthur Humphreys-Owen, although doubtless with some reluctance: Owen was both an Anglican and a landowner.[26] The election results were a surprise. Lloyd George admitted that it was 'a narrow shave'.[27] Humphreys-Owen won, but the Liberal majority fell to only 225, a loss of 600 votes from the general election of 1892. Lloyd George drew the obvious lesson. Had he not campaigned, the Liberal would have lost. 'I was the man who carried the seat', he assured Margaret.[28] Shortly after the election, perhaps spurred by this warning of popular disapproval in Wales of the Liberal government,[29] Lloyd George and three other Welsh MPs declared that the Liberal leadership had broken faith with Wales. They informed Tom Ellis that they would no longer receive the Liberal Whip, in effect establishing themselves as independent Members of Parliament. These rebels, 'the Four', immediately set out for Wales to gather support among their constituents.[30]

Perhaps the general outrage in Wales against its English Liberal allies had an effect. In any case, Asquith introduced the first ever Welsh Disestablishment Bill on 26 April 1894. A sweeping bill, it withdrew ecclesiastical law from the 13 Welsh counties and removed Welsh Bishops from the House of Lords and from the Anglican Convocation. Disendowment provisions were even broader. Tithes, for example, would be vested in county councils thereafter: burial grounds and glebe lands would be under parish councils. The proceeds would be devoted to charitable works, hospitals, schools and the like. By the standards of the day, it was a radical measure.[31] Not surprisingly, considerable opposition to the proposed bill emerged from threatened interests. Anglicans of every stripe, especially the episcopate, denounced it. Conservatives took advantage of the increasing weakness of the government to challenge the bill. They argued that Wales had no separate national existence from England and thus could not be subject to separate legislation. The government majority, which had already reduced by a series of poor by-election results, found it difficult to sustain the bill. It was withdrawn in July 1894.

As the disestablishment struggle was coming to a full boil, Lloyd George's thinking was evolving. He was becoming convinced that the stuttering responses of the Liberal Party would never accommodate Welsh demands. He now put his mind to cultivating grass-roots support for a broader goal than disestablishment – the creation of a Welsh National Party that would follow the Irish example and agitate for Home Rule. An instrument was at hand. The Cymru Fydd (Young Wales) movement, an organization originally established in the 1880s to promote Welsh culture and language, had caught Lloyd George's eye as early as 1891. (Tom Ellis had also been attracted to Cymru Fydd before he joined the Liberal government in 1890.) There were branches of the organization throughout Wales. From Lloyd George's point of view, it would be merely a matter of adding a political plank to the existing aims of Cymru Fydd. He began cultivating public opinion during the summer of 1894. He approached young radical journalists throughout Wales and paid particular attention to the major daily Liberal newspaper in Wales, the *South Wales Daily News*, by scheduling conferences with the Editor and proprietor. He spoke at a huge meeting in Aberdare in June 1894 outlining his plans. The signs were favourable. Lloyd George reported to his wife: 'They go in for a Welsh party. We are winning hands down.'[32] The founding meeting of the revamped Cymru Fydd – now called the Cymru Fydd League – was held two months later. Very quickly branch offices spread throughout Wales, especially in the north. By January 1895, a secretary and general organizer of Cymru Fydd League had been selected (with a £200 annual salary). As Morgan observes, the impetus for the movement came 'almost entirely' from Lloyd George.[33]

Perhaps the new movement for Welsh Home Rule prompted the government to try again with their ill-fated Welsh Disestablishment Bill. In any case, Asquith brought forward a new bill on 25 February 1895 with essentially the same provisions as the old. Conservative opponents were as active against this second bill as they were the first. For example, they proposed excluding from the bill certain border areas that contained a substantial English population. Some doubts about the bill were even expressed by Gladstone, who still retained his seat in the House of Commons. He apparently thought some of the disendowment provisions too severe, especially any attempt to secularize cathedrals. But the most exasperating opposition came from a surprising source. Urged on by the Cymru Fydd League, Welsh MPs began to obstruct the proposed legislation, using the discussion on the bill to advance the ideas of a broader aim – Welsh separatism. Lloyd George, in particular, advocated the establishment of a national council representing Wales as a whole which would manage funds generated by the disendowment of church properties. Already buffeted by numerous close votes on successive parliamentary questions; adverse by-election results; a dogged Conservative opposition; and now blindsided by a somewhat cynical Welsh obstructionism, the government resigned on 21 June 1895 when defeated in a snap vote.[34]

The general election in July was a massive defeat for the Liberals, bringing in the Conservatives, led by Prime Minister Lord Salisbury, who was to lead a strong imperial and Conservative government for the next several years. In fact, it was to be the longest Conservative ministry up to that time, counting from Sir Robert Peel's short ministry of 1834–35. The demoralized Liberals could scarcely mount an effective campaign: 92 English constituencies failed to produce a Liberal candidate. Conservative candidates, raising the imperial flag and promising a strong and active government, swept the field. The new House of Commons had 341 Conservatives plus 70 Liberal Unionists for a total of 411. Only 177 Liberals opposed them. The Irish nationalists held 82 seats.[35]

In Wales, too, there was a loss of Liberal representation as the Conservative tide rose. The Conservative vote rose by 16,000, gaining them six seats from the Liberals, winning a total of nine. The remaining 25 seats were Liberal; but it was nevertheless a shock to the political landscape in Wales, calling into question the relationship between a Welsh national movement and the dominant Liberal Party. Lloyd George himself had left nothing to chance as he campaigned vigorously during the election. As news of Liberal losses in England reached him, he redoubled his efforts. In one instance, he summoned his canvassers in Bangor, warning them that there was a potential electoral disaster in the making and that they were not working hard enough: the entire outcome of his election, he said, depended upon them.[36] As it happened, he won handily enough, defeating the persistent Ellis Nanney by 194 votes, the same number as the general election three years earlier.

Shortly after the election, the House of Commons was again in session. Soon Lloyd George was 'busily obstructing' the Commons procedure by bringing forward a number of Welsh grievances, such as the failure of the Public Record Office to handle properly Welsh historical documents and the lack of Welsh speakers at the PRO.[37]

His aim was obviously to keep Wales before the public eye not only in the principality itself, but also to serve notice to the new Conservative government that he would continue his pursuit of Welsh interests under their ministry as much as he had under the Liberals. Most of his political activity, however, was outside Westminster where he continued to pursue Welsh unity under the aegis of the Cymru Fydd League. If he could complete his task of establishing a branch of the League in every Welsh village and town, he would have an organization in place for consolidating his Home Rule scheme. With much of north Wales already in hand, he began campaigning throughout south Wales in November 1895.

But Lloyd George soon encountered difficulties. Not everyone was fond of the Welsh upstart. For some, he was becoming too brash, too aggressively forward. Others may have been jealous of his quick rise through the political ranks. Some Liberal Welshmen were resentful for his part in the demise of the Rosebery ministry. And some suspected that he was using the League for his own political purposes rather than as a vehicle for greater Welsh aspirations. The greatest threat to the League's success was the opposition that he encountered in south Wales. This was a very different part of Wales from the rural Lloyd George country to the north. In the south, coal was king: industrial production, manufacturing and commerce were not far behind. Indeed, from 1880–1914, only the Ruhr in Germany and the industrial areas of the eastern seaboard of the United States rivalled south Wales in coal mining.[38] Coal miners were already well organized as an economic group: trade union spirit was stronger than nationalist sentiment. Among the prominent leaders was William Abraham (widely known as Mabon), a miner himself, who had been president of the Cambrian Miners' Federation since 1889: he was, in addition, MP for the Rhondda division of Glamorganshire since 1885. Most importantly for Lloyd George, he was a Liberal loyalist who opposed the rebellious notions of his junior colleague in the House of Commons.[39]

An even more formidable adversary to Lloyd George's ambitions in south Wales was D.A. Thomas, whose father had risen from humble circumstances as a grocer to substantial success as a mining speculator. The young Thomas was sent to school at Clifton and, rounding out his privileged status, went up to Caius College, Cambridge, where he earned a second in mathematics. He returned eventually to England in 1887 to operate his father's colliery. A year later he entered Parliament after winning a by-election at Merthyr. He soon proved an ardent nationalist, one of the young Welsh MPs who were strong supporters of Tom Ellis. By 1892, Thomas and Lloyd George were acting in the common cause of Welsh nationalism in opposition to the Gladstonian delaying tactics. Thomas became one of the small band of 'the Four' which included Lloyd George. Thus it would seem natural that Thomas, who had become President of the South Wales Federation, would welcome Lloyd George's initiative in attempting to organize the Cymru Fydd League in south Wales. But this was not the case. Thomas had come to realize the implications of the substantial economic differences that lay between the most populous and wealthiest (and southernmost) counties of Glamorgan and Monmouth and the rest of Wales.

In spite of encouraging letters Lloyd George sent home to his wife during the autumn of 1895, the climax of the League campaign had not yet been reached in south Wales.[40] The crucial confrontation occurred on 16 January 1896 when the South Wales Liberal Federation met at Newport, Monmouthshire. Soliciting what supporters he could, Lloyd George hoped to have a majority of delegates voting for union between the Federation and the Cymru Fydd League. But the meeting proved otherwise. Thomas had packed the meeting with his own supporters, who shouted Lloyd George down when the vote was brought forward. The motion was lost: Lloyd George had been out-muscled. It was the first significant public defeat in his political life. His first response was 'to fight it out'.[41] But the ideal of a united Wales was finished. Disestablishment, too, largely faded from view. Apathy and disenchantment in the Welsh Parliamentary Party for the next several years sapped initiative and energy.[42]

Lloyd George, however – as would prove true of every political set back and personal disappointment in his early years – rebounded quickly. Undeterred by the failure of his attempts at organizing on a local level, he shifted his focus from local to national politics by launching sustained attacks on the Conservative government. He criticized the government for its refusal to develop Pembroke dock; objected to the composition of a Petroleum Committee because it had no Welsh members; hampered a bill to erect new government offices; complained about the late delivery of mail to South Caernarfonshire; urged the Chancellor of the Exchequer to establish an Inland Revenue Office in Wales; opposed the sum of £100,000 for the upkeep of royal palaces and parks; and challenged the details of moneys allocated to the judiciary.[43] In retrospect, the collapse of the Cymru Fydd League freed him from the more insular concerns of Wales as he moved more strenuously to address national affairs.[44]

Some of the most contentious debates in the House of Commons in which Lloyd George was actively involved from the mid 1890s onward centred upon the Agricultural Land Rating Bill, introduced in April 1896. The bill was designed to relieve hard-pressed British agricultural interests (excluding Ireland), which had suffered widely during a serious agricultural depression in the 1880s and 1890s. The bill provided for a reduction of up to 50 per cent in the rates for all land under cultivation. Landlords, whose rents had fallen as a consequence of the agricultural depression, would receive a boon in these proposed subsidies. The idea was of course not merely to relieve landlords; the bill was also designed to encourage landlords to keep land in cultivation and in so doing provide employment for tenants and farm labourers. Lloyd George saw it differently: he, as well as every other politician, was familiar with agricultural distress. But he attacked the bill not as a solution to the problem, but rather as a smash and grab raid on the public purse by entrenched aristocratic landlords. The proposed bill, he claimed, was a shocking example of a conflict of interest: Conservative ministers would benefit substantially from the bill – as much as £67,000 overall, he claimed. Prime minister Salisbury would receive £2,000, Balfour £1,450, and the Duke of Devonshire (a Liberal Unionist serving in the ministry as Lord President of the Council), a sizeable £10,000 from reduced rates on agricultural lands. In short, the bill was 'for the landlords'. The proposed rate reduction would profit them directly: neither the farmer nor the tenant would benefit. Why should landlords, already wealthy, benefit at the expense of others? Other interests were as worthy. He cited the tin-plate industry as an example. There one would find 'misery and actual hunger'; but 'where was the Bill for their relief?'[45] As he put it during the committee stage of the bill in Parliament, the purpose of the bill was to allow 'one class' to benefit 'at the expense of the rest of the community'.[46]

During debates on the bill, Lloyd George demonstrated an extensive knowledge of agricultural practices in the country as a whole. In addition, he also showed a through mastery of the rules of the House in his attempt to amend the bill.[47] Indeed, Lloyd George's parliamentary performance on the Agricultural Ratings Bill had captured wide and favourable attention well beyond the confines of the House of Commons. Even among Conservative-leaning newspapers, there were grudging compliments. The *Daily Mail* declared that Lloyd George was 'far and away the most nimble, bold and hard-working young Radical in the House at the present time'. Particularly notable were his effective parliamentary criticisms of the Conservative government: 'he goes in for harassing the Government all round'. Moreover, in an admiring aside, the *Daily Mail* reported that Lloyd George 'speaks on all manner of questions almost entirely without the aid of notes'.[48]

As Liberals and Conservatives debated the Ratings Bill during the spring of 1896, Welsh MPs were active in attempting to alter the bill in various ways, especially in granting relief to the tenants by creating a land court or advancing state loans to those in need. Lloyd George himself attempted to have Wales removed entirely from the operation of the bill. When these measures failed, Lloyd George again resorted to obstruction. Proposing amendment after amendment, raising objections and suggesting alternative proposals, he peppered his opponents with a steady stream of rhetoric, criticism and raillery. His obstructive tactics brought about an official censure on 22 May from the Speaker of the House who 'named' him and then suspended him for a week for remaining in his seat during a division on the bill.[49] Ultimately, the bill received its third reading, but not until Lloyd George had exhausted his delaying tactics. He pronounced himself pleased with his plan – to drive the government 'into a corner as regards time'.[50]

During the parliamentary session of 1896, Lloyd George was active on another contentious legislative initiative. The Education Bill of 1896, which proposed to increase state aid to sectarian education, raised a fundamental issue: to what degree should state funds be provided to voluntary or sectarian schools. If state money were used to maintain schools, should not also the kind and quality of religious instruction in these schools be regulated? And should such schools require a religious test of their teachers? The nonconformist answers to these two questions were respectively yes and no. In other words, nonconformists would gladly accept state support, but would be loath to use state assistance to support Roman Catholic or Anglican schools. The bill of 1896, however, proposed to do precisely that. Not only Welsh nonconformist MPs but their English cousins too were outraged. Unhappily for nonconformist Liberals of both nationalities, their Irish allies abandoned them to vote for the bill so that the two million Catholics in England would receive the educational benefits of state support.[51] But there was enough of an outcry to force withdrawal of the bill.

Lloyd George's considerable energy was never limited to debates in the House of Commons during his apprentice years. He was always alive to opportunities outside Parliament to keep his name before the public and to strengthen his growing reputation as a champion of the disadvantaged. Thus he followed with interest an emerging labour relations crisis in the mid-1890s at Bethesda, Caernarfonshire, near his own Welsh constituency. Quarrymen at the enormous slate quarries owned by Lord Penrhyn were at odds not only over wages, but also Penrhyn's refusal to recognize the North Wales Quarrymen's Union (NWQU).[52] At that time the Welsh slate industry employed 16,000 men, and Wales had the largest slate quarries in the world. Penrhyn himself had a workforce of more than 3,500. He claimed that since the quarries were on his property, he had the right to deal with them as he chose. In fact, Penrhyn had a strong case: there was little regulatory power that could be brought to bear. Nevertheless, with characteristic flair, Lloyd George began a critical campaign against Penrhyn. Throughout 1897, he advocated the quarrymen's cause at local meetings, advancing 'the right of the people to the land, to the mountains, and to the resources of the earth'.[53] He damned Penrhyn as a representative of 'the forces of oppression and tyranny'.[54] In Parliament, too, he condemned Penrhyn. The quarrymen, he informed the House, 'were fighting … for the principle of conciliation in labour disputes'. But Penrhyn, who 'bullied these men', was attempting to 'intimidate' them 'into submission'.[55] By the end of 1897, the controversy lessened. Penrhyn bowed to public pressure and relented to a slight extent, accepting the right of his workmen to at least present grievances. But he refused to go beyond that, denying any official status to the NWQU.[56]

Although Lloyd George paid special attention to Welsh issues, it is also clear that throughout the 1890s – the first decade of his parliamentary career – he was expanding his political constituency in England as well. Speaking, writing and organizing in both Wales and England, he raised his name recognition by engaging nearly every important issue of the day, including education, land reform and the Irish question. Above all, he energetically advocated the necessity for change and improvement in the life of the nation. It is true that there were failures, perhaps most notably the Cymru Fydd League. Even that failure, however, demonstrated Lloyd George's unusual capacity for expanding his political and social message and establishing a reputation far beyond his own constituency.

If it may be said that Lloyd George was finding his political footing in these early years and enhancing his reputation as a promising politician, it is also true that he was demonstrating some less favourable personal characteristics. During the 1880s and 1890s his interactions with his younger brother William are particularly revealing as an indicator of his later behaviour towards others. Even before he joined his older brother in 1887 to establish the solicitor's firm of Lloyd George and George, William was obliged to help out at his brother's single-handed office in Criccieth. As casework grew, Lloyd George made increasing demands on his brother, even during the time of William's preparations for his own law exams. Once joined with David, William was clearly the junior partner, sometimes serving as a secretary taking shorthand notes of legal proceedings. At other times William worked up the necessary papers for David's advocacy in a particular case. In addition, he managed the firm's accounts – not always easy given his brother's occasional importunate monetary demands. After Lloyd George had entered Parliament, the burden of the work of the firm fell almost entirely on William's shoulders. It is not too much to say that Lloyd George depended for his livelihood in the first ten years of his political career upon William and his North Wales firm.[57]

William was quite aware of Lloyd George's selfish importunities. Time and again, he confided his frustrations to his diary.[58] In August 1890, for example, William questioned David's lengthy stay in London, wondering why he 'doesn't come home now … in order to relieve me'. Making the best of it, he attributed David's absence to his 'sense of duty' to his parliamentary affairs.[59] In December of that year during the parliamentary Christmas recess, Lloyd George returned to Criccieth, but not to aid the overworked William at the firm's Porthmadog office. William was obviously miffed: 'I think this is a good deal too bad.'[60] The following year, also at a time of parliamentary recess, William cut short his own holiday so that David could take the waters at Llandrindod Wells. William was again critical: 'I think it is a little selfish of him to run away in this style as if he were disgusted with the whole business and wanted to throw it off his hands as soon as he could.'[61] A week earlier, Uncle Lloyd had complained about David's sloppy legal work as he went off on a case: 'D.Ll. G. left Brief behind him – all carelessness and mismanagement.'[62]

Certainly it is true that Lloyd George tended to rely heavily upon his brother, not only in their cooperative legal work but also from time to time on political matters as well. During his by-election campaign in 1890, for example, Lloyd George exhorted William to order up posters, to publicize forthcoming speeches and to advise him on canvassing the voters.[63] But it must be remembered that as Lloyd George's reputation widened throughout Wales and as his star rose in the parliamentary firmament, the legal practice benefited. In this sense, the brothers' talents complemented one another. It is also palpably obvious that in these days William admired his older brother. William also acted as a counterbalance to David's wilder schemes and served as sensible and sensitive local agent to David's standing in his constituency. Two notable examples, both of which could have seriously damaged David's reputation, bear this out.

Sometime in 1892, probably through his acquaintance with David Richards, a mining engineer from Harlech, Lloyd George became involved in a speculative gold mining venture called the Welsh Patagonian Gold Fields Syndicate Limited.[64] Richards had spent some time in the Welsh colony in the Argentine province of Patagonia, where he obtained a concession to mine gold. He contacted Lloyd George, presenting a glowing report of untapped riches which only needed capital to realize a fortune. Apart from the lure of substantial wealth from the mining enterprise itself, Lloyd George and George could additionally serve as the legal firm for the Syndicate, gaining additional income. Lloyd George, no doubt in his most persuasive manner, also brought several MPs on board. Tom Ellis, to lend respectability, was recruited as a witness to the document establishing the Syndicate. Capital was raised, shares issued, an office was opened, and as the scheme broadened, a group of French financiers were approached (who turned them down). William, as the voice of realism, had his doubts, however. To his diary in October 1892, he queried: 'what if the gold mine turns out to be a mere illusion of the Patagonian desert?'[65] This warning may have had some effect. The Syndicate sent out a mining surveyor to conduct an independent investigation on the prospects. His report was discouraging. Richards, the original enthusiast for the project, discovered that he had been misled: what little gold there was seemed unlikely to be worth the digging.

Lloyd George, his hopes dashed, wrote to his wife: 'Patagonia is, I fear, a failure. *Don't let uncle or anyone else* know a word.'[66] What his uncle would have said to such a speculative venture can only be guessed – perhaps he would have approved, as he usually did of his nephew's ventures. But to the wider public, such speculation would have raised more than eyebrows. Lloyd George's nonconformist supporters would have likely been uneasy. One can only imagine the delight of his political enemies. Lloyd George's subsequent actions, in what was to be a long-running saga, raised further doubts about his character and judgement. Within a few weeks of his discouraging letter of August 1893 to Margaret, however, another firm, the Andes Exploring Company of Bangor, offered to buy shares in the Syndicate. Word continued to get around and three months later, a group of stockbrokers in Dublin offered to buy shares.

Lloyd George was delighted. As he put it to Margaret: 'It means a present of £120 at the least for me, for it will keep the affair going for 18 months even if we get no further funds.'[67] It must be remembered that at this point there was still no substantial evidence of Patagonian gold. Perhaps the new infusion of funds prompted the flagging hopes of the Syndicate to keep quiet about the earlier reports. The stakes were certainly rising: by the spring of 1894, the nominal capital had increased to £50,000. In any case, the Syndicate, hoping for a more optimistic report, sent out another representative to the Argentine. In March 1894, the Syndicate dispatched W.J. Parry once again (he had made an earlier trip in the autumn of 1893) as agent and manager of the project. His earlier optimism cooling, Lloyd George was apprehensive about the prospects: 'May luck follow him this time. If it doesn't then we shall be at our wits end once more.'[68] As a prominent nonconformist and trained accountant, Parry was a good choice. Matters seemed stalled for several months, however. There is some evidence that only feeble attempts by Parry to work the mine with a handful of labourers failed. The project seemed to languish into the following year. Sometime in 1896 Lloyd George decided to take matters into his own hands and visit the Syndicate's property.

There is some mystery about this voyage. It was an extraordinary journey of many thousands of miles and what Lloyd George could accomplish upon his arrival is not entirely clear. It appears that he believed once again that the prospects in Patagonia had improved and that he wished to see them at first hand.[69] In any case, he and two companions sailed from Southampton on 21 August 1896 in an attempt, as Grigg puts it, to perform a miracle in the Argentine.[70] Once in Argentina, after a voyage of three weeks, the mystery deepened. Lloyd George, remaining largely in Buenos Aires, never visited the Syndicate's territory. He did, however, learn of 'a general scramble going on for our property'.[71] In short, claim jumpers had moved into the territory because it had not been properly worked. Perhaps this discouraged any further travelling during an already extended time away from home. After meeting some local politicos and taking in the sights, the travellers returned, arriving in London at the end of October, having accomplished nothing to rescue the Syndicate. It died a slow death, and was formally dissolved in 1907.

The entire episode was never made known to a wider public. The reasons are obvious. At the very least, Lloyd George would appear inept. Grigg is surely correct when he suggests that Lloyd George's political career could have been damaged if the facts were known. Lloyd George and the promoters of the Syndicate had been at least morally culpable in not revealing fully to its investors the negative reports on the unlikely prospects of finding gold. Poor management and a lack of direction compounded the difficulties. The dangers of speculative business ventures did not discourage Lloyd George, however. Within a year, he was tempted once again when he entered into negotiations to purchase a slate quarry in Caernarfonshire. A year following that he was drawn toward an involvement in an insurance business. Luckily, nothing came of either of these ventures.

Lloyd George's involvement in these speculative schemes may seem surprising and even irresponsible on the face of it. But his motive was clear enough at this stage of his career. He had no significant financial resources. He was only a fledgling lawyer with few clients at that time. Members of Parliament received no salary until 1911. He lacked generous benefactors. He was attempting to maintain a residence in both Wales and London. Election costs were high. So serious was the financial drain upon his meagre resources that he considered abandoning his political career. William, who actively maintained their partnered law firm in Wales, could occasionally offer assistance. In 1897, Lloyd George opened a solicitor's office in London. But these efforts were only barely enough to relieve Lloyd George's financial worries for many years.[72] Given his financial insecurity, it would not be surprising that the lure of turning a profitable trick continued to attract him.

Immediately upon his return from Argentina, Lloyd George discovered that his personal troubles were far from over. Early in October 1896, while he was still abroad, his brother William heard rumours that a Mrs Catherine Edwards, who lived near Mahtafarn in Montgomeryshire, had confessed to her husband that she had committed adultery with Lloyd George and the child she bore in August was his. That Mrs Edwards was a cousin of Margaret, Lloyd George's wife, and that Lloyd George himself had occasionally visited the Edwards home lent credence to the charge. Moreover, his reputation as a lively and amusing companion, especially with women; his many absences from home while attending Parliament or participating in political meetings; and his radical political opinions all told against him to some degree. William quickly sprang into action, sending a note to be delivered as soon as Lloyd George disembarked at Southampton. Lloyd George returned to Criccieth immediately upon receiving the message. Stoutly denying the allegation, Lloyd George promptly set about shoring up his defence, calling upon friends and supporters for advice, and especially relying upon William for specific legal counsel. Ultimately, Mrs Edwards retracted her statement and was divorced by her husband.

Yet a presumption of guilt at the time remained – both then and later among historians. Bentley Gilbert, although admitting his observations were 'pure speculation', suggests that when Lloyd George was travelling back and forth across Wales advocating the cause of the Cymru Fydd League, there were opportunities, as he slyly puts it, to visit Mrs Edwards 'for a moment's comfort'.[73] In his attempt to 'weigh the probabilities', Grigg gives the Edwards case a lengthy analysis. Included in his evidence is a previously unpublished letter from Mrs Edwards to Lloyd George postmarked 15 February 1894 which is, as Grigg rightly observes, 'flirtatious'. Admitting that the entire matter remains 'a puzzle to which no convincing solution can yet be offered', Grigg nevertheless – based largely on the aforementioned letter – concludes that Lloyd George did have a brief affair with Mrs Edwards.[74] Morgan will have none of this. Denouncing the 'obsessive inquiry' concerning the 'sexual proclivities' of Lloyd George, Morgan defends him as 'the complete politician' dedicated to public service, 'not to private lust'. The evidence brought forward (here he names Grigg specifically) is 'inconclusive'. True enough, Lloyd George 'was readily attracted to pretty women', just as many men, even Members of Parliament, often were. But the evidence suggests, for Morgan at least, that Lloyd George 'was a faithful, and in some ways devoted' husband.[75] In the most recent account of the Edwards affair, Hague tends to agree with Morgan. She thinks there 'is no definite answer' as to whether or not there was a relationship between Lloyd George and Mrs Edwards. Hague does believe, however, that 'most likely ... there was a flirtation'.[76]

Far less scandalous – but no less remarkable and more revealing than his putative sexual affairs – were the quirks of Lloyd George's personality as revealed in his letters, especially to members of his family. Most of the content of Lloyd George's letters, as Morgan accurately notes, reveals his political views and tactics.[77] His contempt for traditional elites, whether secular or religious; his involvement and overtures to the newspaper press; his eagerness and ability to marshal public opinion and to manage popular campaigns are all evident. But the unintentional revelations are most striking. In letters to his wife, his uncle and his brother William, he brags, he boasts, he seeks approval. This is particularly noticeable once he became a Member of Parliament. After his London speech before the Liberation Society in May 1890, he lost no time in congratulating himself. To Margaret he wrote: 'I got on beyond my highest expectations.' Moreover, he reported, he had 'roused the audience to such a pitch of enthusiasm that they would hardly allow me to proceed & when I left they rose to their feet & flourished their hats'.[78] His speech the following month at Manchester Free Trade Hall brought another boastful letter to Margaret. 'Your old Dei scored the greatest success of his life', he wrote. He was cheered immediately when he rose to speak; and throughout his speech, there were 'long continued cheers'. When he sat down, the audience 'sprang up as one man & flung hats, handkerchiefs, sticks, hands – anything they could get hold of'. He was 'overwhelmed with congratulation'.[79] Ten days later, he gave his maiden speech in the House of Commons. 'There is no doubt', he assured Margaret, 'I scored a success & a great one'.[80] At the same time, he wrote similarly to William and his Uncle Lloyd. To the latter, he wrote: 'There is hardly a Liberal London or even provincial newspaper which does not say something complimentary about it.' In fact, he writes rather breathlessly, 'I was overwhelmed with congratulations'.[81] Two days later afterwards, he asks Margaret if Uncle Lloyd had seen the complimentary remarks on his speech in the *Pall Mall Gazette*. 'I've had more compliments today', he concludes.[82]

In the following parliamentary session Lloyd George, as we know, was active against the Tithe Bill. After he had spoken, he wrote to Margaret that he had 'scored a great success'.[83] A fortnight later, he wanted to make sure that his uncle was informed of his fight against the bill. 'Last Saturday's Speaker', he wrote, 'refers to me "as a promising young Celtic orator". Now that is rather flattering isn't it?'[84] Throughout the summer of 1891, he was engaged in parliamentary manoeuvres against the Education Bill. As he reported it, he and two other Welsh MPs fought the government into the early morning hours ('we kept them dancing'). At half past two, he raised a discussion on voting money to Church schools. Although they were beaten, Lloyd George was exultant because they had by their obstruction 'prevented the Clergy Discipline Bill coming on'.[85] Once the 1891 parliamentary session was prorogued on 5 August, Lloyd George toured the countryside speaking against the Conservative majority. It was, as Lloyd George recounted it, a personal triumph for him. At a meeting in far distant Wick, for example, he reported that he had 'got on magnificently'.[86] When he was interrupted at Wick, he 'danced' upon the 'carcase' of his opponent, 'to the unbound joy' of his Highland supporters.[87] Several months later, he was again reporting from the House of Commons during the new parliamentary session of 1892. He wrote to Margaret that he had never spoken so well as during the recent debate on the Church Discipline Bill. Not only was he was congratulated by Gladstone himself, but also 'on all hands even by opponents'.[88] The summer's election of 1892 found Lloyd George canvassing throughout Caernarfonshire. In the early hours of one campaign day, he took time to tell Uncle

Lloyd that at Conwy, he 'never spoke better'.[89] When the elections brought in the Liberals under Gladstone, Lloyd George's well-disposed opinions of himself in his letters home did not cease. Prior to the opening of the parliamentary session of 1893, he reported 'an *immense* success' of a meeting in Cardiff. There was, he wrote, a 'splendid reception' when he began to speak: 'all the audience rose & cheered'. When he sat down, 'they rose again & cheered frantically'. A leading article in the *South Wales Daily News* was 'highly eulogistic'.[90]

Lloyd George's fulsome letters of self-praise continued throughout the 1890s. He reported numerous 'mag – nificent [sic] meetings'. At one meeting, he 'never spoke better' in his life: people 'were completely carried away'. In another instance, he 'saved the meeting'. In yet another, he effectively 'sat upon' an opponent. Others he judged 'a smashing triumph'. Or, a common refrain, he declared that during one meeting, he 'made the best speech' he 'ever made' in his life. Similar letters he wrote about his parliamentary speeches. In February 1896, even with the Conservatives now in power, he was 'repeatedly cheered' and received a good report in *The Times*. He had triumphed 'by sheer force of will & clear emphatic speaking'. He urged Margaret to be sure to tell Uncle Lloyd 'all about it'. He claimed equal success in June of that year when he 'completely cornered the Government' in giving 'one of the most successful speeches' he had 'yet made in the House'.[91] How often these remarks were overblown is difficult to say. Certainly on at least one occasion in early 1898, when he wrote William of his 'big hit' during a parliamentary debate over the establishment of an Irish university – a debate which he claimed had advanced him 'most in estimation of Parliament' – it was a clear exaggeration.[92]

To ensure a steady stream of compliments and support from his family, Lloyd George demanded a frequent and lengthy correspondence.[93] An early example occurs within a few months of taking his seat in the House of Commons. In early July 1890, not long after his maiden speech, he praised Margaret – 'my faithful little Maggie' – for her letter; but he also asked her to tell William and Uncle Lloyd that he would be 'very disappointed' unless he received soon 'a long letter from each of them'.[94] Within a few weeks, his tone to Margaret had changed: 'I shall expect a long letter from you tomorrow.'[95] By the end of the year, he became more explicit: 'You don't repay me always for my long letters. When I see two sheets written I am satisfied but I feel disappointed when there is only one sheet.'[96] The following month, the tone was wheedling. 'Be a good girl tomorrow. Don't go to Chapel too often & write me a stunning long letter to make up for tomorrow's gloomy vacuum.'[97] Ten days later, there was a note of comparison: 'Your letters are much shorter than mine.'[98] He was also insistent on daily letters. As he wrote in August 1892: 'Your Friday's letter did turn up late on Saturday night but how came you not to write me yesterday?'[99]

Lloyd George was additionally demanding in requests for materials to be sent to him from home. Forgotten state papers, newspapers, books and articles of clothing are examples. Collars, coats, shirts and a shaving brush were all personal articles he requested from Wales. There was at times a slightly patronizing air: 'I want you to send me *per return*', he wrote in early 1892, 'Rogets *Thesaurus* – you know the thick brown book I have by my side always in preparing speeches. It is a kind of dictionary'.[100] But he was not always gracious when Margaret responded: 'The parcel you sent me this morning compensates for the shortness of your Thursday's epistle.'[101] On occasion, Lloyd George blamed William and Uncle Lloyd through Margaret if items were not sent. 'What a mean and shabby lot you all are', he wrote in late 1892. 'You know how I like to see the local papers when I am from home & yet you do not send me as much as one of them.' Of course, he continued, he did not expect them to read the papers, 'least of all when any speech of mine is likely to appear in them', but he hoped that they would 'take the little care of forwarding them on to me'.[102] Damning by faint praise characterized at least one letter in 1893. 'What a fairly long & thoroughly interesting letter I received from you this morning. Send me more of the same kind & not the short perfunctory ones you are too fond of sending.'[103] Lloyd George's trips abroad – whether for pleasure or business – seemed to heighten his demands. On a holiday in Switzerland in August 1894, for example, he wrote to Margaret that he was 'very disappointed' in not receiving on arrival at his hotel a letter from her, William, or Uncle Lloyd. 'I have just sent to the Poste Restante & there is nothing there. How is that?'[104] During a trip to Canada in 1899, he instructed Margaret to write 'every Tuesday & Friday & as often in between as you possibly can'.[105] The following day, perhaps thinking that he had been too vague about the timing of letters he expected, he sent Margaret a detailed schedule with dates of letters to be sent.[106]

What can be made of this consistent pattern of boastful behaviour and expectations of familial acclaim? Morgan observes that there was not only an element of self-promotion but also of ambition and vanity revealed in these letters.[107] Grigg has identified Lloyd George's 'love of approbation'.[108] Stephen Koss has observed that Lloyd George 'was obsessed with the cultivation of his image'.[109] Perhaps it was simply the boyish nature of a vital young man who found himself doing well in his chosen political profession, and who wished to share his success with his family. Perhaps it was a way of indicating his gratitude for the sacrifices that his family had made and was continuing to make for his success. But family encouragement could be a double-edged sword. It seems that over-praising by his Uncle Lloyd and possibly by his mother as well may have inculcated in the young Lloyd George a continual need for assurance, as we have noted in Chapter 1.[110] Their tendency to indulge, even to pamper, may have created a sense of entitlement which continued throughout his adult life. This could of course sustain him in troubled times. When unchecked, however, Lloyd George's demands could result in unrealistic expectations from friends, family, and political acquaintances.[111]

There is some (admittedly slight) evidence, too, that Lloyd George's family, in addition to coddling the boy, also expected much from him. The most direct evidence may be found in a letter to Lloyd George from his older sister, Mary, in 1890. 'You must not think that we are too hard upon you & expect too much', she begins her letter. But she then clearly sets aside her comment. 'People have such a high opinion of your talents, that they expect you to do something gallant every time there is an opportunity in Parliament.' 'So', she concludes her letter, 'you will pardon us for expecting great things'.[112] Other members of his family also tended to maintain pressure on Lloyd George, which could provoke a sharp response. In reply to a comment from his brother William about his parliamentary performances, he testily replied: 'You wrong me in making a charge of idleness against me.' Through no fault of his own, he had 'failed to catch the Speaker's eye', but was overlooked.[113] To the frequent (and sometimes unwanted) promptings from his Uncle Lloyd to speak more often in the House, Lloyd George had similar retorts. He once wrote to William that he was 'very annoyed' with his uncle for his complaints about not taking part in parliamentary debates. 'Tell Uncle', he demanded, to cease his 'raving ... I can't rush in like a babbling idiot to express my views on every conceivable topic'.[114]

It is also possible that Lloyd George was, in his boastful way, exuberantly exercising a form of triumphalism – a celebration of his defeat over political and personal enemies. There is certainly some evidence of this in the aggressive tone of some of his letters. During the autumn 1895 campaign for a united Cymru Fydd League, for example, Lloyd George vowed to 'smash up' the South Wales Liberal Federation headed by D.A. Thomas.[115] At a controversial meeting the following year in which John Bryn Roberts attended as an opponent of the League, Lloyd George exulted when Roberts was 'beaten' and 'licked' on several points: he concluded that the meeting was overall a 'slap in the eye' for his opponent.[116] After the Newport meeting had gone against the League, Lloyd George was determined to put both Thomas and Roberts 'in the wrong', which he attempted to do by going after them 'hot & strong' at a meeting of Welsh MPs a few weeks after Newport.[117]

In the enthusiasm of political battle, Lloyd George's boastful and combative statements may strike one as unexceptional. Contentious political agendas argued forcefully along party lines were (and are) common enough. But Lloyd George's combativeness, often demonstrated in Parliament and out, called into question early on his motives – not in the electorate as a whole, but mostly among Liberal leaders, and even among some in the Welsh party.[118] The moderate Stuart Rendel, then head of the Welsh parliamentary party, began to have reservations. During the campaign prior to the general election of 1892, he wrote to A.C. Humphreys-Owen that he would not stand on a platform with Lloyd George, because he had been 'most insolent to Mr Gladstone'.[119] Humphreys-Owen, who had never had a high opinion of Lloyd George and who was to replace Rendel as head of the Welsh party, wrote in similar terms later to Rendel that Lloyd George was 'a real irreconcilable'.[120] Tom Ellis was of like mind. He once expressed his reservations about Lloyd George to D.R. Daniel: 'George is very threatening. He means to be on the warpath. His whole attitude is to upset the apple cart!'[121] Both Humphreys-Owen and Ellis were particularly concerned with the Revolt of the Four and the potential dangers to the Liberal Party of a Young Wales movement.

Combative performances were of course not new to the House of Commons: the Irish Nationalists, especially under the leadership of Charles Stewart Parnell, had long been masters of obstruction and the targets of vilification from other members of the House. Lloyd George seemed somehow different from the Irish members, however. He did not speak for a historically united national party. In spite of a surging Welsh national consciousness, Wales was still considered as essentially a part of western England. No geographic barrier separated the two, as the Irish Sea separates England and Ireland. Nor was a religious division between England and Wales as great as that between England and Ireland. In short, Lloyd George's forceful parliamentary speeches were thought of as unnecessary. He seemed unmannerly at the least, or ungentlemanly, or even a ruffian on the loose. Not unlike Joseph Chamberlain, Lloyd George was considered a cuckoo in the nest. But then Chamberlain was a man of wealth and indisputably English.

There is little doubt, as his correspondence clearly reveals, that Lloyd George relished combativeness in the political arena. To stir the pot and to engender conflict was doubtless intentional as a political strategy. It was a way of rallying the faithful while challenging the opposition. But there may be another, less intentional, explanation which can partly account for it. At least one anonymous contemporary of Lloyd George ('M') makes a suggestive case in attempting to explain his caustic debating style in Parliament and his vehement and raging political speeches in the countryside.[122] In the House of Commons, Lloyd George frequently leaned forward, M wrote, 'eager, keen, alert, hand to ear, ready to spring on his prey and rent him to pieces …'. It is the pose of a man seeking attention, M continues, not only for his cause, but also for himself. Like an actor 'who has suddenly taken the centre of the stage and appropriated all he limelight', Lloyd George 'compels your attention'. The important thing 'is that the gaze of the audience should be riveted on you'. The effect is 'of making yourself a storm-centre' which creates 'a pivot about which conflicting factions revolve – this is the power that promises success in the world of affairs'.

Lloyd George's growing sense of entitlement was most manifest in his relations with his wife, Margaret. From the first he had been explicit and straightforward (and quite traditional) in his requirements of a wife. 'Men's lives are a perpetual conflict', he wrote in a revealing letter during his courtship. Thus, 'woman's function is to soothe & sympathize' and 'to pour oil on the wounds – to heal the bruises of spirit received in past conflicts & to stimulate to renewed exertion'.[123] So long as they were together at home in Wales during their first two years of marriage, there were likely enough opportunities for Margaret to serve as Lloyd George's ideal of a submissive helpmate. After their first two children were born – Richard in February 1889 and Mair Eluned in August 1890 – maternal responsibilities would, however, naturally mean some diversion of the amount of attention that Margaret could give to her husband. More significant was the impact of Lloyd George's election to Parliament in April 1890. Lengthy stays in London were now necessary for the new MP.

Lloyd George's initial accommodations were for himself alone during parliamentary sessions. At first he took a small temporary flat at the Inns of Court, Verulam Buildings, Gray's Inn Road. After leaving the Inns of Court, he stayed at various places for the next two years: with friends; at the National Liberal Club; and at temporary lodgings here and there. In the autumn of 1893, he leased a flat at Palace Mansions, Addison Road, Kensington. With a growing family and the desire to have them in London, he sought larger accommodations. He settled eventually on Wandsworth, where the family first rented a house on Trinity Road in 1899.

While in this house, their fifth child, Megan, was born (at Criccieth, as were all the Lloyd George children) in 1902. The following year, they moved to larger quarters in Routh Road, closer to Wandsworth Common. There they remained until the death of their daughter, Mair, in November 1907. Not long afterwards, the Lloyd Georges took temporary lodgings in Chelsea. From there, they moved to Downing Street in 1908 when Lloyd George became Chancellor of the Exchequer in the Asquith government.

As her family grew and her responsibilities increased during these peripatetic years, however, Margaret found it easier and more convenient to be based in Wales. She disliked the crowded conditions and urban atmosphere of London. Moreover, she wanted the most salubrious atmosphere for the children. In 1891, the prospect for Margaret's remaining in Wales increased when her parents sold their house and built two semi-detached houses – one for themselves and the other for their daughter and son-in-law. In that house, their third child, Olwen, had been born in April 1892. In Criccieth, she could indulge her love of gardening, participate in local politics and enjoy her own friends. It was, to her way of thinking, far better for her husband to visit Wales when possible. But Lloyd George firmly discouraged this expectation: 'unless I retire from politics altogether & content myself with returning to the position of a country attorney', he wrote to Margaret, 'we must give up the comforts of Criccieth for life in England'.[124] It was not always possible, he claimed, even at the close of parliamentary sessions, to make the long train ride to Criccieth and leave loose ends behind in London. The goal of his life, from an early age, was to succeed in politics: it was the root of all his ambition. Thus he felt bound by the conferences, committees and parliamentary sittings in London, and obligated as well to attend the innumerable countrywide political gatherings. As he wrote to Margaret in one instance (which can serve for many others), there were continuous 'clamours' for him 'from all parts of the country' which he could not ignore.[125]

For these reasons, Lloyd George believed that he could not spare the time for frequent jaunts to Wales. This accounts for his epistolary campaign, which lasted for many years, to persuade Margaret and the children to join him more frequently in London. These letters home also reveal a sense of loneliness and loss. Only a few weeks after he had gone to London to begin his parliamentary career and before he had delivered his maiden speech in the House of Commons, he confessed that he was 'very lonely' and 'awfully' dejected – so much so that at the time of writing this letter, he 'could not help bursting into tears'.[126] The following month, finding 'this solitude ... unbearable', he asked for a photo of his infant son: 'I want it so badly.' He ended the letter on a note of self-pity: 'I go to my lodgings like a hermit or a prisoner to his cell. Dark, gloomy dungeon my room is.'[127] The following month, in his continued loneliness, he solicited Margaret's assistance by informing her that he was soon to attend a large meeting in Buckinghamshire, but was uncertain of the outcome because she had not vetted a copy of his speech. 'I know', he wrote, that if 'my good angel at Criccieth ... approves I am bound to succeed'. Next year, he continued, 'you must be up with me here altogether'.[128]

Lloyd George continued his plaintive refrain in the months that followed: 'I shall never live in chambers another week alone', he wrote Margaret in 1891. 'It is positively painful in its solitude.'[129] Two months later, he made the same complaint: 'What a desolate hole these chambers of mine were last night.'[130] His complaints continued in the years that followed. In September 1893, he seems to have made a firm decision: 'I am not going to have anymore of this bachelor life. I have had quite enough of it.'[131] Two years later, nothing had changed: 'I am sick of this nomadic life.'[132] Sometimes, he was angry at Margaret for her intransigence: 'I was very annoyed & disgusted when I got your letter putting off your journey to London', he wrote in 1895.[133] But the problem of separation persisted. After opening a solicitor's office in the City of London in 1897, Lloyd George used the opportunity once again to beg his wife to join him permanently. 'Starting business in London must involve a permanent change in our arrangements. You can't leave me in town alone. That would be an act of desertion which I know you are too noble to contemplate – especially as I am about to make an effort not on my own behalf so much as on yours & the kids!'[134] Occasionally, though rare enough, Lloyd George reverted to more tender times in their relationship as in a letter in late 1900 when he addressed his letter to his 'darling & sweet Maggie', thanking her for her recent love letter: 'Write more & more of that stuff. I can take in a prodigious quantity of affection & make good use of it.'[135]

The growing separation between husband and wife has led historians to assume the worst – that the lengthy absences provided an ideal opportunity for Lloyd George's marital infidelities. Pugh believes that Lloyd George, bereft of wife and children, 'was almost bound to succumb to temptation'.[136] Other historians have made similar assumptions about Lloyd George's sexual proclivities. Grigg comments on Lloyd George's 'many … flirtations and casual amours' in the course of his life.[137] Don M. Cregier mentions his 'womanizing'.[138] Gilbert, expanding on his doubts about Lloyd George's innocence in the Edwards case, wonders why it did not 'teach him any lessons about dallying with other men's wives'.[139] Packer, though discounting some rumours, nevertheless believes that Lloyd George's desire for home comforts 'probably' led him into affairs with some women.[140] In what he much too modestly calls a critical biography, Donald McCormick makes the least restrained (and least convincing) case for Lloyd George's libertinism. He argues that Lloyd George, a product of 'the sultry, smouldering evangelism of the Welsh valleys, with its undertones of sexual obsession … undoubtedly undermined the moral structure of British public life'.[141]

Given the substantial number of Lloyd George's purported affairs, amours, flirtations and the like, one may wonder how he had time to do the nation's business. And one may be additionally puzzled – as many historians are – by the fact that these countless assignations with women were not more damaging to his reputation. It may be worthwhile to recall that in the first of these putative episodes – the Edwards paternity case of 1896 – Lloyd George was exonerated. A second case, which began not long after Lloyd George had essentially moved to London, has also been widely reported by historians and biographers. Lloyd George had struck up an acquaintance with Timothy Davies, a well-known member of the London Welsh community. As a wealthy merchant, radical Liberal and a Welshman, Davies would be a natural contact for an aspiring Lloyd George. [142] Lloyd George also doubtless enjoyed the company of Davies's young wife, Elizabeth (or 'Mrs Tim' as she was known), who presided over a comfortable domestic atmosphere and gave him proper meals.[143] Thus, Lloyd George often visited their home in Putney, not far from his own lodgings, then at Palace Mansions, Kensington.

However innocent Lloyd George's friendship may have been with Mrs Tim, it was of no comfort to Margaret that he was a frequent visitor to the Davies home. It should be remembered that Margaret's concerns about her husband's flirtatious manner emerged early in their marriage. As early as 1890, she had penned a questioning letter. 'I am glad you have not seen any girl you would like better than poor me', she wrote, 'but are you sure that you have not seen anyone to flirt with'. A cautionary note followed: 'Remember to be careful in that line or I shall find out.'[144] Margaret's suspicions about her husband did not lessen over the years and apparently reached a climax in 1897–98 over Lloyd George's visits to the Davies home. In May 1897, Margaret chastised her husband for paying too much attention to Mrs Tim. Lloyd George chided her in return: 'What a jealous little wife I have got to be sure!'[145] Matters deteriorated subsequently. In August, hearing a rumour of an early morning visitor to Palace Mansions, Margaret proclaimed her unhappiness and warned him to avoid scandal 'for the sake of your own personal self and your bright career'.[146] Lloyd George responded angrily, addressing his return letter to 'My sweet but stupid Maggie'.[147] Charging her with neglect and intimating that his visitor was on an innocent errand, Lloyd George urged her to drop 'that infernal Methodism which is the curse of your bitter [sic] nature ...'. He praised her on the one hand for being 'a good mother'; but on the other hand he declared that she has 'not always been a good wife'.[148] He concludes with a warning: 'When one of our children offends you what is it you do to him. You admonish him affectionately.' But when he, her husband, offends, she sulks and pouts and makes him wretched. Therefore, he 'must get consolation somewhere & there is plenty of kindness as well as of cruelty in the world'.[149]

It is of course very possible to interpret his relationship with Mrs Tim as a sexual affair, as have many historians. But it is also possible to see how Lloyd George, a man who apparently lacked every domestic survival skill, who could not wash his own dishes and who left clothes and papers strewn about the floor of his flat,[150] would welcome any helpful hand. Moreover, he was comfortable in the company of women, and no doubt enjoyed playing the flirting game. But whether or not he was sexually intimate with women must remain an open question. The evidence seems often based upon hearsay. One can only contrast these unsubstantiated claims with what is known about the case of Frances Stevenson. She was uniquely placed to command both his respect as his confidential secretary and his affection as his devoted mistress.[151] As his secretary from 1913 to 1922, she helped bring efficiency and order to the various administrative offices headed by Lloyd George – at the Treasury, the Ministry of Munitions, the War Office, and ultimately to the office of

Prime Minister. For Lloyd George, the supreme political animal, Frances was the perfect complement. She accepted his boastful self-praise and his need for adulation. She was a woman who understood Lloyd George's complex needs. For this, there is abundant evidence. Little exists for the purported affairs with other women.

4

WITH RADICAL INTENT?

One of the enduring questions about Lloyd George is the quality and the strength of his radicalism. This is difficult to determine largely because of the varieties of radicalism in existence during the late Victorian and Edwardian eras. Certainly the disestablishment of the state church, religious equality, extension of the franchise, educational reform and the improvement of social conditions were primary goals for both English and Welsh radicals within the Liberal Party during the late Victorian era.[1] Most especially, an underlying dislike of privilege as represented in traditional landed society led to a deep mistrust among radicals of such aristocratic redoubts as the House of Lords, the armed forces, the Foreign Office and the diplomatic service. Land reform was a natural corollary of these objectives. With regard to foreign affairs and the military, radicals were united in their detestation of state expenditures for arms and armaments in the belief that an active defence programme would detract from needed expenditures on social programmes. This was especially true of the expensive outlays for the Royal Navy.[2]

With the passage of the Reform Act of 1884 during Gladstone's second term, radical Liberalism gained, it would seem, a significant advantage. In Wales, as in Britain generally, the newly enfranchised included rural labourers and tenant farmers. Miners and steelworkers as well as other members of the working class also received the vote.[3] From these new voters especially, Lloyd George drew his support in winning a seat in the House of Commons.[4] But during the 1890s, the tripartite division of radicals, centrist Liberals and Whiggish aristocrats that made up the Liberal Party was proving discordant. Within the radical wing itself, there were divisions over political priorities. Temperance reformers, nonconformist groups and radicals from the Celtic Fringe (such as Lloyd George) increasingly gave the impression of a congeries of separate interest groups pursuing special causes. Indeed, Liberal radicals were sometimes perceived as 'faddists' – an ineffective and divisive group of dysfunctional idealists.[5] The Gladstonian drive for Irish Home Rule further divided Liberals when Whig grandees and even a few radicals, such as Joseph Chamberlain, bolted from the party to form an alliance with the Conservatives. Moreover, after Gladstone's resignation from his fourth term of office in 1894, Liberal leadership faltered. Lord Rosebery, the strangely conflicted and ineffective successor to Gladstone, was Prime

Minister for little more than a year.[6] Liberal fortunes in the immediate years after 1895 were, therefore, as one historian has noted, a time of 'shrinking horizons' and a feeling of decline.[7]

Lloyd George, who accepted the tenets of Liberal radicalism, was active in his parliamentary career throughout much of the 1890s as an oppositional politician. That is, he adopted a critical stance against existing laws and Conservative legislation. But he realized that he could not build a successful parliamentary career based upon opposition politics alone. He needed a positive, forward-looking programme as well – one that would be radical enough to capture the attention of a significant portion of the newly enfranchised, yet moderate enough to attract those who were less advanced in their political and social views. While still retaining a primary focus on Welsh affairs, he gave evidence of a proactive national radical programme during the parliamentary sessions of 1898 and 1899. He introduced a motion to place elementary public school children in both England and Wales under local management and to provide more facilities for teacher training in colleges free from sectarian control. He also urged more financial support for education in general.

Lloyd George's advocacy of pensions for the working poor is especially noteworthy: it was to become a significant legislative goal for the Liberal Party and the country during the coming decade. Old age pensions first emerged as an issue in Lloyd George's campaign speeches during the general elections of 1892 and 1895.[8] Although he did not consistently follow through with a detailed plan in the next few years, there is no doubt of his genuine interest, rooted as it was in his own encounters of class divisions and traditional privileges during his adolescence and young adulthood. During a speech at Newcastle in April 1899, for example, he alluded directly to these experiences. He reminded his audience that in any English village one could easily find a gentleman driving a four-in-hand along country lanes accompanied by his powdered footmen. This squire would live on an estate 'with his partridges and pheasants' protected by the state's enactment of game laws. He had no need for a pension to cushion his later years. But in that same village, one might see elderly men, broken in health, hard at work, doing menial labour with few resources for their final years of life. The state had a responsibility to them.[9]

In recognition of his advocacy, Lloyd George was appointed to a parliamentary select committee on old age pensions shortly after this speech. He saw two advantages to committee membership. First, he could help right a social wrong. Boasting to Margaret about his contribution to committee work, he wrote that he had insisted on adding several millions to the proposed pension fund: 'it goes all to the poor who really need it'.[10] But secondly (and more cynically), he believed that by increasing the pension fund, he could embarrass the Conservative government, which would be unlikely to accept the committee's recommendation if the costs were two high. As he put it in his letter to Margaret, the larger the pension fund, the greater likelihood 'of putting these bandits who are now in power in a nice fix. They can neither carry out these recommendations nor drop them – not without discredit'.[11]

The scope of Lloyd George's influence upon the committee, however, should not be taken fully at his word. The guiding hand behind the committee was in fact Joseph

Chamberlain, the renegade radical Liberal who was now the strong man in Lord Salisbury's Conservative government.[12] In his earlier years as mayor of Birmingham and as a radical Liberal MP from that city, Chamberlain had campaigned vigorously for radical measures. His famous 'Unauthorised Programme' of 1885 had influenced the young Lloyd George. Of special interest to Chamberlain was a state sponsored system of old age pensions. As a wealthy Birmingham manufacturer, he had witnessed at first hand the plight of aging workers struggling to maintain an adequate income once their most productive years were behind them. Older workers, especially in such fields as agriculture, bricklaying, carpentry, construction, dock labour, or seafaring, could find their active work life severely curtailed as early as 45 or 50 years of age. Unless family help, personal savings, or aid from clubs, Friendly Societies, or unions could offer assistance, the future of these workers was grim. Often enough such working families were driven to selling their furniture and what little possessions they had in order to maintain a precarious existence. Ultimately, some were forced into the workhouse thus becoming paupers at the end of their lives.[13]

Chamberlain made some strides in relieving the burden of the working poor. In 1897, for example, he pushed through Parliament a Workman's Compensation Act for industrial accidents. A parliamentary select committee of 1899 gave some promise for additional action on old age pensions. Lloyd George's respect for his onetime hero and their common interest in old age pensions led to a friendly interview in June 1899. But Chamberlain by then began to have doubts: a state sponsored old age pension plan could be enormously expensive. Moreover, Chamberlain was facing more pressing problems. Since 1895, he had been serving the Salisbury government as Colonial Secretary, an office he used to heighten imperial sentiment at home and to strengthen the bonds of empire abroad. Within a few months of their promising June interview, the political landscape had altered dramatically, bringing Chamberlain and Lloyd George into a conflict that made them implacable political enemies.

The issues that divided the two men originated far from Britain's shores. During the 1870s, relations between Britain and two of its colonies in South Africa, the Boer republics of Transvaal and the Orange Free State, had become strained after the discovery of gold and diamonds in South Africa. Newly enriched and irked by colonial restrictions, the two colonies agitated for greater autonomy within the empire. This, they thought, had been granted them under the terms of the Treaty of Pretoria in 1881, which ended a brief war with Britain in their favour. Thereafter, the two republics conducted a policy of annexation and independent policies throughout that part of South Africa beyond direct British control. From his earliest days at the Colonial Office, Chamberlain was determined to challenge Boer expansionism. He engaged in strenuous diplomatic initiatives, backed by open military threats, to force the Boers to acknowledge their imperial allegiance to Britain. In the Jameson Raid of December 1895, he went so far as to aid and abet a military incursion into the Transvaal. Matters steadily deteriorated after the Raid. An added point of friction was Chamberlain's demand that thousands of British citizens ('Uitlanders'), who had come to the Transvaal to work in the mines, be given full civil rights including the right to vote. To the Boers, this was simply an additional intrusion into their domestic affairs. As diplomatic efforts stalled in the months following, the likelihood of an appeal to arms grew.

Lloyd George viewed these developments with apprehension. Writing to his brother in April 1897, he warned of 'a very serious state of things in South Africa. Chamberlain is making tracks for war'.[14] As relations with South Africa deteriorated over the following months, Lloyd George, perhaps hoping for the best, was diverted by an extended trip to North America. He had accepted an invitation from the Canadian government to visit Canada as a member of a delegation to explore the country with an eye to encouraging Welsh immigration.[15] From the evidence of his letters home, Lloyd George thoroughly enjoyed the journey. In particular, he was astonished at the vastness of the Canadian west. After travelling by train from Toronto to Winnipeg, he wrote to Margaret: 'fancy a forest that ... took the best part of two days to get through travelling at the rate of 30 to 40 miles an hour'. The following week, he went across the prairie ('stupendous') to Regina and then to Alberta and on to Banff in the Rocky Mountains ('Alpine in its magnificence'), followed by a quick trip to Vancouver.[16]

Lloyd George clearly enjoyed North American scenery. But at the back of his mind, South Africa nagged. He began to hear rumours of war between Britain and the South African republics. In early September, he wrote William that conditions seemed 'very grave'. 'If Parliament is summoned', he added, 'I return forthwith'.[17] Several days later, he promised William that if war broke out: 'I shall protest with all the vehemence at my command against this blackguardism ....'[18] In Winnipeg, he secured a copy of the *Manchester Guardian* and some Canadian newspapers: they were filled with reports of increasing tensions. He condemned those who 'have been screeching out for war' and denounced such warmongers as 'wicked'. As he began preparing a speech against the Conservative government's drift to war, he confided to Margaret: 'I am all on fire to be back.'[19] On 4 October, he sailed from Montreal. A week later, while he was still at sea, war had begun between Britain and the Boer republics.

The war was the beginning of a significant transformation and enlargement of Lloyd George's political views.[20] Until then, he had paid little attention to foreign affairs and matters of empire. From time to time, it is true, he had criticized the Salisbury government on its management of foreign affairs, including what he called the unnecessary concessions to the United States during the controversy over Venezuela in 1896 and the weakness displayed to France during the Fashoda incident in 1898. But these were politically motivated comments on relatively minor skirmishes.[21] With the nation fully at war fighting against a determined and resourceful enemy, circumstances were far different and much more was at stake. The South African War forced upon him, as it did upon many others, a rethinking of Britain's imperial role. Most Conservatives and the country as a whole at first remained solidly behind the war effort. Even some Liberals succumbed to war fever. As the war dragged on, however, the country became increasingly divided over its direction. To Lloyd George's enduring credit, throughout the war he steadfastly remained one of its severest critics.[22]

Lloyd George's opposition to the war was not, however, based upon an anti-imperial sentiment. Nor was he, in spite of his passionate and prompt response to the war, a pacifist.[23] There were in fact other reasoned and consistent themes in his criticisms of the war. The first was that wars were costly, doubly so when men and materiel had to be shipped half way around the globe. This led to his second objection – such costs were bound to affect adversely social reforms, including old age pensions, thus delaying their implementation. He also believed that Britain, and especially Chamberlain, had not negotiated with the Boers in good faith and had arranged the diplomatic contingencies so that the Boers were forced into a corner. Additionally, as a Welshman, he felt some sympathy for small pastoral countries attempting to repel an overwhelming imperial aggression. The force of his conviction on these issues lent weight and power to his early condemnations of the war.

Lloyd George's first public statement against the war was made in the House of Commons shortly after his return from Canada. Parliament had been recalled to vote emergency supplies for the war. Although brief, his remarks were highly critical of Chamberlain, who as Colonial Secretary, had 'blundered seriously' in going to war. Furthermore, he charged, Chamberlain had 'deliberately' misled the country in negotiations between Britain and the Transvaal. For this, he was nearly called down by the Speaker. In a restrained apology, Lloyd George had further strong words, hinting at 'criminal negligence' on the part of the government.[24] As he explained it to Uncle Lloyd, he had spoken to an official in the War Office who claimed that 'the troops were in a sad plight', suffering from inadequate equipment in rough terrain. They were also 'weary of the hard work & the experience of being buffeted from pillar to post'.[25] With this information in hand, Lloyd George pitched into the government 'as they have not been pitched into before'. He 'hit straight from the shoulder'.[26] To William he confided that: 'The fiz is out of the Jingo pop.'[27]

A month later, Lloyd George delivered a more comprehensive attack on the war at a Liberal Association meeting in Carmarthen. Condemning the war as 'an infamy', he denounced it as a hindrance to social progress. Money given to fight the war would have been better given to old age pensions. 'There was not a shell exploded', he exclaimed, 'but it carried away an Old Age Pension with it'.[28] In the following two months, Lloyd George paid close attention to the disastrous early months of the war which reached a critical point during 'Black Week' of December 1899: in that week alone, British forces lost three important battles. On 27 January 1900, Lloyd George gave a major speech at the Palmerston Club in Oxford where he recounted Britain's loss of reputation and prestige as a result of the war. He also condemned what he called the New Imperialism, a policy characterized by 'deception' and 'fraud'.[29] In the House of Commons, he sharpened his attack upon Chamberlain as the prime mover most responsible for the war. On 6 February 1900, he condemned Chamberlain for landing the country 'in a great mess'. 'This bloodshed', he declared, 'should be put an end to'.[30]

Speaking in Parliament against the war was obviously safer than making speeches at public meetings where pro-war hecklers could disrupt the proceedings. But the prospect of violent pro-war agitation did not deter Lloyd George. Indeed, his persistent attempts to speak even at the rowdiest gatherings are remarkable. It seemed that he courted furious opposition: he certainly inflamed it. His first seriously disruptive meeting was at Glasgow on 6 March 1900. Reporting to his brother William afterwards (with some pardonable exaggeration and not a little boasting) he declared that it was the worst row at a public meeting he had ever witnessed. There were 10,000 outside the hall, he claimed, 'surging, struggling, fighting, yelling like savages'. Inside, were hundreds 'of the foe' and a 'small Armageddon going on'. For 20 minutes, he withstood 'a shouting, yelping, fighting crowd' until at last he began to recite the casualties from that day's newspaper. At that, a hush descended in the hall. He was then able to speak, 'a splendid hearing', for 40 minutes. At the end he sat down 'amid great cheering'. He had conquered them completely and 'saved the meeting'.[31] But Lloyd George was not safe from assault – even within his own constituency. On 11 April, he spoke at Penrhyn Hall in Bangor in support of the main resolution condemning Chamberlain's South African policy. During his speech, a riot was in progress outside the Hall: ultimately every window was smashed. Afterwards, as he tried to make his way to safety, he was struck a violent blow to his head with a stick. Stunned, he was taken to a nearby café and remained under police protection until the crowd dispersed. Undeterred, he wrote to Herbert Lewis two days later that he hoped to address another meeting within the week: 'One must not allow this sort of ruffianism even a temporary triumph.'[32]

By June 1900, however, it looked as though Chamberlain's gamble had paid off. After a difficult start, British military forces in South Africa had gained ground and had subdued the regular Boer forces. The war was ostensibly over. But Lloyd George did not cease his attacks on the Colonial Secretary, even in the face of his apparent victory. On 29 June he declared in the House of Commons that the entire war had been 'one of miscalculation'. Diplomatic negotiations, preparations for war, and the capacity for Boer resistance had all been underestimated.[33] The following month Lloyd George made his most extensive attack upon Chamberlain's conduct as Colonial Secretary. The history of the past five years in South Africa from the time of the Jameson Raid was, he claimed, replete with a record of facts 'each and every one of them affording good, solid, substantial ground for suspecting the attitude of the right hon. Gentleman in everything that he does in South Africa'. Britain had become overextended during the war and was paying a fearful price in loss of imperial power, declining prestige, destruction of property and civilian and military casualties. Furthermore, Lloyd George charged, the strategy for the war was guided by Chamberlain's plans for a forthcoming general election which would be called to take advantage of the patriotic war fever. As he put it, Chamberlain was determined 'that this war should have one result – that is, a Chamberlain ministry in the next Parliament'.[34]

That Chamberlain was determined to take advantage of the war to press for a political victory at home was true enough. In its capture of Bloemfontein, British forces discovered a cache of letters written to the Boer leaders by sympathetic Liberals. There was little of substance in these letters, but when they fell into Chamberlain's hands, he realized they could be used as a brush to tar Liberal reputations. He therefore publicized their existence without revealing their content. He nevertheless implied that, based upon the evidence of the letters, some Liberal MPs had trafficked with the enemy. This was, as everyone surmised, a likely prelude to any forthcoming election during which the Conservative government would beat the patriotic drum for electoral purposes.

On 8 August 1900, the final day of that parliamentary session, Lloyd George fought Chamberlain's attempted smear with one of his own. He declared before the House of Commons that a recent committee reporting on War Office contracts had identified certain munitions firms, in particular Kynoch's of Birmingham, which had received preferential treatment in the issuing of military contracts for supplying cordite. Kynoch's operated under the chairmanship of Chamberlain's brother, Arthur. When Chamberlain objected that this was argument 'by innuendo', Lloyd George aptly retorted that Chamberlain himself had 'insinuated treason' over the captured letters.[35] It was an effective retort. Elated over his performance, Lloyd George wrote a characteristic letter to William. 'Just given Joe the biggest hiding he has had for years. He squirmed, I got him completely & I lashed him for 20 minutes until he writhed. Our fellows mad with delight. Greatest score yet.'[36]

Several weeks later came the long-awaited announcement of the dissolution of Parliament and the general election to follow in early October. The election, naturally enough, was a referendum on the government's management of the war. This was certainly the main theme of Lloyd George's campaign. In a series of speeches in his constituency in late September, he pounded the Conservative government for its squandered opportunities in pursuing an ineffective military campaign in South Africa. Thus he argued not on anti-war or pacifist grounds, but as a patriot demanding a competent direction of the war. He once again pointed out that wartime priorities had distracted the government from important social priorities, such as old age pensions. He also continued to raise the questionable motives of Chamberlain, claiming in a speech at a Liberal meeting in Navin that the War Office had given favourable contracts to Kynoch's, lining the pockets of the Chamberlains. In a deft reference to the South African war, he conceded that Prime Minister Kruger of the Transvaal may have been an obstinate, even a corrupt politician. To peals of laughter, he added in a thoughtful aside: Kruger might, indeed, 'be as bad as Mr. Chamberlain – and he could not imagine anything worse than that'.[37] Even so, Lloyd George concluded, this did not justify a war.

But, as Liberals had feared, popular support for the war remained high, and the so-called Khaki Election of 1900 returned the Conservative government to power with essentially the same distribution of parliamentary seats as before the poll: 334 Conservatives and 68 Liberal Unionists, opposed by 184 Liberals, joined by their allies, the Irish nationalists, at 82. Lloyd George won, as he always had – not by much. He beat his opponent, Henry Platt, a Bangor banker (who had adopted the title 'Colonel', his rank in the militia) by 2,412 votes to 2,116. It soon became apparent, however, that the war had not ended. Hostilities intensified during the autumn and winter of 1900–01. The Boers were forming themselves into fast-riding, hard-hitting guerrilla bands who struck quickly at their enemies and then retreated into the countryside. In response, British military leaders instituted harsh measures to blunt the new Boer tactics. First, an official policy of farm burning and livestock destruction was instituted to weaken Boer morale and to punish Boer collaborators. This was complemented, secondly, by the construction of blockhouses, manned by British troops, which were connected with barbed wire placed across the veldt in order to pen in the guerrillas. And third, civilians, mainly women and children, were herded into concentration camps which the government justified as a measure designed to protect civilians from the ravages of war, but which soon proved to be centres of infection, disease and high mortality rates, especially among young children.

Lloyd George kept his family up to date with information concerning Boer guerrilla operations. To William, he wrote in late December: 'What a bog they [the government] have landed us in.'[38] The following day, conditions seemed even worse: 'Things in Cape Colony look serious.'[39] Lloyd George also acted more publicly. The inability of the British army decisively to defeat the Boers and the institution of questionable tactics upon a civilian population encouraged Lloyd George in a post-election campaign to step up his attacks on the government's war policy. 'Is it civilized warfare to starve women and children?', he asked in a speech at Bangor.[40] He also reinforced his charges of impropriety on the part of Chamberlain and expanded his attacks by including members of his family. In Parliament, too, he continued his attacks on the Chamberlains and their putative war profiteering. At the opening of the new parliament on 10 December 1900, he claimed that he was not charging corruption against the Chamberlains, but rather suggesting a potential conflict between private interests and public duties.[41] As Chamberlain's chief biographer has noted, there was something to Lloyd George's charges. If there were no evidence of actual corruption, Kynoch's and the Chamberlains had indeed done well out of the war, and at least gave an appearance of impropriety in their supplying wartime materiel to the government.[42] Rumours had continued to swirl during the autumn of 1900 about wartime profiteering. The Liberal press published new revelations, among them the fact that Neville Chamberlain, Joe's second son, was the managing director of the small firm of Hoskins & Sons, Ltd, which had supplied fittings for the Royal Navy. Major shareholders of Hoskins were also members of the Chamberlain family, including Austen Chamberlain, then the Civil Lord of the Admiralty. Additional reports revealed other companies in which the Chamberlains had a large stake and all of which may have enjoyed some kind of contractual favouritism. These exposures caused a minor sensation and additionally stoked the fires of partisanship.[43]

By late 1900, Lloyd George had established a reputation as the foremost critic of the war. His slashing attacks had captured attention both in Parliament and in public meetings throughout the country. Although his speeches were often published in the newspaper press with accompanying editorial comment (not always positive), and his parliamentary deliveries were recorded in *Hansard*, Lloyd George hoped to establish a more reliable and compliant mouthpiece in his anti-war crusade. Controlling a newspaper was the ideal vehicle. Throughout 1900, Lloyd George was centrally involved in organizing a syndicate to buy a prominent London newspaper. If successful, it would be 'a tremendous deal', as Lloyd George reported to Margaret.[44] With the aid of his partners, especially the wealthy chocolate magnate, George Cadbury, in late 1900 he purchased the former pro-war *Daily News* as the instrument of his ambitions. Once the contract to purchase had been signed, Lloyd George wrote exultantly to his brother William: 'It is the sensation of the hour & for the moment I am the centre of it.'[45] Almost overnight, the staff changed hands and a new anti-war newspaper came into being in the capital city where most daily papers supported the war.[46] This was Lloyd George's first successful attempt to shape a national public opinion by using the press: it was not to be his last.

As the war ground on throughout 1901, Lloyd George – fortified by the *Daily News* and bolstered by a growing sense of war weariness in the country – maintained a steady pressure against the government's war policy both in Parliament and out. 'Tell Uncle Lloyd', he wrote to William in March 1901, 'I hope to have another go at the war before Easter'.[47] The following month, he reported to William from Queenborough, Leicestershire, of a 'splendid success' the previous evening at a meeting with 2,000 in attendance. 'I gave them war hot' he wrote, 'and they took it … I am getting a strong hold on English democracy'.[48] Two days later from Wolverhampton – where he had an 'immense success' – he attacked Chamberlain for dragging out the peace process while 'men are dying'. [49] In Parliament on 11 June he queried the government in the House of Commons concerning reports of the destruction by fire of several Boer villages and farms.[50] A few days later, he charged that conditions in the 'camps of detention' were worsening: insufficient food, overcrowding and poor housing (in leaky tents) were the result of 'a deliberate policy'. Worst of all, the government was following a policy 'of extermination against children' in South Africa.[51] In late June, he again criticized the unhealthy conditions in the concentration camps.[52] In early July, he declared that the government was 'now floundering in this morass in South Africa'.[53]

During Parliament's recess in the late summer and autumn of 1901, Lloyd George made extensive public appearances throughout Wales, as well as addressing audiences in Sheffield, Edinburgh, and London – centres of population which would guarantee wide press coverage. In addition, Lloyd George continued to speak at smaller meetings of the faithful in both England and Wales. At the Eivion Liberal Association in late October, he condemned the concentration camps and their 'truly appalling' death rate, especially among children. Britain, he claimed, had used 'its great hulking strength to torture the little child'. Such was 'Chamberlain's charity'.[54] At a Liberal meeting that same week at Llangeitho (where the speeches were all in Welsh), Lloyd George held Chamberlain directly responsible for the War. He condemned the Colonial Secretary for 'his folly in refusing terms which by his own admission were fair and reasonable'.[55]

By the autumn of 1901, Lloyd George had perfected his standard stump speech on the inequities of the government and their failed wartime policy. Typically he would speak for slightly more than an hour, first warming up his audience with some references to a local circumstance or to well known public figures. A light touch, even a few jokes, established rapport with his audience. Depending on the type of meeting, he might make allusions to the Bible or invoke natural phenomena – mountains and storms were common. If in luck, he would be heckled which would provide an opportunity to show his lightning quick repartee. Thus he wound into the main message of the meeting. He employed short and punchy sentences which would remain in the minds of his listeners.[56] Lloyd George's platform skills impressed even the strongly pro-war *Daily Mail*: his 'jaunty self-assurance' and his supreme 'confidence in himself' carried weight. 'You feel as he speaks that he looks down with contempt on all who hold views different from those he expresses, and the fact impresses you'. [57]

Not every meeting would go well, of course. The most famous example was at Birmingham on 18 December 1901. Invited by the Birmingham Liberal Association, Lloyd George was given a most appealing venue – to speak in Chamberlain's domain, the very heart of the government's command centre and of the war effort. Birmingham supporters were suitably riled at the news of the forthcoming speech, and local newspapers encouraged supporters of the war to an active opposition. Concern for Lloyd George's safety was evident in the preparations beforehand. Upon his arrival at New Street station on the evening before the speech, he was spirited away to an undisclosed location. Three hundred and fifty policemen were assigned the next day to the vicinity of the Town Hall where the speech was to take place. Even so, the Chief Constable of Birmingham, in a direct appeal to Lloyd George, informed him that he could not guarantee his safety and urged him to cancel his speech. Lloyd George refused. When he arrived in a closed carriage to the vicinity of the Town Hall the following evening, a large and surly crowd of 30,000 had nearly surrounded the Hall. Somehow, Lloyd George eluded them, slipping in through a side door. Although the meeting was ostensibly a ticketed affair, when the doors were opened legitimate ticket holders were vastly outnumbered as enraged Chamberlainites poured into the Hall. When Lloyd George rose to speak to speak, he could not be heard. The platform was pelted by missiles of every description, including a novel use of bricks bound with barbed wire. Pandemonium inside was the signal for the crowd outside to begin their assault: more missiles were directed to the walls and windows of the Hall. The force of the attack weakened the great glass dome of the building, which began to fall onto the surging crowd inside. Lloyd George, who at first held his ground, was quickly convinced by the Chief Constable that his life was in danger. Disguised in a policeman's uniform, Lloyd George was placed within a flying squad of policemen, who then marched out of the Hall. The police mounted guard over him for the remainder of the evening, and escorted him to his train the following morning.[58] Forty rioters had been seriously injured, two had been killed, and the Town Hall completely wrecked.

Lloyd George himself, if one can rely on his own words, seems to have exulted in all the excitement. As he wrote to William: 'They failed to inflict even a scratch on me.'[59] He had in fact carried the day. If he had been without national name recognition before, he very clearly achieved it after the Birmingham riot. In demonstrating an unexpected courage, he had also earned a reputation for coolness under fire. Three weeks later, at a meeting in Bristol, he turned the riot to his further advantage by upholding the 'great principle of free speech' and blaming the war itself for the rise of intolerance and the use of violence in public meetings.[60] His stature enhanced, Lloyd George continued his anti-war speeches in Parliament into the spring. He gave his last speech on the subject on 20 March, when he once again criticized the government for its role in lengthening the war.[61]

During these early months of 1902 as Lloyd George remained its chief critic, the war was at last winding down. Concluding a war of two and a half years, the Treaty of Vereeniging was signed on 31 May. Lloyd George had been, if not prescient, then consistent and to a degree courageous in his opposition to the war. His emergence as a leading voice of the Liberal Party against the war went hand-in-hand with a palpable stirring within the party itself, best symbolized by Sir Henry Campbell-Bannerman's famous speech on 14 June 1901 when he condemned the 'methods of barbarism' used against the Boer civilian population. It was a phrase that had resonance at the time, summing up the doubts of an increasingly troubled nation. The enforced containment of innocent women and children into concentration camps and the razing of homes and destruction of farmsteads were not soon forgotten.

The war's end did not immediately benefit the Liberal Party, however. Indeed, divisions within the party seemed to have hardened during the course of the war. Anti-war Liberals, the 'Little Englanders', were opposed by the Liberal Imperialists, who believed in supporting the British Empire.[62] In an attempt to heal the rift, the centrist Campbell-Bannerman was chosen to lead the party.[63] Post-war attempts to reach an agreement between the two wings of the party were of prime importance to all Liberals. In none of the high-level discussions over the fate of the Liberal Party did Lloyd George have a role to play. Nevertheless he had undoubtedly contributed to a revitalization of the party during the waning days of the war. His strenuous anti-war, anti-Chamberlain and anti-Conservative tirades enhanced his stature among anti-imperial Liberals. But his vigorous anti-war activities had taken their toll. Writing to William in late 1901, he confessed his weariness at the continual round of meetings in the countryside and of the drain upon his energy that the travelling entailed. Nevertheless, he said, such meetings were necessary to keep up the spirits of those who opposed the war and to 'rebuild a new party & a policy ready for the day when the nation is penitent & willing to be saved'.[64]

Unless, however, Liberals could somehow overcome their electoral failures, greater rewards would be impossible. It was at this juncture that circumstances beyond the control of Lloyd George and the Liberals began to operate in their favour. On 24 March 1902, before the South African War was formally concluded, Arthur Balfour, as leader of the Conservative Party (and within a few days, Prime Minister), introduced a sweeping Education Bill. This was in line with attempts in the previous decade to strengthen the Church of England's hand while reforming education. The bill was designed to rationalize a cumbersome system by abolishing the previous distinction between the nondenominational board schools and the voluntary or Church of England schools. Local committees of county or county borough councils would now administer all schools – whether primary, secondary, or technical – of whatever denomination. The voluntary schools would retain their separate identity, but would also be subject to inspection by the local educational authorities. These authorities also had the power to appoint two out of six managers of the voluntary schools. In return for this intrusion into the management of a private school, financial support for these schools would be underwritten thereafter by local rates in every community.

Balfour's central idea was to put British education on a sounder, more efficient footing as a way of increasing the competitive quality of British citizens compared with its continental counterparts, especially Germany. But Balfour was also determined to preserve the traditional role of the Church of England as the primary educator of the nation's youth.[65] To the first aim of the bill, Lloyd George gave ready assent. Recalling his own experience as a schoolboy, he wrote to Margaret: 'Llanystumdwy School will be now under the County Council & a very great improvement it is.'[66] But the second aim, the preservation of a privileged status for the voluntary schools, could not be countenanced. For example, the bill proposed that the new educational authorities, would be represented by only two of the six managers required of all voluntary schools: the remaining four would be representatives of the school, very likely Anglican clerics. Most important of all was the provision that the voluntary schools, largely Anglican, would be financed by local rates in each community. In majority nonconformist communities, which was true of Wales and some parts of England, this would be very unpopular, especially since under the bill voluntary schools retained the right to continue their particular brand of denominational instruction for all pupils. In short, under the terms of the proposed bill, local nonconformist rate payers would fund voluntary schools but would have neither community control over their management nor a direct say in the religious doctrines taught in those schools. In addition, the majority board of managers of these schools had the power to hire and dismiss any teacher who did not profess the Anglican faith. Worse yet, the same could be true for a Roman Catholic school.

Within weeks, a frenzy arose among nonconformists against the proposed bill. To the nonconformist faithful, the bill seemed 'a wholesale infringement on the principle of religious equality'.[67] Their most strenuous objection was against the proposed use of local rates to fund Church schools: it seemed a restoration of the detested compulsory church rates which were once used to maintain Anglican parish churches, a proviso which had been abolished during the first Gladstone administration in 1868. The energy behind their opposition was fuelled in part by a broad concurrent religious revivalism among nonconformist sects, the consequence of which was a growing cooperation among them for the joint purpose of rooting out moral and social evils. Traditional sectarian divisions were dissolving into a large and effective general nonconformist pressure group, bound together by what became known as the 'nonconformist conscience'.[68] Thus aroused, nonconformists thrust themselves energetically into the greater moral cause of a crusade against Balfour's bill.

Hundreds of local nonconformist rallies took place shortly after Balfour's introduction of the bill. A passive resistance movement, determined to refuse the payment of school rates, mushroomed throughout the country. The National Council of Evangelical Free Churches called for a conference of representatives of the local councils to be held in London on 15 April 1902.[69] Popular ministers such as the Reverend John Clifford of Westbourne Park Chapel, Paddington, the Reverend C. Silvester Horne at Whitefield's Mission and, perhaps the most famous of all, the Reverend R.J. Campbell, whose ministry was at the City Temple, passionately denounced the proposed bill from their pulpits. Sympathetic newspapers, including William Robertson Nicoll's widely read nonconformist *British Weekly*, became a national force against the bill.

The Liberal Party needed only to harness the nonconformist outrage to create an effective political alliance that might challenge the Conservative majority in the House of Commons. No Liberal politician had such a combination of oratorical skills, parliamentary knowledge, expertise in organizing political campaigns and nonconformist credentials as Lloyd George. He was already active in two important nonconformist organizations, serving on the executive board of the National Council and as parliamentary vice-president of the Liberation Society, a venerable organization established in the mid-Victorian era to bring about the disestablishment of the Church of England. Lloyd George was active on other fronts as well. He took pains to cultivate William Robertson Nicoll, urging him, through his influential newspaper, to contribute to a 'more complete understanding between those who conduct the campaign in the Country and the Members who fight the Bill in the Commons'.[70]

Lloyd George's first speech against the bill – at a meeting of his constituents at Pwllheli on 27 March – was delivered only a few days after the bill had been made public. He harshly denounced 'priestcraft' as 'the root of the evil in this country'.[71] The following month, at a packed protest meeting convened by the Swansea Free Church Council, he declared that at last the nonconformists had been given 'a clear distinct issue' around which they could gather and fight for their religious liberty.[72] On 21 May at a Cardiff meeting sponsored jointly by the Welsh National Liberal Council and the Free Church Federation of Wales, he cautioned: 'We are on the eve of one of the most critical decisions for the people of this country.'[73] As the months passed, Lloyd George sharpened his attacks. Playing on nonconformist fears of Anglican proselytizers, he warned (at a meeting sponsored by the Rhondda Labour and Liberal Association) that the bill would 'hand over permanently to the priesthood of the Anglican and Catholic Churches the training of more than half the children of the land'.[74] Lloyd George also claimed to be fearful for the consequences of the nation as a whole if the bill became law. In one of his swings into England, he spoke before the Eastern Counties Liberal Federation, proclaiming the need for a secular education attuned to the modern world. There was a need for 'less catechism and more education' – education that would prepare the youth of the country for the commercial battles of the future. These battles would be 'won by brains, and I don't think', he remarked, 'that the parson can help us there'.[75]

Lloyd George was also active against the bill in the House of Commons. He was vigilant for any opportunity to score points off his opponents, to correct factual errors and to castigate specific provisions of the bill.[76] From time to time, he issued warnings of the consequences should the bill be passed. On 9 July he declared that 'if County Councils were compelled to rate themselves for the purpose of education without management, there would be such strife and contention', perhaps even 'scenes of lawlessness in this country', that had not been experienced 'for a long time past'.[77] Lloyd George was not merely obstructionist, however. On 12 November 1902, Balfour – who had been reluctant to allow any changes in the proposed bill – accepted an amendment brought forward by Alfred Thomas, Chairman of the Welsh Parliamentary Party. It would transfer the educational authority then held by the local county committees – consisting of five members in each county, who were appointed – to the County Councils in Wales, which were elected. Because this conformed to the English system, Balfour was not opposed. The secret that lay behind the amendment, however, was that it had been instigated by Lloyd George, who used Thomas as his mouthpiece. The amendment was in fact a 'booby-trap'.[78]

After the bill became law on 20 December 1902 (as was inevitable, given the large Conservative majority in Parliament), Lloyd George announced in a public address the real intent of the Thomas amendment. The Welsh county councils under the new Balfour Act were given extensive powers of investigation into the existing conditions of the voluntary schools: states of repair, sanitation, lighting and play facilities must all be up to code. Many Church schools had in fact been neglected. Unless repairs were made, the county councils would refuse to sanction their continuation. In addition, the councils would grant rate aid to pay for the needed repairs only if they – the councils – were in turn granted control over their management of the schools. 'No control, no cash' was Lloyd George's motto. Moreover, the school must forego all religious tests in the appointment of teachers.[79] The Welsh National Liberal Council on 25 January 1903 readily accepted Lloyd George's proclamation tying rate aid to control. The Welsh example was received with enthusiasm among nonconformists in England as well.

It was soon apparent that Lloyd George did not intend his proclamation as an ultimatum, but as a negotiating ploy. He hoped for a compromise and entered into discussions with members of the Church of England hierarchy in Wales. Points of negotiation included allowing the teaching of Anglican doctrine a few times weekly in the voluntary schools outside school hours, as well as the possibility of a commonly agreed upon syllabus of religious instruction. Non-negotiable was the provision that the appointment of teachers must remain in the hands of the County Councils of Wales. Lloyd George was able to establish a dialogue on these matters with A.G. Edwards, the influential Bishop of St Asaph. Other members of the Anglican hierarchy, however, were less inclined to treat with Lloyd George and nothing came of the negotiations. Thereafter, Lloyd George returned to his more recalcitrant opposition to the Balfour Act.[80] Thus began in earnest the 'Welsh Revolt'. The seal was set on the policy of Welsh resistance at a well-attended meeting at Park Hall in Cardiff on 3 June 1903. A series of resolutions were passed by acclamation, which reinforced the notion of public control of Welsh schools. County councils were also urged to withhold rate aid from schools that did not comply; and ratepayers in turn were requested to refuse to pay rates to any county council that did not follow this demand. In short, it was a proclamation of popular resistance to the Balfour Act. In his speech to the meeting, Lloyd George was in combative form. 'Why should the clergyman appoint the teacher?' he asked rhetorically. In answer to his own question, Lloyd George declared that the clergyman 'might with equal fitness appoint the exciseman' and in fact clergymen have more in common with excisemen than with teachers, because they both 'have to deal with spirit in bondage'.[81]

Throughout the summer of 1903, Lloyd George travelled widely in England, bearing the news of the Welsh resistance to the Act. In meeting after meeting – many of them sponsored jointly by the Liberal associations and the Free Church Councils – he lashed out at the Conservative government. Although the meetings were enthusiastic, Lloyd George encountered a weakness in the English nonconformist movement. Unity of purpose with Wales had not brought effective organization in England. The English movement lacked the kind of resolute leadership that Lloyd George provided in Wales. The English rather relied upon individual passive resistance in refusing to pay local rates as required by the legislation. Into the autumn and early winter of 1904, nevertheless, Lloyd George continued his campaign, though now more often in Wales, where he focused his energies on the upcoming Welsh county council elections, the key to the strategy of the Welsh resistance. The campaign was wholly successful: the 'progressive' candidates were overwhelmingly victorious in all 13 councils.

Thus challenged, the government had no choice but to respond. After a series of stormy House of Commons sessions, a bill was passed in August 1904 that empowered the Board of Education to assume the role of county councils whenever a local authority was in default of its obligations under the Balfour Act. This Education (Local Authority Default) Act – quickly renamed by Lloyd George the 'Coercion of Wales' Act – sparked a strong counterattack. Lloyd George and his Welsh lieutenants responded by convening a two-day national convention in Cardiff on 6 October. Seven hundred were in attendance, including local education authorities and representatives of the Free Church organizations. In his speech, Lloyd George reminded the assembly that the national flag of Wales bore a dragon rampant, not a sheep recumbent. He denounced further the notion that county councils should act as constables on governmental orders from above: they were bodies responsible to the electorate below. A number of resolutions were then passed reflecting the strong feelings of the meeting. The most important among them stated the determination of Welsh county councils, if the Default Act were applied, to refuse to maintain any elementary schools. Nonconformist parents would withdraw their children from the voluntary schools and educate them privately in chapels and vestries. English representatives from the Free Church Council pledged their support to their Welsh brethren. It was a perfect impasse between the government and a growing insurrection among nonconformists.[82]

Meantime, a second opportunity – quite different from the schools controversy – opened for the Liberals. On 15 May 1903, Joseph Chamberlain, speaking before his West Birmingham constituents, announced that he was embarking upon a campaign for tariff reform. He proposed an imperial union based upon a system of reciprocal preferential tariffs by which Britain and her colonies would establish economic advantages over foreign imports, thus strengthening the empire through material ties of trade and commerce. He promised that under such a system, domestic workers would have higher wages and the government greater revenues, sufficient to fund social legislation such as old age pensions. He also advocated retaliatory duties against some countries that followed a policy of dumping cheap goods upon British markets. In September, Chamberlain resigned from the government to devote more time in pursuit of his campaign.[83]

Chamberlain's campaign posed a fundamental threat to one of the most sacred of Liberal doctrines – free trade – for it was immediately obvious that tariff reform was a return to economic protection. The effect of the campaign for tariff reform galvanized the Liberals far more than any other issue during 1903–05. One would imagine Lloyd George to have been a leading critic of Chamberlain's proposal. But he was already deeply involved with the education issue and was unable to give tariff reform his full attention. Nor was he completely comfortable debating complex economic issues. Liberal leadership against tariff reform was consequently taken by others, especially by another rising star in the party, H.H. Asquith. Persistently following along Chamberlain's campaign trail during the autumn of 1903, Asquith refuted both Chamberlain's economic facts and their theoretical underpinning.

This is not to say, however, that Lloyd George was silent. On 22 May, during a debate in the House of Commons on a private member's bill to provide old age pensions, Lloyd George opened a line of criticism against Chamberlain, categorizing the newly proposed plan for tariff reform as nothing less than a continuation of an imperial policy that had proved so costly during the South African War. Lloyd George further charged that Chamberlain, 'a man of many schemes', was too 'fond of quack medicines'. He tried one thing after another, Lloyd George claimed, only to drop them all for a newer scheme on the horizon. Lloyd George specifically cited the support once professed by Chamberlain for old age pensions which was now apparently thrust aside and abandoned in favour of tariff reform. It was, said Lloyd George, 'a cruel thing to fill the poor with false hopes' and then to dash them to the ground. Chamberlain had simply 'pocketed the votes of the working classes, and forgotten all about old-age pensions'. But Chamberlain, perhaps surprising his tormentor, directly replied on the floor of the House that he not forgotten old age pensions. Indeed, he believed that his recently announced fiscal scheme could so swell the treasury that old age pensions could be funded.[84]

Lloyd George was unpersuaded that tariff reform would benefit social policy, and the very next day continued his line of attack on the Conservatives, and particularly on Chamberlain, during a speech in Cambridge, where he warned that tariff reform would mean a tax upon imported food and raw materials. A fortnight later, he charged at Abercarn that the Conservatives were becoming the party of 'Corn tax and clericalism!' As for Chamberlain, Lloyd George had only scorn: he was a man who had thrown over free trade just as he had thrown over earlier ideas and policies. Chamberlain, he charged, 'seemed to suffer from political spasms'.[85] In the following months, Lloyd George continued to 'go for Joe'. At Oldham on 10 October, he claimed that Chamberlain's plan was nothing less than a return to the bad old days of the Corn Laws when agricultural protection favoured farmers and landlords over the needs of poorer consumers. Soon, Lloyd George predicted, 'lords and dukes and earls and squire and baronets' would be 'running and clucking' towards Chamberlain 'like a flock of fowls when they hear the corn shaken in the tin'.[86] The following month Lloyd George spoke at the Oxford Union, where the question before the House was whether or not to condemn protective taxes contained within the fiscal proposals of tariff reform. As before, Chamberlain was the target. Lloyd George wondered aloud whether or not Chamberlain himself was very serious about tariff policy. After all, he had forsaken others, such as old age pensions. Indeed, said Lloyd George (to the apparent delight of much of his audience), 'the illimitable veldt of politics was littered with his abandoned guns'.[87]

Undaunted by Liberal criticism, Chamberlain initially enjoyed significant success in his campaign for tariff reform in late 1903 and early 1904. Playing upon the uncertainties engendered by a post-war economic downturn and a deep sense of malaise at the diplomatic and military failures during the South African War, he captured the attention of an uneasy public. If Britain and the empire stood firm, Chamberlain declared, a renewed sense of national purpose would follow. Additionally, he promised substantial and widespread social benefits not only for the poor and disadvantaged, but for British workers as well, who would gain from a revived economy. To lure doubters, he created a research and information agency, the Tariff Reform League. Throughout 1903, he steadily made headway in putting together diverse and enthusiastic support. Indeed, by playing the imperial card while simultaneously revealing the ace of greater prosperity at home, Chamberlain had a strong hand in advocating tariff reform.

In early 1904, however, dissident voices among some Conservatives began to question tariff reform. A small but articulate knot of Conservative free traders was doubtful about the protectionist implications of the plan. Other Conservatives, who had never forgotten nor forgiven Chamberlain's early radical days, mistrusted the Colonial Secretary. Equally important was Chamberlain's personal behaviour. A decided certainty of his own convictions, allied to his notable lack of forbearance to any opposition, alienated some potential supporters. As his campaign for tariff reform moved forward, Chamberlain's steamroller tactics began to clash with Balfour's tentative political style. Now Prime Minister, Balfour's attempts to follow a centrist policy by balancing free trade and protectionist factions was anathema to Chamberlain. Never one to stand aside, Chamberlain began to challenge Balfour for the leadership of the Conservative Party.[88]

Additional governmental missteps further invigorated the Liberal opposition, especially among nonconformists. For example, in the early months of 1904 news from South Africa revealed that Alfred Lord Milner, the South African High Commissioner (from 1897 to 1905) and a main instigator of the South African war, had authorized the importation and employment of thousands of Chinese workmen as a source of cheap labour in the mines. Apart from their low wages, they were clearly discriminated against. If they failed to work properly, they could be imprisoned. When not at work, they were restricted to their quarters – essentially substandard all-male compounds. The nonconformist conscience was pricked at what they called 'Chinese slavery'. The National Council of Free Churches drafted a condemnatory resolution, which was soon adopted by numerous chapel congregations throughout the country.[89]

Equally unsettling to nonconformists was Balfour's Licensing Bill of 1904. This was another in a long line of demonstrative examples of the politicization of the drink question. Nevertheless, Conservatives were not unaware of alcohol abuse and attempted to restrict its worst excesses. The 1902 Licensing Act, for example, extended magistrates' control over the sale of alcohol by off licences. Balfour's 1904 proposal, however, seemed to move in the opposite direction by proposing a new procedure for the renewal or refusal of licences to publicans. Normally such licences came up for renewal annually by local magistrates, sitting in special sessions. Under the terms of the bill, if renewal were denied, publicans would be compensated from a special fund raised by a tax on the trade. Furthermore, the bill seemed to reject any notion of a local veto option on licensing. To the temperance movement and its Liberal allies, the bill consolidated an implied alliance between brewers and publicans and the Conservative Party. A religiously intolerant government, it would seem, had now gone so far as to subsidize sin, and to assure that the pub on the corner would remain a temptation to the chapel down the street.[90] Conflict between the Conservatives and 'the Trade' on the one hand and Liberals and their temperance allies on the other created – as *The Times* put it – an 'extraordinary interest' in the bill.[91]

The Licensing Bill also provided an issue that perfectly suited Lloyd George's talents. He had been consistent in his speeches in the House of Commons in upholding temperance demands. He had become one of the two 'Temperance Whips' whose duty it was to ensure the attendance of Welsh MPs during any discussion of a licensing bill in the House of Commons.[92] Since he had consistently denounced the principle of compensating dispossessed publicans, it was not surprising that he condemned the Licensing Bill of 1904 as a 'shameless surrender to the drink industry'.[93] On 7 June 1904, he criticized those provisions of the proposed bill which appeared to grant licences in perpetuity. 'The Government', he charged, 'are putting licences on exactly the same footing as any other freehold'. If passed into law, such an act would undercut temperance reform, and would place the government ever deeper into the hands of the brewing industry'.[94] The government, however, had the votes and the measure passed into law.

By the beginning of 1905, various issues that had been plaguing Conservative governments for several years gave Liberals a potent electoral advantage. The South African war had not only revealed squandered resources and military mismanagement, but it had allowed the Liberals to reaffirm their traditional irenic posture in international affairs. Tariff reform had not only divided the Conservatives, but it provided the opportunity for Liberals to recapture enthusiasm for their free trade policy both at home and abroad. In addition, the nonconformist religious wing of the Liberal Party brought a revivalist moral enthusiasm in their opposition to various Conservative initiatives – their educational schemes, their alliance with the drink trade, and government-sponsored indentured servitude of imported Chinese workers in South Africa.

That the political sense of the country was clearly moving against the Balfour government was much in evidence during a number of successive by-election losses. Indeed, the adverse trend in by-elections can be seen in retrospect to have begun in 1901. At first, the Conservatives could claim with reasonable assurance that such losses were the natural results of electoral slippage after general elections. By 1903, however, with the loss of Newmarket in January of that year, by-election losses for the Unionists had reached seven. Two months later, Will Crooks, the Labour Mayor of Poplar, won a significant victory in the Woolwich by-election in a straight fight with a Conservative, polling 61 per cent of the vote. This was a constituency where a Conservative had been returned unopposed in 1900.[95] Twenty-five seats altogether were lost during the Balfour regime. As Lloyd George noted hopefully in late 1904: 'Time is in our favour as the natural life of this Govt has not much to run.'[96]

With the prospect of victory at the next general election, ambitions among various Liberal aspirants for office rose dramatically, especially after the elusive Rosebery seemed to recede from public life. If Rosebery were determined to remain on the sidelines (his stated position in politics was notoriously fickle), his followers were equally determined that his Liberal imperial ideas should remain strong within the party. Thus, in September 1905, H.H. Asquith, R.B. Haldane and Sir Edward Grey banded together in the so-called Relugas Compact in order to force the centre-left Campbell-Bannerman (CB), the likeliest prime ministerial candidate after Rosebery, to take a peerage and be elevated to the Lords.[97] From there he would serve as Prime Minister while the members of the Compact would effectively govern from the House of Commons as chief officers of the Cabinet.[98] If Campbell-Bannerman refused this arrangement, the ambitious trio would make it clear that they would not serve under him. The ostensible reason for this manoeuvre was CB's age (he was 65), his indifferent health and his faint public image. The more obvious political reason was that the imperial Liberal trio distrusted his ability – given his criticisms of the South African War – to resist the influence of the radical wing of the party.

In none of these high-level negotiations for office did Lloyd George have a role. Nevertheless, he had been the object of overtures by the Liberal leadership. In January 1904, for example, Lloyd George visited Falloden, Grey's seat (in Northumberland), where he was assured that in any future Liberal government, Lloyd George would have a place in the Cabinet.[99] Later that same year, Lloyd George was invited by Rosebery to Dalmeny House in Edinburgh where mutual pleasantries passed between the two politicians.[100] Perhaps this Liberal imperial courting was not too surprising: to capture Lloyd George for the cause of Liberal imperialism would bring a formidable talent aboard. And, after all, Lloyd George himself might be available. If he had begun his criticism of the Boer War as a radical, he seems to have shifted more toward the centre in his later remarks, developing his position as a patriot who wished a competent prosecution of the war. In any case, Lloyd George himself was clearly interested in cultivating all wings of the Liberal Party.[101] After he departed company from Rosebery at Dalmeny in November 1904, he went directly on to Perth to see Campbell-Bannerman.[102]

The slow collapse of the Balfour ministry provided ample opportunities for Lloyd George's caustic wit and anti-Conservative diatribes throughout 1905. Speaking before a Liberal demonstration at Conway Town Hall in January, he noted there were 'rumours of an approaching dissolution', though it seemed that Prime Minister Balfour, 'would rather go on than go off'. This was understandable, Lloyd George continued – to the delight of the crowd – since 'most offenders preferred a year's reprieve to immediate execution'. But, he assured them further, such delays revealed the Conservatives 'hanging desperately' to office and earned them only additional contempt from the people.[103] Within a week, he had travelled to Glasgow to another Liberal gathering which also heard him excoriate the Conservatives. The government's mandate, he claimed, 'was exhausted … Their job, whatever it was, had been done very badly, but they were still hanging about the yard'. To increasing cheers and laughter, he claimed that he would not mind so much, 'but they were keeping their names on the pay-sheet'. More seriously, he damned the Balfour ministry for its self-complacency which had led to unemployment. 'Their incapacity was egregious, their vanity colossal. A Government of that sort was a public danger.'[104]

Keeping his name before the public was a useful tactic in Lloyd George's angling for a position in any forthcoming Liberal government. He also continued his cultivation of prominent Liberals into the early months of 1905. In February of that year, he gave a dinner honouring the Canadian Finance Minister. Also present were such Liberal luminaries as Asquith, Morley and Haldane. 'My first political dinner party', he confided to William, 'So feel excited'.[105] In March, he returned to Wales for another Liberal demonstration, this time at Llanelli Market Hall. There he denounced the Conservative government as doomed men, 'shuffling along to perdition'. To the increasing merriment of his friendly audience, he remarked further that they 'loiter in the condemned cell … and have to be dragged along inch by inch to the place of execution …'. He charged that in their final days, the Conservatives were bringing contempt upon themselves because of their lack of guidance and direction for the country. 'When the crew of a vessel have to cling to the rail with both hands so as not to be swept overboard by the roll of the ship, they cannot be expected to do much in the way of steering.'[106] Two days later, he spoke at a Liberal rally in support of G.H. Radford, the Liberal and radical candidate for Parliament from East Islington. He had just come, he said, from the House of Commons where he had been engaged in attempting to turn out 'the present rather stupid Government'. He also denounced the education and protectionist policies of the Balfour government.[107] The following month, at a meeting of the Liberal Association of Caernarfon Boroughs, Lloyd George reminded his hearers that the Balfour Acts of 1902 and 1904 had not been forgotten. In a future administration, he promised that the Liberals 'would bring the education question boldly to the front'.[108]

Lloyd George's countryside campaign during the first half of 1905 was, if anything, surpassed by his speeches in the latter months of that year as the death throes of the Conservative government became more pronounced. The internecine struggles for leadership between Balfour and Chamberlain over tariff reform and the leadership of the Conservative Party sharpened Lloyd George's criticisms. At the Huddersfield Junior Liberal Association in early May, he again criticized tariff reform.[109] A few days later, at a meeting of the South Wolverhampton Liberal Association in Bilston – within sight of Chamberlain's 'Duchy' – Lloyd George made reference to the Birmingham riot of 1902. He was, he assured his appreciative audience, 'accustomed when he visited the Midlands to receive a warm welcome'. Then he lambasted Chamberlain as the purveyor of 'quack remedies'.[110] Balfour was not forgotten as Lloyd George continued his critical tour. Speaking at the Chester Music Hall, he at first damned Balfour by faint praise, declaring that the Prime Minister was the only distinguished man in the ministry. But then, Lloyd George quickly changed his tack. He defied 'any one to say that he had proved himself a great ruler of a great Empire'. In fact, from the moment that he took office, Balfour had 'muddled every business he undertook'. Worse than that was his Education Act, which had been carried 'by a trick and a fraud'.[111] During a conference of Free Church delegates at Fishguard in September 1905, Lloyd George returned to the education question. In Wales, they did not want the educational standards set 'by second or third rate clerks', nor by such 'an educational dunderhead' as Lord Londonderry, who 'with all the advantages that wealth could confer, could not pass his "Little-go" at Oxford'.[112] Within a few days, Lloyd George repeated his criticisms of the Education Act at Porth in the Rhondda Valley during a conference of Free Church and public authorities. He again charged that Wales was governed by a third-rate clerk in the Education Department – 'just like an Indian district on the borders of the Himalayas'.[113]

Lloyd George's appetite for invective remained unabated the following month. At a meeting of the Kingston-on-Thames Liberal Association in late October, he spoke in support of Robert Whyte, the Liberal candidate for Parliament. Whyte as an MP, he said, would help 'turn out the worst Government that any man in the assembly could possibly recollect'. The government was 'rotten' and 'should be flung upon the dunghill'. To rising cheers, he claimed: 'It was polluting the air.' The remainder of his speech touched on the issues that Liberals were raising throughout the country: the Education Act; Chinese labour in South Africa; and tariff reform.[114] A week later, Lloyd George carried the Liberal message north of the Scots border to Kirkcaldy and its Liberal Association, which symbolically enough met at the Adam Smith Hall in that city. In this speech, he made the most sustained attack yet on Balfour, whom he claimed was 'not a man, but a mannerism'.[115] A few days later, in his last speech as a backbencher, Lloyd George spoke at Glasgow University in support of Asquith's candidature as the Lord Rector of the university. Here he adopted a loftier tone than in his speeches in Parliament or in the countryside. Yet the political message that he had been making for many months was unmistakable. Young university men, he said, must soon meet the test of ranging themselves either alongside 'hopeless reaction' or on the side of 'progress, liberty, and freedom'. Theirs was the choice to make. But he promised that in the Liberal parliament to come, its first duty would be 'to make changes for the better and to cope with poverty and wretchedness'. It would be a great contrast to the present government, which 'would die with their drawn salaries in their hands'.[116]

While Lloyd George was stumping the countryside, there were disturbing signs of internal squabbling among the leading Liberal claimants for office. On 25 November, in a speech at Bodmin, Rosebery, whose influence had been receding, openly criticized Campbell-Bannerman's adherence to a 'step-by-step' approach to Irish Home Rule. For Gladstonian Liberals, who still venerated the memory of their leader and his determination to settle the Irish question, Rosebery's remarks were anathema. Typical was a letter to Campbell-Bannerman from Thomas Bayley, MP for the Chesterfield Division of Derbyshire, who denounced Rosebery: 'He has now repudiated every good cause for which he fought under his late leader, Mr Gladstone.'[117] Even Rosebery's supporters were disappointed and for many it was the last straw. They could no longer tolerate his self-aggrandizing postures which alternated with his disappearances from public life. After this, Rosebery's isolation was complete.[118] In the meantime, Rosebery's three chief lieutenants, still bound by the Relugas Compact, sought an agreement with CB by which he would be sent to the Lords, leaving the real governing to Liberal leaders in the House of Commons. However, Campbell-Bannerman – apparently hearing intimations of the plot – made it plain in an interview with Asquith on 13 November 1905 that that he would remain in the Commons and that the disposition of all offices in the Cabinet would be his prerogative. Rather meekly, Asquith concurred. Grey and Haldane, after several days of intense negotiations, also acquiesced. The conspirators had misjudged their man. The Liberal leadership was now firmly in place, waiting for its opportunity.

So long in coming, the Balfour ministry ended in an unusual fashion. Rather than dissolving Parliament outright, Balfour simply resigned on 4 December 1905, forcing the Liberal Party quickly into office before an election could be held. This rare practice was possibly designed to catch the Liberals off guard and perhaps cause disarray in their ranks as they scrambled to form a government. Within a week, however, Campbell-Bannerman had assembled a strong team. With Rosebery out of the running and the Relugas conspirators brought to heel, CB managed to construct a balanced ministry with himself as indisputable head.[119] Major ministers were: Asquith at the Exchequer; Haldane, War Secretary; Grey, the Foreign Office. Thus the Relugas Compact, if defunct, had been rewarded to a degree. It was also a sign that Campbell-Bannerman recognized the talents of the trio; and also perhaps an indication of the strength of imperial sentiment that remained within the Liberal Party.[120] Other important Cabinet members were: Herbert Gladstone, Home Office; John Morley, the India Office; and John Burns, the Local Government Board. These, and a dozen others who made up the Cabinet, were a desirable mix of Liberal imperialists, centrists and a few radicals. With the inclusion of Burns, there was even a nod toward the working-class vote.

Lloyd George was made President of the Board of Trade.[121] At the age of 42, he was the youngest Cabinet member on a talented governmental team. If Lloyd George had somehow faltered in the previous months, or had been less of a voice for Liberalism, he might not have made the cut. But his reputation as a gifted speechmaker and a fierce defender of the Liberals, especially during his 1905 campaign against the Conservative government, was a strong mark in his favour. He had made important speeches throughout the kingdom, supporting Liberal candidates, castigating the opposition, energizing and helping to unite a broad Liberal front against Balfour's ministry. He simply could not be ignored. He was additionally a voice for Wales, that Liberal bastion, which would expect a suitable reward for its fidelity. And, if Lloyd George were an acknowledged radical, he had also begun to display an emerging centrist streak. Still, Campbell-Bannerman was unenthusiastic. 'I suppose we ought to include him', he is reported to have said while forming his Cabinet.[122] In any case, President of the Board of Trade was not a senior Cabinet level post. Though relatively humble in status, the Board of Trade had its advantages. With its emphasis on the technical details of regulating harbours, railways and shipping, and with its supervisory role in collecting labour and business statistics, the Board of Trade under an energetic President might well be crucial in the coming struggle between tariff reform and free trade. Moreover, the Board of Trade had proved a useful training ground for promising politicians; this had certainly been true of both Gladstone and Chamberlain.

Once the government was in place, Parliament was dissolved on 16 December 1905. Elections began the following month. Although the signs before the election clearly predicted a substantial Liberal victory – even Conservatives thought so – no one was quite prepared for its extent.[123] Not only had the electoral issues worked in the Liberals' favour: increased party funds and an improved organization in the constituencies aided in bringing out the Liberal vote. The Liberal campaign was also more inventive than the Conservative effort. Street rallies by Liberals paraded pigtailed and manacled Chinese in reference to the South African policy of indentured labour. Large and small loaves of bread demonstrated the impact of tariff reform upon working-class food. Liberal hecklers at Conservative meetings were full of fire. Because Liberal newspapers had begun to make some headway against the dominant Conservative London press, Liberals could also get their message out in the capital city more easily than in the recent past. The Liberals, moreover, had a substantial oratorical arsenal in Asquith, Grey, Haldane, Churchill (who had recently crossed the aisle to join his free trade colleagues) and of course Lloyd George. In contrast, there was a noticeable lack of platform talent among the Conservatives.[124]

As he had acted throughout the latter months of 1905 – when he had pummelled the Conservative government on the emerging issues of the day – so in the month-long election campaign, Lloyd George relentlessly denounced Liberal opponents. Early on, during his frequent appearances in his own constituency, his favourite target was the government's religious and educational missteps. At a meeting of the Welsh Campaign Committee at Caernarfon on 2 January 1906, Lloyd George congratulated those who had participated in the Welsh revolt against the Education Act: in so doing, they had 'saved Wales'. He pledged that the Act would be amended as 'one of the first legislative measures' undertaken by a Liberal government. Such an amendment would guarantee complete popular control over schools and would abolish all religious tests. He also promised that a Welsh national council of education would be established, giving Wales control of its own educational system. At the annual convention of the Welsh National Liberal Council held in Caernarfon in the afternoon of that same day, Lloyd George (who chaired the meeting) once again congratulated his audience for their part in resisting the Conservative Board of Education's attempts to 'put under the little Welsh nation'. He additionally promised action on Welsh disestablishment once the Liberals came to power.[125] At Bangor, he broadened his attacks by claiming that tariff reform would adversely affect working men's wages. Joseph Chamberlain, as the author of tariff reform, was a specific target for Lloyd George's sarcasm.[126] Noting that Chamberlain had recently appeared angry during his own campaign rounds, Lloyd George, to the delight of the crowd, remarked that Chamberlain's temper 'was just as bad as his statistics'.[127] Two days later at Pwllheli, addressing a crowd estimated at 3,000, Lloyd George raised the issue of Chinese slavery, charging that the Unionist imperial government had built 'slave compounds' to house the Chinese labourers in South Africa. The Chinese were kept 'like dogs in a kennel'.[128] At a meeting at Criccieth the following day, Lloyd George reminded his enthusiastic audience that he was 'a Criccieth boy'. He again emphasized tariff reform and 'the perils of protection', claiming that if the Conservatives were elected, protection would be the order of the day: the first victims would be working men and their pay.[129]

Lloyd George was also active outside Wales in supporting Liberal candidates. In early January he spoke at Fulham for his friend Timothy Davies, once again emphasizing Chinese slavery and defending free trade. At Croydon, he pointed out the prosperity of the country was due in large part to free trade policies. At Leamington, within the ambit of Chamberlain's 'Duchy', his attempt to speak in support of the Liberal candidate for Warwick and Leamington was at first unsuccessful when a crowd of Conservatives interrupted him. Retreating to the friendlier confines of the Liberal Club, he joked about the Birmingham 'imports' who had infiltrated the Liberal meeting. The rest of his speech was devoted to the Chinese labour question. Rounding out his electoral tour in England, Lloyd George spoke in support of the Liberal candidate for the Altrincham Division of Cheshire on 23 January. After another attack upon Chamberlain, whose 'little game was up' because the country would not be taken in by his 'fiscal reform fiasco', Lloyd George reiterated a fateful promise – that the forthcoming Liberal government was determined to change the Balfour Education Act of 1902; and indeed 'one of the first things' the Liberals would do was to dispose of the great 'denominational quarrels'.[130]

Such overwhelming advantages as the Liberals enjoyed during the election campaign brought a smashing victory for the party. They won 400 seats outright. The Irish Nationalists, a natural ally for the Liberals, provided an additional 83 seats to the Liberal majority. And, in a portentous development as well as a testament to the electoral savvy of the Liberals in this election, 30 Labour Party representatives were elected to the House of Commons. This was the result of secret negotiations between Ramsay MacDonald, the Labour Representation Committee's secretary, and Herbert Gladstone for the Liberal Party. The agreement was that 30 of the

50 candidates put forward by the newly-established LRC would be unopposed by Liberal candidates. This would prevent split votes between the Liberals and the LRC candidates in certain constituencies which might otherwise benefit Conservative candidates. Twenty-four of these 30 were successful. Ramsay MacDonald himself was elected when paired with a Liberal for Leicester. The fact that the LRC was willing to ally officially with the Liberal Party in designated constituencies probably also benefited Liberals elsewhere in unaffiliated working-class constituencies.[131] There were an additional two dozen members of a 'Lib–Lab' group of trade unionists, mostly miners, who would also undoubtedly vote with the Liberals.[132]

Overall, almost half of the 1906 Parliament were new MPs (318 out of 670). This Parliament also contained, at 157, the largest number of nonconformist MPs in its history: this matched the entire number of Conservative MPs returned (157) to the House of Commons. Balfour himself lost at East Manchester. Several other Conservative Cabinet members also went down to defeat. Even these low numbers did not adequately reflect the weakness of a once unified party, for it was deeply divided between Balfour, Chamberlain, and an undecided smaller minority. The battle for the leadership of the Conservative Party continued unabated after the election. In his own re-election campaign for the Caernarfon Boroughs Lloyd George benefited from the Liberal landslide, winning by far the largest margin he had ever achieved: the vote was 3,221 to 1,997. His opponent, R.A. Naylor, an Englishman who knew no Welsh and who ran an ineffective campaign, was clearly overmatched. In fact, Lloyd George scarcely mentioned him during the campaign, preferring instead to issue homilies about representing the people and upholding democracy. How he would balance his new responsibility as a Cabinet member with his reputation in the countryside as a radical rabble-rouser remained to be seen.

5

IN THE CABINET

When the House of Commons met for the first time on 13 February 1906 under the new Liberal government there was considerable enthusiasm and high expectations in the majority party. Almost 20 years of Conservative political dominance had been overturned. The Conservative legislative legacy could now be thrust aside and a Liberal imprint established in Parliament and the country. But in spite of the advantages of numbers and initial good will, the ministry struggled in its earliest years of office. Indeed, historians have often severely faulted the newly elected government. Peter Rowland observes that the Liberals 'had no definite programme' and 'no definite ideas' on entering office: their plans for governing were in fact 'both reactionary and negative'.[1] G.R. Searle adds that the landslide victory swept into Parliament 'a motley crowd of enthusiastic reformers of one kind or another' who ruled over an initial period 'of aimlessness and drift'. Their main legislative priority ('if indeed there was one at all') seemed geared to paying off the vocal nonconformists who had turned out in such numbers to support them.[2] H.V. Emy observes 'a lack of any conceptual framework'[3] within the Cabinet. Martin Pugh thinks that ministers 'became bogged down'.[4] George L. Bernstein calls 1906–08 'The Years of Disappointment' for the Liberal government.[5] Gilbert notes the government's 'sorry performance' in the first three years.[6]

There is some truth to these criticisms, as we shall see. The very size of the Liberal victory and the large number of new MPs could lead to divisions and confusions within the ranks. As one of the junior whips confided to his diary during the second year of the ministry: 'One has to deal with a great mob of new members, most of them absolutely ignorant of the ways of Parliament.'[7] This was especially true of the large nonconformist body, whose denominational diversity guaranteed political fragmentation.[8] In addition, as Chris Cook has pointed out, there was a serious division among the Liberal MPs between those who supported wide-ranging reforms and those who opposed them. In spite of expectations among radical Liberals, the political composition of the Liberal MPs proved to be only moderately liberal.[9] These fissures would have been repaired more easily if Campbell-Bannerman had exercised effective control over the party; but a firm hand rarely characterized his leadership. In addition, his continuing ill health and the death of his wife in August

1906 sapped his interest and energy, lending an acephalous quality to the Liberals in Parliament and to the party organization at large.[10] Within this context of a somewhat unstructured Cabinet, whose meetings were short and infrequent, each Cabinet member was left in some degree to his own devices.[11]

Administrative disorganization within the new government would seem to offer an unusual opportunity for Lloyd George. Given his formidable reputation as a driving critic, a dangerous parliamentary guerrilla and a skilful leader of surprise raids and ambushes upon his foes throughout the kingdom,[12] combined with the absence of any restraining prime ministerial hand, it would be natural enough for him to use his position at the Board of Trade as a springboard for continued political activism, especially against the substantially weakened Conservatives. That Lloyd George would become a responsible member of a Cabinet in command of such technical and complex topics as commerce, transportation and labour relations was, perhaps, initially difficult to imagine. Yet he proved a distinct surprise not only to his Liberal colleagues, but also to historians since. Grigg praises him as 'a patient, open-minded and resourceful pragmatist'.[13] Gilbert is more effusive. He writes that Lloyd George's tenure as President of the Board of Trade displayed 'an unexpected virtuosity at conciliation, and an aptitude for the unspectacular work of bill briefing and minute preparation which with his good humour and courtesy, won general applause'.[14] Morgan notes that Lloyd George 'proved himself to be a firm and resilient administrator, with a remarkable record of legislative achievement'.[15] More recent observations are no less appreciative. Ian Packer praises Lloyd George's legislative record as 'solid', with a capacity for 'skilfully piloting' bills through Parliament and revealing 'unexpected talents'. Packer concludes that Lloyd George's performance at the Board of Trade helped to erase his former reputation as a wild man of the hustings: he became a 'a sober, respectable statesman' at the Board of Trade.[16] Among Lloyd George's contemporaries, even that fierce Tory critic Balcarres seemed surprised when he (grudgingly) jotted down in his diary: 'Lloyd George has done well in his bills': in addition, he was 'civil in the House'.[17]

How can one explain such a sudden shift in Lloyd George's political image? How did the firebrand become a Solon? Was it merely a matter of opportunistic play-acting? A chameleon-like temporary change of colouring with no substantive alteration?

These are difficult questions to answer authoritatively. No doubt in part it was the case, as is often true of populist leaders, that high office brought greater responsibilities. Lloyd George also believed, as President of the Board of Trade, that he had a special responsibility in countering the Chamberlainite tariff reform. Chamberlain used statistical evidence, marshalled by his own Tariff Reform Commission, to make the case for the failures of Liberal free trade policies. To combat Chamberlain on his own ground would be a primary political task of Lloyd George's new office. In this, he was particularly fortunate. The civil service staff at the Board of Trade, like most departments of government, had become increasingly professionalized and efficient during the late nineteenth century.[18] Additionally, the Board had broadened its primary task of statistical gathering into conditions of trade and commerce by creating a Labour Department. Under its first Labour Commissioner, Hubert Llewellyn Smith, the Board of Trade also began to collect accurate evidence on such important issues as unemployment and the quality of work life. Smith brought to his task a deeply felt sympathy for the poor, whom he had first encountered as a student at Oxford where he joined the University Settlement Movement and later worked for Charles Booth on his path-breaking survey of London's poor.[19] Thus the Board of Trade, especially its Labour Department under Smith, stood ready in 1906 to provide the necessary information for any reforming President.[20] And no less importantly, such statistics rightly read could be a counterpoint to the tariff reformers.

As it happened, however, the tide of tariff reform receded somewhat during the first few years of the Liberal ministry due in large part to Chamberlain's removal from active politics. Suffering a massive stroke in July 1906, he was thereafter disabled, lingering until his death in 1914. Thus Lloyd George could turn his considerable energy directly to more constructive reforms at the Board of Trade. In this task, there seems little doubt that Smith influenced Lloyd George. Other members of Lloyd George's first-rate administrative team included his parliamentary secretary, Hudson Kearley, a self-made millionaire businessman and MP for Devonport (later created 1st Viscount Devonport). Lloyd George's two private secretaries, William Clark (later High Commissioner in Canada and South Africa), and the Welshman, John Rowland, who later became chair of the Welsh Board of Health, provided additional support for the reformist inclinations of their chief.

Lloyd George's first significant legislative act as President of the Board of Trade was the Merchant Shipping Bill, which addressed two long-standing problems. The first concerned the conditions of merchant sailors while at sea. Poor food, uncomfortable maritime accommodations and an unsafe working environment were common among the ships of the merchant fleet. Yet compared to other maritime countries, British sailors enjoyed better safety conditions and comfort as a result of a succession of reforms since the 1870s. Any additional reforms, furthermore, with their attendant costs, might put British shipping at a disadvantage to their foreign competitors whose shipping costs were lower. An example was the effect of the Plimsoll Line, required of British ships to prevent overloading. Because foreign vessels were exempt from a required loadline, their cargoes could be piled high onto ships bound for British ports, enabling them to undercut British companies in freight charges. Thus, ship owners had grievances. To counterbalance the needs of sailors and ship owners, Lloyd George proceeded in a novel fashion. Inviting representative ship owners and sailors to the Board of Trade for consultations, he solicited their opinions on forthcoming legislation. A few weeks later, he summoned them again, this time presenting a draft for their written comments and suggestions. Both sides were completely won over. The bill effectively removed the advantages of foreign freighters by requiring them to comply with British standards. In addition, Lloyd George raised the Plimsoll line slightly thus allowing more freight to be handled by British carriers. With these changes, ship owners were quite willing to acquiesce in the cost of proposed reforms to improve the lot of the common seaman.[21]

With this precedent in view, Lloyd George thereafter followed the practice of conferring with deputations during his remaining two years as President of the Board of Trade. Not all of these meetings resulted in legislation, but they were of mutual benefit both to the Board of Trade and to the interested parties in sharing information. Lloyd George invariably promised to examine the issues brought forward and to institute changes when necessary. On their part, the deputations seemed satisfied to secure a hearing before the Board. A few examples follow. In February 1906, the parliamentary committee of the Trades Union Congress recommending cheap workmen's trains met with a railway company deputation. Under the chairmanship of Lloyd George, each side stated its case. The TUC committee was particularly interested in relieving overcrowding at certain hours of the day, which could be remedied by the railway companies' laying on more trains. Lloyd George responded sympathetically, promising 'to go into the matter very carefully'. In an entirely different case the following month, a deputation from the Associated Chambers of Commerce asked the government to enforce more rigorously the Merchandise Marks Act of 1887 which prohibited foreign manufacturers from falsely claiming their goods were English made and selling them both in England and on the continent under that pretence. Lloyd George recommended that local chambers of commerce should be responsible for investigating these cases and then bring them before the Board of Trade for its consideration. Later in the year, a large deputation representing numerous trading interests appeared before Lloyd George, complaining about the railways' increasing reluctance to assume liability for the transport of commercial goods. Lloyd George again responded sympathetically, admitting that it was sometimes 'exceedingly difficult' for small traders 'to fight this great powerful combination of railway companies': he intimated that the whole question of railway rates might be reconsidered 'in the near future'.[22]

Having established lines of communication with various commercial and industrial groups through these common meetings, Lloyd George moved forward with remedial legislation. To gather support for his Census of Production Bill of 1906, for example, he again used deputations as a forum for discussion. The idea behind the proposed legislation was to provide accurate statistics of home industries. Introducing the bill in the House of Commons, Lloyd George pointed out that such a survey already existed for imports and exports but that there was no dependable data with regard to the home industries. 'If trade is going back', he informed the House, 'or it is at a standstill, or not making the progress we expect it to make, the sooner we know it the better'. The census would be compulsory and would require information on the nature of every business, its output, materials used, persons employed, their wages and the type of plant and machinery employed.[23] The proposal met with a favourable response in the House.

There was some opposition expressed, however, by employers concerning the expense and trouble of such a census. Others feared that trade secrets could be revealed. Overall, the bill seemed too intrusive a measure of state control. Lloyd George assured the critics that the idea was not to pry into the workings of individual companies, but to gather aggregate statistics. To put their minds at ease, in July he met a deputation representing important employers' associations, including the Lancashire cotton trades and the London building trades. He had already promised the House of Commons that the act would not be 'inquisitorial'. To the deputation, he made an additional promise. He would establish an advisory committee, which would determine how best to apply the act to particular industries.[24]

Additional legislation designed both to encourage and protect British industry included the Patents Act of 1907. Its most important clause closed a loophole in British patent law. Prior to the act, foreign businessmen could take out patents in Britain and thereafter decline to develop them further. This had the effect of holding the ring for that particular patent with the clear intention of forestalling any British development. Under Lloyd George's Patents Act, foreign patentees were granted only one year to begin working their patents within Britain. Otherwise, they would forfeit them. To some this might seem an unusual interventionist position for a Liberal politician to take. It seemed to strike at free trade principles. Lloyd George denied this. In his remarks to a large and influential deputation in the early days of framing the bill, he declared that the bill had nothing to do with either free trade or protection. It would neither discriminate 'against the foreigner' nor was it an infringement of free trade because it ultimately cheapened production and thus benefited the consumer.[25]

The last of Lloyd George's major legislation at the Board of Trade was the great work of administrative consolidation at the chaotic port of London. Before Lloyd George's reform, governing the port was divided among three authorities (the Thames Conservancy, the Waterman's Company and Trinity House). The economic functions of the port were also divided, shared between three dock companies – London and India, Surrey Commercial and Millwall. Over many years, it had become apparent that modernization and expansion of the facilities of the docks were imperative if London were to maintain its status as a world leader in shipping. Entrenched interests at the port itself, as well as within the London Corporation, the Chamber of Commerce and the London County Council, had to be addressed. Lloyd George well understood the complexities of his task. After some preliminary discussions with the various authorities, he admitted that he could not 'get one deputation to agree with another'. In late 1906, he publicly announced a year's delay in order 'to get those gentlemen to knock their heads together somehow and to arrive at some sort of common understanding' before a bill was submitted to Parliament.[26]

In the meantime, with the special cooperation of his parliamentary secretary, Hudson Kearley, Lloyd George mounted a campaign for change at the port. In May 1907, Kearley and Lloyd George paid official visits to the important continental ports at Antwerp and Hamburg. Upon their return, Lloyd George publicly reported that the up-to-date foreign port facilities would soon leave London behind in the competitive race for the world's shipping: London port must forswear its 'hand-to-mouth' policy.[27] Delays continued but in April 1908, just prior to his appointment as Chancellor of the Exchequer, Lloyd George introduced his bill to the House of Commons. It created a Port of London Authority with the power to make compulsory purchases of riparian land as needed, subject to Board of Trade consent after a public inquiry. The bill received the Royal Assent in December, and within a few months the new Authority took control of the entire port. The first chairman of the Authority was Hudson Kearley, who held the post until 1925.[28]

Lloyd George's first months at the Board of Trade won him significant praise – not least from Campbell-Bannerman. Lloyd George of course quickly related to William the Prime Minister's congratulations of a job well done. 'He wanted to tell me how pleased he was with my success at the Board of Trade. It was the greatest success of the Ministry. My praise was in everybody's mouth. I was known to be an incisive, ready & witty speaker'; and moreover, 'everybody was talking about [the] successful way in which I was managing my Department. I reconciled interests which appeared quite irreconcilable…'.[29] Indeed, Lloyd George's skill as a conciliator was much in evidence during his term of office at the Board of Trade. This was clearly demonstrated in his ability to forge compromises between contending parties, particularly in settling industrial disputes.

Perhaps Lloyd George's most notable success was his mediation of the longstanding disputes between management and labour in the railway system. As the trade union movement continued to grow in numbers and influence among the working classes during the late nineteenth and into the early years of the twentieth century, railway managers became increasingly intransigent, in part because the aging railway system of the country was forcing much needed restructuring and capital enhancement. To save money, railway companies often followed a policy of keeping wages low: railway men had won only a 5 per cent increase in recent years, whereas workers in the building, cotton manufacturing and engineering industries had received increases of 18, 23 and 26 per cent.[30] To redress these inequities, in October 1907 the Amalgamated Society of Railway Servants (ASRS) demanded higher pay, better working conditions and recognition of their union from all railway companies. When the railway directors refused, a deadlock ensued: the ASRS then approved strike action.

With a national railway strike a distinct possibility, Lloyd George followed these events closely. His view was that the railway directors were stubborn at best, pig-headed at worst, and prone to making inflammatory statements against trade unions. In general, he viewed with sympathy the claims of the ASRS. He was also doubtless aware that Richard Bell, leader of the ASRS and Lib–Lab MP for Derby, had attempted on several occasions to enter into discussions with the railway managers.[31] He also learned that Bell would not press for union recognition if the ASRS could be assured of a satisfactory method of discussing with the managers their grievances and some guarantee that their working conditions would be seriously addressed. With this information in hand, Lloyd George decided on a firm policy with the railway managers.[32] On 25 October, he met with 17 chairmen and 12 general managers of railway companies at the Board of Trade. Hudson Kearley, an eyewitness to the meeting, wrote afterwards that Lloyd George completely dominated the discussion, essentially by reviewing in moderate tones the claims and counterclaims of the two sides. Lloyd George additionally pointed out that there was a natural desire for workers everywhere to improve their conditions; but he also stated unequivocally that a railway strike would be harmful to the national interest.[33] He concluded by asking the deputation to select six of their number to meet again soon.

Lloyd George had thus successfully initiated the first stage of the negotiations – as he was the first to claim in a letter to William. 'An excellent beginning', he wrote. The railway managers 'all almost fell on my neck ... I have won their confidence and that is almost everything'.[34] Clearly, the managers had expected a dressing down from the President of the Board of Trade, whose reputation as a radical was well known. They had been surprised by his reasonable approach. But Lloyd George, after his opening gambit of moderation, soon showed another hand. A few days after the meeting, he planted an article in the *Daily Mail* which called for compulsory arbitration in railway strikes. 'That fixed them', he wrote to William.[35] During the next few days, he entered into complicated negotiations with both managers and men. On 31 October, he spent the morning with the chairmen of the six principal railway companies. By 6 November, with delegations from both sides meeting simultaneously at the Board of Trade, Lloyd George could play off each group against the other. When the six railway chairmen, for example, wanted to refer a draft agreement to their shareholders, Lloyd George pointed out that the ASRS delegates could make the same claim – to refer any agreement back to the union as a whole. If this procedure were allowed, an agreement would be unlikely. Thus Lloyd George pressed the six railway chairmen to sign then and there. Lloyd George took the signed agreement straight to the union members who were meeting in a separate room. From them he also demanded immediate signatures.[36] They complied. The threat of a strike was over. To William, Lloyd George once again wrote in triumph: 'Well, it came off, and the whole country is delighted. The papers without distinction of party wild with enthusiastic and amazed satisfaction.'[37]

The general terms of the agreement included a pledge that both sides would adopt a system of conciliation and arbitration in settling disagreements over wages, hours and working conditions. This would be instituted through a network of conciliation boards made up of both railway company managers and employees. There was in addition a built in system of appeals: if all else failed, an arbitrator would be summoned. Although the settlement was never very effective – in part because it had not won union recognition for the ASRS – it did bring the railway managers some way along towards acceptance of collective bargaining with the unions.[38] The role of Lloyd George in the agreement won him almost unreserved praise, which he was quick to exploit.[39] He gave a press conference once the agreement had been signed, and arranged through Campbell-Bannerman (who included a complimentary covering letter) for a special messenger to convey the terms of the settlement to Sandringham.[40]

Scarcely had the railway dispute been settled when another strike was threatened from a different quarter. The Oldham spinning unions, some of whose members – especially the fine spinners – claimed their wages had lagged behind others in the industry. In late November 1907, Lloyd George, accompanied by Llewellyn Smith, arrived in Manchester to intervene directly. Within a fortnight, Lloyd George had managed to soothe tempers between the Master Cotton Spinners Federation and the operative spinners, winning a 9 per cent wage increase for the latter. He had succeeded, as he had in the railway dispute, by separating the contending parties and insisting upon a quick settlement. In thus operating as the crucial connecting link of the negotiations, he was able to control the outcome far more successfully than by moderating face-to-face confrontational meetings.[41]

Throughout his brief career as President of the Board of Trade, Lloyd George worked hard to establish the reputation of the Board as an impartial mediator and of himself as its apolitical head. Speaking at the annual banquet of the Walsall Chamber of Commerce in January 1907, he declared that 'the question of the trade of this country ought to be non-political' and he promised to deal with business problems 'from a purely non-party standpoint'.[42] He reiterated this promise several weeks later at a banquet of the Cardiff Chamber of Commerce, where he proclaimed 'the less the Board of Trade knew of politics the better'. Indeed, he stated more emphatically that 'political controversies' ought to be eliminated as much as possible in matters regarding trade.[43]

In attempting to place himself above party as a member of the Liberal government, Lloyd George could be charged with a certain disingenuousness, as he must have realized. To parry such a criticism, he positioned himself as the protector of British industry and commerce, or, more accurately, as the protector of British imperial trade. 'Commerce', he declared publicly, 'was essential to the greatness of the Empire'.[44] And it was to that end that the Board of Trade should be thought of as a Ministry of Commerce. At the Colonial Merchant Shipping Conference held in March, Lloyd George once again played the imperial tune by suggesting that the conference adopt resolutions that would form the basis of settling any issues that may arise 'between the Mother Country and the Colonies', especially those relating to shipping. He also recommended 'uniformity in merchant shipping legislation' within the Empire.[45] Thus Lloyd George first declared as an operating principle that on important imperial matters he would, as a member of the Cabinet act without party prejudice.

Partisanship was much in evidence, however, in Lloyd George's approach to three interwoven and important domestic issues that bedevilled the Liberal government during its early years – education, the role of religion and the schools. As one of the main campaign issues prior to the general election of 1906, education was quickly brought forward for action. At its first Cabinet meeting in December 1905, a committee on education was appointed. Chaired by the Earl of Crewe, the new Lord President of the Council, the committee met for two months in order to draw up a new education bill to replace the Balfour Act of 1902.[46] At first, the sense of the committee was that the guiding principles should be (as the election campaign had pledged) only two: popular control over schools; and no religious tests for teachers. But soon other questions emerged. How would the government bring privately-owned schools into a national system and not be liable to charges of confiscation of property? When would religious instruction take place – during school hours, or afterwards? Should religious instruction be offered two days a week, or every day? These questions were not easily resolved. Lloyd George, who seems to have been the dominant member of the committee in its later stages,[47] complicated matters further when he insisted on the establishment of a Welsh central committee that would in effect have independently managed educational matters in Wales.

Lloyd George's attempt to make Wales a special case was symptomatic of the weakness of the proposed legislation as all denominations attempted to graft their particular programme onto the bill.[48] The Cabinet, in its hope of bringing the long-simmering education debate to a close, was willing to compromise. Clause 4 of the bill, for example, empowered education authorities of any borough or urban district with a population of more than 5,000 – if four-fifths of the parents requested it – to provide denominational instruction every day of the week. This would satisfy the Roman Catholic schools, which tended to be grouped in urban areas. But it clearly offended many nonconformists, who were firm on secular schools and non-denominational religious instruction. Clause 4 also tended to alienate Anglicans. Because many Anglican schools were in the numerous villages throughout the country, Anglicans would not benefit from the daily religious instruction provided by Clause 4 and would have the right of denominational teaching in its schools for only two days a week. Furthermore, not all Catholics supported Clause 4, on the grounds that religious education should not be under the control of any secular authorities. In short, the government, in hoping to draw support from the various interested bodies, so weakened the bill that none were satisfied.

The bill also encountered difficulties during parliamentary debates from the time of its introduction on 9 April 1906. Augustine Birrell, President of the Board of Education in the Cabinet, proved to be a poor advocate. This was not surprising: he had made only minimal contributions in drawing up the bill. It was, he complained privately, primarily Lloyd George's bill which the Cabinet had accepted and forced upon him.[49] When the bill, in its fractured form, reached the House of Lords, there were also some who opposed it strictly on religious lines.[50] But most of the opposition came from the dominant Conservative peerage whose numerous additional amendments were designed to weaken the bill. The task of the Conservatives in the House of Lords was eased by an ineffective response from the (admittedly small) Liberal minority in the House of Lords.

In the meantime, a strong Anglican reaction against the bill emerged in the countryside. Hundreds of protest meetings, petitions and sermons demanded Anglican religious teaching in the schools and denounced undenominational teaching as against their collective conscience – thus turning upside-down the nonconformist argument. Nonconformists were not behindhand in staging their own protests against any attempt to allow denominational teaching at state schools during school hours. Lloyd George was active among them in cultivating the nonconformists and attempting to rally their support. Shortly after the bill had been introduced by Birrell in the House of Commons, Lloyd George was the principal speaker honouring the eminent Baptist minister, Dr John Clifford, at the Bloomsbury Central Church. Lloyd George hailed Clifford, perhaps the foremost proponent of an uncompromising nonconformist educational bill, as his friend and as the man who, during the last general election, had led the Free Churches 'to victory in one of the greatest struggles in which they had ever engaged'.[51] The following month, speaking at the City Temple Hall, Lloyd George again praised the work of the Free Churches: they 'represented the main stream of the religious life of the English-speaking peoples of the world'. Indeed, he assured his audience, nonconformity 'was growing in power'.[52] In July, he spoke before the Liberation Society, reminding them that at that very moment, the Liberal ministry was 'engaged in emancipating the schools'. [53]

As the House of Lords made increasingly clear its intention of severely amending the Commons bill, Lloyd George's message to the country toughened and intensified. Speaking at Denbigh in August 1906, he warned that the Lords 'were going to cut up the Education Bill'.[54] Thereafter, in the final months of the year, this became his recurrent theme. In late September, at a public meeting in Llanelly, he charged that in opposing the bill, the House of Lords 'was taking up its quarrel with the people of the country'.[55] A month later, at Spaulding, he expressed outrage at the Lords' amendments to the bill on the grounds that the general election had given a mandate to the Liberal government to change the Balfour Act of 1902.[56] At a demonstration under the auspices of the Gloucester Liberal Association in November, he declared that the Lords 'had been at their old trick of defacing the coinage of democracy'. The Lords, he further claimed, had 'no method, no plan – nothing but the frenzy of ignorant prejudice'. He claimed additionally that the Lords 'had hit out with a blind fury' and in a 'frenzy of ignorant prejudice ... it was the prejudice of petrified Toryism'.[57] The next month at the Palmerston Club in Oxford, when it was clear that the bill had earned more enemies than friends, Lloyd George again blamed the House of Lords for wrecking the bill. The bill had been 'stripped and wounded, and left half dead' by the Lords. So 'waylaid and mutilated' had the bill become that the government could no longer accept it. The House of Lords was not merely acting in an 'arrogant' fashion, it had in fact begun a process, if continued, would destroy the British constitution.[58] These attacks upon the House of Lords were not without precedent: Gladstone himself had done so when the Lords struck down his Home Rule proposals. But Lloyd George's sustained and violent attacks seemed somehow more threatening, emanating as they did from a noted radical. Ultimately Lloyd George drew a series of rebukes from King Edward VII himself. But as Campbell-Bannerman explained it to Francis Knollys, the King's private secretary, Lloyd George was, as President of the Board of Trade and in his parliamentary conduct, 'most conciliatory'. CB did admit, however, that in his speeches in the countryside, 'the combative spirit seems to get the better of him'.[59]

By December, it was clear that the Education Bill, laden with amendments hostile to its intent, was unacceptable to the government. On 12 December, the House of Commons rejected the Lords' amendments by an overwhelming majority (416:107). In the following week, the Lords voted to retain these amendments. The bill was effectively dead. Two further attempts to legislate education bills, in 1907 and 1908, also fell apart, victims of the same pressures that had doomed the original bill. Repercussions of the failed legislation were inevitable, both in Parliament and throughout the country, in the months that followed. A Cabinet reshuffle sent Birrell to Ireland as Chief Secretary replacing Bryce who was shipped off to America to become the British ambassador in Washington. Reginald McKenna took Birrell's place at the Board of Education.[60] There was, however, a positive outcome of the education fracas for Lloyd George. Wales was granted, perhaps in recognition of his hard work for the Education Bill, its own department within the Board of Education. The new department had a permanent secretary who reported directly to the President of the Board. Equally important to Lloyd George was that the patronage of this department lay in his hands. The first of his appointments was his old friend and former election agent, A.T. Davies, to be Permanent Secretary.[61]

The Liberal government realized that the victory of the Conservative majority in the House of Lords must be addressed. Rather than appeal to the countryside in an election against the Lords – the bill seemed too divisive and the constitutional question too complicated for such a tactic – Campbell-Bannerman moved a resolution in the House of Commons on 24 June 1907 to restrict the power of the House of Lords to alter or reject bills sent them by the Commons, in effect a suspensory veto. This initiated a fierce debate revealing the pent-up feelings among many Liberals at the failure of the Education Bill and the frustrations they felt at their inability, in spite of a large majority, to control the legislative agenda. Lloyd George was at the forefront of the criticism. He charged that for three-quarters of a century the House of Lords had so mutilated bills 'as to take the life out of them'. In a tone of genuine anger, he claimed that the Lords were 'ill-informed'; that they lacked the necessary experience to legislate properly; and that they were 'not in touch' with the best interests of the country. In an often-quoted passage, he asserted that the Conservative Lords were simply the lap dogs of the Conservative Party. The House of Lords was Balfour's poodle: 'It fetches and carries for him. It barks for him. It bites anybody that he sets it on to.'[62]

In the meantime, Lloyd George had kept up the pressure against the Lords by intensifying his country campaign. At a January meeting sponsored by Caernarfon Liberals celebrating Lloyd George's 44th birthday, he claimed that the Education Bill, 'killed by the Lords', would have been a good bill for Wales and well as for England. But the 'foul blow' delivered by the peers in a 'petty and spiteful piece of vandalism' had postponed a nation's hopes.[63] A week later, Lloyd George took the chair at the annual luncheon of the Newcastle-on-Tyne Liberal Club where he admitted Liberal frustration 'by a House which was chosen by nobody, which was representative of nobody, and which was accountable to nobody'. At an evening meeting he again held forth against the Lords. Denouncing their 'insolent tactics', he claimed that the Peers were determined to defeat any legislation that affected the privileges of their class. The Liberals, on the other hand, affirmed fair play for all classes 'and special privileges for none'.[64] Several weeks later, Lloyd George addressed a meeting of Liberals in Nottingham where he advocated a reform of the second chamber in order to guarantee a selection of men 'of superior judgment and intelligence'.[65] In late March, he spoke to the Berkhamsted Liberal Association: there he described Balfour and Lord Lansdowne 'as a couple of conspiring conjurers'.[66] Two months later, he declared at a dinner of the City Liberal Club, Walbrook, that something 'had to be done' about the House of Lords.[67]

The strength of Lloyd George's campaign against the House of Lords, by 1907 in its second year, has been a matter of some comment then and now. The provincial press noticed a dichotomy between Lloyd George's moderation in Parliament and his angry words in the countryside. In a leading article, the *Sheffield Independent* observed that Lloyd George sometimes presented 'the curious dual phenomenon of a fiery Hotspur on the platform and a shrewd go-ahead administrator in the office and the legislative chamber'.[68] W. Watkin Davies, a supporter of Lloyd George until the later years of his Premiership, saw his stump speeches as almost a visceral reaction: the House of Lords represented 'all those social and political abuses which he hated most – the hereditary principle, snobbishness, the rule of the rich, monopolies, and landlordism'. Thus, each time the Lords challenged the House of Commons, 'the smouldering fire within him burst into flame, and the suave and patient bureaucrat of the Board of Trade became the eager agitator'.[69] Grigg seems to think that it was a calculated tactic: 'his vehemence on public platforms made those who had to deal with him in his official capacity all the more ready to appreciate his moderation as a Minister'.[70] But Lloyd George's public performances also provided ammunition for his political enemies. In a letter to *The Times*, F.E. Smith noted that Lloyd George appeared to undergo a 'transition' when he left 'the grave scenes of Ministerial activity' for the provinces, where he reverted to a form of radicalism. Lloyd George seemed to be involved in a 'struggle of personalities' in which, Smith hoped, 'Dr Jekyll, and not Mr Hyde, may ultimately be found triumphant'.[71]

A primary reason for Lloyd George's pummelling the Lords was that they were a convenient scapegoat. They could be blamed for any failure of the Liberal legislative programme. This certainly seems to have been the case when Lloyd George attempted to address a growing concern among many nonconformists, especially in Wales, at the delay of the government in legislating the disestablishment of the Church in Wales.[72] The triennial conference of the Liberation Society on 1 May 1907 openly expressed its concern over the laggardly efforts on its behalf. Lloyd George was absent, crying off for a Cabinet meeting, but sent a letter stating that Prime Minister Campbell-Bannerman had 'definitely promised' to take up Welsh disestablishment 'at the earliest possible moment'.[73] Two months later, when presiding over a meeting of the New Reform Club in London, he reiterated the ministry's support for disestablishment, but claimed that delay may be necessary until an opportune moment arrived: it was, he said, 'very largely a question of strategy when one was attacking a great citadel'. The fact was that if a bill proposing Welsh disestablishment went to the House of Lords, 'it would be thrown out'.[74] He followed this same argument at a meeting in Pontypridd three weeks later. Disestablishment 'was coming', he promised, but it was 'a question of ways and means'. Indeed, disestablishment would have been brought forward in the next legislative session but for the action of the Lords in rejecting the Education Bill, which (he seemed to suggest) should assume priority over disestablishment.[75]

With little action on the horizon from the Liberal government and Lloyd George equivocating, patience finally ran out among the Welsh on the question of disestablishment.[76] Lloyd George was brought to book at a convention of Welsh nonconformists in October 1907 at Cardiff. Two thousand were in attendance. Apparently feelings ran high as unanimous resolutions were passed, expressing 'deep concern' at the slow pace of the disestablishment movement and urging the settlement of the question 'at the earliest practicable date'. Additionally, a resolution before the meeting threatened the withdrawal of support from parliamentary candidates at the next general election unless they placed Welsh disestablishment 'in the very forefront' of their campaigns. At this declaration, Lloyd George was on the defensive. In his address to the convention, he first reviewed the good intentions of the government toward Wales and its sincere belief in religious equality. The Education Bill proved that; but the Lords 'with great contempt' threw it out. Real progress on disestablishment would never be made, he continued, until they had 'dealt with' the problem of the House of Lords. In fact, he promised that the Prime Minister would soon, if the Lords continued their policy, 'secure a mandate' to remove 'this obstacle' in the interest of democracy and Liberalism. In the meantime, he pleaded for patience: 'do not fire at us from behind', he urged. In his final peroration, he appeared choked with emotion as he reminded them of his sacrifices for Wales. He asked rhetorically if they thought he would sell out the land that he loved. A silence fell. After the pause, he answered his question in Welsh: 'God knows how dear to me Wales is.'[77] The crowd rose as one, many in tears. An incipient Welsh revolt was at an end.

Had the crowd that day in Cardiff been aware of other events, however, they might have entertained different feelings from the adulation they expressed for Lloyd George at the end of his speech. There is some evidence that he was not as fierce an opponent of the Church of England's privileges as he seemed. As early as February 1906, he had been in private communication with A.G. Edwards, Bishop of St Asaph. He asked the Bishop whether or not the Welsh Church would cease opposition to a Welsh disestablishment bill, if it were so drawn up in 'very mild and kindly' terms. This might mean, Lloyd George implied, that the Church could retain everything – buildings, houses, glebes – but would forego tithes. Shortly afterwards, Lloyd George met with the Bishop and the Archbishop of Canterbury in the House of Lords. There Lloyd George revealed the government plan of appointing a Royal Commission on the state of the Church in Wales. The clerics did not oppose in principle and a fortnight later, the Cabinet appointed such a commission, the report of which, as Lloyd George informed the Archbishop, could lead to a bill 'of a moderate kind'.[78] Lloyd George was himself actively involved in selecting the Commission's members. Unfortunately, the Commission proved slow to work, not beginning until October 1906, and eventually meandered off course never to fulfil its obligations.[79] In the meantime, the government went forward on its many other active legislative proposals, not all of which, as we have seen, became law. In short, the slow pace of disestablishment cannot be blamed wholly on the House of Lords.

At the very height of his growing ministerial reputation, Lloyd George suffered a devastating personal loss. On 29 November 1907, only days after he had effectively prevented a national railway strike, his eldest daughter, Mair, died of a ruptured appendix at the age of 17.[80] She had succumbed during an emergency operation carried out in her father's study at the Routh Road home of the Lloyd Georges in London. By all accounts, Mair had been his favourite child. Described as sensitive and sweet natured, and musical as well, she had increasingly become a companion to her father, occasionally accompanying him on the piano when he sang Welsh songs. She was also intelligent and ambitious, planning on an undergraduate career at Cambridge to study mathematics. Lloyd George took the loss deeply and could not easily cope with the immediate aftermath of his daughter's death. Both his wife and brother William were left to manage funeral arrangements in Criccieth. Later, while Lloyd George was in France with the two boys on a recuperative tour, Margaret and William moved the family residence to Chelsea: Lloyd George was unable to return to the house where Mair had died.

The impact of Mair's death upon Lloyd George has divided historical opinion. Gilbert thinks there was a 'childish selfishness' to his grief. Rowland is also critical: one is 'tempted' to the conclusion, he writes, that in Lloyd George there was 'a certain amount of almost Micawberish self-dramatisation' in his lamentations. Grigg on the other hand sees Lloyd George more genuinely saddened – 'almost demented with grief'.[81] William's account of his brother's sorrow substantiates its genuine quality and reveals how 'very deeply' Mair's death affected him.[82] In the days following her death, Lloyd George wrote to William of his inability to sleep, and of his attempts to remain busy to prevent 'brooding'. He suffered, too, from pangs of guilt for not doing more during Mair's illness. Not calling in a specialist earlier, he wrote from Nice, 'has caused me the greatest & most prolonged torture'. His trip abroad gave little solace. 'If I get my mind onto something else even for a short while I feel as if I had been guilty of treason to my little darling to have forgotten her or let her out of sight for an instant.'[83] Letters to Margaret echoed those of his to William. He wrote of their common grief, and of his reliance upon her 'brave spirit', which had a calming effect upon his own 'turbulent & emotional nature'.[84] But it may very well be that the most significant impact of Mair's death was upon the relationship between Lloyd George and his wife. It proved difficult thereafter for either of them to rise above mutual recriminations about the circumstances of her death: the delay in summoning a doctor; and the consequent emergency operation performed at the family home, without customary hospital support staff.[85]

The Lloyd Georges were in Chelsea for only a few months. Campbell-Bannerman, whose health had steadily deteriorated, resigned as Prime Minister to be succeeded by H.H. Asquith in April 1908. Asquith, who had some reservations about Lloyd George, nevertheless chose him to become the new Chancellor of the Exchequer.[86] A move from Chelsea to 11 Downing Street was now obligatory for the Lloyd Georges. As Chancellor, Lloyd George had arrived at the inner circle of Liberal politics and near the apex of government power. Not unnaturally, he could not restrain the need to point out to William the significance of his achievement. 'I am Chancellor of the Exchequer', he wrote, '& consequently second in command' in the Liberal government. He had been, he assured William, 'overwhelmed with congratulations'. Even the Conservative papers were 'almost adulatory'. When he put in his first appearance in the House of Commons as Chancellor, both sides received him 'with great cheers'.[87]

Lloyd George's relationship with the new Prime Minister and his ability to work in harness with him, however, faced potential difficulties. Although Asquith's accession was widely expected, some radicals in the party had reservations because of his support of the South African War. Others disapproved of his intrigues against Campbell-Bannerman during negotiations at the Relugas Compact. Nor was Asquith a fervent democrat: he was stoutly against the emerging suffragette movement and votes for women. Nevertheless, Asquith was one of the foremost debaters in the House of Commons. His sound and innovative budgets as Chancellor of the Exchequer gave him additional stature. His 1907 budget, particularly, was a pioneering effort in making the distinction between earned and unearned income, the latter of which was taxed at a higher rate. In that same budget, instead of remitting taxation because of an unexpected surplus, he set aside £1,500,000 to fund old age pensions. Immediately after he became Prime Minister, he proved to be decisive in pruning dead wood and moving other ministers into more suitable positions.[88]

Under Asquith, as was true with Campbell-Bannerman, Lloyd George thrived. His legislative skills and reformist bent, revealed during his tenure at the Board of Trade, came into full flower at the Treasury. It was this record that made him, in the words of one historian, 'the outstanding constructive statesman' of the twentieth century.[89] His first task, given him by Asquith, was to pilot through the House of Commons a proposed bill on old age pensions.[90] As we know, old age pensions had been for many years a primary goal of both political parties. The Conservatives under Chamberlain's guidance had at least given it a nod in the 1890s. Lloyd George, too, had a long-standing aim of providing for the working poor in their old age. This was not merely a matter of social equity for Lloyd George: he also had a political motive in mind. As he stated in a speech before a convention of Welsh Liberals, the Liberal Party must become more active in coping seriously 'with the social condition of the people', including widespread poverty, destitution, and 'the national degradation of slums'. They had to attack boldly the causes of such wretchedness – the drink trade and the 'vicious' land system among them. They must also find the revenues 'to provide an honourable sustenance for deserving old age'. If Liberals did not respond adequately, and here lay the political mandate, 'a real cry would arise in this land for a new party' which would address these social issues.[91]

A variety of schemes providing relief to the elderly had been in place for many years. Clubs, trade unions and some employers made contributions to the retirement years of their members. Perhaps the largest of all the support groups for retired workers were the Friendly Societies, such as the Oddfellows and the Foresters. Originally established to promote fellowship and conviviality for working men, these societies evolved during the nineteenth century into organizations whose members paid into a common fund to receive sickness and funeral benefits. By the early years of the twentieth century, however, it had become increasingly clear that these piecemeal provisions for the elderly were inadequate. Asquith himself, as Chancellor of the Exchequer in the Campbell-Bannerman government, had expressed sympathy for old age pensions in the early days of the Liberal administration; but he had also expressed reservations over their cost. The government's delay spurred significant protests. Labour by-election victories over sitting Liberals sounded a clear warning. At its annual meeting in September 1907 the Trades Union Congress added its voice in demanding action.[92] The moment had arrived for a definitive commitment on the part of the Liberal government for a state-sponsored pension plan.

In the speech from the throne on 19 January 1908, the Liberal government pledged its support for pensions. Thereafter, events moved with deliberate speed. In April, Asquith had replaced CB as prime minister. The following month, Asquith laid the foundation of the legislation when he announced the provisions of a pensions bill. Lloyd George, as the new Chancellor of the Exchequer, moved its second reading in the House of Commons on 15 June 1908. Although there was some opposition in the House among those who believed that the bill had not gone far enough, it passed without much difficulty. In the final stages of his management of the bill through the Commons, Lloyd George kept his brother apprised of its progress – and of his own role in its passage. On 18 June, he led the House in the debate on the bill and, he wrote to William, it was 'generally admitted that I did it uncommonly well'. A fortnight later, he reported 'a very distinct triumph' in his conduct of the bill '& that is the general impression'.[93] Perhaps surprisingly, the House of Lords also accepted the bill – on the likely grounds of appeasing working-class voters. The bill received the royal assent six weeks later on 1 August 1908.

Scheduled to begin on 1 January 1909, the Act was non-contributory and provided 5s. weekly to British citizens over 70 years old who earned less than £21 annually. For those who earned larger incomes, there was a sliding scale that dropped the benefits incrementally, falling to a 1s. benefit for those who earned as much as £31 10s annually. This was undoubtedly a modest beginning and there were also noticeable restrictions.[94] Persons deemed idle or subject to drunkenness were disqualified, as were lunatics. Those convicted of a crime who had served prison time were disqualified during the length of the sentence and for ten years afterwards. Claimants had to prove their age, and they could not simultaneously receive relief under the Poor Law. To establish their claims, prospective pensioners had to fill out a form at the post office where they would collect the pension. The form would be sent to a local pension officer who visited the homes of all claimants to check the accuracy of the information provided. Pension officers would then send the forms to the Pension Committee appointed by local councils who would review them. At that stage, pensions were then either approved or declined. Refusals were at first fairly high – as much as a quarter of the applicants were denied pensions. These restrictions and disqualifications have led one historian to observe that the act was as much backward- as it was forward-looking because it was clearly based upon the model of the old Poor Law.[95] Nevertheless, the introduction of the Act was in itself important as a first step in providing some security for elderly workers.[96]

A second important measure for this legislative session was a new Licensing Bill – part of the nonconformist triad of education, disestablishment and temperance.[97] The first two had been defeated and the government was therefore especially keen on succeeding with the third. Asquith had introduced the Licensing Bill in February 1908 before he became Prime Minister. Intended to supersede the Conservative 1904 Licensing Act, the new proposal would reduce licensed premises by as much as one-third throughout the country during the next 14 years. After that date, the number of licensees would be restricted to a fixed ratio of the population and would be validated by local option.[98] Those losing their licences would be compensated by a tax upon the remaining licensees. New licensing hours would also be established.

Although Lloyd George was not directly involved in the drafting of the bill, it represented his own strongly-held views on temperance. In speeches before the countryside he denounced the drink trade as contributing to an impairment of the nation's vitality and sapping of its energies. Drink was also a major contributor to the unemployment problem. 'A nation suckled on alcoholism', he declared to a London audience in 1907, '[is] doomed'.[99] The following year, at a convention of temperance organizations sponsored by the United Kingdom Alliance, Lloyd George condemned the alliance between brewers and peers and accused the Conservatives in general of trying to swim 'back to power on liquor'. The Liberal Party 'stood for the victims of the drink' against 'the sordid menace of the brewer'.[100] Intemperance was, he declared at a ceremonial laying of a foundation stone of a new congregational church in Fulham, 'a gigantic evil'.[101] At a meeting sponsored by several temperance societies in Edinburgh, he charged that the drink trade 'constituted a peril to the State'. It was a trade 'that lured myriads of citizens into excesses' and a trade that bred 'poverty, disease, crime, and vice'. The government was determined to challenge this 'powerful, ruthless, relentless foe' primarily by restricting the number of public houses 'especially in the poorer quarters of the cities' which had become 'beer-sodden swamps'.[102]

Lloyd George's temperance campaign, however, may have told against him and the proposed Licensing Bill. Prone to oratorical excess on the stump, his hortatory remarks very likely created a backlash among the inhabitants of the 'beer-sodden swamps'. Press accounts suggest as much. The Association of Conservative Clubs, with a membership of more than half a million, carried on a vigorous campaign against the bill. The clubs, licensed to sell drink, had a large working-class clientele. To sabotage the bill, the clubs sponsored a circular that claimed that under the bill the police could raid their premises if teetotallers complained.[103] On the wings of popular displeasure, Conservatives took heart in resisting the bill, broadening their opposition by claiming that it was a violation of property rights. They also argued against it as an infringement upon the inherent right of the working class to enjoy themselves. Furthermore, the bill seemed to single out brewers unfairly for discrimination. Encouraged by the anti-bill sentiment and a series of by-elections unfavourable to the Liberals, Conservatives sensed that the ministerial tide was ebbing. Conservative MPs tactically forced delays in the House of Commons to prevent its consideration until after the summer recess. When the bill finally reached the House of Lords in December 1908, Conservative peers successfully denied it a second reading.

In spite of the fact that significant planks in their reformist platform had fallen at the hands of the Conservative majority in the House of Lords, the Liberal ministry enjoyed some successes. Old age pensions were the most notable. Other reforms are worth mentioning. For example, the Education (Provision of Meals) Act of 1906 allowed (but did not compel) local education authorities to provide meals for children in any public elementary school in their area. Although some charitable organizations and Conservative groups at large hotly opposed this reform on the grounds that it directly interfered with parental responsibility and was thus a dangerous departure from the tradition of limited state activity in private matters, enough parliamentary support in the House of Lords helped carry the measure. A corollary to this act was the Education (Administrative Provisions) Act of 1907, which created a school inspection service to guarantee better health among school age children.[104] In 1908, the government passed the Children's Act, which made the neglect of children an offence at law. In addition, a (slight) recognition of the rights of women, soon to become a major national issue, was granted in the Qualifications of Women Act of 1907. Since 1894, women had had the right to sit on district and parish councils: this was now extended to county and borough councils. As a final example of successful Liberal social reform measures, the Coal Mines Regulation Act of 1908 reduced the working day allowable for miners to eight hours.

Clearly, the Liberal ministry – if it did not achieve all its objectives – was able to advance on several fronts, especially in social legislation. Many historians have credited the influence of ideas in accounting for the reformist record of the Liberal government. Most particularly, New Liberalism has been cited as the intellectual forcing ground and overarching coherent framework for the diversity of the Liberal reformers.[105] New Liberals, including such social thinkers as L.T. Hobhouse and J.A. Hobson, advocated a stronger role of the state in redressing social wrongs. New Liberals thought of themselves as part of a progressive alliance, one wing of which was the emerging Labour Party. New Liberalism was not limited to intellectual circles only: it reached a wider audience through such progressive newspapers as the *Manchester Guardian* and the *Daily News*. It is, nevertheless, always difficult to trace the positive impact of ideas either on social consciences or on political action. As Bernstein notes, it is simply 'not clear' to what extent New Liberalism influenced the Liberal Party's social policies.[106] He does believe, however, that New Liberalism 'helped create a climate' for change. Jose Harris agrees that ideas formed the 'legitimizing framework' of social thought in that era.[107]

How strongly these various reformist strands influenced Lloyd George as he pursued his legislative programme is also unclear. Given his radical past and his loathing of privilege and the status quo that supported it, he had a natural tendency towards social and political change, as we have observed. Thus, a good case can be made that he was exceptionally attuned to all these potential reformist influences at the beginning of the Liberal ministry and in the years of its life thereafter. Already a parliamentary veteran when he became Chancellor of the Exchequer, Lloyd George was fully aware of the various cooperating strands of reform that underlay a national support for a grander scheme of reformist legislation than had yet been proposed.

He had developed a method of managing men in contentious negotiations in his work as President of the Board of Trade. He very likely had a nodding acquaintance the ideas of the New Liberals, and shared their objectives of reform within the existing social system, though he was not interested in following closely abstract notions of reform. In short, there was a strong reformist context in the nation as a whole, within which Lloyd George operated during 1906–08, and later in 1909–11. Without the reformist context, Lloyd George would likely have been a lonely voice in the wilderness. There is no doubt, however, that his role was critical in operating within that context to legislate practical applications of reformist ideals. He could draw the conclusion that the time was ripe for an extension, perhaps even an unparalleled extension, of the state in righting the wrongs of society. His observant eye, sure hand, administrative guile and superlative rhetoric were all necessary for the success of the broad reformist programme that had begun to unfold in the Liberal ministries of Campbell-Bannerman and Asquith.

6

ROBBING THE HEN ROOST

The Old Age Pensions Act was a natural lead-in to greater social reforms. Once productive workers had been assisted in their old age to a reasonably secure retirement, it made sense to assist those who needed coverage for illnesses and disabilities incurred during their active work lives. To gather information about the practical problems in extending the principle of old age pensions to the promotion of productive workers' welfare, Lloyd George travelled to Germany on a fact-finding tour shortly after the Old Age Pension plan had received the royal assent. Beginning in Bavaria, Lloyd George and a few companions then toured through Stuttgart and Frankfurt, ending up in Hamburg and Bremen. Apart from exploring social questions and giving a number of press conferences, he took the opportunity of meeting in Berlin the German vice-chancellor, Bethmann-Hollwegg, to discuss the growing naval rivalry between the two countries.[1] Upon his return, Lloyd George issued a press release. In it, he explained that he had explored with his German hosts the possibility of grafting a contributory system relating to disability and illness protection onto a noncontributory system such as the recently passed Old Age Pensions Plan. He generally found that German employers and workers were well satisfied with a contributory system.[2] He was most impressed by the comprehensive nature of the German state insurance system. It touched 'the great mass of German people in well-nigh every walk of life'. He reported, too, that in Germany old age pensions were only a part of an overall plan. When a German worker fell ill, 'state insurance comes to his aid'. When a worker became disabled, 'again he gets a regular grant whether he has reached his pension age or not'.[3]

The drift of Lloyd George's thinking was becoming clear. In an important speech several weeks later at the National Liberal Convention for Wales held in Swansea, he hinted more substantively that he was considering a broad extension of state insurance for the benefit of the British worker. 'The new Liberalism', he declared, would never abandon the traditional Liberal determination to establish freedom and equality; nor would it relinquish the Liberal habit of steady and sure approach to reform. But in addition, it must bring forward measures 'to ameliorate the conditions of life amongst the multitude'. He promised that the recently passed Old Age Pension scheme 'was but the beginning of things'. When poverty 'was due to circumstances over which a man had no control, the State should step in'. He was particularly concerned with those who, 'through no fault of their own', could not earn their daily bread. No country, he added, could lay claim to being a civilized society should they allow 'the aged and infirm, the broken in health, the honest unemployed' to starve.[4]

Lloyd George also began discussions about this time with a recently appointed Cabinet colleague, Winston Churchill, who had taken Lloyd George's old post at the Board of Trade. During the autumn of 1908, the two Liberal colleagues formed a partnership in which they jointly devised a comprehensive social welfare programme. Churchill had only recently left the Conservatives over their tariff reform policies, and had all the enthusiasm of a recent convert for his new party. It was an unusual partnership. Although there were some similarities between the two men – they were both radical and rebellious at this stage of their careers – startling differences were also apparent.[5] Churchill had been born at Blenheim Palace, the monumental country house given by a grateful nation nearly two centuries earlier to his ancestor, John Churchill, the first Duke of Marlborough and the hero of the late wars against Louis XIV of France. Following his patrilineal heritage, Churchill, after schooling at Harrow and Sandhurst, accepted a commission with the 4th Hussars in 1895.[6] He had a cavalier attitude about service in the military. Using his family's influence in the next few years, he was able pull enough strings to travel widely to various global hot spots. Shortly after his commission, he went to Cuba, where he first saw military action during the Cuban revolt against the Spanish government. There he also developed a life-long fondness for Havana cigars. Next, he served as a subaltern in India. Later, he became a soldier and adventurer in Africa, fighting at the great battle of Omdurman in the Sudan in 1898. Leaving the army, he became a newspaper correspondent during the second South African War. He was captured and became a prisoner of war. Escaping, he obtained a temporary commission as a lieutenant with the South African Light Horse and returned to the front. Throughout these adventures, he had kept an eager public informed through his newspaper articles. When he disembarked at Southampton on 26 July 1900, he was the man of the hour. His timing was perfect. Two months after his return to England, he used his reputation to political advantage by standing as a candidate for Oldham, a seat in East Lancashire, during the Khaki election of 1900. Campaigning on the virtues of Tory imperialism, he won in a close election. At Westminster, he joined a small band of young Conservatives in Parliament, among them Earl Percy, eldest son of the Duke of Northumberland; Arthur Stanley, a younger son of the Earl of Derby; and Lord Hugh Cecil, youngest son of the Prime Minister, Lord Salisbury.

How this military adventurer and child of privilege became a close friend and loyal partner with Lloyd George in advocating some of the most significant reform measures of the twentieth century may at first seem surprising. But Churchill, who on the surface often appeared to the world as 'a hyperactive, hotheaded and rather alarming teenager',[7] had been preparing for another life during his foreign escapades. On his travels abroad, his mother had sent him by post some of the great intellectual classics: Gibbon and Macaulay; Plato and Aristotle; Malthus and

Darwin; Adam Smith, and many others. He discovered within himself a powerful and retentive mind and an immense curiosity. Upon his return to England, his circle of acquaintances gradually widened. He became acquainted with Lord Rosebery, whose imperial leanings did not exclude an interest in social reform. In addition, Churchill discovered urban poverty by reading Seebohm Rowntree's pioneering study of poverty in York. The fact that nearly 20 per cent of the population of York dwelt in poverty and that the workhouse or prison were their only recourses made his hair 'stand on end'.[8] Perhaps his discovery of social inequalities on such a scale contributed to his alienation from the Conservatives. In addition, he had serious doubts about the efficacy of the Conservative tariff reform platform. It was, he believed, a fundamental error in trading policy.

In May 1904, Churchill crossed the floor of the House of Commons, taking a seat next to Lloyd George. It was a symbolic gesture. He had cast his lot with the Liberals. In fact, the two men had already been in contact regarding their common interests in social reform. In the summer of 1903, Churchill had invited Lloyd George to Blenheim. After Churchill's break with the Conservatives, he appeared with Lloyd George for the first time on a public platform at a free trade meeting in Caernarfon in October 1904. In the months that followed, Churchill became one of the most popular free trade orators. He was not far behind Lloyd George in castigating the Conservatives and their enchantment with tariff reform. As a reward for his apostasy, and no doubt in recognition of his first hand knowledge of and interest in the empire, he was made Under-Secretary at the Colonial Office (without Cabinet rank) in Campbell-Bannerman's ministry. His new parliamentary seat in northwest Manchester, won at the general election of 1906, brought him into proximity with the radical C.P. Scott, editor of the *Manchester Guardian*. He had also made the acquaintance of Fabian socialists such as Beatrice and Sydney Webb, who schooled him further on the importance of social legislation.[9] The Webbs introduced him to William Beveridge, whose influence strengthened his resolve as a reformer.[10] In March 1908, just prior to the resignation of CB and the creation of the Asquith government, Churchill published an article in *The Nation* which outlined a comprehensive programme for relieving the plight of unemployed workers: labour exchanges and wage boards for sweated industries were two specific remedies he advocated. In attacking unemployment as his specific contribution to the growing Liberal reform movement, Churchill chose shrewdly. He addressed a growing problem that undermined the security of Britain's working class. Attempting a solution might reap political rewards from grateful workers.[11]

When Asquith became Prime Minister in April 1908, he made Churchill President of the Board of Trade after moving Lloyd George from that post to become Chancellor of the Exchequer. Thus the stage was set for a partnership with Lloyd George.[12] At the Board of Trade, Churchill was assigned the specific task of tackling the growing problem of unemployment.[13] The first of Churchill's legislative accomplishments was the Trade Boards Act of 1909, which established cooperative boards of both employers and workers to fix minimum wages for the small garment workshops in the East End of London and in Leeds and Manchester as well. A more substantial act, also passed in 1909, empowered the Board of Trade to establish labour exchanges throughout the country where needed. This facilitated the search among unemployed workers for appropriate jobs. In addition, a fund was established to assist workers travelling to jobs where work had been found by the exchanges. The exchange offices also provided facilities for (non-alcoholic) refreshment: some offices also provided lavatories where workers could make themselves presentable before travelling to work. Within four years, there were 430 labour exchanges throughout the country.[14]

There was an obvious connection between the insurance plan that Lloyd George had begun to envision relating to workers' sickness and disability and Churchill's concern with the effects of cyclical unemployment. Conversations between Lloyd George and Churchill led to a cooperative effort. Churchill would delay any proposed legislation until Lloyd George had devised his own insurance scheme and the means to pay for it. This was the background of perhaps the most famous Finance Bill of modern parliamentary history. The provisions in the bill were to meet fiscal needs not for the coming year only, but rather to fund for the future the recently legislated Old Age Pensions Act and the anticipated costs of new social insurance programmes to be enacted into law.[15] These new social responsibilities assumed by the state created a substantial budget shortfall, estimated at £16 to £17 million. This was, as Lloyd George declared, a 'financial emergency'. But it was not unexpected: as Lloyd George had warned the House of Commons the year before, it would likely be necessary to rob someone's hen roost in the coming year to pay for new social programmes.[16]

Lloyd George's landmark 1909 budget was clearly not a fiscal document only: it was also inextricably connected with projected social reforms. As the budget developed over time, its provisions became increasingly radical in scope. But the main outline of the budget itself was not a radical innovation. Lloyd George followed Asquith's lead as Chancellor in three important respects. First, Asquith had introduced the principle of taxing on the basis of income differentiation: those with higher incomes would pay higher taxes. Secondly, Asquith established the principle of financial continuity by planning ahead, beyond a single year's fiscal needs.[17] And thirdly, in his budget for 1908, Asquith had set aside a sum of £4 million for old age pensions. If he followed Asquith's innovations in crafting the Budget, Lloyd George nevertheless made the Budget his own by taking the initiative in carrying it through the Cabinet and the House of Commons, and later defending it in the country at large.[18]

As the weeks passed in negotiating the terms of the Budget, Lloyd George kept his brother informed of his progress. He admitted that it would be 'a stupendous task to got it through the House of Commons' because it was a 'gigantic scheme'.[19] Lloyd George was not exaggerating. In working up both the general principles of the Budget and the immense number of intricate details, Lloyd George exasperated and intrigued his colleagues in equal measure. Given the Treasury's entrenched Gladstonian views on strict economy and their firm free trade notions, Lloyd George tended to ignore Treasury officials and to rely upon men of his own stamp such as Sir Robert Chalmers, Chairman of the Board of Inland Revenue. In addition, the radical Charles Masterman, Parliamentary Secretary to the Local Government Board, was particularly helpful in assisting Lloyd George in preparing the land value taxes. In spite of their expertise and the aid of other advisors, Lloyd George encountered considerable opposition in part because of his idiosyncratic working habits. He constantly demanded from heads of departments numerous revised drafts of the Budget heedless of their other work. To many officials, he seemed irresponsible in his inattention to details. Charles Hobhouse, then serving as Financial Secretary to the Treasury, complained that his relationship with Lloyd George was 'very uncomfortable'.[20] During Cabinet discussions of the draft budget, extending over 14 meetings from mid-March to late April 1909, Lloyd George faced additional difficulties. Examining the draft line by line and clause by clause, Cabinet members often voiced reservations, criticisms and concerns. Several Cabinet members were fearful that middle-class Liberals would be frightened by the notion of increased direct taxes. Others distrusted Lloyd George's projected budget deficit, suspecting that he was demanding more taxes than necessary. Still others disliked the impact of the new land taxes upon the landed classes, a substantial number of whom were Liberals. But there seems to have been a fair amount of give and take during the Cabinet review: Lloyd George often gave ground when pressed.[21]

Presenting the Budget to the House of Commons on 29 April 1909, the Chancellor declared portentously that it was 'a war Budget ... for raising money to wage implacable warfare against poverty and squalidness'.[22] In a speech of more than four hours, he set out the proposals by which this war could be won. Taxes would be raised on unearned incomes and at the higher end of earned incomes. On incomes over £5,000, a supertax would be levied beginning at the £3,000 level. Additional taxes were placed on existing death duties, stamp duties on conveyances of sale and liquor licences. Tobacco, cigarettes and cigars all had their duties increased. A tax on petrol and required motorcar licences reinforced the impression that Lloyd George was proposing a redistributive tax scheme by disproportionately increasing taxes on the wealthy. This impression was substantiated by the introduction of taxes upon land, including duties on the value of mineral property and on the capital value of undeveloped land worth more than £50. In addition, a tax was levied upon the assessed capital value of improved sites. And finally there was a proposed tax of 20 per cent on the increased value of any real property sold or inherited after 30 April 1909. As a necessary complement to these land taxes, Lloyd George proposed a national valuation of real property (separate from buildings improvement) based upon site value.

The Budget speech was – as virtually every historian has noted – a failure in its delivery. So complicated and so lengthy was it that Lloyd George, in contrast to his usual extempore style, had to read it all. At one point, his voice failing, he was forced to take a half-hour recess.[23] But once the content of the speech was perused and understood, its implications were unmistakable and the responses predictable. Liberals generally favoured it, as did members of the Labour Party. Irish Nationalists were more reluctant, disliking the increased levies on whisky and tobacco. Conservatives were up in arms. The centrepiece of their campaign against the

Budget openly declared that it was an initial step toward a socialist war on property. Indeed, the 'leftward lurch' of the Budget was manifest in its tax provisions.[24] Approximately 75 per cent of the tax increase would be paid by the wealthiest 10 per cent of the population.[25] The heir apparent to the tariff reform movement, Austen Chamberlain, the eldest son of his more famous father, claimed that Lloyd George's Budget was 'a portent of oppressive taxation and social revolution'.[26] Lord Lansdowne, the leader of the Conservatives in the Lords, denounced the Budget as 'a new departure of the most dangerous kind'.[27] Conservatives also challenged the constitutionality of the Budget on the grounds that it was less an instrument for raising revenue than it was a device for manoeuvring around the House of Lords' objections to social legislation. Lansdowne specifically charged the ministry with 'tacking' extraneous matter onto the Budget Bill. Outside Parliament, Walter Long, president of the Budget Protest League, mobilized Conservatives in the countryside.[28] Other important interests favourable to the Conservative cause made their voices heard. City bankers, merchants, businessmen, brewers and landowners engaged in protest meetings and petitions against the Budget. *The Times* summed up its objections by condemning it as a 'Socialist Budget'.[29]

The main Conservative assault upon Lloyd George and the Budget, tactically speaking, was launched in the House of Commons. To coordinate their opposition, the Conservatives organized four committees, each of which was assigned a specific section of the Budget. During debates, each committee would thus have in hand a well-prepared response. The ultimate aim was to wear down Lloyd George through constant badgering and delay – on occasion extending the debate well into the evening hours. The Conservatives had some early successes. Defending such a complicated budget proved to be difficult for Lloyd George.[30] The Conservative whip, Balcarres, noted with glee Lloyd George's 'lamentable flounderings and confusions' throughout May and June which showed, he thought, that the Chancellor had not 'the faintest notion of his much vaunted plan'.[31] But as the weeks wore on, the tone changed. After one 18-hour sitting in the House, Balcarres wrote dismayingly: 'Our men are really worn out by these constant sessions of twelve and fourteen hours ….'[32] By September, he observed, almost admiringly: 'Our expectation of wearing out Lloyd George has … failed ….'[33]

By the summer of 1909, the Liberals began to organize more effectively in favour of the Budget. Churchill headed up the Budget League to rally popular support for the Budget. This organization proved superior to its Conservative counterpart by coordinating an active press campaign with constituency meetings throughout the country. It was also able to raise substantial contributions from the party faithful.[34] By mid-summer, some 140 newspapers had subscribed to the Budget League's 'Weekly Column'. In addition, the League printed and distributed widely numerous pamphlets and leaflets, cartoons and posters. Cabinet members as well were drafted to speak at selected meetings. Among these was one of the most notorious speeches ever given by Lloyd George. Speaking to a crowd of 4,000 at the Edinburgh Castle, Limehouse, in the East End of London on 30 July 1909, Lloyd George pulled no punches.[35] Alternately ridiculing and excoriating the Conservatives and the House of Lords, he portrayed them as heartless 'shabby rich men' who begrudged 'a fair contribution towards the less fortunate of their countrymen'. These were men who by the accidents of birth and privilege had taken advantage of their position as extensive landowners both in town and country to insist upon high charges for the use and development of such land. Capitalists, farmers, miners – all worked on the land, but did not reap its full benefits because landlords insisted on more than their fair share through ground-rents, fees, premiums, fines and reversions. The Welsh coalfields (and here Lloyd George begged the indulgence of his cheering London audience) were good examples. Landlords received millions through the extraction of minerals in lands that they owned. What had they done to deserve such royalties? Had they deposited the coal? Had they taken the risks of the capitalist operator? Had they used their brains as did the engineer? And what about the miners: had the landlord taken the risks to his life in extracting the coal beneath the ground? Here was the greatest risk of all, said Lloyd George. He then painted in graphic colours a mine into which he himself had recently descended a half-mile down. He walked, he said, 'underneath the mountain'. Rock and shale pressed in all around: the earth 'seemed to be straining ... to crush us'. Dangers everywhere were apparent. 'You could see the pit-props bent and twisted and sundered until you saw their fibres split. Sometimes' he continued, 'they gave way, and then there is mutilation and death'. Or, a spark may ignite and 'the whole pit is deluged in fire, and the breath of life is scorched out of hundreds of breasts by the consuming fire'.

In spite of the dangers to the men who risked their lives to create the wealth of the landlords, these same landlords rejected the idea of adequately providing for them. As Lloyd George told it in a metaphorical allusion, when he and the Prime Minister came knocking at the doors of the great houses, they were refused entrance and the great landlords 'turn their dogs on to us, and every day you can hear their bark'. The ownership of land was more than merely 'an enjoyment', Lloyd George declared, it was 'a stewardship'. And if the landlords refused the responsibilities that landownership brought, he warned, 'the time will come to reconsider the conditions under which land is held in this country'. After all, the proposed land taxes were 'fair, just, and moderate'. In his concluding remarks, Lloyd George reminded the meeting (to loud and prolonged cheering) that he was a child of the people, and that he would never add 'one grain of trouble to the anxiety' which the people 'bear with such patience and fortitude'. The Budget was designed to relieve their burdens, not to compound them. Almost anticlimactically, the meeting passed a resolution in favour of the Budget.[36]

Reaction to the speech was swift. *The Times* condemned Lloyd George for 'openly preaching the doctrine that rich men have no right to their property, and that it is the proper function of Government to take it from them and divide it among the less fortunate'. His 'studious misrepresentations', his 'violent invective', his 'sophistry' and his 'pitiful clap-trap' were also singled out for comment. It was, thought *The Times*, especially dangerous to bring this message before 'an ignorant and easily deluded audience' such as that at Limehouse.[37] In the days that followed, letters to the editor from important Conservative leaders flowed in to the offices of *The Times* with the same sense of outrage. Sir Edward Carson claimed that Lloyd George's speech revealed the true purpose of the Budget – not to secure needed revenues for the state, but rather to end 'all rights in property'. It was clear that Lloyd George was not attempting to legislate for a budget, 'but for a revolution'.[38] Walter Long, speaking at a Unionist fete at Christchurch to a crowd estimated by *The Times* at 20,000, declared that Lloyd George spoke like 'a demagogue, seeking to set class against class'.[39] Andrew Bonar Law echoed this sentiment, claiming that an extreme section of the Liberal Party, led by Churchill and Lloyd George, had captured that Party and was now attempting to impose taxes upon the nation which would make private property of all kinds in the kingdom 'utterly insecure'.[40] Lloyd George's Limehouse speech, he believed, had no other object than 'to excite the hatred of class against class, enlisting the poor under his banner by promising to lead them on a crusade of spoliation against the rich'.[41]

Lloyd George's comments even flushed out a brace of dukes and an earl. The Duke of Westminster, specifically mentioned at Limehouse as an example of how landlords took advantage of others, considered legal action. The Duke of Rutland, speaking before a Conservative demonstration at Melton Mowbray, declared that it was 'no longer any use believing in the existence of a Liberal Party' because it was obvious that the Party had been taken over by the Socialists – 'the most violent, the most illogical, and the most illiberal set of men in the world'. The Earl of Lonsdale, at a Conservative demonstration at Clifton, Westmorland, thought that Lloyd George simply did not understand the land question. Lonsdale defended large estates as the source of labour employment: such estates would be at risk if the Budget Bill were to pass. It would be 'absolutely impossible' for him to maintain his own should the bill become law. And, like Rutland, he feared the triumph of Socialism.[42]

None of this criticism deterred Lloyd George. He was convinced that 'a mighty smashing wind' was sweeping aside all opposition to the Budget. 'There was undoubtedly a popular rising', he wrote William, 'such as has not been witnessed for over a generation'. Should the House of Lords vote down the Budget, Lloyd George could not imagine what might happen: but he could speculate. 'I wonder whether they will be such fools – I am almost wishing that they should be stricken with blindness.'[43] In any case, Lloyd George did not cease his country-wide campaign. In a strongly critical speech against Budget opponents at Newcastle-on-Tyne on 8 October 1909, he denied Conservative claims that the proposed taxes were an attack on industry.[44] In fact, he said, during the lengthy debates on the Budget of the past few months, trade had improved, industrial investments had remained steady and even brewery shares had gone up. But there had been, he noticed, 'a great slump in dukes'. Dukes, he claimed, had once been high in the market, especially the Tory market, but even the Tory press had come to the conclusion that they were of 'no value'. And, he reminded the delighted crowd, dukes were expensive to maintain: 'a fully equipped duke costs as much to keep up as two Dreadnaughts; and dukes are just as great a terror and they last longer'. In contrast to ducal resistance, he assured the crowd that many Liberals in the House of Commons who spent night after night working on the Budget were also men of wealth, perhaps not as rich as a duke, but rich enough and willing to pay thousands of pounds in new taxes because they believed that 'wealth should pay its fair share'. The new land valuation, he claimed, would make public what the fair value land should be. Never again would landlords charge enormous fees and fines, and demand unjust rents and reversions.

Lloyd George promised that the Budget Bill would soon go to the House of Lords for their approval. What would the Lords do, he asked? 'The more irresponsible and feather-headed among them' wanted to throw it out. But it must be remembered, he warned, that the British Constitution had clearly established 'through centuries of struggles and of strife, even of bloodshed ... that the Commons, and the Commons alone, have the complete control of supply and ways and means'. The Constitution must not be 'torn to pieces'. Should that happen, the Lords would be 'forcing revolution'. In his rousing peroration, punctuated by delighted laughter from the crowd, Lloyd George predicted that the people would begin to ask: 'Should 500 men, ordinary men, chosen accidentally from among the unemployed, override the judgment – the deliberate judgment – of millions of people who are engaged in the industry which makes the wealth of the country?' The people will also ask a second question: 'who ordained that a few should have the land of Britain as a perquisite, who made 10,000 people owners of the soil and the rest of us trespassers in the land of our birth?' And a third question must follow: 'who is responsible for the scheme of things whereby one man is engaged through life in grinding labour, to win a bare and precarious subsistence for himself ... and another man who does not toil receives every hour of the day, every hour of the night, whilst he slumbers, more than his poor neighbour receives in a whole year of toil?'

As was true after Limehouse, so after the Newcastle speech; criticism was quick to follow. Sir Edward Carson again condemned Lloyd George – this time as 'a demagogue and a farceur' whose 'violence and vituperation' were designed 'to rouse the baser passions of man' purely for electoral reasons.[45] Two days later, Walter Long, speaking in Glasgow to members of local Conservative associations, derided Lloyd George's Newcastle speech as 'fiction' and 'a distortion of facts ... packed full of inaccuracies'. He also repeated the charge that was becoming increasingly common among Conservative critics – that Liberals 'had gone over bag and baggage to the policy of the Socialist party'.[46] A more measured response was offered by Lord Curzon during a large Conservative demonstration at Leeds.[47] After a nod to the dangers of plunging 'downhill into Socialism and revolution', he turned his primary attention to the constitutional question before the country. Assuring his audience that the House of Lords was a body of moderate men who would always act for the public good, Curzon reviewed the traditional rights of the Lords not only to amend financial bills, but also to reject them – though he admitted this had rarely been done. He also (like Lansdowne) condemned 'tacking'.[48] Lloyd George, however, had an answer to Curzon. In an article in the *Nation*, partially published in *The Times*, Lloyd George wrote that the purpose of a budget was to include projects for the future 'earmarked from the outset' as important legislative goals. Thus he rejected the Conservative charge of 'tacking' for political purposes as the motivation for the Finance Bill.[49]

On 4 November, the Finance Bill cleared the House of Commons and was sent on to the Lords. For his work on the bill to this point in its progress, most historians have given Lloyd George high marks for his parliamentary skills. From an early, halting start in late April, he had developed a mastery of its contents and had been receptive to amendments during the long sessions in the House of Commons. Even his parliamentary opponents had been favourably impressed by his conciliatory tone in the debates in the House of Commons.[50] He had also received, as was his custom, numerous deputations from such groups as the Tobacconists' Protection Association; the London Stock Exchange Committee; the Cigar Manufacturers' Union; the Licensed Grocers' Associations of Dundee, Glasgow and the West of Scotland; the Coventry Chamber of Commerce; the Motor Union of Great Britain and Ireland; the Garden City Association; British grain distillers; and London brewers, among many others. In all these discussions he listened, promised to give consideration to their concerns and, where possible, to meet their complaints.

Lloyd George's speeches out of doors were a different story, however. His tirades at Limehouse and Newcastle seemed harsh, uncompromising and deliberately provocative. Gilbert believes that Lloyd George's public campaign for the Budget, which began with the Limehouse speech, 'may have been designed precisely to force the Lords to throw out the Budget, so allowing him to shift the emphasis in party debate from the relatively straightforward one of progressive income taxes versus import duties to the more favourable ground of the peers against the people'. As for the Newcastle speech, it was a 'deliberate provocation' to noble landlords.[51] Packer agrees: Limehouse and Newcastle were declarations of class war on landowners and the House of Lords.[52] On a slightly different tack, Grigg thinks that Limehouse (described as the 'most famous and possibly most effective speech of [Lloyd George's] life') was intended to energize Liberal supporters and to demoralize the Conservative opposition. But Grigg also observes that Lloyd George 'must have known' – 'or at least hoped' – that his speech at Newcastle would make rejection of the Finance Bill 'even more likely than it was already'.[53] For Pugh, Lloyd George's speech at Limehouse was nothing less than a bold Machiavellian move. With the speech, Lloyd George 'stoked up the controversy' which had a dual effect of not only ensuring that the Liberals 'would be wedded to radicalism', but also that the Conservatives 'would be drawn into a trap'.[54] If the Conservatives in the Lords passed the bill, they would demoralize their party: if, on the other hand, they vetoed the bill, the general election sure to follow could return a mandate for curtailing the powers of the House of Lords.

Such reasoning is suggestive. Lloyd George's early antipathy towards landed privilege, and his experiences as a young MP had only strengthened his views of the Lords as a bastion of retrograde conservatism that hindered social and political progress. But there is little evidence that he had worked early on to devise a budget that the Lords would reject out of hand. This would be too simplistic a motive for a man as cunning as Lloyd George. The most likely series of events is that once having devised the budget, and then defending it in temperate fashion during debates in the House of Commons, he reverted to his standard practice of operating as a partisan in his speeches out of doors in order to ginger up the faithful and to generate support. Limehouse, he naturally hoped, would put the Conservatives and the Lords on the defensive. As he put it in a letter to William shortly after Limehouse: 'General feeling here is that they will make a show of fight and then collapse.'[55] The following day, he again wrote to his brother, this time quoting Lord Northcliffe: 'He told me that the Budget has completely destroyed the Tariff Reform propaganda in the country.' Northcliffe added that the Conservatives 'had all miscalculated the popularity of the Land Clauses'.[56] A fortnight later, Lloyd George reported 'a mighty smashing wind' 'against the opposition. He then speculated openly what would happen should the Lords reject the Finance Bill once it passed into their hands. He confided to William: 'I rejoice at the prospect', but he wondered if they would be 'such fools'. [57]

In September and October, the Cabinet had begun to discuss the consequences of a Lords' rejection of the Finance Bill, and had instructed the law officers to examine the legal aspects of such action.[58] By the time Lloyd George made his Newcastle speech in early October, therefore, the prospects of rejection had been fully considered by the Cabinet. At that point, Lloyd George may well have drawn the conclusion that another strong attack upon the Lords could goad them into overplaying their hand. As he confessed to William after the Newcastle speech: 'I deliberately provoked them to fight.'[59] Once the bill had gone to the Lords, Lloyd George saw with some certainty the dilemma of the Conservative peers. The Lords were, he wrote, 'very sick. They know now they are in the trap but they cannot get out'.[60] In short, it would seem that Lloyd George did not have in mind, nor was he guided by, an initial original intention to trap the House of Lords. It evolved over time; but it was not a guiding reason for crafting the Budget.[61]

After nearly a month of intense debate and discussion, on 30 November the House of Lords rejected the Finance Bill, declining to give it a second reading by a vote of 350:75.[62] A few days later, on 3 December, Parliament was prorogued and a general election was called for the last two weeks of January 1910. Thus the bill entered into another phase, essentially a national referendum on the Budget. At nearly two months' duration, it was the longest election campaign in modern British history.[63] Although the Liberal election campaign was not officially begun until Asquith's Albert Hall speech of 10 December, Lloyd George had engineered his own campaign kickoff a week earlier at the National Liberal Club in London. His speech was somewhat surprising. There were a few jabs at the House of Lords: especially noteworthy was his claim that its unrepresentative quality made it 'an effete oligarchy' in contrast to the House of Commons. Most of the speech, however, simply set out the claims that the Commons best represented the people of the country.[64] A week later brought an even more restrained speech. Before a very large crowd estimated at between 7,000 and 8,000, Lloyd George addressed his constituents at Caernarfon. Primarily he discussed the main points of the proposed Budget. This was no doubt informative and instructive both to his constituents and to the national audience, whom he also addressed. Overall, however, it was not the scintillating and scathing electoral diatribe one had come to expect from him when on the stump.[65] The moderate tone of these early speeches was soon to change, however, as the campaign heated up.

The Liberal election campaign began well. The foremost trio of Liberal speakers – Asquith, Churchill and Lloyd George – was unmatched. By joining together the issues of tariff reform and rejection of the Budget, it was possible to portray the Conservatives as determined to tax the bread of the workers instead of taxing the privileged and the wealthy. Conservative obstructionism could be more broadly portrayed as an alliance against the people – an alliance made up of peers, Conservatives and the food taxers. Lloyd George took the lead. On the afternoon of 21 December 1909, he declared at Cardiff that the 'people were sick of this garrotting of Liberal Bills'. The evening of that same day he was in the port city of Swansea, stating that 'he could not imagine any place interested in British shipping supporting Tariff Reform'.[66] The following day at Llanelly, he praised free trade as beneficial to the tinplate industry of that region. He concluded his speech by a direct attack upon Lord Midleton, who had condemned Lloyd George a few days earlier for creating 'dissension and division' among all classes with his wild talk. Claiming that Midleton was 'a muddler', Lloyd George noted that Midleton was a Mr Brodrick before he went to the Lords. Doubtless, Lloyd George suggested, Midleton had taken that aristocratic title hoping that the public would forget that he was the same Brodrick at the War Office during the South African War who wasted substantial amounts of public money.[67]

During the next several days, Lloyd George continued his election tour throughout Wales before departing for London and other English constituencies. Very often during these numerous campaign stops in England and Wales, Lloyd George travelled in a special train to save time. As recalled by Watkin Davies, these trips were not unlike a triumphal procession. Wayside stations were packed with people hoping to catch a glimpse of the famous orator as he sped past. Occasionally the train, sometimes consisting of a single saloon carriage and an engine, would slow down at the platform and come to a brief halt: Lloyd George would come to the window of the carriage and make a few remarks to the crowd before the train would then gather steam for the next rendezvous.[68]

January 1910 was very much like the previous month in Lloyd George's campaign tour. During a lengthy address before the London Liberal Federation on 31 December, he once again praised free trade and condemned the great landlords who 'have escaped their fair share of the burden of taxation'.[69] In the following fortnight, he spoke at Reading, twice again in London, and at Peckham. In a speech at Plymouth, he parried the criticisms of Lord George Hamilton made a few days earlier at Uxbridge when Hamilton had made patronizing comments about 'this little Welsh solicitor' and his 'sneering tone' while electioneering.[70] Lloyd George replied that his own ancestors were a part of Britain a thousand years earlier: he wondered aloud 'where Hamilton came from'. Like most aristocrats, he mused, Lord George Hamilton was probably 'something of a mongrel'.[71] At Wolverhampton, Lloyd George reiterated a claim he often made – that the Lords had no qualifications whatsoever for becoming a member of a legislative body. 'They merely required a certificate of birth to prove that they were the first of the litter. Why, they would not choose a spaniel', he said to laughter and cheers, 'on that principle'.[72]

On their part, Conservatives had not been caught off guard by the general election. For several years, they had been rethinking their electoral strategy.[73] First, they had retooled tariff reform, shifting its emphasis from an instrument of imperial unity – which it had been in Joseph Chamberlain's day – to more domestic concerns. Taxing the foreigner by imposing tariffs upon certain imported manufactured goods and raw resources would provide sufficient funds for Conservative reform measures. This would obviate the need for direct taxation as proposed by Lloyd George's Finance Bill. Thus the land taxes and super tax would be unnecessary (pleasing the landlords) as would any taxation upon tobacco and beer (pleasing the working class). The Conservatives also brought to fruition several years' pondering the implications of a growing Labour Party, and especially its significance in presaging some form of Socialism. Throughout the lengthy election campaign of December 1909–January 1910, they sought repeatedly to associate Lloyd George with Socialism. Sir Gilbert Parker, Conservative MP for Gravesend, for example, not only condemned Lloyd George for his 'music-hall methods' but also for leading the socialist and extreme radical wing of the Liberal Party towards 'State landlords, State ownership, and State tyranny'.[74] George Wyndham also denounced Lloyd George personally – 'a playful, pathetic, romantic Celtic Chancellor of the Exchequer'. But his main criticism was that Lloyd George 'was aiming at the nationalization of the land of England, and that was what the Socialists desired'.[75] Privately, Austen Chamberlain echoed this opinion: 'This budget', he wrote, 'is Socialism, the alternative is Tariff Reform'.[76]

The Conservative dual message of tariff reform and the dangers of Socialism increasingly gained a hearing. Conservatives were also heartened by the recovery of their leader Arthur Balfour, who had been ill for several weeks. Unintentionally, Lloyd George's vehement campaign style may also have contributed to rising Conservative morale. He had ruffled too many feathers. Indeed, Lloyd George's comments had troubled even some traditional Liberals. Sir Alfred Pease, a mine and colliery owner and brother of the Liberal whip, Jack Pease, withdrew his support from the government in part because of Lloyd George's haranguing of the upper classes. Alfred Emmot, the Deputy Speaker, grew increasingly disenchanted with Lloyd George. Lewis Harcourt, in a post-election comment to Asquith, thought that 'all over the country' Lloyd George had 'done us much harm, even with the advanced men of the *lower* middle class'.[77] The British journalist J.A. Spender believed that Lloyd George's rousing the working class may have worked well in the North, but had alienated the middle classes of the South. Even one of Lloyd George's Cabinet colleagues, Walter Runciman, President of the Board of Trade, feared that Lloyd George's speeches had lost the Liberals many middle-class voters.[78]

The Conservative rally, however, fell short. The final election results showed a virtual tie in England, with the Liberals winning 275 seats and the Conservatives 273. A sharp geographical division in the country had emerged, with the North overwhelmingly Liberal and Labour – largely because of the organized artisans and skilled workers – while in the South, professional and shopkeeping classes combined with casual workers and clerks to vote Conservative. The Liberals in England had lost slightly more than 100 parliamentary seats compared with the 1906 election. Many of these voters, however, had been typically Conservative in sympathy and were returning to the fold after their temporary desertion in 1906. If the Liberals fell into a tie with the Conservatives in England, they were more successful in relying upon their allies, Labour MPs and the Irish Nationalists, to maintain their legislative supremacy. Labour lost 13 seats compared to 1906, but still retained 40, while the Irish had held steady, losing only one seat to remain at 82. These seats, when added to the Liberals MPs produced a total of 397 for a majority of 124 over the Conservatives.[79]

The Irish, however, were not a sure bet for the Liberals. For 15 years, since the last Gladstonian attempt at Home Rule in 1893 had failed, Irish Nationalists had been without a Liberal champion for their cause. Hopes had risen during the Liberal landslide of 1906; but they were dashed when social reforms and conflicts with the Conservatives sidetracked any possible Home Rule initiatives. Their patience running thin, Nationalists under John Redmond began a campaign to press Liberals into action.[80] Almost a year prior to the election of January 1910, Redmond had made it plain to both Asquith and Lloyd George that unless the Liberal government took seriously the question of Irish Home Rule, Irish MPs would consider supporting the Conservatives. Allied to this warning was Redmond's insistence that the Liberals must make the curtailing of the veto power of the House of Lords a first priority. Otherwise, even if Home Rule were passed by the Commons, it would be struck down by the Conservative majority in the Lords. When it became clear in November 1909 that a general election was imminent, Redmond repeated his warning. This no doubt prompted Asquith to include a Home Rule promise during his important speech at the Albert Hall on 10 December, which officially began the campaign season.[81]

With the Irish at least tentatively on board and a safe majority in hand, the Liberals faced the opening of the new Parliament on 21 February 1910 with some hope of success in pursing their primary objectives – forcing the Lords to pass the much debated Finance Bill and enacting some scheme for reducing the veto power of the Lords.[82] After all, they had beaten the Conservatives in a general election twice in a row and had withstood a powerful electoral counterattack during a lengthy and bruising campaign. Nevertheless, there was a sense of pervasive discouragement at the loss of so many English seats.[83] The Cabinet also remained distracted by continuing pressure from the Irish, who were now demanding immediate action. Redmond tightened the screws by issuing an ultimatum to the Liberals on 24 February 1910, a few days after Parliament had opened. That same day, the Irish fired a shot across the bows by abstaining from a tariff reform amendment proposed by the Conservatives, reducing the Liberal majority to only 31.

The Irish were doubtless responding to a startling revelation by Asquith a few days earlier at the opening of Parliament that he did not have an agreement from the King to create sufficient peers to override the Conservative majority, should they prove to be recalcitrant over the Budget in the forthcoming parliamentary session. This was a particularly damning admission in that he had clearly implied in his Albert Hall speech a few months earlier that he had just such an agreement from Edward VII.[84] An emerging division among Cabinet members over tactical matters was also damaging to the Liberal government. Some favoured an immediate and thoroughgoing stripping of the Lord's veto power. Others desired a more limited reform in the composition of the Lords, rather than any alteration in their traditional powers. In their view, to weaken the Lords might suggest a movement toward a single-chamber legislative system, unlikely to be popular in the country at large and sure to raise the hackles of the Lords even higher. Debates in the Commons offered no respite as Asquith was forced to hedge and delay about the ministry's intentions. In response to opposition badgering, he developed a stock phrase that he often used in years to come: 'Wait and see.'

By mid-April Asquith's doggedness enabled him to regain his position in the Cabinet and the Commons. On 13 April, he sought a guarantee from Edward VII that the King would exercise his royal prerogative and create enough peers to overturn the Unionist majority in the House of Lords on the pending Finance Bill. (Lloyd George had lobbied hard for this guarantee in order to square Redmond with the ministry.) On the following day, 14 April, Asquith introduced three resolutions forming the basis of a parliament bill which would at last address the powers of the House of Lords. First, the Lords would be denied the authority either to amend or reject a money bill. Second, the Lords could no longer delay other bills: such bills would automatically become law if passed in three successive parliamentary sessions by the House of Commons, provided that at least two years had elapsed from the time the bill had been introduced and its final approval by the Commons. Third, the duration of Parliaments was reduced from seven to five years. A week later, the Finance Bill, somewhat revised, passed its Third Reading in the Commons: the following day, after only a three hours' debate, the House of Lords passed the bill without a division. The People's Budget became law less than a fortnight later when it received the royal assent.

By giving the Finance Bill an easy ride, the Conservatives cut their losses and accepted the election as a referendum on the Budget. But they were holding firm on the emerging Parliament Bill. Turning down that bill would, as they well knew, likely bring about a dissolution and another general election. The risk seemed worth taking: perhaps another appeal to the electorate could provide a referendum against the Parliament Bill. Only a week after the passage of the Finance Bill, however, Edward VII died, bringing to the throne George V. The consequences of this event were incalculable. All parties were concerned about dragging the neophyte king into a constitutional morass. From several quarters came a novel suggestion to ease the path of the new king and to create a cooling off period in an attempt to assuage bitter party feeling. An agreement was entered into whereby Liberals and Conservatives together would engage in a constitutional conference concerning the proposed Parliament Bill specifically, and the state of the parties in general.

The Conference extended from 17 June to 29 July and again from 11 October to 10 November 1910, with 22 meetings in all. Four representatives from the Liberals

(Asquith, Lloyd George, Birrell and Lord Crewe) and four Conservatives (Balfour, Austen Chamberlain, Lansdowne and Lord Cawdor) made up the membership. Such a lengthy attempt at the highest level aimed at discussing the most important political and constitutional issues of the day suggested some hope of success. Because its proceedings were secret, it is difficult to follow precisely the scope and intent of the discussions. Nevertheless, there was considerable good will at work as both sides attempted to reach an accommodation. Balcarres confirms this, noting in his diary that all eight Conservative and Liberal representatives had 'sincerely striven' for an agreement. Even Lloyd George, he reported, had 'behaved well' and 'done his best to be accommodating'.[85] But the Conference was never able to bridge significant gaps in the differences between the opposing parties. Its most interesting result was to prompt an unexpected response from Lloyd George. During the ten-week adjournment of the Conference, he crafted a memorandum which urged a coalition government, comprised of Liberals and Conservatives alike.[86] Such a government would solve cooperatively outstanding problems of finance, social reform and the governing institutions of the realm.

Apparently the first to read the memo was Churchill. Enthusiastic about its contents, he recommended the memo be shown to his friend, the Conservative F.E. Smith, who was also taken with it. Thereafter, the memo was circulated among important Liberal and Conservative leaders, including Asquith, Balfour, Birrell, Bonar Law, Chamberlain, Crewe, Elibank, Haldane and Grey. The general interest among Liberals was perhaps not surprising.[87] More surprising was the favourable Conservative response. F.E. Smith, for example, believed the time was ripe for a non-partisan approach to politics. In a letter to Austen Chamberlain, he confided his belief that he could not remember within the past two decades a time 'when so many men in England were sick of mere party cries and faction. A great sigh of relief would go up ... if a strong and stable government were formed'. Smith also declared his satisfaction with 'LG's honesty and sincerity. He has been taught much by office ...'.[88] Chamberlain, too, was intrigued by Lloyd George's plan. Replying to Smith the following day, he hailed Lloyd George's 'momentous proposal'. Although he had some reservations about any cooperative settlement on the Irish question, he also believed that Lloyd George's proposal in general had been made 'in perfect good faith'. He was particularly pleased with Lloyd George's position on the navy, national defence and imperial preference.[89] The same day as his letter to Smith, Chamberlain wrote another letter to Lord Cawdor, one of the Conservative four attending the Constitutional Conference. In it, he reported a conversation with Bonar Law, who saw two very important concessions in Lloyd George's coalition plan. The first related to trade and tariff reform. Lloyd George was wiling to give a tariff preference to the colonies based upon the existing rate of duty. In addition, he was prepared to accept the findings of an impartial commission on the fiscal question, even if (Lloyd George implied) such a commission were to advocate tariff duties as a viable instrument for the preservation of the empire. In short, Lloyd George seemed ready to modify the free trade position of the Liberals in favour of tariff reform. Second – as Chamberlain reported to Cawdor – Lloyd George would consider settling the

Irish question on the basis of a form of devolution rather than Home Rule, a clear abandonment of the official Liberal position.[90]

In the meantime, a few days before Chamberlain's letters to Smith and Cawdor, Lloyd George gave a major address to the Liberal Christian League in London. The speech came hard on the heels of a cancelled address before the Welsh Liberal Council, which would likely have been one of Lloyd George's 'fighting' speeches. The Liberal Christian League, on the other hand, was billed as a non-political speech, delivered as the Constitutional Conference was reconvening. The speech offered a hand to the Conservatives by praising Joseph Chamberlain as one who had 'rendered outstanding service to the cause of the masses'. Chamberlain had, as Lloyd George reminded his audience, called attention to 'real crying evils festering amongst us, the existence of which the governing classes in this country were ignorant of or overlooked'. Lloyd George then developed at length the idea of 'social waste' with its attendant elements of poverty, unemployment, crowded urban conditions and under utilization of the land. In his concluding remarks, he once again referred to Chamberlain and to his boldness in addressing social conditions. That lesson still applied, he said. 'The time has come for a thorough overhauling of our national and Imperial conditions.'[91] The speech was obviously designed to state in public what his coalition proposal in private had been driving at – a temporary suspension of party allegiances with an eye to creating a national government to deal with domestic and foreign emergencies.

Clearly, Lloyd George's contemporaries took his proposals seriously and saw potential merit in his broad aim of party collaboration to solve the nation's outstanding problems. Some historians since have agreed. Gilbert believes that Lloyd George was honestly working his way forward to solve common problems as well as to regain a momentum for social reform by compromising with the Conservatives.[92] Rowland thinks that Lloyd George was driven by feelings of frustration at the slow progress of social reform and that something 'really imaginative', not simply 'a collection of half-hearted proposals', was necessary to break the deadlock.[93] Kenneth Morgan also sees Lloyd George – concerned with the serious issues dividing the country and driven by his dislike for partisan politics – as acting in the national interest. Morgan thinks additionally that Lloyd George's ideas drew widespread support – if only for 'a fleeting moment'.[94] Addison's account of the coalition plan gives Lloyd George full marks, calling the attempt 'a genuine invitation to the Conservatives to negotiate a deal' with no 'public posturing on his part'.[95] Grigg essentially agrees, but with a caveat. Lloyd George's 'energy and vision', as demonstrated in his attempted coalition, made him 'a good patriot, but not a good party man'.[96]

Other historians have been more critical of Lloyd George and his motives. As David Dutton observes, Lloyd George's motives for proposing a coalition are at least debatable. Dutton himself thinks that Lloyd George may have played 'something of a double game' in advocating somewhat different plans to each side during Conference discussions.[97] G.R. Searle fills in the details of Lloyd George's apparent trickery.[98] Charging him with duplicity and deviousness, Searle suggests that Lloyd George told the Liberals one thing and the Conservatives something else. There were in fact two memoranda setting out his proposals. Lloyd George gave copies of his 17 August memorandum to the Liberals, whereas with the Conservatives he only talked from that memorandum, making extemporaneous comments from it. These verbal comments amended the written memo, tilting it towards Conservative views. This was followed up by additional comments to both F.E. Smith and Bonar Law which further substantiated ideas favourable to the Conservatives. Searle believes that this 'opportunistic shuffling around from week to week' which characterized his negotiations with both sides was nothing more than 'the result of a conscious desire to deceive and confuse'.[99] Searle strengthens his case against Lloyd George when he discusses a second memo dated 29 October 1910. This memo – about which Searle admits little is known – seems at odds with the 17 August 1910 version. Searle thinks that in the October memo Lloyd George shifted his ground decisively against granting concessions to the Conservatives. Indeed, the October memo was, as Searle puts it, 'designed to appeal to a Liberal reader'.[100] Robert J. Scally essentially agrees with Searle in claiming that Lloyd George 'played a shell game with at least two differing versions of his plan'.[101] But Gilbert has an entirely different reaction to the October memo. He sees it as a natural corollary of its August predecessor – the sum of the two memos offering 'astounding concessions' to the Conservatives.[102]

It is not easy to reconcile these opposing historical viewpoints because of the secrecy surrounding them, but a direct appeal to the memos themselves suggests, if not a reconciliation of views, at least a possible interpretation of their provenance. The earlier August memo was largely a justification of the need of a coalition: it was pitched in general terms. The lengthy opening paragraphs set out the dangers surrounding the kingdom and the empire, both of which faced the threat of foreign competition. Internal political divisions, exacerbated by nearly equal numbers of both major parties in Parliament, had created a stalemate. A national reorganization devoid of partisan rancour attracting the most talented men could restore strong and stable government at home while guaranteeing a firmer response to dangers abroad. To that end, Lloyd George suggested (again in broad strokes) a coalition government which would address such important issues as the poor law; the problem of excessive drinking; national insurance; a national defence strategy (which might include a consideration of 'compulsory training'); and imperial unification.

The later October memo was much shorter and more specific. Examples are: the settlement of the Welsh Church issue on the basis of the Irish Disestablishment Act of 1869; easing the denominational controversy in education by legislation based upon Birrell's 1906 Act; a national scheme of insurance against unemployment, sickness and invalidity (including provision for widows and orphans) to be passed by Parliament within a year; and a reduction in the number of public houses where they were too numerous in certain districts. Both memos, if not identical, share many of the same provisions. Both memos address the same issues. Both include balanced solutions that will appeal equally to Liberal and Conservative alike. And both engender a spirit of compromise. For example, the August memo had recommended that national defence should be 'thoroughly looked into' with an eye to securing both efficiency and economy (a bow to the left). Even the question of 'compulsory training' should not be shirked (a bow to the right). The October memo repeated the need for adequate defensive preparations, including 'all necessary steps' for the defence of the empire at home and abroad (a Conservative credo). This was coupled with an injunction to make every effort to use diplomacy in securing international understanding with a hope of halting 'the alarming growth' of armaments (a clause sure to warm the hearts of Liberals). On Ireland, Lloyd George also attempted to please both parties. The August memorandum indicated that the Irish Question would be considered as a non-party issue, thus reducing the influence 'of extreme partisans', whether Nationalist or Orangemen. The October memorandum was somewhat more detailed on Ireland. Recognizing the Conservative opposition to full Home Rule for Ireland, Lloyd George proposed a scheme first advanced by Joseph Chamberlain in 1886 – a form of devolution granting significant authority to Ireland while retaining some ties to the mother country. On another supremely important issue, tariff reform, the August memorandum pledged an official enquiry into the 'various problems connected with State assistance to Trade and Commerce'. This was of course, a coded implication of a willingness to modify the Liberal free trade doctrine relating to trade and tariffs. The October memorandum reiterated and strengthened this proviso by additionally stating that a preference was 'to be given' to colonies on existing duties when practical. On the mainly Liberal issues of Welsh Church disestablishment, education, social reform and licensing Lloyd George held firm. But the undoubted sense of the two memoranda was one of establishing negotiating positions with an eye for eventual compromise.

In sum, the two memoranda can be viewed as separate drafts, with the latter draft emerging as a more specific legislative programme. The specificity of the later memorandum would be a natural consequence of discussions with members of both parties designed to flesh out the more general comments of the August memorandum.[103] If this is so, the charges that Lloyd George may have been involved in deception by showing different versions of his coalition plan to the Liberals and the Conservatives cannot be sustained. Indeed, as we have seen, although there are some differences of detail and form between the two memoranda, there are none of substance. Viewed in this light and remembering that both Liberals and Conservatives found something of worth in the coalition plan, we can reasonably conclude that Lloyd George made a good faith effort and was seen to do so by his contemporaries.

Why, then, did the coalition plan fail? There are a number of possible answers. There were in the first instance difficult structural problems in crafting a coalition government: for example, who should assume what offices? More important was the attitude of the rank and file party members on both sides. Die-hard landed Conservative backbenchers were deeply suspicious of the secret proceedings of the conference, as were the unyielding radicals of the Liberal left. In addition, both Labour and the Irish Nationalists, who had been excluded from the Conference, harboured doubts about Liberal goodwill.[104] Conservatives of every stripe were doubly suspicious of Lloyd George, who had directed scathing comments and partisan jabs at them for many years. Any role that he might play in a coalition government would likely be damned in their eyes from the outset. Perhaps Lloyd George's fundamental error was his secrecy in advocating the coalition plan. It was never formally brought forward to the conference: individuals were notified of it in random fashion. This is reminiscent of his bargaining tactic of keeping two sides apart and in the dark when he was President at the Board of Trade. Although this had worked well enough in negotiating between labour and management, it had limited appeal to intransigent political opponents.

Having said this, it is worthwhile to ascertain, if possible, the proximate cause of the failure of the negotiations of both conference and coalition – worthwhile because the failure added to party antagonisms and led directly to the second general election within a year. Lloyd George himself laid the blame at Balfour's door.[105] In his *War Memoirs*, written many years after the events, Lloyd George claimed that initially Balfour was 'by no means hostile' to the coalition proposal: this was also true, he writes, of the 'ablest members' on the Conservative side. In a crucial meeting between Balfour and Lloyd George in October, however, Balfour indicated that before he decided on the coalition plan, he needed a consultation with Aretas Akers-Douglas, former Conservative Chief Whip, who had the pulse of the party. Balfour further confided to Lloyd George that he could not repeat the experience of Sir Robert Peel, who had defied the dominant protectionist opinion in the Conservative Party by leading a coalition of Liberal, Whig and Tory MPs against the Corn Laws in 1846, thus officially establishing free trade. Peel thereafter was a man without a party and without influence until his death several years later. When Akers-Douglas confirmed Balfour's reservations, coalition negotiations ended shortly afterward and the conference itself came to an end.[106]

If Lloyd George's comments can be trusted and if Balfour said what Lloyd George recorded, Balfour had misled Lloyd George. Writing many years after the fact, Austen Chamberlain remarked that the central issue for the Conservatives throughout the Conference was not free trade versus tariff reform, but rather Home Rule for Ireland – the shadow of which 'hung over us all', as Chamberlain put it. In fact 'Home Rule barred the way'.[107] This was certainly true of Balfour. In a lengthy letter to J.L. Garvin in late October 1910, Balfour poured out his opposition to any form of Home Rule for Ireland, delivering a crushing response to Garvin's own letter of a few days earlier which had urged a moderation of views toward Ireland and the acceptance of a form of federalism, or devolution, or Home Rule all round as it was also called. Some form of devolution, Garvin thought, was inevitable.[108] But Balfour would have none of this, and his opposition 'sealed the fate of the federal solution and the fate of the Lloyd George plan'.[109] Federalism for Ireland, Balfour believed, could lead to an undesirable federalism for the empire as a whole; and it could excite in Ireland (and in Scotland and Wales as well) sentiments for separation. Balfour also raised the spectre of Ulster, whose Protestant majority would never accept a dominant Catholic Irish rule. Balfour's anti-Irish sentiments may have surprised Garvin, but would not have surprised those who knew Balfour from his days as Chief Secretary for Ireland in the late Parnellite era, when he was known as 'Bloody Balfour' for his coercionist policies. In short, it would appear that

Balfour, holding such views as he did upon Ireland, could never negotiate with Lloyd George on that crucial aspect of the coalition proposal. And without a resolution of the Irish question, the coalition plan could not go forward.[110]

Could Lloyd George have been culpable in some way of sabotaging his own coalition plan and if so, to what purpose? It is not beyond imagining that Lloyd George may have used the coalition plan to weaken the Conservative Party. On a downward slope since the latter stages of the South African War, Conservatives had become prone to factionalism in both Parliament and the country.[111] Balfour's rejection of Garvin's proposal on Irish federation revealed a wider rift within the Conservative Party on this issue. (Garvin had no status at the Conference, but his newspaper was a powerful instrument.) Lloyd George surely knew the differences of opinion on Ireland between Garvin and Balfour, emblematic of a growing division of opinion among Conservatives over the fate of Ireland. Simply by opening the question of Irish Home Rule and keeping both men equally informed of his proposed coalition plan, Lloyd George could sow mistrust and create mischief among them.[112] Whatever decision Balfour would make—either for or against considering Irish Home Rule – would alienate Conservatives of one kind or another.[113]

As is often the case when negotiations fail, pent up frustrations and a cycle of mistrust could cause a backlash into hardened positions. So it was with the failure of the Constitutional Conference and the coalition plan. A rapid sequence of events related to issues held in abeyance during the conference led to another legislative showdown between the two Houses of Parliament. On 10 November, after Asquith reported officially to the Cabinet that the Conference was stalled, the Cabinet decided on a snap general election, based in part upon the slight swing to the Liberals at the Walthamstow by-election of 1 November.[114] The following day and again on 16 November, Asquith held conferences with King George V and obtained from him a pledge to create sufficient peers to push through the House of Lords legislation limiting the veto power of the Lords. That same day, the Lords read the Parliament Bill, which had been passed by the Commons many months earlier, for the first time. On 21 November, at the second reading of the bill in the Lords, the Conservative majority presented its own plan for settling differences between the two Houses of Parliament. In recognition that some reform was inevitable, the Lords entertained a proposal to expand its membership beyond the existing hereditary privilege by including some who would sit *ex officio* and others who would be nominated by the Crown. Other suggestions included a provision for a joint sitting of both Houses in the event of legislative differences. If, however, more serious matters of legislation, such as a constitutional question (Home Rule would be an obvious example), could not be settled between the Houses of Parliament, a referendum would be held among the electorate at large.[115] These proposals were, however, unacceptable to the Liberal government. The Liberals, for example, opposed referendums because of their cost and complexity. On 28 November 1910, Asquith dissolved Parliament. The polls opened five days later.

At first blush, it may seem that the referendum proposal would be an enticing election ploy for the Conservatives. It could remove the public image of the

Conservatives, and the House of Lords particularly, as elitist anti-democrats. Indeed, Balfour sought immediately to turn the referendum proposal to advantage in an important speech at the Albert Hall on 29 November. There he pledged that if the Conservatives won the election, tariff reform and its attendant food taxes would not be levied until these issues were put before the electorate. Unfortunately for the Conservatives, Balfour's pledge proved divisive within Conservative ranks. The Albert Hall Pledge raised an immediate outcry especially among the Chamberlainites, the purist wing among the tariff reformers. They disliked the referendum because it would imply that tariff reform was not the settled policy of the party. Austen Chamberlain, titular head of the tariff reform movement since his father had been removed from the field of battle by a stroke in July 1906, was wholeheartedly against those 'fools' and 'wobbly Tariff Reformers' who were prepared to compromise.[116] Balfour was also roundly criticized not only on his specific referendum proposal, but also for the fact that he had not widely consulted his compeers before his public announcement of a referendum. The lack of unity among Conservatives prompted a gloomy view of their election prospects from Balcarres, the Conservative Chief Whip. Even before the campaign was fully underway, he registered 'discomfort' about the controversy within the party over tariff reform, fearing that 'divided counsels' would be distracting to their efforts.[117]

In contrast, the Liberals seemed reasonably united behind their double campaign slogans of restricting the veto power of the House of Lords and opposing the referendum. As had been true in earlier elections, the Liberals had the edge in platform speaking; and as before, Lloyd George was among the most active. He gave his speeches in characteristic fashion. Speaking up to 90 minutes at many meetings was not uncommon. Even at such length, his speeches never failed to capture his audiences. They were often dense in detail about the issues of the day, but nevertheless enlivened through his deft use of topical allusions to people and places. His humour and his ability to improvise and to turn hecklers to his advantage never undercut his ability to stay on message. During the campaign of December 1910, he kept up his barrage against tariff reform, against the referendum and against the aristocracy as a bastion of unlawful and benighted privilege. He also argued for justice for Ireland. His most celebrated speech of the campaign, at the Paragon Music Hall, Mile End Road in East London before a crowd of 5,000, was characteristic.[118] The first part of his speech was a comprehensive defence of the People's Budget and the iniquity of its veto by the House of Lords. As for the proposed constitutional referendum, he denounced it as a sham. The Lords would block every radical bill, sending it on to the country as a referendum measure, designed to delay its effect. Additionally, every referendum would cost up to £2 million, adding unnecessary expenses to the Budget. Once the people had decided at an election which issues should become law, 'no man, be he great or small, shall have the right to stop them'. The present election, Lloyd George informed his listeners, would make it 'impossible' thereafter for 'an hereditary House ever to reject' another budget.

Attacks on the aristocracy, as always with a Lloyd George audience, drew the most fervid response at Mile End.[119] He reviewed the origins of the English aristocracy, much to their discredit. It was, said Lloyd George, an ancient aristocracy; indeed, it was 'like cheese – the older it is, the higher it becomes'. The first aristocrats, he claimed, were French filibusterers who sailed over in a few shiploads from Normandy. They promptly set about killing all owners of property they could find. Having done that, they levied heavy duties upon the remainder of the population. Their descendants have been busy since 'cutting each other's throats'. A second wave of aristocrats was created when 'a certain number of people' took advantage of the turmoil of the Reformation 'to appropriate to their own uses land and buildings which had been consecrated to feed the needy and to attend the sick'. Thereafter the poor had no recourse, and there were many years of discontent, hunger, famine and rebellion. 'And now', Lloyd George confided to the crowd, 'you and I are paying rates in order to make up revenue which has been appropriated by those noble people who reject our Budget'. They are the very people, he went on, who 'hurl at us the epithets of robbers, thieves, spoliation because we dare put a tax of a halfpenny upon the land they purloined'.

If short on historical accuracy, this was good electoral stuff and tended to rouse the faithful while unsettling the opposition.[120] Of course, sometimes Lloyd George had to make exceptions to his general condemnations of the aristocracy. While campaigning in Scotland, he was the guest of the Master of Elibank, the Liberal Chief Whip and the tenth baron of a venerable Scots dynasty dating from the seventeenth century. To him Lloyd George paid tribute as one of the ablest whips ever serving the Liberal Party. He also singled out for praise Lord Crewe, leader of the Liberal opposition in the Lords; and perhaps surprisingly, he complemented Lord Lansdowne, the Conservative leader in the Lords, as 'a man of eminent ability'.[121] But, he said, there were scores of others who had never earned a living in any profession and who did not know the care and worry of work, who did not sow, did not reap, did not mill the grain, nor did they bake the bread that others ate. These men, whose lives were far from the common lot of mankind, should never hold exclusive power over others.

This message was repeated at other campaign stops. In Newport, he declared from the door of his dining car on the train to Cardiff: 'With the next push the House of Lords topples over.'[122] At Cardiff, he claimed that the referendum would simply be a barrier to legitimate legislation and would perpetuate the 'bondage of landlordism'.[123] At Ipswich, he made two separate speeches: the first to a crowd of 4,000 packed into the Palace Skating Rink; and afterwards to another large crowd at the Corn Exchange. His message was the same as elsewhere: the referendum scheme 'would be in the way of reform'.[124] Returning to Scotland a few days later, he affirmed at Glasgow his belief that the election was primarily to remove the 'long standing obstacles in the path of progressive and Liberal legislation' – obstacles created by 'an unrepresentative hereditary Chamber'.[125] The final stages of the election found Lloyd George primarily in Wales, campaigning hard for Liberal candidates at Llandrindod, Nevin, Pwllheli, Criccieth, Wrexham, Conway and Bangor.[126]

Lloyd George himself did not of course remain unscathed as Conservative candidates made him their special target. Bonar Law set the tone only a few days after the failure of the Constitutional Conference at a meeting of the Constitutional Club in London. There he warned that in the coming election, the people must decide 'whether we were to have revolution or reform'.[127] At a meeting convened a few days later by the Battersea Conservative and Unionist Association held at the town hall, F.E. Smith – one of the few Conservatives who could approach Lloyd George's ability as a stump speaker – condemned what he called 'Lloyd Georgeism', defined as 'the preaching of class hatred for party purposes'.[128] A fortnight later, Smith elaborated on his criticism during a speech in support of the candidate for East Islington.[129] He claimed that during the previous election of January 1910, Lloyd George had 'raced all over England chasing his own vulgarities'. In that election, Smith also charged Lloyd George with conducting a 'campaign of incomparable scurrilousness'. He was attempting the same tactic during the present election but, Smith declared, he was 'a beaten demagogue': the more the Chancellor spoke, the greater the chance of a Conservative victory because his 'campaign of class hatred' would fail.

As historians have noted, the most striking feature about the campaign was its similarity to the January poll of the same year. In both cases, voter interest was high, political speeches were in abundance and the final results were virtually identical. After the votes were tallied, the distribution of parliamentary seats in England and Wales was very close: the Conservatives at 274 and Liberals, 270. But as had been true at the January 1910 election, parties usually allied to the Liberals made the difference. Labour returned 42 seats and the Irish Nationalists 84, which gave the Liberals a comfortable majority of more than 120 seats in the House of Commons.[130] Although Balcarres tried to console himself with the thought that the election was perhaps a Conservative moral victory, he had to admit the prospects were bleak for the party: 'to me', he wrote in his diary, 'the outlook is black'.[131] This election was, after all, the third in a row lost by the Conservatives. The Liberal legislative programme, including the curtailment of the power of the House of Lords, seemed impregnable.

Lloyd George had largely neglected his own constituency, spending only a few days campaigning against his opponent, a young barrister, Austen Lloyd-Jones, who was a non-Welsh speaking Anglican. The result was a foregone conclusion: Lloyd George won easily by 3,112 votes to 1,904 votes. His vigorous campaigning throughout Wales, Scotland and England, however, had affected his health. Towards the end of the campaign, his voice began to fail. To recoup and recover his strength, he departed immediately after the election on 20 December for the South of France, upon the recommendation of his doctor. At first accompanied by Margaret, his young daughter Megan and John Rowland, his Welsh private secretary, Lloyd George was joined after Christmas by Alec Murray, the Master of Elibank, and the new Attorney General, Rufus Isaacs. Shortly after the New Year, the party settled for a time in Nice. There, Sir John Bradbury, principal clerk at the Treasury, and William John Braithwaite, an assistant secretary in Inland Revenue, joined them. It was obvious that the rest cure was rapidly turning into something more serious. Indeed, Braithwaite had come straight from Germany, where he had completed a survey of the German health insurance system. On the afternoon of 3 January 1911, in an informal session on the pier at Nice, gave his report orally to Lloyd George. The various complicated strands of what was to become the National Insurance Act of 1911 were coming together.

7

TRIUMPH

During the time away from his official duties while recuperating, Lloyd George had also begun work, as we have noted, on the national insurance scheme. He therefore took little part in the continuing battle over the Parliament Bill.[1] Brought forward on its first reading on 21 February 1911, the bill sped through its second reading within a few days. Not until May, however, did it receive its third reading and then move on to the Lords. Its provisions were unchanged from the original bill sent to the Lords prior to the general election of December 1910. A preamble stated that the ultimate goal was to reconstitute the House of Lords in some fashion to make it less based upon hereditary privilege. There followed three short clauses: abolition of the power of the Lords to veto money bills; a delay of no more than two years for other bills; and reduction of the maximum duration of Parliament from seven to five years.

As the Liberal government had moved forward, Conservatives remained divided and indecisive over a passable strategy against the bill. Many Conservatives regarded the results of the December 1910 election as merely another obstacle to be surmounted in their quest to keep the Lords sacrosanct, rather than accepting it as a national referendum on the bill. Some in the party sought to discount the Liberal majority in the House of Commons by arguing that the government was kept in place only by an Irish minority who had bargained with the Liberals for a quid pro quo: Irish support for the Parliament Bill would be rewarded with a Liberal Home Rule Bill. They claimed that the Liberal government, given its reliance upon the Irish Nationalists in the House of Commons, was essentially un-English. Other Conservatives, especially among the peerage – driven by their frustrations and sense of impotence – began to organize their numbers in the House of Lords in order to block the pending Liberal Bill. These 'Diehards' have attracted historical attention in an attempt to understand why a substantial number of Conservatives had become increasingly extremist after 1906, even destructively so, in their political behaviour.[2] The Diehards were undoubtedly distressed by the decline of aristocratic influence in the country and by the threats posed to them from the invasive Liberal reformist programmes. In addition, they were uneasy about the spread of democracy and sincerely believed that the Liberals were harbingers of a socialism that could mean the death knell for the privileged landed society of which they were the natural leaders. They were particularly concerned about military and imperial affairs, doubting the Liberals' capacity to stand firm for the navy, army and the empire. The Parliament Bill, in attacking the House of Lords as the symbol of aristocratic power, was the last straw.

The majority of moderate Conservatives in the Lords, however, attempted to draw the teeth of the Parliament Bill by instituting a reform. On 8 May Lansdowne proposed reducing the peers in the Lords to 350, with the members chosen through a combination of elections and appointments. The measure failed almost immediately.[3] Matters worsened for the Conservatives in July when they learned for the first time that Asquith had secured from the King an agreement to create sufficient peers in the Lords to override any veto of the Parliament Bill.[4] Balcarres, who became Chief Whip that same month, reveals fully in his diary the despair gripping the Conservatives.[5] Even before the Parliament Bill had been resubmitted to the Lords, he reported that the party was 'low-spirited' and 'in perilous danger of a collapse'.[6] As Whip, Balcarres was actively concerned about the morale of his troops. At first he supported the Diehards as a useful ginger group for a divided party. But when the Diehard movement became increasingly truculent and entrenched, Balcarres realized that the party could 'really be split asunder' by their actions.[7] This was a distinct possibility. A number of moderate Conservatives had decided to act in direct opposition to the Diehard group in the Lords. They were determined to support the Parliament Bill in order to prevent 'swamping' in the Lords by newly created Liberal peers.

Apart from gloomily following this development in the Lords, Balcarres grew increasingly disenchanted with the existing Conservative leadership, especially with Balfour. Tense and frequent conversations between the Chief Whip and Balfour's role as party leader proved unsatisfactory. Complaints came from several other sources, substantiating a growing criticism of Balfour. He was thought detached, secretive, ineffectual and a perpetual trimmer. Most damning of all, he had presided as party leader over three consecutive Conservative electoral defeats. His weariness of such criticism and of the internecine party strife were doubtless the reasons that lay behind Balfour's decision to depart for Gastein on a rest cure only a few days before the final vote in the Lords on the Parliament Bill.[8] While Balfour was abroad, the critical vote in the Lords on 10 August approved the bill by a close vote of 134 to 117. The majority was made up of 81 Liberal peers, 37 Conservatives, the two archbishops and most of the bishops. The minority was comprised mainly of Diehards (also known as Ditchers; that is, willing to die in the last ditch for their cause). But the largest number of peers, some 300 Conservatives (Hedgers), led by Lansdowne, abstained.[9]

The passage of the Parliament Bill brought the question of Conservative Party leadership to a head. The rank and file as well as numerous party leaders believed that Balfour had failed to give a firm lead in the struggle over the Parliament Bill. A 'Balfour Must Go' campaign, led by disaffected Conservatives and given voice by the editor Leo Maxse in his monthly *National Review*, was vigorous and effective.

The Diehards formally organized themselves as the Halsbury Club in October, pledged to the removal of Balfour as party leader.[10] Balfour was not unaware of the growing opinion against him. Even before the Parliament Bill had passed through the Lords, he had hinted to Balcarres that he was thinking of resigning as leader of the party.[11] By late September, this notion had grown in him. In conversations with Balcarres, he confessed that his lengthy service for the party was nearing its end: at the age of 63, he felt tired and stale and ready for resignation.[12] By then the most important question surrounding Balfour's resignation had come to the fore: who would succeed him? By November, the difficulty of filling Balfour's shoes became the only impediment to his resignation.

In contrast to the internecine struggles of the Conservatives, the Liberal government was solidly united behind their reform measures, with Lloyd George as the chief spokesman. Addressing the needs of the working class was becoming the most important plank in the Liberal government's platform for social legislation. The broad idea was to guarantee some support and specific benefits to the working class in times of particular difficulty. The Labour Exchanges Act of 1909 had tackled the problem of temporary unemployment. The passage of an old age pensions plan had aided the elderly. By logical extension, the state also had a responsibility toward the working class who had not yet reached retirement age and whose livelihood – and that of their families – depended upon a steady job and good health. Plans to guarantee state aid to unemployed workers and those stricken by illness could now go forward after the passage of the Parliament Bill.

Unemployment was the first priority. Through the combined efforts of such civil servants as Beveridge and Llewellyn Smith, in association with a Cabinet committee overseen by Churchill, three guiding principles of a proposed bill emerged to assuage the difficulties of job reductions. First, the bill would be narrow in coverage, applicable only to those trades commonly subject to cyclical downturns, such as building, shipbuilding and iron founding. No provisions were made for dockworkers, for example, for whom casual labour was customary.[13] Second, a national scheme would work in tandem with the trade unions so that their own unemployment plans would not be jeopardized. And third, unemployment insurance would be contributory. Every worker in an insured trade would have 2½d. deducted from the weekly pay packet; employers would add 2½d. more, and the state would add 1d. benefits including 7s. per week for 15 weeks of unemployment (after a one week waiting period) in the insured trades. Perhaps surprisingly, given its further extension of state responsibility into the social realm, unemployment insurance encountered little resistance from the Conservative opposition and followed a relatively uneventful path to legislation, becoming law in December 1911.[14]

The main battle erupted on health insurance. No doubt anticipating the difficulty, Lloyd George himself took the lead in managing the bill through the House of Commons.[15] He rightly understood that there were greater entrenched interests opposed to a state sponsored health insurance plan than to state aid for unemployment. Among the most vehement of these were Friendly Societies and industrial insurance companies. Friendly Societies were opposed to any state scheme competing with their own social insurance programmes, as has been noted in the controversy over old age pensions.[16] Knowing this well in advance, as early as November 1908 Lloyd George had initiated the first of many meetings with representatives of the Friendly Societies. Constructive negotiations resulted in a tentative accord by which the facilities of the Societies would be incorporated into a national scheme of insurance. Soon afterward, however, exigencies of the Parliament Bill forced a recess and suspended contact between Lloyd George and the Friendly Societies until mid-1910. After a brief informational meeting in June 1910, progress was delayed further by the abortive Constitutional Conference of that year.

Simultaneously with his discussions with the Friendly Societies, Lloyd George had also begun conferring with the industrial insurance companies, potentially a far more formidable foe.[17] These privately-owned companies were well capitalized and influential among the working-class population. Some idea of their wealth can by gauged by the holdings of the Prudential, the largest of the 75 insurance companies; it owned more freehold properties in the kingdom than any other corporation and had an annual premium income of about £7 million. The sole mission of the companies was to provide death benefits. Working-class families took great pride in a 'good death', characterized by a respectable funeral and perhaps a pageant for the neighbourhood of the deceased. Funeral benefits provided the necessary funds for these ceremonies. Over 30 million funeral policies had been written by 1910. Policyholders kept up the payments on their policies through some 70,000 full-time door-to-door sales agents who made weekly collections. These agents, known and respected by their clients, could exert a powerful influence against any health insurance plan.

Lloyd George approached the companies with care in his attempt to persuade them to be a partner in a national insurance scheme. When he renewed his talks with the leaders of the Friendly Societies in late 1910, he also began conferring with insurance company representatives. The results were not entirely satisfactory. Neither organization liked the notion of compulsory payments by workers into a state fund: such a scheme could make their own functions redundant. They were also leery of provisions for widows and orphans which Lloyd George believed essential in addressing the impact of a husband's and father's death upon their families. But such provisions could extend the liabilities of the companies and the societies well into the future.[18] Friendly Societies were also concerned that their role as ethical guides to the working class could be undermined by state intervention. This was voiced by T. Barnes, Grand Master of the Manchester Unity of Oddfellows during a meeting of its representatives with Lloyd George at the Treasury. Friendly Societies were not merely insurance agencies, he pointed out: they were also moulders of 'the character of the English people'. Barnes believed further that 'any system of compulsory State insurance must necessarily undermine existing voluntary institutions'.[19] Under sharp questioning from Lloyd George, however, Barnes admitted he was opposed to any government insurance provision for the 10 million workers then outside the Friendly Society system. Lloyd George firmly rebutted that view: 'We must consider the millions who ... cannot keep up their contributions and who find it all they can do to shift along and buy bread for their children.' This was, he continued, 'one of the subjects we cannot let rest'. Furthermore, the 'vast majority' of people had come to the conclusion that the poverty stricken 'cannot live on *laissez-faire* policy'. Lloyd George ended on a more conciliatory note, praising the work of Friendly Societies and promising to give Barnes for his eyes only a copy of the provisional bill that very day.

In early 1911, the debate over national health insurance intensified. The industrial insurance companies made the startling suggestion that they be included in any scheme of state insurance. By such means, they no doubt hoped to influence the development of the insurance programme. As negotiations continued, Lloyd George bent with the wind. Widow's pensions were dropped, but in compensation, the sickness benefit was increased. Both industrial insurance companies and Friendly Societies would become 'approved societies'; in effect, they would act as agents of the state in administering and funding the new national insurance scheme. To the financially strapped Friendly Societies, this could be a boon; as an approved society, they were thus eligible to receive substantial state funds to be used as payments for their members.

After extensive consultations and conferences, Lloyd George introduced the bill on 4 May 1911 to the House of Commons. Under its provisions, all workers, men and women, aged 16 to 70 who earned less than £160 annually would be compelled to insure themselves against illness through approved societies. (After 70, old age pensions would begin.) Men would pay 4d. and women 3d. each week to an insurance fund: employers would be required to add 3d. and the state 2d. to the fund. Workers earning more than £160 could voluntarily join the plan, but would be required to pay the employers' contribution as well as their own. Benefits included 10s. weekly for men (7s. 6d. for women) for 13 weeks beginning on the fourth day of illness. Thereafter for the next 13 weeks, benefits would be reduced to 5s. weekly for men and 3s. for women. A disability benefit of 5s. weekly began when the sickness benefits ran out and could last indefinitely. Medical benefits included care from a general practitioner employed by an approved society. A maternity benefit of 30s. would be paid directly to the insured worker's wife at the time of childbirth; if both husband and wife were contributors, the payment doubled. Tubercular patients had the right to treatment in sanatoria, the construction of which would be financed by a grant of £1.5 million to local authorities. Administration of the provisions of the bill was fairly straightforward. The approved societies would be self-governing and could even distribute surplus funds among their members in the form of new or increased benefits. Local health committees representing the approved societies, the post office and local sanitary authorities were to administer the sanatoria benefit. A central insurance commission would administer the plan throughout the kingdom.[20]

Not surprisingly, Lloyd George thought his presentation to the House a success: it was in fact 'a smashing triumph', as he wrote to William. 'All parties now engaged in lauding it.' The bill, he believed further, had 'transfigured politics'.[21] In this instance, Lloyd George's opinion was not far wrong. The scheme was initially greeted favourably by most politicians and by the press.[22] *The Times* endorsed the proposed bill as 'a great object' in alleviating the twin misfortunes of illness and unemployment 'among the poorer classes of the community'.[23] Praise from at least one Conservative leader was also forthcoming. Austen Chamberlain thought the scheme was 'bold, sound and comprehensive and in many respects original'.[24] But the bill soon began to generate unfavourable second thoughts. Perhaps most surprising was the opposition from a small group of Labour MPs and trade unionists who spoke for those workers who disliked the mandatory contributions taken from their wages. Even 4d. weekly, they claimed, might strain workers at the lower end of the pay scale. Furthermore, workers in those trades covered by the unemployment scheme of national insurance, had to pay an additional 2½d. weekly. In effect, these flat-rate insurance contributions were not unlike regressive direct taxes.[25] To soften this criticism, Lloyd George engineered a trade-off by which he would sponsor a bill granting payment for Members of Parliament, in return for which Labour would agree to support the National Insurance Bill.[26] There was also stout opposition to health insurance from a body of Irish MPs on the grounds that the medical benefit would be superfluous to Ireland where workers already had free doctor's care under the Poor Laws and voluntary hospitals. On this point, Lloyd George agreed. The Irish medical benefit was deleted from the bill and Irish workers' contributions were reduced.

The strongest opposition to health insurance, however, came from the British Medical Association. Lloyd George had paid little attention to the doctors during formative stages of the bill: such neglect came to haunt him after the bill became law. The BMA was particularly perturbed by Lloyd George's original idea of allowing the approved societies (in most cases these were Friendly Societies) to administer medical benefits granted by the bill. Doctors opposed this well-established practice in the belief that competition among them for contract work with the Friendly Societies would drive down fees charged to patients. Doctors desired a state-managed system of patient panels providing a better income.[27] They also wanted adequate representation on any and all committees concerned with the administration of medical benefits. The small size of the medical benefit limiting doctors' compensation under the bill was an additional grievance.

Lloyd George reacted in characteristic fashion. He appealed directly to the medical profession by asking to speak at a special conference in London summoned by the BMA to oppose the bill. After speaking at length, he entertained questions from his angry audience.[28] Throughout, his overall tone was accommodating. Declaring that the bill was a work in progress, he invited their suggestions for its improvement. Their recommendations, he promised, would be entertained by appropriate administrative bodies created by the bill, such as the Health Committee and the Insurance Commissioners. Lloyd George's conciliatory approach was followed by a more extended appeal in a speech at Birmingham before a crowd of 3,000 comprised of representatives from leading Friendly Societies, trade unions and labour organizations, as well as some medical professionals.[29] Lloyd George directed his speech primarily at the beneficiaries of the bill – those hundreds of thousands of families, as he put it, who led precarious lives and whose breadwinners were too often swept away by tides of ill fortune, hurling their families into destitution. This bill would avert 'myriads of ruined homes and broken hearts'. He emphasized that the bill was not a 'final solution': it was, rather, the first of a series. With this bill, he added: 'We are not done with fighting poverty and misery.' He concluded with one of his most famous and felicitous analogies. 'I am', he said, 'in the ambulance corps. I am engaged to drive a wagon through the twistings and turnings and ruts of the Parliamentary road'. Some have claimed that his wagon was overloaded, while others saw it as too lightly laden. But he had packed it carefully with as much as he could carry and he wanted to drive as fast as he could because he could 'hear the moanings of the wounded' and he wanted to carry relief quickly to them as they lay stricken. 'I ask you', he concluded to a cheering audience, 'to help me to set aside hindrances, to overcome obstacles, to avoid the pitfalls that beset my difficult path'.

But Lloyd George's rhetoric did not silence critics of the bill. The BMA remained a redoubtable foe and continued its opposition throughout 1911. As a result, the original medical benefit, the control of approved societies, was removed and transferred to local health committees. Perhaps emboldened by this victory, the BMA continued to press its advantage. Even after the bill became law on 16 December 1911, doctors demanded additional perquisites and changes in its provisions. Chief among them was a capitation fee for each panel patient of 8s. 6d. Pressuring the government further, the BMA called upon all doctors working under the terms of the new act to resign unless their demands were met.[30] On this issue, Lloyd George remained firm; but he did suggest at a meeting with the BMA in June 1912 that a systematic survey be conducted of doctors' existing remunerations in order to determine a baseline for further negotiation. The following month, the survey revealed that all doctors averaged annually 4s 5d per patient. Thus the government's proposal of 6s. per patient was a generous increase: the BMA's demand of 8s. 6d. appeared unreasonable and grasping.[31] Lloyd George took this opportunity both to offer a compromise and issue a threat. If doctors should ever boycott the act, he warned, the administration of medical benefits would be returned to such approved societies as the government may designate. On the other hand, he proposed an increase in annual capitation fees per patient from 6s. to 7s. 6d., with an extra 1s. 6d. for the provision of drugs. In a last burst of angry denunciation, at a meeting on 21 December 1912 BMA delegates once again urged all doctors to refuse medical care under the act. But an uproar from grassroots medical practitioners, many of them in poorer areas of the kingdom, soundly rejected this advice. The 'revolt of the doctors' was at last at an end.

Through adroit stratagems and a series of hurried ad hoc compromises, Lloyd George's plan of state-sponsored national insurance had triumphed. If the plan retained some unpopular features, Lloyd George himself enjoyed a personal popularity and a national recognition for his efforts. Although a change of mood and tactics emerged in the later months of 1911 among Conservative opponents when they began to attack the bill, Lloyd George's luck held. Conservatives could not sustain their opposition as their energies were sapped by the continuing debilitating battle over the Parliament Bill, which was then making its way through the House of

Lords during simultaneous debates on national insurance in the Commons. When successive by-elections went against the Liberals in November, however, it seemed at last that the Conservatives would gain some traction. But Balfour's decision to resign the party leadership, made public on 8 November, roiled the waters. Once again, the Conservatives were placed on the defensive.

By December 1911, the final stage of the National Insurance Bill was making its way through the House of Commons. Lloyd George assured his brother that he was 'quite ready for smooth or storm. I have had both on the Bill but I am nearing the harbour'.[32] A week later, after the House had passed the measure, he reported that the debate in Lords was 'going on quietly'.[33] A few days afterward came the joyful news to William: 'Insurance Bill received Royal assent!' Expressing delight at this victory during a most 'strenuous session', Lloyd George now hoped 'for rest & relaxation'.[34]

The struggle over health insurance has been widely chronicled by contemporary observers and historians; of these, William Braithwaite's diary is the most informative.[35] At the most crucial moments during the passage of the bill, his diary entries convey a sense of the controversies encountered and overcome. Indeed, few accounts exist in such detail of the development of a major legislative act – its conception, analysis and construction. Throughout, Braithwaite portrays Lloyd George as the central lynchpin of the bill, always at work conferring with officials, seeing deputations and remaining on top of any potential legislative hurdles. Braithwaite was particularly impressed with Lloyd George's 'uncanny art' of receiving and disarming deputations. He 'invariably allowed' the first speaker to present his points fully, helping him along with sympathetic questions. His own replies were to the point and 'full of fun', inducing a companionable atmosphere. He promised even 'the most unlikely proposals … full consideration'. Meetings thus conducted by the Chancellor often 'broke up for informal chatty conversation', everyone 'fully satisfied that it would probably get almost all that it had asked for'.[36] In the most unlikely places – in hotel dining rooms, on the golf links, in restaurants – as well as at the Treasury, Lloyd George would consort with a gaggle of advisors on the details of the bill. Braithwaite himself had been the centre of early discussions of the bill on the boardwalk at Nice, where he met and reported to Lloyd George and others immediately upon returning from an exploratory trip to Germany in early January 1911. Within a week, Braithwaite was back in London, attending one of Lloyd George's working breakfasts at 11 Downing Street.[37] From that moment on, national insurance gathered steam.

Historians since have largely agreed, even if at times grudgingly, that Lloyd George's achievement was momentous. Rowland, while noting that there were numerous omissions in the National Insurance Act and that it had been drafted 'in haste and confusion', nevertheless praised it as one of Lloyd George's greatest achievements. Morgan gives more credit to Lloyd George's handling of the complex details of the bill, hailing it as 'masterly'. Packer, admitting that Lloyd George's habits of work were 'erratic', also finds much to praise in Lloyd George's achievement. It was he who 'took all the initiatives to start the scheme'. Searle, in categorizing the health insurance plan as 'a fiendishly complex measure' which was undertaken in a 'lighthearted manner' by that 'master of improvisation, Lloyd George', nevertheless notes that no other government had ever attempted such a grandiose scheme.[38]

In the meantime, Lloyd George's manifold talents were put to an additional test during the summer of 1911. Several months earlier, a series of disputes in the South Wales coalfields had led to an increasing number of work stoppages and strikes which threatened the Liberal government far more seriously than any action taken by the Conservatives. Viewed retrospectively, the strikes were part and parcel of a generalized labour unrest characteristic of the years immediately preceding World War I.[39] The background to the unrest lay in the momentous changes in Edwardian capitalism created by Britain's declining position in world markets, which in turn led to a reduced rate of economic growth. Slowing productivity and lower profits inclined employers to increase workloads and to institute a strategy of 'speed-up'.[40] Smaller crews on longer trains, systematic undermanning on ships and shorter turnabout times on the docks were common practices. Elsewhere, coal production became dependent on deeper and more dangerous mines. Not surprisingly, industrial relations became strained. Indeed, in some cases, employers simply refused to enter into collective bargaining with unions. Employer demands created a new spirit of militarism, especially among rank and file union members, who were demanding higher pay, shorter hours and better working conditions. Not only did the frequency of union-sponsored strikes increase, there were also larger numbers of sympathetic stoppages among other workers and allied unions. Growing labour solidarity thus created a new self-confidence among the unions.[41]

The first significant strike, as we have noted above, occurred among coal miners in South Wales. After months of wrangling, the owners of the Cambrian Combine mine in the Rhondda Valley locked out its workers on 1 September 1910. Sympathy for the strike in the next several weeks led to mass picketing and rioting. Pitched battles between police and miners occurred in Tonypandy, the main town in the Rhondda. Over 500 were injured and one striker was killed. While the dispute lingered, in Southampton a general strike of seamen and firemen erupted. Spreading quickly to the principal ports of the country, other workers were drawn into the conflict, including dockers and carters. By August 1911, the Port of London had been brought to a standstill, with 80,000 workmen on strike. Perishable cargoes began to rot in the heat of summer, and other foodstuffs were undeliverable. In that same month, a wildcat railway strike in Liverpool spread to other cities, including London.

The likelihood of a rail strike was particularly serious and prompted governmental intervention for the first time.[42] The initial response, however, was ill advised, even inflammatory: they gave the railway management a written *carte blanche* to call in troops when they considered it necessary.[43] In addition, at a meeting with railway managers and men, Asquith (with Sidney Buxton, President of the Board of Trade, in attendance) revealed an unsympathetic attitude towards the striking railway unions. The executive secretaries of the unions, therefore, after conferring with the TUC and the Parliamentary Labour Party, issued a general strike order on 17 August.

In response, Churchill as Home Secretary ordered up nearly 60,000 troops to be dispersed to all threatened strike areas. Tensions continued to rise. Troubled sections of the country were placed under martial law. Two railway strikers were shot dead at Llanelli in South Wales.

As events threatened to spin out of control, Lloyd George volunteered his services and began the work of negotiation. He was a natural choice, having been instrumental in establishing the conciliation boards in 1907. But as the unions pointed out, the boards had failed primarily because the railway managers refused either to recognize the unions or to meet with them.[44] Thus collective bargaining had become impossible. Setting up headquarters at the Board of Trade, Lloyd George worked towards an agreement by which conciliation boards would be strengthened. For the intermediate future, a Royal Commission would determine what additional changes might be made for the better. If the two sides did not agree voluntarily to accept the findings of the commission, Lloyd George threatened legislation to enforce the findings. Within two days, his whirlwind negotiations and his firm yet accessible manner seemed to calm the two sides.

At that point Lloyd George increased pressure upon both railway management and men by employing an unusual argument: he used scare tactics. Referring to events in Morocco (along the southern rim of the Mediterranean) during July and early August 1911, where a diplomatic standoff between Germany and France had raised international tensions, Lloyd George intimated that the prospects for war were very real and that should it occur, the railways would be called upon to play an important role in the transport of military goods and materiel. This appeal to patriotism may very well have contributed to the settlement of the strike. For the railway unions, it was a major victory. They had won the right for their oft-repeated demand for face-to-face talks with railway managers on the issues that divided them. These talks in themselves also helped legitimize union demands, encouraged further a sense of union solidarity and endorsed industrial action as a sound strategy if all else failed. For his part, Lloyd George interpreted the settlement as a distinctly personal triumph. To his wife, he wrote (in characteristic fashion) that it had been the hardest struggle of his life but, he assured her, he had won. Quoting from an anonymous friend who called it 'a miracle', he could only modestly agree: 'it certainly looks like it'.[45] That same evening, still enthused by his success and by his desire for approbation, Lloyd George barged into the War Office where Haldane was busily coordinating the military arrangements against the strike. 'A bottle of champagne!' he exclaimed. 'I've done it! Don't ask me how, but I've done it! The strike is settled!'[46]

But the most serious strike of all was yet to come – potentially even more disruptive than the railway dispute. For the first time in history, a national coalminers' strike was threatened early in 1912.[47] Their demands were 'the 5 and 2' – five shillings a man minimum for each shift and two shillings for a boy. At stake were not only an increase in wages, but also the principle of establishing a minimum wage for workers. The importance of coalmining as a test case for the battle over minimum wages was shrewdly chosen: coal was the chief source of energy for industry and for domestic use. The consequences of a shut down of all coalmines in the country were incalculable but easily imagined. Lloyd George thought that industry would be brought to a standstill within a month. As Postmaster General, Herbert Samuel began laying in extra coal stocks for the Post Office's power stations. George Askwith believed that such a strike would likely mean 'terrible bloodshed', especially in South Wales.[48] An initial meeting in late February 1912 between representatives of the Miners' Federation and four members of the Cabinet – Asquith, Lloyd George, Grey and Buxton – adjourned without agreement. The strike was called on 1 March: within a short time, more than a million men had walked out of the mines.

Once the strike was in motion, the ministerial negotiating team entered into talks with both mine owners and miners. There were also informal discussions among mining leaders, politicians and other public figures. Throughout the discussions, ministers held firm that minimum wages could not be set by legislation. With the miners also refusing to budge, little advance was made in settling the strike. The Cabinet may have been surprised by the tenacity of the miners; indeed, George Riddell believed that the ministry had been 'staggered' by the strike.[49] Lloyd George himself seems taken aback by the miners' determination. He had at first discounted their demands. To William he wrote that it was 'just as well' the strike had been called because they would very soon be brought to their senses and would be more 'amendable to reason. For the moment they are not'.[50] By mid-March, however, at a time when Lloyd George thought 'things were going very badly' with no end in sight, he instigated a meeting between Riddell and Vernon Hartshorn, a leader of the Welsh miners.[51] Together, the two hammered out a draft proposal for settling the strike. Riddell presented it to Lloyd George the following morning; he in turn gave it to Asquith. Several days of contentious discussion between Lloyd George, Riddell and Hartshorn followed, with the minimum wage remaining the most difficult issue. In an effort to move forward, Asquith introduced a Coalmines Bill on 19 March, which divided the coal mining regions into 22 districts. In each district special boards, made up of both management and men, were created; they would be empowered to determine minimum wages and conditions of employment for that district.

Parallel to this legislative activity, a number of 'most serious Cabinets' were held.[52] Cabinet discussions, however, revealed divided counsels. Some were against any legislation at all, including that old Gladstonian, John Morley. Grey advocated a government subsidy to compensate the coal owners for any losses they may incur until an inquiry could be completed on miners' grievances. Lloyd George, on the other hand, was willing to give in to the miners' demands 'absolutely'.[53] It appears that Asquith, displaying unaccustomed decisiveness in the Cabinet, took the lead in directing his colleagues toward legislative action.[54] On 27 March, the third reading of the Coalmines Bill was carried and two days later quickly ratified by the Lords. Although the government avoided setting a national wage scale, it had nevertheless established the precedent for legislating minimum wages for workers. Satisfied, coal miners began returning to work within a fortnight.

This was not the end of the strike wave, however. Labour troubles continued to hound the ministry. During the summer of 1912, another transport strike centring on the Port of London broke out, over the hiring of a non-union foreman. Attempts to widen the strike to other ports failed, and the strike ended quickly. Throughout 1913 and into the summer of 1914 there were a number of smaller, more successful local strikes where workers won concessions. These included London cab drivers, Yorkshire dyers, Lancashire cotton spinners and agricultural labourers, London printers and High Wycombe furniture makers.[55] Less successful was a strike in Dublin in 1913–14 led by James Larkin's conglomerate Irish Transport and General Workers' Union. Riots and arrests, combined with employer intransigence and perhaps overreaching by Larkin, eventually broke the strike in early 1914.

Throughout the pre-war labour unrest, the Liberal Ministry toiled mightily to maintain a sense of purpose and to serve as guardians of public order. Nevertheless, they had occasionally been caught flat-footed and were forced to pursue ad hoc measures in attempts to curb the continuous flow of the strike waves. The issues were unusually complex, however, and even today historians struggle to ascertain causes and to separate the important concerns of both employers and employees. Eventually, the Ministry was able to deal with the unrest effectively enough by granting some redress to strikers' grievances. Lloyd George has been given substantial credit for his role in managing the unrest. Although he was not always successful, his capacity for negotiation and his sympathies with working men were instrumental in settling some strikes.[56] Had war not broken out in 1914, however, there is some question as to whether or not the ministry could have continued to keep the lid on worker dissatisfaction.

A more surprising success enjoyed by Lloyd George in a wholly different field of endeavour was the aforementioned Moroccan crisis, which had flared up during the railway strike. Even before the strike had been settled, Lloyd George had taken an active role in this, his first public intervention in a matter of foreign policy. He had been led to do so by the overtly hostile actions of the German government in sending a gunboat, the *Panther*, as a challenge to French influence in northern Africa.[57] As an exercise in imperial realpolitik, Germany's action was a reminder of her similar challenge several years earlier.[58] At first glance, the contretemps between Germany and France did not seem pertinent to British concerns. But there were at least three vital interests. First, a German presence in that part of Morocco was a potential, if unlikely, threat to British trade routes. Secondly, and more importantly, a secret treaty of 1904 had pledged British support to any future attempt by France at establishing a protectorate in Morocco. This was a belated effort to compensate France for the long-standing British dominance in Egypt. Thirdly, and most important of all, this exertion of German naval power, however small in this instance, was another reminder to Britain of Germany's determination over the previous several years to counter the might of the Royal Navy with an expanded naval programme of its own.[59]

On 21 July, Lloyd George gave a public address that was clearly intended as a warning to the German government. Speaking at the Mansion House before a blue ribbon audience of bankers and merchants of the City of London, he was loudly cheered for his remarks on the necessity of maintaining the prestige of Britain among the great powers of the world. If Britain and her vital interests were ever held to be of 'no account in the Cabinet of nations', he explicitly vowed 'peace at that price would be a humiliation intolerable for a great country like ours to endure'. National honour, he continued, 'is no party question'.[60] His speech may have been vague in not referring to specific countries,[61] but his intent was clear. A minister of the crown, known for his radical and anti-war tendencies and known, too, for his pro-German sentiments from his earlier fact-finding tours to that country, had indirectly warned off Germany from any incursions into Morocco. Although the speech was at the initiative of Lloyd George, he was speaking officially. He had conferred with Grey at the Foreign Office who had vetted his speech: Asquith and possibly Churchill had also been consulted.

Lloyd George had, however, alienated some of the more radical and pacifist members of his own party. The Liberal radical wing was already strongly opposed to what they considered an outdated notion of the balance of power – the need for nations to jockey constantly for offensive and defensive alliances to maintain their own position *vis-à-vis* potential enemies. Such a system, they believed, made for international instability that could lead to powerful blocks of states confronting one another with hostile intent. In its place, the radicals advocated more limited alliances based on compromise and conciliation, designed to reduce tensions rather than to foster them.[62] An active radical press held fast to these ideals and exerted considerable influence. Chief among these newspapers was the *Manchester Guardian*, whose editor, C.P. Scott, became the special target of Lloyd George's attempt to allay any negative impact among radicals of his Mansion House speech.[63] Urgently requested by Lloyd George on 21 July to refrain from writing about the speech, Scott was summoned to London. The following morning, Scott arrived for breakfast with Lloyd George: Churchill was also in attendance. In his diary Scott describes Lloyd George's plea for a sympathetic response to his speech; if the government and the *Guardian* were seen to be at odds, 'it would smash the party'.[64] Lloyd George then justified his speech as a way of deterring any future German mischievous actions which could escalate international tensions. His appeal seems to have had some effect. The *Guardian* leader, published a few days later, struck a balanced tone, upholding legitimate British interests while suggesting that France should not be encouraged to think that Britain would unfailingly support their imperial schemes.[65]

Lloyd George's motives for the Mansion House speech have been difficult to decipher. K.G. Robbins has observed that the speech was perhaps the most surprising development of a surprising summer and that it had never been entirely explained.[66] Grigg suggests that Lloyd George was never truly pacifistic nor a Little Englander and that his true colours as a 'patriotic radical of the Left Centre' were revealed during the crisis.[67] Dockrill believes that Lloyd George was in fact pro-German and had strenuously advocated an Anglo-German understanding; but the Germans had not responded effectively, especially in refusing to reduce their naval programme. Additionally, their forward moves in Morocco seemed designed to take advantage of Britain's domestic difficulties.[68] This explains the tone of 'intense indignation' of Lloyd George's speech. Michael Fry thinks that a political motive was at work: firmness against Germany would prevent the Conservatives from charging the Liberal government with weakness.[69] Keith Wilson has presented the subtlest analysis in suggesting that the speech was in fact a warning to both Germany and France that any resolution to the Moroccan problem must not ignore British interests.[70] Another motive, as we have noted above, was Lloyd George's eagerness to settle a domestic issue – a potentially serious work stoppage – by raising the spectre of war and the importance that unimpeded rail traffic would play in the crucial task of supplying coal to the Royal Navy.[71]

If Lloyd George's motives seem murky, so are the consequences that historians have drawn from his role during the Agadir crisis. Paul Kennedy believes that Lloyd George's actions over Agadir shifted the power balance in the Cabinet toward a pro-French policy, thus making serious accommodation thereafter between German and Britain more difficult.[72] Rowland is more accusatory, terming the Mansion House speech as not only 'reckless', but that it also 'wreaked … terrible damage' upon Anglo-German relations.[73] Searle, however, credits the speech as persuading the Germans to back down from their Moroccan claims thus bringing resolution to an indecisive Cabinet.[74] Gilbert thinks that Agadir was a turning point in Lloyd George's career by introducing him to military thinking and defence policy – issues which, perhaps surprisingly, he found interesting.[75]

There is merit to most of these suggestions. It is certainly true that Lloyd George had for several years viewed Germany as a model for Britain in utilizing state intervention to improve internal transportation through rationalized rail lines when he was President of the Board of Trade. After he became Chancellor of the Exchequer in Asquith's government in April 1908, Germany became a guide to his own efforts in creating social programmes such as unemployment and health insurance. Aside from his relations with Germany, which served as an introduction to his interest in foreign affairs, was another, more important reason that can help explain his diplomatic initiatives in 1911: he always had a strong propensity to expand his role beyond his official position. This we saw, for example, during his actions in settling strikes when President of the Board of Trade. We also saw this tendency at work during the summer of 1908 when he fancied himself as a diplomat. His conversation with Metternich in July 1908 was followed by a fact-finding tour in Germany the following month when he was quoted twice (once in the Viennese *Neue Freie Presse* and once in the *Berliner Tageblatt*) as advocating Anglo-German discussions on naval armaments. This unauthorized intervention in foreign policy was not well received at the Foreign Office.[76] Lloyd George's tendency to use the foreign press to advance his own ideas on diplomatic policy occurred again in December 1910, when several French newspapers published interviews on his opinions about Franco-German relations. This initiative also brought a rebuke.[77] An additional example of Lloyd George's growing interest in foreign policy occurred in early 1911, when he and others in the Cabinet began pressing Grey for an accommodation with Germany. They persuaded the Cabinet to establish a sub-committee on foreign affairs to examine this possibility and to keep themselves informed about foreign policy. As Lloyd George explained it to Arthur Murray, Grey's Parliamentary Private Secretary, as Chancellor of the Exchequer he was called upon to provide for naval estimates, yet he 'was kept in the dark' about the 'essential features of our Foreign policy'. Indeed, he 'knew nothing' of 'what was going on'.[78]

Well before the Moroccan crisis, then, Lloyd George was insinuating himself unofficially into matters of foreign policy. These efforts had met with indifferent results. But with his Mansion House speech, he had rapidly gained a reputation for steadiness and resolution, suffused with an anti-German tinge. The Foreign Office finally had something to praise in Lloyd George's behaviour. Sir Arthur Nicolson pronounced himself 'pleasantly surprised' when he reported with approval to Sir Charles Hardinge that Lloyd George had 'grasped the situation thoroughly'.[79] The speech won the approval and respect of others in high places. William Tyrrell, Grey's private secretary, wrote not long after the speech to Cecil Spring Rice: 'Don't ever forget to teach your children to keep alive the memory of Lloyd George who by his timely speech has saved the peace of Europe and our good name.'[80]

Lloyd George's new 'realist' diplomatic posture had an immediate consequence: it gained him an entrée into a round of repercussive discussions in the months that followed the crisis. The most important of these was a special all day meeting on 23 August 1911 of the Committee on Imperial Defence to review British strategy. Although the importance of the CID itself is a matter of historical dispute, the August 1911 meeting of the CID has a strong claim to our attention.[81] First of note was that only a minority of Cabinet members were summoned: Asquith himself, Grey, Haldane, McKenna, Churchill and Lloyd George. Known pacifists and radicals such as Morley, Loreburn, Harcourt and Crewe were excluded. Also in attendance were the First Sea Lord, Sir Arthur Wilson; Brigadier Henry Wilson, the Director of Military Operations; and some other officers. The meeting revealed not only a dangerous lack of coordination between the navy and the army, but also that the Royal Navy was unprepared for any potential cross-Channel intervention in the event of war.

In contrast to his Royal Navy namesake, Brigadier Henry Wilson proved to be knowledgeable and articulate about the prospects of a continental war and the role that British forces should play. Fluent in French and thoroughly familiar with the topography of France, Wilson insisted that the balance could be tipped in France's favour by six British divisions operating with the French army if German troops should invade.[82] Even before Morocco, Wilson had been engaged in conversations with French military authorities regarding the mobilization and transport of a British expeditionary force to France. Once the *Panther* appeared off the Moroccan coast, the conversations had an added urgency and by late July there was a *de facto* military convention between France and Britain who coordinated their forces in expectation of any German attack. Thus the August 1911 CID meeting placed 'an imprimatur upon continental involvement' on the side of France in the event of a German invasion.[83]

This conference was also important for the first meeting between Lloyd George and Wilson. The general was impressed by the keen interest taken by Lloyd George in military matters: he recorded in his diary that there had been 'much questioning' of his proposals at the meeting, especially from Lloyd George.[84] Indeed, immediately after the meeting Lloyd George was spurred to quick action in familiarizing himself with relevant diplomatic correspondence. On 25 August, he wrote to Churchill that the Foreign Office papers were 'full of menace'.[85] He feared that the 'thunderclouds' were 'gathering'. Moreover, he was 'not at all satisfied' that Britain was prepared for every eventuality. 'I am inclined to think', he confided to Churchill, 'the chances of war are multiplying'. Then Lloyd George launched into a full-scale tactical and operational mode, suggesting in the event of war the possibility of sending 150,000 British troops to support the Belgian army against the Germans. The Anglo-Belgian forces could then 'pivot' on the 'great fort' at Antwerp and, supported by British 'command of the sea', thus become 'impregnable'.

That Lloyd George had become bellicose towards Germany was confirmed by several sources. A few weeks after the August 1911 CID meeting, Wilson summed up in his diary a long talk with Lloyd George confirming a shift in the latter's thinking about military and foreign affairs. Wilson had impressed upon Lloyd George the 'absolute necessity' for mobilizing the same day as the French in the event of German aggression. Lloyd George seemed to agree and, as Wilson recorded it, Lloyd George was 'quite in favour of a war now'.[86] This is confirmed by Nicolson's letter to Hardinge dated 14 September 1911. He wrote that Lloyd George (along with Haldane and Churchill) were 'perfectly steady – I might almost say eager – to face all possible eventualities, and most careful preparations have been made to meet any contingencies that may arise. These three have thoroughly grasped he point that it is not merely Morocco which is at stake'. He added, in confidence, that 'preparations for landing four or six divisions on the Continent have been worked out to the minutest detail'.[87] At least one important member of the Conservative leadership was more than surprised at Lloyd George's new views on Germany. Austen Chamberlain wrote that Balfour had been 'rather shocked' by a conversation with Lloyd George in which the later was 'very bellicose' about Germany.[88] In a more informal setting, Charles Masterman and his wife Lucy, while visiting Lloyd George at Criccieth that summer, found him perusing a map of the Franco-German frontier. For the diversion of his guests, he suggested various tactical deployments in the event of war with Germany, pointing out likely lines of German advance. In addition, as Lucy remembered it: 'We spent an amazing amount of time planning wars, considering combinations, alliances and contingencies.'[89]

Lloyd George's new warlike attitude seems startling, almost shocking. What had become of his radical Liberal views and his irenic ideals? Michael Fry suggests that these discussions of diplomatic options and military stratagems at the highest level contributed to what Fry has called his 'evolvement' as a man and as a politician over the years.[90] Indeed, as we have begun to notice, especially since the beginning of his tenure as a Cabinet minister, there was in Lloyd George a natural progression of interests and challenges. Moving from Wales to London, from radical to realist, from provincial politician to Cabinet member, he shifted from ideological positions to more empirical approaches in domestic issues. It must be remembered that his position during the Boer War, for example, seemed to alter from his initial outrage at the British bullying of a smaller power to a condemnation of a war badly fought and incompetently managed by Joseph Chamberlain and the Conservative government. This was no less true in foreign affairs, where his thinking by 1911 can best be described as a synthesis between his earlier ideals and his growing acceptance of British national interests abroad. This was clearly enunciated in his famous Mansion House speech where he signalled to Germany that their territorial claims could be legitimated, but not at the expense of either international peace or of Britain's own foreign policy aims. By issuing a diplomatic warning, he believed that a peaceful outcome would thus be more likely guaranteed than any threat of retaliation.[91] The Moroccan crisis was in fact settled without recourse to arms. British firmness apparently paid off. In early November 1911, France and Germany signed an accord which gave France a protectorate in Morocco while Germany received compensations in the French Congo. Although some uneasiness remained among the parties concerned, relations between Britain and Germany took a favourable turn over the next two years.[92]

8

SCANDAL AND FAILURE

Once the diplomatic skies had cleared after the Moroccan crisis, Lloyd George's attention was diverted to matters closer to home. Fresh from his triumphs on financial and social reform and his successful venture into foreign affairs, Lloyd George had high hopes for new victories. The time seemed ripe to implement his long-held belief that land reform was crucial to right the wrongs imposed by the traditional landlord-tenant relationship in the country. The Irish Question, too, was attracting his attention.[1] And he expected to play a continuing role in arbitrating labour disputes. However, the year 1912 found Lloyd George the target of a scandal on such a scale that his survival as a minister of the crown lay in the balance. Thereafter a series of events diminished further his political career and threatened his personal reputation in the ensuing two years.[2]

The initial misstep was Lloyd George's participation in a stock scheme that promised large returns for little effort − a temptation for quick riches that was particularly attractive to Lloyd George, as we have already observed, during his earlier involvement in the Patagonian gold-mining adventure. The Marconi scandal, however, had a greater impact, involving not only the Chancellor of the Exchequer, but other high-ranking Liberals as well, including the Attorney General, the Postmaster-General and the Liberal Party whip.[3] The affair began in 1910 when Godfrey Isaacs was appointed Director General of the Marconi Wireless Telegraph Company in England. Developing an interest in international finance, he had met the great Italian inventor Marconi through an acquaintance with Marconi's brother-in-law. Suitably impressed, Marconi himself had offered the position of Director General to his young protégé. Quickly realizing the potential of wireless telegraphy, Isaacs submitted to the Colonial Office a plan to establish throughout the empire an 18 station telegraphic system. Referred to a House of Commons committee, the plan was then reviewed by a second committee under the chairmanship of Herbert Samuel, the Postmaster General. Negotiations on a contract between the committee and the Company were slow but ultimately successful in establishing an initial chain of six stations. By the spring of 1912, public shares were offered in the Company.

At approximately the same time, Isaacs, also a director of the American branch of the Marconi Company, was in the United States giving evidence in an infringement suit against the failing United Wireless company. The entrepreneurial Isaacs soon discovered that if sufficient capital were raised, United Wireless could be purchased, thus adding to the growing international Marconi business. New stock options were therefore offered for this specific purpose: Isaacs himself agreed to place half a million shares with American and British brokers. The Marconi Company – in its American and English branches – now had a monopoly on trans-Atlantic wireless telegraphy. Immediately upon his return to England, Isaacs arranged a lunch at the Savoy with his two brothers, Harry and Rufus. Offered shares by Godfrey, both brothers bought some, Rufus hesitating for several days to insure that there was no conflict of interest in his official position as Attorney General.[4] Shortly afterward, Rufus offered 1,000 shares each to Lloyd George and Alexander Murray, Chief Whip of the Liberal Party.[5] Both men accepted. In addition, Murray purchased additional stock for the Liberal Party, presumably for his use in his second official position as Patronage Secretary of the Party.

To this point in the affair, little complaint can be made about the advisability of these officers of state capitalizing on private information. In those days, informal contacts between brokers and buyers were not uncommon. Meanwhile, however, in the spring of 1912 another development proceeding parallel to the purchase of Marconi stock had begun to capture public attention. Questions were raised in the House of Commons by the Conservative opposition about the contract talks between Marconi and the government for the proposed wireless stations to be constructed throughout the British Empire. The lack of forthcoming information encouraged speculation that the government had something to hide. A few of the more disreputable members of the press added fuel to the fire by suggesting that there was a Jewish conspiracy concocted by Samuel and the Isaacs brothers to line their own pockets at the expense of the nation.[6]

It is true that Postmaster-General Samuel had been somewhat remiss in not keeping the House informed about the progress of the talks. To counter the rumours, therefore, he explained the substance of the negotiations before the House on 7 August 1912, just prior to the parliamentary recess. But the delay in offering information to the House so late in the session, thus precluding any possibility of discussing the contract, raised further suspicions. During the late summer, questions continued. In October, after the recess, the government was forced into appointing a select committee on the Marconi contract. A debate in the House of Commons on 11 October ranged widely over the particulars of Samuel's handling of the contract. Such topics as the government's failure to investigate other wireless companies than Marconi's and the absence of any committee to advise on technical aspects of various wireless systems fully engaged both sides of the House.

Throughout the debate Lloyd George had remained silent. But when George Lansbury, Labour MP for Bow and Bromley, rose to introduce a related topic – rumours of possible speculation and corruption in Marconi stock by persons unknown – Lloyd George sprang from his seat. In a brief and heated exchange, Lloyd George angrily denied any such activity on his part.[7] Lansbury seemed perplexed by this outburst, as was the House generally. Within a few moments, denials by Rufus

Isaacs that he, too, had speculated in the British Marconi Company added to the tone of Lloyd George's remarks and in so doing, changed the direction of the Marconi affair. Their defensiveness merely reinforced suspicions that financial speculation among some Liberal ministers had taken place. Investigative reporters were soon at work, exploring a possible financial malfeasance at the heart of the Liberal government.[8] Chief among these was the Tory Leopold Maxse, proprietor of the *National Review*, who wielded considerable influence as we have seen in his campaign against Arthur Balfour's leadership of the Conservative Party. Maxse articulated a growing public question: did Lloyd George and Isaacs have something to hide, as their parliamentary performance on 11 October so strongly suggested? And were there others who had taken advantage of insider information?[9] Indeed, as we now know, there was some point to Maxse's charge. Lloyd George had not passively kept the thousand shares given to him by Rufus Isaacs. He had speculated, selling high and buying low in search of a quick return with little risk – a classic 'flutter'. It at last became clear even to Lloyd George and his implicated colleagues that it would be wise to admit their participation in the stock scheme sooner rather than later.

Before the still-sitting select committee, therefore, Rufus Isaacs testified in late March 1913. Cross-examined for two and a half days, he revealed that he and the two other ministers had bought shares on favourable terms, not in the English Marconi Company, but rather in the American Marconi Company at a time when such shares were not yet traded publicly. This belated admission cast a wholly different light upon his October 1912 statement before the House in which he had denied any transaction with 'that' (unnamed) company, a misleading statement because it suggested Isaacs was referring to the English branch of the Marconi Company. Lloyd George's testimony followed. He portrayed himself as a poor man with few resources who had hoped to build some equity capital for his old age. He had not intended to deceive. This seems to have satisfied his detractors. But in early June, the committee learned for the first time that the Master of Elibank was additionally involved in the Marconi stock scheme. To make matters worse, Elibank had resigned his position as Liberal Party whip several months before the news broke and had left England for South America, where he was engaged in business interests for Lord Cowdray, now his employer.[10]

Each phase of the scandal had revealed additional prevarications and obfuscations on the part of the ministers involved. Even Liberal Party members and the Liberal press were increasingly disturbed by the incriminating disclosures.[11] Although leader columns of the *Manchester Guardian* publicly supported Lloyd George, C.P. Scott's private communications told a different story: he urged Lloyd George to express 'complete frankness and an unreserved expression of regret' for his actions.[12] An opportunity for candour and an apology occurred shortly after the select committee's report on 13 June 1913. Stacked with a Liberal majority, the committee had unsurprisingly let the actions of the errant ministers off lightly. But danger yet lay in the upcoming parliamentary debate on the report, scheduled for several days later in the House of Commons. Conservatives were bound to exploit the issue. The Cabinet therefore prepared carefully to orchestrate the forthcoming debate.[13]

Asquith sent a draft proposal to Lloyd George (after it had been vetted by Grey) with suggested talking points. Lloyd George and Isaacs then coordinated their remarks by preparing their speeches together.[14] Following this, Asquith held a conversation with both Lloyd George and Isaacs. A day later, Lloyd George and Isaacs rehearsed their final version before the Cabinet.[15]

As expected, the parliamentary debate of 18 and 19 June was prefaced by a Conservative resolution of censure. Both Isaacs and Lloyd George admitted some culpability, the latter characterizing his own actions as thoughtless, careless and mistaken. Matters might still have gone badly against the government had not Asquith staunchly supported his colleagues. He reviewed their case before the House and found no evidence of serious charges. He also appealed to the House not to censure the ministers; for if they did so, their resignation would become mandatory and their political careers would likely be at an end. In addition, he made a startling admission – that he had known for a year about the stock purchases under investigation and had even been informed by Elibank of his questionable use of party funds. In so doing, Asquith made the debate effectively a matter of confidence. Thus the Conservative resolution was defeated by 346 to 268, a comfortable enough margin.

The favourable House of Commons vote enabled Lloyd George to go on the attack against the Conservatives. At a speech before the National Liberal Club, he claimed that he had done nothing to dishonour his position as a member of government. Those who had tried to make something of his investments in Marconi shares, he assured his cheering audience, had engaged in an 'unctuous and fatuous man-hunt'.[16] He blamed the Conservatives. They had, after all, lost three consecutive elections – a difficult blow to those who thought themselves 'the governing classes'. They were humbugs, 'steeped in smugness and self righteousness'. Their actions during the Marconi investigation, he claimed, were merely a further example of wealth and privilege still unjustly dominant in politics. Lloyd George's exuberant counter-attacks signalled the end of the immediate crisis.

Lloyd George had escaped possibly the greatest threat to his ministerial career. It seems that he never fully understood the seriousness of his actions. Indeed, he had accepted the proffered shares in an offhanded manner, in the way that he usually managed his personal finances. The fact that he had not made a profit from the questionable purchases meant to him that no harm had been done. The historian Frances Donaldson has generally agreed with Lloyd George's sophistry. She wrote that the scandal was 'an isolated incident' without 'much historical significance' and that there was a 'benighted innocence' among the participants in the scandal.[17] But most historians have taken a different view. Grigg indicated some sympathy for Lloyd George when he attributed his action to a perennial sense of insecurity about financial matters. But for Grigg, this was no excuse. It was not seemly for a Chancellor of the Exchequer 'to gamble in shares'. Not only had Lloyd George acted 'unwisely', he had committed an impropriety 'only a little short of corruption'.[18] Cannadine thinks it was 'a definite abuse of public position'.[19] Gilbert believes that Lloyd George had genuinely been 'in great danger' because he was already regarded by many as 'a charlatan genius', too free with the truth to be trusted.[20] Moreover, his outsider status at Westminster as a Welshman, a putative radical and one born below the privileged elite made him a special target. As Searle observes, what drove the 'Marconi muckrakers' forward was their anger at 'ill-bred Radicals' attempting to enrich themselves at public expense.[21] There is little doubt that Lloyd George ought to have exercised more than the usual care in any matter concerned with private moneys and public finance, given his office as Chancellor of the Exchequer. This was certainly the point behind Packer's judgement that Marconi had shown Lloyd George to have little regard for caution or the 'rules of conventional political morality'.[22] A family member must have the last word. William George was always loyal to his brother, yet even he could not refrain from a muted criticism. In spite of the official House of Commons exoneration, William wrote, Lloyd George should never have allowed himself 'to become involved in such a charge at all'.[23]

The Marconi scandal was at the very least a failure of judgement by a nationally known politician who should have known better. Potentially a greater blow to Lloyd George's reputation was a programme he was soon to launch relating to one of his highest priorities – reform of the land. It is easy to understand why the land question would be important to him. As we know, the impact of his experiences as a boy and a young man in a Welsh village dominated by elite landed proprietors left him with a deeply-rooted animus against privilege. His antipathy to landed property was reinforced by his early years as a solicitor when he gained a first-hand knowledge of the workings of the land laws. Rating appeals, rent collecting and conveyancing were at the heart of his work. The lessons he drew were that landed proprietors earned but did not work; they profited while others paid taxes; and they exploited those beneath them. Driven by this 'single-minded antagonism',[24] Lloyd George's actions in tackling the land question can be seen as motivated not only by a sympathy for the disadvantaged rural population: a personal vendetta may also have been at work.

Of course, the land scheme was not merely Lloyd George's own. A solid core of radical Liberals believed that privileged landlordism was an anachronistic semi-feudal practice which could no longer be justified in a modern world. Radicals emphasized the obligations, rather than rights of property. Landed property, they believed, must play a more responsible role in promoting the overall good of the community. This idea was strengthened by the belief that landlords, simply by virtue of the fact that they held land, were receiving unearned rewards. As land increased in value over time, so did their income. To induce landlords to pay their fair share of taxes, the idea of taxing site values took hold. Site values would be set at the fair market price at the time of valuation. A separate valuation of all buildings and improvements upon that land would also be fixed. Thus it would be possible to establish two different tax schedules – one that would apply to the landlord and his holding and another for his tenants.[25] This would apply not only to the traditional aristocratic grandees, but also to landlords of every stripe, such as commercial holders of land in urban areas.

Lloyd George's views were in accord with these radical beliefs. But he understood that such ancient privileges could be attacked only obliquely. Thus his land campaign began stealthily. Tucked away in his famous People's Budget of 1909 were several small land value duties, including a 20 per cent tax on the future unearned increment in site values, and a half penny tax in the pound on the site value of undeveloped land.[26] Their purpose was not to enhance revenue, but rather to establish the principle (however surreptitiously) of land evaluation as a necessary precursor to the taxing of it.[27] Lloyd George was clearly acting upon precedent within a Liberal frame of reference. Since Gladstone's time, Liberals had been advocating changes in the system of rural landholding in order to reduce the power and influence of Tory magnates in the countryside.[28] Such a programme could also lead to a political advantage. If Liberals were to capture and maintain the traditional deferential voters in the countryside – farmers and agricultural labourers – Liberal electoral fortunes could soar. Indeed, during the run up to the general election of 1906, rural radicalism among Liberals was much in evidence. The landowner as social parasite preying upon the common people was a common refrain in Liberal electoral appeals.[29]

Indeed, even prior to Lloyd George's land scheme, the Liberals had some success. Once in office, the Campbell-Bannerman ministry early on had passed a Land Tenure Act which established comprehensive schemes for compensating tenant farmers' improvements made during their tenancies. A Smallholdings Act followed, designed to aid agricultural labourers establish themselves as landowners.[30] In 1907 and 1908, the House of Commons passed two Scots Land Valuation bills which proposed de-rating buildings and using land sites alone as a basis for taxation: they were, however, struck down in the Lords. Liberals were also involved in urban land reform as the radical wing of the party in London made much of the fact that titled owners held some of the most valuable town and city land.[31] Under Asquith there was increasing interest in using the land, based upon site values, as the basis for taxation particularly within urban areas. But the complexity of the issue and the ministry's substantial reform initiatives elsewhere postponed any far-reaching land reform. It was not until Lloyd George's inclusion of land value duties in the People's Budget that the logjam was broken.

Such an intervention by the state into the fortunes of the great landowners could raise a firestorm. By including the land value duties within a finance bill, therefore, Lloyd George hoped to avoid a veto from the Lords on such a touchy subject. In the event, however, as we have seen, the People's Budget was contentious and provoked considerable opposition from the Lords. But with the ultimate passage of the Budget, site value rating gained legitimacy. In 1910, Commissioners of the Inland Revenue were charged with undertaking a systematic valuation of all land within the kingdom, showing both total value (which would include improvements) and site value (minus improvements). Site values, thus officially and accurately identified, could form the basis for any future taxation. In that same year, a Land Value Office was established within the Inland Revenue Department.

Lloyd George's political distractions over the next few years, however, precluded any further action on the land question. By 1912, he gave signs of renewed attention to the land. In a newspaper interview in May of that year, he advocated a minimum wage of £1 a week for agricultural labourers.[32] Later that same month, he discussed at some length a land campaign with one of his most constant confidantes, George

Riddell.[33] He was determined to 'break down the remnants of the feudal system'. He believed that the land and the state of agricultural labourers were 'at the root of the whole social evil'. The land campaign was of such importance that he was considering resigning his office to carry it out. When Riddell expostulated, Lloyd George countered that radicalism needed 'a great stimulus': it had fallen 'into the abyss of respectability and conventionality'. Writing to William, he hinted that the land campaign might also reap electoral benefits: 'We want to come back on a great land resolution next time.'[34]

In that busy month of May 1912, Lloyd George created a Land Enquiry Committee as an advisory group to help him plan and develop strategy for the land campaign. They were additionally charged with collecting information from both urban and rural sources. The chair of the Committee was A.H.D. Acland, a former Liberal MP who had served as Vice-President of the Council during the last Gladstone government. He had been a friend and supporter of Lloyd George since the 1890s. The staff for the land inquiry eventually included some 70 employees.[35] This was a wholly private group, with no official connection either to the ministry or to the Liberal Party. Its allegiance was to Lloyd George only. It was also self-funding: several members of the committee were wealthy philanthropic Liberals. The incestuous nature of the Committee was less important to Lloyd George than its loyalty and its ability to pay for itself. Its charge, given directly by Lloyd George, was to enquire further into the land question and, most importantly, to recommend policies. This body, as a creature of the Chancellor, was to operate independently of the official Inland Revenue Department, already at work on similar tasks.

To downplay the partisan nature of the committee, Lloyd George recruited Seebohm Rowntree, whose study of poverty in York, published in 1901, had made his reputation as a respected social investigator. But even Rowntree's participation could not mask the political dimensions of the committee's work.[36] Because of its examination into such sensitive matters as land use, tenure and game, Tory landlords in the countryside could easily become the targets of Lloyd George's legislative recommendations. That Conservatives were up in arms against the committee early on was evident to Baron de Forest, another member of the committee. As he put it to Lloyd George, 'the Tories will endeavour and will possibly succeed in arousing a good deal of popular prejudices against the secrecy of our methods. There is already a loud cry against 'backstair enquiry'.[37]

There is little doubt that Lloyd George regarded the committee as more than a neutral collector of social and economic facts. After Asquith had given him permission to move forward to gather information, he wrote to his brother that the purpose of the land campaign was 'to rouse the public conscience on the evils of the land system'.[38] To J. St G. Heath, secretary of the committee, Lloyd George confided that one of his primary objectives was to establish accurately the number of landowners in Britain. 'On this point', he wrote, 'I am anxious to obtain statistics showing what a considerable portion of the land of this country belongs to a small number of owners'.[39] The following month, Lloyd George restated to George Cadbury the aims of the land campaign in general and specifically the role of the

Committee. The campaign, he wrote, would be 'a real uplift in the conditions of life not only of hundreds of thousands of agricultural labourers but of the working people in the towns as well'. But, he added, another benefit of the campaign was that 'in attacking the land we are attacking the citadel of the privileged aristocracy'.[40]

The political dimension of the land campaign was also evident in the means by which it collected evidence. To ascertain local conditions, the Committee used questionnaires. These were distributed by Liberal MPs and land agents, who often selected local Liberals to fill them out. It was not surprising that Conservatives denounced the findings as partial and unrepresentative of actual conditions.[41] The separate urban land committee likewise depended for information upon local residents, the majority of whom were committed Liberals. But the complexities of urban landholding mandated a more expert body of informants and the responses from local surveyors, architects or solicitors – not all of whom were Liberals – moderated the partisan aspect of the urban report to some extent.[42]

As the Land Enquiry Committee began its work, Lloyd George took additional steps to insure the success of his land campaign. In October 1912, during a contentious debate in the House of Commons, he defended the Land Enquiry Committee.[43] Writing home to Margaret the following day, he exulted over the 'glorious row' in the House. The introduction of the land question in the House and the response to it from the opposition, he predicted, was only a prelude 'of the savage passions' that would be raised once the campaign itself was underway.[44] Lloyd George, however, was also encountering some resistance among his Cabinet colleagues and others in   · his own party. He had to convince them of both the political advantages and of the social utility of the land campaign. This had to be carefully done. Over time, he contacted members of the government singly and in small colloquies but exercised caution in presenting his ideas before the Cabinet as a whole.[45] He also engaged other allies, seeking their advice.[46] By the summer of 1913, there was sufficient support for the land campaign that Asquith placed it on the agenda for the first Cabinet meeting of the autumn parliamentary session (14 October 1913).[47]

In the meantime, Lloyd George busily continued to woo his colleagues. During the summer recess, he co-opted McKenna, the most likely Cabinet critic of the land scheme, by engaging his assistance in writing a Cabinet memo on the subject: Grey, Haldane and himself were the other members of the group.[48] In September, Lloyd George secured Asquith's approval of the land campaign. By then, the Land Enquiry Committee was nearly ready to report its rural findings – not, however, without some prompting on the part of Lloyd George. In August 1913, he had written to Seebohm Rowntree suggesting that he select 'a few parishes where the wages of the Agricultural Labourer are low and his housing bad, but where the landlord lives in a fine house and keeps up a great style'. He had a further idea for finding such places – by looking at some choice samples of great houses portrayed in the pages of *Country Life* and investigating their neighbourhoods. He needed this information, he wrote, for speeches he was soon to make.[49] Lloyd George was also busily courting the newspaper press. To C.P. Scott, he wrote that it was 'of first class importance' that the *Manchester Guardian* endorse the land campaign because of its influence with the intellectuals of the Liberal Party.[50]

The rural report, released on 11 October 1913, pleased Lloyd George. Its most important findings were the indisputable facts of low wages and the appalling state of housing conditions among agricultural labourers. With the report now in hand, Lloyd George officially opened the land campaign with two major speeches in Bedford on 11 October 1913 – three days before the first Cabinet meeting of the new session of Parliament. This could hardly have been a coincidence, and indeed there is some evidence to suggest that he had scheduled the Bedford meeting in order to pressure any waverers in the Cabinet to support his land reform campaign.[51] His performance at Bedford was a considerable feat of persuasion and justification.[52] In his first speech of two hours and 20 minutes before a crowd of 2,500 (later that evening he spoke to 4,000 more), Lloyd George emphasized the importance of the land to everyone in the kingdom. From the beginning of life to its end, the land was 'woven into its texture … The cradle is rocked on the land, and the grave is sunk in the land'. In between life and death, the land 'enters into everything … the food the people eat, the water they drink, the houses they dwell in, the industries upon which their livelihood depends …'. Yet most of the land in the kingdom was in the hands of a few. These landowners exercised, he claimed, 'gigantic powers … terrible powers' in creating 'the greatest of monopolies' in the country. Continuing his attack upon 'landlordism', Lloyd George declared that: 'A landowner can devastate the countryside, he can sweep every cottage away and convert it into a wilderness.' With their powers, landowners can 'destroy the cottages, drive the peasantry away to exile, convert the land into a desert'. Citing the Highland clearances during the nineteenth century as an example, he noted that in the north of Scotland were 'the remains of the old crofts, but the crofters are not there. The land is trodden by deer'. The system of landlordism, in administering 'this vital commodity' with 'almost unfettered control', had been 'a ghastly failure': it had produced under-cultivated farms, low wages, bad houses and had driven workmen abroad to Canada and elsewhere. Low wages for farm labour were, Lloyd George declared, especially disgraceful. Agricultural labourers, as skilled as any industrial employee, often worked longer hours than others and yet were paid lower wages. If wages were bad, their housing was 'atrocious – inadequate, insufficient, insanitary [sic], rotten'. Added to this was substantial overcrowding. The existing land system was responsible for all these conditions. Land ownership should be, he continued, 'not merely ownership. It is stewardship'. In contrast to unacceptable conditions in rural villages were the magnificent parks and houses of the landowners nearby. On those privileged estates, Lloyd George pointed out, land that might be given to cultivation was often used for sport. This was harmful to farmers, especially tenant farmers, who complained about crop damage by game raised for hunting. What had been the response? In recent decades, landlords had removed even more land from cultivation and tripled the number of gamekeepers. Farmers were also burdened by the workings of the tenurial system, which denied compensation for any improvements they made on the land. This had the effect, as Lloyd George declared, of discouraging entrepreneurial farming practices.

In his concluding remarks and in his evening speech, Lloyd George suggested remedies for the existing landlord system – a system fundamentally flawed by abuses of power. He admitted that governments have been loath to act: 'we have handled the land question as if we were handling a hedgehog. We were afraid of gripping it'. But now, he declared, it was time 'that we should handle it firmly and deal with it boldly, thoroughly'. The state had to intervene as a steward of the land, a role that landlords had neglected. Lloyd George had not at this point, however, devised a specific programmatic approach to the land and could only speak in general terms – of the need to secure a living wage for agricultural labourers, better housing and enough land for possible gardens and allotments. For farmers, he advocated protection against the appropriation of the increased value of the land due to the work of improvement by tenants themselves. The state, too, should have greater powers for the acquisition of land for the people. Lloyd George also promised more information later on urban land, the report on which had not yet been completed by the Land Inquiry Committee.

Historians have tended to dismiss the impact of the Bedford speech.[53] Lloyd George himself believed, however, that the speech was effective as a first step toward the ultimate goal of land reform.[54] Riddell agreed, suggesting that the real importance of the speech was to give a quiet warning to the public at large that the government intended to abolish 'the unfettered ownership of land'.[55] Whether or not the Cabinet grasped this radical point fully is unclear. There was certainly no indication of Cabinet division in its three lengthy meetings from 14 to 16 October. Indeed, Hobhouse recorded in his diary that the meetings were 'friendly, harmonious, unanimous'. Asquith pronounced them 'the most business-like proceedings he had ever seen at Cabinet'. At the end, Lloyd George's proposals 'were all agreed upon'.[56] Lloyd George was well satisfied. At the conclusion of Cabinet discussions, he wrote to William: 'Cabinet over. My plans adopted. Hurrah.'[57] Thereafter, the Cabinet rarely discussed the rural land campaign.

Now that land reform became an official policy of the government, Lloyd George once again went before the county, this time in Swindon, to unveil specific operational proposals.[58] A new Ministry of Lands would be created, replacing the Board of Agriculture. Duties of the ministry would include managing the machinery of land valuation established under the People's Budget of 1909. Lloyd George reported that the work of valuation was well along. Once complete, the nation would have 'a sort of Domesday book – a full record of its most valuable asset'. The new ministry would also have control and supervision of the nation's land generally and would oversee disputes between landlord and tenant. Powers of reclamation and the development of uncultivated land also fell under the ministry. Another new body, the Commissioners of the Land, would not only manage the revision of eviction notices, but also award compensatory damages in cases of capricious evictions of farmers from their tenancy. Commissioners could additionally regulate compensations for improvements made by tenants in the event of the sale of such land. It could also order rebates of rent, enabling farmers to pay labourers higher wages. Moreover, the Commissioners could fix the price of land when acquired for any public purpose. The overall idea, as Lloyd George summed it up, was 'to assume a complete control of the monopoly in land in this country'.[59]

For Lloyd George and the Liberal Party, a successful land campaign would not only be a capstone to the Liberal reforms initiated since 1906. It might also, as we have noted, reap political rewards by capturing Tory voters in the counties. There was potentially another political advantage: land reform could cut the ground beneath a burgeoning Labour Party. That Labour was making inroads among agricultural labourers was well born out by events in Norfolk in 1910–11, where a farm labourers' strike at St Faiths had caught the attention of the Norwich Trades Council, dominated by the Independent Labour Party. Through supportive demonstrations and donations, the Trades Council won the allegiance of the Eastern Counties Agricultural Labourers' and Small Holders' Union, which had originally been established under Liberal auspices. By the spring of 1911, the Union had fallen away from Liberalism and came under the influence of the ILP.[60] The Lib-Lab Pact – so useful to both the Liberal and Labour parties since the election of 1906 – was indeed showing signs of wear.[61]

In essence, Labour agreed substantially with Lloyd George's land reform and was loath to oppose him outright. On the other hand, they hoped to draw attention to themselves as an independent agent with a tradition of agrarian radicalism. A leader in the *Glasgow Forward* (the voice of the local ILP and an advocate for land reform) put the dilemma concisely. 'It is clear that the great Liberal Showman will fight the next election on Land Reform … Mr Lloyd George has chosen his ground well.' But, the *Forward* continued, a heavy duty now rests upon the Labour Party to make its own voice heard against 'landlordism'.[62] In response, the Labour leadership established a land inquiry in August 1912, a few months after Lloyd George had created his own like-minded Committee. Labour's report, published in January 1914, revealed a 'remarkable congruity'[63] with Lloyd George's similar document. The only major difference between the two reports, though an important one, was Labour's emphasis upon the ultimate public ownership of land.

Viewing the rural land campaign up to 1914, a case can be made that it was a striking example of Lloyd George's coherent reformist vision. Indeed, Lloyd George's leadership of the land campaign has since drawn praise from historians. Emy was impressed by both the scale of the reform and Lloyd George's continuing determination to increase government expenditures for the collective good.[64] Offer writes that the campaign 'was masterly in conception, simple in structure and incisive in effect'.[65] Pugh, while admitting that if there were a slightly chaotic impression in the planning of the land campaign as it moved forward, reminds us that this was not uncommon when Lloyd George manoeuvred for political advantage.[66] It seems fair to conclude that Lloyd George had demonstrated his usual energy, capacity for organizing and political skills in devising the land campaign.

These encomiums were more deservedly true, however, of the rural than of the urban campaign, which followed an uneven course. Although there were some tentative plans to devise a programme of urban leasehold reform and to empower local authorities to provide adequate housing in urban areas, the primary effort remained focused on rural issues. The urban report by the Land Enquiry Committee was delayed several months after the rural report was published, and its recommendations were never fully presented to the Cabinet.[67] Town meetings designed to generate support for urban land reform were poorly organized and sporadic at best: thus its intended audience of urban middle-class leaseholders was never drawn fully into the campaign. Urban land reform therefore drifted, largely unattended, into the early months of 1914. By the summer of that year, international tensions were engaging the ministry to the exclusion of domestic programmes, including the more promising rural land campaign. In short, all the energy and expense of the land campaign, in spite of Lloyd George's careful planning, came to naught, overcome at last by events beyond even his energetic efforts.

In an entirely different political arena during the early years of the twentieth century, Lloyd George also played an important role, one that was far more ambiguous than his forthright campaign for land reform. The issue of women's suffrage emerged by 1910 as an important political topic. Women had long been active in the public sphere as philanthropists, teachers and workers outside the home. Gradually women gained significant legal rights, such as the 1857 Divorce Act and the Married Women's Property Acts of 1870 and 1882. Gradually, too, women became increasingly involved in political affairs, beginning with women's auxiliaries to both Conservative and Liberal parties. Women also began to make their way – having won the vote at the local level – onto local school boards and the boards of poor law guardians. It was only natural for women to claim the right to vote in parliamentary elections as the next step forward.

But proponents of women's suffrage faced an entrenched opposition. As Brian Harrison has demonstrated, anti-suffragism was a powerful force and drew from a wide variety of sources: anti-democratic sentiment; traditional views on the subordinate role of women in family and society; economic interests such as the drink trade which feared the women's temperance vote; and above all, the belief that separate spheres between the sexes had been ordained by God or dictated by nature.[68] Those who held to the inviolability of separate spheres were especially disturbed by the logical extension of suffragist aims. They feared that suffragist women might ultimately want not only the vote; it was possible that they had a far greater goal in mind – to alter the sexual culture of Britain. This could ultimately mean a change in the relations between men and women, and the obliteration on every social and cultural front of those boundaries between the sexes that held been traditionally buttressed by the notion of separate spheres.[69]

As the opposition to women's suffrage remained obdurate over the years, suffragists all over the country in almost every region had reached such a level of disappointment and frustration after decades of failed peaceful demonstrations and publicity campaigns that they were ready for a more activist effort. In response, they began to organize on a national scale. Two important women's organizations gained prominence – the National Union of Women's Suffrage Societies (the

National Union) and the smaller and more militant Women's Social and Political Union (WSPU).[70] These organizations, with their intelligent and dedicated leaders and their energized base of support, were determined to bring the issue of women's suffrage to the forefront of national politics and to pressure the government of the day – whether Liberal or Conservative – to a resolution.[71] However, it was in the Liberal government that suffragists placed their greatest hopes. After all, Liberals were the heirs of a proud reforming tradition. Surely they would take heed of suffragist grievances and act accordingly. As early as the parliamentary election of 1906, suffragists made their presence known through heckling and harassment at Liberal election meetings. It was all within the tradition of extra-parliamentary opinion making. The idea was to prod Liberal candidates into an acknowledgement, at the very least, of suffragist claims to full citizenship.

But Liberals, too, had their share of anti-suffragist sentiment, most significantly among members of Asquith's own Cabinet, many of whom had earlier supported important social and political reforms as part of the progressive Liberal parliamentary agenda. Indeed, so fiercely opposed were some Liberal Cabinet members that they assumed leadership positions in the anti-suffragist movement. Hobhouse, for example, once declared in a public speech that if women became involved in politics, it would limit their 'capacity and inclination for maternity' and would lead to 'their unwillingness and incapacity to manage their home'.[72] Hobhouse also organized parliamentary resistance to suffrage proposals in the House of Commons. Lewis Harcourt was like-minded and a close ally of Hobhouse. Jack Pease, the Chief Liberal Whip during the early years of the Liberal government was an anti-suffragist, as were John Burns, Reginald McKenna and Herbert Samuel. Churchill claimed to favour women's suffrage in principle but he refused, as he once put it, to be 'henpecked' on the matter.[73] Birrell was a self-proclaimed supporter of women's suffrage, but became more circumspect after being attacked on the street by a band of vigorous suffragettes and suffering a dislocated knee (as well as a damaged amour-propre). Most important of all the anti-suffragists was Prime Minister Asquith. The remainder of the Cabinet – including Grey, R.B. Haldane, Walter Runciman, Sir John Simon and Lloyd George – were at least nominally in favour of some form of women's suffrage; but they could hardly go against the Prime Minister and their anti-suffragist colleagues without endangering the government's hold on office.

When a crowded legislative agenda gave the appearance that the Liberal government was dragging its feet on the cause, suffragists intensified their actions. Cabinet members became particular targets, among them Lloyd George. He may have been singled out because of his reformist reputation and his self-proclaimed support of women's suffrage. But he had not actively pursued the cause of votes for women as a member of the new Liberal government. Suffragette impatience found a voice in Sylvia Pankhurst's complaint that Lloyd George came to them 'empty handed with only a bevy of fair, indefinite words in his mouth'.[74] They wanted 'Deeds, not Words'. If Lloyd George were pressured hard enough, perhaps he would be inclined to make a stronger case for women's suffrage in the Cabinet. An early example occurred in February 1908 when Lloyd George – at that time President of the Board of Trade – was the principal speaker at a London demonstration for free trade. The meeting was repeatedly interrupted by both suffragist outbursts throughout and the noise created by their ejection. But the meeting had the effect of forcing Lloyd George to commit himself publicly to women's suffrage.[75] Suffragist demonstrations against Lloyd George were not confined to London. A few months later, at a meeting in Edinburgh in support of the Licensing Bill, sponsored in part by the British Women's Temperance Association, several suffragists called out from various parts of the King's Theatre, demanding votes for women. Their ejection often prompted screams of protest from the demonstrators: accompanying shouts from the audience added to the din.[76] At a particularly raucous meeting in London two months later, Lloyd George was again harassed from all parts of the hall. Some of the demonstrators had even obtained seats on the platform. One suffragist had tied herself to her seat, making ejection difficult.[77] It was a sign of hardening opinions among suffragists.

Lloyd George did not take kindly to these interruptions. In a letter to Mrs Emmeline Pethick-Lawrence, he condemned 'this stupid rowdyism', noting that he had invited women suffragists to put questions to him at the end of his speeches. Instead they had persisted in provoking disturbances that not only harmed their own cause, but also damaged 'the sacred cause of free speech'.[78] The most sensational confrontation of the year between Lloyd George and the suffragists occurred on 5 December 1908 at the Albert Hall during a demonstration meeting in favour of women's suffrage.[79] Sponsored by the Women's Liberal Federation, some 8,000–9,000 were in attendance. Signs of trouble were apparent at the outset when numerous women, sitting in the front row, quietly removed their cloaks to reveal their attire – facsimile prison dress – intended as a protest against the imprisonment of suffragists. Scarcely had Lloyd George begun to address the audience when a woman in the highest balcony of that vast auditorium began to make a speech of her own. As stewards closed in to eject her, they were held off for a time by a dogwhip, which she flicked at them until overpowered and removed after a struggle. Shouts of her sympathetic supporters throughout the Hall continued for some time. When Lloyd George again attempted to speak, chants from around the Hall of 'Deeds, not Words' prevented his being heard. He sat down for several minutes to allow soothing chords from the organ to restore order. Rising again to speak, he chastised the demonstrators for their 'lunacy and hysteria', claiming that their actions were 'doing infinite harm to the cause of women'. These comments released a flurry of catcalls from the audience. This led to a verbal set-to between Lloyd George and the suffragists scattered throughout the Hall. The tumult was so great he was once again forced to take his seat. At one point during the fracas, he was provoked to exclaim 'he would not stand being bullied'. Only near the end of his speech, after nearly two hours of continuous commotion, was Lloyd George able to make some uninterrupted remarks. Admitting that the Cabinet was divided over women's suffrage, he declared that the suffragists must convince the public of their cause. He then stated that his own opinion was that 'it was fair, just, and equitable that the suffrage should be granted to women'. This only brought further comment from the crowd who were impatient with banal generalities and weak promises. 'Give us a government pledge' was their cry.

The Albert Hall meeting was significant in revealing the power that suffragists could exercise in their cause. In this instance, it effectively denied Lloyd George his primary political venue – the open meeting – for capturing public opinion. It also disclosed a petulant side to his personality. Normally Lloyd George could manage hecklers, but not in this case. As one commentator who was present put it: 'The little man lost his temper badly.'[80] These interruptions had an immediate impact upon Lloyd George's future meetings. A week after the Albert Hall meeting, a public notice in *The Times* proclaimed that he would no longer address meetings at which women were present.[81] This proscription was not always successful. At a meeting in Liverpool in late December 1908, Lloyd George spoke at the Sun Hall, Liverpool. His agenda was primarily a defence of the Liberal reform programme. On friendly territory and with only receptive supporters applauding him, one would expect Lloyd George to be at his usual best. But the suffragettes, if denied entrance, were not to be entirely outdone. From a house opposite the hall, they employed a megaphone to shout slogans which could be heard inside, forcing the closing of all doors and windows 'to keep out the battlecry of the women'. This had the unfortunate effect, as *The Times* noted, of making the interior of the Hall 'insufferably hot'. [82]

In the years that followed these early demonstrations, Lloyd George frequently found himself – no less than other Liberal politicians – a target of the bolder suffragettes. Public meetings throughout the country where Cabinet members were to speak became guarded affairs. Police barricades, street blockages and beefed up security forces attempted to control protests.[83] But it was difficult to exclude all protestors: it was almost impossible, for example, to screen male sympathizers, who could more easily gain entrance than their female accomplices. And inevitably, some women successfully intruded. At the inaugural meeting of the newly formed Gladstone League in March 1910, for example, Lloyd George was questioned from the floor by a Liberal suffragist, who wished to know when the government would bring in a parliamentary bill to grant the franchise to women. Stating once again his support for such a bill, Lloyd George chastised the women's movement for 'arousing feelings of anger and indignation' among the population by their protests. Furthermore, he said, 'no Parliament likes to be henpecked'.[84] Barbed comments such as these on the part of Lloyd George won him no favours among suffragists. Their frustration at the slow pace of women's suffrage occasionally led to more aggressive acts directed at him personally. In December 1909, as a car carrying Lloyd George to a meeting in London drew up to the curb, two suffragettes leapt inside: one locked the door and other seized the Chancellor by the shoulders and shook him while she exhorted him to action for the cause.[85] Two years later there was a more serious assault when 'a young male associate' of the suffragettes hurled his leather book-filled attaché case through the open window of Lloyd George's car, striking his head and bruising his face.[86]

As frustrations rose generally among suffragists, the more militant among them escalated their tactics.[87] By 1909, the first hunger strikes by imprisoned suffragists had begun. To break the deadlock between protesters and the government, a Conciliation Committee, chaired by the Conservative Earl of Lytton was established in February 1910. Comprised of 54 MPs from all parties, the Committee drafted a bill, based upon the municipal franchise, which would grant the parliamentary vote to single women who were householders or who possessed a £10 occupation. So narrowly defined an enfranchisement would have added about a million women voters. In early July 1910 the proposed bill was debated in the House of Commons where – to the surprised anguish of both the National Union and WSPU – it was opposed by none other than the radical Chancellor the Exchequer, Lloyd George. But, as his speech to the House of Commons indicated, he was not opposed to women's suffrage. He was, however, opposed to this bill as it was drafted because it excluded the possibility of an even wider extension of the franchise. It was a faulty bill, as he informed the House, which could not be amended 'either for restriction or extension'.[88]

The Times commented that his negative vote, largely on procedural grounds, caused Lloyd George to be 'now regarded by the suffragists as a traitor'.[89] Indeed, his opposition to the Conciliation Bill and his apparent inability to move the government to a decisive vote for women's suffrage have brought considerable obloquy down upon him from suffragist historians. Sandra Stanley Holton has castigated his role as that of 'cynical wheeler-dealing'.[90] Claire Hirshfield claims that Lloyd George followed a 'duplicitous strategy' in his policy on women's suffrage.[91] Grigg notes that Lloyd George 'cannot escape his share of responsibility for the Liberals' disastrous mishandling of the women's suffrage issue'. He observes further that although Lloyd George was 'a genuine suffragist, he never gave the issue the very high priority it deserved' and was 'ready enough to fall in with Asquith's delaying tactics'.[92]

Better explanations for Lloyd George's behaviour than crude cynicism or a careless duplicity lie at hand, however. Three fundamental reasons for his apparent equivocations may be advanced. The first was that the government was under severe pressure because of the continuing struggles over other important Liberal reform initiatives. Lloyd George's People's Budget, the establishment of the National Insurance programme and the reform of the House of Lords sapped considerable Cabinet and parliamentary energy. Second, as we have noted, was the division of opinion within the Cabinet on the question of women's suffrage. Any attempt by Lloyd George and his suffragist allies to force the question might mean Asquith's resignation and the fall of the government.[93] Thirdly, and not the least important reason, was that Lloyd George – although a suffragist in principle – viewed its implementation primarily in political terms.[94] His opposition to the Conciliation Bill was clearly based upon political calculation. He thought the bill was fundamentally a Tory contrivance because it would enfranchise relatively affluent women occupiers and householders, women who would likely vote Conservative. If such a bill succeeded, he believed it could mean electoral 'disaster to Liberalism'.[95] Lloyd George believed therefore that any bill granting the franchise to women must be wide enough to bring in working men's wives, who would be likely to vote Liberal, as a targeted electoral group.[96]

Lloyd George was not alone in gauging the political consequences of the Conciliation Bill, and his suspicions of the Conservative Party's support for it were not far wrong. Conservatives as a whole supported the bill as a means of offsetting any Liberal stratagem for changing the election laws to their advantage prior to the general election of 1915. Liberals could, for example, abolish the plural voting system and university seats, both of which were inherently tilted toward Conservative voters. They could also remove the requirement of a 12-month residency for all voters, which tended to disenfranchise transient working men, who were likely Liberal voters.[97] In short, Lloyd George (and some Liberals) feared any franchise bill too narrowly defined, whereas the Conservatives feared too broad a bill.

In spite of Lloyd George's opposition, the Conciliation Bill passed its second reading by a substantial margin. But the bill was immediately consigned to a quiet death when it was sent to a Committee of the Whole House where it could only be revived by persuading the government to provide the time for further discussion. This the government refused to do.[98] Thus a second Conciliation Bill was brought forward in May 1911. In order to attract more support, the bill had been altered somewhat: it abolished the £10 qualification clause and changed the title to indicate the inclusion of a broader franchise (from 'A Bill to Extend the Parliamentary Franchise to Women Occupiers' to 'A Bill to Confer the Parliamentary Franchise on Women'). Mollified by a step in the direction of expanding the electorate beyond the first Conciliation Bill, Lloyd George voted for the bill, joining a substantial majority of 167.[99] A few weeks later, however, the Cabinet decided not to proceed further with the bill in the current parliamentary session. As Lloyd George explained it, the importance of the bill required more time for consideration than was available in the present parliamentary session and it would be given its second reading in the next parliamentary session in 1912.

This postponement, not surprisingly, was met with keen disappointment by both the National Union and the WSPU. On 17 June 1911 a combined procession of some 40,000 suffragists – militants and moderates together – marched in protest at the delay. But that same day Asquith made public a letter to Lord Lytton, chairman of the Conciliation Committee, which confirmed the promise of a week long debate on the Conciliation Bill during the following 1912 parliamentary session. On that promise, suffragists held their fire during the summer months of 1911 and into the autumn of that year. But events in November prompted renewed action. On 7 November, Asquith announced that the government would bring forward a bill within the next few months that would enact manhood suffrage. An opportunity for an extensive scheme for women's suffrage would also be provided for through the device of friendly amendments. In short, there was to be a two-track approach to women's suffrage for 1912: one through the Conciliation Committee; and the other from the government itself.[100]

Though the government now seemed to promise two chances at women's suffrage, many suffragists – as well as the militant suffragettes – were suspicious. Having been fobbed off twice before, they were in a state of disbelief about the government's public statements.[101] They feared that the government's proposal, by tacking a women's suffrage measure onto a bill that also widened considerably the pool of male voters, would rally all opponents of a democratic franchise, especially from the Conservative side of the House. To demonstrate their displeasure, suffragettes resumed militant tactics. More than 200 suffragettes rallied outside the Houses of Parliament on 21 November 1911. Another detachment, armed with stones and hammers, began to break windows of government buildings including the Home Office, the Local Government Board and the Treasury. The National Liberal Federation was also attacked, as were newspaper offices and a number of business establishments, such as Swan and Edgar's, Dunn's Hat Shop, a chemist, a bakery and several other small businesses. It was the first time that private businesses were hit. Two hundred and twenty women were arrested, as were three men.

Concerted efforts to disrupt Liberal meetings, especially with Cabinet members present, began again in earnest. Asquith was driven from a speech at the City Temple on 28 November by suffragists who shouted and blew police whistles to drown out his address. Lloyd George himself had already been a target of the protestors at Bath a few days earlier. Ostensibly to speak on the government's programmes of National Insurance, land reform and the need for an extension of the suffrage, Lloyd George found instead a sustained opposition from suffragist hecklers. As *The Times* put it: 'Cabinet ministers have seldom been subjected to a more deliberate attempt to break up a meeting.'[102] Even before the meeting had begun, windows of the neighbouring post office were broken and police barriers set up against the agitators were rushed. Though Lloyd George declared his support for women's suffrage several times, persistent disruptions, carried out mainly by male suffragists, spoiled his presentation.[103] The meeting is best remembered, however, for what was likely an unintended inflammatory comment by Lloyd George. In seeking to justify the government's new enfranchisement scheme, he claimed (twice) that the Conciliation Bill had been 'torpedoed'. By this he meant that the conciliation plan 'for a limited suffrage', which would have been 'grossly unfair to Liberalism', could now be replaced by 'a broad and democratic' suffrage for women. But the implication that Lloyd George had been a party to wrecking the Conciliation Bill did not sit well with those suffragists who had worked hard for its passage.[104]

These violent actions by the more militant suffragists spurred Lloyd George to complain despairingly to C.P. Scott of the *Manchester Guardian* that the attacks were 'ruinous' to the cause of women's suffrage.[105] Nevertheless, during the latter weeks of 1911 and the early months of 1912, attacks on private property continued, including another large-scale smashing of windows of businesses and shops in the West End. Letterboxes were set ablaze by the simple expedient of lighting pieces of paraffin-soaked linen and dropping them through the slots. Lloyd George deplored such actions. To William, he condemned the perpetrators as 'lunatics' and 'raving mad'.[106] He well knew that violence begat violence. WSPU meetings were disrupted. Crowds broke the windows of the Women's Press. Perhaps because of this increased suffragist militancy and retaliation by anti-suffragists, or perhaps because the previous all-party support now waned in the face of the anticipated Liberal franchise proposal, the Conciliation Bill failed in the House of Commons in a close vote on 28 March 1912. This spurred additional acts of protest by the WSPU. The more moderately inclined National Union for its part made overtures to the Labour Party with the intention of sending a warning to the Liberals, should they continue to be unreliable allies. Through a newly created Election Fighting Fund, the National Union also declared its financial support for Labour candidates who stood for Parliament against anti-suffragist Liberals.[107]

Violence and disruptive actions continued throughout the latter part of 1912. In May leading suffragists were convicted of conspiracy and imprisoned. The following month, hunger strikes began among all goaled members of the WSPU – 79 in all. In July, suffragettes who travelled to Dublin ahead of a planned visit there by Asquith were successful in throwing a hatchet into the carriage in which the Prime Minister and John Redmond were travelling. The weapon missed Asquith but grazed Redmond's ear. An arson attempt at the Theatre Royal where Asquith was to speak resulted in firing the curtains in one of the boxes. A small explosion was also set off. In that same month, two suffragettes were apprehended at the wall surrounding Nuneham House, the residence of Lewis Harcourt, a foremost anti-suffragist in the Cabinet. They were caught with flammable material in their possession.[108]

In the midst of the growing furore among the suffragists, the ministry's own measure, the Franchise and Registration Bill, reached the committee stage at the end of January 1913. There were four anticipated amendments, each of which would create substantial numbers of newly enfranchised women. However, when one of the first of the amendments came before the House for debate on 23 January – to the apparent surprise of all – the Speaker ruled it out of order on the grounds that proposed amendments for women's suffrage significantly altered the intent of the bill.[109] The government had no option but to withdraw it. Once again, the sense of betrayal was manifest among suffragists of every stripe. Liberal suffragists were especially demoralized by the succession of promises and failures which could be laid at the door of their own party. Resignations among the leaders of the Women's Liberal Federation followed: its membership also shrank. The more action oriented suffragettes, however, responded to the Liberal rebuffs with a renewed sense of determination. They in effect declared war upon the Liberal government through a series of rapidly escalating incidents.[110] Suffragettes burnt down a refreshment kiosk in Regent's Park. The tea pavilion at Kew Gardens was torched. Suffragettes damaged racecourses and golf greens around the country. Lloyd George's new house under construction at Walton Heath was damaged by a bomb. Random violence and what were essentially terrorist actions were accompanied by a form of passive resistance as imprisoned suffragettes continued the use of hunger strikes (first initiated in 1909), which in turn generated widely publicized forced feedings. When these actions by prison officials began to generate negative publicity, Parliament passed in April 1913 the Prisoners' Temporary Discharge for Ill Health Act – popularly known as the Cat and Mouse Act – which abandoned forced feeding in prison and simply released those suffragettes who became ill through hunger strikes. This was a circumscribed freedom, however: suffragists were free until they were required to return to prison at an appointed date, presumably in better health. But few of the freed suffragettes adhered to their end of the bargain. Hence the game of cat and mouse began as the authorities sought to track them down.[111] Several weeks after the passage of the Act, with violence unrelenting, Emily Wilding Davis became the first martyr to the cause when she threw herself in front of the King's horse and was trampled to death on Derby Day, 31 May 1913.

The efficacy of these militant tactics have been a matter of contention. Suffragettes themselves proudly defended their militancy as necessary measures to gain their political objectives. They called upon historical precedents in justification of their actions – such as Charles Stewart Parnell's campaigns in winning concessions from the British Parliament. Other libertarian influences cited were Wat Tyler, John Hampden and the Chartists. Even Magna Carta was brought into play as an ideal that the suffragettes ostensibly followed.[112] As Emmeline Pankhurst put it, suffragettes were no more violent than men: 'bomb throwing shooting and stone throwing' she wrote, were 'time honoured masculine political arguments!'[113] Sympathetic historians have also viewed suffragette militancy as legitimate and within the traditional context of British radicalism.[114] They have argued that suffragettes could rightly claim that they were driven to such extremes because women were denied the full rights of citizenship. Without legal status as voters, suffragettes had little choice but to act outside the law and to disregard notions of propriety.

Other historians have taken a dimmer view of the increasingly militant tactics of some suffragettes. Although Martin Pugh thinks that their early tactics were effective in bringing the issue of women's suffrage to the public and in attracting funds and new members, he believes that in its later phrase militancy alienated both the public and Parliament and had a discouraging effect upon suffragism as a whole.[115] Harold L. Smith also praises suffragists' initial tactics as reasoned and calculated to obtain reasonable ends, but that ultimately militancy was counterproductive.[116] Constance Rover is largely sympathetic to suffragist aims, holding the government accountable for not granting more parliamentary time to women's suffrage before 1912. But she, too, thinks it unfortunate that the suffragettes resorted to violence after the failure of the 1912 vote on the Conciliation Bill.[117] Andrew Rosen, the historian of WSPU militancy, also faults the ministerial equivocation on women's suffrage; yet he regrets the fact that within the WSPU after 1911 there was an 'incipient stage of what was to become a most Manichean outlook' towards politicians.[118]

There seems little doubt that the increasingly violent actions by militant suffragettes throughout 1912–13 had consolidated and strengthened anti-suffrage opinion in the public at large. Attacks upon private property were widely deplored. Concerns rose that the escalating violence could even lead to the assassination of public officials.[119] Within Parliament, too, suffragette militancy had a negative impact by strengthening the hand of anti-suffragists. Balcarres condemned the 'suffragette folly' of window smashing which, he thought, merely punished harmless tradesmen for the shortcomings of the Liberal government.[120] Austen Chamberlain, who frequently complained to his stepmother about the suffragist movement as a whole, gleefully reported that window smashing was alienating opinion not only in the House of Commons but among the public as well.[121] There is also evidence that the not insignificant Irish Nationalist representation in the House of Commons was becoming uneasy at the violent turn of the suffragette campaign. With 84 seats after the election of December 1910, the Irish Nationalists, it will be remembered, held the balance of power in the House of Commons. They had voted strongly for the Conciliation Bill of 1911, but turned dramatically against the bill in 1912. As John Dillon explained it to C.P. Scott, there had been 'an immense change in Irish feeling' toward anti-suffragism.[122] Lloyd George agreed. In a letter to H.N. Brailsford, he pointed out that 'the militants' could not have adopted a better plan to destroy their own cause than the 'their outrages' they have perpetrated.[123]

In spite of the considerable antagonism generated by suffragette militancy, some historians believe that it paved the way for eventual suffragist success. Indeed, if war had not intervened, Holton believes that votes for women might have become law perhaps as early as 1915.[124] Other historians cite as evidence of an increasingly favourable climate for a suffrage bill movement an apparent weakening of Asquith's opposition. This view is based upon a meeting between the Prime Minister and a deputation of women from the East End of London held on 20 June 1914. The meeting had come about at the request of Sylvia Pankhurst, who had begun to break away from the autocratic grip of her mother Emmeline and sister Christabel in their leadership of the WSPU. By establishing the East London Federation of the suffragettes (ELF), Sylvia hoped to create a more democratic and socialist approach to women's suffrage than that of the WSPU. The deputation to Asquith was in fact made up of six women members of the ELF.[125] Asquith, it seems, had only reluctantly agreed to the meeting.[126] But once the meeting was under way, he was, according to some commentators, more conciliatory than usual. Sylvia herself thought so. There was 'an unmistakable softening in his long hostility', she wrote, 'almost he seemed to declare himself a convert ...'.[127] There is some agreement with her conclusion: Les Garner also believes that Asquith had an 'apparent change of heart'.[128] Martin Pugh also thinks that Asquith had given 'an unusually conciliatory response' to the deputation.[129]

Perhaps Asquith had these political concerns in mind and had at last determined to come to terms with the suffragists. But evidence for this is slim. A close examination of Asquith's remarks to the deputation reveals a noncommittal position. He declared that he had 'listened with the greatest interest' to the deputation and promised a 'very careful and mature consideration' of their remarks. He would also take the economic conditions of women in the East End 'into careful consideration'. Should the franchise be given to women, if the change 'has to come' he said, it must be made 'thoroughgoing and democratic in its basis'.[130] Beyond these platitudes and his patronizing tone, Asquith offered neither a promise of action nor a tactical calendar.[131]

The Prime Minister's indifferent response stands in strong contrast to his Chancellor of the Exchequer. Lloyd George, as we have seen, was certainly against militant suffragism, chastising their interruptions at meetings and condemning their violent attacks around the country. In July 1912, he confided to Riddell that the suffragettes had 'lost their opportunity' and had 'ruined their cause for the time being' by their tactics.[132] But the militants had neither discouraged nor alienated him from what he considered the just claims of the more moderate suffragists. 'Although I hate the militants', he wrote to William, 'one must not allow that to deflect judgement in a great question of principle'.[133] Indeed, he was quite willing to establish a working relationship with the National Union. As we saw in the case of Helena Swanwick, he was even willing to seek her advice on his public pronouncements on women's suffrage. He attempted to establish common ground with Millicent Fawcett by warning her that the militants were 'alienating sympathy from the women's cause in every quarter', including some Members of Parliament who had formerly been 'steadfast in the support of Women's Suffrage'.[134] He also engaged in lengthy negotiations in 1913 with Catherine Marshall (who was then the National Union's Parliamentary Secretary) concerning his active commitment to women's suffrage.[135] In addition, Lloyd George had begun negotiations with both George Lansbury, the leading Labour Party suffragist, and Sylvia Pankhurst, head of the East London Federation. To them, he pledged that he, Grey and Simon would refuse office in any future Liberal ministry that did not seriously take up women's suffrage. Lloyd George may well have had in mind a coalition of suffragist sympathizers both in and out of any future ministry that would guarantee the passage of a comprehensive democratic suffrage bill, including the enfranchisement of a broad spectrum of women.[136] What definite plans Lloyd George and the government may have had to settle the suffrage question during the latter months of 1914 is unknown. In late July of that year, scarcely a month after Asquith's meeting with the deputation of women from the East End, the threat of a general European war had thrust aside all plans for any enactment of women's suffrage.

In the immediate years prior to the Great War, we have seen that Lloyd George had a mixed record. He had experienced a series of uncompleted plans, derailed programmes and possible scandal in the years following some of his greatest achievements. Of all the circumstances that could have threatened Lloyd George's political career and ruined his personal reputation during the years 1912–14, however, none was more potentially dangerous than his intimate involvement with a young woman half his age. The story is now widely known, not least through the diaries and autobiography of Frances Stevenson. The two were brought together at first by chance. Frances was hired to tutor Megan Lloyd George, the youngest of the Lloyd George children, during the summer of 1911. An accomplished young woman, Frances was intelligent, lively, fluent in French and musically inclined. She was teaching at Allenswood, a girls' boarding school in Wimbledon, when she was engaged by the Lloyd Georges to tutor Megan. Frances began that summer, staying with the family at Criccieth. So successful was she that at summer's end, Megan was sent to Allenswood for further schooling, where she could remain under the wing of Frances.

Thereafter, there were casual interactions between Lloyd George and Frances when he visited Megan at school. As the bond between Megan and Frances strengthened, Frances was occasionally invited to Downing Street, where she was welcomed as a guest. Lloyd George, always on the lookout for talent to use for his own ends, began to assign her specific tasks. He asked her to translate a book on land reform in French. This was followed by more work in connection with the land campaign. Gradually, a professional relationship turned increasingly personal. They began to confide in one another. She revealed that she found teaching tiresome, and had begun shorthand lessons to prepare for a possible job in journalism. He revealed that his marriage to Margaret was less than satisfactory: he was often lonely in the absence of his wife. She began to look forward 'avidly' to seeing him.[137] He began to take her to tea, and then to restaurants. They began writing to one another almost daily. By then, Lloyd George had broached the possibility of her becoming one of his secretaries at the Treasury. At about the same time, he gave her a copy of Katherine O'Shea's book on Parnell. The lesson was obvious; Parnell had destroyed his political career by marrying his mistress. That road, Lloyd George made clear, he would not take. If Frances would accept him on those terms, they could have a future together. By January 1913, they had become lovers.[138]

Lloyd George made it clear from the first that he had no intention of giving up Margaret. The impressionable Frances accepted these terms and became resigned to following a double life. The relationship was mutually beneficial. For Frances, being on the inside of government and politics at the highest level was exciting and fulfilling. She was, as one historian has observed, 'a consummate political secretary'.[139] For Lloyd George, apart from his reliance upon her efficiency, hard work and discretion in matters of state, there was doubtless the equal excitement of enticing a young and attractive paramour. He also discovered, perhaps to his surprise, that Frances supplied a need that he had always, not often consciously, felt. Frances was his loyal and inveterate booster. She praised and flattered him at every turn. After his parliamentary speeches in the House of Commons, which she would often attend, she sent a cheery note down from the Gallery. She also followed up speeches he made in the countryside with similar praise. To her, Lloyd George could confide his worries and doubts, sure in the knowledge of her support and sympathy. As Frances tellingly observed: 'He had made me realize that I was necessary to him'.[140] Thus Frances supplied the need for affirmation and praise that Margaret had never been able to give.

9

IMPERIAL MATTERS AND FOREIGN AFFAIRS

Lloyd George's need for relaxation and relief from the complexities of his private life and from the toils of public endeavours were met by his growing affinity for foreign travel. Some of his trips abroad can be seen as related to business or professional interests. As early as 1891, however, he also began to travel on holiday for relaxation to Europe fairly frequently: Switzerland, Austria, Italy, and France were his favoured spots. These holiday jaunts were most often taken in late summer and early autumn after Parliament had risen. He was usually accompanied by parliamentary friends or Welsh acquaintants, rarely by Margaret. Twice he went with his brother William. Sometimes he would be away during Christmas while his family remained in Wales. In December 1897, for example, he went to Rome where he saw the Pope; and a year later, again at Christmas time, he went on a Mediterranean cruise which weighed anchor at Tangiers, Algiers and Tunis among other ports. On another cruise, during August 1905, he travelled on Rendel's yacht off the western coast of Scotland.

On a holiday to Scotland in 1895 (with Margaret this time), he discovered golf. Enthusiastic from the beginning, he proclaimed it 'a glorious game' and 'an excellent diversion'.[1] It soon became his most important pastime. But golf for Lloyd George was more than a game. Like many other politicians at the turn of the century, recreational golf provided ideal opportunities for relaxed conversation, gossip and deal making. Golf may also have played a part, if a minor one, in fostering a connection between the Liberal elite and the Welsh firebrand within the Liberal Party. A letter to Lloyd George written in early 1905 suggests as much. Sir Arthur Crosfield, of the Crosfield soap manufacturing firm in Warrington, had parliamentary aspirations. To that end, he invited Lloyd George for a long weekend to Hoylake, where he was promised 'comfortable quarters'. An added attraction was the nearby golf club which, Sir Arthur claimed, 'cannot be beaten in the United Kingdom'. In addition, Sir Arthur hoped that Lloyd George would be his guest during his next visit to Cannes, where he had been asked to take the Captaincy of the Cannes Golf Club. Sir Arthur promised 'plenty of good matches day by day and first class easy motoring through most delightful scenery into the bargain'. He assured Lloyd George he would have 'a rattling good time'. For all this, there is an implied *quid pro quo*: he hoped that Lloyd George would lend his oratorical support to further his parliamentary candidacy in Warrington.[2]

Golf in fact knew no political boundaries.[3] A.J. Balfour, as a Scot, was perhaps naturally taken with the game and became one of its keenest adherents. At the other end of the political and social spectrum, the Liberal/Labour MP Henry Broadhurst, a former stonemason, was also a golfer. Lloyd George pursued his golf even during some of his busiest parliamentary moments. He became a member of the Walton Heath Golf Club in 1907, where he managed to play once or twice a week. Other members of the Club at that time were Cosmo Bonsor, former Tory MP for Wimbledon; the Hon. A.E. Gathorne-Hardy, the son of the well known Tory, Earl Cranbrook; and the Liberal Earl of Crewe, who served as Lord President of the Council in Henry Campbell-Bannerman's Liberal Ministry. A mixed lot politically, but certainly all were of the elite. By the eve of the Great War, the club membership included six Cabinet members, 24 MPs, 21 lay peers, and two bishops.[4] So popular had Walton Heath become for Members of Parliament that it has been called 'the chief scene of Ministerial activity' after Westminster.[5] The golf played there was neither skilled nor serious, but it did provide considerable opportunities for mobile meetings among politicians. Even if the ball went into the heather, as it not infrequently did, players often abandoned it: they preferred losing the hole to missing the talk.[6] The golf club was owned by a syndicate headed by George Riddell, an eager golfing companion, who would on occasion take Lloyd George to the Club in his chauffer-driven motor car. Later on, Riddell purchased for Lloyd George a house at Walton Heath so that he did not have far to go to play the game.

Lloyd George's need for relaxation was never more in evidence than in his dealings with Ireland. Indeed, the Irish Question was to become the most trying of all unresolved problems facing the Liberal ministry in the final years of peace prior to 1914. The initial step was taken by John Redmond once the Parliamentary Bill of 1911 had restricted the powers of the House of Lords, thus removing (it was thought) their consistent opposition to an Irish Home Rule Bill. Redmond made it clear to the Liberal government that they must honour their promises to Ireland which had been enunciated in Asquith's Albert Hall speech as long ago as December 1909. In April 1912 the Liberal government complied by bringing forward a Home Rule Bill for Ireland.[7] Although the bill created a bicameral Irish Parliament. comprised of a Senate of 40 members and a House of Commons with 164 members as well as an executive drawn from that Parliament, it did not establish an autonomous body. The primacy of Westminster was affirmed. Under the terms of the bill, the executive would be headed by a Lord Lieutenant with extensive powers of veto and control over legislation. Provisions were also made to retain 42 Irish MPs in the Westminster Parliament. Certain areas were declared outside the purview of the proposed Irish governmental structure and were reserved for the Westminster parliament, such as matters relating to the Crown, the making of peace or war, foreign and colonial relations, and trade and navigation. To soothe any potential ruffled feathers of the predominantly Protestant population in Ulster, a special section guaranteed freedom of religious practice.

If the Liberal government hoped that Ulster would be satisfied with this bow towards religious tolerance, it was gravely mistaken. Ulster was destined to become not only the major obstacle to the Home Rule Bill: it was also the centre of bitter partisan strife and the focus of constitutional struggles which threatened the structure of parliamentary government.[8] Since the seventeenth century, Ulster had defended its minority Protestant status against the more numerous Catholic Southern Ireland. Determined never to be ruled by a Dublin parliament, Ulster was zealously vigilant to any alteration in their political ties to a greater Britain. Thus, when the Parliament Act of 1911 weakened the powers of the House of Lords – the traditional opponents of Home Rule – Ulster Unionists quickly understood the implications. Within a month of the passage of the Parliament Bill, the first of a series of Ulster protest meetings took place. On 23 September 1911, 50,000 men gathered at Craigavon, the estate of Captain James Craig, to demand that Ulster remain an integral part of Britain.[9]

Realizing the potential of this spontaneous upsurge of opinion, the Conservative opposition at Westminster quickly seized the opportunity of making Ulster the means of killing the Home Rule Bill. They believed, as they had believed in their opposition to the previous two Liberal attempts at Home Rule in 1886 and 1893, that Ireland must remain an imperial possession. Their deeply rooted suspicion was that Home Rule was but a half-way house to separation from Britain.[10] The majority of the Ulster population shared these imperial sentiments. Standing four square with Ulster could bring an additional advantage to the Conservative Parliamentary Party at Westminster: opposition to Home Rule could help unite the Conservative Political Party.[11] If Conservatives could be brought together over Ulster, they could possibly be brought together over tariff reform, still a divisive issue within the party.

Ulster provided an additional advantage to the Conservative Party – a chance to reinvigorate its leadership. Andrew Bonar Law, who had replaced Balfour as party leader in 1911, was of Ulster stock.[12] His father, a nonconformist minister and a native of County Antrim, emigrated to Canada, where Bonar Law was born. As a young man, Bonar Law moved to Glasgow, where he made his way in merchant banking and later bought a partnership in a substantial iron merchant firm. This was to be the foundation of his wealth. Meanwhile, his father had retired to Ulster in 1877 and Bonar Law often visited him there. Bonar Law's Scots covenanting tradition, combined with his personal sympathies and familiarity with Ulster, made him an ideal spokesman in support of that province's demands.

The crisis of Home Rule and the Ulster question came at an opportune moment for Bonar Law to establish his credentials as leader of the Conservative Party. In early April 1912, Bonar Law travelled to Ulster to begin a campaign against the proposed Home Rule Bill. Speaking to an immense crowd of 100,000 Ulstermen on 9 April 1912 at Balmoral near Belfast, he pledged his assistance to Ulster's opposition to Home Rule. A week later, in his formal response to the introduction of the bill in the House of Commons, he declared that only coercion could force Ulster into the arms of a Dublin-based Home Rule Parliament. In July, Bonar Law raised the rhetorical stakes even higher. During a speech at Blenheim Palace, he claimed that the Liberal government had no constitutional right to impose its will on a free people. Indeed, he regarded the Liberals as leading an illegitimate government. They were, rather, a 'revolutionary committee' which had 'seized by fraud' a 'despotic power'. This being so, he pledged that the Conservatives would 'use any means' to deprive the government of the power which it had 'usurped'. As for himself personally, he could 'imagine no length of resistance to which Ulster will go' in which he should 'not be ready to support them ...'.[13] Embedded within this somewhat tortuous sentence was an unmistakable pledge: Bonar Law supported Ulster unconditionally.

Bonar Law's unyielding public statements on Home Rule and particularly on Ulster were unquestionably inflammatory. As events unfolded, however, Bonar Law – while retaining his public posture as the staunch defender of Ulster and a fierce opponent of Home Rule – found himself occupying a curious middle ground. There were others within the party, such as Walter Long and Lord Willoughby de Broke, who were even more extreme and who pressed hard for a rigid, uncompromising position against Home Rule, even to the point of opposing any negotiations with the Liberal government. A knot of Unionists in Southern Ireland, many of whom were wealthy landed members of the Anglo-Irish ascendancy, also remained firm against Home Rule, fearful of what might happen to their lands and estates under a Dublin parliament.[14] This has led Jeremy Smith to defend Bonar Law's 'high risk strategy' as a legitimate way of holding together all wings of the Conservative Party while simultaneously denying the Liberals an important victory. Smith believes that Bonar Law's ultimate goal was to force an unresponsive Liberal government into negotiations that might lead to a constructive compromise.[15] How well this strategy worked can now be examined.

Bonar Law's most significant opponent in the Home Rule controversy was, of course, Prime Minister Asquith, who held firm in leading the Liberals to a successful conclusion of the first parliamentary circuit in the House of Commons: the Home Rule Bill received its third reading on 16 January 1913. Sent to the Lords, the bill was as expected overwhelmingly rejected two weeks later. Under the specifications of the Parliament Act of 1911, bills rejected by the Lords could be resubmitted by the Commons, but without any alteration or deviation whatsoever in the language of the bill. This was done in July 1913 when the House of Commons passed the Home Rule Bill a second time only to have it again rejected by the Lords. This lengthening of the legislative process exacerbated tensions. Conservative politicians, led by the severe and unswerving Bonar Law, kept up their relentless criticism of the bill. Bitterly divisive debates within the House of Commons found a reflection in speeches throughout the countryside as Conservatives began demanding a direct appeal to the nation on Home Rule, either through a general election or a referendum.

Within Ulster itself, anti-Home Rule sentiment had risen to new heights, spurred by Captain Craig's continued opposition and now abetted by Edward Carson's bellicosity.[16] Providing the liaison between Ulster and Parliament, Carson travelled back and forth from London to the province reinforcing the bonds of parliamentary Unionism and the anti-Home Rule movement in Ulster, which was now fully aroused. Ulster activists began developing sophisticated anti-Home Rule propaganda, using flyers, pamphlets, photos and moving pictures to make their case. Pro-Ulster demonstrations carried Ulster's cause to England and Scotland as well, especially in the heavily Irish communities of the north.[17] There is no doubt that retaining Ireland within the Union was becoming a popular cause throughout Britain as Conservative leaders banged the imperial drum and raised sectarian sentiment against Irish Catholicism to good effect.[18] In Ulster itself, plans for a provisional government were laid. A solemn oath and covenant, based upon the sixteenth-century Scots covenant, circulated widely throughout the province (and in England as well) pledging its signers to defend Ulster citizenship within the United Kingdom and to 'defeat the present conspiracy to set up a Home Rule Parliament in Ireland'. Most ominous of all was the establishment of the paramilitary Ulster Volunteer Force, which claimed nearly 100,000 men by the end of 1913. Retired British army men and officers made up its ranks. Drilling, recruiting and route marches demonstrated that the province was moving towards a war footing.[19] These were all the signs of a revolution; but a curious revolution it was – not a rejection of the existing governmental structure, but an affirmation of its legitimacy and a demand for its continuance. Ulster was determined to maintain the status quo.

The Liberal government's response to these measures seemed laggardly. But they were neither digging in their heels nor negligent. Difficulties were only too apparent. Evidence existed that small caches of arms and ammunition were secretly being brought into Ulster, but accurate information was scarce and police reports were inconclusive. Additionally, Birrell's indecisive management as Chief Secretary for Ireland was inadequate to a resolution of the crisis.[20] By late 1913 tensions had undeniably risen. Asquith was now convinced that firm action must be taken, especially with the news that Southern Ireland had begun to stir. In November 1913, with the establishment of the Irish Volunteers in Dublin as a counterfoil to the UVF, a clash of arms between the opposing sides became ever more likely. The Volunteers represented more than a new military force: they became the spearpoint of a new political vision. They began to question the constitutional niceties of the official Irish Nationalist party at Westminster led by John Redmond. They especially condemned the 'emasculated representative politics of Home Rule', with its delays and compromises.[21] Thus, the Volunteers soon fell under the influence of the Irish Republican Brotherhood (the Fenians), dedicated to an independent republic of Ireland, shorn of any attachment to Britain. Particularly unsettling to the leaders of both the Conservative Party and the Liberal government was the growth of the Volunteers not only in Southern Ireland, but in Ulster as well, especially in the catholic areas. The potential political, religious and cultural conflict was no longer merely sectional. The prospects of civil war were very real.

What role in these complicated developments relating to Home Rule expectations and Ulster intransigence did Lloyd George play? Not surprisingly, his interest generally in federalism and specifically in Welsh self determination and his own widely recognized skills as a negotiator put him in the forefront in the Liberal ministry's attempt to defuse the Irish crises.[22] In the months before the introduction of the Home Rule Bill in the Commons, he was appointed to a committee with several other Cabinet members to frame Home Rule legislation. In February 1912, several weeks before the bill was brought to the House of Commons, Lloyd George revealed the fruit of his own thinking. He proposed to the Cabinet that every Irish county, whether North or South, should have the option of contracting out of the Home Rule provisions.[23] At this early stage in the evolution of the Home Rule Bill, several Cabinet members were opposed to the scheme. Birrell took the lead in refusing to countenance it for obvious reasons: it would hardly do for the Chief Secretary of all Ireland to support a measure that essentially excluded part of that country from the operations of a Home Rule bill. He would be seen by most of the Irish, especially in the South, as a turncoat.[24] Any special consideration to Ulster was therefore dropped from the final bill.[25]

Thereafter for many months Lloyd George retreated from an active participation in the Home Rule/Ulster controversy. This was partly due to his distraction brought about by the Marconi scandal.[26] After the scandal receded, he turned his full attention to the land campaign, now his most important priority. Once the land campaign was up and running, Lloyd George again stepped forward and became essentially Asquith's second-in-command, directing the fortunes of the government's Home Rule policy.[27] Returning to his original idea of allowing specified Irish counties (that is, Ulster) to contract out of any Home Rule arrangement, Lloyd George added a modification of that plan: designated counties in Ulster could opt out of any Home Rule plan, but only for a specified time, say five or six years, after which they would automatically be incorporated into a greater Ireland.[28] The hope was that such a delay would allow tempers to cool and that Ulster would recognize over time the advantages of a union with Southern Ireland under a Home Rule arrangement.

The proposal could additionally provide the framework for a possible compromise. If the Conservative parliamentary opposition at Westminster would accept Home Rule for Southern Ireland, the government would accept the exclusion of the whole of Ulster on a temporary basis for a specified length of time. In fact, during the ongoing secret talks between Asquith and Bonar Law, Asquith tentatively advanced the idea, intimating that he would bring it forward to the Cabinet for their consideration. Bonar Law was receptive.[29] At an important Cabinet meeting on 13 November 1913, Lloyd George's plan was accepted in principle. Details needed to be worked out. Of first importance was the definition of Ulster: which counties of the province should be designated as excluded from Home Rule? Equally important was to bring around the Irish Nationalist Party, which had to be squared with the loss of Ulster, however temporary. The Conservative leadership, too, had to be convinced of a temporary exclusion plan. Following the Cabinet meeting of 13 November, both Asquith and Lloyd George in separate interviews with Redmond put the case for Lloyd George's county option proposal.[30]

Negotiations continued into the early months of 1914. In mid-February, Lloyd George proposed a slightly different exclusion plan by which a plebiscite could be called by 10 per cent of the parliamentary electors of any county. The resulting vote, if successful, would legitimize an exclusion for six years, at the end of which that county would become part of Ireland as a whole. Lloyd George kept his brother informed of the negotiations. On 14 February, he wrote: 'This morning had long & interesting talk with Irish leaders. P.M. has left it to me to negotiate with them.' Several days later, he wrote: 'Getting on well with the Irishmen'. And later still: 'Believe the Irish MPs will accept my plan.'[31] But as the talks dragged on, the prospects of compromise faded. Many Irish Nationalists were opposed even to a temporary exclusion and Conservatives were adamant against the ultimate inclusion of any Ulster counties, even if long delayed, into Southern Ireland. In spite of these objections the government nevertheless placed the new exclusion plan before the House of Commons on 9 March in the form of a White Paper. But Conservatives, under the leadership of Carson, rejected the plan outright. Thereafter a series of attempts to reconcile differences were attempted, but these, too, ended in failure.

Especially alarming throughout the early weeks of 1914 were the police reports from Ulster. Guns and ammunition smuggled into the province from Britain and elsewhere continued unabated. As the evidence of illegal activity mounted, the government had no choice but to take some action as a precaution against any overt military operations on the part of Ulstermen. On 11 March 1914, two days after the Conservative rejection of the exclusion plan, the Cabinet decided to protect the military arms depots in Ulster from any unwarranted seizure. J.E.B. Seely, Secretary for War, gave instructions to this effect to Lieutenant-General Sir Arthur Paget, Commander-in-Chief of the army in Ireland. At the same time, Churchill (in his capacity as First Lord of the Admiralty) ordered a battle squadron of the Royal Navy dispatched from Gibraltar to the naval station at Lamlash on the Isle of Arran off the coast of Scotland, only 70 miles from Belfast across the North Channel. Meanwhile, Paget in Dublin, in attempting to carry out his orders, prefaced his instructions to his commanders with alarmist comments on the potential violence they may encounter in leading their men to assigned posts in Ulster. Additionally, he stated that any who refused orders to march north would be dismissed. Moreover he declared that any officers who felt divided loyalties and were unable to carry out their mission to Ulster should resign. As a result, some 58 officers of Brigadier-General Hubert Gough's Third Cavalry Brigade stationed at the Curragh Barracks, southwest of Dublin, resigned their commissions. It transpired that Seely's orders to Paget had been misinterpreted and Paget's own instructions to his subordinates had been garbled. The upshot of this episode was that the government appeared to be both secretive and incompetent. It also revealed the underlying pro-Ulster sentiment among many regular army officers. Asquith's countermanding of Churchill's naval manoeuvre merely added to the general confusion and suspicion of the government's motives. Were they planning a coup against the Ulster anti-Home Rule movement?[32]

A few weeks later, the government's reputation was further damaged. On the night of 24–25 April, a cargo of some 30,000 rifles along with ammunition purchased in Germany was off-loaded from the coal-boat *Clydevalley* at Larne, County Antrim, north of Belfast.[33] Under cover of darkness, and with the aid of the Ulster Volunteer Force, the weapons were carried away by squadrons of motor cars to various hide-outs in the province. It had been an impressive feat of organization, including transshipment at sea and outfoxing customs officials. The UVF had sent an unmistakable warning to London – a warning that could be backed by a fully armed and motivated military force.[34] This series of events caused even Lloyd George to lose confidence in the possibility of a peaceful solution. 'In the thick of the Irish crisis', he wrote William in July. After a conference with Bonar Law, Lloyd George discovered that he, too, was not optimistic. 'He is hopeless of peace', Lloyd George confided to his brother.[35]

Because there was no effective government response in the weeks that followed the Larne demonstration, a reaction in Southern Ireland was inevitable. It took the form of a mimetic action. The Irish National Volunteers staged its own gunrunning on 26 July at Howth, north of Dublin. Carried out brazenly in daylight, its purpose may have been to draw public attention to the concurrent right of Irish Nationalists, no less than Ulster, to arm in self-defence.[36] If it had been designed as a provocative act, the Howth plot was successful: it turned deadly when a Dublin riot against British troops searching for the contraband weapons resulted in three rioters killed and 38 others wounded. The Irish Nationalists made political capital of the disparate response of the Liberal government between Ulster and the south: Asquith appeared to be treating Southern Ireland more harshly than Ulster. At the very least, Asquith seemed dangerously slow in responding to an accelerating crisis.

There were two immediate consequences of the rival gunrunning episodes. First was military: the prospect of serious clashes between the two antagonistic armed forces now seemed imminent. The second was political: Irish Nationalists in Parliament withdrew their support for the Amending Bill, which would have legislated the policy of exclusion. This was devastating to the government's Home Rule plan. The public posture of the two hostile sides in Ireland was now complemented by a heightened contentiousness between the Conservative opposition and the Liberal government in London. In an attempt to overcome the impasse, a conference called by the King gathered at Buckingham Palace from 21–24 July. Asquith and Lloyd George represented the government side with Lansdowne and Bonar Law for the opposition. Redmond and Dillon sat for the Irish Nationalists and Carson and Craig for Ulster. Expectations were low. Bonar Law thought there was very little chance of any agreement. Asquith himself, while advocating the conference, seems to have had little illusions, hoping that it would at least delay potentially more dangerous actions from either side in Ireland.[37] Not surprisingly, the conference foundered, ostensibly over the issue of which counties could be recognized as having the right of self-exclusion.[38]

In the meantime, Cabinet divisions threatened the government's unity at this critical juncture over another matter. This ministerial conflict also brought into high relief a growing separation between Lloyd George and Churchill which almost led to an open break between the erstwhile political allies. The issue between them was naval expenditures. The general tendency of the Liberal government in its early years was to hold down such expenditures – which indeed fell three years running from 1906 by about 15 per cent when compared to the Conservative government's 1904–5 expenditure. This was consonant not only with the Gladstonian tradition of peace and retrenchment, but was supremely important to the radical wing of the

Liberal Party who were staunch in their pacifist beliefs and opposition to military expense.[39]

Outside pressures, however, began to impinge upon the government's naval policy. Most significant was the rise of Germany as a clear threat to British naval dominance. In the quarter century following unification in 1871, Germany witnessed remarkable progress. Its population rose from 41 million to more than 62 million. Income per capita showed a similar advance. Urban growth and industrial progress added to Germany's economic power. Not far behind was its political and economic expansion abroad: it was becoming imperially minded. Germany's *Weltmach* had a natural corollary – a navy commensurate with its ambitions.[40] The German Navy Acts of 1898 and 1900 were designed to fulfil those ambitions. Clearly, Germany aspired, if not to close the gap entirely with the Royal Navy, to become at least a respectable second.

In 1906, under the leadership of Admiral Sir John Fisher, First Sea Lord, the Royal Navy took a calculated risk to maintain its naval dominance. In that year, the HMS *Dreadnought* was launched, the first of a new line of capital ships – larger, faster, and more heavily armed than any previous British battleship, and so superior in firepower and design that it rendered earlier ships in its class obsolete. But Germany quickly began to construct its own naval vessels based upon the *Dreadnought*: they could now compete with Britain on nearly equal terms in building comparable capital ships. When the German naval plans became public knowledge, a clamour from the Conservative Party for additional construction, seconded by the Conservative press, put the Liberal government on the defensive. The Sea Lords, who actively lobbied for an increase in forthcoming naval estimates, soon joined Conservative demands for additional naval revenues.[41]

The outcry placed Lloyd George particularly in an uncomfortable position. As Cabinet minister at the Board of Trade under Campbell-Bannerman in the early years of the government, he had sought to restrain the growth of naval expenditures. He had in fact opposed the *Dreadnought* on the grounds of expense.[42] When he became Chancellor of the Exchequer in April 1908, he had an additional reason to oppose untoward increases in either military or naval expenses: these could jeopardize a domestically oriented budget. Money spent on military matters meant less would be available for social services such as old age pensions and a national insurance system. Therefore, Lloyd George tried to deflect German naval acceleration in order to reduce the likelihood of an echoing British response. He had, as we have seen, attempted direct contacts with the German government, both in discussions with the German ambassador in London, Count Metternich, and with officials in Germany during his expedition to explore the German insurance scheme in 1908. Unhappily, he had no success in striking a responsive chord: at home, too, his personal diplomacy was not well received.[43]

By the end of 1908 Germany was clearly determined to close the gap on British dreadnought construction by an accelerated building schedule: they laid down nine dreadnoughts to Britain's ten. If Britain continued at that pace of construction and the Germans maintained theirs, the German navy would achieve near parity with the

Royal Navy dreadnoughts by 1912. To the naval establishment, there was no other option but to match and then exceed the German production of dreadnoughts. The Sea Lords, therefore, operating through Reginald McKenna (then First Lord of the Admiralty) requested a new shipbuilding programme of six dreadnoughts. This would mean an increase of £3 million in the next year's budget. Early in 1909, a number of contentious Cabinet meetings attempted to thrash out a decision. As the debates continued, however, the Admiralty upped the ante, claiming that six dreadnoughts were insufficient: only eight would do.

Lloyd George and Churchill led the attack against the naval enthusiasts during these months of public debate. Churchill, then President of the Board of Trade, gave a series of speeches in which he denounced the 'windy agitations of ignorant ... and excited hotheads' who were intent upon 'wasting the public money upon armaments'. Churchill claimed these notions were 'a part of a showy, sensational, aggressive and Jingo policy'.[44] Lloyd George agreed. In a letter to Churchill, he criticized 'McKenna's fatuous estimates', and in another he told Churchill that he believed 'the Admirals are procuring false information to frighten us'.[45] At one point during Cabinet discussion of the naval estimates, both Churchill and Lloyd George threatened resignation. Behind the two men stood the strong cadre of radical Liberal MPs, supported by the radical press, who were dead against an enhanced naval programme. In a letter to Asquith in early February 1909, Lloyd George reminded the Prime Minister of the pledges they had made to reduce the expenditure on armaments built up by the previous Conservative government. If these pledges were not honoured, he warned, scores of their most loyal supporters in the House of Commons would become disenchanted with the government. Equally serious would be the loss of support of 'millions of earnest Liberals' in the countryside.[46]

But Lloyd George was not unmindful of the German threat and was willing to compromise to a degree. Rather than responding to the ' very crude & ill-considered' Admiralty demands, Lloyd George proposed 'a steady programme' to replace the scatter shot 'jumpiness' so characteristic of naval budgets.[47] A measured approach to naval finances would, he believed, avoid such 'extravagant and ill-digested' estimates that presently lay before the Cabinet. Asquith's reply to Lloyd George's 'important' letter agreed that a more businesslike and yet flexible approach would be best. He, like Lloyd George, favoured a naval programme 'which, while adequately securing our naval predominance at any given moment, would be elastic, adaptable to circumstances ... and not ... a "shot", or guess, more or less in the dark'.[48] He thus moved toward the acceptance of at least some increase in the naval estimates. More significantly, he agreed to an immediate production of four dreadnoughts with a possibility in the future of laying down four more. The Cabinet accepted this on 24 February 1909.[49] Two months later, during his presentation of his great reformist budget to the House of Commons, Lloyd George brought forward the agreed upon naval expenditure. In justifying the expense, he declared that: 'whatever the cost, no great country can afford to shirk its responsibilities for the defence of its coasts against every possible invader'.[50] Thus Lloyd George and other Liberal 'realists' in the Cabinet exerted sufficient pressure upon reluctant radicals to bring them aboard the new programme for an enhanced navy.[51]

But the naval issue did not die quietly and continued to be a divisive issue within the Cabinet. As we have seen in Chapter 7, Lloyd George's belief that a strong navy was essential to the maintenance of the Empire and the protection of trade was again fully revealed in his firm attitude to the German threat to Morocco in 1911. For Churchill too, Morocco had been a watershed. Upon the revelations of Admiralty slackness at the important August CID meeting that followed Morocco, Churchill replaced McKenna as First Lord of the Admiralty. He was thereafter, as one of his biographers has observed, 'a changed man'.[52] Indeed, immediately upon his appointment, Churchill set about mastering all aspects of naval administration and policy. Touring shipyards, witnessing gunnery practice, viewing the fleet and spending considerable time at sea, he sought information at every level.[53] He was especially taken with the Admiralty yacht *Enchantress*, which became a floating salon for the First Lord when he frequently invited official guests and on which he also entertained his extensive circle of friends.[54] As an ex-lieutenant of Hussars and a close student of military history, Churchill was now in his element.

When Churchill, in his new role as navy advocate, enthusiastically began an extensive programme of naval reforms, with all its attendant expenses, there was an inevitable clash with Lloyd George, a more moderate navalist and keeper of the Treasury purse. The conflict began in earnest during the preparations for the 1912–13 budget. Churchill pressed strongly both in Cabinet and Parliament for a large increase in naval estimates. This was not an easy task, given the Liberal Party's traditional irenic posture towards world affairs. Indeed, Churchill's naval plans found greater support from the Conservatives than from his own colleagues. To counter his Liberal opposition, Churchill proposed a naval holiday to Germany (and to all nations) as a form of arms reduction.[55] When Germany rejected the proposal, he was free to go full steam ahead on his naval expenditures.

Potential opposition in the Cabinet remained, however, especially with Lloyd George. As Chancellor of the Exchequer, Lloyd George had to balance the competing claims of various Cabinet members for revenue: an enhanced naval programme could be the most expensive of any. Discussions – often heated – continued intermittently during Cabinet meetings from mid-1912 into 1913. Lloyd George was clearly exasperated. He fully realized the need for a strong navy, but as he complained to his brother, Winston had become 'Navy mad'. As usual, Winston regarded 'the office which he presides over for the time being as the pivot upon which the Universe attends'.[56] The two friends continued quarrelling, perhaps fuelled in part by personal rivalry; but there were genuine differences of opinions on matters of state. There is some indication that to relieve the impasse, Lloyd George and Churchill struck a personal bargain some time in 1912. In return for Churchill's support for his land policy, Lloyd George would give more money for the navy.[57]

As the debate over the naval estimates lengthened, however, Churchill's estimates continued to rise. In his second presentation to the House of Commons as First Lord in March 1913, he proposed five new dreadnoughts, eight light cruisers, 16 destroyers, and an unspecified number of submarines. The total exceeded £46 million, an increase of more than £1 million over the previous year. In the months following, Churchill suggested further additions to the naval budget, rumoured to be as high as six million pounds. To Lloyd George, this upended his bargain with Churchill. Relations between the two once again became strained as the debate wore on during the winter of 1913–4.[58] Indeed, Lloyd George complained to Riddell in mid-December 1913 that in spite of his bargain with Churchill over expenditures, Churchill had 'not kept' his end of the bargain: he had become 'extravagant ... with other people's money'.[59] A few days later, Lloyd George – using Riddell as a conduit – urged the diarist to advise Churchill 'to fall in with the views of the Cabinet'.[60]

Matters continued to deteriorate throughout the following month. Churchill maintained that his naval estimates had been prepared 'with the strictest economy'.[61] But Lloyd George held firm, intimating to Riddell he would resign unless Churchill reigned in his naval estimates.[62] Lloyd George's private comments to C.P. Scott of the *Manchester Guardian* substantiate this line of his thinking. In late January 1914, he wrote Scott that he was considering resignation – a serious act, he emphasized in his letter, because it would 'wreck the Government, the Liberal Party & the prospect of carrying Liberal measures for 10 years to come'.[63] By early February 1914, however, the dispute was suddenly settled, largely through the intervention of Asquith, who supported the First Lord. Churchill agreed to a slight reduction in the estimates and he also reluctantly agreed in advance to a reduction in naval expenditures for 1915–16; but he gained another two dreadnoughts and succeeded in his demands for an enhanced budgetary share for the navy in 1914–5.

To preserve his domestic priorities in the budget and to meet the new naval estimates, Lloyd George insisted that taxes must be raised. This had already emerged as a likely possibility as early as November 1913 when planning for the 1914 budget had begun during a working dinner at 11 Downing Street.[64] In addition to Lloyd George, also present were Asquith, Grey, Crewe and Haldane. Both financial and political issues were discussed. It was at this meeting that Lloyd George announced a potential budget shortfall of £3 million if Churchill's naval estimates went through and if the Board of Education received the £2 million it had requested. Once Churchill's estimates had been added to the normal annual budgetary increase, Lloyd George found it necessary to request nearly £10 million in new revenue.

For the first time since the 1909 People's Budget, therefore, Lloyd George proposed higher taxes. The 1914 budget retained the 9d. tax in the pound for earned income under £1,000, but taxes thereafter gradually rose to 1s. 4d. for earned incomes over £2,500. The upper rate on unearned incomes was also to be 1s. 4d. in the pound. The previous supertax, beginning at an income of £5,000, was now lowered to £3,000 and a higher rate of taxation was imposed. Inheritance taxes were also increased. Some new taxes affected the lower income communities, such as new taxes on tobacco and spirits, but primarily this was a budget tilted against higher incomes even more than the 1909 budget had been. In addition to an increase to income taxes, Lloyd George extended the landed tax clauses enacted in 1909. Most interestingly, he proposed urban site value rating in an attempt to tap the profits of undertaxed land in urban settings.[65] Lloyd George also proposed direct government grants for local authorities to provide better housing and improved facilities for education, poor relief and asylums.

Because the machinery for the new site rating system had not yet been legislated, Lloyd George's budget provided temporary grants to local authorities. But this was conditional on the passage (as yet not assured) of the legislation to install the permanent site rating and grant system. Thus there was a general sense of puzzlement, even from those Liberals who approved the extension of social reform in the proposed budget, about the complex nature of the intended reforms. Indeed, one might well ask why Lloyd George pushed forward so rapidly with a somewhat muddled and crowded budget, even to the extent of asking for money to fund a system not yet in place. This may have been due to the fact that the budget had been rushed to completion without sufficient care to examine its finer points. This was likely the result of major distractions. Preoccupations over the naval estimates and the continuing unravelling of the Ulster resistance to Home Rule lost valuable time for the government. This would be especially true of Lloyd George, who was deeply involved in both issues.

In any case, Lloyd George's presentation of the budget before the House of Commons on 4 May 1914 has been universally condemned. We would expect opposition from such Conservative stalwarts as Balcarres, who lamented the fact that the Liberal government seemed to think that 'rich people are inherently vicious and should be taxed out of existence'.[66] Robert Sanders, then a junior opposition whip, was more critical of the speech, terming it 'singularly ineffective' and 'impossible at all' to understand the proposals on local taxation.[67] Even among Liberals – especially those who remembered fondly the Gladstonian precepts of low taxation and limited government – there was a sense of alarm. Shortly after the budget presentation, a group of wealthy old school Liberal backbenchers met both Asquith and Lloyd George to complain about the budget.[68] Among Lloyd George's staunchest supporters, critical voices were also raised. George Riddell confided to his diary that the budget was 'an ill-digested production'.[69] Asquith himself reported that the budget debate 'collapsed' as Lloyd George landed the House in a 'morass of obscurity'.[70] Historians have been equally unkind. Mallet and George, in what may be an understatement, wrote that Lloyd George's complicated budget 'coupled with a noticeable lack of clarity in the budget speech, prevented any immediate effective criticism, which, however, was not lacking in the subsequent debates'.[71] Murray has condemned the budget as 'an administrative nightmare' and Lloyd George's nearly three-hour speech as 'a disaster'.[72] Morgan calls Lloyd George's performance 'a parliamentary fiasco'.[73] Gilbert agrees, labelling his budget address, delivered in an almost inaudible monotone, as 'a new pinnacle of ineptitude' for Lloyd George.[74]

Matters were further complicated by the looming legislative deadline of the 5 August recess. There was insufficient time for a thorough debate of the budget due to a mystifying miscalculation concerning the legislative timetable. To meet this difficulty, Lloyd George redrafted the budget, but in such a way as to exacerbate the problem by merging incompatible subjects. For example, the local authority grants became a part of the finance bill. Thus the budget could be criticized not only for raising more money than it could spend, but also it could be ruled out of order.[75] As criticism rose on both sides of the aisle, Asquith mused – not entirely tongue in cheek – that 'the rational course is to drop the whole thing' with the exception of certain essential expenditures, such as the Royal Navy. But – he admitted – to do so 'would be very nauseous & even humiliating to Ll. G'.[76] The Cabinet did, however, scrap parts of the budget, including the local authority grants. This was announced to the House of Commons on 22 June 1914, enabling the government to reduce slightly some proposed taxes.

Cobbling together the budget in the face of heavy criticism and finally devising some sense of closure on financial issues did not, however, restore confidence in the government.[77] Nor did it alleviate the dangerous conditions in Ireland. The stalled Home Rule Bill had only intensified the uncompromising attitudes in both Ireland and Britain. Rising tensions over Ulster in particular had led, as we have noted, to a high level conference, chaired by the Speaker to insure impartiality, at Buckingham Palace in late July 1914. As we have noted, too, the conference failed. When the Cabinet met on the final day of the Conference (24 July) in a post mortem, the Foreign Secretary Lord Grey raised an even more sobering topic just as the Cabinet was about to adjourn. Grey reported that a potentially serious development in the Balkans was nearing a crisis. Austria had just issued a 48-hour ultimatum to Serbia over the assassination a month earlier on Serbian soil of the Archduke Franz Ferdinand, heir to the throne of Austria. The diplomatic standoff between Serbia and Austria-Hungary now seemed certain to escalate. There was even the prospect of a wider war, Grey reported, with the additional danger that other powers might intervene. Grey's prophecy was quickly confirmed. Only 11 days later, Britain declared war on Germany.

10

A NIGHTMARE WORLD

The outbreak of World War I has drawn the attention of some of the best historical writing, both in quality and quantity. This cannot be entered into detail here. For our purposes, the emphasis must lie in the decision of Britain to intervene in the rapidly developing series of diplomatic and military events on the European continent during the late summer of 1914, especially the role of Germany in those events.[1] In retrospect, it can be seen that in the years prior to 1914 British and German rivalry had intensified. As we have already noted, Germany was undergoing a vigorous economic development – not unlike Britain a century earlier. But this had come at a notable social cost. Rapid industrialization had produced a political crisis, threatening an outdated constitutional structure led by a quasi-absolutist monarchy and a privileged elite.[2] In more specific terms, the challenges of an emerging social democracy, industrial unionism and Liberal notions of a broadly based suffrage encountered stiff resistance from King Wilhelm II and his closest advisors, who were eager to pursue expansionist dreams and increased armaments without recourse to a national debate. Ignoring any pretence at securing popular support, ruling circles relied upon selective and reliable engines of public opinion, such as nationalist organizations which energetically campaigned for a greater Germany. These groups were not unfavourable to a pre-emptive war in order to distract the population from growing social divisions. The same could be said of those German industries and businesses connected to a vigorous naval armaments progamme such as shipyards, the iron industry and bankers who provided loans needed by the government to finance construction. A 'glamorous' naval policy[3] could also help tamp down divisive trends by instilling a national pride in the navy and, in a broader sense, promote greater patriotism among all Germans. A strong navy could also be used when necessary as a bludgeon for 'diplomatic bullying'.[4]

No less important in understanding the mood of Wilhelmine Germany was its 'pathological fear' of encirclement.[5] Revanchist France had been eager for decades to right the wrongs of the Franco-Prussian War. Nor could Germany ignore events to the East and the growing military strength of Russia since 1905. After that year, when Japan had won surprised attention from the West with its crushing defeat of the Russian Navy in the Russo-Japanese War, Russia had expanded both its navy and its army significantly. Especially unsettling to the Germans was Russia's construction of new strategic railways up to the German frontier.[6] The British entente with France and Russia (the latter to protect Britain's Asian interests) gave additional cause for discomfort among policy makers in Germany. Germany's own alliance with Austria-Hungary, a declining power locked into adjacent Balkan power struggles, was less a source of strength than a diplomatic weakness. All in all, the prospect of a short but decisive war by striking preemptively against France and then turning East to teach Russia a lesson gained appeal among the small group of men who made policy in Germany.

Britain, too, was undergoing a series of upheavals in the pre-war years – though primarily in the domestic sphere. The struggle over women's suffrage; strikes and union militancy; contentious divisions between political parties; and uncompromising attitudes on Irish Home Rule all come to mind. Like Germany, Britain was also intensely nationalistic, experiencing a significant surge of imperial sentiment during the late Victorian and Edwardian eras. This was hardly surprising given Britain's role in global affairs. As MacKenzie has convincingly argued, there was a growing popularity of the armed forces and an exalted pride, especially in the navy. The tales of manly heroes and their brave actions around the globe was pervasive in popular literature, theatre and the newspaper press. An active patriotism and a feeling of imperial pride were thus inculcated in the population at large.[7]

British nationalism in the Edwardian era should be set within the broader debate on what G.R. Searle has termed 'the Edwardian obsession' with standards of national efficiency, the inadequacies of which had been revealed during the Boer War.[8] The humiliating military defeats in the early stages of that war dealt a blow to the complacency of British national superiority. But the lesson drawn was not the danger of imperial overextension; rather, Britain was determined to reshape society in order to carry out its global imperial project more effectively. How to improve the health and physical fitness of its citizens for service in any future war became a primary topic for politicians and social theorists alike. By raising standards of public health and making education compulsory, young men would become fit for military service. Army reforms would emphasize the military canons of discipline and drill. Some advocates, in a break from traditional military thinking, believed in a larger British army and supported national conscription. Moreover, such actions could also have an added advantage in the civilian work force. By increasing discipline and order, workers would become more efficient and thus more productive. Curiously enough, given their rivalry, Britain looked to Germany as an examplar of the role of the State in promoting national efficiency through educational reforms, the advancement of science and technology and, not least, the professionalization of its military. Thus, a paradoxical mood grew in Britain: an admiration for German national organization existed side by side with a deeply rooted Germanophobia.[9]

Given these underlying causes of rivalry, only a flashpoint was necessary to spark an armed conflict. To the German leadership, the assassination of the Austrian Archduke Franz Ferdinand in Sarajevo on 28 June 1914 was not only a direct threat to Germany but it also provided a unique opportunity. If Slav intransigence against

Austria continued, a weakened Austria itself could be at risk, raising the spectre of disorder along yet another of Germany's frontiers. Support from Germany could encourage Austria towards a short and decisive war against the Serbs, thus removing their threat to Austrian stability before Russia could act. Moving quickly with an overwhelming force could keep military action localized and prevent a wider war. That at least was the hope. But events moved more rapidly than Germany had planned. On the day of Austria's declaration of war against Serbia, 28 July, Russia began a partial mobilization of its Western military districts. This was followed two days later by Russia's general mobilization. Germany claimed that Russia, an ally of France, was actively preparing for war. The prospect of a two-front war for Germany activated military plans already in place. France was to be attacked in force while smaller German detachments held the eastern front. Once France was quickly defeated, entrained troops would be dispatched to the Russian front where the full force of battle-tested German troops would carry the day.

In the meantime, what of Britain's reaction? From 24 July to 4 August the Cabinet met ten times. Their response to the rapidly unfolding European drama has been thoroughly analyzed. Many historians have been critical of the Cabinet's delay and hesitancy in reaching a decision. Colin Nicolson condemns the Cabinet's 'tentative attitude' and 'extraordinary procrastination'.[10] Williamson agrees, criticizing the Cabinet's 'continuing dalliance' throughout the crisis.[11] Historians have tended to blame above all the actions and policies of the Foreign Secretary, Earl Grey, during the crisis. Nicolson charges that Grey's ambiguous statements confused friend and foe alike.[12] Williamson condemns Grey's 'failure of perception' that inhibited Britain from taking a more active role for peace during the earliest stages of the crisis.[13] Most critical of all is Keith Wilson's judgement: Grey was secretive, deceptive, rigid and misled the public and Parliament.[14] Steiner treads a middle ground. She claims that Grey realized the gravity of the Austro-Serbian crisis from the start and worked hard to avert any adverse impact upon the Balkans or upon Austria. But she also notes that Grey seemed detached and unwilling either to solicit or follow the advice of his professional staff at the Foreign Office. More importantly, writes Steiner, Grey simply 'followed the wrong course' during the July crisis.[15]

Grey, however, has his defenders. Michael Fry, for example, thinks that Grey had intentionally attempted to devise 'an efficacious uncertainty' to keep the contending powers guessing about Britain's role: the longer the delay, the less chance for war.[16] Stephen J. Valone is sympathetic to Grey's careful diplomacy, supporting his determination to maintain primarily British interests against a rapidly deteriorating European rush towards war.[17] In his biography of Grey, Keith Robbins also staunchly defends the Foreign Minister, praising his 'tactically adroit' methods in his attempts to localize the pre-war conflicts. Robbins additionally praises Grey's ability to manage the 'delicate balance of opinion' as the Cabinet struggled to come to a decision on whether or not to wage war.[18] Asquith has fared somewhat better at the hands of historians, although he has also been charged with being dilatory in managing the Cabinet on the eve of war. His 'wait and see' policy had often exasperated some; but to others, it was a sign of a careful and judicious mind. Churchill, on the other hand, was imperious and eager for action from the first. As he confessed in a letter to his wife, with a surprising touch of self-knowledge: 'Everything tends towards catastrophe & collapse. I am interested, geared up & happy. Is it not horrible to be built like that?'[19]

It is certainly true that the ministry's response to the rising tensions on the Continent was initially tardy. Converging problems in Ireland distracted the Cabinet's attention.[20] Not until 29 July did the Cabinet become fully engaged with the prospect of war between Austria and Serbia. As Herbert Samuel put it in a letter to his wife that day: 'We nineteen men round the table at Downing St may soon have to face the most momentous problem men can face.'[21] By then, Austria had already moved swiftly and decisively by issuing its punitive ultimatum to Serbia, breaking diplomatic relations with that country, and mobilizing its army.

The Cabinet meeting on the morning of 29 July heard Grey's condemnation of Austria's conduct as 'brutal recklessness'.[22] But Grey also pledged to continue his efforts at mediation and the policy of a 'free hand' toward the continental powers. This could best be promoted, he believed, by Britain's role as a mediator between the two power blocs – Austria-Hungary and Germany on the one hand, and France and Russia on the other. However, as Asquith explained it to Venetia Stanley, there were pressures on Britain and complaints from each of the opposing power blocs. Germany pressed for a declaration of neutrality, while Russia and France insisted on a pledge of support from Britain.[23] Some attention at the Cabinet meeting was also given to the question of Belgium, with whom Britain and other powers had a treaty guaranteeing that country's neutrality. An equally important issue was whether or not Britain should respond favourably to any request from France for support. The Cabinet, 'from our selfish point of view' (as Pease put it), decided that they must 'do the best' for British interests.[24] In the afternoon of 29 July, Grey spoke to both the German and French ambassadors in London, emphasizing that whatever actions Britain might take would indeed be solidly based upon British interests. In spite of its public neutralist posture, however, the ministry on that same day initiated military procedures in the event of diplomatic failure. The Cabinet directed the Army and Navy departments to put themselves in readiness for the 'precautionary period' which precedes a possible outbreak of hostilities. Additionally, on the evening of 29 July, the First Fleet left Portland, passing through the Straits of Dover under cover of darkness with lights extinguished, arriving at Scapa Flow, its preliminary war station, on the morning of 30 July. At the same time, the Second Fleet began assembling at Portland.[25]

On 30 July, no Cabinet was held, but Asquith reported to Venetia that the European situation was 'at least one degree worse than it was yesterday'.[26] He wrote additionally that the contending powers continued to press for some action from Britain. The next Cabinet meeting on 31 July reaffirmed Britain's reluctance to support France outright.[27] This was satisfactory to the neutralists or 'waverers' who were still in command of the Cabinet.[28] Waverers at this time included Morley, John Burns, Lewis Harcourt, Lord Beauchamp, Sir John Simon, Herbert Samuel, J.A. Pease, Walter Runciman, T. McKinnon Wood and Lloyd George. Hard-liners, apart from Grey, were Churchill, Asquith, Haldane, Birrell, Lord Crewe, McKenna and Masterman.

On 1 August, the Cabinet also sanctioned Grey's message of warning to the German ambassador against any violation of Belgian neutrality. The defeat and occupation of Belgium would give Germany access to the Channel, an action completely unacceptable to Britain. That evening, London learned that Germany had declared war on Russia. Early the next morning, 2 August, Churchill, with Asquith's approval, ordered full naval mobilization. Later that morning, news arrived that German troops had entered Luxembourg and would soon – no one doubted – be entering Belgium.

At 11:00 a.m. on 2 August, the Cabinet convened for what proved a difficult meeting. Grey was by now ready for tougher measures. He declared that since the French had been relying upon the entente to the extent that they had kept their northern coast undefended, the Cabinet must act to prevent a possible German naval attack on France's vulnerable shores. The Cabinet therefore authorized the British fleet to intercept the German navy should it enter the North Sea or the Channel. As for Belgium, again no decision was made, although Grey told the Cabinet that in his view the British obligation to Belgian neutrality was 'binding'.[29] As the discussion went forward, the meeting became contentious. Grey 'became more pro-war', threatening resignation if the Cabinet refused to support Belgian neutrality.[30] Conversely, Morley threatened resignation if Britain went to war. The Cabinet was in danger of an irreconcilable division.[31] Samuel thought there was a danger that a domestic political crisis was about to be 'super-imposed on the international and financial crises' because 'Grey expressed a view which was unacceptable to most of us'.[32]

Although the meeting ended in some disarray, the waverers had ceded an important point. They had agreed that if the German navy moved against France, it would trigger a British response. In short, the Cabinet had agreed upon a *casus belli*. Once such a principle had been established (German naval aggression against France), it was possible to extend that principle to another case (German military aggression against Belgium). There was, of course, an important difference between the two. In the first, only naval action was required; but in the second, it was clearly understood that protecting Belgian neutrality would inevitably mean the dispatch of a British expeditionary force to the continent – a far greater commitment than a purely naval response.

After the stormy morning Cabinet meeting of 2 August, the evening session went more cordially. Grey reported his conversation with Cambon, which had taken place in the interim between the two Cabinet meetings. The French ambassador heard the welcome news of British naval support for France against a hostile German fleet in the Channel and the North Sea. Grey, however, indicated that this decision was subject to parliamentary approval. Furthermore, Grey turned down Cambon's request for two brigades of British troops. The Cabinet still hesitated in reaching a firm decision on the Belgian issue. Nevertheless, two waverers, Samuel and Walter Runciman, President of the Board of Trade, indicated that they were willing to consider the violation as a provocation and a potential *casus belli*.[33] At the Cabinet meeting on the following morning, 3 August, three other waverers – seeing the drift of things – submitted their resignations: Sir John Simon, the Attorney General; Lord Beauchamp, First Commissioner of Works; and John Morley, Lord President of the Council. John Burns, President of the Board of Trade, had already resigned. (Later, Simon and Beauchamp retracted, leaving only Burns and Morley out of the Cabinet.)

In the meantime, opinions from outside the Cabinet continued to press forward. As the crisis had developed, the Conservative opposition had been kept up to date on a daily basis by Grey's communications to Bonar Law. Sir Henry Wilson, Director of Military Operations, had also been frequently briefed. However, there was a concern among some Conservatives and Wilson as well that the Cabinet was behindhand in its deliberations. When Cambon, the French ambassador, informed the Conservatives that the Liberal Ministry was reluctant to support France openly, Conservatives were stirred to action, joining hands with Wilson who thought that the Ministry was 'doing nothing'.[34] The result was a brief letter from Bonar Law to Asquith on 2 August urging the government to uphold the honour of France and Russia and pledging 'unhesitating support' toward that end. This letter was read to the Cabinet at the morning meeting on 2 August. The following morning, 3 August, Bonar Law and Lord Lansdowne met with Asquith to reinforce their message.[35] They 'laid great stress upon Belgian neutrality', as Asquith reported to Venetia.[36] Asquith was noncommittal and fended off any suggestions for an immediate declaration of war against Germany. At that time, he was still busily working for unity within the Cabinet – a matter of delicate negotiation and timing – and would not be rushed precipitously into war. Furthermore, he knew by then through the Foreign Office that Germany had issued an ultimatum to the Belgians. This information brought the remaining neutralists into the growing Cabinet inclination for action against Germany. But at this time, the Cabinet had moved only as far as accepting a role of the British navy on the outbreak of war: an expeditionary force to France had not yet been sanctioned. Even so, the tide of opinion for neutrality had ebbed.

The Cabinet was now on its way to a unified decision. The time had come for the government to inform the House of Commons of its deliberations. On the afternoon of 3 August, Grey gave what most historians believe to be have been the speech of his life.[37] He began by stressing the government's earnest desire to preserve peace. But, he observed sorrowfully, it had not been possible to achieve this. Concerned to find precedents for Britain's actions in the present state of affairs, Grey reviewed the first and second Moroccan crises. As a result of those disputes between France and Germany, he reminded the House, military and naval conversations had begun between France and Britain. These conversations, Grey took pains to point out, did not require either country to assist the other in the event of an unprovoked attack by a third power. Thus, even now, on the eve of a war, the government remained 'perfectly free' from any commitment to intervene and, Grey added, '*a fortiori*, the House of Commons remains perfectly free'.[38] Having assured the House that there was no secret treaty or public responsibility to aid France at a time of its present need, Grey proceeded to outline the 'long-standing friendship' with France and what obligations may flow from that friendship.[39] Should an aggressor attempt to take advantage of the 'absolutely undefended' coasts of France by sailing down the English Channel, Britain could scarcely stand aside 'looking on dispassionately, doing nothing!'[40] Grey then told the House that the Cabinet had informed the French ambassador that the British fleet would protect French coasts should conditions make it necessary.

There was, Grey stated, 'a more serious consideration' – the preservation of the neutrality of Belgium. Only a few days previously, Grey informed the House, he had telegraphed both the French and German governments asking them if they were prepared to respect the neutrality of Belgium: France responded positively; Germany had declined. Indeed, that very day, Grey continued, he had received information that Germany had offered friendly relations with Belgium, but only on condition of their facilitating the passage of German troops through that country. It was obviously an ultimatum that the Belgians refused. 'We have great and vital interests' in Belgium, Grey declared.[41] If Belgium fell, so would other small states. Holland and Denmark would be next. Should this happen, there would be opposite Britain on the Continent 'the unmeasured aggrandizement' of a powerful country.[42] The balance of power then existing in Europe would be jeopardized. There was but one option left to keep out of the impending war – to issue immediately a declaration of unconditional neutrality. But Grey advised against that course because Britain had now 'made the commitment to France'.[43] There was also the consideration of Belgium and Britain's responsibilities to the Treaty of 1839, which guaranteed that country's neutrality. The dangers of not acting were greater than those that would accompany Britain if she did not take a stand on these issues that he brought before the House. After Grey had finished his speech and the cheers had died down, he went to the Foreign Office. There he looked out the window to see the lamps being lit in St James's Park as the summer's light began to fade. Only then did he proclaim his famous elegy: 'The lamps are going out all over Europe: we shall not see them lit again in our life-time.'[44] The following day, he telegraphed an ultimatum to Berlin, protesting the invasion into Belgium and requesting a reply. None came. At 11:00 that evening, Britain was at war with Germany.

Discussions on peace or war had been led by three prominent Cabinet members: Asquith presiding over the meetings; Grey keeping the diplomatic lines open and informing the Cabinet of each new development; and Churchill speaking readily for war. The role of Lloyd George throughout these momentous discussions is more obscure.[45] As the leader of parliamentary radicals, Lloyd George had the credentials to play a constructive role in maintaining peace. At least half the Cabinet were radicals of various hues, though they were all united by a neutralist sentiment. If they held firm under Lloyd George's leadership, they could perhaps prevent Britain from an active role in any war. But Lloyd George had also, as will be remembered, reacted sharply against German ambitions over Agadir in 1911. Did the Agadir spirit linger on in the Chancellor of the Exchequer? Lloyd George's behaviour early on suggests that it did. Hobhouse records that at first 'LG was very strongly anti-German'; but when it became clear that the Liberal papers were anti-war, 'he veered round and became peaceful'.[46] His Francophone secretary, Frances Stevenson, confessed to being 'desperately unhappy' that Lloyd George seemed at one point to be against supporting France in its hour of need.[47] Grigg also observes that Lloyd George was initially 'somewhat uncertain how to act'.[48] Nevertheless, it was clear that Lloyd George's influence in the Cabinet would be crucial to any decision on waging war or maintaining neutrality.[49]

It seems, then, that Lloyd George's initial uncertainty was shaped by his concern to balance the demands of his radical and nonconformist allies against what he perceived as a significant military threat from Germany. The anti-war forces had busily rallied their forces against war through newspaper articles, pressure groups and personal contacts with Cabinet members.[50] Such influential supporters of neutralism as C.P. Scott of the *Manchester Guardian* and Robertson Nicoll of the *British Weekly* urged caution on Lloyd George. Indeed, Scott went so far as to issue a blunt warning to Lloyd George: if war came under a Liberal government, that would be 'an end of the existing Liberal combination' and a new party based on radicalism and Labour would come into existence.[51] Within Parliament, Arthur Ponsonby, MP for Stirling Burghs, who had been instrumental in organizing the Liberal Foreign Affairs Group in the House of Commons, was notably active in pushing the radical policy of neutrality against any who would advocate intervention on the Continent in the event of war.[52]

But there were countervailing pressures on Lloyd George. Most important among them was Churchill, who actively attempted to guide his friend towards a pro-war position. Churchill arranged a military briefing for Lloyd George given by one of General Wilson's aides, Lieutenant-Colonel A.H. Ollivant, who had been seconded to Churchill at the Admiralty.[53] Additionally, Churchill personally pressed his friend to be active in the cause of intervention during those hectic final days of peace. In one of his Cabinet notes to Lloyd George on 1 August, Churchill urged his friend thus: 'Remember your part at Agadir. I implore you to come and bring your mighty aid to the discharge of our duty.'[54] That Lloyd George had been frequently consulting with Churchill is alluded to by Morley, who had a discussion with Lloyd George on 3 August, just prior to the Cabinet meeting of that day. Morley informed Lloyd George that he was sending in his resignation. The Chancellor seemed taken aback and asked if Morley had considered the news 'of Germany bullying Belgium'. Replying in the affirmative, Morley responded with: 'war is not the only reply …'. In reflecting upon this conversation, Morley later recorded his impression that Lloyd George 'must have begun the day with one of his customary morning talks with the splendid *condottiere* at the Admiralty, had revised his calculations, as he had a perfect right to do; had made up his mind to swing round, as he had done about the *Panther* in 1911 to the politics of adventure; and found in the German ultimatum to Belgium a sufficiently plausible excuse'.[55]

Lloyd George, operating as the supreme political animal that he was, found himself in a dilemma. No one knew quite what the Cabinet's decision would be on matters of peace and war, even after several days of discussion. Perhaps war could be averted. But if Lloyd George supported the neutralists, and war were to break out with Germany seizing the imitative and winning a quick victory in France, Britain would be placed in an untenable diplomatic and military position. On the other hand, if Lloyd George supported those in the Cabinet calling for war, he risked alienating his radical and nonconformist base. Moreover, should Lloyd George declare for war too early, and war were somehow averted, his followers would also be displeased. His aim seems to have been to wait as long as possible before declaring his intentions. This may explain why he rarely spoke during the early Cabinet meetings in late July. Instead, he worked behind the scenes, mainly by meeting informally with groups of radical ministers. As Morris observes, Lloyd George listened to his colleagues' opinions, 'but never unequivocally declared his own'.[56] During the crucial day of 2 August, for example, there were three informal meetings of the neutralists. The first, before the Cabinet met, was held at Lloyd George's official residence, 11 Downing Street. In attendance, apart from Lloyd George, were Pease, Harcourt, Beauchamp, Simon and Runciman. After some discussion, they all agreed that they 'were not prepared to go to war now'; but they also agreed that 'in certain events we might reconsider position [sic] such as the invasion wholesale of Belgium'.[57]

After the disputatious Cabinet meeting, there was again a meeting of the neutralists, this time at Beauchamp's, where that morning's six ministers were joined by three others – Samuel, McKinnon Wood and Morley. According to Morley, the tone at this meeting was 'on the surface' against any involvement in a continental quarrel. Lloyd George as well as Simon declared themselves willing 'to resist at all costs the bellicose inferences from the entente'.[58] And yet, there was something in Lloyd George's statement that did not quite sit well with Morley. Perhaps he thought Lloyd George's statement unconvincing. In any case, he was left wondering: 'What exactly brought Lloyd George among us, and what the passing computations for the hour inside his lively brain, I could not make out.'[59] Lloyd George's motives, he mused, 'were a riddle'.[60] The third meeting, this time after the second Cabinet of the day, was once again held at 11 Downing Street. Pease does not discuss this meeting in detail nor who was in attendance, but presumably most of the Cabinet neutralists were present.

It is fairly clear that Lloyd George was the guiding force during these meetings and that he used them to consolidate his leadership over the neutralists, who were all men of lesser stature and experience than he. By occupying a central, if undeclared, position between the Cabinet hawks and doves, he could exercise considerable influence. On 1 August, the eve of the all-important Cabinet meetings, Asquith wrote to Venetia Stanley in praise of his Chancellor, contrasting him to the remaining radicals of the '*Manchester Guardian* tack' who were insisting on a neutralist policy toward France and Belgium. These radicals he thought, represented 'the bulk of the party'. Lloyd George, who was also 'all for peace', nevertheless was 'more sensible & statesmanlike'.[61] It was apparently not until the evening of 2 August, when he was dining at George Riddell's house in Queen Anne's Gate – after three successive meetings of the neutralists – that Lloyd George finally spoke out for Grey's policy. According to Riddell, he 'spoke very strongly' regarding the inviolability of Belgian neutrality.[62] This he announced the following day in the Cabinet. He had previously, he said, differed from Grey, 'but the invasion of a neutral state made all the difference with him'.[63] That same day, Riddell – likely prompted by Lloyd George – went to Hampstead to see Robertson Nicoll, editor of the influential *British Weekly*, who was preparing a petition against intervention. As Riddell put it, he 'fully explained the situation to Nicoll', who then backed off, agreeing with Riddell that there was now 'no alternative but to support France'.[64]

To hold together the Liberal Cabinet was of course a personal objective for Lloyd George as well. Already a risen star, Lloyd George had seen his brightness in the political firmament recently dimmed. Only two weeks before the Austro-Serbian crisis reached its climax, Riddell observed of Lloyd George that '[h]is stock stands low with the party. The Budget has been a fiasco, and badly managed'.[65] Morley agreed with this assessment. In puzzling over Lloyd George's motives during Cabinet discussions on peace and war, Morley wrote that Lloyd George was well aware that 'his "stock" was dangerously low ...'. Morley then mused that 'peace might be the popular card' to play to regain support among the Liberal rank and file. Additionally, should the government become fatally divided over the war issue and be replaced by the Conservatives, Lloyd George would be out of office: 'the break-up of Government and Party might well make any man pause quite apart from demagogic calculations'.[66] Following along the line of Morley's thought, K.M. Wilson has advanced the idea that political motives among neutralist Cabinet members may have played a part in their shift toward intervention. If the Cabinet could not reach a unified conclusion about peace or war and were forced to resign, a Conservative government might come to power – something that no Liberal, much less a neutralist, would want. If war should come, neutralists believed (guided in part by Lloyd George) that it would be better managed by the Liberals than by a war-mongering Conservative government.[67] There seems little doubt that Lloyd George had stealthily and self-interestedly (yet in his lights also for the nation's sake) helped Asquith, Churchill, and Grey to bring round his comrades in the Cabinet to accept the need for supporting France and defeating Germany.

Lloyd George's role in the reversal of Cabinet opinion has not found favour with many historians. Keith Wilson writes that Lloyd George exhibited a 'failure of courage' throughout the crisis. Lloyd George, he claims, acted with his eye on the main chance: he was opportunistic and had 'no convictions', which contrasted 'starkly with the resolution displayed by Grey, Asquith and Churchill'.[68] Gilbert, who believes that by his later actions in unifying the Cabinet, Lloyd George 'saved the nation', nevertheless accuses him of playing a 'double game'.[69] Hazlehurst thinks that the Cabinet 'waverers' (with whom he links Lloyd George) were indulging in self-deception and sham when they decided to use Belgium as an excuse for intervention in order to cover up their 'humiliating *volte face*'.[70] Most recently, J. Paul Harris has been critical of Lloyd George and the neutralists for their 'extreme reluctance' to make up their minds, thus delaying Grey's early 'honourable and rational' policy of intervention in support of France and Russia.[71] On the other hand, a few historians defend Lloyd George outright. Fry, for one, characterizes Lloyd George's behaviour as a 'quest for a policy synthesis'.[72] Morgan, in attempting to explain Lloyd George's apparent change of opinion on intervention, stresses Lloyd George's 'agony of conscience' in attempting to make up his mind between war or peace.[73] It may, however, be more accurate to suggest that it was an agony of advantage.

Lloyd George's influence was not the only contribution to the reversal of opinion in the Cabinet. Several issues had been brought to bear upon the Cabinet neutralists: the march of events, especially unremitting German bellicosity; the threat of resignation by Grey and Asquith unless France and Belgium were supported; and the letter from Bonar Law pledging opposition support must all be taken into account. Radical opposition was also collapsing in the countryside. The cry of the inviolability of Belgian neutrality no doubt took its toll. Additionally, the currents of patriotism were running swiftly. Grey's famous speech likely had some effect. Balcarres thought so, as he marvelled at the reversal of mood among Liberals in only 24 hours. Listening to the House of Commons debates on 3 August, he believed that a great majority of the radical rank and file was 'intensely hostile to the government' and that if a vote were taken that evening, the government would have been supported by only 50 of its usual adherents. The following day, however, Balcarres thought that Grey's 'long explanation' had 'greatly changed the situation' and that 'no efforts had been spared to maintain peace …'.[74] The decision having been made, the Liberal ministry had now to prepare the nation for war. Perhaps to the surprise of many, it was to this task that Lloyd George gave his most determined leadership and for which he was to earn his greatest acclaim.

11

'THE RIGHTEOUSNESS THAT EXALTETH A NATION'

As Chancellor of the Exchequer, Lloyd George's first obligation in the earliest days of the war was to deal with the financial markets, in turmoil over the prospect of international hostilities. The initial difficulty lay in the City of London, the centre of British finance: it was also by 1914 the financial capital of the world. The City was the home of the London Stock Exchange, the Bank of England, and the chief offices of the network of 'ordinary' or joint stock banks with 9,000 or so branch offices throughout the country. There were in addition acceptance houses (or merchant banks) which financed international trade and discount houses which managed bills of exchange. Although each of these institutions was highly specialized, they were joined together in the common function of providing investment capital, issuing money, and granting credit on a global scale in the early days of the war.

Even during the final days of peace, the threat of war had led to serious financial disruptions. Major stock markets were affected as heavy selling in internationally traded securities caused a sharp drop in prices.[1] Following the example of several European bourses, the London Stock Exchange closed on 31 July for the first time in its history. Other instruments of international credit simultaneously came under pressure. London financial institutions held bills of exchange worth some £350 million. Foreign borrowers (such as Germany) would be unable to remit on time their balances owed in the event of war. This crisis in foreign credit could be replicated internally if there were a panic reaction and a consequent rush for liquidity among the general public withdrawing money from local banks. Should this become widespread, local bank reserves would be depleted, forcing a call upon the Bank of England to meet the requirements of banks throughout the country for ready cash.[2] There was in fact a general movement among depositors to withdraw substantially from their accounts, exacerbated in part by the need for cash during the upcoming Bank Holiday. Some local banks responded to the demand by refusing to pay out gold, offering only notes and silver.[3]

The Bank of England, concerned about the possibility of a drain on its reserves, and viewing the wider threat of a possible collapse of international credit, requested authority from the Prime Minister and the Chancellor of the Exchequer to issue additional notes to meet unexpected demands. Acting quickly, Lloyd George and Asquith authorized the Bank to exceed the legal issue.[4] Lloyd George was also energetic on several other fronts. He extended the August Bank Holiday for several days; issued a Postponement of Payments Act which established a month's moratorium on the payment of outstanding bills; and created new paper currency, allowing banks to redeem these notes at their discretion.[5] This latter provision effectively took Britain off the gold standard, relieving the pressure on circulating coinage. Furthermore – in order to restore liquidity after the moratorium – the Bank of England, supported by the Treasury, could thereafter purchase bills of exchange. Thus the state became the guarantor for the future financing of international trade. These comprehensive actions bolstered the confidence of the financial community and the public at large.

There had been some initial uncertainty about Lloyd George's knowledge and competency concerning the technical aspects of the financial system. As Chancellor of the Exchequer, he had always been more interested in public finance as a tool for supporting his social reforms. The inner workings of the City had not captured his attention. If his knowledge were imperfect, nevertheless he employed his greatest strengths as a politician and conciliator in calming the jittery financial markets. Meeting continuously from 2 August through 6 August at the Treasury, Lloyd George brought together representative experts from finance and industry. Among his important advisers were Rufus Isaacs, now Lord Reading and Lord Chief Justice; Sir Walter Cunliffe, Governor of the Bank of England; Sir John Bradbury, Permanent Under-Secretary to the Treasury; and Sir George Paish, who was joint editor of the *Statist*. In addition, Lloyd George drew upon the expertise of two former Conservative Chancellors of the Exchequer, Austen Chamberlain and Michael Hicks Beach (now Lord St Aldwyn), a former Conservative MP and Chancellor of the Exchequer under Salisbury.

Predictably, Lloyd George's opponents saw this co-option of some opposition leaders as a sign of his weakness and inability to manage his own portfolio. The Conservative Balcarres derided Lloyd George as someone who knew 'very little about finance' and thus was forced to employ Chamberlain, who, he claimed, was 'practically acting as chancellor of the exchequer'.[6] But this was to underestimate Lloyd George's capabilities. As a practicing solicitor, he had some basic understanding of economics. As a neophyte speculator and overseas investor (with, admittedly, mixed results) he had gained at least a fundamental and first-hand knowledge of how trade, finance, and investment intersected. There is no doubt, however, that during the August 1914 crisis he relied mostly upon his quick intelligence and his skill at assimilating relevant information. Charles Hobhouse, a Cabinet colleague and a frequent critic of Lloyd George's work habits, acknowledged in late August that the Chancellor had 'been much overworked of late'. Hobhouse also recounted praise that Runciman had bestowed upon Lloyd George. Although knowing little of financial questions, of commerce and trade, bills of exchange or acceptors, Lloyd George had, according to Runciman, mastered the problems of each. He had 'captivated the bankers' and the measures taken were proving 'wise, prudent and farseeing'. Lloyd

George's performance had been, Runciman concluded, 'marvellous'.[7] The financial journalist Hartley Withers, who gave a detailed contemporary examination of the crisis, echoed this view outside government circles. Unacquainted with the machinery of the City, Lloyd George was neither tied nor bound by precedent. Thus he was ready, Withers wrote, 'to take advice and quick to act upon it' with a sure boldness that saved the banks from a potential financial disaster.[8] When such praise reached Lloyd George's ears, he promptly informed his family. To William, he wrote that his financial plan – 'the boldest financial experiment any Government ever launched' – had brought congratulations from the Rothschilds for his 'masterly' manner in tackling 'the greatest difficulty that has ever occurred in the finances of this country'. Prime Minister Asquith had also given him credit (according to Lloyd George) for executing 'the greatest success' the government had ever had.[9] To Margaret he was no less effusive: his arrangements to prevent a financial panic 'have been a complete success'; in fact, his actions had resulted in the 'first great British victory of the war'.[10]

An equally important example of Lloyd George's dispatch in shoring up British financial and economic security was his proposal to create a scheme of state insurance against the risks of wartime shipping. It was designed not only to safeguard commerce and the continual flow of trade in general, but also to protect and guarantee the necessary importation of vital foodstuffs. Although this was a scheme long in the making, it was not until Lloyd George took up the measure and brought it to the House of Commons on 4 August 1914 that it was adopted.[11] By its terms, the state would reinsure 80 per cent of all war risks on ships leaving port after war had been declared. This was, as one historian has noted, a major shift in government policy.[12] And indeed, the implications were unmistakable even to contemporaries. As Christopher Addison noted with satisfaction in his diary, it was 'probably the most Socialistic measure, after [National] Insurance, to which this Government has ever been committed'.[13]

Lloyd George presented his first wartime budget as Chancellor of the Exchequer to the House of Commons on 17 November 1914. By necessity, it was supplementary to his earlier budget in May. And naturally enough, it was a difficult budget to craft inasmuch as it had to foretell to some degree of accuracy additional military funding. The House of Commons had already acted, voting for a credit for £100 million (and later allowing the government to borrow as needed on the security of the Consolidated Funds). But it was not enough. Lloyd George therefore proposed two major sources of wartime revenues. The first was to increase taxes. At the top end of the scale, both the income and the supertax were doubled. Lower income levels paid higher excise duties on beer, wine, spirits and tea. The second major source of revenues would come from borrowing. He proposed a war loan of £350 million through a bond issue supported by the Bank of England. All in all, it was a budget relatively lenient on the taxpayer, relying instead on war loans, thus postponing a considerable financial burden for later generations to pay.[14] Given the sense of the emergency that the war had generated concerning financial and budgetary matters,

Lloyd George's proposal had an easy passage through the House of Commons – 'criticism was very indulgent', as one account has it.[15]

Meanwhile the German military steamroller had advanced unchecked during the early weeks of the war. Deploying seven of their armies in the West and sending the eighth eastward, German forces rapidly overran allied French, Belgian and Russian defences. The 100,000 well-trained professional soldiers of the British Expeditionary Force (BEF) sent as reinforcements to the French and Belgian armies were clearly overmatched. Paris itself was threatened by the leading units of the German army, which had moved to within 30 miles of the city. By late August, however, the fortunes of war were shifting. Germany's rapid offensive manoeuvres, at first so successful, were beginning to outrun supplies and to exhaust its troops. French and British forces under General Joffre halted their retreat and began to regroup. On 6 September, the Allied armies moved forward all along the battle line. Operating on interior lines of communication and supported by the arrival of reinforcements brought forward from Paris by a task force of 1,200 Parisian cab drivers, the Allies first halted and then began to push back against the combined German armies. By 11 September, the Allies had won a victory, though not a decisive one, over the retreating Germans. The German armies had been stopped but not defeated. Indeed, from their new defensive positions, the Germans soon struck back at the Allies. The French countered. In the weeks that followed, both sides continued attempts to outflank the other as the armies moved inexorably towards the North and West in what has been called the 'Race to the Sea'.

Lloyd George could draw his own conclusions as he watched carefully the unfolding military drama across the Channel. The strength and dash of the German army was at first undeniable and inescapably impressive. But the response and retaliation of the allied forces as they rallied at the Marne was encouraging. Both sides gave indications at this juncture of equally matched forces that forecast at least the possibility of a long war. In addition, the sheer size of the armies and the scale of operations gave additional signs of an extended war: a battle line of 25 miles in length; 14 armies; thousands of guns, horses and wagons; over two million men – a military concentration, as one historian has noted, never before seen.[16] Added to this was the developing struggle in the East, where Russia had assembled an army of six million against a smaller but formidable German army. It is possible that these battlefield circumstances suggested to Lloyd George that the initial weeks of a war of mobility was giving way to a war of stability and stagnation.[17]

Lloyd George also understood the necessity – if a lengthy war were likely – of rallying the nation. At the Queen's Hall on 19 September, with the echoes of the Battle of the Marne still reverberating, he proclaimed a 'new patriotism' for the kingdom and for the empire. He had prepared well in advance what he called 'a rattling good speech'[18] – and so it proved. A note of poignancy was added to the gathering by its chairman, Lord Plymouth, whose son was among the earliest to die in battle. Quoting Kipling's famous lines, 'Who dies if England lives?' in his opening remarks, Plymouth set a mixed tone of pathos for the fallen and denunciation of the enemy which characterized the meeting. An audience of thousands, mainly London

Welsh, heard Lloyd George repeatedly criticize Germany's contempt for international treaties, and specifically for its violation of Belgian neutrality.[19] Germany had not only broken a treaty, he declared, it had also pillaged and plundered Belgium. Worse yet, Belgian men had been 'slaughtered ... and her women and her children, too'. This 'massacring' and 'shooting down of harmless people' were the actions of a 'barbarism' inconsistent with civilized nations. Lloyd George also condemned Austria for its attack upon 'gallant, brave' Serbia – a 'little nation' that had done its best to meet the demands of a larger country. It was Germany, however, especially the 'Prussian military caste', that was the main target for Lloyd George's attack. The Prussian Junker, he claimed, was 'the road hog of Europe'. Small nations in the way were 'hurled to the roadside, bleeding and broken; women and children crushed under the wheels' of a 'cruel car'. Britain itself had been 'ordered out of his road'. But that 'old British spirit' was still alive and British hearts, he promised, would tear 'that bully ... from his seat'. It would not be an easy task, however. Britain would need all those qualities that its people possessed – 'prudence in council, daring in action, tenacity in purpose, courage in defeat, moderation in victory' – to win the day. Thus 'a great opportunity' was before the country, an opportunity that 'only comes once in many centuries to the children of men'. It was the chance to join in 'the glory and thrill of a great movement for liberty that compels millions throughout Europe to the same noble end ..., a great war for the emancipation of Europe'.

It has been said that the Queen's Hall speech and the plaudits it earned could only have been given by Lloyd George.[20] Such a speech was certainly beyond the capacity of the reserved Asquith, or indeed any member of the Cabinet, save perhaps Churchill. It was, in fact, a prime ministerial speech, a speech to the nation, to rouse its enthusiasm against the foe, and – more importantly – to energize recruiting efforts in a country that relied upon only a small professional army, whose numbers, it was soon clear, were insufficient to play its new role as a substantial military force on the continent. So powerful was its appeal to British nationalism that few opposed its message. It even drew praise from the anti-Liberal, traditional patriotic right wing of British politics.[21]

The question naturally arises: had Lloyd George become a jingo? Or at the very least, a hawk among Liberal doves? Or was this speech a natural culmination of his growing anti-German sentiment, which had begun at Agadir? Or was Lloyd George, as was often the case, shrewdly calculating what political advantage he could derive from unexpected circumstances? Grigg poses the question starkly: was the speech 'a masterpiece of genuine patriotism, or a masterpiece of hypocrisy?'[22] Grigg points out that at first Lloyd George was reluctant to make such a speech, even at the urging of Riddell.[23] Grigg explains this by suggesting that Lloyd George, like many politicians and military leaders, believed that the war could conclude quickly and thus might not require a substantial addition of British troops to their continental allies. Perhaps only a few divisions would suffice. If this should prove so, Lloyd George's warlike attitude could be quickly forgotten in a brief, victorious war waged by Britain, France and Russia against Germany. In short, it would seem that Lloyd George was cautiously waiting for some sign that would indicate the direction and duration of the war. It came during the first Battle of the Marne in early September 1914. That battle determined the timing of his Queen's Hall speech. In his valediction at Queen's Hall, he added a word of caution. 'We have been too comfortable', he declared, 'too indulgent ... perhaps too selfish'. We may have forgotten as a nation, he continued, 'the great peaks of honour ... Duty, Patriotism' and especially 'the great pinnacle of Sacrifice'.[24] He would sound this warning often in the months and years that followed.

Lloyd George, then, like many in the ministry, hoped for an abbreviated encounter of arms. Indeed, within the Cabinet, only one member was certain of a lengthy war – the newly appointed Secretary for War, General Horatio Kitchener, Britain's senior field marshal. An imperial hero who had won the battle of Omdurman in 1898 and played a decisive role in the Boer War, Kitchener had also served as Governor General of the Sudan, Commander in Chief in India and had been British agent and Consul General in Egypt since 1911. Given his background and experience, Kitchener seemed an ideal choice. With a first-rate military reputation and an unforgettable face on a famous war poster, he was well positioned to lead the nation's war effort. Politically, too, this was an astute appointment, neatly deflecting any possible criticism from the Conservative ranks had the choice been a Liberal. In effect, he was given vast authority to manage the war from its outset.

But historians, with few exceptions, have been unkind to Kitchener. Gilbert claims that Kitchener was 'not simply' a difficult Cabinet colleague, but rather 'an impossible one'.[25] Grigg agrees, calling Kitchener's lack of fitness to serve as a Cabinet minister 'total' and his term of office 'disastrous'.[26] Pugh puts him down as 'no administrator'.[27] Even Cassar, the most sympathetic of biographers, admits that substantial weaknesses – his autocratic manner, inability to delegate authority, secretiveness and inarticulate speech – made him an ineffective Cabinet colleague.[28] Yet at first the Cabinet seemed in awe of the famed war hero and allowed him considerable leeway. When he announced at the Cabinet meeting of 10 August that the war would likely last three years and that the size of the BEF must immediately be expanded from its current seven divisions to 24, he had the full attention of the government. In the weeks that followed, Kitchener's stature rose as the first battle of the Marne proved the mettle of the Allied forces. His reputation also invigorated recruitment, as the drive for volunteers for the New Armies, which would supplement the professional soldiers of the BEF, was proving enormously successful.

Indeed, Kitchener's solid qualities were in marked contrast to another Cabinet secretary, Winston Churchill, who suffered a sharp blow to his reputation when his singular actions during the early months of the war called his judgement into question. Not content, it would seem, with holding the office of First Lord of the Admiralty, he personally involved himself with the fighting on the Belgian front. On a fact-finding mission to Antwerp, he ordered up three brigades of the Marines and the Royal Naval Division to repulse the German siege of that city. He also offered, in a telegram to Asquith, to resign from the Admiralty so that he could be appointed the authorized army commander at Antwerp, with appropriate military rank. When Asquith refused, Churchill returned to London.[29] Among many of the casualties at the fall of Antwerp a few days later were the British reinforcements called in by Churchill.

In the meantime, Lloyd George had been largely absent from Cabinet meetings in the early weeks of the war. Mastering the financial duties and problems of a wartime Chancellor of the Exchequer left him little time for other Cabinet work. When he returned to more frequent attendance in October, Lloyd George quickly took issue with some of Kitchener's pronouncements. The first of these was a skirmish over nonconformist chaplains who, Lloyd George claimed, should have equal status with Church of England chaplains on the battlefield. Kitchener eventually concurred. But Kitchener was less easily convinced that Welsh speaking should be allowed either on parade or in military quarters. More importantly, Lloyd George questioned the War Office's resistance to the idea of forming homogenous Welsh army divisions. Kitchener refused either to consider the question or to enter into any discussion about its feasibility, informing the Cabinet that he 'would tolerate no interference' with his war plans. This brought a stuff rebuke from Lloyd George, who informed Kitchener that he 'was not an autocrat but only one out of a body of equals …'. Furthermore, Lloyd George informed the general, 'his attitude showed his sterility of ideas, and ignorance of British conditions and that he must expect and would certainly get criticism of his doings'.[30] Lloyd George got his way. Eventually the 38th (Welsh) Division was formed and fought with honours at the battles of the Somme and elsewhere on the Western Front.

Having pricked the Kitchener bubble, Lloyd George made peace with the general for a time. Overall, it seems that Lloyd George's quarrels with Kitchener had an unintended but welcome effect upon the Cabinet as a whole. By calling down Kitchener and denouncing his autocratic methods, Lloyd George shifted Cabinet opinion away from their attitude of acquiescence and toward a more critical view of Kitchener and his methods. It had already been clear for some time, even among those outside the government, that Kitchener's ability to manage the war almost on his own was proving an impossible task. Exhausted by his lengthy work schedule and worn down by his responsibilities, Kitchener by October seemed unwell. Balcarres thought him worried and overwrought, caused by his assuming too many responsibilities on his own. Given his inability to delegate authority, Kitchener created administrative backlogs.[31] The result was a continuous state of confusion, which led Balcarres to confer on the General the title 'Lord K of Chaos'.[32] The following month Riddell corroborated Balcarres's observations when he recorded in his diary that he had heard Kitchener was increasingly 'showing signs of age' and that the strain of managing the war was beginning to tell on him.[33]

The weakening of Kitchener gave added opportunities for Lloyd George to take an increasingly active role in military matters, including recruitment, wartime industrial relations, and the productive capacity of military arms, ammunition and supply. He was also beginning to assume a role in the development of strategy. It may seem surprising that Lloyd George, as Chancellor of the Exchequer, should have been so prominent in addressing military matters. There are a number of likely reasons for his 'restless intervention' as one historian has called it.[34] Perhaps above all was that he surely knew his days as a reformer would be in abeyance during wartime: there was no possibility, for example, of continuing his land scheme. Furthermore, apart from making war budgets, a Chancellor of the Exchequer's official duties were restricted in times of war. Without a more promising outlet for his talents, he could be shunted aside should the war drag on. Not to be ignored, too, was Lloyd George's restless itch for achievement and accomplishment, and the consequent favourable acknowledgement and praise from his friends, peers and family. There may have been a personal reason for his strong reaction against the Secretary for War. Kitchener, though of relatively humble birth, represented part of that privileged establishment that had excluded Lloyd George as a young man and as a striving Welsh outsider.

A more immediate reason for Lloyd George's activism on the military front, however, was his growing conviction that the War Office under Kitchener was mismanaging the war effort. This was most strikingly in evidence during in the earliest weeks of the war when it became apparent that munitions supplies could not keep up with the consumption of shot and shell used by the British artillery. The BEF's 18-pounder field guns were firing an average of 14 rounds per gun per day, but were receiving daily from Britain only seven rounds per gun.[35] At this rate, the stockpile of munitions at the front would soon run out. The lack of artillery firepower against the Germans could be the deciding factor in the war. Lloyd George's concern was echoed among other Cabinet members. Hobhouse recorded in early October that Kitchener seemed 'unable to look forward' in redressing the problems of supply: he noted additionally that it was only at Lloyd George's insistence that Kitchener increased the order for new guns.[36] Hobhouse also observed that Lloyd George and Grey forced Kitchener to examine the insufficiency of supplies.[37] Within 48 hours, on 11 October, a committee (the 'Shells Committee'), which included Kitchener, Lloyd George, Churchill and Haldane, was charged with investigating munitions production. The Committee, at the initiation of Lloyd George, immediately increased the standing order of 18-pounders and shortened the contract delivery period.[38]

The following week, Lloyd George went to France on a fact-finding tour. There, his fears of a lengthy war were confirmed. Upon his return, he reported to his wife: 'It is *stalemate*. We cannot turn them out of their trenches & they cannot turn us out'.[39] Lloyd George immediately set in motion plans to procure additional arms, including substantial numbers of rifles from the United States. This was an independent action on his part and an end-around of the War Office's own Master General of the Ordnance, General Stanley von Donop, who was responsible for arms purchases.[40] Lloyd George's whirlwind of activity placed him at the centre of the government's war effort. In recognition of this, Asquith invited him to become a member of a small and secret body, the War Council, which was designed to review the conduct of the war. Other members included Grey, Kitchener and Churchill, as well as some service chiefs as the Council expanded over the next several months.[41]

Although wartime strategy was an absorbing concern early in the war, Lloyd George was also drawn into important domestic issues. Chief among these was the impact of the war upon industrial productivity and labour relations. More specifically, he remained concerned about the continuing lag in the supply of munitions. The reasons for this were not at first clear, although War Office procedures, as noted above, were likely contributory. By February 1915 complaints were beginning to reach Lloyd George from various quarters that the primary cause of low productivity was absenteeism among the workforce brought on by widespread drunkenness. In the following month, the national press carried numerous letters that seemed to confirm substantial alcoholic consumption among war workers. In a letter to the Earl of Derby, Lloyd George complained that munitions supplies were being 'seriously retarded' because of the growing habit among workmen 'of throwing up their tools about the third day in every week to drink the rest of their time'.[42]

Thus was set in motion a curious episode – an anti-drink campaign that hearkened back to the temperance campaigns of Lloyd George's early career. But his rationale for embracing the anti-drink programme was different from his peacetime efforts. Now, he claimed, it was not merely a moral matter, but rather a necessary measure to promote national efficiency during wartime.[43] In so stating, he seems to have accepted the premise of those who blamed the workforce for effectively sabotaging the war effort.[44] Collecting data from a number of sources, including the directors of armaments firms and shipbuilders, Lloyd George proposed a scheme that would prohibit all alcoholic beverages in certain work areas as well as a general limitation of the hours for the sale of beer. Symbolic of the campaign was Lloyd George's solicitation of the 'King's Pledge' from George V, a promise on the part of the monarch to abstain from drink for the duration of the war.

Lloyd George's detestation of excessive drinking seems to have been genuine. He wrote excitedly to his brother William in March and early April 1915 about his work on the drink crusade.[45] He also discussed his plan several times with Riddell, although that sceptical newsman remained unconvinced. Additional doubts emerged, with a few exceptions, among his Cabinet colleagues.[46] Although Asquith was at first supportive, praising Lloyd George's proposal as evidence of his 'versatility of interest & mind', he had second thoughts a week later, believing that the Chancellor had 'completely lost his head' over the matter.[47] Within two days, however, Asquith changed his mind once again, encouraging Lloyd George to work with others, perhaps on a scaled down measure. Soon after, Asquith observed approvingly that Lloyd George was engaged in his 'usual process of "roping in" everybody' to win them over.[48]

Indeed, Lloyd George was moving into a second phase of his anti-drink campaign, the nationalization of public houses. Should such a scheme go through, it would give the government the power to manage the trade as it saw fit. If the buyout were generous enough, public ownership might be attractive to brewers who had been facing severe economic problems prior to the war.[49] He commissioned a report from Sir William Plender, a chartered accountant, on the costs involved. A Cabinet committee was formed to look into the matter. Lloyd George himself began talks with the brewers and leaders of the Conservative Party about its feasibility. He was, as he wrote to his wife in April: 'Up to the eye in *Liquor*.'[50] He seemed to be having some success: even Bonar Law was inclined at first to accept the idea. But other Conservatives had reservations and the scheme quickly foundered. Lloyd George was tenacious, however, and, after dropping the nationalization scheme, tried yet another tack. This time, he sought legislative control over the liquor trade with the power to regulate, close down, or acquire the liquor industry in those areas of importance to the production and transport of war materials. This provision was more successful and was enacted through an amendment to the Defence of the Realm Act (DORA), which he introduced to the House of Commons on 20 April 1915.[51]

Lloyd George made one additional attempt to restrict alcohol consumption. On 4 May 1915, he introduced his last budget as Chancellor of the Exchequer. In it, he proposed to continue financing the war by borrowing rather than increasing taxes. In addition, he proposed substantial tax increases on the liquor trade, doubling the taxes on whisky and wines as well as levying substantial increases on heavy beers. This raised a storm of protest from Conservatives. The former Conservative Chancellor of the Exchequer, Austen Chamberlain, declared that the taxes on alcohol were an 'excrescence', and the levies on beer were 'not taxation, but annihilation'.[52] Bonar Law declared that the liquor trade would be roused 'to a perfect passion of excitement and resentment' against the proposals.[53] Arthur Henderson, speaking for the Labour Party, was also dismissive of the claims of 'over-drinking'.[54] Equally severe criticism came from the Irish Nationalists, normally Liberal allies, who deplored the tax threats to Irish brewing and distilling. John Redmond declared that the taxation of beer would additionally have a negative impact upon agriculture by effectively destroying Ireland's most important cash crop, barley. Such criticism forced Lloyd George to surrender the drink taxes.

The general thrust of Lloyd George's final budget has generally been given poor marks by historians. Mallet and George seem to think that the 'unsparing criticism' directed at Lloyd George for his failure to increase taxation was justified when public opinion was 'fully prepared' to accept such a rise in taxes.[55] Grigg, too, is critical of Lloyd George's timid response to the escalating cost of the war, which stood at £360 million by the end of March 1914. Given the financial gap, it was 'a miserable anti-climax of a Budget'.[56] Gilbert believes the budget 'not only uninteresting, but lifeless' because the Chancellor 'proposed nothing'.[57] But more recently, Martin Daunton has taken a favourable view. Although the financing of Britain's previous wars had relied largely on increased taxes, as Daunton notes, Lloyd George went against the grain by borrowing for good reasons. Lloyd George was fearful, as were many others, that the effects of war within the next several months could exacerbate trade disruption causing mounting unemployment and falling incomes. A tax increase would only accelerate a possible economic downturn.[58]

In spite of Lloyd George's reasoned approach to his taxing policy and his energetic attempts to tackle production bottlenecks, he was clearly having difficulty during the early months of 1915 in finding his feet on domestic matters, including those relating to his official duties as Chancellor of the Exchequer. His involvement in the drink trade seems particularly curious, even dysfunctional, especially as it became an issue in his proposed war budget of 1915. His desire for retaining radical and nonconformist support for temperance measures cannot be ruled out.[59] But there seems to have been little mention of this by Lloyd George or his contemporaries.

Instead, there was a general air of puzzlement about the Chancellor's intentions. In Lord Beaverbrook's famously subjective account of the domestic politics of wartime Britain, Lloyd George's actions appeared to be 'a strange vagary'. The mind of the Chancellor of the Exchequer, Beaverbrook thought, seemed to have flown 'off at a tangent' as he became 'obsessed' with the problem of drink in the workplace. Yet once the plan for state control began to falter, Lloyd George quickly dropped it. Beaverbrook thought this was a sign of Lloyd George's genius for 'theatrical management' by which he always withdrew a failed work just before it was 'hissed off the stage'.[60] Although Beaverbrook's reputation as a historian is open to question,[61] his characterization likely had resonance with some contemporaries who viewed Lloyd George's drink campaign as either opportunistically playing to his non-conformist temperance gallery, or simply fishing in troubled waters. Other historians who have written more recently have also been puzzled by the campaign. Owen describes it as a 'curious political adventure'.[62] Grigg believes that Lloyd George was simply 'carried away' by his desire to increase vital wartime productivity and had not thought through the issue before 'plunging into feverish activity'.[63] Morgan throws up his hands, noting only that Lloyd George advanced his plan 'for reasons that are still obscure'.[64] Biographers of Bonar Law have also had something to say because of Lloyd George's attempt to solicit Conservative support for his plan. Blake thought the drink campaign 'a curious by-product' of Lloyd George's 'effervescent mind' and 'a somewhat chimerical scheme'.[65] Adams concurs: it was a 'quixotic proposal'.[66]

Such comments may unintentionally suggest that Lloyd George had entered upon his scheme, zealously to be sure, but perhaps in a light-hearted manner – perhaps even hypocritically or insincerely, as a means of targeting a convenient scapegoat for lagging production of war materiel. Evidence carefully considered suggests otherwise. To understand his behaviour in this instance, we must look more closely at his motives. Viewed retrospectively and in a larger sense, Lloyd George may have had in mind the notion that restricting alcoholic consumption was only a first step in the greater aim of interjecting the state into the lives of its citizens to enhance wartime production. Perhaps, as Gilbert suggests, Lloyd George was simply 'feeling his way' towards that end.[67] Turner concurs. He believes that the drink campaign was less about drink than about infusing the population, especially the working classes (who performed the crucial productive tasks for munitions manufacturing), with a seriousness of purpose hitherto lacking. State control of the liquor trade could signal to the country that emergency measures on the domestic front were now necessary to winning the war.[68]

That Lloyd George had come to believe in the necessity of steeling the nation to greater wartime effort was clearly evident in an 'epoch-making' paper presented to the Cabinet on 24 February 1915.[69] In it, he set out the case for legislation to commandeer those engineering factories capable of increasing munitions. Additionally, he wanted government authority to arbitrate all trade disputes, enforced by punishment clauses against those who refused. Essentially he declared 'a manifesto for total war'.[70]

A few days later (28 February 1915), in one of his great wartime speeches, he fleshed out his ideas on a nation at war.[71] Beginning in a solemn and admonitory tone (the usual jokes were few), Lloyd George told the crowd that the German Army, 'like a wild beast', had 'fastened its claws' deep into French soil, and was now rending and tearing 'the living flesh of that beautiful land'. Paris was 'a changed city': its gaiety and vivacity were gone. Only through 'a long agony' could it be restored. The lesson was plain to the British people. They must be prepared to sacrifice and to endure 'a prolonged struggle' to avoid a similar fate. A great army must be raised, and was indeed being raised: 'our men', Lloyd George observed, had 'flocked to the standard'. But, he continued, there was at the moment a greater need: 'we need arms more than men'. Any delay in producing them was 'full of peril for this country'. He then specifically singled out industrial disputes as a chief cause of delay. The government must have the authority in wartime to settle such disputes, if necessary by compulsory arbitration. Nor could the country tolerate absenteeism in the workforce. Here he specifically condemned 'the lure of the drink' which prevented some workers operating full time and at their peak efficiency. This must be dealt with, if necessary, by the powers of the government, just as industrial disputes must be settled quickly. In a period of war, he warned, 'there is suspension of ordinary law'. It was important to remember 'output is everything in this war'.[72]

Lloyd George gave specific examples of the negative effect of industrial disputes upon crucial wartime productivity, mentioning most specifically the recent Clydeside work stoppages. In February 1915, just prior to the Bangor speech, a series of unofficial strikes had broken out at the concentrated engineering and shipbuilding industries along the banks of the Clyde in Scotland. By 20 February some 10,000 men had withdrawn their labour. Particularly significant was the fact that the strikes were not union sanctioned: rather, a group of shop stewards became the workers' spokesmen. They insisted that accelerating food prices and higher rents were outpacing wages. Workmen were also convinced that their employers were making enormous profits from the war, and that these should be shared more equitably with their employees. Eventually, the men won a small concession; but the larger issue of settling labour disputes without harmful work stoppages had not been resolved.

That Lloyd George was serious about the government's determination to exercise its full authority over wartime production, even to the point of government control, was illustrated by his speech in the Commons on 9 March 1915. In it he introduced an amendment to DORA that would enable the government to take over any factory or workshop needed for war production. The bill quickly passed into law. Although Lloyd George was not averse to using the stick of state intervention, he had not abandoned the carrot of personal negotiation. On 17–19 March, he convened a meeting of trade union officials, some leading politicians (including Arthur Balfour) and several members of the army and navy. In what has become known as the Treasury Conference, he hoped to strike a deal with trade unionists. In return for the unions' pledge to suspend strike action for the duration of the war; to agree in principle to arbitration during labour disputes; to accept less skilled workers in manufacturing firms; and to support the employment of women in the war industries, he vowed to control excess profits among armament manufacturers. These proposals were met with a mixed response, however. The Amalgamated Society of Engineers, the most important skilled union in the production of munitions, was initially cool to the idea. Nevertheless, the Conference provided an opportunity for the Chancellor to play to his strengths of conciliation and management of conflict. The Conference concluded with a written statement promising some support to Lloyd George's proposals. Perhaps most importantly, it set another precedent on the road towards an expanded state intervention during wartime industrial disputes.[73]

While the government continued to press forward in harnessing domestic industrial capacity for the war effort, the military progress of the Allies remained discouraging. On the eastern front, German armies enjoyed continued success against depleted and poorly supplied Russian forces. Beginning in January 1915, the German army advanced all along the 800 mile front from the Carpathians to the Baltic, driving the Russians before them. In the West, attack and counterattack on both sides merely consolidated the stalemated trenches. The most disquieting news from the Western Front was the continuing shortage of artillery ammunition. At the battle of Aubers Ridge on 9 May 1915, three corps of the British army were driven back from an abortive offensive manoeuvre with heavy casualties because of a lack of high explosive shells. Field Marshall Sir John French, then overall commander of the BEF, claimed that he had been urgently requesting more shells from the War Office for several months. Immediately after Aubers Ridge, French sent two of his staff officers to plead his case before influential politicians, including Lloyd George. French also instigated a damaging report in *The Times* about the shells shortage. Written by Lt Col. Charles Repington, military correspondent of that newspaper, the report reached a wide and influential audience. On 17 May Repington met with Lloyd George to discuss the tactical consequences for the battlefield of an insufficient supply in armaments. At the same time, the influential press baron Lord Northcliffe began to use one of his newspapers, the *Daily Mail*, to expose what soon became known as the 'shells scandal'.[74]

This was not the only bad news for the Asquith government during the spring months of 1915. A lack of progress on the Western Front and the precarious position of Russia had prompted a rethinking of grand strategy. In January 1915, Russia – already pressed by Germany from the West – requested help from Britain to deflect the advance of the Ottoman Empire. Ottoman naval forces had begun naval bombardments of Russian cities on the Black Sea, and their military sorties had fought overland through the Caucasus into neighbouring Russian territory. Churchill, then first Lord of the Admiralty, was eager to respond.[75] The Ottoman regime, which he perceived as corrupt and despotic, would be a pushover. Thus British forces began a campaign as though it were no more than 'a large-scale punitive expedition against a recalcitrant native regime …'.[76] Operating under the notion of the inherent superiority of white Christian peoples against a coloured Muslim nation, the War Council decided that a 'ships alone' policy should do the trick. Elements of the Royal Navy would steam into the Dardanelles, blast the Ottoman forts guarding their passage, and then – once the guns had been silenced and defence forces had fled – the way would be clear for the British fleet to sail into the Sea of Marmara and on to Constantinople.[77] Thus began one of the most notorious of all Allied military failures during the war.[78]

The East Mediterranean Fleet, under the command of Vice-Admiral Sackville Carden, began bombarding the outer Ottoman coastal fortifications on 19 February 1915. As the 18-ship flotilla (including four French vessels) moved up the Dardanelles towards The Narrows, however, its position became increasingly vulnerable. A number of extensive minefields lay ahead. The fortified Ottoman defensive batteries were proving difficult to root out. Mobile howitzers changing their positions up and down the shore were hard to spot. These difficulties prompted the Cabinet to complement the Navy's stalled attacks by enlarging the expedition to include a land attack led by General Sir Ian Hamilton. To soften anticipated resistance ahead of the military expedition, the Navy attempted a major operation on 15 March. This proved overly ambitious. Three capital ships were sunk; others were seriously damaged.[79] Nevertheless, late the following month, on 25 April, Allied landings began. British units disembarked at five sites on Cape Helles, the southern tip of the Gallipoli Peninsula. A French force landed at Kumkale on the opposite shore, but soon re-embarked to join the British forces at Helles. A third group, the Australian and New Zealand Army Corps (ANZAC), landed farther north along the Peninsula near Sulva Bay. In all, some 75,000 Allied troops were put ashore.

The difficulties of an amphibious landing at that time in the history of warfare were not well understood. Although some beaches had a relatively smooth embarkation, others witnessed a nightmare of confusion. As one account has observed: 'Ships lost their way; troops were landed in the wrong place; arrangements for soldiers to land by way of improvised temporary wharves failed; and supporting firepower proved either inadequate or nonexistent.'[80] Once ashore, troops were subject to continuous machine gun and rifle fire from the embedded Ottoman forces on the heights above.[81] In the eight months that followed, Allied forces were pinned to their small beachheads. Successive attempts by the British military to break out of their perilous enclaves were consistently beaten back by the Ottomans, whose tactical resilience continually surprised Allied troops. Ottoman officers such as Colonel Mustafa Kemal and the III Corps commander Esat Pasha also led their defensive deployment superbly. Inaccurate maps and an uneven terrain added to Allied difficulties. Logistical problems mounted: among the most severe was the inadequate supply of water. The promised naval support fell short: ship-based artillery proved both inaccurate and inadequate. Command at both higher and lower levels faltered. Morale declined. Supporting ships failed to clear the mined waters nearby, which hindered Allied mobility. In May a greater danger appeared when German submarines sank two vessels of the Royal Navy.

Continued bad news from the stalemated Western Front, the Russian imbroglio in the east and the on-going struggle for a foothold in the Dardanelles inevitably had an adverse effect upon domestic politics. Questions began to surface about Asquith's leadership of the war effort. Lloyd George expressed his own doubts to Riddell as early as March 1915 when he complained that the Prime Minister was 'too easy'.[82] The following month Asquith publicly stated his belief in the adequacy of shell supplies at the front. In response, Lloyd George again privately voiced his negative opinion of Asquith to Riddell, labelling Asquith's remarks as 'unfortunate'. In fact, shell production was 'deplorable'.[83] To Miss Stevenson in May 1915, Lloyd George added specific criticisms of the faltering land and sea operation against Ottoman military forces: 'we should never get through the Dardanelles'.[84] Lloyd George's opinions echoed the views of a number of increasingly disenchanted Liberals. There were even some Conservatives who had begun to compare Asquith unfavourably to Lloyd George's energetic pursuit of the war, citing his Bangor speech, his willingness to control labour and his concerns about munitions production.[85]

There is, however, no evidence that Lloyd George conspired to challenge Asquith's leadership within the Cabinet. The initiative may have come from the Conservative leader Bonar Law.[86] On the morning of 17 May, Bonar Law sought out Lloyd George at his Treasury offices for a consultation.[87] Both men quickly came to the conclusion that a political tipping point had been reached and that the government could not go forward as it was then constituted. A fresh approach and a firmer direction in the prosecution of the war were badly needed. From this recognition emerged the idea that a new government must be constituted – a government along national lines, drawing upon all the talents from both political parties. After some initial hesitation, Asquith accepted the sense of the Lloyd George/Bonar Law initiative. He immediately sent out a confidential memo to Cabinet members, informing them that a new departure was necessary.[88] He then quickly set about recasting the Cabinet. This news fell like 'a bombshell', as Addison put it.[89] No one had expected it: both Liberal and Conservative MPs were caught unawares. At the end of the day, Lloyd George confided to his brother: 'Big things in course of determination & I am in the thick of it.'[90]

The day after the decision had been made, the new coalition government was announced to a startled House of Commons. Among the significant changes was the removal of Haldane, Lord Chancellor, to be replaced by another Liberal, Lord Buckmaster. Bonar Law replaced Harcourt as Colonial Secretary. Harcourt, in turn, was effectively demoted to the First Commissioner of Works. Churchill, too, was reduced to Chancellor of the Duchy of Lancaster, far removed from his previous office at the Admiralty, now taken over by A.J. Balfour, a significant Conservative addition to the Cabinet.[91] Another important Conservative gain was the appointment of Austen Chamberlain as Secretary for India. Additional Conservatives in the new Cabinet included Sir Edward Carson as Attorney-General in place of Simon; Lansdowne as Minister without Portfolio; Walter Long as President of the Local Government Board; and Selborne as President of the Board of Agriculture. Lord Curzon became Lord Privy Seal. A bow to Labour was made with the appointment of Arthur Henderson as President of the Board of Education. A few other positions were shuffled among Liberals, such as Simon's replacement of McKenna at the Home Office, while McKenna became Chancellor of the Exchequer. The most important Cabinet change, as it proved, was Lloyd George's agreement to surrender his post as Chancellor of the Exchequer to accept an entirely new office, Minister of Munitions.[92] Overall, of 23 members of the new Cabinet, 12 were Liberals, nine were Conservatives, one Labour and one non-party, Lord Kitchener.

The dramatic rapidity of the Cabinet changes and its new political composition brought condemnation from leading members of the Liberal Party, especially those who were excluded from the new government. Charles Hobhouse, whose position as Postmaster-General was dropped from the new Cabinet, was angry at the outcome and painted a gloomy picture overall of Liberal prospects. He believed that the coalition government meant the 'complete' disintegration of the Liberal Party.[93] Among backbench Liberals, the mood was equally dark: their party leader, cooperating with the opposition and a few Liberal insiders, had secretly engineered a coalitionist coup. Scarcely more than half of the Cabinet were now Liberals. Addison recorded in his diary that Liberal MPs 'were furious about the coalition'.[94] Not only were Liberals troubled by the speed and secrecy of the Cabinet changes. Lloyd George informed his brother that: 'Both parties [were] disturbed & perplexed by the move. They know nothing of the facts that moved us to take the step & the worst of it is we cannot tell them as it would give dangerous information to the Enemy.'[95]

The role of Asquith throughout the coalition crisis was paramount – far more so than Lloyd George's. Asquith had to bear the ultimate responsibility for the break up of the government, soothe savaged egos and reconstruct the government with his political foes. This was not an easy task for the Prime Minister. As Jenkins notes, Asquith's 'old Liberal mandarin spirit' militated against accepting Conservatives as ministerial equals.[96] In addition, as Jenkins has it, Asquith was suffering from a private grief. Only days before the fall of the government, his intimate epistolary confidante, Venetia Stanley, announced to him that she was marrying Edwin Montagu, a rising Liberal star soon to play an important role in coalition politics. This news was a severe blow to Asquith. Brock suggests, however, that the unsettling news gave him an added emotional empathy which he was able to utilize to political advantage in explaining to the party the steps he had taken to bring in Conservatives to the government.[97] At a meeting of rebellious Liberal MPs on 19 May, Asquith won them over by an uncharacteristically humble performance, complete with tears. As related by Alexander MacCallum Scott, who was present, Asquith, 'speaking with deep feeling … flung himself on our mercy'. Intimating that he had information that he could not divulge because it touched upon national security, he declared that coalition was 'inevitable'. He needed their confidence in his judgement: otherwise he could not continue and must resign. Asquith then left the room to 'an overpowering ovation'.[98] Koss presents a different Asquith, one more decisive and with a firm notion of what he hoped to achieve by a coalition government. Koss believes that Asquith's reasons were primarily political – to defuse Conservative backbench demands, supported by a vociferous Conservative press, for a more vigorous pursuit of the war. This could best be accomplished by accepting a number of Conservatives into a coalition ministry, thus co-opting them. By acting vigorously, Asquith preserved his own position within the Liberal Party and, with luck, with the nation at large. In portraying Asquith in command, Koss also dismisses the notion that he was 'reeling' under the emotional stress induced by Miss Stanley's betrothal.

Indeed, Koss claims that Asquith had always been able to keep his private affairs from impinging upon his public duties.[99]

If the Liberals seemed to rally after initial confusion, Conservatives also gained something by the coalition. For Bonar Law, as suggested above, the national interest declared a fresh approach to the war. Conservative rank and file had believed from the beginning of the war that their opinions should have more weight in governing circles. Conservatives in Parliament also believed that they had a special vested interest in the war: 140 Conservative MPs had joined the forces since the war began, far more than the Liberals. For the Conservatives, too, the all-party truce imposed at the beginning of the war was nothing less than a gag order. Such outspoken men as W.A.S. Hewins, Conservative MP for Hereford, believed from the first that the nation's entire economic resources 'must be put on a war footing'. Months later, on the eve of the May crisis, Hewins's opinion had hardened. On 6 May 1915, he wrote in his diary that the government was now 'discredited', having failed to prosecute the war effectively.[100]

Dissatisfaction among Conservatives, given tongue by Hewins, had risen to the point that they were now willing, so Bonar Law believed, to demand a public debate upon the course of the war, a move which would inevitably be divisive in the public at large no less than in Parliament.[101] Should this happen, the impact upon an effective pursuit of the war would be incalculable. Now as partners (even if junior partners) in the Cabinet, Conservatives had an official voice and a set of policies that could no longer be ignored. In addition, the very fact of coalition making had seen some of their favourite Liberal targets in the Cabinet either removed, such as Haldane, or chastened as in the case of the turncoat Churchill. Perhaps most of all, after a decade out of power, their days in opposition were over: they were now partners in governing.[102]

A change in government made little difference in the progress of the war itself. That the shell shortage continued to affect battlefield proficiency was clear from the Battle of Loos in September 1915 – up to then, the largest land battle in the history of British warfare. The main initiative behind the attack came from the desire to satisfy both French and Russian demands that British forces play a more active offensive role. Even before the battle, it was widely recognized that armament shortages (as well as strong German defensive positions) could weigh heavily against success. General Sir John French, Commander in Chief of the BEF, predicted 'some terrible losses'.[103] General Rawlinson, Commander of the First Army, which would carry out the attack, agreed: 'I fear heavy losses', he confided to his diary.[104] Kitchener himself, in visiting Haig several weeks before the attack, emphasized the need to do all they could to help their Allies, 'even though, by doing so, we suffered very heavy losses indeed'.[105] It seems quite clear that at the highest levels of command, a policy of heavy casualties to achieve victory had been established by late 1915.

In an attempt to make up for the tactical battlefield disadvantages and the recurring armament shortages, British commanders decided on the use of poisonous gas against the Germans in advance of the ground attack.[106] But the gas attack went awry: it proved largely ineffective, shifting with the wind and blowing over both

German and British trenches indiscriminately. Scarcely any ground was gained, and in little more than two days, the British suffered 60,000 casualties.[107] Lloyd George, in reporting the battlefield results to his brother William, had little doubt of the outcome. 'The attack was I fear premature. We were not ready for it. We shall gain a few miles here and a few kilometres there. Just enough ground to bury the dead who won it.'[108] Several days later in summation, he wrote again to William under the shadow of Loos: 'We have committed every military & diplomatic blunder our enemies could have wished for.'[109] Years later, in retrospect, Lloyd George recalled that some weeks after Loos, he saw photographs of dead Highlanders, 'lying in swathes in front of a single German machine-gun ...'.[110] From that time forward, he claimed, began the seed in his own mind of the necessity for civilian responsibility in managing the war, even if it meant overriding contrary military opinion.

A discouraging record in the European theatre was echoed during British operations in the eastern theatre of the war. Having made little progress against the Ottomans during the later months of 1915, the Allies had no choice but to evacuate their troops – a far smoother operation than had been the invasion. Chased out of Gallipoli, the British military (and by extension, the government) lost considerable prestige. The government's reputation was further tarnished by the findings of a Royal Commission 'to pick over the bones'[111] of the Gallipoli campaign. Historians since have held General Hamilton accountable for his command of the military operation. Travers, for example, believes that he was 'something of a lightweight ... a commander-in-chief who did not really command'.[112] But the government itself was held ultimately accountable for the failed operations. Asquith has been particularly faulted by his biographers for allowing the service chiefs too free a hand and in not asking the hard questions of military and naval feasibility during the early planning of the operation.[113] Ultimate responsibility for the failure has historically rested squarely with Winston Churchill for whom the Gallipoli operation became, as one account has termed it, an 'obsession'.[114] His removal from the Admiralty was a crushing political and personal defeat.[115] It was widely thought that his career was over.

Lloyd George's precise role in the Gallipoli decision is not entirely clear, but he did in fact lend some support to the campaign. Grigg thinks that Lloyd George gave his blessing to the naval operations 'on the spur of the moment'.[116] Woodward believes that Lloyd George, while supporting the naval operation, was opposed to sending in troops unless the Navy succeeded in its mission. Should the Navy fail, Lloyd George wanted 'immediately ... to try something else'.[117] Lloyd George himself claims that he 'stood alone' in initially opposing the Dardanelles campaign.[118] As soon as the Council had approved of the scheme, however, he acquiesced, ceasing 'to challenge the wisdom of the enterprise', and even began to advise sending troops in 'sufficient numbers' to Gallipoli with 'an adequate equipment of guns and ammunition'.[119]

The Dardanelles was not the only battleground in the east which lured a misbegotten British campaign. In Mesopotamia, then a part of the Ottoman Empire, a series of stunning and unexpected reverses also called into question British military leadership.[120] It all began well enough. In November 1914, a combined Anglo-Indian expeditionary force captured Basra, the port city at the head of the Persian Gulf. The object was twofold: to secure British oil interests; and to ensure strategic security in the region. Before long, however, military ambitions resulted in what can best be described as 'mission creep'. After enjoying some initial success in navigating upstream on the Tigris River towards their objective, Baghdad, British forces began to encounter the hazards of desert fighting, including intense heat, insect plagues and an unfamiliarity with the terrain – distinct disadvantages in a war of rapid movement. Logistical problems in supplying food and water added to their troubles. Sunstroke, fever and dysentery also began to take their toll.

A final insult to the unsuspecting British was a military one: they were out-generalled by their Ottoman foes. After a decisive defeat at Ctesiphon, south of Baghdad, in November 1915, the British withdrew to Kut, where they remained, besieged by a large Ottoman army, for five months. A second British expedition sent from Basra attempted to relieve their trapped comrades. But this expedition also failed, defeated in three separate encounters with the Ottomans along the riverine battlefields south of Kut. With diminishing supplies, increasing debility of the troops and little hope of either a breakout or another relief force, the Kut garrison had few options. In April 1916, they surrendered to the now vastly reinforced Ottoman army surrounding them. Nearly 9,000 (3,000 British and 6,000 Indian troops) were taken into captivity. It was, as one historian has claimed, a surrender like none other in the history of the British Army.[121] The captives were forced to march through the desert to Baghdad. Some were left in that city, while others were sent to Mosul and Anatolia, where they remained prisoners of war until the cessation of hostilities.

A third major failure in the eastern theatre of operations in 1915 also had potentially far-ranging consequences. While the Dardanelles and Mesopotamian campaigns were still on-going, a Balkans operation was initiated. This time, Lloyd George took the lead, convincing the War Council of his views at its meeting of 13 January 1915.[122] This was, as Woodward puts it, 'a great personal triumph for Lloyd George'.[123] The proposed strategy was to secure as military partners the countries of Rumania, Serbia and Greece, with a possibility of Bulgaria as well. These states, acting with Britain and France, could directly threaten Austria on its southern flank. A successful campaign in the east could knock Austria-Hungary out of the war and deal a deadly blow to the German war machine. At the very least (it was thought), Germany would be forced to send sufficient men and materiel to Austria, and in so doing would weaken its forces on the Western Front. This could effectively break the stalemated western trenchlock in the Allies' favour.

Sanctioned by the War Council, Lloyd George set out to expedite the Balkan campaign. Meeting with both Asquith and Kitchener, and then summoning the Greek ambassador, Lloyd George led the way in preparations for sending an army corps to the Balkans. Lloyd George also met in London with the French War Minister, Alexandre Millerand, to lobby for an Allied invasion in the Balkans. To shore up support among the French, he travelled to Paris in early February 1915 where he spent several days with members of the French government. Negotiating without instructions from his own government, he engaged in a 'whirlwind diplomacy' with President Poincare, Prime Minister Viviani, Foreign Minister Delcasse and the influential Aristide Briand, the Minister of Justice.[124] Before returning to London, Lloyd George also met with Generals French and Robertson to win approval of his Balkan scheme. Possibly misinterpreting their response, Lloyd George believed that he had received from them a cautious approval.[125] A few days later, however, Sir John French – who had opposed all along a Balkan venture – raised his objections at the War Council of 9 February 1915. Moreover, General Joffre had convinced the French government to tread cautiously. And Russia, which had been invited to participate, could provide only 1,000 troops. Nevertheless, with Lloyd George 'speaking often and forcefully',[126] the Council approved sending a division of British troops to the Greek port of Salonika in support of a larger Balkan force to be used against Austria.

But delays throughout the early months of 1915 prevented the dispatch of Allied forces. Primary impediments lay not only in the ancient rivalries and suspicions among the Balkan states but also the threatening encroachment of the Central Powers.[127] Serbia was increasingly under duress as German and Austrian troops began massing for an attack. Bulgaria was tilting ever more towards the Central Powers. Even Greece wavered in its support of the Allies. Nevertheless, on 5 October the first Anglo-French units disembarked at Salonika. Allied troops soon moved into Serbia as reinforcements against an enemy invasion. By December, however, they had returned to Greece, beaten back by Bulgarian, German and Austrian forces. In spite of this defeat, Lloyd George continued to work tirelessly to maintain an Allied presence in Salonika, which could serve a bridgehead for possible future incursions against the Central Powers in the Balkans. This was not, however, to occur until the later stages of the war in 1918.

There is no doubt that military failure haunted the Allies throughout 1915. Asquith's coalition government of Liberals and Conservatives was no more efficient than Asquith's previous all-Liberal government. Military losses throughout 1915 also tarnished the reputations of many Allied military commanders. But in retrospect, the only politician from any party who gained an enhanced reputation from the government restructuring in May 1915 – in spite of his own misjudgements – was Lloyd George. His tenure at the Ministry of Munitions was a success. In an important sense, Lloyd George had fortuitously emerged as the natural choice for that position. The shells scandal came at a time when politicians and parliamentarians alike were demanding a firmer response to a growing realization that Britain was facing a brutal land war of unknown dimensions and duration.[128] Defeat, stalemate and the Dardanelles and Balkans adventures had contributed to an urgent need for a concerted national response. In addition, since his appointment to the Shells Committee in October 1914, Lloyd George had been an ardent advocate of expanding armament production. When that Committee seemed moribund and the need for a more authoritative body became obvious, Asquith in March 1915 began considering a new office – which he thought might be called 'Director of War Contracts' – to be headed by Lloyd George.[129] As an interim measure, Asquith appointed a Munitions (War Supplies) Committee on 8 April with Lloyd George as its chair.[130] These interim offices led naturally to Lloyd George's appointment as Minister of Munitions in Asquith's coalition Cabinet of May 1915.

The Ministry of Munitions had two daunting tasks – to establish a new department of state from scratch and to increase the manufacture and shipment of heavy munitions so desperately needed at the front. The original idea was that Lloyd George would serve as head of the ministry on a temporary basis only, perhaps for a few months, until the problems of arms production and delivery had been solved: he would then reclaim the Chancellorship. But it was soon obvious that this would be no short-term job. Indeed, the munitions shortage had not been the fault of one man, Kitchener, as many had assumed. Rather, the shortages had come about at least in part because of false assumptions by military planners drawing from their experiences in the Boer War. In that war, pitched battles were fought over a vast area by rapidly moving ground forces. The need for light, mobile artillery that could fire shrapnel accurately in support of advancing infantry was among the tactical lessons learned. The war in Europe, however, demanded saturation barrages of unimagined duration and intensity launched at embedded and entrenched enemy troops. Only heavy guns firing high explosives could be effective.[131] Kitchener himself had realized the changed nature of artillery in the earliest days of World War I, but he was unable to unlock the productive capacity necessary to redress the problem.[132]

In searching for a solution, Lloyd George did not act alone. Moreover, he drew upon existing precedents and practices.[133] But he brought to the new ministry his own diligence and style of management. He was as always ready to improvise, to consider advice from any source and to work inhuman hours until tasks were completed. But even his systematic approach to problems and his untiring energy would be sorely tried. This he knew well enough. As he confessed to his brother after a few weeks: 'I am griping [sic] this job but will need all the grip I can give it.'[134]

His initial task was to increase munitions production as quickly as possible. There were two principal state-owned munitions works: the Royal Ordnance Factories, which manufactured small arms and gunpowder at several locations; and the Royal Arsenal at Woolwich, which manufactured most types of heavy armaments, such as guns and mountings and heavy shells.[135] The Royal Aircraft Factory at Farnborough was primarily for research and development: manufacturing was carried out elsewhere under contract. In addition there were a number of private firms, such as Vickers Armstrong and Cammell Laird. Placing orders at these firms required strict adherence to a cumbersome chain of command which moved through various divisions of the War Office. Lloyd George immediately simplified the authorization needed to expand production by cutting through traditional red tape. In the early days of June 1915 he also went on a rapid tour to advertise the aims of the new ministry and to recruit men of 'push and go' who could serve as administrative heads of the various departments created by the new ministry. He was less interested in technical experts than in men who had proved themselves successful in business and administration and who could manage large labour forces. Some recruits were, of course, leaders in technical fields, such as Ernest W. Moir, head of an engineering firm who was placed in charge of machine-gun production, and Alfred Herbert, director of a machine tool firm responsible for supplying his product to the ministry. Others, however, were businessmen, such as Samuel Hardman Lever, one of Britain's best known chartered accountants, who ran the Ministry's Finance Department, and Leonard W. Llewellyn, managing director of the Cambrian Coal Combine, who directed the Raw Materials Department. Eric Geddes, who was to serve Lloyd George loyally for many years, left the managing directorship of the North Eastern Railway to manage artillery production. Lord Moulton, a well-known scientist and jurist who became Director-General of Explosives Supply, exemplified how far Lloyd George would reach for talent. Sir Maurice Sheldon Amos, Professor of Comparative Law at the University of London, led the Priorities Department of the ministry.

Once Lloyd George had attracted a talented team, his next priority was to organize the productive capacity of the entire nation to supply the necessary munitions. Here he relied upon James Stevenson, former managing director of the distilling firm of John Walker and Company. Stevenson, as the new Director of Area Organization, divided the country into ten Munitions Areas. Each area would have a Board of Management, who would act as unpaid agents of the ministry and were responsible initially for gathering information on the industrial capacity in their areas. They would then be instructed, directly from the ministry, to manufacture what was needed for the war effort. In some cases, this meant the conversion of factories from domestic products to war materials. In others, purpose-built factories were constructed where there was an adequate labour supply: this was characteristic of the National Shell Factories, which produced the badly needed heavier shells. Complementary industries were the National Filling Factories, responsible for filling the empty shells with explosives and fuses.[136]

Assembling managerial teams at both local and national levels and converting workplaces as well as constructing new ones involved enormous challenges. Finding sufficient skilled labour to put the new wartime factories into production was no less problematic. Indeed, labour shortages had occurred even in the early months of the war: by mid-1915, the problem of sufficient labour had grown to the point of putting the entire scheme of the new ministry at risk. This was in large part due to the number of workplace volunteers who had streamed into the armed forces during the first year of war. If unrestricted recruitment were to continue, essential military production could be severely affected.[137] Both the War Office and the Admiralty attempted to place some classes of workers out of bounds for military service though a preferential badging system, designed to confer prestige upon those workers who remained at their civilian jobs and had not joined the forces. But badging did not always work: men continued to enlist and recruiting officers sometimes ignored the system in their need for fighting men.[138]

In short, there were insufficient men to staff both critical wartime industries and the ranks of the fighting forces. Matters became critical when dozens of new factories designed for munitions production were scheduled to open in the summer of 1915: thousands of new workers had to be found. Under Lloyd George's leadership, the ministry targeted the one remaining untapped reservoir of workers – women. Women already had a lengthy history of working outside the home, making up one quarter of the workforce before 1914, primarily in domestic service and the textile and clothing trades. But women workers historically were unaffiliated with trade unions, whose regulations were designed to protect male workers' wages and conditions of work. A mass of cheap semi-skilled non-union labourers flooding factory floors, most of whom would be women, could 'dilute' the work force, jeopardizing labour rights won over the years by the trades unions. In the face of Labour opposition, the ministry had to act circumspectly. A precedent was already in place dating from the Treasury Conference held in March 1915, which had sanctioned the use of semi-skilled workers and women. But that agreement had been voluntary. Lloyd George and the new ministry now believed that the time had come for new legislation to utilize women workers in crucial war work projects.

Scarcely a fortnight after his appointment to head the new ministry, Lloyd George began his campaign for turning the whole of Britain, both men and women workers – citizens all – into a workshop for war. During his tour in early June, he reiterated this theme in four significant speeches. At Manchester on 3 June 1915, he spoke to a meeting of engineers against the backdrop of the recent Russian defeat in Galicia.[139] The German victory, 'a great success' as Lloyd George admitted, was due to the organization of its workshops and to its superiority in munitions production. Britain, too, he warned, must better organize its productive capacity. To advance that goal, the state must be active. 'I come', Lloyd George stated, 'as an emissary of the State'. Because the government alone had the necessary facts at its command, it must take a lead. Most particularly, he continued, it might become necessary for the government to employ conscription to fight Britain's battles. By this he meant compulsory service in producing the needed materials of war. Up to now, the country had 'too much of the haphazard, leisurely, go-as-you-please methods'. Different principles must be extended 'to the whole field of industrial organization', especially to Labour. In short, 'we must have greater subordination in labour to the direction and control of the State'. A 'great industrial army' must be formed, whose job was not unlike its military counterpart – to defend the country against foreign foes.

The following day found Lloyd George at Liverpool where he spoke to a variety of audiences: in private with a number of businessmen; with employers mostly connected with engineering; and to the Liverpool Dock Battalion, a uniformed group of more than 500 dock workers on parade, hailed as an example for a disciplined work force in wartime.[140] Lloyd George's primary message was an appeal for the relaxation of trade union restrictions during the war, and in that regard he mentioned especially the need for more women in the workplace. The following week at Cardiff at a meeting of employers and workers in the South Wales engineering and metal trades, Lloyd George presented the technical needs of high explosive shells in destroying German entrenchments, machine-gun emplacements and barbed wire defences. Once again, he spoke of the equality of status and of sacrifice that soldiers and workers bore in the battles to come. 'Plant the flag on your workshops', he declaimed. 'Convert your lathes and your machinery into battalions which will drive the foe from the land which he has tortured and devastated and trampled upon and disgraced.'[141]

The final meeting of the four was held at Bristol, where Lloyd George spoke to representatives of the engineering trades from throughout the West Country, including Bath, Gloucester and Exeter – an audience of 1,000. Here again, Lloyd George made his plea for labour organizations to suspend their rules to allow women and unskilled workers to supplement skilled labour in war production – in other words, to allow 'dilution' of the workforce. Unity of the home front by all workers could produce enough munitions so that 'the incessant hammering of British guns' would crack the German steel barrier. Then, in his best oratorical style, Lloyd George concluded: 'you will hear the cheers of the British infantry as they march through their shattered entrenchments to victory, and in that hour the engineers will know with a thrill that the workshops of Britain have won a lasting triumph for the righteousness that exalteth a nation'.[142]

To lend weight to his campaign for a greater governmental role in the industrial life of the country, Lloyd George planted a somewhat alarmist article in William Robertson Nicoll's nonconformist *British Weekly* (10 June 1915). Warning that the next three months of the war would be 'extremely critical' for the Allies, Robertson Nicoll pointed out that the Germans, already better armed with munitions of war, would likely increase their offensive power in the future. The Germans might even attempt an invasion of Britain. To meet this impending military crisis, the nation must be roused. Praising Lloyd George's recent speeches at Manchester and Liverpool, Robertson Nicoll applauded him especially for his intended use of the principle of compulsion. This 'compulsory power', he wrote, 'must be extended to the whole of industry – to employer and workman alike'. In sum, the new Minister of Munitions must be given the opportunity, without delay, to address the munitions shortfall. 'To carp at him in the midst of his mighty task should be regarded as a work of an enemy.' Indeed, if Lloyd George found himself 'hampered by conditions' imposed upon him by either the government or the House of Commons, he would 'refuse to go on'.[143]

The article was clearly designed to remove any opposition to Lloyd George's policy at the ministry – under his threat of resignation – and to prepare the way for a quick passage of new legislation. Only ten days after his speech at Bristol, Lloyd George introduced to the House of Commons the Munitions of War Act, which moved quickly through Parliament, receiving the Royal Assent on 2 July. Although the act did not legislate industrial conscription in the strict sense of the term, it travelled fairly far along that path by fixing wages and salaries; suspending trade union rules; mandating arbitration; declaring strikes illegal; and by its Clause 7, binding workers to their jobs for the duration of the war unless freed by their employers. In addition, the Minister of Munitions could declare any factory a 'controlled establishment' if it were thought necessary to the war effort: such a declaration brought it directly under the control of the ministry. These severe restrictions seemed to be directed far more against labour than management, whose only restriction appeared to be a clause limiting wartime profits in the munitions industry. Perhaps this act led Grigg to claim that Lloyd George acquired 'almost dictatorial powers' while he served as Minister of Munitions.[144]

In the months that followed, Lloyd George often felt compelled to bring the full force of official reprimand into play to keep munitions makers up to the mark. Addressing the Leeds National Factory assigned to make shells, for example, he made his displeasure at their performance abundantly clear. He declared his 'disappointment' at their lagging 'contemptible output'. 'To put it quite frankly', he continued, 'either this factory is being muddled, or this system is a complete failure'.[145] In another instance, he chastised one of his department heads for a report that was 'profoundly disquieting'.[146] To another, he declared their plan for labour dilution 'insignificant and unsatisfactory'.[147] When he discovered that an official circular was sent without his knowledge to munitions factories suggesting holidays at Easter and Whitsuntide, he ordered it countermanded 'at once' on the grounds that output would be too diminished.[148] Higher officials in the Ministry of Munitions were not immune. In July 1915, Lloyd George sacked Sir Percy Girouard, a Kitchener protégé. 'He was not an efficient organizer', was the succinct reason given.[149]

Lloyd George's hard charging tactics did not always bear fruit. The path of industrial relations proved especially difficult. Only a fortnight after the passage of the act, the South Wales coal miners struck over wages and working conditions.[150] When Lloyd George's pleas failed, he resorted to a series of threats – including proclaiming the mines a controlled industry. But this proved ineffective: virtually the entire work force of 200,000 downed tools. Although the Munitions of War Act prohibited strikes, such a unified action on the part of so many workers made prosecution impossible. In addition, the critical need for coal (used in the production of high explosives and as fuel for the newer dreadnoughts) forced the government to settle the strike on generous terms by exerting pressure upon the colliery owners.

A far more contentious episode occurred several months later on the Clyde, the most important munitions centre in the country. The Clydeside industrial complex, with Glasgow at its heart, contained 370,000 workers in shipyards, mines, iron, steel and chemical manufacturing. There was additionally some textile and food production, as well as a high concentration of transport workers.[151] 'Red Clyde' workers already had a reputation for industrial militancy. In February of 1915, an unofficial strike in Glasgow – called by shop stewards, rather than by the Amalgamated Society of Engineers – demanded an increase in wages. A new, more militant organization emerged from the shop stewards' initiative, the Clyde Workers' Committee (CWC), which soon began to enlist large numbers of engineers. To Clydesiders the Munitions Act, with its restrictive clauses, suggested collusion between government and the bosses, a conspiracy to keep wages low and hours long. When Lloyd George imposed dilution of the workforce in late 1915, a wave of resentment swept the Clyde.

Lloyd George discovered these conditions first hand when he visited the region in late December 1915. Speaking in St Andrews Hall, Glasgow, on Christmas morning before a boisterous crowd of 3,000 workers and CWC activists, Lloyd George and the chairman of the meeting, Arthur Henderson (the only Labour MP in the Cabinet) were accorded a rough reception. Henderson was met with booing, hissing and interruptions of every sort as he opened the meeting. In attempting to put to rest the rumour that dilution was an employer's plan, Henderson claimed that it had in fact been promoted by several leading trade union leaders and taken up by the Ministry of Munitions. In his remarks, Lloyd George fared no better. When he rose to speak, a chorus of boos and a boisterous rendition of the 'The Red Flag' delayed his remarks. Interruptions were constant throughout his speech. In trying to reassure the crowd, Lloyd George claimed that the government's purpose was 'to put skilled men on skilled work'. Light work, 'which requires neither strength nor skill ... should be performed by women'. As the interruptions continued, Lloyd George moved from persuasion to exhortation. More than a half million casualties on the battlefield have already occurred, he said. It was essential to staunch the flow of the wounded and dying. He appealed to the workmen of the nation: 'help us quickly; help us thoroughly', he urged. From this plea, Lloyd George tried to frame a promise. If the workmen came forward now, they would 'strengthen their claim at the end of the war ... for a redress of any grievances they may suffer to-day'. Even this met an unfriendly response. Finally, Lloyd George adopted a threatening tone. 'All this chaffering about relaxing a rule here and suspending a custom there is out of place.'[152]

The meeting was such a disaster for Lloyd George and his policy of dilution that London papers were apparently persuaded by the Press Censor to publish only a heavily sanitized version of the events. [153] However, a small socialist paper, the *Forward*, published a complete account of the meeting, including the crowd reaction. Stung by these public revelations, Lloyd George, along with some of his closest advisors, decided to suppress the paper. This drew down on him considerable criticism, however, including questions put forward in the House of Commons, where he was forced to defend himself in an equivocating fashion that has drawn criticism since.[154] For Lloyd George, the lesson learned was that he would not thereafter take a visible role in enforcing dilution. He did, however, fully support actions carried out by local dilution commissioners as they enforced the provisions of the Munitions of War Act against recalcitrant Clydeside workers. Leaders of the CWC were arrested; some were deported from the region.[155] The CWC was thus broken up and the process of dilution went forward. Within a few months, several thousand women were employed in various engineering works on the Clyde.

Concomitant with the question of industrial compulsion as it was developing in late 1915 was an equally serious matter involving the general role of the State in providing sufficient men to fill the military ranks. In the early months of the war, high volunteer rates had kept the army better supplied with men than with munitions. The ideal of a volunteer army was strongly supported – for a variety of reasons – by orthodox *laissez faire* Liberals, the Labour Party, trade unionists and Irish Nationalists. The Cabinet itself was very largely voluntarist. But by late summer 1915, the static trench warfare on the Western Front and its voracious appetite for men and materiel demanded increasing numbers of new recruits. Among Conservative MPs especially, agitation for a military conscription bill gathered steam. Within the Cabinet, Conservatives found a ready ally in the belligerent Churchill. More surprising, perhaps, was the support of the Minister for Munitions.

It was no sudden conversion for Lloyd George. As early as 1910, in his coalition plan of that year, he had strongly suggested that compulsory training on the model of the Swiss militia should be one of the items 'to be thoroughly looked into'. Since then, there had been occasional positive references to conscription. In a private conversation with Riddell and a few others in late 1912, for example, Lloyd George divulged – 'within the four corners of this room' (as he put it) – that he favoured universal military service. But he also admitted that it could never be carried 'except in the case of some great national emergency'.[156] Once the war was underway, he was more forward in his advocacy. His June 1915 speeches and Robertson Nicoll's *British Weekly* article had hinted at his conscriptionist views. Indeed, the entire thrust of his work as Minister for Munitions and its harnessing of the nation's productive capacity for war was only a step away from a military draft. In August 1915 he was reportedly 'pushing hard' for conscription during a Cabinet meeting.[157] A week later, at a War Policy Committee, he stated unequivocally that delay in adopting some scheme of military compulsion brought the nation closer 'to disaster'.[158]

By October 1915 Asquith faced a surging conscriptionist tide in the Cabinet, with Lords Lansdowne and Curzon, Walter Long and Churchill, as well as Lloyd George making the case that 'our voluntary system of recruiting' could no longer provide sufficient troops for the needs of the army.[159] Privately, Lloyd George unburdened himself to Frances Stevenson with stronger comments. Denouncing the 'grave', even 'desperate', situation, especially Asquith's laggard pursuit of the war in general and his delay in addressing conscription in particular, Lloyd George also complained that it was impossible to get the Prime Minister to do 'anything'.[160] Indeed Asquith's efforts to resolve the conscription crisis had a labyrinthine quality that was difficult to follow. He appointed committee after committee during the conscription debate, perhaps as a delaying tactic in an attempt to introduce conscription slowly. Or perhaps it was a device designed simply to keep him in the game with the hope the conscriptionist chorus would die down.[161]

Asquith's hand was finally forced in late November, 1915 when a by-election at Methyr Tydfil returned John Stanton, a conscriptionist, over the official voluntarist Labour candidate. Lloyd George was reportedly 'jubilant' at the outcome.[162] Asquith had now no option but to fashion some measure of conscription. On 5 January 1916 he introduced the Military Service Bill (the 'Bachelor's Bill') in the House of Commons. Inducting only able-bodied single men and widowers without dependent children, it quickly became law by an overwhelming vote of 403:105. By conceding partial conscription, Asquith hoped to satisfy somewhat conscriptionist demands without alienating Liberal supporters.

Asquith's hesitant policy over conscription prompted a broader dissatisfaction over his uncertain direction of the war. Lloyd George's own reservations about the Prime Minister had been expressed privately to his brother months earlier: 'He has muddled everything up to the present', he wrote. 'I fear a great split in the Cabinet.'[163] By early 1916, Lloyd George's pessimistic mood had deepened. He seemed to his friends uncharacteristically rudderless and dispirited. Addison thought him not 'in good form', 'overdone' and 'nervy'.[164] Riddell noticed after one of his 'breakfast parties' that Lloyd George 'was feeling tired out' and had to telephone for a doctor.[165] Scott reported that Lloyd George was looking 'worn and old' as he continued to express his 'profound dissatisfaction with the whole conduct of the war'. [166] Frances Stevenson, ever solicitous, observed that Lloyd George was often tired, needed a rest and was 'rather depressed ... about things in general'.[167] He even considered resignation because, as he confided to Riddell, Asquith had 'no plan, no initiative, no grip, no driving force'.[168] He informed C.P. Scott of the *Manchester Guardian* of his 'strong and increasing dissatisfaction with the conduct of the war'.[169] To his brother William he also wrote despairingly: 'Things critical in Cabinet. I am afraid we are blundering into defeat. Blunder after blunder. There is no handling of the situation. Our chief has no decision or drive.'[170] There was little doubt that his dissatisfaction with Asquith's leadership and the lack of progress in the war was contributing to his malaise. Most critical of all was the need for more men under the colours. The Bachelor's Bill was only a partial solution.

Under continuous pressure both within and without the Cabinet, on 2 May 1916 Asquith introduced in the House of Commons legislation for the general conscription of all eligible adult males. By the end of the month it had become law. The only opposition came from 27 Liberal and ten Labour MPs. There were some positive outcomes to this decision. A vastly simplified conscription scheme had triumphed over a complicated and difficult compromise. Lloyd George, pleased with the conscriptionist legislation, did not resign. If Asquith did not escape obloquy, he at least remained Prime Minister. Yet the government, kicked about by the House of Commons for its continual fumbling of recruitment, had gained no points. Asquith's authority had been further weakened.[171]

For our purposes, the greater question is the role of Lloyd George throughout the conscription controversy, especially during the spring of 1916. What was his game? Was he using conscription as a stick to beat Asquith with the idea of replacing him as Prime Minister? Hankey for one had heard rumours that during Asquith's trip to Paris and Rome in late March to consult with the Allies, Lloyd George (along with Carson and Churchill) was cooking up a political plot against the Prime Minister. Alerted by Hankey, Asquith co-opted Lloyd George by inviting him along for part of the journey.[172] It is also certainly true that Lloyd George led Riddell to believe that he might be willing to form a new party.[173] Perhaps he intended to break up the ministry and seize the premiership.[174] But more likely, Lloyd George was not seeking higher office for himself; rather, he was simply attempting, as he often said, to put pressure on Asquith for more 'grip' in his approach to the war. He wanted military conscription to complement industrial compulsion.[175] Only in this way could Britain organize the nation fully to meet wartime exigencies. But to the dismay of the Asquith government – even as it struggled to find the key to victory over the Germans on the Western Front – an unexpected armed rebellion much closer to its shores was soon to prove an additional and equally deadly threat to Britain's military capacity.

12

PRIME MINISTER IN WAR

On 24 April 1916, a day before the parliamentary secret session on conscription was to begin, Irish insurgents stormed the Dublin Post Office and declared an independent Ireland. Centuries of Anglo-Irish conflict lay behind the Easter Rising of 1916.[1] The heightened desire for Home Rule in Southern Ireland in recent years and the Ulster resistance in the north to that ideal were crucial in creating a fertile ground for rebellion. Most of all, the Rising's leaders recognized the opportune moment when the British imperial government – distracted by the demands of war on the continent – could not turn its full attention to its nearest point of weakness. Even after the Rising had begun, the Asquith Cabinet, preoccupied with the conscription controversy and lacking detailed information on the assault, was initially unsure of its response. Within a week, however, British forces on the ground, assisted by a heavy bombardment of artillery and a gunboat operating on the Liffey, reduced the rebel strongholds and forced their surrender. Shortly afterwards 15 rebel leaders were tried and executed by drumhead military courts, actions performed without either the knowledge or the sanction of the Cabinet. Thus it was that the Rising's leaders – among them Clarke, Connolly, McBride, MacDermott, MacDonagh, O'Rahilly, Pearse and Plunkett – became martyrs to their countrymen for the nationalist cause.

The immediate aftermath of the Rising was draconian.[2] The British government decreed martial law for Ireland, administered by a military governor. Arrests, trials and deportations became commonplace, as were reprisals against innocent civilians, including murderous attacks by British soldiers. But the effect only insured a broader sympathy for the Rising among the Irish. County councils throughout Ireland passed resolutions condemning British harshness. There were widespread reports of priests praising the rebel martyrs. In England itself, opinions were more mixed. Some Liberals, in tune with the historic Liberal connection with Home Rule for Ireland, believed that a peaceful and equitable settlement even after the Easter Rising was still possible.[3] Most Conservatives, especially the fervent unionists among them, were aghast at the attempted revolution against British authority, especially when it emerged that the insurgents had solicited German assistance. Conservatives therefore opposed any conciliatory moves towards Ireland as concessions to rebellion, and were more determined than ever to resist Irish Home Rule.[4]

Once it had grasped the basic facts, it must be said that the Liberal government acted with reasonable dispatch in managing the crisis. Accountable ministers in Dublin were removed: these included the Viceroy, Lord Wimborne; the Irish Chief Secretary, Augustine Birrell; and Sir Matthew Nathan, Permanent Under-Secretary. Unable to find a new Chief Secretary in a hurry, Asquith himself went to Dublin (11– 18 May) where he spent long hours 'sitting in Dublin Castle', gathering information and attempting to shore up a floundering administration.[5] Asquith became convinced that the old colonial system of governing Ireland was at an end and that Home Rule legislation for Ireland, which had been put into cold storage when war broke out, must be revived. Upon his return, Asquith continued to demonstrate unusual decisiveness. He asked Lloyd George to become Irish Secretary in order to tamp down separatist sentiment in Ireland and to fashion an agreement that would also settle the outstanding differences between Ulster and the south. Although Lloyd George refused the Secretaryship, believing that his work at Munitions was unfinished, he agreed to accept the role of mediator between Irish Unionists, led by Carson, and the Nationalists under Redmond.[6]

Employing what Turner has called 'shuttle diplomacy' – that is, not seeing the two sides together in one room, but rather in separate meetings – Lloyd George made rapid progress in late May and early June.[7] The draft agreement proposed an immediate reintroduction of the pre-war (but suspended) Home Rule Bill, thus granting Home Rule to the 26 southern counties. Six northern Ulster counties would be excluded, remaining directly under Westminster governance. In addition, the number of both Irish and Ulster MPs at Westminster would be unchanged. The new Irish Home Rule Parliament in Ireland would consist of a House of Commons made up of the Nationalist MPs who sat at Westminster, and an Irish senate to be nominated by the Lord Lieutenant of Ireland.

Some confusion emerged over the negotiated terms, however. Carson, the most prominent Ulster supporter, understood that the six county exclusion would be permanent: indeed, Lloyd George told him that the Cabinet had so agreed. Redmond for the southern Irish, on the other hand, was led to believe by Lloyd George that the Ulster exclusion was temporary – only for the duration of the war. Whether or not Lloyd George intended to mislead the Irish leaders is a matter of controversy. Perhaps, driven by a purely instrumental need for a quick solution to an important matter, he thought that both sides would be willing to set aside their differences and to compromise without paying much attention to the finer points of the proposal. After all, each side would gain what it wished: Ulster would remain within the Union and the Irish Nationalists would win Home Rule. But when it emerged that the principals in the proposal had been given contradictory promises and that Lloyd George had been essentially acting on his own without Cabinet sanction, there was a chorus of complaint from Conservative unionists. Walter Guinness, for example, condemned Lloyd George's 'usual adroitness' in offering 'bribes and baits all round' to secure Irish Home Rule.[8]

More important was the reaction among Conservative leaders. Carson proclaimed himself 'astounded' at Lloyd George's actions and maintained he had been 'disgracefully treated'. Curzon also believed that the unionists had been 'tricked'.[9] Selborne went so far as to resign from the Cabinet, explaining to the House of Lords as he did so that Lloyd George had acted beyond his authority: he was 'not a plenipotentiary'. Moreover, to inaugurate such an important constitutional change as proposed by Lloyd George in time of war would be 'perilous'.[10] Balcarres, who replaced Selborne at the Board of Agriculture, was sympathetic to Selborne's reasons for resignation. To his diary he confided that the Cabinet had been 'bamboozled into a hopeless commitment on the Irish question'.[11] Walter Long and Lord Lansdowne, Conservatives in Asquith's coalition government and strong Unionist sympathizers, also castigated the proposals.[12] Long, speaking for the indignant southern unionists, was sure that 'Ll. G. has sold us'.[13] He and Lansdowne were determined to defeat the proposals, even though some Conservatives in the Cabinet, such as Bonar Law and Balfour, favoured them.[14] Lloyd George was taken somewhat aback by the flurry of negative response: 'Irish situation getting hotter and hotter', he reported to his brother.[15]

Lansdowne's speech in the House of Lords on 11 July 1916 was the climax of the campaign against the Irish proposals. He argued against any experimentation in Irish government at a dangerous time in the life of the country: instead, he advocated a firmer hand under the existing constitutional framework. At a Cabinet meeting several days later, Lansdowne toughened his message, claiming that Home Rule would be a surrender to force and would encourage more violence in Ireland. This view carried the day. Asquith and Lloyd George acceded to the Cabinet majority.[16] Thus the old imperial system of governing Ireland from Dublin Castle was reaffirmed. Returning as Viceroy was Lord Wimborne. Replacing the disgraced Birrell was H.E. Duke, the new Chief Secretary.[17] Administratively speaking, Ireland remained as it had been before the Easter Rising. Unknown as yet to the British government, not far beneath the surface of imperial politics, the fires of resentment continued to burn. But in Ireland, as many well knew, much had been changed by the Rising. Indeed, in the words of one, they had 'changed utterly'.

Lloyd George's intervention in this latest Irish crisis had failed, and failed badly.[18] Gambling on a quick and cobbled together solution for the most intractable problem in British politics, he seems to have overreached himself. In so doing, he was exposed politically: open to criticism from on all sides, he became more isolated and mistrusted than ever.[19] One wonders why he undertook the task at all. The consequences of failure were obvious even to him.[20] But with Lloyd George, the political dimension should never be forgotten. By settling Ireland and providing Home Rule (at least to most of Ireland), he could keep his ties to the historic Gladstonian Home Rule wing of the Liberal Party. By burnishing his reputation as a solver of problems, he would also strengthen his position within the coalition, perhaps even with an eye to attaining its ultimate leadership.[21] But there is another reason for his willingness to take on the task. In public statements, private meetings and political discourse Lloyd George was consistent in declaring that the war was going badly and that every effort should continue to be placed on driving the nation forward to a final victory over Britain's enemies. Any distraction to that effort, political or otherwise, should be rebuffed or settled quickly. As he put it to Carson during the initial stages of the negotiations after the Easter Rising, 'we should get Ireland out of the way in order to press on with the war'.[22]

In the meantime, another opportunity for Lloyd George to expand his Cabinet authority opened tragically and unexpectedly. On 6 June 1916, during a time when Lloyd George was still intensively involved in the Irish negotiations, news reached London that the armoured cruiser, HMS *Hampshire*, which had the previous morning sailed out of Scapa Flow westerly through the Pentland Firth and then north along the west coast of Hoy, had struck a German mine off Marwick Head. Heavy seas, which had prevented proper escorts, also made lifeboats difficult to launch, or, once launched, to keep afloat. Within 15 minutes, the ship sank by the bows. On board was Earl Kitchener, along with a complement of a dozen staff and servants, bound to Russia along the northern route. He had been dispatched on a high level mission to discuss strategy and war aims. Of the 655 men on board, only 12 survived, none of whom was a member of the Kitchener party. Kitchener's body was never found.[23]

While the public reacted to the news with shock and dismay, the government worked swiftly behind the scenes to find a new Secretary for War. Only two candidates seemed likely – Bonar Law and Lloyd George. Within a few days of the General's death, the two men met at the home of Max Aitken, who acted as interlocutor.[24] There, it is claimed, Bonar Law recognized that Lloyd George was better suited to the job than he and withdrew from consideration.[25] For Lloyd George – given his critique of the direction of the war, and his belief that civilian authority should be given greater play in the conduct of it – the new Cabinet office was a natural step upward. He was not only critical of Asquith's wartime leadership: he had also come to believe that the military conduct of the war was deeply flawed, leading to 'inexcusable' failures of strategy and command. There were, he said, 'no brains at the top' and General Haig, was 'not an able man'.[26] At the War Office, he could make a direct impact upon military operations, an area in which, as we have seen, he had been interested from the beginning of the war. After several meetings between Lloyd George and his more intimate advisors, Lloyd George accepted the position officially on 6 July 1916.

The great irony of his taking the War Office, as Lloyd George was well aware, was that Kitchener had been gradually stripped of much of his power as Secretary for War. Lloyd George's criticisms had undoubtedly contributed to the weakening of Kitchener's authority and reputation. His role had been reduced to administration and recruiting, essentially peacetime duties. The important duties of the War Secretary, such as signing operational orders and directing battlefield operations, had been shifted to General William Robertson, who became Chief of the Imperial General Staff in December 1915. During the five months that he was Secretary for War, Lloyd George again and again attempted to reclaim the former influence of that office and to override Robertson. But he had little success: Robertson proved extremely jealous of his prerogatives. He became the sole military adviser to the War Council. Simultaneously, he discontinued briefings to ministers, substituting instead only a weekly summary.[27] Moreover he steadfastly refused to consider any change in the Western strategy. This was in direct conflict with Lloyd George's long-held views that an eastern strategy should be employed. Within a few weeks of accepting office, Lloyd George indicated his support in a War Council meeting for a French plan to attack Bulgaria in order to protect Rumania. This was met with an immediate challenge from Robertson. Disagreement between Robertson and Lloyd George over war aims in the Balkans and the primacy of the Western Front continued to fester throughout the summer of 1916.

Lloyd George's conflict with army top brass soon widened beyond his disputes with Robertson. Civil-military relations became increasingly strained during one of the most controversial battles of the war – the Somme offensive by British and French forces in late June 1916.[28] The Somme operation was prompted by the need to counter the effects of a major German operation, which had begun in late February 1916, against the great fortress of Verdun. Thorough preparations were made weeks beforehand. The Somme sector (named for the river which traversed it) was chosen in part because of its gently rolling, open landscape and firm chalky subsoil, an aid to massive troop movements. New railheads were built to move and supply troops for the battle; wells were dug for fresh water; thousands of miles of cable were laid both below and above ground for communication purposes. In addition, although it was primarily a British Army operation, the French gave strong support.

Action began with several days' artillery bombardment over a 20,000-yard front. After what was considered sufficient softening up, Haig ordered 14 divisions forward on 1 July. Some units went rapidly over the top in small groups to reach the German trenches. Others, however, moved forward through no man's land, where they met dense machine gun fire at close range. Only then was it learned that German machine gun emplacements had been largely undamaged by British artillery. Of approximately 120,000 British soldiers who took part in the first day's assault, 19,000 were killed outright and another 38,000 were either wounded or missing.[29] Haig had hoped British forces would break through the German trenches, allowing a follow up by cavalry, which would then ravage at will the enemy's defensive system. But this never happened – neither on the first day nor in the weeks and months that followed. As the battle lengthened into a stalemate, tactics shifted from an all out intensive attack to smaller, more defined objectives. Little ground was gained, however, and casualties mounted. The Somme became a slogging match, finally ending in the rains and mud of autumn, which made continued operations nearly impossible. Overall, some 650,000 British and French were killed and wounded compared to 500,000 Germans. The struggle lasted for 141 days, ending inconclusively on 19 November 1916.

The impact of the Somme upon the domestic front as the battle raged month after month was palpable. Casualty lists and the long lines of the returning wounded brought to the home front the perils of an interminable war. The Somme seemed to presage even greater casualties if the conflict continued as a war of attrition, of hammering away at the German defences with a consequent staggering loss of life among the Allied armies.[30] Not only were the survivors, the wounded and their families experiencing the appalling implications of such a policy: members of the government, too, were affected. Asquith himself, who lost his son Raymond during the Somme offensive, was thereafter (some thought) never quite the same.[31] Bonar Law has been described as in a state of continual worry about the fate of his own sons during the campaigns of 1916 – a concern tragically borne out in the following year, when his two eldest sons were killed in action.[32] Maurice Hankey, the indispensable secretary and adviser to the great, lost his brother Donald.

Even as the casualty lists lengthened, the government had remained supportive of the campaign. The official word was optimistic. Asquith assured Haig as late as September 1916, many weeks into the epic struggle, that the government was 'well pleased' with the operations.[33] But Lloyd George was less pleased. As casualties rose, Lloyd George's doubts rose proportionally. On an official visit to France in early September 1916, he visited General Foch at the French headquarters. In a celebrated interview with the General, Lloyd George raised questions about the casualty rates of Allied forces: he particularly solicited the General's opinion on the heavy British casualties. He also asked Foch's opinion about the ability of British generals.[34] A few weeks later, Lloyd George sent Field Marshall Sir John French (then the General Office Commanding-in-Chief Home Forces) on a mission to General Joffre to inquire about French artillery and tactics. Lloyd George was clearly seeking specific information about the causes of a flagging military operation, which he claimed lay within his purview as Secretary for War.

Historians since have supported Lloyd George's reservations about British military leadership during the Somme. The Somme has become the symbol for British military leaders' incompetence which led to useless human slaughter and suffering. The primary target of criticism has been General Haig. Some historians have seen him as a deeply flawed individual – a man whose 'notorious inarticulacy' and 'remarkable inability to communicate', as well as his 'angry, suspicious nature', made him unfit for command.[35] In addition, Haig often seemed detached and removed from the battle. Once his troops were engaged, he was guilty of 'chateau generalship'.[36] Apart from his personal foibles, it has also been claimed that as a cavalryman, Haig had little understanding of artillery and lacked expertise in the complexities of artillery-infantry cooperation.[37] Consequently, he stubbornly ordered waves of attacks upon unyielding German defensive positions. Other historians, Prior and Wilson among them, agree that Haig had 'performed badly' on routine matters of command. He seemed rarely able to impose his authority on the battlefield. His conception of warfare 'was rooted somewhere in the nineteenth century' and he was 'in denial about the reality of warfare on the Western Front'. Furthermore, he lacked 'the deadliness, the fixity of purpose, or the type of mind' that could make the precise calculations of munitions and guns needed to achieve substantial results on the front line.[38]

In his wide-ranging critique, J.P. Harris agrees with other critics that the 'truly horrific day' of 1 July 1916 on the Somme was largely a failure of Haig's 'limited knowledge and understanding of artillery'.[39] Harris also condemns Haig's characteristic 'extreme optimism', which led him to believe that a breakthrough of the German field fortifications was imminent.[40] As the Somme campaign continued into the summer and early autumn, British military efforts fell into 'a multiplicity of piecemeal operations' which, Harris believes, indicated 'a breakdown of command and control'. [41] In addition, Haig's lack of talent for 'positive planning and clear direction' was often at fault.[42] Harris also believes that Haig's 'almost maniacal stubbornness' militated against what could have a more productive flexibility in tackling the German trench system.[43] Overall, a more graduated, patient and systemic step-by-step approach, such as Rawlinson's 'bite and hold', would have worn down German defenders at far less cost to British soldiers.[44] As it was, Haig 'squandered' the fighting power of his army. [45]

Haig, however, has his defenders. Among the stoutest of these is John Terraine, who makes the case for the General's indispensability in winning the war. Although admitting that the first day of the Somme was 'an almost unmitigated disaster', Terraine believes that as the battle wore on, the German Army 'suffered irreparable harm'.[46] As far as Haig's detachment from the front lines, Terraine points out that Haig was firmly against placing any high command officers directly in harm's way, too close to the fighting. Complementary to this principle, Haig also believed that as Commander-in-Chief, once he had outlined broad strategic plans, it was then up to the direct commanders on the ground to implement them. Haig's persistence, even in the face of appalling casualties, was not the result of ignorance, incompetence, or callousness: it was a calculated strategy. To pound the enemy unceasingly, to interdict supplies, to prevent their rest and reorganization, to offer no respite to the German forces was his aim. Overall, Terraine believes that the Somme was 'an unquestionable Allied victory' which paved the way for the final defeat of German forces.[47]

The Asquith government, including Lloyd George as the new Secretary of War, could not have known at the time the complexities of battlefield successes and failures as they developed during the Somme and as portrayed in the scholarly skirmishes decades later. The perceptions of the government were framed by the lengthening casualty lists and the virtual stalemate on the ground. The Somme was seen as the climax in a series of losses, surrenders and botched campaigns since the war began. By the end of 1916, it was clear that Britain was not winning the war. At best, it was an uneven record. On the Western Front, the Germans had taken everything that the Allies had thrown at them and had not yielded. In the eastern theatre, the Ottoman Empire had won not only defensive battles, such as Gallipoli, but also had successfully gone on the offensive in Mesopotamia. Britain's Balkan strategy had also reached stalemate after substantial losses inflicted by the enemy.

Perhaps the greatest disappointment for Britain in the contest of arms was the chequered exploits of the Royal Navy. Although there were some promising naval actions early on – at the battles of Heligoland Bight in August 1914, the Falkland Islands in December 1914 and the Dogger Bank in January 1915 – countervailing German naval victories offset these gains. A single German submarine sank three armoured cruisers off the Dutch coast in September 1914 with a loss of 1,600 British sailors. In the same month, a small cruiser, the *Pathfinder*, was torpedoed and sunk just off the Firth of Forth. A month later, the battleship *Audacious* went down after striking a German mine near the Irish coast. On 1 November 1914, a German cruiser force overwhelmed a British squadron off the Chilean coast. In December 1914, German cruisers bombarded the coastal towns of Hartlepool, Whitby, and Scarborough, inflicting 500 civilian casualties.[48]

The most significant naval action of the war was the celebrated battle of Jutland of 31 May–1 June 1916. This was an engagement of epic proportions. British vessels totalled 149, including 28 dreadnoughts. Germany had 100 ships, including 16 dreadnoughts.[49] During the encounter, the British Grand Fleet lost three battle cruisers and eight destroyers while the German High Seas fleet lost two battleships, four cruisers and eight destroyers. Although the Germans broke off contact in retreating, the British suffered far greater casualties (6,945 to 2,921). German gunners also proved more accurate and demonstrated a higher level of skill in night-time action than their British counterparts. In returning to base, Vice-Admiral Reinhard Scheer claimed the victory, serving champagne on the conning bridge of his flagship, *Friedrich der Grosse*. In Britain, there was shock that the navy of Drake and Nelson had not overwhelmingly prevailed. Naval officers and men of the Grand Fleet were no less disappointed: the best that could be offered was a 'partial victory', not the smashing of the German fleet that had been expected.[50] The deep sense of disappointment at the time was heightened symbolically five days later when HMS *Hampshire* went down with Kitchener aboard.

An even more disturbing development in the war at sea was Germany's unrestricted submarine warfare, which began in August 1916. German submarines were soon sinking 643,000 tons a month – a direct threat to the importation of essential foodstuffs, especially wheat, to Britain. Balcarres, as President of the Board of Agriculture in the Cabinet, bore special responsibility for food supply, began to confide in his diary in late 1916 that the country was 'short of food and going to be still shorter'.[51] In early November, after an official visit to the War Office, Balcarres wrote that Lloyd George was 'getting nervous' and 'anxious' about the food supply. Balcarres noted additionally that Lloyd George had told him that some 'heroic remedy … a gigantic effort must be made' to cultivate more land.[52] The following day, Balcarres made the same report to Asquith. But here, he was disappointed: Asquith seemed 'ill and frail – also weak and undecided', offering only a hope of a 'generous providence' as a check to German submarine activity.[53]

As if these naval and military failures were not enough, financial pressures relating to the costs of war were also becoming serious. During his term of office as Munitions Minister, Lloyd George had been instrumental in engaging the vast resources of the United States to the aid of the Allies.[54] He established the first resident British mission in the United States, whose job it was to purchase arms and munitions and to oversee their manufacture and shipment across the Atlantic. Payment for these weapons of war was maintained through such devices as gold shipments from Britain and loans raised in the United States. The need to import food and other supplies added to the tally. This financial arrangement initially worked smoothly enough. But the unexpected duration of the war and its extraordinary materiel absorption meant that before long Britain was heavily indebted to the

United States. By the spring of 1916, as confidence in the pound waned, the declining exchange rate of the pound against the dollar raised concerns. By November 1916, the British Treasury needed £5 million a day to pay for the war, nearly half of which was being raised in the United States. Britain also found itself in the position of financially supporting its allies, especially France and Russia, thus additionally straining British resources.

Given these military and financial difficulties, it should not be surprising that some in the Cabinet began to question whether or not continuing the war was desirable, or even possible. In a Cabinet paper dated 13 November 1916, Lord Lansdowne wondered aloud if the manpower and the industrial resources of Britain could stand additional strains in pursuing the war. Not known as a pacifist (indeed, he had taken a hard line in Irish matters), Lansdowne had begun to doubt the strategy of the 'breakthrough' which lay behind the 1916 military campaigns. He proposed lending a friendly ear to any offer of peace or mediation which might shorten the war. It should not be thought, however, that Lansdowne was alone among ranking politicians who had doubts about the possibility of victory. Lloyd George himself expressed his own fears, most fully and intimately to Frances Stevenson. Terming the Somme 'a ghastly failure', Lloyd George could not readily see a way out.[55] He believed that the military were 'running the country on the rocks'.[56] In a depressed mood, he thought everything was 'in a muddle' and that it was 'too late to do anything'.[57] To Riddell, he confided that he was 'very apprehensive concerning the military position' and was doubtful 'of the wisdom of the advance on the Somme' where the losses had been 'very serious'.[58] On one occasion, Riddell found Lloyd George 'very gloomy': indeed, he confessed that he had 'not felt so depressed before'.[59] Lloyd George did not hide his feelings from more public figures. Hankey recounted a lengthy discussion with Asquith who mentioned that Lloyd George was 'very depressed about the war, very disappointed with the lack of imagination of the General Staff, and very disgusted at the heavy losses involved in the offensive on the Somme'.[60]

Lansdowne's memo was likely the final straw for Lloyd George, who had become convinced that defeatism and acquiescence to a stubborn and stalled military leadership could not win the war. On 20 November 1916, he met with Edward Carson and Bonar Law to discuss his ideas for pursuing the war more effectively. This meeting, as Turner puts it, 'hatched the plan' for a new war committee of only three men whose sole responsibility would be to guide the war effort – effectively displacing the preponderant military influence.[61] Lloyd George was clearly the animating force behind the triumvirate. Bonar Law was a natural ally as the official leader of the opposition party with a seat in the Cabinet. Carson's reputation in the House of Commons as an independent-minded dynamic leader with strong Unionist tendencies had made him popular, especially among Conservative backbenchers. Moreover, he had favourably impressed Lloyd George during their negotiations over Ireland and their agreement on the need for conscription. By the summer of 1916, Lloyd George and Carson were meeting occasionally to discuss the conduct of the war. In July, Lloyd George spoke of Carson 'in glowing terms' to Riddell: Carson, he said, was a 'man of resolution, good judgment, and inspiring personality'. Lloyd George confided further that the nation would probably 'prefer Carson to Asquith'.[62]

The formation of the triumvirate took place at a time when, as Balcarres describes it, 'a wave of anxiety' was sweeping through 'the inner circles' which, he feared, would soon be reflected in the public mind.[63] Clearly something had to be done. On 22 November 1916, a Cabinet meeting discussed Lansdowne's memorandum. Lloyd George differed from its implications and thought that 'a knock-out blow' was possible against the enemy.[64] During each of the following two days, the War Committee discussed the need for a restructuring of executive machinery in order to conduct the war more effectively. Within the Cabinet meetings, too, there was a growing concern about the prosecution of the war. Balcarres noted the heightened tension. Balfour, for example, 'looked ominously depressed ... almost bent double by anxiety'.[65] Balcarres himself thought the situation was 'indeed terrifying': the ministry seemed paralyzed by indecision.[66] That same day, Bonar Law, after a number of meetings with Carson and Lloyd George, wrote to Asquith proposing a smaller War Committee with Lloyd George as its chair. The time had come for a crucial change in government that would eventually break the administrative log jam and find the key to winning the war.

The days of late November and early December 1916 were a maze of hurried meetings, private conversations and anxious letters among the political leaders of all parties. Lloyd George on the one hand and Asquith on the other, with Bonar Law as intermediary, were at the centre of events. Lloyd George took the lead in twice suggesting the formation of a small committee meeting continuously with the responsibility for managing the war. Its members would include the triumvirate plus Asquith. But the Prime Minister, fearful of the loss of his own power, turned down these proposals.[67] In the meantime, Bonar Law met with the Conservative members of the coalition Cabinet and other Conservative leaders. They were nearly unanimous that Asquith must go. The climax of the negotiations was a twofold action. First, Lloyd George threatened to resign from the government unless it was restructured. In his letter of resignation, he declared that: 'Vigour and vision are the supreme need at this hour.'[68] Secondly, in a surprising turn of events, Balfour came out for Lloyd George. Balfour, ill in bed during the convoluted negotiations described above, had played no role in them. On 5 December, he dispatched two letters to Asquith. In the first, he supported a new war council chaired by Lloyd George. 'I am quite clear', he wrote, 'that the new system should have a trial under the most favourable possible circumstances'.[69] There was a hint of resignation in Balfour's tone. In response, Asquith dashed off a hurried note, asking him to reconsider. But later that same afternoon not only did Balfour renew his threat, he also repeated his advice to Asquith that the experiment of giving Lloyd George 'a free hand' was 'worth trying'. 'We cannot,' he warned, 'go on in the old way'.[70] This support for Lloyd George, given by the First Lord of the Admiralty (as Balfour then was) proved decisive. Asquith resigned that afternoon.[71]

Asquith's resignation closed the option of reconstructing his ministry and opened the way for an entirely new government. King George V therefore invited Bonar

Law, as leader of the opposition, to form an administration. But the confusing series of intrigues, resignations and potential intra-party conflicts posed a constitutional dilemma. How should the new ministry be formed? Bonar Law thought that dissolution of Parliament might be necessary to legitimize such a proceeding, but the King was doubtful. To hold a general election during wartime could only sow further doubts and divisions upon the proper conduct of the war. Additionally, an election would alarm and confuse the country. Bonar Law then left the King with the issue unsettled to discuss the matter with both Lloyd George and Asquith. The crucial question came down to Asquith: would he serve under either Bonar Law or Balfour? To this, Asquith replied that he would not. The following morning, 6 December, Lloyd George and Bonar Law – after a brief discussion with their fellow triumvir, Carson – sought out Balfour for his advice. The First Lord of the Admiralty, still recumbent and convalescing at Carlton Gardens, recommended that the King call a conference at Buckingham Palace to sort out matters.[72]

In the afternoon of 6 December, the conference was convened. Present were the King, Stamfordham and the following ministers: Asquith, Bonar Law, Lloyd George, Arthur Henderson (spokesman for Labour) and Balfour, who rose from his sick bed to chair the meeting. There is general agreement that the conference was inconclusive. Asquith refused to serve under anyone else as Prime Minister; and both Lloyd George and Bonar Law held firm that Lloyd George should chair any new war council.[73] Within two hours, Bonar Law reported to the King that he could not form a government. Lloyd George was then summoned, offered and accepted the commission to form a government. To this task Lloyd George now bent his considerable energy.

The political events of late November and early December have led some historians to claim that all along it had been Lloyd George's intention to replace Asquith and install himself as the Prime Minister. Donald McCormick, for example, claims that Lloyd George's 'plots' forced out the Asquith government.[74] Colin Clifford thinks that a 'Monday Night Cabal', of which Lloyd George was a member, harboured the same ambition. This 'nest of vipers' eventually 'sucked into their intrigue' a coalition of politicians and journalists who sought the destruction of Asquith.[75] The idea that Asquith had been brought down by underhanded means was, of course, a natural reaction from his family and close friends. Violet, Asquith's favoured daughter, wrote disparagingly of Lloyd George's 'consistent treachery' after her father's fall from office.[76] John D. Fair, however, reverses the causal arrows, suggesting that the outcome of the crisis can best be understood as 'a Conservative *coup d'etat*' by which Conservative leaders took advantage of a 'dextral swing' of public opinion generated by the war to install themselves in power under the aegis of Lloyd George.[77] In this sense, Lloyd George was as much a pawn as Asquith. Other historians defend Lloyd George's actions as an attempt to invigorate the war effort while retaining Asquith as Prime Minister. Pugh and Packer argue that Lloyd George, in spite of his poor opinion of Asquith's administrative skills and wartime leadership, did not wish to replace him but rather hoped to work around the Prime Minister to alter the government's strategy for winning the war.[78] Morgan insists that throughout Lloyd George acted openly: there were no secret meetings or conspiratorial alliances.[79]

This is not to say that Lloyd George simply stood aside and hoped for the best. He obviously was – as we have seen – in the thick of the fight for a new approach to winning the war. There is, however, some evidence that he was additionally very active in cultivating public opinion throughout the crisis in his favour through the manipulation of the newspaper press. It has been argued that the press during the early years of the war had displaced Parliament as a leader of public opinion. Parliament's influence had been steadily declining since 1914. Its members, depleted by the Services and diminished by the increasing centralization of power at the Cabinet level, had lost to a considerable degree their former capacity for leadership. Newspaper owners, editors and journalists filled the gap.[80] When, therefore, newspapers began a campaign against the Asquith government's feeble prosecution of the war, they provided a background for change that undoubtedly aided Lloyd George. The press campaign revealed a remarkable consensus – that a change in the government's decision-making process was essential if the war were to be won. This opinion was widely held, irrespective of editorial allegiances. On 29 November, the Liberal leaning *Daily Chronicle* deplored the government's 'inability to make up its mind'.[81] On the afternoon of that same day, another Liberal paper, the *Westminster Gazette*, virtually echoed the *Chronicle*, pointing out that there was 'an appearance of delay and indecision' in the government's actions. The government, it claimed, too often 'discloses half-baked schemes before it is ready to take action on them, [and] it leaves the public a good deal in the dark about certain of the fundamentals of war'.[82] Perhaps most surprising of all was the opinion of the strongly Conservative *Morning Post*. A few days prior to the *Chronicle* and *Gazette* publications, it praised Lloyd George specifically as 'a power which makes for victory' and 'a force to which the nation may adhere, which the nation may follow'.[83]

The question naturally arises: how much did Lloyd George seek and engage newspaper support in his own political campaign to displace Asquith? As we know, Lloyd George had cultivated the press throughout his political life and met frequently with journalists and proprietors, both to solicit their opinions and to pass on to them information favourable to his own prospects. There is little reason to doubt that he pursued the same tactics during the December crisis. He was in direct contact with Max Aitken, owner of the *Daily Express*, Lord Burnham of the *Daily Telegraph*, Robertson Nicoll of the *British Weekly* and Riddell as usual. Riddell was also central in relaying information to Lloyd George from Robert Donald, editor of the *Daily Chronicle*.[84] Lloyd George also met frequently with Scott of the *Manchester Guardian*. On 3 December 1916, for example, Scott lunched with Lloyd George at Walton Heath. Afterwards, Scott motored back to the War Office with Lloyd George. En route, Lloyd George was critical of Asquith, charging him essentially with dereliction of duty. Asquith came to Cabinet meetings 'with no policy' in hand; merely summed up what others said and generally postponed any decisions. It was, Lloyd George declared, 'a futile method of carrying on a war'.[85]

The most promising newspaper alliance that Lloyd George developed was with the influential Lord Northcliffe, owner of *The Times*, the more popular *Daily Mail*, the *Evening News* and a number of other papers and journals.[86] The two men had first met in 1909 at the height of the battle for National Insurance when Lloyd George had favoured Northcliffe with a preview of the famous People's Budget before it was introduced to the House of Commons. Although Northcliffe was to oppose the National Insurance scheme, relations between the two men for a time remained amicable. On occasion, Lloyd George and Northcliffe met privately, with the former giving the press lord valuable information for his use in scooping other newspapers.[87] But as the war progressed, Northcliffe increasingly adopted a public position of support for the generals against the politicians, even after the disasters of the Somme had become evident. 'Hands Off the Army' was Northcliffe's warning. 'The man on the spot knows best' was his credo. Thus he supported the decisions of Haig and Robertson against Lloyd George's criticisms.

Yet there was a bond between Lloyd George and Northcliffe – their common belief that the war must be waged more effectively. As the events of early December 1916 rapidly unfolded, Lloyd George, in a series of meetings, used his position as a ministerial insider to dangle before Northcliffe the prospect of revealing momentous news for his eyes only. To a newsman of Northcliffe's stature, this was tempting bait.[88] If Lloyd George should succeed in either reconstructing the government along more purposeful lines, or in deposing Asquith, it would be foolish for Northcliffe to be at odds with him. For his part, Lloyd George could certainly use the influence of the great press lord to strengthen his own political position. As Cecil Harmsworth noted in his diary for 3 December: 'Alfred has been actively at work with Ll.G. with a view to bringing about a change.'[89] When Asquith resigned on 5 December, both *The Times* and the *Daily Mail* made it clear that this was a desirable solution to the problems of waging a successful war.[90]

With the broad support of the press and the acquiescence of important Conservative leaders, Lloyd George confidently accepted the King's commission to form a government. Some pitfalls remained. There were numerous reservations from all points of the political compass – including mistrustful Conservatives, doubtful Labourites and a host of Asquithian Liberals.[91] Yet the task of Cabinet making appeared, on the face of it, unexpectedly easy. This was initially due to a sound tactical approach on Lloyd George's part. Balfour was the first to be asked: he quickly accepted the office of Foreign Minister, without a seat in the small War Cabinet but with a promise of frequent attendance. Once Balfour was in harness, the new government was attractive to Conservatives. The irascible Walter Long, well respected among Conservative backbenchers, was tempted by the offer of any position but that of the Admiralty or the Foreign Office. He chose the Colonial Office.[92] With Balfour and Long in the new government – both Conservatives, but two very different men – other Conservatives were willing to serve as ministers.

The War Cabinet itself, increased from three to five, also attempted to strike a balance. Not surprisingly, Lloyd George as Prime Minister held no other office. Bonar Law, leader of the Commons and Chancellor of the Exchequer as well, was the other inevitable choice for the War Cabinet. Two other positions in the War Cabinet were surprises, however. Lord Curzon, reliably pompous and whose privileged mannerisms Lloyd George professed to loath,[93] nevertheless had impressed Lloyd George with his assiduous work habits, his general knowledge of the world and his dispatch in Cabinet meetings during his term of office as Lord Privy Seal throughout the May 1915 coalition. Curzon was, thought Lloyd George, 'useful in council'.[94] Perhaps most importantly, Curzon was one of the few members of the House of Lords willing to serve in a coalition government led by Lloyd George. Thus, Lloyd George made him the Leader of the Lords, with the title of Lord President of the Council. Most surprising of all the five members of the war council was the selection of Alfred, Lord Milner. As High Commissioner of South Africa and Governor of the Cape Colony and an advocate of an imperialism based upon 'race patriotism', Milner had been a fierce opponent of all pro-Boers (including Lloyd George) throughout the second South African War. Since then, he had held no official position; but his reputation as an accomplished bureaucrat, renowned for his administrative expertise, made him a valuable member of a government committed to comprehensive planning in war and peace.[95] Adding to the lustre of Milner's reputation was his advocacy of what he called 'reasonable socialism' – that is, utilizing the state for eliminating poverty and regulating trade, all to be sure for the benefit of the empire.[96] Milner's imperial credentials were especially attractive to the more ardent Conservatives, some of whom had lobbied hard for Milner's inclusion in the War Cabinet.[97]

The final addition to the War Cabinet was the Labour leader, Arthur Henderson, who had served as the token Labour representative in the previous coalition government. Before Henderson would accept, however, Lloyd George was compelled to strike a bargain with representatives of the labour movement. Speaking to Labour MPs and the National Executive Committee of the Labour Party on 7 December, Lloyd George not only promised Henderson a seat in the War Cabinet: he also pledged himself to establish new governmental departments for Labour. He additionally promised two under-secretaryships. These concessions were generally well received, and the meeting ended harmoniously. Miss Stevenson, apparently at the meeting taking notes, recorded that the men were at first sulky and hostile, but went away 'laughing and friendly': it was 'a great success' she concluded.[98]

Surprisingly, one of the original triumvirs, Carson, failed to gain membership in the new War Cabinet. Reasons for this remain obscure. Lloyd George was to claim later that he had been forced to reassign Carson to the Admiralty, a position outside the War Cabinet, because of the objection of (unnamed) 'Conservative ministers' who resented his promotion to the War Cabinet.[99] Pugh, however, believes that Lloyd George thought Milner's abilities and sensitivity to working-class aspirations were more attractive than Carson's allegiance to 'the dead-end of Ulster Unionism'.[100] There is also some evidence that King George V preferred Carson at the Admiralty, vacated by Balfour when he accepted the position of Foreign Secretary.[101] Carson's stand down did not affect the final political composition of the War Cabinet, which had grown from three to five: one Liberal; one Labour; and three Conservatives.

Lloyd George's insistence upon a small War Cabinet was designed to create a new administrative machinery for the more efficient prosecution of the war. To further this aim, Lloyd George established a Cabinet Secretariat. He appointed Maurice Hankey, formerly Secretary of the CID, to bring order to Cabinet proceedings, the meetings of which had never been systematically recorded. Lloyd George knew his man. A complete workaholic and fastidious in both his personal habits and public duties, Hankey – aided by several assistant secretaries – was dedicated to any task at hand. As well as taking minutes of every meeting, he created an administrative system which prepared agendas; solicited requisite papers from other departments; and attended to all necessary correspondence.[102] He also drew up important position papers for the Prime Minister and for the Cabinet as a whole.

A separate secretariat, and one often confused with the Cabinet Secretariat, was a group of advisors popularly known as the 'Garden Suburb', named after its headquarters established in the 10 Downing Street garden. This group has been the subject of some speculation for its unofficial status and its secrecy. It has been criticized, for example, as a nest of Milnerite ideologues determined to steer Lloyd George into dangerous imperial waters.[103] Hankey himself viewed it with suspicion.[104] Composed of some half dozen Lloyd George supporters, it operated as an independent administrative intelligence department for the Prime Minister by providing him with information relating to the various departments of state. They also helped devise policy on any topic deemed essential by Lloyd George. Sometimes its members provided the substance for Lloyd George's speeches. There are occasional examples of members briefing the press to put a favourable spin on the Prime Minister's policy, or to prepare the public for a controversial subject under review.[105] Most importantly, the Garden Suburb, as a direct arm of the Prime Minister, aided him in maintaining control over an expanding role of the state in wartime. Thus the Garden Suburb can be readily contrasted with the more mechanical and formal work of minutes, memoranda and agendas of the Cabinet Secretariat.

Over time, there were a number of other administrative bodies which revolved around Lloyd George as wartime Prime Minister. These included a War Policy Committee of Lloyd George, Curzon and Milner. A fourth member, General Jan Smuts, the South African Minister of Defence, was added in 1917. The Committee's main task, as an adjunct to the War Cabinet, was to serve as a watchdog over the army high command. The so-called 'X' Committee, comprised of Lloyd George, Milner and General Henry Wilson, involved itself in strategic decisions. Both these committees made strategic decisions without reference to the War Cabinet. In addition, there were occasional meetings of an Imperial War Cabinet, in which representatives from Canada, South Africa, Australia and New Zealand would convene in London. Beyond these were other special ad hoc committees related to specific tasks, such as the Tonnage Priority Committee to allocate shipping space. Two other important ad hoc committees were the War Priorities Committee and the Aerial Operations Committee. Their task was to allocate resources between manufacturing departments.[106] Lloyd George maintained his own personal secretaries, including the loyal and loving Miss Stevenson. The Welsh speaking J.T. Davies and William Sutherland, formerly Clerk at the Board of Trade, also worked closely with the Prime Minister.

Lloyd George was clearly instrumental in reshaping government institutions to promote a more efficient and energetic pursuit of the war. Such a wide-ranging and powerful committee structure tied to the Prime Minister, however, raised fears that he could become a dictatorial war leader. But there were substantial limits to Lloyd George's authority. Even in the formation of his War Cabinet he had been under considerable political pressure, particularly from Conservatives, who not only formed a majority in the War Cabinet and the ministry, but in Parliament as well. Indeed, Conservative influence was greater than initially apparent. Balfour, Carson and Lord Derby (the new Secretary of State for War), although not members of the War Cabinet, often attended its meetings, adding substantially to the Conservative presence in that important body. Other potential sources of opposition to any despotic inclinations on the part of the Prime Minister included the Labour Party, which now had a voice in the War Cabinet with the appointment of Henderson. George Barnes as Minister of Pensions and John Hodge as Minister of Labour rounded out the Labour presence. The aggrieved Asquithians and the Irish Nationalists, not surprisingly, remained detached from the government.

Unity of action, however, did not come easily in the new coalition government. There was at the heart of the new administration a fundamental division on military strategy. Lloyd George had bought Conservative support at a high price: that he would not interfere with either military planning or the personnel of the Supreme Command.[107] Haig and Robertson would remain in place – whatever reservations Lloyd George may have about them. Other demands made by Conservatives in return for their support of Lloyd George's government included the exclusion of both Northcliffe and Churchill from the government, and the promise of no further attempts to settle the Irish question and no advances to be made on franchise reform. But it was soon evident that Lloyd George did not intend to follow this agreement strictly, especially the pledge to abstain from interfering with military command.

In January 1917, at an inter-allied conference in Rome, he pushed forward a plan to aid the Italians in their struggle against Austro-Hungarian forces by providing a substantial supply not of British troops, but of British artillery. Thus, Lloyd George hoped to put into practice his long held belief that opening an Eastern Front could weaken Germany. Indeed, as Woodward points out, the plan was 'neatly conceived' because it provided for a delay in future attacks against the German forces to give the Italians a chance for military success.[108] It was an optimum chance 'to square the strategic circle'; that is, to secure a victory with the least loss of life, especially of British forces, which remained a fundamental aim of Lloyd George's strategic thinking.[109] British generals, however, torpedoed the scheme, fearing that even a temporary loan of several hundred guns could drastically weaken the Western Front. They consistently argued that all available British forces should continually focus on the main German armies.[110]

In the meantime, plans were moving ahead for a spring offensive in the West. General Robert Nivelle, the hero of the defence of Verdun and newly appointed commander in chief of the French army, had replaced the aging General Joffre in December 1916. Nivelle, confident and articulate (in both French and English – the latter from his British mother), had persuaded Haig and Lloyd George that a combined thrust by British armies in the north and the French armies to the South could overwhelm German defences and achieve at long last the desired 'breakthrough'. Haig agreed, with a caveat: the BEF would assist a Nivelle offensive if at a later stage French forces would in turn support a long-held plan of his own – a large scale offensive in Flanders with the idea of taking the Belgian ports then held by the Germans. As more detailed planning went forward, however, cracks in the agreement for a Nivelle offensive appeared. Haig seemed slow in responding, delaying his preparations on the grounds that the French railway system was inadequate to the logistical task required of the BEF. Lloyd George, given his growing reservations about the British military leadership, was inclined to believe that Haig was dragging his feet. He was increasingly drawn to the notion of placing Haig and the BEF under French command. He passed this information on unofficially to French authorities, including Nivelle. On 24 February 1917, during a War Cabinet meeting, Lloyd George's objective of giving Nivelle supreme command during the forthcoming offensive was given an official imprimatur. Two days later, during a conference at Calais to resolve the conflict of military leadership on the Western Front, Haig and Robertson were informed of the drift of things. Haig was to be essentially reduced to the status of an adjutant-general, with the British commanders receiving their instructions directly from French headquarters during the forthcoming offensive.

Surprised and shocked at the news, the British generals vigorously objected and forced a watering down of Lloyd George's original intent before the Calais meeting adjourned. Any subordination of Haig to Nivelle would now be temporary and Haig retained the freedom to direct operations on the British side of the planned offensive. This did not resolve tensions between Nivelle and Haig, but they were ultimately able to work in harness. Lloyd George fared less well. As the news of his manoeuvres against his own high command made the rounds, both his secrecy and his favouritism towards the French were strongly censured. Conservatives were particularly outraged, including some members of his own government. Lord Derby (then holding office as Secretary for War) made threatening noises of resignation. Should this have happened, the government itself could have been at risk.[111] King George V himself was particularly incensed. He personally informed Lloyd George that as constitutionally designated head of state and of the army, he objected to any secret arrangement by which the BEF might be put under foreign command. The Prime Minister had no choice but to back away from his intrigue. At an Anglo-French conference on 12–13 March in London, Lloyd George informed Nivelle in a private interview that Haig had the full confidence of the War Cabinet. Furthermore, he declared that the British army should not be 'mixed up with the French army'.[112]

Lloyd George's first essay at high strategy as Prime Minister proved unfortunate. Historians are in accord with contemporary criticism. Woodward condemned Lloyd

George's actions as 'rash', 'devious' and ill advised in his attempt to establish 'a faulty system of supreme command'.[113] French essentially agrees: Lloyd George 'far exceeded his brief'.[114] Trevor Wilson, rarely a Lloyd George enthusiast in any case, charged him with 'grasping at straws' in operating within a framework of 'confusion between means and ends'.[115] Even the friendlier Grigg declared that, given the political sensitivities involved, Lloyd George's attempt to elevate the commander of one of the component national forces to be supreme allied commander was 'a practical absurdity'.[116]

Lloyd George's miscalculations, the clash of commands between France and Britain and the escalating civil-military conflict at home could have been resolved by Nivelle's promised 'breakthough' against the German armies. Victory would have salved all wounds. But this did not happen. In March 1917, the German army — having learned of the Allied plan through captured documents — had been busily executing a strategic retreat, shortening their salient between Arras and Soissons by about 25 miles. This was the first stage of a developing concept among German military thinkers, an 'elastic defence in depth'. By withdrawing into less lengthy and thus less exposed positions, the German armies were strengthened by denser formations. The new defensive posture, the Siegfried Stellung (or Hindenburg Line), was not merely a reconfiguration of the trench system: it added an elaborate network of barriers. Built during the winter of 1916–17 the construction project, Operation Alberich, was undertaken in great secrecy. Alberich enlisted more than half a million German solders and civilians to construct several interlocking lines, ranging from initial tank traps and barbed wire to much more elaborate steel reinforced concrete blockhouses.[117] In addition, there were significant retraining programmes, emphasizing tactics of infiltration and envelopment, designed to smother attacking forces whose momentum would be slowed by the deep German defensive system.[118]

So it proved. Although the British Army had gained much needed experience in recent months and had more arms and ammunition since the Somme, the Nivelle offensive begun on 9 April 1917 effectively came to a halt within a few days. Fighting continued for several weeks longer, until mid-June, with no further advances. To the south, Nivelle's French forces fared even worse as they attempted to butt against the newly constructed Hindenburg Line: the French lost 100,000 men with no significant ground gained. More ominously, rates of desertion and outright disobedience among French soldiers reached alarming proportions as the fighting sputtered to a halt. On 10 May, Nivelle was relieved of command, to be replaced by Marshall Petain as commander-in-chief of the French Army. Committed to restoring the morale of the French army, Petain proved far more defensively minded than Nivelle. He favoured only a series of limited objectives for the remainder of 1917 in order to reduce casualties.

The military impact upon the Allies as a result of the failure of the Nivelle offensive was only too obvious. For Lloyd George, the consequences of failure were also apparent. Having supported Nivelle in the hope of averting Haig's more extensive campaign in Flanders, Lloyd George was now at a 'fatal disadvantage' in any future disagreement with Haig, the Commander-in-Chief of the BEF.[119]

In a 'chastened mood', Lloyd George realized that his authority over any strategic decisions 'had been lowered'.[120] Fully aware of his exposed position, Lloyd George cautiously began a well-recorded *volte-face* even before Nivelle's dismissal. At an important War Cabinet meeting on 1 May, just prior to an inter-Allied conference in Paris, he put forward the idea of limited offensives for the remainder of the year. This would, he hoped, preserve both men and materiel and relieve a growing shortfall of available troops. The War Cabinet, however, overwhelmingly rejected Lloyd George's proposals and urged him to press the French to continue offensive operations. Lloyd George obeyed as instructed. But during the Paris conference, the cautious Petain made it plain that he was unwilling to take part in any future large-scale operations. For the remainder of the conference, Lloyd George's remarks were notable for his praise of the British high command. Haig was naturally pleased. He pronounced Lloyd George's two speeches at the conference as 'excellent'. Haig also noted with particular approval Lloyd George's declaration that 'he had no pretensions to be a strategist' and that he would leave that subject 'to his military advisers'.[121] After the conference, Lloyd George visited Haig at GHQ in Montreuil. While there, the Prime Minister was on his best behaviour. General Charteris recounted that Lloyd George was 'most charming' and fascinating 'in a way I have never known any other man fascinate'. He was, as Charteris added, 'amazingly sharp-witted, and full of energy, fire and go'.[122]

Perhaps Charteris could take a mild view of Lloyd George, knowing that Haig had already begun preparations for a major military operation. This was the third Ypres campaign or, as it is often called, the Flanders campaign. It is also sometimes referred to as Passchendaele, named for the village where some of the fiercest fighting occurred. The planning clearly had in mind a major offensive. In a complicated double manoeuvre, British forces would engage in both an amphibious attack on the coast to clear the German-held naval bases at Blankenberghe and Ostend, while ground forces simultaneously pushed outward from the Ypres salient northward toward coastal Belgium. Haig presented his plan on 19 June before the recently established War Policy Committee. (The WPC, consisting of Lloyd George, Curzon, Milner and Smuts, with Hankey serving as secretary, had been created to conduct a wide-ranging review of British domestic, military and diplomatic policies.) Portraying Germany as near the end of its capacity for continuing the war, Haig predicted that the enemy was 'within 6 months of the total exhaustion of her available manpower'.[123] The following day, at a second meeting of the WPC, the testimony of the First Sea Lord, Admiral Jellicoe, supported Haig's plan. Removing German-held Belgian ports, he maintained, would enable the destruction of German submarine bases.

To influence the WPC further towards a favourable decision, Haig apparently withheld from the Committee information regarding the state of the French army. Before his meetings with the WPC, he had received authoritative reports that French morale had sunk to new lows after the failure of the Nivelle Offensive. There had also been outbreaks of strike activity, and of soldiers fraternizing with the strikers. The similarity with the recent events in Russia was alarming. Haig confided to his diary that 'the situation wants careful watching'.[124] Circumstances in France were even worse than Haig knew. From late May into June, approximately 40,000 French troops were involved in demonstrations that affected 49 divisions to some degree – in other words, nearly half the operational French divisions. In suppressing the disturbances, the authorities sentenced nearly 3,000 men to forced labour, some for as long as five or more years. Six hundred twenty-nine more were condemned to death, of whom 75 were actually executed.[125] Had the WPC been fully aware of events in France, or if they knew even as much as Haig knew, they would likely have been disinclined to sanction his military plans. French military support during the Flanders campaign would have been viewed as doubtful.[126] Acting on the basis of the information provided, the WPC gave the green light to Haig, convinced that a victory was necessary not only to shore up French morale, but also to raise the spirits of a war weary Britain as well.[127] Still smarting from the failed Nivelle adventure, Lloyd George reluctantly agreed with the consensus of the WPC.[128]

The Flanders campaign had in fact already begun with a spectacular explosion under the German-held positions on Messines Ridge south of Ypres on 7 June, even before the broader operation had been sanctioned by the WPC. British sappers had placed nearly a million pounds of explosives in 19 separate mines: the sound of their detonation, it was said, could be clearly heard in Downing Street.[129] Some 10,000 German troops were likely killed outright, and another 7,000 were captured. Additional artillery barrages sought to soften up the survivors. But even a thorough shelling could not fully penetrate the defensive depth of the new German positions. The shelling did, however, churn up already soggy ground, destroying the drainage system of lowland Flanders. Intermittent rain throughout the campaign quickly turned the earth into a quagmire as Allied troops began their advance on 31 July. Once again, an Allied military offensive stalled, forcing the abandonment of a 'breakthrough' as heavy casualties mounted.[130] Not until 10 November was the ruined village of Passchendaele captured by Canadian troops. This was the furthest point gained by the three and a half month long offensive, a distance of approximately five miles. Estimates of casualties for the entire campaign vary: one account puts it at 200,000 for the Germans, 250,000 British, and a smaller number for the French.[131]

Such a high casualty rate with so little gain inclined the British high command to try again, and soon, for a victory in order to restore morale. Ten days after the cessation of hostilities at Passchendaele, General Byng's third army launched an attack in the south towards Cambrai, which had been in German hands since the early days of the war. As had often been true in the past, initial success was encouraging. Using massed tank formations for the first time on dry and level ground, British forces at first overwhelmed German defences. Nearly 500 tanks, many of them the new model Mark IV with more powerful engines and increased fire power compared with earlier tanks, surged forward with six divisions of accompanying infantry on 20 November 1917. They were strongly supported by accurate artillery fire and fourteen squadrons of the Royal Flying Corps. Within 24 hours, some of the forward Hindenburg Line had been breached as British troops penetrated more than four miles toward Cambrai. But heavy tank losses through mechanical failure coupled with a devastating fusillade, especially from German machine guns, stalled the attack. In the week following, German reinforcements moved forward and on 30 November they counterattacked. Using novel infantry tactics perfected in Italy and the eastern front against Russia, German infantry assaulted in groups, infiltrating through weaknesses in the British line and bypassing points of resistance to advance against artillery positions in the rear. After falling back and regrouping, the British (now operating defensively) halted the German attack: by 7 December both sides were once again stalemated. The cost of Cambrai was high. Britain had suffered 45,000 casualties, including one third of its tank personnel and two-thirds of its tanks.[132]

Historians' post mortems of Passchendaele and Cambrai have been severely critical of British military leadership, with Haig once again bearing the main responsibility. Poor choice of battle ground for an offensive; an inability to adapt to adverse weather conditions; and a misunderstanding of artillery usage have all been cited as causes of the failure.[133] But as Prime Minister, Lloyd George must also share at least part of the blame. Woodward states that Lloyd George's role in the War Policy Committee decision to sanction the Flanders offensive 'does him no credit'. His courage, Woodward believes, 'did not match his strong convictions': he could have followed his instincts and overruled the military.[134] Prior and Wilson essentially charge Lloyd George with dereliction of duty. In an echo of Woodward, they note that the Prime Minister had serious doubts about the campaign and indeed had made them known to the War Cabinet. Yet while openly 'proclaiming the futility' of the proposed plan, he 'failed to raise a finger to stop it'.[135] Prior and Wilson argue moreover that Lloyd George could have overridden his ministers because his own position as Prime Minister was unassailable throughout 1917: he had the power to decide upon strategy without fear of serious dissent from the political elite.[136] Even Grigg does not offer praise. Claiming that Lloyd George felt 'the anguish' of the Flanders Campaign for the rest of his life, Grigg notes that he had 'in effect given carte blanche' to Haig and the generals for the campaign.[137] Perhaps, as David French has observed, Lloyd George may very well have been motivated by the hope that if the generals could somehow manage a victory without excessive casualties, it would be a significant morale booster – not only for Britain but for France as well. The Allies needed a victory.[138] It was worth a chance.

The plight of the Allies in late 1917 was evident not only on the Western Front. In the East, the fall of the Czar in March, which had ushered in the moderate Russian revolution, was losing ground to the more radical Bolsheviks. Elsewhere the Austrian army was pressing hard on the Italians and was soon to achieve an overwhelming victory at Caporetto in October. Although there were some successes on peripheral battlefields, such as General Allenby's campaign in Palestine, Anglo-French forces in the Balkans continued to falter. Shipping losses to German submarines remained unacceptably high. The prospect of significant American direct aid seemed distant. On the home front, the streams of wounded soldiers from Flanders once again brought to the civilian population the human cost of the war, as it had during the Somme. Another blow to morale was the air war initiated by giant German Gotha aircraft attacks against the civilian population of London. Precautions taken against attacks from the air had their own disruptive and even dangerous consequences, as darkened streets could be unavigable at night where lightning restrictions were enforced. Coal supplies began to run short and, even more alarmingly, so did food stocks. It was not surprising that home front morale was sagging by the end of 1917.[139]

For Lloyd George, these adverse circumstances were only too apparent. The lessons of the Somme and Passchendaele could no longer be denied. A new military command with realistic strategic aims and more effective tactical operations, he believed, was imperative. Nor was he alone is his determination to shake up the military establishment. Lord Northcliffe, formerly one of Haig's staunchest supporters, turned against the general as the casualty lists lengthened during the Flanders offensive. Others who sought change included Milner and Smuts within the War Cabinet; and most important of all, Sir Henry Wilson, who had first caught Lloyd George's eye several years prior during the Agadir Crisis in 1911. Since then, Wilson's native intelligence, knowledge of French and love of intrigue had carried him far. He had continued as Director of Military Operations until the outbreak of war in 1914. Then he became Sub-Chief of the BEF in 1915 and thereafter served as Chief Liaison Officer with the French Army. By 1917, he had become the primary (though unofficial) military advisor to Lloyd George. Sharing the Prime Minister's reservations with the high command's military strategy, Wilson helped to craft a surreptitious means of bypassing their authority.

The plan was to create a small supranational body which would replace to some degree individual Allied commanders' authority in order to coordinate battlefield tactics more effectively. Such a need had been evident from the early days of the war, but initial attempts to establish coordinated military strategy and tactics had foundered on mutual suspicions between Britain and France.[140] Both Lloyd George and General Wilson had taken part in these early efforts: both now had additional reasons to resurrect the scheme. Wilson's ambitions to play an important role among military decision makers had only been whetted since 1915. Lloyd George had always believed in the greater efficiency of centralized authority, as his political career had demonstrably shown. The waste, duplication of effort and tragic loss of men and materiel during wartime could be reduced by better organization and more nimble administrative procedures. Lloyd George was, furthermore, attracted to the Francophone Wilson for his intelligence and for his reformist frame of mind. Equally important was Lloyd George's conviction that Wilson would be a far better military adviser to the War Cabinet as a Chief of the Imperial General Staff than General Robertson. To effect the changes of military-civilian relations at this stage of the war, Lloyd George realized, would require careful implementation.[141]

Luckily for Wilson and Lloyd George, in France too the idea of a unified command system was gaining ground. At an Anglo-French conference on 7–8 August 1917, General Foch proposed such a scheme. The following month, Lloyd George engaged in secret talks with French war minister Paul Painlevé. The outline of an Inter-Allied War Council with a permanent staff soon emerged. Wilson would serve as the British military representative. In October, conversations between British and French representatives on the proposed Council continued at Chequers, the new prime ministerial retreat. This was followed by a paper written by Wilson and circulated among members of the government and the general staff alike. Lloyd George and Wilson were soon joined by General French, the former CIGS who had preceded Robertson and who was also highly critical of both Haig's and Robertson's leadership.

With the ground thus thoroughly prepared, Lloyd George could await an opportunity to make public his plan for a unified command structure. It came in late October 1917 with the defeat of the Italians at Caporetto – an event that completely surprised the British military leaders. Lloyd George, laying blame for the debacle upon the general staff's earlier refusal to assist the Italians, persuaded the War Cabinet that it was time for the creation of a new unified command system. On 2 November, the Cabinet accepted Lloyd George's proposal in principle: it also approved of Sir Henry Wilson as the British representative on the permanent staff of the proposed supreme war council. The following day, bolstered by the Cabinet's support, Lloyd George left for Paris to lobby further for his proposal. On 4 November, he met with Haig, who had been summoned to hear of the proposed plan.

It was a contentious meeting. Lloyd George declared his 'firm intention' to establish a unified war council (including a transnational general staff).[142] Frances Stevenson wrote in her diary that Lloyd George 'made it quite plain' to Haig 'that the time had come when he was going to assert himself, & if necessary let the public know the truth about the soldiers & their strategy'.[143] But Haig was not persuaded. As he recorded in his diary: 'I gave several reasons why I thought it could not work, and that it would add to our difficulties.'[144] Undeterred by Haig's reservations, Lloyd George next travelled to Rapallo for an important inter-allied conference where he again spoke for his plan. The climax of the two-day conference (6 and 7 November 1917) was the official establishment of the Supreme Allied War Council (SAWC), to be headquartered at Versailles.[145] Returning to Paris, Lloyd George for the first time gave a public address on the Rapallo Agreement.[146] The new Supreme Council, Lloyd George promised, would have 'real power in the co-ordination' of the Allied military effort. Up to this point in the war, he stated, there had been 'no authority responsible for co-coordinating the conduct of the war on all fronts and in the absence of that central authority each country was left to its own devices'. There had been thus far only 'an appearance of a strategic whole'. In reality, the Allied generals had merely 'all sat at the same table and, metaphorically, took thread and needle' and sewed their various plans together, then presented them 'as one great strategic piece'. But as strategy, it was 'pure make-believe … it was a collection of completely independent schemes pieced together'. Stitching, he declared, 'was not a strategy'. The result had been that the Allies had fought four wars separately, rather than one war together. To prevent further disasters, he continued, the Allies must, with 'promptitude and completeness … break with our past and for the first time realize in action the essential unity of all the Allied fronts'. The only solution was 'a permanent council whose duty it will be to survey the whole field of military endeavour with a view to determining where and how the resources of the Allies can be most effectually employed'. This was, he concluded 'the only sure pathway to victory'.

This startlingly candid speech immediately struck a responsive chord. Leaders in *The Times* over the next two days were fully supportive. Lloyd George's call for unity was 'absolutely sound'. Too often, the various Allied military conferences had been 'spasmodic, irregular' and summoned 'in haste to deal with a sudden crisis'.[147] In the meantime, Lloyd George and his private secretary, William Sutherland, devised a press campaign promoting SAWC. Even members of the War Policy Committee were brought into play. Smuts was sent to C.P. Scott and other newspaper editors for unofficial briefings.[148] This brought fruitful results: the *Daily Telegraph, Evening Standard, Daily Chronicle* and *Manchester Guardian*, among others, gave their support. But not everyone was convinced. Some charged Lloyd George with dictatorial designs, while others balked at any hint of the British High Command serving under French generals. In the House of Commons, Asquith hoped to make capital of Lloyd George's apparent public break with the British military command. Haig and Robertson were also busy in their own interests, engineering a press campaign against the idea of a unified command.

Nevertheless, SAWC went forward. In late November, Lloyd George travelled to Versailles to authenticate further the newly established body, especially the powers of its permanent military representatives (of whom General Wilson was now one).[149] The military representatives were to examine the Allied military position as a whole and to make recommendations about operations for the forthcoming year. The powers of the military representatives were soon expanded by their incorporation into an Executive War Board, charged with administering a general reserve of all Allied forces, which could be used as needed during battlefield encounters with the enemy.[150] The Board had the power to assign Allied troops held in reserve to any Allied commander. This was designed to resolve the recurring problem of national commanders' occasional refusal to lend support to one another during battle on the grounds of endangering their own armies.

With SAWC under way, Lloyd George turned his attention to harnessing the British high command. On 11 December, he asked War Minister Lord Derby to sack both Haig and Robertson. Derby refused, but did agree to request from Haig the replacement of some important command subordinates, such as General Charteris, Haig's Intelligence Officer, and General Kiggell, his Chief of Staff. Other staff changes included the Quartermaster-General, the Engineer-in-Chief and the Director-General of Medical Services.[151] These changes were an indication that Lloyd George was beginning to gain the upper hand against the high command. Early in the new year, the Prime Minister intensified his efforts. Because Haig's popularity remained high among the public at large, General Robertson was a likelier target. Robertson had strongly opposed the creation of SAWC, even to the point of boycotting its formal inauguration at Rapallo in November 1917. He discerned clearly the threat to his own position as CIGS and his role as official advisor to the War Cabinet on military strategy. After several weeks of complicated manoeuvring,

Robertson was removed, demoted to the Eastern Command on the home front.[152] The new CIGS brought in fresh from Versailles was General Wilson.

The next official to go was Derby at the War Office. Too cosy with the military establishment, Derby was packed off to Paris as the British ambassador.[153] Replacing him at the War Office was Lord Milner – a far more loyal and effective supporter of the Prime Minister. The Royal Navy was not immune to the changes at work among high-ranking officers. Eric Geddes, who had proved his administrative skills in matters military by sorting out transportation problems on the Western Front, became Controller of the Navy in May 1917. Two months later, he had replaced Carson as First Lord of the Admiralty.[154] By the end of the year, Geddes had removed Admiral Jellicoe, the First Sea Lord, replacing him with Admiral Rosslyn Wemyss.[155]

Thus Lloyd George's intentions to subordinate the military command to civilian authority gained ground. This development was matched by the first undeniably significant Allied military victory in some time. Equally important to Lloyd George, it occurred in the eastern theatre of operations. By opening a front in Palestine, Lloyd George at last hoped to provide for an alternative to 'the attritional grind' of the Western Front.[156] To capture the Holy Land from the Ottoman Empire would also be a significant public relations coup for the government and a boost to public morale during a time of unrelieved Allied failures.[157] Initially, however, the Egyptian Expeditionary Force, led by General Sir Archibald Murray, was unsuccessful. After crossing the Suez Canal into Sinai and twice failing to capture Gaza in March and April 1917, Murray was replaced in June 1917 by General Sir Edmund Allenby, formerly commander of the Third Army on the Western Front.[158] In an interview with Allenby at the time of his appointment, Lloyd George made it clear that he wanted not only a significant victory, but also a symbolic one. The Cabinet expected, Lloyd George informed the general, 'Jerusalem before Christmas'.[159] In a spirited campaign (enlivened by several cavalry charges) that has been called a model of mobile warfare, Allenby brought his troops within sight of Jerusalem by early December 1917.[160] On 9 December 1917, Jerusalem fell to Allenby's forces. The following day, Lloyd George announced the victory in he House of Commons. He had received his Christmas gift for the nation with two weeks to spare. Allenby's victory represented only the military arm of Lloyd George's Middle Eastern strategy. He also opened diplomatic avenues. By 1917, he had been instrumental in crafting a policy for Palestine that that he believed would additionally strengthen Britain's hand in the Middle East – politically as well as militarily – both during and after the war. This policy, as we shall see, would have some initial success, but eventually it proved to be destructive to his imperial aims and to the life of his postwar government.

In his global reach to win the war, Lloyd George was also instrumental in bringing the United States into a more active role in the fighting on the Western Front. American assistance had not come easily. President Wilson was initially unenthusiastic. Wilson's official policy was to maintain neutrality and to act when possible as a mediator. Gradually, however, pro-war public sentiment in America aided by German intransigence (in, for example, launching unlimited submarine warfare) gave an opening to the Allies. At last, on 6 April 1917, the United States declared war on Germany. Wilson called the United States Congress into a special session to hear his proposed war resolution. Within two days, both the House and the Senate overwhelmingly approved. American troop deployments remained agonizingly slow, however. By January 1918, only 150,000 American troops had been sent. Moreover, their fighting quality was still unknown.

After nearly a year and a half as Prime Minister, Lloyd George had gone a long way in his plans to subordinate the military to civilian leadership, to energize the service establishments and to expand the wartime alliance to include the United States. But his achievements and his wartime leadership were soon severely tested. On 21 March 1918, the German army launched its most dramatically successful offensive of the entire war.[161] The battle began with Germany outnumbering the Allied divisions by 200 to 169. The disparity in numbers was due in part to the collapse of Russia and its withdrawal from the war: German troops on the Eastern Front could now substantially reinforce its western theatre of operations. Attacking at the most vulnerable spot in the Allied lines – from near Arras in the north to La Fere further south – 'Operation Michael' struck hard, especially at General Gough's Fifth Army, which defended the longest defensive sector (42 miles) with the fewest troops, only 17 divisions. General Byng's Third Army, also of 17 divisions, was strung out along 26 miles. At the juncture where the British Fifth Army joined the French Sixth was an additional weakness in the allied defensive line. Against all these targets, the Germans had marshalled more than 6,000 guns and 35,000 trench mortars supported by 1,000 airplanes and 76 German assault divisions. Additional German divisions assumed a defensive position further south to prevent reinforcements by other French armies.

After German artillery prepared the way, their infantry punched through. Substantial gaps quickly appeared in the British lines of defence, especially those held by Gough's undermanned Fifth Army. German troops then infiltrated behind remaining pockets of entrenched and isolated British soldiers. Overwhelmed, the Allies quickly retreated. Within a day, retreat had turned into a rout, with nearly 40,000 British casualties and 20,000 taken prisoner. A week later, more than 1,000 artillery pieces had been lost. German strategy was becoming clear: to separate the British forces from the French armies; then to roll up British troops and force them toward the Channel; and finally to defeat the French armies, now isolated from their British allies. An irreversible German breakthrough severing the two Allied armies seemed imminent.

At first, the scope of the German offensive was unclear to British high command. Haig noted with some equanimity in his diary on the evening of the assault: 'Our men seem to be fighting magnificently.'[162] The following day he wrote: 'All reports show that our men are in great spirits.'[163] The next day, however, brought a different observation from the general. Visiting Gough at Fifth Army headquarters, Haig learned that the Fifth Army had been driven back beyond the Somme. Allied action of some sort was imperative. Haig's response to the rapidly deteriorating conditions of the British army has been variously described. It had long been held that Haig

– accurately sensing the danger – recommended, during a hastily summoned conference of British and French wartime leaders and generals at Doullens, that a unified command under General Foch be immediately established to rally the Allied forces against the German advance. Thus Haig's cool headed and selfless effort was 'crucial' to the eventual slowing of the German offensive, as the Allies under a unified command system went on in the final months of the war to achieve victory.[164] But others have taken issue with this interpretation, pointing out that instead of acting as a calm and self-possessed enabler in finding a solution to shore up the Allied defence, Haig was in fact 'considerably shaken' because he believed that the BEF was 'in a desperate position' and 'near to disaster'.[165] The real impetus for a concerted allied response to the Germans seems in fact have been the French, with Petain energetically mobilizing available reserves and Foch emerging as the natural choice for a supreme Allied commander.[166]

Staring military defeat in the face on such a scale would likely have shaken better generals than Haig; and certainly he was not the only British military or civilian leader fearing the worst in late March 1918. The new CIGS, General Wilson, was also deeply perturbed. In his diary for 22 March, he wrote: 'I don't understand why we are giving ground so quickly, nor how the Boches got through our battle zone apparently so easily.'[167] News from the front was no better 24 hours later: 'An anxious day. The Fifth Army seems to be beaten ....' Plunging into a round of discussions with Lloyd George and then the War Cabinet, Wilson urgently pressed the need for reinforcements by extending the conscription laws.[168] The following day brought news of additional German advances, adding to Wilson's dismay. 'We are very near a crash', he concluded.[169] He was soon on his way to Doullens via special train from London and a destroyer across the Channel. Hankey, too, was deeply worried as his diaries for 22 and 23 March attest: 'the situation was menacing', he wrote, and 'we could not but fear a debacle'.[170]

Lloyd George's response was outwardly reassuring. Wilson entered in his diary on 24 March that Lloyd George had 'on the whole been buoyant'.[171] Hankey reported that Lloyd George was 'very anxious' but 'more sanguine' than he, Hankey, was.[172] Privately, however, Lloyd George was less optimistic. To Riddell he confided that the news was 'very bad' and feared that it meant 'disaster'.[173] Nevertheless, the Prime Minister seemed energized by the German juggernaut: he quickly took charge.[174] His immediate task was to reinforce the beleaguered BEF. More than 220,000 men were rushed across the Channel in the next several weeks. Two divisions in Palestine and one in Italy were transferred to the Western Front. Workers in such vital industries as munitions, mines, and docks were drafted. Boys as young as 17½ were added to the conscription lists: at the other end of the age scale men as old as 55 became eligible for war service.[175] Lloyd George also issued a personal and urgent appeal to President Wilson, requesting 300,000 American troops within the next three months. A less effective measure – and a sure sign of the desperation driving the government – was an extension of conscription to Ireland (a policy which was never enforced after strenuous objections from Irish Nationalists).

But the German offensive, if somewhat slowed from its initial rapid pace, continued inexorably forward. On 9 April, preceded by a 'violent artillery storm' followed up by 'the dreaded rolling barrage',[176] German infantry struck north in Flanders toward the Channel, hoping to push the BEF toward the sea. Operation Georgette (the battle of the Lys) was immediately successful as BEF forces reeled backwards at the onslaught. Dunkirk, a crucial port in supplying the allies with men and materiel, was soon threatened by advancing German infantry. Further South, the Germans fought into the Mt Kemmel region in an attempt to surround Ypres. So desperate did the Allied position seem that General Haig was prompted to issue a controversial 'Backs to the Wall' communiqué to the troops, urging the British to stand firm and 'fight it out'. Every position, he claimed, 'must be held to the last man: there must be no retirement'.

German success at arms brought the inevitable recriminations in Britain between civilian and military authorities. On 8 April, the War Cabinet discussed the desirability of removing Haig. But, as Hankey recorded it, conversation on the topic revealed a consensus that 'we have no general of very outstanding merit' who could replace him.[177] By default, Haig remained. The military high command had, of course, an entirely different view. Haig's position, as it evolved under the duress of the continued German onslaught, was that the politicians were to blame for not providing enough manpower. Haig was additionally convinced that the Prime Minister was 'looking for a scapegoat' for the retreat of the Fifth Army.[178] Before long, there were rumblings in both the press and Parliament echoing Haig's views. On 8 April, the *Morning Post* began to feature articles that suggested that the government had failed to supply the army's needs. Other newspapers began to track the story in the following weeks.

Worse was yet to come. On 7 May there appeared in several newspapers an authoritative account condemning the government for its mishandling of manpower on the Western Front. Written by Major-General Sir Frederick B. Maurice, who had formerly been Director of Military Operations at the War Office, this public letter charged the government with purposely withholding needed troops for the BEF.[179] Lloyd George denied this assertion, claiming that the BEF had sufficient troops on the ground to blunt a German offensive. His implicit message was that poor British generalship was at fault. Lloyd George's response ruffled military feathers, leading to a simmering undercurrent of criticism in both press and Parliament. Lloyd George began to suspect a military conspiracy against him and his government.

There was a slight truth to this. General Robertson, who had been forced out as CIGS, had certainly encouraged the Prime Minister's critics, perhaps in an attempt to reclaim his former position.[180] On 9 May, Asquith – hoping to take advantage of the growing furore over troop strength – moved in the House of Commons for an investigation by a select committee of the House. This gave Lloyd George an opportunity to put the matter to rest. Practically charging General Maurice with insubordination, Lloyd George also condemned those in the House who brought forward 'distracting' controversies that slowed the progress of winning the war. Using information from Maurice's own department when he had been DMO, Lloyd George produced evidence that apparently supported his contention that there was indeed an increase in troop strength during 1917 and that the high command could not legitimately claim otherwise. He concluded by making Asquith's motion a vote of confidence: it lost by 293 votes to 106.

Coalition government supporters were generally well pleased. Riddell's congratulations can stand for many: 'you really smashed them this week,' he declared to the Prime Minister.[181] Addison was in agreement. Terming Asquith's performance 'miserable' and criticizing him for 'condoning Military anarchy', Addison commented additionally that Lloyd George 'had really an easy job' in demolishing the former Prime Minister.[182] Hankey, who had helped prepare Lloyd George for his speech, joined the chorus, praising the Prime Minister for his 'superb parliamentary effort'.[183] Balcarres, then serving in a minor post as Lord Privy Seal in the ministry, thought the Prime Minister's response was 'crushing'.[184] But not everyone associated with the coalition government approved. J.C.C. Davidson, then Private Secretary to Bonar Law, was present in the House of Commons when Lloyd George gave his exculpatory address. Years later, he remembered clearly that there was considerable 'heart-searching' on the part of many Conservatives that day, many of whom distrusted Lloyd George.[185] Yet there was also, Davidson believed, a reluctance among them to approve of Maurice's actions in making public military matters which were best kept secret. Scott summed up the views of many when he observed that, whatever 'his faults', Lloyd George was 'at least an incomparably better war minister than Asquith' had been.[186] In the end, it was Lloyd George's personal appeal and the threat of a dissolution that won wide support in the final vote.

Questions nevertheless remain about Lloyd George's role in the Maurice affair. Woodward believes that there is little doubt that Lloyd George misled Parliament during the debate of 9 May.[187] It appears that Lloyd George, before his statement to the House of Commons, had in hand the most recent troop estimates from the Adjutant-General. This clearly showed that fighting troops (or what was called 'rifle-strength') were 100,000 *less* in January 1918 than a year earlier. To cook the numbers, Lloyd George had added some non-combatant troops to the January 1918 list, thus increasing the total number of troops ('ration strength'). The diary of Hankey – who was in on the deception – is conclusive. In spite of his assistance prior to the Prime Minister's speech, Hankey felt the prick of conscience. He knew full well that Lloyd George had seen the Adjutant-General's report prior to his statement in the House.[188]

Why did Lloyd George apparently lie publicly on such an important matter? For military apologists, such as Terraine, it was merely another example of Lloyd George's duplicity.[189] But there may have been extenuating circumstances, as argued by some historians. Roskill defends Lloyd George by suggesting that the War Office had produced so many confusing and even contradictory statements about the army's strength that he 'can be forgiven for getting muddled'.[190] Woodward, after declaring that Lloyd George had 'misled' Parliament, observes that although Lloyd George did in fact hold back some troops, it was an instance of a concerted policy to force Haig to curtail the 'reckless depletion' of manpower.[191] Indeed, this was not simply a humanitarian consideration. By mid-1917, declining manpower for the military could not easily be made up by combing out workers from important wartime domestic industries such as shipbuilding, munitions and aeroplane construction. Shortages there would adversely affect critical war production. More recently, and from a surprising source, comes an exculpatory (if grudging) defence of Lloyd George. Cassar writes that Lloyd George 'did not have to lie'. There was a good case to be made for adequate numbers of British troops on the ground. Cassar points out that rifle strength was not the only criterion to measure fighting strength. Labour units – responsible for building entrenchments, roads and railways and bringing to the front supplies and arms – often stood in for regular troops on combat duty.[192]

Nevertheless, was Lloyd George justified in lying to the House of Commons – a serious breach of parliamentary decorum? Grigg certainly believes so. Admitting that Lloyd George was guilty of 'using the figures that suited him best', Grigg thinks that the Prime Minister had a larger issue before him: the principle of civilian control over the military.[193] Pugh believes that Lloyd George treated the matter of troop strength purely as a political question.[194] That is, to Lloyd George's way of thinking, political opponents aided by some military malcontents had decided to bring down the government weakened by military failure and parliamentary unrest.[195] Riddell's diary provides evidence of the Prime Minister's frame of mind. Responding to Riddell's congratulations after the 9 May debate, Lloyd George agreed that he did 'pretty well', commenting gleefully on the failure of Asquith's parliamentary performance: 'Old A looked very sick. He crouched low down on the bench and kept moistening his lips ....' Several days later he informed Riddell 'of the political intrigues' which were 'on foot against him'.[196] Thus Lloyd George's prevarications in the House of Commons were in the service – to his way of thinking – of a greater good. He needed a triumph to quell the ministry's parliamentary and military opposition whose actions could weaken not only the mood and morale of the country, but more importantly of the armed forces. It had been a tight squeeze; but as Jones rightly notes, the conclusion of the Maurice debate strengthened, rather than damaged, the Prime Minister.[197]

In the meantime, the German offensive had continued. The third German offensive, followed by the fourth (Operations Blucher and Gneisenau) in late May and June, once again tested Allied resolve. Prior to its advance, the German army had been reprovisioned and rested. The assault began in Champagne. Concentrating more than 5,000 guns against the slightly fewer than 1,500 British and French, the Germans enjoyed their most favourable artillery ratio ever on the Western Front.[198] Overwhelming the Allies, the German armies advanced to within 56 miles of Paris, taking 50,000 prisoners of war and forcing the evacuation of up to a million Parisians.

The renewed German offensive rattled the British government once again. Hankey recorded on the very day of the attack the 'bad news' – the Germans 'seem to have gone through our strong positions like paper'.[199] The following day nothing had changed: the news remained 'deplorable'.[200] Two days later, it was still '[v]ery bad news': the Germans had entered Chateau-Thierry.[201] The ministry now had to think the unthinkable: should they begin planning for the withdrawal of the BEF from France? To consider such an option before the Cabinet as a whole was risky. Any security lapse on such a topic could strike a severe blow to the morale of the country.

Thus began the formation of the X Committee, a small group meeting outside the formal constraints of the War Cabinet. Standing membership of the Committee included Lloyd George; the recently appointed CIGS, General Wilson; and Milner – with Hankey as its secretary. Leo Amery took minutes.[202] Others were summoned from time to time as needed. By meeting separately from the War Cabinet, often just prior to those meetings, the smaller body could devote itself more quickly and in secret to sudden emergencies. One of its earliest discussions was against a general retreat in the face of the German offensives, unless battlefield conditions worsened. The X Committee continued to meet regularly after the initial crisis of the early German spring offensives. In the months that followed it became the instrument by which Lloyd George was able to take greater control of the strategy of British forces on the Western Front.[203]

On 9 June 1918 began the fourth German offensive, the Gneisenau. Its object was to extend the recent gains of the Blucher, thus drawing more tightly the noose around Paris. A quick gain of six miles seemed to assure its success. But within forty-eight hours, Foch launched a counter-attack at Chateau-Thierry and Belleau Wood. A month later, on 15 July, the final of the German spring offensives, the Friedenssturm (or Peace Assault) began east of Reims between the Aisne and Marne Rivers. But as during the Blucher, the Allies counter-attacked with artillery and infantry – this time even more quickly than had been the case during the Gneisenau. Although initially somewhat hindered by the fighting retreat of the Germans, the Allied advance was the beginning of final stages of the war against Germany.

The great German offensives during the spring of 1918 were brought down in part by their own aggressive and rapid advance. The leading German units had penetrated so deeply into France that they were nearly 100 miles from a friendly railhead. Logistical problems mounted. Where German infantry had succeeded beyond expectations, artillery and ammunition were slower to follow. Exposed salients thrust into allied territory proved vulnerable.[204] With that fifth and final offensive, German military weakness was becoming palpable.[205] Their initial advantage of numbers was declining as enormous casualties mounted.

The Allies, too, had faced manpower shortages no less severe than the rampaging German army. The Allies, however, had at last a decisive advantage – the growing numbers of American troops in support of the beleaguered British and French forces.[206] The United States as a neutral power had already been selling substantial war materiel to Britain, as we know. Now at war, American ground troops and naval forces added to the scales against the enemy. Naturally enough, not all went smoothly at first. There undoubtedly remained problems of integration with Allied units at the front, and General Pershing, commander of the American Expeditionary Force, was universally disliked by his British counterparts.[207] Moreover, American troops early on gained the reputation of being enthusiastic but unskilled in warfare. Yet the American 2nd and 3rd Divisions played important supporting roles in stemming the German tide at Chateau-Thierry and Belleau Wood in May and June 1918. Most daunting of all for the Germans was their realization that American forces were a deep well of reserve strength.

The Allies, thus assured of a bountiful manpower source, were also beginning to draw upon another advantage as they counter-attacked the Germans. They finally reaped the rewards of experience. Emblematic was the battle of Amiens on 8 August 1918.[208] Feinting towards the North, British and French forces in tandem with a Canadian and Australian corps advanced to the German lines, led by more than 400 tanks.[209] (Only one American regiment participated in the Amiens operation.) Allied aircraft had a superiority of four to one. The artillery barrage, more accurate than in the past and with sufficient munitions, preceded the attack. Battalion firepower had also been enhanced by increasing the number of Lewis guns, trench mortars and grenade-throwing rifles.[210] Equally important was the complete surprise that Rawlinson's Fourth Army gained over German defenders. Tanks, troops and supplies movements towards enemy lines took place at night. To reduce noise, roads were covered in sand or straw and wheels were bound up in rope or sacking.[211] Attacking in early morning, aided further by a fortuitous low-lying mist, British troops rammed through German defensive positions. Within a few hours, the Germans had been pushed back seven miles. Their casualties were heavy. The high number of German prisoners of war taken – a sure indicator of a loss of morale – was an equally important sign of victory. By September, British forces were attacking the main defensive fall back position of the German armies – the Hindenburg Line. If the Allies broke through, all of Germany would be open to the rush of foreign troops. The Germans attempted an orderly retreat and in some cases were successful in holding actions against the Allied forces. But these were isolated incidents. The Allies were well on their way towards victory.

For the BEF particularly, it has been argued that their success at arms in late 1918 can be attributed to a substantial learning curve at all levels in the forces.[212] Even J.P. Harris, a frequent critic of Haig, believes that Haig led 'the most combat-effective' of the Allied armies at this point in the war.[213] As the Allies took the offensive in August 1918, Haig was energetically active in widening the British offensive, 'setting the whole front in motion with a series of massive offensive blows'.[214] Thus, Haig's contribution to the final stage of this long war, as Harris sees it, was 'crucial', even 'vital'.[215] This suggests that Haig's style of conducting warfare had finally come into its own. He had long sought the opportunity of a breakthrough as a way to roll up the German defensive trench system. No longer bound by a static, punch and counter-punch system of war on the Western Front, Haig seemed more comfortable in a war of mobility, a war that as a cavalryman he had been trained for. 'Breakthough' rather than 'bite and hold' was now the optimum military course.

Emblematic of the new steamrolling tactics was General Rawlinson's Fourth Army, which led the successful battle at Amiens and was the vanguard of the counterattack against the German spring offensives of 1918.[216] Rawlinson, an early proponent of bite and hold tactics, was now free of such a cautious posture and benefited from the fortuitous coming together of a number of military advances enjoyed by the Allies. Chief among these for the British forces was the overwhelming firepower they enjoyed over the German armies. British heavy industry was now providing artillery, tanks, machine guns and mortars, along with ammunition supplies of unimaginable quantity compared to the early years of the war. The Fourth Army, as was true of the BEF as a whole, was also benefiting from a gradually evolving 'all arms doctrine' by which artillery, aircraft, infantry and tanks operated well together using enhanced communications systems. Above all, the British Army had developed a scientific approach to gunnery that had enhanced accuracy to a much greater degree than their German counterparts. Thus British counter-battery action, 'with crushing intensity'[217] knocked out German artillery positions with far greater effect than ever before. British soldiers could thus advance more rapidly in tactical operations with less loss of life. With these military advantages in hand, the Allies were well prepared for their sternest test in pursuit of the retreating German armies – the Hindenburg Line. In September, the British First and Third Armies attacked the central sector, while Rawlinson's Fourth breached the strongest section of the Line. Once the Hindenburg positions had been lost, the Germans had few defensive options remaining.[218] Scarcely capable of sustained resistance, the German armies began to disintegrate. Reserve troops thrown into the lines against the rapidly advancing Allied forces were disorganized and ineffective. German soldiers readily surrendered. Although some severe clashes occurred between isolated German forces and the Allies, these did not prevent the Allies' inexorable advance.

The impending defeat of the German Army had severe consequences not only for the German military machine: it was also a catalyst for unrest among the civilian population within Germany, which had suffered for years under the Allied blockade of German ports. Foodstuffs and the basic necessities of life rapidly diminished. As early as 1915, such critical items as fat, sugar, bread and soap had been rationed. In the following year, potato stocks fell. Coal and clothing supplies were short. Fertilizer and fodder for farm animals were equally affected. Civilian morale was badly affected as ordinary Germans turned against established authority.[219] The same disaffection was felt among German military forces. At the seaport city of Kiel on 4 November, German sailors mutinied against their commanders and incited a revolutionary takeover of the local government. Within days, several provincial capitals had fallen to revolutionary cadres, some of whom advocated a socialist republic. In the meantime, the German Commander in Chief, Erich Ludendorf, began a series of exchanges between Berlin and Washington with the object of effecting a ceasefire based upon President Wilson's famous Fourteen Points. By then Germany's allies had begun surrendering. Military losses, declining rations and shortages of other provisions led Bulgaria to sign an armistice agreement on 30 September.[220] Austria-Hungary also appealed to President Wilson for an armistice. Its army was surrendering wholesale to the Italians and its fragile political divisions began to splinter into constituent ethnic groups, made up of Poles, Czechs, Slovaks and Germans. The old multinational Hapsburg Empire was in tatters. On 2 November 1918, Kaiser Karl I signed an armistice. A week later, the Kaiser Wilhelm abdicated and a German republic was proclaimed.

The war, now effectively over, was soon to be once again at the centre of European and world affairs during the Paris Peace Conference. Lloyd George would once more play a central role, as he had during the war years – perhaps even more crucial a role than during the war itself. At this juncture, then, it is important to summarize his contributions to the winning of the war. The historical judgements have been nearly unanimously favourable. To Peter Rowland, Lloyd George was 'The Nation's Saviour' and 'The Man Who Won The War'.[221] Rowland believes that by supplying the guns and ammunition, the tanks and aircraft, Lloyd George won the war on the ground. By encouraging the introduction of the convoy system to safeguard shipping from German submarines and providing Britain's allies with needed shipping, he won the war at sea. Gilbert agrees: for him, Lloyd George was clearly 'the organizer of victory'.[222] Even the frequently sceptical Trevor Wilson admits that 'from the outset' Lloyd George revealed 'a prescience regarding the needs of the conflict'; and in sounding 'a note of stern resolve', he achieved the necessary stature to lead the country in wartime.[223] Not surprisingly, Thomas Jones – one of Lloyd George's strongest supporters, who wrote a laudatory biography – has perhaps the highest words of praise. The source of Lloyd George's wartime leadership, Jones believed, 'lay in the fire and zeal which burned within him', and in his radiating 'authority and force' which carried all before him. As Prime Minister, he always arrived in the Cabinet room 'acutely observant', 'with his batteries fully charged', and was soon often issuing 'a whirl of lightning instructions'.[224]

Can it be that Lloyd George played such a decisive role in the war? After all, as we have observed above, numerous players and performers in the stage of war made important contributions. How significant could one individual have been? Tom Jones is suggestive here when he speaks of Lloyd George's supreme confidence in his own ability to find a solution to any difficulty. This was so because the Prime Minister was 'endlessly adjustable and accommodating'[225] – a trait that we have often noted in his political life. As Roger Chickering has written in agreement, Lloyd George's 'mercurial energies, adaptability, and disdain for routine thought' led him 'to embrace improvisation as a principle of government', clearly evident during his tenure as Minister of Munitions and during his term as Prime Minister.[226] This was in direct contrast to the regimented approach of the generals who managed the German military machine. Keith Grieves further suggests that Lloyd George – by appointing like-minded men in positions of power – made sure that others followed his tendency to avoid static hierarchies and existing administrative practices. Thus, these new decision makers, by merging military and civilian spheres, created a streamlined and integrated war effort. The nation in arms emerged, but under civilian leadership.[227]

But Lloyd George's style of wartime leadership did not emerge immediately. If it can be legitimately claimed that the British military leaders followed a progression of ideas and actions, indeed a learning curve, in their pursuit of victory during the Great War, so it also seems true in the case of Lloyd George. As we have noted, Britain's military command had gradually adapted the tools of warfare to conditions on the ground, in the air and at sea. But not every battle was the same: not all clashes of arms were alike. The lessons learned in one operation could not be strictly applied to another. Circumstances such as weather, supply and unanticipated actions of the enemy all differed from battle to battle. Within the framework of operational tactics and grand strategy as they developed over time, a certain flexibility was essential. So it was with Lloyd George's leadership in war. A solid core of Lloyd George's wartime ends and principles can be identified: to win the war unconditionally; to preserve the British Empire; and to maintain British influence in the world at large. These reveal his firm patriotism and determination to retain secure global power in the postwar era. To achieve these, he had to be nimble in carrying them out and in facing successfully the unexpected twists and turns of a vast global military operation.

13

PRIME MINISTER IN PEACE

The tenor of the peace negotiations was established at the outset by the stringent terms of the Armistice.[1] Germany's territorial gains since 1914 were to be surrendered on both her eastern and western borders, including the evacuation of all territory on the left bank of the Rhine. The German army relinquished substantially its arsenal, including 5,000 artillery pieces; 30,000 machine guns; 2,000 aircraft; 5,000 locomotives; and 160 submarines. Most of its battleships and battle cruisers were to be interned in either a neutral or an allied port. In addition, the British economic blockade would continue in place. These measures were all designed to discourage any further military action on Germany's part should the Armistice be broken. Finally, and most portentously, the Armistice stipulated that Germany would be bound to pay for war damages incurred by the Allies. On 11 November 1918, after four days of discussions, the Armistice was signed in Marshal Foch's special train, parked in an isolated stretch of the Forest of Compiegne. How much of its provisions would be incorporated into a peace treaty remained to be seen.

As the terms of the Armistice demonstrated, events were moving towards a punitive and uncompromising peace to be imposed by the Allies upon Germany. In Britain, even before the final days of the war, a coalition of influential imperial idealists, Conservative newspaper barons and (what Douglas Newton calls) 'economic warriors' joined together to insure that Germany paid heavily for the war.[2] The economic warriors were comprised of protectionists, moderate tariff reformers and business pressure groups, such as the Federation of Business Industry (FBI). They were determined to keep postwar Germany out of world markets to the advantage of British commerce. Additionally, they sought to impose a heavy indemnity upon Germany. Lloyd George cannot have been unaware of these intentions. Nor could he have been unaware of the general sentiment among Britons for retribution against Germany. So many lives lost and so much treasure spent must be redeemed. Under intense pressure from the vengeful postwar determination among the victors to exact a stringent peace treaty upon Germany, Lloyd George often found himself in an awkward position. He believed that Germany ought to be punished, but not to an extent that would hinder its return to a peaceful family of nations in the postwar world.

For Lloyd George to implement a just but fair peace, it was important to insure his position as primus inter pares in the coalition government. The first task towards this goal was to win the general election of December 1918, the first election to be held under the Representation of the People Act of February 1918.[3] For Lloyd George, as Prime Minister, the election provided both a challenge and an opportunity. If he succeeded, he could enhance his own popularity as the man who won the war. He could rise above the Conservative coalition ministry, perhaps rise even above party. He hoped that a new Parliament would sanction his policies, giving him a free hand at the forthcoming peace conference. For this, he sought electoral legitimacy. His coalition government had come to power essentially as the result of a political coup against Asquith in December 1916 with the dedicated aim of winning the war. A parliamentary victory would validate and strengthen his position as the head of the coalition government and his hold upon postwar political power at home. As C.P. Scott put it after an interview with Lloyd George, 'he felt the need of a mandate …'.[4] Moreover, a successful election would place him at the forefront of peacemaking – to Britain's advantage in Europe and in the world at large. Most particularly, and perhaps surprisingly, Lloyd George was determined both to consolidate and to expand the British Empire as a powerful global entity in the immediate postwar years.

To ensure a victory for the wartime coalition in the forthcoming general election was the Prime Minister's initial task. Even before the Armistice, during the spring and summer of 1918, tentative negotiations among the interested parties attempted to sort out the terms of any new postwar government.[5] It was not smooth sailing: some Conservatives were vehemently opposed to any further alliance with Lloyd George. They were eager to throw off the shackles of coalition government and to re-establish party affiliation. Eventually, however, most Conservatives came round. Bonar Law – now virtually Deputy Prime Minister – was convinced that the coalition under Lloyd George must be maintained and he so argued the case among his Conservative colleagues.[6] With the Conservatives in principle lending their support to the continuation of the coalition, an electoral pact was sealed ahead of the forthcoming election. Details were left to Freddie Guest, Lloyd George's chief whip, who conferred initially with Sir George Younger, Chairman of the Conservative Party, and later with Robert Sanders, Deputy Chairman. The coalition's campaign platform included the following planks, designed to appeal to a broad spectrum of the electorate: better social and economic conditions and higher wages for British citizens; the right to levy a duty on imported articles; disestablishment of the Church of Wales; and maintenance of the British Empire.

Most controversial in the government's election preparations was its designation of an approved list of parliamentary candidates. These were divided mainly among Conservatives and Lloyd George Liberals: the Liberals were given 150 candidates; Conservatives were overwhelmingly larger at 364. Asquithian Liberals, Labour MPs and the Irish nationalists were excluded. All approved candidates were notified by an official letter (or 'coupon' as Asquith derisorily called it), signed by Lloyd George and Bonar Law. For many Liberals then and for Liberal historians thereafter, the electoral pact of 1918 and the Coupon Election of that year represented the ultimate betrayal by Lloyd George. He could be excused perhaps for entering into a coalition of Conservatives in 1916: it was an emergency wartime measure. But for Lloyd George to engage in a fully-fledged cooperation with the Conservatives in an election battle against his own party was unforgivable. Among historians, Trevor Wilson has been the harshest critic. Wilson believes that Lloyd George's primary reason to employ the coupon was 'to destroy the Liberal party'. As a Prime Minister 'of no fixed political abode', Lloyd George thus abandoned the Liberals in throwing in his lot with the Conservatives.[7]

In a curious episode, Lloyd George provided evidence of his own ambiguous views on Liberals and Liberalism during the delicate balancing act he performed prior to the election. In remarks to Liberal MPs at Downing Street on 12 November, he enthusiastically reaffirmed his Liberalism. Indeed, he declared that the nation needed the Liberal Party more than ever in order to enact necessary peace-time reforms, including a bold housing and land programme: 'let us utilize victory', he declared, 'to get the necessary impetus for reform' and especially to improve 'the condition of the people'.[8] 'Now is the great opportunity of Liberalism', he continued. 'Let us rise to it!' He then emphasized his own unflagging Liberalism. 'I was reared in Liberalism. From the old leaders of Liberalism I learnt my faith.' He could never leave Liberalism. Yet within a few days, he issued the coupons and soon thereafter began a series of speeches highly critical of opposition Liberals. Denouncing these 'wild inconsistencies', Wilson believes that Lloyd George's 12 November speech was an unprincipled exercise in 'political calculation'.[9] There is some truth to this charge. The pro-Liberal tone of Lloyd George's Downing Street address on 12 November was unmistakable. The Liberal Lord Buckminster, in a letter to C.P. Scott, noted it with surprise, wondering how the Prime Minister's speech could be reconciled with the Conservative leaning coalition government.[10] Indeed, the speech had startled Lloyd George's coalitionist Conservative allies. As Sanders wrote in his diary: 'Our people became suspicious at once.'[11] At an impromptu meeting shortly afterward with Balfour, Bonar Law and Sanders, the Prime Minister was apparently called to account. Sanders recorded that Lloyd George seemed to offer half an apology. He admitted he had spoken 'impromptu' and indicated that 'he had a difficult job' and was trying 'to make things easy for his Liberal supporters'. Yet on the same day that Sanders recounted this incident, Lloyd George assured a delegation of Manchester Liberals that he remained a Liberal and should the coalition win the election, he would carry out a Liberal programme.[12]

Clearly Lloyd George was operating from political calculation. But to what end? That his aim was the destruction of the Liberal Party is unlikely. Perhaps he believed that talented Liberals could be swayed to serve in a postwar government. The truth may be that Lloyd George was not clear in his own mind where his political course should lie. He was well aware that the coalition he led, largely dominated by the Conservative Party, had little love for him. He could no longer look to the Asquithian Liberals, who considered him a traitor. Nor was an association with the emerging Labour Party possible. Thus there remained only the coalition Liberal rump – not large enough to sustain a still vital and relatively young Lloyd George in office. In effect, he had increasingly become a man without a party and must perforce keep all his options open.[13]

There is some evidence that suggests Lloyd George was indeed thinking of turning the fluid state of the political parties to his own advantage. He entertained the idea of establishing a centrist party which would bring together like-minded Liberals and Conservatives. As early as May 1918, a cadre of Lloyd George's supporters began to organize to that end. Their programme included the continued vigorous execution of the war; a role for the state in economic development; a broadened social programme that would address unemployment and the needs of transportation and housing; and the creation of a Ministry of Health. Traditional Liberal creeds such as free trade, nonconformism and temperance were omitted or downplayed.[14] The implication was clear: the traditional Liberal Party, in spite of its reformist traditions, had been revealed by the war as fatally suspicious of the power of the state as a force for mobilizing citizens in times of emergency. Perhaps, too, the old Liberal Party would be unable to face the equally severe challenges of a postwar age. The Liberal leadership had become hidebound, symbolized by Asquith, its fallen leader. Certainly Lloyd George believed, as he told Riddell, that the Liberal Party was 'a thing of the past'.[15]

To give a public face to his centrist campaign, Lloyd George turned to the newspaper press to rally potential Liberal supporters.[16] C.P. Scott of the *Manchester Guardian* was an obvious target for a trial balloon. At a breakfast meeting with Scott in late October Lloyd George presented his views on free trade, an article of faith dearly held by Scott.[17] Lloyd George pledged to uphold the general principle of free trade. He would, however, act to prevent 'dumping' – an important enough reservation to give pause to Scott. On Ireland, he took a harsher line, maintaining the need for conscription in that country for wartime service abroad if necessary. This also did not please Scott, who believed that such a policy would destroy any hope of a peaceful resolution of the Irish question. At the conclusion of their meeting, Lloyd George assured Scott that he was open to some kind of reconciliation with the Asquithian Liberals, even suggesting that there might be a place for Asquith in a new coalition government.

Perhaps Lloyd George believed that he could no longer rely upon the somewhat testy and self-righteous Scott to get his ideas out to the newspaper reading public. In any case, securing a more pliable conduit for Lloyd George's opinions was under way. He had already established close relations with various important pressmen throughout his career, including Riddell of the *News of the World*, William Robertson Nicoll of the *British Weekly* and Sir Henry Dalziel and his *Reynolds News*.[18] But even these men occasionally spoke their independent minds: the Prime Minister now wanted a newspaper of his own which would be wholly loyal and a mouthpiece for his ideas. In an unusual move, he engineered through wealthy backers the purchase of the *Daily Chronicle*, the third largest of the major newspapers of the day.[19] With such an influential newspaper firmly in hand, Lloyd George had a powerful instrument of public opinion which he could operate as he wished. And more specifically, such an instrument would be invaluable in advocating his plans for a centrist party.

Bearing in mind Lloyd George's background of fluid political and party affiliation, it is possible to understand better his actions during the general election of 1918. He sought not only to solidify his position in the electorate at large, but also to strengthen his hand within the more circumscribed confines of Parliament. And, no less importantly, he had to appease to some degree the growing coalition of Conservative forces within the business community and the imperial spokesmen who held out for a harsh treaty against Germany. Thus the tenor of Lloyd George's public statements during the course of the election campaign hardened against the defeated Germans. This dismayed the Prime Minister's former allies, such as Scott, who thought Lloyd George began 'very well' in his quest for 'a just peace' but noted sadly that he later went 'downhill'.[20] Coalition candidates, however, applauded Lloyd George's change of tack. Leo Amery reported that he had 'gradually cut down' on social reform in his speeches 'to a few generalities' and was going 'wholeheartedly for a strong policy including punishing the Kaiser as well'. He praised Lloyd George's speeches as a model – 'full of zeal' and 'a great help' in this brand of electioneering.[21] Balcarres also commented on Lloyd George's change from his original conciliatory speeches, which had fallen 'rather flat'. Having 'pulled himself together', the Prime Minister became more effective by revising his speeches to include indemnities from the enemy and punishment of the Kaiser for war crimes.[22]

Thus, contemporary sources seem agreed on Lloyd George's altered message during the course of the election campaign. There has also been a consensus among historians. Koss has written of Lloyd George's 'blistering invective' as the election drew to its conclusion.[23] Trevor Wilson has denounced Lloyd George's 'cheap election stunts'.[24] Even Morgan, who thinks that Lloyd George's earlier speeches 'were in the main low-keyed' as he attempted to educate the public on the need for reconciliation with Germany, nevertheless admits that his later speeches showed 'a tendency to be carried along by he floodtide of jingoism'.[25] Turner believes that 'by the end of the campaign there was a marked convergence between Lloyd George and the more robust elements in the Conservative Party'. [26] Turner in addition has a qualifying comment, remarking that Lloyd George's election tactic must be placed within a political perspective: the Prime Minister was largely motivated by a concern that he could be outflanked by Conservative hard-liners who advocated even more brutally than he for a harsh peace.[27]

Closely read, Lloyd George's speeches reveal a more sophisticated message than merely pandering to the crowds, or struggling to find some convenient centrist haven among the electorate to perpetuate his term of office. The speeches in fact represent a series of synchronized interlocking goals: to celebrate victory in war; to announce postwar reconstruction plans; and to convince Liberals, radicals and Labourites that his Conservative coalition partners could be trusted to follow the path of needed reforms. Only incidentally did he discuss the possible terms of a peace treaty and punishment for the Germans. In his opening speech of the campaign at Central Hall, Westminster, for example, Lloyd George claimed that the war had been 'a revealing war'.[28] In its 'lurid glare', all the faults of the old system stood out, especially 'the faulty organization of our national life, the wasteful use of our national resources in men and materiel'. The war, he continued, operated 'like a ploughshare and a harrow': it had 'turned up and rent the soil of Europe'. Now was the time to replenish that soil: 'If you do not sow, weeds will grow.' Immediate action was necessary 'to begin on the task of reconstruction'. Problems of national health, poor housing and inadequate transportation must all be addressed. Ensuring that the coalition government remained in office, staying the course and finishing the job could best achieve these goals.

On 25 November, Lloyd George was at Wolverhampton where he piped a more patriotic tune.[29] On the navy: 'never has the record of the British Navy been so glorious'. As for the army, their 'dauntless courage' was beyond praise. Now it was time, he continued, 'to make Britain a fit country for heroes to live in'. Within a few days, he was at Newcastle-on-Tyne, where he developed a more partisan tone.[30] In a morning address, he once again brought forward 'the principles upon which this country is to be reconstructed during the next five years'. This was coupled with a warning to reject those 'who did nothing but carp and criticize and harass' the coalition government. In his afternoon speech, he turned more directly to the enemy, promising never again to allow suspected German spies (thumping the Speaker's table for emphasis) to remain in Britain. As for punitive damages against Germany, he addressed the issue of 'indemnity', declaring that Germany 'must pay the cost up to the limit of her capacity to do so'. Later on in the same speech, he emphasized this point: Germany 'ought to pay, she must pay as far as she can'.

He pursued this theme at his next speech in Bristol, where he declared: 'By the law of every civilized country in the world the party who is guilty of the wrong pays the costs.'[31] To which a voice in the crowd shouted out: 'In full.' 'Certainly in full', the Prime Minister responded; and then in almost an aside, 'if they have got it'. In conclusion, Lloyd George returned to the topic of reconstruction and the role of the coalition in supporting it. The coalition, he reminded his audience, had worked together during the war 'in perfect unity and harmony for one common purpose – the saving of our native land'. They were now committed as eagerly 'as any Liberal or Labour man ... to work for these great social reforms which ... are necessary for this country'. In his final speech of the campaign – at the public baths of Camberwell before a largely working class audience of 2,000 – he defended the achievements of the coalition government in wartime.[32] Mentioning the Conservative Bonar Law, without whose assistance he 'could not have done my work in this war', Lloyd George praised him further as 'loyal, a most true comrade' and a 'sagacious counsellor'. He then appealed directly to his audience, warning them that the Labour Party was at present 'being run by the extreme pacifist, Bolshevist group' whose policies, had they been adopted during the war, would have assured a German victory. It was crucial to the country, he continued, to vote for the coalition government in the coming election. Vote for 'the present team', he concluded.

There is little doubt that Lloyd George's election addresses were carefully crafted to appeal to a wide spectrum of the electorate. He did not merely trade upon popular sentiment for revenge against Germany. He also pledged to work for a new Britain, one designed to reward the nation as a whole for its wartime sacrifices. In that promise, he also made the case for the continuation of his ministry, even though its composition would normally have been antipathetic to Liberals and Labourites alike. As he had phrased it in his first election speech at Westminster, 'when you have great, gigantic tasks that will affect not merely the structure of the Empire and the fate of he world, but which come home to every man in his own household and workshop, in the life and health of his children, you really do not want a strong opposition. This is a time rather for the criticism of experts and not of partisans'.[33]

Given the retributive mood of the electorate; the dominant electioneering tone by the majority coalition MPs, especially Lloyd George; and the electoral contract between the coalition government and the couponed candidates, the election results were a foregone conclusion. In the new House of Commons, 526 of 707 MPs were supporters of the coalition and only 181 opponents, including 57 Labourites.[34] Seventy-three Irish Sinn Féin MPs refused to attend at Westminster. Fewer than 30 Asquith Liberals remained. Asquith himself lost his seat at East Fife, a constituency he had held for 32 years.[35] Indeed, the entire opposition Liberal front bench was defeated, including (apart from Asquith) McKenna, Runciman and Samuel. For this small body of independent Liberals, as they now were, their defeat has been variously labelled 'a shattering defeat', 'an unmitigated disaster' and for Asquith, 'a personal humiliation'.[36]

With the Liberal opposition not only down but out, and with an overwhelming political sanction for the coalition, Lloyd George could turn his attention immediately to the peace process with the mandate he had sought. His role as peacemaker was undoubtedly strengthened by his electoral success. This gave him a certain self-confidence and influence at the Paris Peace Conference that bode well for British interests. But Lloyd George was also fully aware that the new coalition Parliament was dominated by Conservatives, some of whom were hard-liners who would look over his shoulder at every opportunity. He was also mindful of the entrenched strength of those influential spokesmen who held anti-German views and were determined to make Germany pay. Additional pressures would likely come from some dominion leaders, who might circumscribe Lloyd George's range of actions, especially on reparations.

The most vociferous of the dominion spokesmen was Prime Minister William Morris Hughes of Australia. A Welshman, 'Billy' Hughes had spent his youth in Llandudno before emigrating to Australia. A member of the Imperial War Cabinet, he was not easily intimidated and was not shy of making his demands directly to the Prime Minister.[37] Hughes was particularly eager to secure compensation for Australia in the peace process, frequently reminding the allies of the contributions Australian troops had made to the war effort. Hughes also strenuously plumped for imperial preferences and tariff protection for the dominions. To these forces – vengeful anti-Germans at home and self-aggrandizing imperial leaders abroad – Lloyd George was in addition soon to face revanchist allies.

Peacemaking began on 18 January 1919 when more than 1,000 diplomats and statesmen gathered in Paris to begin the months' long negotiations to settle the postwar fate of many nations. Added to these were thousands more essential staff and service assistants, such as printers, messengers and typists. In addition, there was an enormous number of chauffeurs, security personnel and custodians. All had to be quickly housed, giving rise to almost insoluble problems of inadequate accommodations and poor working conditions. Conference proceedings were inevitably affected. Because official minutes of the numerous ad hoc commissions required a fortnight for printing, the primary decision makers were often delayed in their deliberations.[38] Thus, the intense work of important officials in such trying conditions very likely undermined their efficiency and possibly affected their decisions on vital matters. But most important of all in evaluating the Paris Peace Conference were the handful of important delegates and their strengths and weaknesses in managing the supremely difficult negotiations on matters of war and peace.

President Wilson of the United States was perhaps the most eagerly awaited presence at the conference. His Fourteen Points had already begun the peacemaking process. But this early intrusion into the peace process had not been well received by Lloyd George, who believed (with some justification) that the President was ill informed about conditions in Europe and was naively entering into complicated matters of European history and culture inadequately prepared. Lloyd George was particularly incensed by Wilson's habit of *ex cathedra* diplomatic initiatives, without consulting his allies. Particularly egregious was Wilson's entering into private negotiations with German officials during the final stages of the war. As Lloyd George put it to Riddell, Wilson 'must act in accord with the French and British, who have borne the burden of the day'.[39] Lloyd George's view was shared by his closest advisors. Riddell flatly distrusted the Americans, as he confided to Lloyd George as early as December 1917. 'They resent our command of the seas', he believed, and it was obvious that 'the Americans will endeavour to clip our naval wings'.[40]

President Clemenceau of France, the doughty warrior of 78 years, was the principal host. His antipathy toward Germany was widely known. His aims at the Peace Conference were relatively straightforward: revenge, compensation and security. This was not surprising given the destruction of French property and land and the loss of life – a quarter of all Frenchmen between the ages of 18 and 30 had died in the war, a higher proportion of its population than that of any other belligerent.[41] French demands were thus understandably inflated. But Clemenceau's avowed border rectifications were viewed by both the United States and Britain as extreme and the ensuing conflict led to considerable tension in the early weeks of the Conference. There was in fact little love lost between Clemenceau and Wilson. Conflicts between Clemenceau and Lloyd George were also not uncommon. Bad blood between the two had begun over the disposition of French and British troops during some of the heaviest fighting in the war. Festering resentments popped up throughout the conference and finally burst into the open over conflicting Anglo-French designs in the Middle East.

Lloyd George, the victor of an overwhelming electoral mandate to secure the peace in British interests, effectively moved to Paris for the duration of the conference. Establishing a residence in a rented flat in Rue Nitot, Lloyd George (with an entourage including Hankey, Riddell and Philip Kerr nearby) was at the centre of events as they unfolded. Balfour, as Foreign Secretary, occupied the flat above. As head of the British Empire delegation, Lloyd George was accompanied by over 200 clerks, military staff and aides, most of whom stayed at the nearby Hotel Majestic. In attendance, too, at the Majestic was Lloyd George's daughter, Megan, and Frances Stevenson, who served as Megan's sometime chaperone. Stevenson was officially installed as one of the Prime Minister's personal secretaries, a function which she had faithfully and efficiently undertaken for many years. There is some evidence, however, that Stevenson was also treated as Lloyd George's unofficial wife.[42] Indeed, there were momentary breaks in the hard work of the Conference when Lloyd George and Frances could spend time together, taking walks, day trips out of Paris and dining with friends.[43] But, as Frances recorded in her diary, they had to exercise care and discretion to avoid scandal: 'D. thinks it better that I should not be seen dining with him in public. I think he is right.'[44]

As the Conference got underway, it was soon clear that peacemaking would not be easy.[45] Administrative chaos, clashes of national interests and personalities and struggles for dominance among the powers continually threatened the proceedings. Larger events outside the Conference also intruded: collapsing state systems and revolutionary movements threatened the smooth operation of its proceedings.[46] The first order of business was to devise an efficient administrative system. The original Council of Ten (comprised of two delegates each Britain, France, Italy, the USA and Japan) proved too cumbersome and, because it met publicly, tended to move slowly as it received delegations from various countries. At Lloyd George's insistence, a new Council of Four (Lloyd George representing Great Britain, Wilson for the United States, Clemenceau for France and Orlando for Italy) came into being. Meeting more than 200 times, often informally and secretly, the Council of Four utilized other groups, individuals, or expert commissions to suggest solutions or to draft responses to particular issues as they arose. A second body, the Council of Five, composed of the foreign secretaries of the Four plus Japan, was an important subsidiary body. Absent from any active participation in the conference were representatives of the defeated nations: Germany; the Austro-Hungarian Empire; Bulgaria; and the Ottoman Empire. Bolshevik Russia was not invited.

During the six months of its existence, the Peace Conference was dedicated largely to settling five major issues: boundary settlements; the disposition of German colonies; the establishment of the League of Nations; reparations; and the famous (or infamous) Article 231, the war-guilt clause. The tenor of its deliberations could be gauged even before the meetings had officially begun. Clemenceau led a campaign to re-annex those parts of Alsace and Lorraine that had been taken by Germany during the Franco-Prussian War.[47] Clemenceau also demanded that the Rhineland, which extended along the west bank of the Rhine from Alsace northward to the Dutch border, become a client state under French influence. Indeed, at one point, there was even some talk that the French-German border be restored to its 1814 extent – a time when Napoleon's empire extended deep into German territory. These territorial demands represented France's strong desire to protect its eastern boundary with Germany by creating a buffer zone. In addition, France also claimed significant economic compensation. Having lost important coal mines – deliberately destroyed by the retreating German army – the French demanded annexation of the Saar with proprietary rights over its coal.

Both Britain and the United States, while agreeing to the restoration of Alsace and Lorraine, refused to consider other, more extensive, border rectifications. Lloyd George was particularly adamant. To Riddell, he confided that the French demands were 'absurd' and that he would not agree to them.[48] A compromise was arranged by which Allied troops would occupy the left bank of the Rhine and its appropriate bridgeheads for 15 years before withdrawing. In addition a 50-kilometre strip on the Rhine right bank would be demilitarized. Moreover, Britain and the USA gave guarantees of support to the French against any German attempt to reoccupy the Rhineland. French demands over the Saar were also settled with a compromise. The yet-to-be-formed League of Nations would initially assume sovereignty of the Saar, while France would enjoy the right to exploit its resources. After 15 years, a plebiscite would offer alternatives to Saar inhabitants: to remain under the League or to become either French or German citizens. If the decision went for Germany, that country could purchase the mines from France.[49]

In the midst of these difficult negotiations, during which Britain and the USA strove to reduce French territorial demands, Lloyd George – concerned at the persistent attempts to establish a harsh peace – attempted to set out a more moderate tone towards Germany. Gathering together his most trusted advisors, including Hankey, General Wilson and Philip Kerr, Lloyd George spent a working weekend in late March 1919 at a hotel in the Paris suburb of Fontainebleau. Assigning his advisors to play specific roles at the peace conference (Hankey took Britain, and Wilson was both a German officer and a female French civilian), Lloyd George led the discussion. Kerr then drew it all together and typed up a conclusion.[50] The document, marked 'Secret' and dated 25 March 1919, was the famous Fontainebleau Memorandum. Lloyd George presented the memorandum two days later at a meeting of the Council of Four.[51] The memorandum argued against French demands for a punitive peace as advocated by Clemenceau. An overly harsh peace, Lloyd George warned the Council, would stir up German patriotism. Such a treaty could even drive Germany toward Bolshevism, then a distinct possibility. Therefore he cautioned against any mandatory transfer of German territory 'to the rule of some other nation'. Embedded within the Fontainebleau Memorandum were also direct references to reparations. 'Our terms may be severe', the memorandum stated. They may even be 'stern and even ruthless'; but so long as they were just, Germany would have no right to complain. Once reparations had been imposed, the Allies would open to Germany 'the raw materials and markets of the world on equal terms with ourselves … to enable the German people to get upon their legs again. We cannot both cripple her and expect her to pay'.

In the discussions on the memorandum among the Council of Four during the days following, Lloyd George spoke directly to Clemenceau, reminding him that the Allies were soon to demand 'a very hard peace on Germany'.[52] Under the terms of the proposed treaty, Germany would lose much of its imperial trappings: it would have neither colonies nor fleet. A great part of its natural resources, such as iron and coal, would be stripped away. Lloyd George believed that Germany would not only accept these terms, but would also accept additionally 'a very heavy indemnity'.[53] What would 'wound them most', however, would be the compulsory transfer of millions of Germans to become the subjects of other countries.[54] Such an action, he warned, might so alienate German sensitivities that they would refuse to sign the treaty.

The transfer of German citizens to other states was a direct reference to a growing problem that was emerging with the collapse of old empires and destruction of established state boundaries, especially in Central and Eastern Europe. The Austro-Hungarian Empire, for example, was completely dismantled into the roughly ethnically divided sovereign states of Austria, Hungary and Czechoslovakia. Other parts of that empire were reallocated to Rumania, Italy and the new state of Yugoslavia. Poland, now created as an independent country, also gained territory from the old empire. Most of the new Poland, however, was fashioned from parts of eastern Germany and western Russia. Estonia, Latvia and Lithuania, originally detached from Russia under the Treaty of Brest Litovsk, also gained independent status by the Treaty.

Britain, under the leadership of Lloyd George, often took the lead in revising the new national boundaries. Like Woodrow Wilson, Lloyd George generally favoured the notion that peoples and provinces were not to be bartered and treated like pawns in a vast geopolitical game. Mindful of the conventional trampling of the rights of ethnic minorities by coercive majorities, the two statesmen laid special emphasis in attempting to group together similar peoples to make new sovereign states. This was certainly the ideal in supporting Yugoslavia, a South Slav state, now freed from their Austrian overlords. But the ideal was not always possible. The new Czechoslovakian state, for example, would be economically and strategically vulnerable without the Sudeten border lands containing rich mineral resources and mountain defences: yet the Sudetenland also contained some three million Germans. The same problem emerged in Poland – now an independent state for the first time since the eighteenth century – which contained within its borders as many as two million Germans. The Poles, however, had a reasonable request for a clear route to the Baltic Sea, a Polish Corridor, which could only come at the cost of traditional Prussian lands. France firmly supported a strong and independent Poland as a barrier to the spread of Russian Bolshevism westward. More importantly, any gains which Poland could make at the expense of Germany would weaken that country to the eventual benefit of France.[55] Lloyd George rejected this reasoning. Fully aware that the German minority within Poland could become a magnet for irredentist claims, Lloyd George argued successfully for a narrowing of the Polish Corridor and for making Danzig a free city under the League of Nations, rather than a Polish one. He was also persuasive in providing plebiscites in certain areas, including Upper Silesia, some of which voted to remain German.[56]

As negotiations over boundary settlements became increasingly complex, so too did another contentious issue – the reparations question. Lloyd George himself certainly believed that Germany should face serious economic consequences in order to deter any future military adventurism on the Continent.[57] This view he held even before the war had been won. At his notable Caxton Hall speech in January 1918 – widely recognized as a restatement of British war aims and a tentative olive branch to the German government – he made it clear that the first order of business in any peace negotiations would be the restored independence of Belgium 'and such reparations as can be made for the devastation of its towns and provinces'. Although he did not claim specific reparations for Britain at that time, he affirmed the principle. 'Reparation means recognition', he stated. 'Unless international right is recognized by insistence on payment for injury done in defiance of its canons it can never be a reality.'[58] His campaign speeches during the general election of 1918 often carried the same theme.

In short, it is undoubtedly true that Lloyd George expected payment of some kind from Germany, as did every Allied leader. This was not merely a matter of keeping down an enemy through punitive measures. Both France and Britain had incurred substantial debts in the war, and Germany could be a main source of finance in their repayment. The question that quickly emerged, however, was the amount that the Allies could realistically demand. As we have seen during the coupon election campaign, popular sentiment in Britain believed that 'Germany Must Pay' (as the slogan went) for the entire costs of the war. Parliament often reflected this view. But many responsible statesmen realized the impossibility of imposing a war debt of this magnitude upon Germany. They generally used the term 'reparation', which reflected a more limited intent than 'indemnity'. Reparation was usually defined as compensation for damage done to civilian property by military action. An indemnity, on the other hand, may be seen as a financial penalty imposed on the defeated powers for a war they had lost: thus its financial imposition could theoretically be much more extensive than a charge for property alone. It was not uncommon, however, for the terms to be used interchangeably, often leading to a substantial misunderstandings.[59] Lloyd George himself was guilty of this. As early as the Caxton Hall speech in January 1918, he had spoken of reparations. But during his Wolverhampton speech in November 1918, he stressed 'indemnity'. In the Fontainebleau Memorandum, he again spoke of 'reparation'. During discussions in the Council of Four he would on occasion switch the terms. On 24 March 1919, for example, he spoke of 'reparations'; but a few days later, he used the word 'indemnity'.[60]

Lloyd George's vacillation is not easily explained. Perhaps he was confused about their meaning, but this is unlikely.[61] It is more likely that he knew the differences between the two terms, and he used them variously depending upon circumstances. Given the popular anti-German mood in Britain at the end of the war, for example, it made sense to make some bow toward indemnities during his election speeches. Other reasons are not far to seek. Newton, for example, believes that Lloyd George could, by speaking in favour of harsh indemnities during the coupon election of 1918, discredit the emerging strength of the Labour Party and its inclination toward a negotiated peace. The influence of the Conservative right, especially among the Conservative dominated coalition, must also, Newton argues, have played a role.[62] Lloyd George may indeed have been attempting to sooth the right and retain their confidence, especially in Parliament; and he was certainly not above attacking Labour unfairly, as evident in his Camberwell speech in December 1918.

But there may have been a more fundamental concern on his part. Lloyd George was quite well aware that in any distribution of German payments – whether reparations or indemnities – Britain could be at a disadvantage. Britain could not claim extensive war damages upon civilians and property (that is, reparations) as could both France or Belgium: unlike those two countries, no part of Britain had been either occupied or destroyed by the Germans. Lloyd George needed some justification, therefore, to claim substantial payments to Britain for its wartime losses. But he also understood that if Britain (or the Allies) claimed too much, it would damage Germany's ability to achieve an economic recovery, thus jeopardizing its capacity to honour any payment schedule imposed by the Allies. If Germany were forced to pay beyond her limit, moreover, her value as a postwar trading partner with Britain would be imperilled. Thus his hedging before the crowds during the election campaign of 1918: he agreed that Germany must pay, but only up to its capacity to pay.

In late November 1918 Lloyd George had appointed a committee, chaired by the Australian Prime Minister Billy Hughes, to examine the specific prospects of Germany's ability to pay. But the committee, made up of Conservatives and economic protectionists, ignored its charge. Instead, it widened its scope to include Germany and its allies. It also failed to address adequately the Central Powers' ability to pay. Instead, it focused on 'the measure of the Indemnity which the enemy Powers *should in justice* pay'.[63] The report, issued on 10 December 1918, recommended an enormous indemnity of £24 billion to be paid in annual instalments of £1.2 billion. This was far above the more modest Treasury estimates of between £900 million and £3 billion. Lloyd George himself was taken aback by these sums.[64] Since the Hughes Committee was a body appointed by him and sanctioned by the Cabinet, it had official status and could not be ignored. Nevertheless, he referred to it only obliquely during the election campaign in December 1918.[65]

The Hughes Committee did not, however, have any power to bind the delegates at the Paris Peace Conference to its instructions. Soon after the opening of the Conference, Lloyd George led the way to establish a more formal body for examining reparations. This new Commission on the Reparation of Damage was composed of delegates from five major Allied powers and seven smaller ones. The work of the CRD proved inconclusive, however. There was no agreement on the fixed sum that Germany had the capacity to pay.[66] Deadlocked, the question of reparations was referred to the Council of Four in late March 1919 for resolution. A new committee, designed to resolve the varying estimates, also failed to win approval. Deadlock forced the topic once again back into the lap of the Council. But discussions there became so convoluted and divisive that Lloyd George was led to an exasperated outburst: 'We can't really say what Germany's capacity to pay will be!'[67] Nevertheless, it was Lloyd George himself who led a way out of the impasse. He proposed a permanent postwar inter-Allied Reparations Committee with the power to establish Germany's capacity to pay: this must be accomplished by 1 May 1921. In addition, Germany must make a preliminary payment of £1 billion in gold by that same date. By postponing the issue, the Council could move forward to other issues.

By this time, Lloyd George had found his justification for claiming a substantial payment from Germany not only to Britain but also to the Dominion states such as Australia, Canada, South Africa and New Zealand – all of whom had given substantial blood and treasure to the war effort but whose territories had not suffered directly from the German war machine. Lloyd George's solution was to claim reparations based upon the future costs not only of pensions for returning service men, but also allowances to dependents of the disabled and deceased veterans.[68] In this interpretation, pensions and separation allowances could be counted as civilian damages. This claim for non-material war damage stretched to the limit the widely understood meaning of reparations. Nevertheless, with French support, Lloyd George prevailed over President Wilson's initial refusal to grant the request. The matter was settled during a Council of Four meeting on 1 April 1919. Thus was written into the final Treaty Article 231 (the 'war guilt' clause), which forced Germany to accept a broad responsibility 'for causing all the damage to which the Allied and Associated governments and their nationals have been subjected as a consequence of the war imposed upon them by the aggression of Germany and her allies'. With this admission of guilt, the way was now clear for the determination of a precise sum that could be assessed at some future time against Germany.[69]

Lloyd George had won a significant battle within the Council. It was none too soon. In Britain, complaints about the delays in making the treaty were beginning to stir. A rising tide of suspicion about his intentions on peacemaking was also apparent. The Fontainebleau Memorandum of late March 1919 was a particular target, as were the conciliatory boundary settlements on the German Polish border. Members of the Conservative Party and the right wing press (those 'irrepressible Germanophobes on the British Right' as Newton called them) continued their demands for a 'stupendous war indemnity', as did wealthy mercantilists and industrialists – the same economic warriors who had loudly voiced their demands at the time of the Armistice.[70] Hostile newspaper comment, especially in *The Times* and *Daily Mail*, were also active in reporting that the Prime Minister had become soft on reparations. An angry Lloyd George, who had always followed the press carefully, admitted to Riddell that the attacks in the press were 'most harmful'.[71] Especially dangerous to the Prime Minister were the murmurs of discontent among his coalition partners in Parliament. On 8 April, a telegram signed by some 370 MPs urged him to stand firm on making Germany pay for the war. There was no option for the Prime Minister but to return to London to face his critics.

On 14 April 1919, Lloyd George left Paris for London. He was, Frances Stevenson recorded, 'in excellent spirits', having made up his mind to attack his detractors '& declare war to the knife'.[72] Two days later, Lloyd George addressed the House of Commons.[73] He used the opportunity to set out his European policy for the immediate postwar period. There were two main themes. The first was to discourage any thought of overthrowing the revolutionary Bolshevik regime in Russia. He admitted that Russia was 'in a state of complete chaos, confusion and anarchy'. Russia was 'like a volcano which is still in fierce eruption'. That being so, Britain must exercise caution.[74] With regard to Germany and its fate at the Peace Conference – the main theme of his speech – Lloyd George reminded the House that he had 'never swerved one iota' from his previous pledges on a peace treaty. 'We want a peace which will be just, but not vindictive.' To those who criticized his role in Paris, he chided: 'I would rather have a good peace than a good Press.'

Rowland claims that Lloyd George entered the chamber 'with the light of battle blazing in his eyes', and left it 'wreathed in smiles'.[75] Exaggeration aside, there is evidence that Lloyd George not only had the sympathy and attention of the House, but that he had once again demonstrated his mastery of the moment. Miss Stevenson reveals that Lloyd George was 'very pleased with himself' after the speech.[76] More neutral observers confirmed Lloyd George's triumph. Austen Chamberlain, member of the War Cabinet (and soon to be Chancellor of the Exchequer), whose relations with the Prime Minister have been described as 'at best equivocal', expressed the most fulsome praise.[77] Lloyd George, he thought, was 'grave, restrained & moderate in expression voice & gesture throughout ... He marshalled his speech admirably, showed good sense, reticence where reticence was required & courage. I never liked him better ...'.[78] Newton seems to sum up the general historical opinion: the speech was 'superbly crafted to shore up Lloyd George's leadership of the Coalition'.[79]

By couching his speech in broader terms than merely defending his actions at the peace conference, Lloyd George was able to strengthen his political position as head of the coalition. He articulated the broader context of British policy in the postwar era. His subtext was that he remained firm on the need for a just retribution and punishment for Germany: but he also was willing to settle European conflicts by showing the softer side of diplomacy. 'We have had quite enough of bloodshed', he declared before the House of Commons. In short, this speech may be seen as the first official pronouncement of Lloyd George's evolving post war strategy of appeasement as a valid diplomatic policy.[80]

After his triumphal appearance in the House of Commons, Lloyd George returned immediately to the peace conference. During the last two weeks of April, the Council wrapped up several important lingering issues, such as the disposition of the boundaries of newly created states; the settling of the Rhineland crisis; and the compromise over the Saar. On 29 April, the German delegation arrived at the Conference. A week later, they received the draft treaty in a solemn ceremony in the great hall of the Trianon Palace. With ill grace, Count Brockdorf-Rantzau, head of the German delegation, rejected the notion that Germany bore chief responsibility for the war. Within 48 hours, a more considered response (but no less recalcitrant) from the German delegation sparked the most serious crisis yet encountered by the peacemakers. Recoiling at the harshness of the treaty, especially the reparations clauses, the German delegates and their government balked. They objected to the war-guilt clause; to the confiscation of her merchant shipping, coal and other resources; to the extensive powers of the proposed Reparation Committee; and to the (as yet unnamed) fixed sum of the reparations. They once again denied that they alone were the cause of the war. They also objected to an imposed peace and called for a settlement negotiated between the two sides. For three weeks a series of diplomatic notes and counter notes passed between the Allies and their defeated enemies. The Germans offered proposals, among them the establishment of a German Commission to negotiate with the Reparation Commission and an offer of a total reparation payment of 100 milliard marks (conditional on their retaining merchant ships and most pre-Armistice territories).[81] These were unacceptable to the Allies. The Germans threatened to reject the treaty: the Allies in turn threatened to invade Germany.[82]

At this point, Lloyd George stepped into the breach, influenced no doubt by the news of the desperate economic conditions in Germany which were gradually becoming known to the peacemakers during the early months of 1919. Convincing reports of general privation and even starvation, attributable in part to the continuing Allied naval blockade, spread concern and alarm among the conferees. To help stabilize the infant German republic and stop the slide toward Bolshevism, some of Lloyd George's advisors – Hankey, Kerr and Smuts among them – had already begun advocating a toning down of demands, especially on reparations. Their reservations were confirmed upon a final reading of the draft treaty, which now drew together all its cumulative, harsh pronouncements. Influenced in part by their opinions and by the German response to the terms of the draft treaty, Lloyd George summoned members of the Cabinet and the Dominion Premiers to a conference in Paris in late May. This British Empire Delegation (as it was known) quickly came to a general agreement that some aspects of the proposed treaty should be altered. The most fervent revisionists were General Smuts of South Africa who had increasingly spoken in moderate tones during the peace process, and George Barnes, the Labour MP, Minister without Portfolio in the Cabinet. Even Churchill, as War Secretary, fearing that resumption of the conflict would mean an invasion of Germany with a depleted army, advocated leniency. Other members of the delegation agreed to some necessary revisions. Perhaps the most influential of all was the opinion of the CIGS, General Henry Wilson. As the Prime Minister's preeminent military advisor, Wilson carried considerable weight. He, too, favoured a moderation of peace terms. Confiding to his diary on 29 May, he noted the sense of the first meeting of the British Empire Delegation was 'that the Boches had made a good case, and in several particulars an unanswerable case'. The result, he thought, was unfortunate. 'The Frocks [Wilson's pet name for diplomats and politicians] are in a beastly mess.'[83] Nevertheless he was also persuaded that the treaty must be modified, even though this would put Lloyd George 'in a very difficult position'.[84]

On 2 June 1919, Lloyd George – reporting on the proceedings of the British Empire Delegation to the Council of Four – 'exploded his bombshell'.[85] In lengthy opening remarks, he emphasized the importance of British public opinion, which desired peace 'above all else' and was less inclined to 'attach excessive importance' to the specific terms of the peace treaty. Should the treaty provisions fail, public opinion would not support resuming the war 'without the most compelling reasons'.[86] In addition, so strongly did some members of the delegation feel about the draft treaty that they could not sign as it stood. The reparations question was especially troublesome.

Clemenceau immediately countered that he was also bound by public opinion; and France was in favour of the draft treaty. Germany's previous hegemonic position in Europe, with its threat to French sovereignty, had to be removed through the reduction of its territory and the restriction of its military. Germany's economic power must also be addressed.[87] President Wilson, who remained ominously silent during Lloyd George's announcement on 2 June, was more vocal at a meeting the following morning with the American Commissioners Plenipotentiary. There he declared against any changes in the proposed treaty: in addition, he also castigated the British for attempting to alter its terms. British efforts to recast the treaty made him, he declared, 'very sick' and 'very tired'. Furthermore, he condemned the British as 'all unanimous ... in their funk'.[88] Intra-Allied conflict over the draft treaty was resumed on 3 June when steady bickering between Wilson and Lloyd George continued. For several days longer, the argument over the Upper Silesian plebiscite and reparations raged. Lloyd George claimed that he was only following the precepts of Wilson himself in fostering the principle of self-determination. Wilson at first opposed on the grounds that such a plebiscite would naturally fall to the advantage of the Germans who had ruled that province for so long: in short, he wished to subjugate the substantial German minority to Polish authority. Lloyd George, however, won the argument.[89]

But reparations remained stubbornly perplexing. Lloyd George reminded the Council that no question had cost such time and work; and yet they were unable to determine a reasonable fixed sum. [90] He argued again for postponing the setting of such a sum. 'If we fixed it today,' he told the Council, 'the figure would be too high, and the Germans would sign less than ever'.[91] He therefore proposed an inquiry into an appropriate sum to be established by a team of both Allied and German experts. The following day, Lloyd George altered his proposal: immediately after the treaty was signed, the Germans would be invited to prepare their own reparations estimate to be presented to the Allies within four months.[92] The Allies would promise to respond within two months.

By mid-June, however, the Allies were becoming impatient with Germany's determined antagonism to other aspects of the draft treaty and had begun to think about contingencies in the event of their refusal to sign. On 13 June, Lloyd George took the lead in threatening to resume the blockade if Germany refused to sign the draft treaty as amended. When President Wilson protested, Lloyd George insisted that they 'shorten this dreadful period of waiting'.[93] If peace did not come promptly, he feared 'chaos'.[94] Indeed, there were already disquieting signs of altercations among newly created states and the remnants of old ones as Rumanians, Czechs, Hungarians, Estonians and Latvians, among others, engaged in armed struggles to establish themselves as viable ethnic unities within reshaped boundaries. Impelled by a sense of urgency, the Council of Four devised a stick and carrot approach to intensify the pressure on Germany. On 16 June, Marshall Foch came before the Council to review a military option should Germany refuse to sign: his mission was 'to compel the German government to sign the peace' by invading Germany.[95] But when Foch seemed at one point to raise reservations about the planned expedition, Lloyd George quickly chastised him for his irresolution by firmly declaring: 'We must be prepared to advance rapidly, resolutely, in such a way as not to give the impression that we are too weak to obtain decisive results.'[96] When the council again discussed Foch's reservations the following day, Lloyd George reinforced his determination to go forward, declaring that Foch 'must march on Berlin in order to compel Germany to sign the treaty'.[97] To encourage Germany to sign, the council also offered as a carrot the following concessions: a plebiscite for Upper Silesia; the promise of negotiating a fixed sum for reparations at a later date; a promise to admit Germany to the League of Nations at an early date; and the possibility of a shortened occupation in the Rhineland. Five days only were granted for the German response. Should Germany refuse to accept the newly revised treaty, war would resume. On 22 June, the German delegates indicated a willingness to sign, with the proviso that the war-guilt clauses be omitted. Within hours, the Council of Four refused, reminding the Germans that only 24 hours remained on the deadline.

On that same day, the Council received important news from several fronts. Philip Schiedemann, the first Chancellor of the new German Republic, resigned in protest against the Treaty's terms. Friedrich Ebert, the President of the Republic, then appointed Gustav Bauer as the new Chancellor to lead a coalition of Social Democratic and Centre parties pledged to sign the treaty. In addition, Count Brockdorff-Rantzau, head of the German delegation at Versailles, who had so enraged the Allied delegates when receiving the draft treaty in early May, was replaced. The German delegation then notified the Council that it was now willing to sign the treaty, but without the war guilt clause. The Council also learned, to its stupefaction and anger, that Vice Admiral Ludwig von Reuter, Commander of the German High Seas Fleet – then interned at Scapa Flow, off the Northeastern coast of Scotland – had ordered his crews to scuttle the entire fleet.[98] This event prompted another exasperated threat on the part of Lloyd George – 'to march right to the seat of the German government'. He also offered three divisions of British troops 'within a very short time' and the possibility of two more 'if necessary' for the German expedition.[99] The council was understandably not in a compromising mood and gave Germany only 24 hours to accept the treaty and its British revisions or face invasion. As President Wilson put it: 'we can no longer accept any reservation or evasion'.[100]

Scapa Flow was the centre of the Council's discussions over the next few days. To the general condemnation among the Allies, Lloyd George led the way with aspersions upon German honour: 'this is not a civilized nation that we have to deal with'.[101] But it was difficult to find any justification for punishing an enemy who destroyed its own fleet. President Wilson believed that Scapa Flow was a violation of the Armistice but was stumped as to the correct response and fearful that any untoward act of retaliation would renew hostilities. Clemenceau concurred with Wilson, but seemed more inclined to engage in punitive action. Lloyd George at first entertained the possibility of retaliation by occupying a major German city once the treaty had been signed. Later, perhaps influenced by his advisors, he rejected this option and suggested instead that the consequences of Scapa Flow should fall under the general topic of reparations, and thus be relegated to some future judgement by an appropriate authority.[102]

After many months of difficult and delicate negotiations among the world's leaders, the peace conference as it related to Germany came to a formal conclusion with the signing ceremony in the Galerie des Glaces at Versailles on 28 June 1919. The signing of the treaty brought no obvious relief to postwar tensions. The ceremony itself was disappointing, badly managed, and its solemnity marred by the crowds of pressman and sightseers.[103] More to the point, the consequences of the peace were as yet unknown. Numerous questions remained. Would Germany accept the Treaty fully? How would France, its nearest enemy, respond? Would the Allied victory and its enforced peace treaty contribute to a settling of European rivalries and conflicts? The United States, too, posed questions. Across the Atlantic there were already hints of a desire to retreat from the military and diplomatic battles of Europe. Would America remain in play as an ally in enforcing the treaty and keeping the peace in the intermediate future? Lloyd George had played a dominating role at Paris. As Prime Minister, he had made his mark successfully on a European-wide scale during years of war and a time of peace. How would he now utilize his prestige and power in a postwar world?

Before these questions can be addressed, a final analysis of Lloyd George's role at the peace conference is essential. Only then is it possible to understand both his strengths and the weaknesses as a political leader in postwar Britain. This is a complicated issue. Contemporaries and later historians have frequently disagreed. There is considerable evidence to show that Lloyd George pursued a mediative policy at Paris in the settlement of boundaries. His Fontainebleau Memorandum has been hailed as a moderate manifesto. He was also able to amend the more extreme territorial claims of the French and the Poles against the defeated powers. He took the lead in advocating independent homelands for a variety of national groups. On the reparations question, however, Lloyd George has received less favourable appraisal. This has led to a general condemnation of his overall performance at the peace conference. The classic comment was John Maynard Keynes's excoriating evaluation of the Prime Minister.[104] Keynes was the official Treasury representative to the peace conference until his resignation in June 1919 over what he perceived as harsh reparations demanded from Germany by the victorious allies. Although he supported reparations, citing especially the 'enormous' losses to British shipping, he also believed that the material damage in German occupied territories in France and Belgium during the war was the subject of 'excessive exaggeration' by the Allies. Keynes attributes this harsh and unfair exaction primarily to Lloyd George who was, he thought, too much under the influence 'from certain quarters' (which Keynes identifies as Billy Hughes and Northcliffe's press) during the coupon election of 1918. In the latter stages of that campaign, Keynes believed that Lloyd George's 'debauchery of thought and speech progressed hour by hour' as he ratcheted up his attacks upon Germany. Admitting that the Prime Minister never said that Germany should pay for the whole cost of the war, Keynes nevertheless believed that the effect of his speeches led 'the ordinary voter' to think so. Once at the Peace Conference, Lloyd George further exercised 'patriotic greed' in demands for a high indemnity.[105]

Subsequent historians have followed along in Keynes's wake. Trachtenberg, for example, states categorically that 'Lloyd George at no point opted for a moderate stand on reparation'.[106] Indeed, Trachtenberg believes that Britain under Lloyd George's leadership 'proved the stumbling block to a relatively moderate settlement'. This can be attributed in large measure to the Prime Minister's personal eagerness for a punitive peace – the reason for which, Trachtenberg thinks, was directly related to the moral conviction he had as a member of the moderate political left which emphasized 'justice and not reconciliation'.[107] With slightly different reasoning, Sharp tends to agree: 'it would be unwise to underestimate the Calvinism in the prime minister's soul' as he sought not vengeance but justice in upholding oppressive reparations.[108] One of the harshest critics has been Antony Lentin, who berates both the behaviour and the character of the Prime Minister in broadening his attack beyond reparations. Lentin condemns Lloyd George for acting 'out of pure expediency'; for 'living politically from hand to mouth'; and for 'his lack of principle'. Lloyd George, Lentin believes, thought of the treaty as nothing more than an 'improvisation' entered into perhaps unconsciously because he was 'drawn to power like a moth to a candle', worshipping success 'for its own sake'.[109]

Lloyd George does have his defenders, however. The sympathetic Morgan maintains that Lloyd George 'was the most persistent advocate of moderation throughout the entire conference'.[110] Dockrill and Goold find that Lloyd George's views on reparations tended to shift towards moderation as the conference went forward.[111] Pugh does not believe that Lloyd George was extreme in his views on reparations. He maintains that Lloyd George had two reasonable aims: to attain 'a respectably large total sum for German liability'; and to ensure that Britain won its share of that sum.[112] Packer has a more mixed view. Although he thinks that Lloyd George's position throughout the conference 'was contradictory and sometimes duplicitous', Packer also declares that Lloyd George, 'the great conciliator', had an outstanding achievement in ensuring 'that there was a peace settlement at all'. Indeed, the Versailles treaty 'was the apex of Lloyd George's career'.[113]

Most surprisingly, and in a telling reversal, Antony Lentin seems to have changed his mind entirely about Lloyd George. In his newer work, he finds much to praise in Lloyd George: his ebullience; his 'breezy indifference to convention' – even his 'cheerful adultery' with Frances Stevenson.[114] Lentin goes on to write that at the conference Lloyd George's personal qualities aided in his success: his 'electric rapidity of apprehension, a ready and inexhaustible well of inventiveness, an air of assurance, a warm enthusiasm, a hypnotic flow of language' were all contributory. Additional laudable qualities were his 'combination of charm, psychological insight,

resource, forcefulness, daring, pugnacity'. Formerly critical of Lloyd George's
changeable tactics, Lentin now finds that 'weathercock volatility was not necessarily
proof only of unreliability', but rather it meant 'a commendable readiness to
examine complex problems from different angles and in the round'. In short, Lloyd
George 'was quite prepared to think again, once apprised of the full facts'. Overall,
Lloyd George's 'instincts were for genuine peace'. No hypersensitivity or false pride
inhibited Lloyd George from rectifying obvious errors, unlike Woodrow Wilson.
'His ultimate purpose, behind many of his tergiversations, was serious and wise.' 'If
Versailles remained a bad settlement, Lloyd George recognized at least some of its
faults and saw to it that they were mitigated.' Lloyd George was above all moderate:
'No one at Paris spoke more tellingly against over-harsh, humiliating terms that would
drive German to extremes.' When the German representatives to the conference
presented counter-proposals to the Treaty, Lloyd George was 'instantly responsive'.
As to the specific issue of reparations, they were 'a valid objective, not a mere vulgar
response to popular clamour'. Yet Lloyd George, as a twentieth-century politician –
'unlike some grandee in the era of pocket boroughs' – had to pay attention to 'the
clamour of a new Parliament'. Although Lloyd George may have erred in delaying
the regulations for the German payment of reparations and in insisting on Article
231 of the treaty, he was not acting out of vengeance, but rather he was 'preoccupied'
with 'public sensibilities at home'. In so doing, he 'consolidated his mastery over
the House of Commons', thus securing his power base. Lentin concludes that to
the last, Lloyd George's thoughts 'were of peacemaking: of preserving, promoting
and presiding over the destinies of Great Britain and securing her place among the
nations'.

There is in fact a reasonable case that can be made for Lloyd George's
resolute pursuit of an equable peace and a fair share of reparations for Britain,
while simultaneously retaining his own precarious position as head of a coalition
government, many of whose members stoutly opposed his policy. It must first be
recalled that the peacemakers were involved in the most complicated issues of the
day; or arguably, of any day. As Hankey (who was often there) has observed, the
evaluation of damages in various countries; the financial capacity to pay on the part
of the defeated enemy, especially Germany; the kinds of control and guarantees that
the Allies wished; and the jockeying for financial advantage among the victorious
powers – all these issues simply 'baffled' the council.[115] The sequential commissioning
of various committees and their inability to come to a resolution was proof of this.
As we have also seen, circumstances of great moment in Europe and around the
world could change dramatically almost from hour to hour, often forcing upon the
council quick decisions, sometimes without the luxury of adequate information.

It is important to emphasize that Lloyd George, like his Allied compatriots, had
to bear in mind their respective publics and to take into account the impact upon
domestic opinion of all their decisions. Within the confines of the secret negotiations
of the Council of Four, Lloyd George not infrequently admitted this dilemma.
At the important meeting of the Council of Four on 29 March which discussed
reparations, he spoke of the necessity 'from the point of view of British domestic

politics', of 'not abandoning our claim to the totality of war costs while admitting the obligation imposed upon us by the practical necessity to limit ourselves to a more modest demand'.[116] In other words, it was important to uphold explicitly the *right* of substantial reparations, but not necessarily to exercise that right. He reiterated his position a week later when he clarified his middle ground on reparations. 'I have fought against those who go on repeating that Germany can pay all that the war cost', but he also made it clear that Germany should pay 'the extreme limit of the possible'.[117]

At every step of the way, Lloyd George managed – as he had all his political life – to keep every option open, and to hear every side of the argument before him. Margaret MacMillan, who is somewhat troubled by Lloyd George's seeming inconsistency and vacillation, nevertheless believes that in the confusion and dynamic atmosphere of the Peace Conference, he was steadily working out his own ideas to achieve a moderate yet realistic peace. He was also 'feeling his way politically', testing the boundaries of the possible both at the peace conference and in the domestic sphere at home. As a politician, therefore, he was 'obliged to weigh what was just against what was practical'.[118] Bearing this in mind, he could with consistency advocate moderation in the Fontainebleau Memorandum as a general policy statement without in any way diminishing the justified demand of heavy reparations.

Perhaps it was this tendency of Lloyd George's – to keep options open and his willingness to change his views based upon shifts of circumstance – that also accounts for his apparent reliance upon hard-line advisers throughout the reparations discussions. His selection of the Hughes Committee is a case in point. From what we know of Lloyd George's opinion on reparations, he did not agree with Hughes's views. But by bringing Hughes into the decision making process, Lloyd George hoped to manage the Australian's inconvenient forthrightness. Skidelsky, for example, frankly states that the appointment of Hughes as chair of the War Cabinet committee on reparations was designed 'to muzzle him'.[119]

Lloyd George knew well enough that British public opinion was following closely only certain issues, such as reparations, as the Peace Conference continued its deliberations. This gave him freedom of action to operate more moderately on other issues. Boundary alignments in distant Eastern Europe, for example, would not seem to affect Britain directly. He could, therefore, act with more freedom and a fair impunity from domestic criticism to ensure that German citizens would not be victimized by the ambitious annexations of near neighbours. But on the matter of assigning to Germany blame for the war, on payments for war damages to Britain and on expanding the British Empire at Germany's expense, he had to bear in mind not only a demanding public, but also his Conservative allies who made up the bulk of his parliamentary support. All in all it would seem that Lloyd George can be more easily characterized as suitably flexible rather than a man without principle. With the ever-shifting political circumstances on the Continent and the threat of revolutionary movements very real, Lloyd George as well as other Allied leaders had little choice but to adapt. This is not to say that Lloyd George was unprincipled, or wishy-washy or prone to exhibiting an unattractive flaccidity at the peace conference. Indeed, one historian has chastised him as 'rude and overbearing' in dealing with some representatives at the conference: in fact, he sees Lloyd George ending the conference as 'the bully' of the Council of Four. On the other hand, he admits that Lloyd George 'was the most successful member of the Four'.[120] A reading of the official notes of the Council of Four meetings supports this view. Lloyd George seemed often to be the guiding hand of the council, urging them forward, keeping them focused on the topic at hand and incisively dissecting (and thus clarifying) a multitude of complaints, special pleading and unreasonable demands from government officials and individuals at the highest political level. To settle satisfactorily every argument and altercation would have been impossible. But Lloyd George rose to the challenge more often than not. His intention – as was true all his political life – was to strike a balance, to achieve compromise and to settle irreconcilable views. In Paris, as in all his conciliatory challenges, his aim was to move forward over a potential battleground to reach the best solution possible between opposing forces. As Keynes himself once shrewdly observed, not unkindly, Lloyd George's career demonstrated his 'incurable love of a deal'.[121] His capacity for deal making was clearly in evidence at the Paris Peace Conference. His conciliatory role was to be tested once again after his triumphant return to Britain.

14

RECONSTRUCTION AND RESISTANCE

The year 1919 did not only witness Lloyd George's leadership on a global scale in settling the peace after a victorious war. It was also a year noted for his initiatives in addressing the domestic needs of postwar Britain. The demobilization of tens of thousands of army, navy and air personnel and their reintegration into civilian life was the most immediate problem. New housing was another: a major building programme was critical not only for returning servicemen and their families. Wartime exigencies had delayed repair and renovation on existing houses for millions of others. No less important was forward thinking on conditions of work, job opportunities in a re-tooled peacetime economy and labour-management relations during a time of rapid change. Education, too, had to be addressed. New schools, expanded teaching staffs, and revised curricula for students in a postwar world were all essential.

For his part, the Prime Minister had been thinking ahead for some time about the needs of a postwar Britain. In doing so, he built upon the work of the Reconstruction committee created during the waning hours of the Asquith administration in December 1916.[1] Utilizing some of the former staff and committee reports of the first committee, Lloyd George created a new government department, the Ministry of Reconstruction, headed by Christopher Addison, a long-standing Lloyd George loyalist.[2] One of the most successful and farsighted (and among the earliest) of all the reconstruction projects was H.A.L. Fisher's Education Act of 1918. Lloyd George had plucked Fisher from academic life – he was a distinguished historian then serving as Vice-Chancellor of Sheffield University – to serve as President of the Board of Education in his coalition government of December 1916. Fisher proved to be an able Cabinet minister and an effective spokesman for the extension of education. He strongly believed that longer schooling years could improve the occupational prospects for all children. Moreover, industry and business would benefit from better-prepared entry level workers. Additionally important, he believed, was the inculcation of discipline among children and adolescents through steady schooling. Compulsory schooling to age 14 was an important component of the Act. To ensure school attendance, hours of employment for children under 12 were abolished and for those over 12, hours were restricted. Medical treatment and inspection were to be provided in all schools maintained by Local Education

Authorities (LEAs). Physical training, including the provisions for equipment, playing fields, school baths and swimming pools, was also provided for. Other clauses in the Act dealt with the supply, training and appointment of teachers. Some clauses addressed the compulsory purchase of land necessary for LEAs in building new schools. The contentious religious issue, so divisive in the past, was left largely untouched. Fisher was not only active in drafting the bill. During the parliamentary preliminaries, he toured industrial centres to spread the news about the proposed legislation. Although only an average speaker, his tours were highly successful in drumming up support.[3]

No less important as an agenda item for the new Ministry of Reconstruction was adequate housing for the working class. Lloyd George had declared during the election campaign of 1918 that Britain must provide a 'land fit for heroes'. The war had thrown into high relief the inadequate and shoddy working-class housing. As the war wound down, demobilization of servicemen exacerbated housing shortages. The number of new houses needed was imposingly high: 300,000 within a year after the war. Such an unprecedented building programme could only be achieved by state aid. Addison, who had at first encountered the depth of this problem when at the Ministry of Reconstruction, continued his efforts to solve the housing issue when he became the President of the Local Government Board in January 1919. Strongly encouraged by Lloyd George, Addison quickly outlined plans for the government's Housing Bill. Approved by the Cabinet on 1 March 1919, the Housing and Town Planning Act became law in July. It required local authorities to provide houses where needed; and it empowered the Treasury to guarantee the costs of loans entered into by local authorities.

The creation of a new governmental agency, the first Ministry of Health and Housing, in June 1919 was a further indication that the Lloyd George government was moving directly to ease the social consequences of wartime dislocation and the economic needs of a population in distress after a long war. Additional reforms included increases in old age pensions and the extension of unemployment benefits. The history of social legislation in this postwar era, Morgan believes, was 'without parallel' since the days when Lloyd George pushed forward his pre-war social reforms.[4] Moreover, Morgan argues that Lloyd George's role was central to the postwar reforms: the Prime Minister's 'activity and energy were remarkable'. He seemed everywhere, acting as 'a kind of minister of all departments'.[5] Not to be forgotten of course was the electoral reform act of 1918, probably the greatest of all the reconstruction initiatives, enfranchising as it did many of those who also benefited under the social advances brought forward by the government.

One of Addison's earliest achievements was to implement administrative machinery, approved by the Cabinet in October 1917, by which joint industrial councils (more commonly termed Whitley Councils after the deputy speaker of the House of Commons, J.H. Whitley) were authorized at every level – whether on individual shop floors or in industry-wide settings. These councils, made up of both employers and union leaders, would decide on important matters on each side of the industrial equation, such as wages and workplace control. The basic premise was to encourage a system of free play among the parties involved in collective bargaining, with state intervention occurring only in times of imbalance between the two sides. The hope was that such an arrangement would provide the opportunity to head off any potential conflict that could cause a crisis in industrial relations in the country at large.[6]

In spite of the movement forward of reconstruction, there was a palpable undercurrent of unrest and dissent against the Lloyd George government – an 'uprising of Labour' as it has been called.[7] Reasons are clear enough. Primarily, the war had fostered a new self-confidence among working Britons, engendered especially by the growth of trade unions. At the beginning of 1911, trade union members numbered 2.6 million, second only to Germany. By the end of the war, they numbered 8.25 million. For the first time, more than half the male population was union organized. Women unionists, too, had gained in numbers. Unionism on this scale brought not only a broader consciousness of the importance of labour in the life of the nation: it also strengthened common demands for higher wages, better working conditions and ultimately for more political power. Wartime control of some sectors of the economy, especially coal mining and the railways, had spurred the case for nationalization.[8] The emergence of union confidence and its growing sense of power can be gauged by the fact that 1918 witnessed the highest number of stoppages of any previous year with the exception of 1913. The number of working days lost in 1919 was second only to those lost in 1912. Union members were clearly determined to engage in direct action to secure their economic and social goals.[9]

The government, while willing to conciliate the unions, was not always agreeable to their demands. One of the most dramatic examples of both the spirit of an aroused trade unionism and the government's determination to temper it occurred as the war was winding down. During the summer of 1918, the London Metropolitan Police engaged in an unexpected strike over long hours and low pay (policemen in fact earned considerably less than London dockmen). Caught by surprise, Lloyd George called an emergency War Cabinet meeting and then met police representatives, including an officer of the National Union of Police and Prison Officers (NUPPO). Bringing news of the government's sympathy with their pay demands, Lloyd George also 'by studied ambiguity' seemed to concur with NUPPO's demands that it be recognized as a legitimate union.[10] But this proved to be merely a tactical manoeuvre. The Prime Minister's later actions clearly indicated that he had been stalling for time: he was opposed to a unionized police. He appointed Sir Nevil Macready (then Adjutant-General of the Army) to head the police with a specific charge to undermine union activity. Lloyd George's motives became more explicit in a telephone message to Bonar Law in January 1919, when he emphasized the importance of establishing 'the authority of social order'. Unless 'the Guardians of Order' were brought to heel, he said, 'the whole fabric of law may disappear'.[11]

Members of NUPPO, however, continued to organize for the right of recognition. After the Cabinet's refusal to do so in March 1919, NUPPO organized a demonstration of some 9,000 police in Trafalgar Square. A few weeks later, Macready effectively banned police strikes. This was sweetened with a government announcement of a substantial pay increase for policemen. But this did not satisfy police activists. The prospects of a showdown grew. Lloyd George remained adamantly opposed to a police union. 'It seems to me,' he informed Edward Shortt, the Home Secretary, 'to be contrary to the fundamental principles of discipline for a semi-military body like the police to join a trades union'.[12] In July, the government introduced the Police Bill in the House of Commons, which in effect outlawed police unions. NUPPO nevertheless went forward, calling a national strike on 31 July. The response was mixed. In London and Birmingham, only a few came out. On Merseyside, more than half were involved: 51 per cent in Liverpool to 82 per cent of a much smaller force in Bootle. In these areas, rioting and looting took place. Troops and special constables were called in, as were two cruisers and a battleship, which sailed up the Mersey for demonstration purposes. The strike quickly collapsed.

In other instances, the government was more inclined to act favourably towards labour demands, put forward as they were by the traditional unions of civilian workers. Not long after the Armistice had been signed and into the early weeks of 1919 extensive strike threats came from the great industries – mining, textiles, engineering and shipbuilding, as well as transport, especially the London underground and the railways.[13] Here, too, low pay and long hours were at the heart of union demands. Lloyd George often took the lead in settling these disputes. When cotton workers demanding higher wages went on strike in December 1918, Lloyd George invited both employers and workers to Downing Street where a settlement was reached. Railwaymen had the same issue, demanding an eight-hour day as early as August 1917. They delayed any industrial action, however, until the end of the war. When strike action seemed imminent in early December 1918, the War Cabinet under Lloyd George's leadership accepted the eight-hour principle. But on the London Underground, meals were excluded from the eight-hour day provisions, essentially forcing drivers to work longer hours if they wished to consume food. In early February 1919, London tube drivers went on strike. The strike was quickly settled by allowing meal times within the eight-hour working day. At about the same time, more serious disruptions of Glasgow and Belfast engineering workers began: their grievances also centred on hours of work. Striking in late January, they were soon joined by shipyard workers on the Clyde, as well as Scots coal miners and iron moulders. In this case, the government used more muscle: mounted police, followed by a show of military force to discourage rioting, put down a massive demonstration – one estimate was as high as 10,000 – in Glasgow.

Potentially the most serious threat to industrial peace came from the miners, whose working conditions were the most dangerous of perhaps any occupation. During the war, the shortage of mine labour and the demand for naval coal spurred a wages growth and an enhanced sense of entitlement. In postwar reconstruction, the Miners Federation of Great Britain – largest and wealthiest of all unions – became a strong advocate for higher wages, lower hours and (particularly important for miners) better conditions of work.[14] Most specifically, the MFGB demanded a 30 per cent increase in wages; a six-hour day; and public ownership of the mines.[15] The possibility of support from the Triple Alliance – a consortium of miners, transport workers and railwaymen's unions founded in 1914 – gave added strength to the miner's demands.[16] Faced with such a potent workers' combination, the government responded quickly by forming a Royal Commission of inquiry, half of whose members the MFGB either nominated or approved. Chaired by Mr Justice Sankey, the commission set about their task with admirable dispatch.

The developing struggle between management and labour had become so serious by February 1919 that Lloyd George was forced to return to London from the Paris Peace Conference to take personal charge of mediation. As a first step, he sponsored the National Industrial Conference of nearly 1,000 employers, unionists, civil servants and Cabinet ministers to consider ways of developing further practical proposals of mutual cooperation in industrial relations.[17] A representative number formed a Provisional Joint Committee which, after convening for several weeks, drew up a list of reforms relating to rates of pay, hours of work, unemployment and methods of negotiations – all those outstanding issues that lay at the heart of the on-going industrial unrest. Although there were some minor advances towards smoother industrial relations as a consequence, there was no new legislation tackling the principal issues of shorter work weeks and a national minimum wage. The dashed expectations of the National Industrial Conference and the Provisional Joint Committee have often been laid at the Prime Minister's door. Wrigley, for example, believes that Lloyd George's reasons even for calling the conference have 'never been satisfactorily explained'.[18] Perhaps Lloyd George simply lost interest in the project. Or he may have been facing difficulties with his Conservative coalitionists who were averse to any state intervention in solving industrial disputes. More damning was the suspicion that Lloyd George had put forward the conference merely to keep the unions talking, rather than agitating. Lowe discounts this, doubting that neither the Prime Minister nor the government was 'guilty of premeditated duplicity', but he does fault them for failing to take a 'bold political stand' which might have won over enough support to generate a productive social policy that could have had lasting effects on British industrial relations.[19] The most likely reason, however, was that Lloyd George was distracted by his unremitting work at the peace conference. In any case, by the autumn of 1919, the National Industrial Conference was essentially moribund, although it lingered on until 1921.

Lloyd George's waning interest in the work of the National Industrial Council does reveal, at the very least, a certain weakening of his conciliatory stance towards labour demands as the winter crisis of 1919 continued into the spring months. While on leave from the peace conference, he addressed the House of Commons on the labour unrest in combative terms: 'we are determined', he declared, 'to fight Prussianism in the industrial world as we fought it on the continent of Europe with the whole might of the nation'.[20] Should there be a miners' strike, for example, or a shutdown of the entire transport system, the government would need to intervene strongly against them. Even Morgan admits that Lloyd George had become 'increasingly strident' in his comments.[21] In the Cabinet and the halls of government, alarmist talk 'filled the air'.[22] To some historians, Lloyd George's actions and speeches were, as Desmarais has it, signs of 'a new inhumanity' and an insensitivity to the problems of labour. Indeed, Desmarais believes that in the immediate postwar era Lloyd George had one primary goal – 'to be done with unrest at home and abroad': furthermore, 'he was not overly concerned with the means to obtain that end'.[23] In substantiating this view of Lloyd George as a politician 'who would yield matters of principle for political gain', Desmarais cites W.S. Adams in support.[24] But in fact, Adams had a much more suggestive and nuanced view of Lloyd George's attitude towards labour and labour disputes. To make arrangements between the two sides, Adams pointed out that Lloyd George had to convince employers of the need for concession while simultaneously persuading (or sometimes coercing) employees that these concessions approached their demands. This flexible dual tactic of concession and coercion, applied discriminately 'according to the needs of the situation' by Lloyd George, was often successful.[25]

Other historians have echoed Adams's view of Lloyd George's management of the industrial disputes of 1919. Pugh notes Lloyd George's tendency to talk tough, while giving ground to labour demands.[26] Morgan praises the overall government effort as 'more flexible and sophisticated' than may at first appear.[27] Wrigley agrees that Lloyd George's firm line with 'overmighty trade unionists' was balanced by promises to redress all legitimate grievances – as he had done in his speech of 11 February to the House of Commons.[28] Indeed, a careful reading of Lloyd George's February speech reveals not merely a warning, but also a promise to labour. There were, he declared, legitimate causes of concern expressed in the continuing outbreaks of labour unrest – genuine fears of unemployment and poor housing. The government would carefully examine every grievance: 'it was', he further declared, 'the business of the Government to remove them'.[29] There is little doubt, then, that Lloyd George pledged himself and his government to be proactive in redressing the genuine complaints of labour. But there was also little doubt that the government could show a strong side. Essential services had to be protected from severe disruption: it was the duty of the State to do so.

Perhaps the best example of Lloyd George's tactical approach during the labour unrest can be found in the outcome of the coal industry inquiry. Within a few weeks of its appointment, the Sankey Commission issued an interim report in March. The Commission had met in public and its proceedings, open to all, soon developed into a bruising adversarial contest between mine owners and the MFGB.[30] Contrary to what one might expect, the union members by far had the best of it. Thoroughly prepared and more powerfully argued, unionist spokesmen clearly demonstrated not only a formidable knowledge of the industry, they also directed their rhetoric to political ends by marshalling an effective public opinion campaign against the mine owners. In addition, they elevated their demands to an economic, and ultimately, to a moral plane, by demonstrating the appalling housing conditions of mining communities and the dangerous conditions of mining operations. Lloyd George observed privately that the Commission's hearings were 'arousing the social conscience in a way that no inquiry of modern times had succeeded in doing'.[31] That the Commission's interim report issued on 20 March 1919 recommended a substantial increase in wages, a decrease in weekly hours worked, and a limitation on mine owners' profits was a foregone conclusion.

The second Commission report, on the possibility of nationalization of the mines, had a different outcome, however.[32] This was due in part to a recovery of the mine owners, who were much more aggressive in pursuing their interests than in the early sessions of the commission. As the weeks passed into the summer, they were aided by a waning of public interest in the mines question.[33] There was also a growing hostility at large to the notion of a sweeping nationalization of the mines. The Sankey Commission itself gave only a lukewarm recommendation for nationalization in its final report of June 1919. Direct pressure upon Lloyd George was crucially determinant. He was presented with a petition signed by some 300 MPs – the majority of whom were Conservative supporters of the coalition government – in opposition to public ownership of the mines. This sense of public opinion was corroborated by Lloyd George's private discussions with coalition Liberals. The Cabinet, too, perhaps exasperated by a regional strike in South Yorkshire in July, leaned against offering any further concessions to the miners.[34] Indeed the Cabinet, apprehensive that the Yorkshire strike could spread beyond its borders, began to make preparations for that eventuality. Lloyd George ordered, with Cabinet approval, the return of all coal carrying British ships at sea to home ports. Anticipating other shortages in the event of a general miners' strike, the Cabinet enforced restrictions on such important supplies and services as electric lighting, gas and water. Churchill, acting as Secretary for War, recalled two divisions from the army of the Rhine and put two others on standby.

With preparations in hand, Lloyd George announced to the House of Commons on 18 August 1919 that the government had decided against proposals to nationalize the coal mines. Nevertheless, he also attempted to mollify the miners by declaring the government's support of public ownership of mining royalties to create a fund for ameliorating the social and working conditions of mine workers.[35] He also accepted the idea of worker representation, if not in the direct management of individual mining pits, at least on area boards. As Supple notes, in other times or circumstances these proposals would likely have been considered radical.[36] But the heightened expectations among miners, and especially among union leaders, caused a deep sense of disappointment in the Prime Minister's actions – a disappointment that continued to fester among them in the near term.

Coal miners were not the only source of continuing labour discontent. The National Union of Railwaymen, dissatisfied with inequitable pay scales within its ranks, pressed the government throughout 1919 for a redress of their grievances. More than 40 meetings between government officials and the NUR officers failed to reach a settlement. On 26 September 1919, the NUR struck. Worker response to the strike call was virtually complete. Reports from around the country to strike headquarters indicated an unprecedented stoppage of all rail traffic. From Derby came reports that the normal daily run of 130 trains was down to three on the first day of the strike. Elsewhere, steamboat service was interrupted, as were the mails. Beer brewing ceased in Edinburgh and Burton on Trent because of a shortage of barrels. Collieries closed down in Leeds. Miners were idled in South Wales.[37] Clearly, the effect was not merely an inconvenience or delays for commuters and casual travellers. These disruptions bore out to some degree Beatrice Webb's worried comments in her diary that there never was 'a strike of anything like this in magnitude ... which has burst on the world so suddenly'. Her anxieties at the outcome were likely enough shared by many: 'We are all at sea as to what will happen in the next few days.'[38]

Curiously enough, however, the nine days' strike ended with little attendant violence. Perhaps this was a reflection of the government's confidence. They had prepared several months in advance. Hankey, who had been the quintessential organizer of agendas and planning during the Paris Peace Conference, joined an unofficial anti-strike committee of the Cabinet, led by Eric Geddes, who had just become Minister of Transport, a new Cabinet office. In his diary entry of 29 September 1919, Hankey reported the extensive operations in place to alleviate the impact of the strike: these included the use of motor lorries, coastal shipping and canals for deliveries and haulage; aircraft for mail and urgent journeys; and an emergency communications system made up of aircraft, wireless and even pigeons. In addition, non-strikers and volunteers were utilized to keep rail traffic rolling. Government propaganda was published through the uninterrupted distribution of newspapers. 'We are', he noted in his diary, 'meeting the strike with a very powerful organization'.[39]

Lloyd George's role throughout the strike is somewhat difficult to decipher. At first, he seemed abrasively antagonistic, publicly describing the strike as 'an anarchist conspiracy'. He further declared that railwaymen were 'being used by extremists for sinister purposes'.[40] His statement reflected a view widely held by prominent Conservatives. Auckland Geddes, President of the Board of Trade (and brother of Eric), believed that if the strike succeeded, it would mean 'Soviet government in this country'.[41] Robert Sanders, who had spent some time in his Conservative constituency during the strike, found that '[t]he feeling was certainly strong against the strikers there'.[42] Yet within a few days, the Prime Minister was setting a more moderate tone, which led to a mood of near friendliness between the opposing sides. Hankey reported continuous contact between the Prime Minister and J.H. Thomas, the General Secretary of the NUR. Unofficial private conversations also brought the sides together. There was even some hilarity at meetings of ministers and railwaymen at Downing Street. At one point, the Transport Workers' Conciliation Committee burst into renditions of 'Cockles and Mussels' and (perhaps more appropriately) 'The Red Flag'.[43] Once an amicable tone between the contending parties had been established, Lloyd George stepped forward to take direct charge of the negotiations. He quickly accepted the NUR's wage demands and promised additional benefits in the future, including the establishment of National Wages Boards where both men and management could hold joint consultations.[44]

It may very well be, as Wrigley has suggested, that Lloyd George changed his tune, singing softer notes when it appeared that public opinion was moving in favour of the railwaymen's demands, which had been moderately pitched and widely publicized in newspapers and in cinema advertisements.[45] Bagwell seems to agree: the government, he believes, 'capitulated' under pressure.[46] But he exonerates Lloyd George from any charge of dithering, recalling that he had been sympathetic to railwaymen even when he had been at the Board of Trade many years earlier.[47] There is something to this. Lloyd George had long looked to the development of an active transport policy, especially railways, as a way of regenerating the rural economy by creating garden cities where labour could live and commute by cheap transportation to jobs inside the metropolis. By such means economic growth and social betterment could both be promoted.[48] Perhaps this accounts for Lloyd George's somewhat ambivalent feelings about the strike – his understanding and appreciation of railwaymen were at odds with his responsibilities as Prime Minister to maintain the public peace. In any case, the railwaymen had not only won their case for wage increases but they had also won public approbation for their moderate demands.

However sympathetic Lloyd George may have been to various sections of the Labour movement, there is strong evidence that he never fully sympathized with the aims of their organized associations, especially the unions. He was wary of union strength and suspicious, too, of their claims to speak for their members. In a series of conversations with Riddell during the NUR strike, Lloyd George's attitude emerged in sharp relief. Riddell, who was impressed by the NUR's adroit use of propaganda, believed that Lloyd George's initial description of the strike 'as a Bolshevist movement' was 'a mistake'. Riddell attributed the remark to the fact that Lloyd George 'does not understand or sympathise with working men'. Lloyd George's point of view was 'that of the solicitor or shopkeeper'. For his part, once the strike had ended, Lloyd George claimed that the effect of it was to break up the Triple Alliance because the NUR had accepted the government's terms to the exclusion of the miners and transport workers. As Lloyd George put it to Riddell: 'we have detached the railway men. I think the result of the strike will have a most salutary influence'.[49]

That the Prime Minister was consciously attempting to divide the unions is entirely plausible in explaining his behaviour towards the Labour movement.[50] His frequent references to the Bolshevik threat – and by its implication tainting the British Labour movement – can of course, be seen as merely an election ploy, or as a palliative sop to his Conservative coalition partners. This was the view of the sceptical Beatrice Webb, who had strong suspicions about Lloyd George's motives. She thought that the strike had been 'subconsciously desired' by Lloyd George as 'a good stunt' for the next election, which could be called 'on the issue of Bolshevism' as well as on 'the extremists of the manual working class'.[51] But it is also possible that Lloyd George was genuinely fearful of the influence of militant unions. At the end of his talks with Riddell, he revealed his belief that some unions had ulterior motives. The miners' claim for nationalization, for example, cloaked a hidden purpose. Their real object, he believed, was 'the appropriation of the mines for their own benefit': they wanted '"guildism" or syndicalism'.[52]

Given the general labour unrest and the unsettled postwar European conditions, the government believed it prudent to take precautions. Under Lloyd George's leadership, the government devised a two-pronged tactical approach: first, to isolate the militant workers and their leaders; and then to conciliate the majority of moderate union members by operating through selected trade unionist leaders. Among the targeted moderate Labour leaders were Frank Hodges, Robert Smillie and J.H. Thomas.[53] As Hinton has observed, the government was largely successful and 'showed considerable skill' in avoiding confrontations and in finding allies among these trade union leaders, who in turn mediated among their respective union members.[54] The government was nevertheless determined to be vigilant for any future unionist activity which they considered a threat to the domestic peace. The NUR strike of September 1919 was both a warning and an impetus to establish a permanent body to counter and to control strikes. An emergency Strike Committee was formed, endowed with extensive executive powers. Chaired by Eric Geddes, its members included among others Churchill; Walter Long; George Roberts, the Food Controller; and Sir John Maclay, Minister of Shipping. Within a short time, this committee changed its name (to the more innocuous sounding Supply and Transport Committee) and broadened its authority by appointing a subcommittee of civil servants, the Supply and Transport Organization (STO). These two committees became the leading edge of a governmental wide systematic effort to preserve public order during any future strikes. The government also established an extensive information file not only on union leaders and labour opinion, but also on the strength (or weakness) of militant groups. To that end, the government utilized an expanded intelligence service, including the Intelligence Department of the Ministry of Labour and the home reports of Military Intelligence. There is also some evidence of a secret propaganda agency designed to incite public hostility against trade unions and the political left wing, should circumstances warrant.[55]

These examples of apparent secretive underhanded acts on the part of the Prime Minister must have been a disappointment to those who remember Lloyd George as a champion of labour. Evidence suggests, however, that Lloyd George was under considerable pressure. Some decision makers, in a state of near panic, were determined in the aftermath of the railway strike of September 1919 to show a firm hand. Among the most distraught was General Henry Wilson (who was still CIGS), who favoured a military option against strike action. Additional strikes, he predicted, would 'be a direct threat and attack on the life of the nation'.[56] He believed further that the government had committed a 'criminal folly' in not dealing more forcefully with previous strikes and strikers.[57] Giving action to his fears, Wilson initiated with his General Staff plans to counter mutiny and revolution in Britain, including a proposal to concentrate 18 battalions to protect London from strikes and social disorder.[58]

Several Cabinet members shared Wilson's alarm. A meeting of the Cabinet held on 2 February 1920 fully revealed their perturbed state of mind.[59] Thomas Jones recounts Wilson's opening remarks to the Cabinet as painting 'a very lurid picture of the country's defenceless condition'. Following on, the Home Secretary, Edward Shortt, outlined proposals that would raise a special military force of 10,000 soldiers to be available for any national emergency. First Lord of the Admiralty Walter Long

1 Early portrait of an ambitious politician, 1898 (© National Portrait Gallery, London)

2   At his ease as a young parliamentarian in 1905 (photo by Ernest H. Mills/Getty Images)

3   The young family in November 1910

OCT. 28. 1912.

THE NEW DAVID.

[The Florence Nightingale—or was it Sarah Gamp?—of Liberalism.]

THE NEW DAVID, whose methods have this advantage over those of the original David that they entail no suffering on Goliaths.

4   A dashing Lloyd George as portrayed by Will Dyson in the *Daily Herald*, October 1912

DELIVERING THE GOODS.

5   Riding to the rescue as Chancellor of the Exchequer, but soon to be Minister of Munitions of War

6   The Council of Four at the Paris Peace Conference, January 1919

7   In October 1919, a triumphant Prime Minister addresses a crowd from Mansion
     House in the City of London (photo by Hulton Archive/Getty Images)

8   On the high wire in 1926

9   Lloyd George advocates his land scheme at Kingsway Hall in November 1926
(photo by Fox Photos/Getty Images)

10   Lloyd George uses to advantage new technology to keep his name before the public
in 1931 (photo by Jimmy Sime/Central Press/Getty Images)

11   Lloyd George and Churchill in Morocco, 1936 (National Library of Wales)

THE CABINET BUILDER

"Quite effective in its way! I hope the one I've just made will do as well."

12   A lesson for an old friend and colleague

13   Lloyd George celebrates his 80th birthday with Frances Stevenson and his daughter Lady Olwen Carey-Evans looking on (photo by Bert Hardy/Picture Post/Hulton Archive/Getty Images)

14 Lloyd George and admirers in late 1944 amid the Kale at Churt, his farm in Surrey (photo by Time Life Pictures/Pix Inc./Getty Images)

lamented the state of 'peaceable manpower' in the country, which was 'without arms'. For himself, he said: 'I have not a pistol less than 200 years old.' Robert Horne, Minister of Labour, revealed that considerable quantities of munitions 'including hand grenades' had entered Glasgow from Ireland. Auckland Geddes, President of the Board of Trade, suggested that any shortage of manpower could be supplied by the universities, who, along with clerks and stockbrokers, would rally to the government's side should a serious outbreak occur. Bonar Law supported this idea, referring to stockbrokers 'as a loyal and fighting class'.[60] Churchill warned of 'a revolutionary attempt to seize the reins of Government'. Jones notes that at one point during the meeting, Lloyd George and General Wilson engaged in 'some altercation' over the precise figures of available troops needed to suppress any outbreak of violence. Jones's overall evaluation of the meeting was that Lloyd George 'played the role' of taking revolution seriously; but in reality, the Prime Minister 'did a lot of unsuspected leg-pulling' because he discounted the prospects of an imminent revolution. Rather, Lloyd George suspected that the War Office and General Wilson were crying wolf in order to increase the size and influence of the army. To be sure, the lack of any sense of urgency in the Prime Minister riled Wilson. He continued to condemn Lloyd George (in the pages of his diary) for not standing out, 'right out, against the Unions' – the consequences of which were that 'the forces of disorder' were 'steadily strengthened'.[61]

It was Lloyd George's task as Prime Minister somehow to tamp down the alarmists while simultaneously devising sensible contingency plans in the event of a serious strike that could in fact threaten public order. The Prime Minister could not openly flout the constitution and bring to bear such illegal methods as using military forces to break up strikes. Nor could he simply ignore the threat of subversive industrial action. Under Lloyd George's leadership, the ministry acted without panic, introducing restrained legislation to deal with severe strikes. To that end, the ministry sponsored the Firearms Bill of August 1920, which for the first time created a national system of gun licensing and control. Two months later, the Emergency Powers Act solved the knotty problem of providing a sufficient force to supply essential services by authorizing servicemen to be employed on non-military duties. And finally, upon the advice of Geddes, Lloyd George appointed – without consulting the Cabinet – 11 Commissioners in England and Wales who would superintend strike management on a regional basis.[62]

Demands by labour on the domestic front were not the only source of antagonism between it and the government. Labour leaders had begun to think well beyond their traditional roles as the voice of the British worker. In the final year of the war, Labour leaders as well as the rank and file followed the Russian Revolution closely. The Bolshevik-led second stage of that revolution in November 1917, with its promise of a better life for workers and peasants, strongly attracted British Labour. But the increasingly violent turn of the Revolution within Russia and its explicitly declared intent to undermine capitalism won it no friends among Western governments. When Russia left the war at the Peace of Brest-Litovsk in March 1918, a sense of betrayal was especially widespread in Britain and France. The Allies therefore decided on a preventive strategy. In the latter half of 1918, detachments of Allied troops were sent as reinforcements to the northwestern Russian port cities of Murmansk and Archangel. The Allies also involved Japanese military forces, who were to advance from Vladivostok across eastern Russia towards their Western military objective. A Czechoslovak Corps, then in Siberia, and a lesser American force which would complement Japanese forces, were also driving westward.[63] In addition, substantial White Russian armies began to organize throughout Russia against the Red Bolsheviks.

The declaration of the Armistice between the Allies and Germany on 11 November 1918 and the defeat of the Central Powers left the Allied/Russian confrontation unresolved in various theatres of operation. Indeed, political, diplomatic and military problems were heightened. Scarcely a week after the Armistice, British forces operating from Mesopotamia occupied Baku, Azerbaijan, and the oil fields nearby. The railway from Baku (on the Caspian Sea) to Batum (on the Black Sea) was also captured. The following month, a French expeditionary force came ashore at Odessa, protected by an Anglo-French fleet patrolling the Black Sea. In the Baltic Sea, Royal Naval squadrons battled elements of the Soviet Navy intermittently from late 1918 into 1919, with later confrontations extending beyond those years.[64] These military and naval operations around the perimeter of Bolshevik-held central Russia gave clear evidence that the Allies were intending a strategy of containment against the new regime. But it soon became apparent that the growing strength of the Bolshevik army – which contrasted sharply with their disparate and poorly organized White opposition – would necessitate a far larger interventionist strategy than the Allies were prepared to pursue.

It was this realization that gave an opportunity for cooler heads to prevail. Among the most noteworthy was Lloyd George.[65] But he had to exercise care in order not to ally himself too closely with the more outspoken non-interventionists such as British Labour, which tended to regard the new Russian revolutionary government sympathetically. On the other hand, Lloyd George had to take into account the strong anti-Bolshevik sentiment held by Conservatives and other right wing groups. The Cabinet itself was divided. Whereas Bonar Law and Balfour tended to follow Lloyd George's lead, Curzon, Long and Milner were strongly Russophobic.[66] The most vehement opponent of any accommodation with Russia was the new Secretary for War and Air, Winston Churchill, who had been appointed to the War Cabinet in the reshuffled government following the general election of December 1918.

Churchill made clear his intentions at his first War Cabinet meeting on 23 December 1918. He believed that Allies should launch a massive intervention into Russia 'with large forces, abundantly supplied with mechanical appliances'.[67] This policy found no favour with the Prime Minister. Lloyd George pointed out that there was evidence of growing Bolshevik support within Russia. The Bolsheviks could, he believed, soon become the legitimate government of Russia. Furthermore, Lloyd George believed that it would be impossible to find sufficient troops to confront the energized Bolshevik armies.[68] Cabinet discussion became heated over Russian policy. Churchill was confident that the Bolsheviks represented only 'a mere fraction' of the Russian population; and that the Allies would be fully justified in using force to establish a democratic government.[69] Lloyd George once again reminded his persistent Secretary for War that adequate troops for an invasion force were not available. Even if conscription were enacted, 'he doubted whether the troops themselves would go'.[70] He was, therefore, 'definitely opposed to military intervention in any shape'.[71]

Within a fortnight of this exchange, Lloyd George was in Paris for the opening of the peace conference. While there, the Prime Minister instructed the Foreign Office in London through its principal embassies to call upon all interested parties to help end the fighting in Russia. He also proposed inviting all contending parties in Russia to meet with the representatives of the peace conference to establish a permanent settlement. When Clemenceau refused to host the Russians, the venue was changed to Prinkipo, an island in the Sea of Marmora: the proposed meeting was scheduled for 15 February 1919. Thus was the Russian question officially changed from a potential military operation to a diplomatic effort. But both Russian parties – the Bolsheviks and their White Russian opponents – turned down the proposal.

With Lloyd George preoccupied at the peace conference, Churchill took the opportunity to rebut publicly his Chief's conciliatory demarche towards Russia.[72] In a speech before the House of Commons on 3 March, Churchill explained that British forces, as well as some Allied detachments, remained 'on those wild northern coasts locked in the depth of winter' and that 'we must neglect nothing for their safety and well-being'.[73] Clearly Churchill was signalling his determination to continue operations in the Murmansk-Archangel region. To that end, he argued that additional troops must be sent to establish a security perimeter for the evacuation of all British forces in northwest Russia. Knowing that the dispatch of war weary veterans would be unpopular with both the public and the troops themselves, Churchill organized through the War Office a new volunteer force – the North Russian Relief Force. The stated object of the NRRF, as advertised publicly, was for the defence of existing positions, rather than offensive operations. But the real mission was indeed offensive. As Sir Henry Wilson noted in his diary on 23 April 1919 after consultation with Churchill: 'Winston and I discussed a good punch towards Viatka to join with Kolchak before we cleared out'.[74] Viatka, more than 600 miles southward from Archangel, would be reached by the River Dvina and rail. By then, the NRRF would have joined forces with the White Russians under General Kolchak. If successful, a further invasion deeper into Russia in support of White Russian troops would be possible.

However, misfortune dogged the British forces from the first. Low water in the Dvina hindered a British flotilla, essential for transporting artillery. Units of White Russian soldiers under British command mutinied, murdering their British officers. When British forces attempted to repel Bolshevik troops in the Murmansk region between the Finnish border and Lake Onega, poor planning and execution, compounded by a breakdown in discipline, ended their foray. Farther afield, by the autumn of 1919 both Generals Kolchak in the East and Denikin in the South were continually on the defensive against advancing units of the Red Army.

Despite the declining fortunes of the White Russians, Churchill remained their staunch supporter. He attempted time and again to regain the initiative. He seemed convinced that Bolshevism would fall before their combined opponents. Indeed, examining a map of disposition of military forces in July 1919 lends some credence to his optimism.[75] The main body of Bolshevik supporters lay in central Russia, centred on Moscow. They were surrounded not only by Denikin, Kolchak and the Allied forces, but also by the Ural Cossacks to the South, and the White Finns, the Poles and General Yudenich's army in the Baltic States in the East. What Churchill overlooked, however, was the advantage of Bolshevik internal lines of communication, their unity of command and the morale of the Red Army. Perhaps most important was that the Red armies were under direct control of the Bolshevik political leadership, which could inspire their troops with an advanced social programme as well as encouragement to revolutionary military ardour. The White armies, in contrast, represented the status quo, the right and right-centre of the political spectrum.[76] As the realization dawned in the British Cabinet that the Red Army and its Bolshevik leaders were steadily gaining in military strength and political mastery, they became increasingly sceptical of Churchill's exhortations.

During the misadventure of the Allied intervention in Russia, Lloyd George acted 'boldly' throughout.[77] Or so Morgan claims. But in fact, the Prime Minister was quite circumspect. He fully recognized the strong anti-Bolshevik sentiment among the coalition Conservatives and was careful not to alienate them. He tended to mute any direct reference to Russia in public remarks. In so doing, he could plead the trials of making the peace treaty in Paris (where he was for the first half of 1919), which took up most of his time. Once the Treaty of Versailles had been signed, he could devote more attention to the Russian problem. An early (and public) sign of his policy of accommodation towards Russia occurred at a Guildhall address in November 1919. Observing that the war with the Central Powers was over, Lloyd George made it plain that war in Europe could not be finally concluded until there was peace in Russia. The armed struggle then raging in that country promised to be 'prolonged and sanguinary'.[78] Given the struggle between the Whites and the Reds, Britain could not 'afford to continue so costly an intervention in an interminable civil war'. He warned his audience further: Russia was 'a quicksand'. Yet the Prime Minister also hinted at a possible solution in bringing the two sides together. He suggested reviving the Prinkipo proposal. This was, however, poorly received in certain quarters. *The Times*, for example, believed that Lloyd George's proposal was 'a slap in the face' to anti-Bolshevik forces because it elevated the Bolsheviks to equal partner status with the White Russians in any negotiations.[79] Several days later, in one of his rare appearances at question time in the House of Commons, Lloyd George read out a more considered statement. To counter any idea that he was 'soft' on Bolshevism, he professed his own 'horror' at the principles and practice of Bolshevism in Russia: 'the chariot of Bolshevism', he declared, was 'drawn by plunder and terror'.[80] Although most could agree on 'the pernicious character' of Bolshevik doctrines, he continued, it was less easy to devise a way of dealing with it. Armed intervention would be 'lunacy'. Some other means must be found. *The*

Times was again critical, claiming that 'the simple issue' was whether or not the anti-Bolsheviks would be supported in their battle against 'an odious and bloody tyranny'. In a significant caveat, however, *The Times* admitted that 'armed intervention ... cannot now be contemplated'. Perhaps only 'moral and material ... support may be feasible'. [81]

Lloyd George's statements of November 1919 were read by the Soviets as a possible avenue to explore peace overtures. In fact, tentative contacts between the Bolsheviks and the British had begun more than a year earlier when the two governments held talks with the aim of exchanging prisoners.[82] This represented a shift in Foreign Office policy, which had initially assumed that the Soviets would fail, thus restoring their Liberal reformist predecessors, a more amenable government. Once the Foreign Office realized that the Bolsheviks were consolidating their power, however, and that British citizens remained in Russian prisons, it was forced to reconsider. In the spring of 1919 the first prisoner exchange was carried out on the Finnish/Soviet border. Further communications led to an agreement, in a document signed at Copenhagen in February 1920, between Britain and Russia to discuss the status of remaining prisoners.

The moving force behind the Copenhagen Agreement was Lloyd George.[83] Given his premise that any further military intervention in Russia was futile and that the Bolsheviks had finally gained the upper hand, he turned his attention to fostering trade between Britain and Russia.[84] In the same month as the Copenhagen Agreement, Lloyd George gave an official statement of his policy in the House of Commons. He began by restating his belief that 'you cannot crush Bolshevism by force of arms'. To attempt this would quickly 'arouse the patriotism of the Russian people'.[85] There was a better way. The Russian people were now in the depths of winter: they were cold, unclothed and hungry. They lacked basic means of transportation and sufficient agricultural machinery to till and harvest the soil in the upcoming months. Britain could supply these. In return, Britain would benefit from badly needed imports of agricultural commodities. Mutual self-interest could benefit both parties. An Anglo-Russian trade agreement might have another by-product: it could 'bring an end to the ferocity, the rapine, and the crudities of Bolshevism surer than any other method'. Britain could, to its advantage, he concluded, 'fight anarchy with abundance'.

The Bolshevik government responded to this entreaty. In late May 1920, Lloyd George was host to Leonid Krasin, the Soviet Commissar for Foreign Trade and Transport. Negotiations proved difficult, however. [86] They frequently stalled on such nettlesome issues as further prisoner exchanges and the disposition of the pre-revolutionary Russian debt owed to both the British government and private individuals. Opposition within the Cabinet also delayed proceedings. Chief among the opponents was – not surprisingly – Churchill, who remained adamant against any accommodation with the Bolshevik government.[87] Lord Curzon also lent his considerable talents against a Russian agreement unless guarantees were met: he had in mind most specifically the continuing Bolshevik revolutionary propaganda directed against not only Britain, but the British Empire as well.[88] The Soviets, too, had their reservations. They were reluctant to promise the cessation of revolutionary propaganda and they remained uneasy about the prospects of British confiscation of Soviet goods or gold should British creditors gain support for such claims. Indeed, at the highest levels of the Soviet government there was substantial mistrust of British intentions. Communicating with the Soviet Trade Delegation in London, Lenin himself raised a warning: 'That swine Lloyd George has no scruples or shame in the way he deceives. Don't believe a word he says and gull him three times as much.'[89]

Lloyd George was nevertheless doggedly determined to reach a conclusion on trade. By-passing his Cabinet opponents, he allied himself with Robert Horne, President of the Board of Trade, and Austen Chamberlain, Chancellor of the Exchequer – the two Cabinet officers most associated with facilitating international trade.[90] As Chamberlain explained it to his sister Ida, trade with Russia was 'right & indeed necessary'. All Europe, including Britain, urgently needed Russian wheat, flax, butter and other commodities. To refuse trading with Russia 'would be to increase the distress of all who suffer from want, short supplies & high prices'.[91] Bonar Law was also strongly in favour of the agreement. Lloyd George and his supporters were aided by Krasin, who was helpful in bringing the negotiations to a conclusion. Touring Britain during the final months of 1920 and conferring with businessmen and bankers, Krasin placed orders worth millions for such goods as textiles, shoes and machinery – those industries hardest hit by the postwar depression.[92]

The Trade Agreement was eventually signed on 16 March 1921. It guaranteed that the established privileges of trading nations would be granted to both signatory parties, such as privileges and protections pertaining to masters, crews and cargoes. It also prohibited any form of blockade of trading routes, and it sanctioned the mutual residency of official trading agents. But the agreement addressed far more than trade. British and Russian prisoners were to be released 'immediately'. Both parties explicitly allowed representatives of each country residing in the other to communicate freely and to be exempted from any compulsory services. Defending the agreement a week later in the House of Commons, Lloyd George emphasized that it was 'a purely trading agreement' recognizing the Soviet government 'as the *de facto* government of Russia, which undoubtedly it was'.[93] Lloyd George informed the House, too, that the Soviets were changing from their 'wild extravagant Communism' to more sensible governing principles. They had made an important discovery – that 'you cannot patch up locomotives with Karl Marx's doctrine'.

For Britain, there was a further primary political and diplomatic goal enshrined in the agreement. The preamble prohibited both parties from engaging in propaganda in their respective countries and territories. The Soviet Union was explicitly enjoined to refrain from such action in India and Afghanistan – a demand reinforced by a supplementary letter from Sir Robert Horne presented to Krasin at the time of the signing of the treaty.[94] To make its import clear, the British government immediately made the letter public. Horne's warning letter may seem at first an offensive gesture, a gauntlet gratuitously thrown at the Bolshevik government and a questionable tactic if the British were serious about a trade agreement. However, there was in fact little doubt that the Soviet Union had laid plans not only for subversive activities in

Britain but also in India and its borderlands. The British Secret Intelligence Service had irrefutable proof: its staff of dedicated code breakers had been systematically decrypting their communications for some time.[95] Many Cabinet members, especially Curzon and Churchill, were outraged at these reports. Lloyd George, however, who seemed 'normally unruffled by Bolshevik intrigues', viewed Russian efforts at subversion as amateurish and without consequence.[96] To the forefront of his mind was the trade agreement – of such importance to a revived British economy that he was willing to overlook evidence of Bolshevik chicanery. He was, nevertheless, prompted by negative Cabinet response to reveal some specific examples of Soviet bad faith by leaking them to the press. Thus, he agreed to make Horne's letter public.

Throughout the lengthy negotiations over the Trade Agreement, the British Labour movement had continued to question the government's policy towards the Soviet Union. Suspicions over the government's intentions reached a flashpoint when armed hostilities broke out between Poland and the Soviet Union over the contested boundary between the two countries. As the war escalated in the early months of 1920, with each side enjoying reciprocal successes, the possibility of a British intervention once again emerged. In the Cabinet, not surprisingly, both Churchill and Curzon favoured active support for Poland. There were also hints from the government that it was willing to allow munitions exports to Poland, acting under the terms of the Treaty of Versailles by which the Allies had vowed to protect hard-won Polish territorial integrity. So long as the Poles enjoyed military success, however, little action on the part of the British government seemed necessary.

However, when the Soviets gained the upper hand in the summer of 1920 and the Red Army advanced rapidly westward, discussion in the British Cabinet began to solidify in favour of overt support for Poland. If Russia won a great victory, the postwar *cordon sanitaire*, designed to establish a firebreak between Eastern Europe and revolutionary Bolshevism, could be breached.[97] To bring peace between Poland and Russia, Lloyd George busily explored all options. He proposed a cease-fire based upon the Curzon Line, originally devised by the Paris Peace Conference as the eastern boundary between Poland and Russia. He sent Hankey as his personal emissary on an emergency inter-Allied fact-finding mission to Poland.[98] He also took a lead during the international conference at Spa in July 1920 to confer with the wartime Allies on the Russo/Polish War.[99] In addition, he issued a warning to the Soviets from the floor of the House of Commons in late July. Admitting that Polish aggression against Russia was 'reckless and foolish', he nevertheless insisted that such actions did not justify a nation 'being wiped out'. An independent Poland was essential 'to the whole fabric of peace'.[100] A few weeks later, Lloyd George, again speaking from the House of Commons, declared in measured terms that 'the Allies cannot be indifferent to the existence of Poland'.[101] Although the Allies would not send troops, they were willing to furnish Poland with the necessary equipment 'out of the stores at their disposal' to stem the Russian tide. Furthermore, should the Soviets persist, the Allies would equip General Wrangel, the White Russian commander who had succeeded General Denikin. Whether or not Lloyd George's remarks carried conviction is unknown. Perhaps, as one historian has suggested, the best that could be said is that he hoped to win time and allow the possibility of a battlefield stalemate.[102] If so, he was rewarded for his patience. After the Battle of Warsaw was won decisively by the Poles, a convincing Polish counter offensive began in mid-August 1920 against the overextended Bolshevik army. Within two months an armistice between the two sides was declared. The British government's policy of firmness and watchful waiting had been rewarded.[103]

But in his attempt to find a middle ground on the Soviet question, Lloyd George had followed a potentially dangerous course. Some British anti-Bolshevik elements were suspicious of Lloyd George's motives. To their way of thinking, the Prime Minister not only lacked resolve in his interactions with the Bolshevik government, he also seemed overly solicitous towards the Soviet negotiators. This view was strongest among certain British military leaders. Chief among these was the CIGS, General Henry Wilson. Wilson had often been critical of his civilian superiors during the war. His postwar opinions, too, were less than laudatory. By 1920 he had begun to edge into a conspiratorial frame of mind. In his diary of 15 January 1920, he wrote: 'I keep wondering if L.G. is a traitor & a Bolshevist, & I will watch him very carefully.'[104] The notion that the Prime Minister could possibly be a traitor became increasingly pronounced in Wilson's mind. 'I wonder', he wrote in May 1920, 'is L.G. allowing England to drift into Bolshevism on purpose?'[105] On 23 July 1920, the refrain continues: 'Is L.G. a traitor? I have often put this query in my Diary.'[106]

Particularly disturbing to Wilson was the presence of Soviet emissaries in Britain who ostensibly sought peaceful relations between the two countries, but whose secret activities suggested otherwise. When the Russian trade representative, Krasin, returned to London in August 1920 after consultations on trade in Moscow, he was accompanied by Lev Kamenev, a far more politically inclined operative. President of the Moscow Soviet and Head of the Moscow Communist Party, Kamenev was also a member of the Central Committee of the Party. Not long after his arrival in London, Kamenev became heavily involved in establishing like-minded British contacts. In addition, he was instrumental in subsidizing the *Daily Herald*, a Labourite newspaper. Nor was there any doubt that other Bolshevik influence peddlers were actively engaged in building a British Communist Party, with the ultimate aim of subverting the government.[107] Although their pursuits were heavily monitored by the British Secret Service, and the Labour movement was in general immune to Soviet blandishments, Wilson remained in a state of alarm.

On 18 August, Wilson confided his suspicions about the Prime Minister to both his deputy, General Sir Charles Harington, and Lieutenant General Sir William Thwaites, Director of Military Intelligence. Later that day, he also conferred with Churchill, who was, as Secretary for War, Wilson's immediate superior. According to Wilson's diary, he succeeded in convincing Churchill of the Soviet danger and of Lloyd George's complicity. 'He [Churchill] said it was quite true that L.G. was dragging the Cabinet step by step towards Bolshevism ....'[108] Churchill's official response to Wilson's prompting was realized in a letter to Lloyd George. In it, while advocating the expulsion of the Soviet emissaries, he avoided mentioning Wilson's fears of Lloyd George's loyalty. In the meantime, Wilson had found favourable responses from Sir Basil Thomson, Director of Special Intelligence, Home Office; the Second Sea Lord, Admiral Sir Montague Browning; the Deputy Chief of the Naval Staff, Vice Admiral Sir Osmond de B. Brock; Rear Admiral Hugh F.P. Sinclair, Director of Naval Intelligence; and Air Marshall Sir Hugh Trenchard, Chief of the Air Staff. Of the latter, Wilson wrote in his diary that: 'Trenchard ... thinks, like Basil Thomson, that LG is a traitor.'[109] Luckily for all concerned, events in Eastern Europe outran conspiracy theories hatched in London by foremost members of the Services – even though Wilson's parting shot in his diary at the end of 1920 showed a suspicious mind still at work: 'Is he a Bolshevist?' queried the worried General of the Prime Minister.[110]

How much Lloyd George suspected of Wilson's conspiratorial behaviour is unknown. There were others in the Cabinet however who, if not conspiratorial, also believed that Krasin and Kamenev should be expelled. Lloyd George reasoned with them. Admitting that there was a case for expulsion because of their 'perfidy' and 'trickery', as the Secret Services had revealed, he nevertheless believed that more information of value could be obtained by keeping them in place. Declaring the Bolshevik propaganda 'crude', he doubted that British workmen would be taken in by it.[111] But Lloyd George also realized that some action should be taken against the Russian envoys. As luck would have it, Kamenev had arranged to return to Moscow at an opportune time. Prior to his departure, Kamenev requested an interview with the Prime Minister. Given a free hand by the Cabinet, Lloyd George, accompanied by Thomas Jones, Hankey and Bonar Law, met with Kamenev on 10 September 1920. As Ullman discloses, Kamenev had a bad time of it. Charging Kamenev with a 'gross breach of faith' for interfering in British internal affairs, Lloyd George specifically mentioned the *Daily Herald* affair and Kamenev's attempt to co-opt influential Labour leaders. Most significantly of all, Lloyd George claimed that Kamenev had deceived him in a diplomatic note of 7 August 1920, which had suggested that in the event of a Russian victory over the Poles, peace terms would be mild: Polish independence would be maintained. But in fact, the Soviets intended to establish a communist regime in Poland. In effect, Poland would become a client state to the Soviet Union.[112]

Because of his firmness in dealing with Kamenev, Lloyd George appeased somewhat the anti-Bolshevik sentiment of the Conservative right wing in Britain. But the Prime Minister was also faced with thunder from the political left. Critical Labour voices in Britain had risen throughout the months of the Russo-Polish conflict. Lloyd George's anti-Bolshevik public utterances raised suspicions that he planned a military alliance with Poland to overthrow the Bolshevik government, still popular among many Labourites. In August 1920, a combined meeting of the TUC and Labour MPs in the House of Commons formed a Council of Action whose task was to prevent the government from once again becoming involved in a continental war of 'unlimited sacrifice of blood and treasure'.[113] To that end, the council committed itself to a general strike unless the government backed down. Thus, the Labour movement immediately became an anti-war movement that quickly won nationwide support.[114] Local Councils of Action were set in motion, ultimately numbering between 300 and 400. Interviews with Lloyd George, letters to the principals in the dispute, delegations to France to consult with the French Socialist party and domestic demonstrations were all a part of the Council's programme. The most visible example of direct action was the London dockers' refusal to load the *Jolly George*, bound for Poland with suspected munitions on board.[115]

These actions on the part of Labour suggested to some disturbed opponents that the Council of Action's activities too closely resembled a government in being, operating perhaps unconstitutionally against existing ministerial policies.[116] The Council of Action raised a number of questions among its opponents. Was a general strike a seditious offence? Could a broad work stoppage be an insurrection? Would the Councils be, as some nervously asked, the beginnings of British Soviets? Lloyd George himself had his doubts about the constitutionality of the Councils. At a contentious meeting in August 1920, Ernest Bevin claimed the right to query Krassin and other Russian emissaries then in London. Lloyd George strenuously opposed this notion, declaring that such a meeting would entwine domestic politics with on-going diplomatic discussions.[117]

Labour's suspicion about Lloyd George's foreign policy was not its only concern. A change in the economic weather and government's response to it also raised warning flags. Wartime exigencies had forced government spending at a rapid rate for the materiel of war. With peace came a pent-up demand for consumer goods. Freed from government controls and in need of plant renewal and equipment replacement, business expanded rapidly. Employment consequently rose dramatically. But as the boom continued unabated into 1920, evidence mounted of increasing speculative ventures – even in such solid industries as shipbuilding, textiles and engineering. Treasury and Bank of England officials had sounded the alarm early. In 1919, the Bank urged Austen Chamberlain, as Chancellor of the Exchequer, to impose a tighter monetary policy. The Bank's requests fell upon receptive ears. Chamberlain believed his major task was to discourage the belief, engendered by wartime exigencies, that there was scarcely any limit to available credit.

The ministry was fully supportive of a retrenchment policy. A new Finance Committee of the Cabinet met in August 1919 to consider emergency measures. Among its decisions was a decree that the Treasury thereafter must approve any charge proposed by ministers of the government. In addition, the Permanent Secretary of the Treasury became Head of the Civil Service, with the right to advise the Prime Minister on the appointment of senior officials to all departments. Thus encouraged, Chamberlain – in his second budget speech in April 1920 – raised taxes on excess profits as well as the duties on beer and spirits with an eye for debt reduction. He also raised the bank rate to 6 per cent and then to 7 per cent. Lloyd George reinforced the Treasury view by sending round a circular letter threatening to dismiss any Cabinet member who refused or was unable to reduce expenditure.

The climax of discussions on the economy occurred at emergency Cabinet meetings in September 1921 held at Gairloch, Scotland, where Lloyd George had been sent by his doctor, Lord Dawson, for a late summer holiday as treatment for exhaustion.[118] Lloyd George initially proposed borrowing funds (as much as £250 million) to be expended on public works projects, such as roads, canals and trains to ease rising unemployment. But the possibility of an unbalanced budget did not please the Treasury.[119] Exerting pressure upon the new Chancellor of the Exchequer, Sir Robert Horne (who had replaced Chamberlain a few months earlier), the Treasury made its reservations officially known. The central tenet of the Treasury view was that State expenditure, if financed by borrowing, would divert money from potential private industrial investment and thus hamper economic recovery.[120] Operating from a position of strength, the Treasury made it difficult for either the Cabinet or the Prime Minister to ignore their advice. A fortnight after Gairloch, Lloyd George announced to the House of Commons that only £38.3 million could be used as a stimulus for increasing employment. So small an amount meant that a public works programme to ease unemployment was severely restricted.[121] In sum, by the end of 1921 the government, in combination with the Bank of England and the Treasury, had put the brakes on the boom.

As the slow down initiated by the government took hold, two serious consequences became apparent. The initial consequence was, inevitably, to increase unemployment. In 1914, unemployment had registered at 3.3 per cent: throughout the war it was negligible. But by 1921 with the collapse of the boom, it reached 11.3 per cent, one of the highest rates of the century.[122] As the jobless rate rose, emergency measures were called for. A number of committees set out to examine the causes and consequences of mass unemployment, among them the Cabinet Committee on National Expenditure, chaired by Eric Geddes, the wartime efficiency expert. Geddes's report, popularly known as the 'Geddes Axe', recommended stringent cuts on government expense ranging from military forces reduction to education to social services.[123] The second consequence was a downgrading of the government-sponsored policy of postwar reconstruction. Christopher Addison, who had become the first Minister of Reconstruction in July 1917, had – as we have seen – energetically set out to establish priorities through a large number of committees, which were to explore the possibilities of postwar progressive programmes. A first priority was the settlement of veterans of the war into peacetime work and affordable housing. But the promised plan of 'Homes fit for Heroes', a fundamental plank in the reconstruction platform, ran into innumerable snags. Unexpected delays, the high cost of building materials and the economic downturn took their toll.[124]

The path of Lloyd George's decision making on economic policy throughout the slump is not entirely clear. Although he had proved sensitive to the plight of the unemployed, he was also clearly influenced by pressure from the Treasury and other tight money advocates. But another circumstance was also at work. What had initially gone largely unnoticed – and was proceeding simultaneously along with the Prime Minister's altered fiscal priorities – was the fact that Lloyd George's political views were shifting. As Riddell's diary entries in late September and early October of 1919 indicate, Lloyd George had already begun expressing in private a growing anti-Labour attitude.[125] This was directed less at labouring men and women than at the militant trade unions. Perhaps the continuous labour unrest had taken its toll. Added to this were the persistent pressures from the Treasury and the loud chorus of his

Conservative critics. Equally important were the small but noticeable indications that Lloyd George, soon after his return from the Paris Peace Conference, had begun reviewing his own political position.[126] The wartime coalition, it was easy enough to see, could not last forever. The coalition, essentially a centrist bloc between Labour and hard right Conservatives, had served its purpose well. But the coalition was only a temporary expedient: war and the rigours of peacetime economic adaptation would eventually smooth themselves out. At that point – with the Liberal Party in apparent decline – political parties might revert to traditional Left and Right configurations, but in an altered form. Labour versus Conservative was the likeliest outcome.

Such a strong dichotomy of rival political parties might offer an opportunity for a third grouping – a centrist party which could draw from the moderate men of both left and right, as had happened during the war. After a meeting at Criccieth in mid-July 1919 with several of his closest intimates, including Churchill and Hankey, Lloyd George apparently commissioned Churchill to give a public address on the need for a new centre party.[127] Within a few days, Churchill gave a speech in which he presented the idea in a public forum: it was an obvious trial balloon.[128] Recalling Lloyd George's previous effort of a coalition plan in 1910, Churchill declared that earlier effort 'was, in effect, the exact counterpart of the coalition government now in power'. Such a long-standing notion of political centrism on the part of the Prime Minister, Churchill seemed to imply, both validated and legitimized such a proposal now brought forward. The important issue above all, Churchill emphasized, was that 'the moderate elements in both parties must not pull apart'.

In the months following, Lloyd George continued to seek advice from supporters and important politicos. After a dinner hosted by Lloyd George in late November, C.P. Scott recorded that the Prime Minister had spoken in praise of coalitions: there was no other option, he had declared.[129] On 6 December 1919, Lloyd George was in Manchester, attempting to reclaim the loyalty of rank and file Liberals, while simultaneously defending the coalition. Addressing the Manchester Reform Club – 'that haven of north-of-England Liberalism'[130] – Lloyd George paraded his Liberal credentials. He also expressed his 'deep pain' that there had been a parting with many in the Liberal Party with whom he had been working for years 'in the same common cause'.[131] Defending the coalition government as a necessary measure to 'preserve the national unity', he also defended the extension of that government into peacetime. During a time of postwar 'tumult and unrest', he declared, a coalition government could act 'more effectively, more thoroughly, and what is very important now, more speedily'. Emphasizing, too, the progressive nature of the government, he urged his audience to give allegiance to it: 'Don't let us sulk and fret over trivialities and personalities while great and gigantic events are fashioning.'

Although there was no mention of it in his Manchester address, Lloyd George was clearly laying the groundwork for a grand scheme of political centrism by reminding Liberal Party members of the advantages of the wartime (and now peacetime) coalition. Several weeks later, in early January 1920, at a strategy session attended by Lloyd George, Bonar Law, F.E. Smith, Addison and Churchill among others, the prospect of a 'fusion' of like-minded Liberals and Conservatives was discussed more explicitly at length.[132] Sanders, who was also present, understood from the sense of the meeting that fusion was designed 'to strengthen resistance to Labour'. A general consensus at the meeting favoured fusion, although there was some disagreement on timing: several 'thought that a good excuse such as a big strike ought to be awaited'.[133] As his consultations had gone forward, threats against the government posed by several by-election losses to the Labour Party hastened Lloyd George's decision to act. The government could not continue to sustain these losses, he confessed to Riddell: something must be done to ginger up coalition support. To that end, he told Riddell that he had decided to go forward on a fusion between the two wings of the coalition, shorn 'of the most reactionary members'.[134] He had at last decided, after several months' reflection, to follow up on the Churchill kite of July 1919. By March 1920, Lloyd George's plan for fusion was widely known. Balcarres observed in mid-March that fusion was 'the order of the day'.[135] Yet, suddenly – almost shockingly – within a few days it collapsed. Balcarres put it bluntly: fusion 'seems off'.[136]

What had happened? To Trevor Wilson, the answer was easy. Lloyd George's 'unblushing opportunism' was simply too obvious.[137] But Morgan takes issue with this explanation. Lloyd George, he believes, 'simply botched' the opportunity to establish a genuine centrist government by his performance at two crucial meetings in March – the first on 16 March with Liberal ministers of the coalition government, and the second with Liberal MPs two days later.[138] In both instances, Liberal stalwarts insisted upon a commitment to traditional Liberalism. Some expressed reservations that would surely arise in the constituencies. Nor was Lloyd George's message particularly progressive. In fact, as Morgan notes, the Prime Minister was 'not now in a progressive mood'. He seemed to have been 'soured' by the continuing industrial conflicts. By adopting 'a strongly Conservative stance', Lloyd George failed completely.[139] His quest for a centre party was stillborn.

During Lloyd George's quest for a fusion party and his continuing preparations for possible strike action, he was also mindful of opportunities throughout late 1919 and early 1920 to head off confrontations with the unions through negotiations and agreement. For example, the Prime Minister kept the line open to the NUR following the September 1919 railway strike, as we have seen. At about the same time, dockers won the right to bring their claims for hours and wages to a public court of inquiry, established by the new Industrial Court Act of November 1919. The Act enabled the Ministry of Labour to appoint ad hoc courts as a way of settling industrial disputes. Ernest Bevin put forward the dockers' case, heard in February and March 1920. In 20 public sittings, Bevin won his spurs as the 'Dockers' KC'. Through his advocacy, the Dock, Wharf, Riverside and General Labourers' Union secured an important verdict: a daily minimum wage, the establishment of a permanent joint industrial council and the abolition of casual labour.[140]

With the settlements of the railwaymen and the dockers, two of the three sections of the Triple Alliance were satisfied, at least temporarily. Only the miners remained. Their case was more complicated. Since the early days of Lloyd George's administration, the government had controlled coal in order to foster the smooth running of this vitally important wartime industry. By 1920, the government was moving firmly in the direction of decontrol; that is, of returning to the coal owners their pre-war management of their mines.[141] This prospect had roused miners' opposition which in turn had spawned the Sankey Commission, with the possibility that the mines would instead be nationalized. When this failed, miners – fearful that private management would act firmly in their own interests – preemptively demanded higher wages. Characteristically, Lloyd George was active in personally negotiating with mining leaders; but ultimately he failed and the miners struck on 16 October 1920. The government in response brought into play the Emergency Powers Act. This in turn spurred supportive action from the railwaymen, who threatened to come out in support of the miners unless their demands were met. A provisional agreement was soon reached which essentially granted miners their demands. The agreement also established an increase in productivity as a criterion for higher wages. In addition, a bargain for a national pooling of both wages and profits was devised by which less advantaged miners would gain equally with all others.

But difficulties continued in the months that followed. The slump, which had affected much of the economy, finally caught up with the coal trade in late 1920 and early 1921. The average price for export coal plummeted. The government, still in control of the mines, was faced with increasing deficits as prices dropped. It therefore decided to decontrol several months earlier than originally planned, thus returning control to the owners, who were now faced with an unprofitable industry. Facing a loss in profits, owners terminated earlier contracts with the miners, offering much lower rates of pay. When the miners refused, owners ordered a national lockout. The very next day, 1 April 1921, the miners' federation announced a work stoppage.

The initial response of the ministry was a carefully designed alternating strategy of conciliation and coercion. To Lloyd George, the most effective tactic would be simple and straightforward: 'Our line', he informed the Cabinet, 'is to be moderate and conciliatory'.[142] On the other hand, the ministry again invoked the Emergency Powers Act: army units and naval ratings were ordered on immediate alert. Miners in the meantime had begun soliciting aid from their partners in the Triple Alliance to join the strike in sympathy. Should this happen, a general strike of all workers would become likely. But on Friday, 15 April, railwaymen and the transport workers decided against supporting the miners. This day in labour history has since been known as 'Black Friday' – the day that union solidarity suffered a fatal defeat.[143]

The coal strike lasted for three long months, during which mining communities suffered increasing privation. As the strike progressed, Lloyd George's attitude hardened. At a ministerial conference on 12 April he declared that after lengthy negotiations with the miners, there was little left to discuss.[144] An urgent telephone plea the following day from J.H. Thomas of the railwaymen's union for further talks left Lloyd George unmoved. 'I think we had better have the strike', he responded. 'Let them kick their heels for a week or a fortnight. It will help the moderates against the extremists.'[145] To a conference of his ministers several hours later, Lloyd George justified his action. 'I believe you can prick the bubble', he declared. 'These men have always had the idea they can strangle the community.'[146] Lloyd George had succeeded in dividing the Triple Alliance.

Yet, several days after the strike had begun, he once again attempted to break the impasse in a conference with the miners' and owners' spokesmen; but they were 'miles apart', as Thomas Jones reported it.[147] However discouraging, Lloyd George initiated further conversations from mid-May onwards between the union and the mine owners, but once again without success. In the following month, perhaps at last convinced by the severity of the strike, both sides met in lengthy discussion with Lloyd George and came to an agreement. To break the deadlock, Lloyd George offered a £10 million government subsidy to miners for the purpose of slowing down the pace of wage reductions among them on the condition that they return to work.[148] The miners had little choice: they accepted.

The effects of the failed miners' strike were several, but two were especially important. The first was a general weakening of the aspirations of a unified Labour movement. The Triple Alliance was, as Lloyd George had hoped, severely weakened by the ambivalent attitude of its constituent members towards strike action. The prospect of strike-induced unemployment dampened enthusiasm among railway men and transport workers. The abandoned miners and their consequent defeat, combined with the continuing economic slump, brought to an end the postwar labour unrest as the unions retreated from their former aggressive stance. But it was not a happy peace. The second effect was the impact upon Lloyd George's reputation as a defender of labour. As Morgan convincingly argues, Lloyd George had thrown himself energetically into labour's cause upon returning from the Paris Peace Conference.[149] Reconstruction was foremost in his mind. 'Homes fit for Heroes' was no idle promise. He actively pursued satisfactory compromises between labour and management to such a degree that he seemed an auxiliary Minister of Labour. Taking personal charge of major disputes, he invited deputations and delegations of every stripe to Downing Street for consultations, setting the stage for the compromises between opposing sides that had long been his trademark since his days as President of the Board of Trade. That he withdrew at labour's supreme hour of need was an ironic development for this great social reformer. For him now, the primacy of social order trumped the needs of labour. Or so it certainly seemed to labouring men.

15

THE IRISH REVOLUTION

In spite of the background of labour unrest and the frequency of major strikes, these were not the most serious threats to pubic order in postwar Britain. The most violent scenes of action were in Ireland. The aftermath of the Easter Rising of 1916 had deepened the divisions between Irish separatists and the British government. Martial law had consolidated anti-British sentiment throughout much of Ireland – most strongly, of course, in the South. No less important to the hardening of anti-British sentiment was the canonization of the Dublin martyrs by the Catholic hierarchy as they offered commemorative masses throughout the country. The effect was to instil within Irish political circles a cold and determined resolution that the Irish nation – as it was now becoming – must be united in establishing self-government as its primary goal. Initially, separatists in the main had believed that only through parliamentary devices could this realistically be accomplished. Now, however, local political apathy that had been characteristic during the time of the ascendancy of John Redmond's Irish Parliamentary Party was rapidly becoming a thing of the past.[1]

The instrument of national aspirations was the emergence of a political party thoroughly dedicated to Irish independence. Sinn Féin had been a loosely organized group characterized by strongly separatist inclinations since its establishment by the journalist Arthur Griffith in 1907. But it had lain fallow since its early days, overshadowed by Redmond's more moderate and more successful national Parliamentary Party. Gradually, however, support for Redmond was undermined by events: Ulster and the Home Rule crisis; the advent of war in Europe; and the fear and hatred of the threat of compulsory military service for Irishmen who would be forced to aid the British war effort. These developments, brought to a head by the 1916 Rising and the British response to it, provided the opportunity for Sinn Féin to become the repository of fresh hopes for a new Ireland.[2] By imprisoning hundreds of suspects after the Rising, the British government created a school for subversion as Irish prisoners educated one other in the arts of dedicated political opposition and revolution.[3] When Lloyd George released these prisoners upon his accession as Prime Minister in December 1916, he returned to Ireland a leadership hardened and strengthened in their dedication to the cause of Irish independence.

Sinn Féin's first electoral victory at the North Roscommon by-election in January 1917 showed its potential strength and popularity. Standing as an advanced nationalist candidate, in effect sponsored by Sinn Féin, was Count Plunkett, the father of Joseph, one of the Dublin martyrs.[4] A local curate, Fr Michael O'Flangan, was a leading Sinn Féin operative. This sanction by the Church, unofficial though it was, gave an added thrust to the campaign. Upon defeating the official Redmondite candidate, Plunkett declared that he would not take his seat at Westminster. This became the model in other by-elections that followed in the months to come: successful Sinn Féiners, upon their election, declined to attend the imperial Parliament. Spurred in part by their continuing victories in successive by-elections, Sinn Féin became a popular movement.[5] At the South Longford by-election in May 1917, Joe McGuinness, one of the Easter rebels and still a prisoner, was elected, helped no doubt by Dr William Walsh, the Catholic Archbishop of Dublin, who spoke out against a partitioned Ireland, and by implication in favour of Sinn Féin's all-Ireland separatist platform.[6] The most notable of all the 1917 by-elections was at East Clare in July. The seat fell vacant when Major Willie Redmond, the brother of John Redmond, was killed on the Western Front. Clare was by all accounts the most rebellious area in Ireland, as well as one of the most populous constituencies. The Sinn Féin candidate was one of the newly released prisoners of state, Eamon de Valera. As the senior surviving commander of the Rising, de Valera had impeccable credentials. He had little trouble at the poll in this, his first election contest. The final of these early by-elections that heralded the advance of a Sinn Féin wave was held in Kilkenny city in August 1917. The outcome here was as it had been in the three previous – this time with W.T. Cosgrave, also a veteran of the Easter Rising, as the victor.

The impact of these elections was clear enough. Moderate and radical separatists, uniting together in the Sinn Féin movement, were rapidly undermining the Home Rule Nationalist Parliamentary Party of Redmond. Sinn Féin's enthusiasm and organizing skills, combined with sufficient fighting funds, overwhelmed their opponents. In an attempt to counter this potential danger and diversion from the war effort, Lloyd George proposed a nationwide Irish Convention, whose purpose was to allow leading Irishmen to craft their own solution to an all-Irish self-government and to settle issues in both North and South.[7] Meeting from July 1917 to April 1918, the convention held court at Trinity College, Dublin. But it was undercut from the start: Sinn Féin boycotted the proceedings; and there was eventually no meaningful outcome. Perhaps if the Prime Minister had devoted sufficient time to its proceedings, more progress would have been possible. Indeed, there is some question about how much real interest Lloyd George had in the convention. Grigg thought that it was merely a delaying tactic,[8] which is consistent with what we know was Lloyd George's primary goal at this time – setting aside all other problems for the successful prosecution of the war.

As the influence of Sinn Féin gained strength throughout 1917, Lloyd George's government was faced with an additional Irish problem, one more directly concerned with winning the war. The horrifying loss of life on the Western Front had begun to tell against British manpower available for the trenches. Within a month of his becoming Prime Minister, Lloyd George sounded out H.E. Duke, the Chief Secretary for Ireland, on his 'latest views' on the possibility of Irish conscription. 'The military authorities', he continued, 'are again worrying me on this subject, and it is clear we shall soon have to discuss the best methods of utilizing the manpower of Ireland'.[9] Duke, in reply, agreed that there was a large number of 'able bodied young men' in Ireland 'who could and ought to serve'.[10] But the government well knew that any attempt to impose conscription upon Ireland in its present mood would be difficult, if not impossible. Lord Wimborne, then the Lord Lieutenant of Ireland, sounded a note of caution. Noting the growing strength of Sinn Féin, he believed that the present state of Ireland gave 'cause for anxiety'. Especially unnerving was the 'immense' influence among the younger Catholic priesthood, many of whom had 'seditious proclivities'.[11]

Lloyd George and the government were concerned not merely about the political consequences of Sinn Féin. A growing agitation on the land among distressed small farmers could provide an opportunity for a broadened economic and social appeal as well. In early 1918, Wimborne reported to Lloyd George that there were increasing signs of a serious defiance of the law particularly in the West and South of Ireland. He cited incidents of cattle driving and unlawful tillage of land by gangs of farmers operating against the larger graziers and more substantial landowners.[12] In some cases, property was damaged; in others, hayricks were set alight. There were clashes between police and demonstrators. If these acts of intimidation were successful and extended widely across Ireland, the social structure of the country could be at risk. That these rebellious farmers may well have had something in mind beyond a mere redistribution of land can be illustrated by an example in Connacht where fields were commandeered by as many as 500 men, marching in military order, carrying spades and waving the tricolour.[13]

The government could not but be concerned about these hints of an agrarian revolution. But the government's attention towards Ireland remained firmly directed towards conscription. Little resistance was anticipated in Ulster, where volunteers for the war effort had enlisted in force. Southern Ireland was expected to be less forthcoming, especially given the palpable rise in anti-British sentiment fanned by Sinn Féin. In the end, the government had no choice. The exigencies of war and the need for manpower ruled out the potential dangers of further inflaming Irish opinion. The German offensive, begun on 21 March 1918, was the catalyst. Four days later, the Cabinet extended conscription to Ireland. On 9 April, Lloyd George introduced in the House of Commons a Military Service Bill which included Irish conscription. In an attempt at conciliation, the government also promised a measure of Irish self-government. The bill received the royal assent on 18 April.[14]

The impact in Southern Ireland was immediate. While on mission to Dublin, Lord French – soon to become Lord-Lieutenant of Ireland – reported that the country was 'thoroughly roused by bitter animosity and resolution to oppose conscription'.[15] The following day, in a 'Secret and Personal' letter to Lloyd George, French wrote that the Catholic bishops, the Lord Mayor of Dublin and the entire group of parliamentary nationalist MPs were 'openly preaching absolute rebellion'.

It was his 'firm conviction', French added, that Ireland 'should be at once put under complete Martial law, and that a purely Military Government should rule it'.[16] French's alarm was not misplaced. Resistance to conscription had quickly spread throughout Southern Ireland. A one-day general strike (Ulster was excluded) set the tone for civil disobedience. Within a short time, hundreds of thousands had signed an anti-conscription pledge and had contributed to a national defence fund. Passive resistance of this sort was not the only option, however. Irish Volunteers and Sinn Féin prepared for armed rebellion. Recruitment began; stocks of food were set aside; and public speakers roused the population.[17] Events at Westminster mirrored those in Ireland. The Irish Parliamentary Party, now led by John Dillon after Redmond's death, withdrew to Dublin and there joined the anti-conscriptionist crusade.

The government quickly realized that some action must be taken. Options were limited, however. Perhaps in frustration, the government was led to a belief that the anti-conscriptionist campaign was associated in some fashion with the German enemy. More than 70 Sinn Féin leaders, including de Valera, Griffith and W.T. Cosgrave were arrested. But it transpired that the putative plot was apparently set afoot by Captain Reginald Hall, chief of naval intelligence in London. Recalling Casement and his treasonable activity in 1916, Hall manipulated the details of a counterfeit plot and released them to credulous government authorities, including Walter Long. Only after the public pronouncement of the plot and the ensuing arrests was it realized that – in Hankey's words – the evidence was 'of the most flimsy and ancient description'.[18] Hall, summoned by the Cabinet, was treated to a 'scathing' rebuff for his fictitious account of a German-Sinn Féin plot.[19] By then, however, Irish suspicions had intensified.

At about the same time, Lord French replaced Wimborne as Lord Lieutenant of Ireland. Edward Shortt, a Liberal who favoured some form of Home Rule, also replaced the Chief Secretary for Ireland, H.E. Duke. There was some hope that French's Irish ancestry and his military credentials would help smooth troubled waters, as would Shortt's moderate views. When anti-British hostility continued during the summer of 1918, however, French responded harshly. Egged on by Walter Long – who had become the official liaison between the Cabinet and Dublin Castle – a number of counties and cities were 'proclaimed' – that is, persons arrested there would be tried by special juries.[20] In some districts suspicious gatherings were banned. Meetings of the Volunteers and Sinn Féin were specifically declared illegal. To enforce these edicts, more troops were sent to Ireland, further lessening the numbers that could be sent to the front. But these suppressive actions backfired. As Lyons points out, Sinn Féin became more intransigent.[21]

Lloyd George's conscriptionist policy towards Ireland has puzzled historians. Townshend thinks it 'hard to comprehend'.[22] Granting extensive powers to Lord French during a time of ticklish relations with Ireland was bound to exacerbate tensions. Ward is harsher in his judgement, charging Lloyd George with a failure to control, to understand, or to inform himself about Irish conditions.[23] Even Morgan, normally a resolute defender of Lloyd George, thinks the burden of blame must be directly assigned to him. Major decisions about Ireland in 1917 and 1918 were his own, and none other. The results were, Morgan believes, 'disastrous'.[24] Pugh, however, takes a different tack. He attributes Lloyd George's Irish decisions to an underlying political weakness. He had less authority than most prime ministers because his Premiership was founded upon a coalition – a coalition whose main purpose was to win a war. This aim Lloyd George accepted wholly.[25] Even the critical Ward modifies his views (perhaps unintentionally) when he observes that the Prime Minister was 'simply too busy with the war' over Germany and Austria to understand fully the implications of an enforced conscription in Ireland.[26] Whatever his motives, Lloyd George must be held ultimately responsible for Lord French's rigid military rule as it extended into the summer of 1918.

Signs of continuing trouble for the British government occurred in June when, at the East Cavan by-election, Arthur Griffith, even though a prisoner, won the seat handily. As another of the Sinn Féin by-election victories, Griffith's success could well seen as a portent of strong Sinn Féin showing in any future general election. Indeed, the new Irish electorate, widened by the Representation of the People Act of February 1918, was soon to prove its loyalty to Sinn Féin. The act had increased the Irish electorate from approximately 700,000 to nearly two million. Sinn Féin was well aware of its opportunity at the polls and began campaigning from mid-summer onward.[27] Even though official British harassment continued against Sinn Féin campaign workers, this tactic proved counterproductive. Thirty-four incarcerated Sinn Féin candidates stood for the general election of November 1918, as did six others who were evading arrest. The Redmondites, whose eponymous leader died in March, were disheartened and demoralized by the swelling Sinn Féin tide: they managed only token campaigns. Sinn Féin's emphasis on republicanism and the heroism of the Easter rebels ensured their electoral success. They won 73 seats to the Redmondites' six. Twenty-six seats went to the Unionists of Ulster.

The new Sinn Féin MPs, however, did not make the trek to Westminster. Meeting in the Mansion House, Dublin, on 21 January 1919, they proclaimed themselves the Dáil Éireann (Parliament of the Irish Republic). None of the invited Unionist MPs of the North nor the few remaining Redmondites attended. Conducting their first business primarily in Irish, the Dáil approved a constitution and ratified the new nation as an Irish Republic. Beginning in 1919 and thereafter, the Dáil and Sinn Féin and its military counterpart, the Irish Republican Army (as the Irish Volunteers had become), began to act as entities independent from Britain. The Dáil, for example, carried out a successful drive for finances by raising a national loan. They established a land bank and a land commission. They created an alternative system of local government that effectively bypassed the old system of corporations and county councils established under British rule. They also reshaped the judicial system by creating new courts and a legal hierarchy displacing the old.[28]

To some historians, these actions represented a revolution in Ireland. Fitzpatrick has no doubt that there was a 'revolutionary convulsion' in Ireland from 1918 through 1921.[29] Foster writes that by 1919, the Irish revolution 'was an established fact'.[30] Townshend believes that most Sinn Féiners and Irish Volunteers 'certainly felt themselves to be revolutionaries'.[31] That Irish republicanism could be a distinct revolutionary threat occurred to English and Irish contemporaries as well. The course of events in Russia was much in their minds as a cautionary tale. In the opinion of Walter Long, for example, Irish republicanism was 'another word for Bolshevism'.[32] Lord Oranmore and Browne, an Irish peer, believed that the increased land agitation in the West of Ireland, was 'virtually a form of Bolshevism'.[33] Even the more moderate were concerned about the potential radical political shift in Ireland. The Earl of Dunraven had warned Lloyd George as early as 1918 that he had never 'seen the law so openly derided' in Ireland, 'or the people in so dangerous a mood'. He, like Long, saw in the 'increasing lawlessness ... a faint reflection of conditions in Russia which may tend to spread'.[34]

Whether or not there was a widespread self-conscious sense of revolution in Ireland against British rule by early 1919, there was no doubt that the new Irish republic was rapidly following up its proclaimed independence by challenging British rule directly. At the same time that the Dáil advanced their civilian authority into formerly British spheres of governance, the Irish Republican Army began a guerrilla war against the British military presence in Ireland. On the very day of the Dáil's first meeting, a band of IRA men killed two members of the Royal Irish Constabulary at Soloheadbeg in County Tipperary and carried away a cache of gelignite. Thereafter, the IRA systematically began assassinations of anti-republicans: the RIC became special targets. Attacks upon police barracks followed. IRA 'flying columns' began a series of ambushes of police patrols. A plot to assassinate Lord French in December 1919 almost succeeded.

As violence spiralled upward throughout 1919, the British Cabinet offered no certain response. At Dublin Castle there was, as one historian has observed, 'seldom a consensus on what steps to take'.[35] The drift in Irish policy was due partly to the absence of Lloyd George at the Paris Peace Conference throughout the first half of the year: 'no constructive policy' could be developed 'in the PM's absence' was Thomas Jones's informed opinion.[36] The result was that an ad hoc response to Irish disruption took the place of a coordinated policy. Harsh tactics tended to prevail. The British government detained thousands of potential suspects; declared martial law in several counties; and reinforced British troops in Ireland. Lord French, perhaps still incensed by the attempt on his life, had further hardened his views. Drawing lessons from the Boer War – in which he had served – French believed that it was time to apprehend Irish insurgents and their families and put them inside concentration camps. Such as operation was, he believed, 'the only way' to 'settle this business here'.[37]

More fatefully, the government reinforced the Royal Irish Constabulary (RIC) by recruiting the undisciplined 'Black and Tans' and 'Auxilliaries', who often unofficially engaged in retaliatory actions. These irregular forces were intended to reinforce the hard-pressed RIC. But they quickly became hated targets of the IRA. November 1920 was a particularly murderous month. A flying column of IRA ambushed two truckloads of Auxiliaries returning to their barracks at Kilmichael in County Cork: all were killed.[38] Not long after, another ambush near Cork City caused more Auxilliary casualties. That same night, hordes of Auxiliaries and Black and Tans looted and wrecked Cork, burning the city's centre to the ground. In counterpoise, on 21 November IRA death squads systematically assassinated 14 suspected British intelligence agents, most of them army officers, in their Dublin homes. That same day, in direct bloody reprisal, a force of Black and Tans opened fire on a crowd of Gaelic football fans during a match at Croke Park: 12 died and many more were wounded. During 1920 as a whole, 176 members of the RIC were killed and 251 wounded. The British army also suffered substantial casualties: 54 soldiers died and 118 were wounded. The government, under heavy pressure, was therefore forced to pass another telling piece of legislation, the Restoration of Order in Ireland. This Act gave exceptional power to General Macready, the British military commander in Ireland, who thereafter had the authority to arrest and imprison without trial any suspected member of Sinn Féin. Prisoners could be tried by courts-martial. [39]

Even before the crescendo of violence had reached a climax in late November 1920, Lloyd George and the government had come to the conclusion that a new approach to Irish governance was imperative. Political events and armed confrontation in Ireland had outrun existing legislation. The Home Rule Act of 1914 – already on the Statute Book – had been suspended for the duration of the war and would automatically come into effect when all peace treaties had been signed. In October 1919, Lloyd George had accordingly appointed a committee to look into the prospects of a new Irish initiative. His choice of its chairman, Walter Long, may not have been initially encouraging to the Irish, but it had the advantage of reassuring backbench Conservative MPs, Ulster Unionists and southern Irish Loyalists as well. Behind this screen, with his rightist anti-Irish flank covered, Lloyd George could operate more freely in searching for an Irish solution.[40] As Long pursued consultations both in and out of government circles, a legislative package took shape during the early months of 1920.[41]

Much had happened since 1914 of course and any new Government of Ireland Bill had to take this into account. No longer would Home Rule apply to all of Ireland: there were now effectively two Irelands. The new Bill thus provided for two separate Parliaments, each in full control over internal administration, including finance. An all-Ireland Council would deal with common problems between Ulster and Southern Ireland. A united Ireland could only come about if the two Parliaments agreed. Ulster itself was redefined as containing only six of its nine counties. The excluded three were rejected because of their Catholic majority – an anomaly when compared to the Protestant majority of the new six county Ulster. This was granted at the express wish of the Protestant Ulster leadership (including Sir James Craig), which was loath to have such a large Irish Catholic population within Ulster's borders.[42] Under these terms, the bill became the Government of Ireland Act in late December 1920. But it was not an act for the unification of Ireland; indeed, it effectively recognized partition. And because it retained the notion of Home Rule for the southern counties, it was an Act dead on arrival at the time of its passage. Only self rule – not Home Rule – would now satisfy Sinn Féin and the IRA.

The difficulties encountered in devising the Act and its ultimate failure was emblematic of the countervailing pressures upon the government that were rising to a climax in 1920. From every quarter, the government was buffeted by conflicting opinion and advice. A public debate among academics, labour leaders, leading churchmen and newspapers revealed the intense interest regarding the state of Ireland.[43] Much of the opinion – while unsure about the prospects of an independent Ireland – was nevertheless heavily critical of British reprisals upon Irish citizens. In particular, this 'war of reprisals' had attracted the attention of the world's press, which was proving largely sympathetic to the Irish. The new Republican government also carried out a propaganda campaign in Britain. Through press releases to British journalists and the encouragement of pressure groups among sympathetic members of the public, the new Irish government emphasized their peaceful intent and their determination to foreswear violence and agitation in mainland Britain.[44]

Equally important to the Irish cause was the courting of British and foreign correspondents to visit Ireland to see for themselves the beginnings of a new nation. Articles questioning the harshness and legitimacy of British forces in Ireland began to appear.[45] Speaking in the House of Commons against the Irish crackdown, critics condemned especially 'the Tans' and 'the Auxies'. The legitimacy of the Irish cause was impressed upon the metropolis with the death of the republican leader, Terence MacSwiney, the Lord Mayor of Cork, who died of a hunger strike in Brixton Prison in October 1920. His funeral cortege from the prison to Euston Station where he began the journey home to Ireland passed through streets lined with Sinn Féin flags. As the *Manchester Guardian* acknowledged, among many in the crowd were English onlookers, some curious and some reverent, but all of whom greeted the demonstration 'with respect',[46] The *Daily News* described the event as 'an image of all Ireland'. MacSwiney's death and funeral was 'being repeated in Irish town after Irish town and in Irish village after Irish village'.[47]

The events of 1920 revealed some changes of opinion among leading politicians and ranking military leaders. Walter Long, for example, was seconded by Bonar Law, in his belief that an arrangement had to be made to secure some form of Irish autonomy.[48] Other Conservative Unionist spokesmen, however, held fast in their opinion that any loosening of the bonds of union with Ireland would be another nail in the coffin of the British Empire. General Wilson was among the foremost spokesmen against Irish demands. He had pushed hard for Irish conscription in 1918. Two years later, his views on Ireland were unchanged. Lloyd George was his main target, although other Cabinet members were also called into account. Confiding to his diary that the Prime Minister was 'funking' Irish policy, Wilson believed that unless the government held firm against Sinn Féin 'we shall be kicked out' of Ireland.[49] This was a refrain often repeated in his diary entries. To Churchill (who was then Secretary for War), Wilson complained that the existing Irish policy 'was suicidal' and that the government must either take stronger measures in Ireland or retire. But, he cautioned, if the government retired from Ireland, we shall have 'lost our Empire'.[50] Nor was Wilson shy about facing down the Prime Minister himself. After a lengthy conversation with both Lloyd George and Bonar Law in late September 1920, Wilson charged them both with a failure to govern. Later in the secrecy of his diary, he wrote that neither man 'had the faintest idea of what to do'.

He reserved his severest criticism, however, for Lloyd George: 'We drift from bad to worse, and always under the guidance of Lloyd George.'[51] Lest it be thought that Wilson's views were extraordinary and hypercritical, it should be noted that even the usually staunch Hankey had gradually changed his mind on Ireland from conciliation to coercion.[52]

Others in governing circles were almost in despair about the prospects of any solution and were uncertain what position to take. Among these was Austen Chamberlain, whose somewhat pompous and wooden appearance belied a genuinely sensitive and reflective approach to Ireland. Chamberlain believed that Ireland had too often been ignored and left to its own devices: in this, he blamed primarily Asquith and the pre-war Liberal government – not a surprising opinion from his Conservative perspective. Nor was it surprising that Chamberlain had supported Irish conscription. Beyond this, however, he was generally hesitant in suggesting a harsh policy towards Ireland. Confiding to his sister in June 1918, he wrote: 'I am mightily troubled about Ireland & cannot see any way through the difficulties that confront us.'[53] The following month was no better: 'As to Ireland I can see no light.' Worsening conditions in Ireland during the following months increased his doubts. After a Cabinet conference on Ireland in mid-1920, he admitted that Ireland was in revolution, and that the whole subject was 'most puzzling & most distressing'. He confessed despairingly: 'I don't see my way clear'. By late 1920, however, Chamberlain's views on Ireland had hardened. The policy of official reprisals, he now believed, had lessened the attacks on the RIC: 'Govt is getting the Murder gang on the run by degrees.' Yet in the months that followed, Chamberlain once again changed his mind. This time, he was in a position to make a significant difference in the settlement of Ireland. In March 1921, after persistent ill health, Bonar Law resigned from the coalition government. Chamberlain replaced him as leader of the party. This event coincided with Chamberlain's realization that, after all, there had been little progress made in Ireland. To his sister, Ida, in April 1921, he wrote: 'the suspicion, distrust & dislike are so strong on both sides that I do not know how to take a new step'.

The most important opinion of all, of course, was that of the Prime Minister. He had taken the lead in 1916, as will be recalled, in attempting to devise a satisfactory solution to the divisions between Ulster and Southern Ireland based upon an acceptable formula of Home Rule. This had failed. Lloyd George had, however, retained the notion of a sustainable Home Rule at some point in the future. But after the election of 1918 and the rise of Sinn Féin and the IRA, he gradually became convinced that Home Rule was no longer an option for the southern Irish. This realization came slowly to Lloyd George as it did to most British politicians. Well into late 1919, Lloyd George was praising the ideal of Home Rule. 'Home Rule was an absolute necessity' he insisted in a conversation with Riddell.[54] As the Anglo-Irish War dragged on, however, Lloyd George appeared to change his mind – not once, but twice. He seemed first a hard liner, wholly opposed to what he considered the illegal actions of unchecked bands of armed assassins. Lloyd George's occasional public pronouncements in the latter half of 1920 indicated his intransigent mood.

At a public meeting in Caernarfon in October, he strongly defended government actions against Irish attacks: 'Policemen and soldiers do not go burning houses and shooting men down wantonly without provocation.' Admitting there had been reprisals – 'some severe hitting back' – he claimed that such retaliation was justified as a natural consequence of 'scores of policemen' who have been shot in the back by armed civilians. 'That is not war', he assured the crowd, 'it is murder'.[55]

As violence continued unabated into the early months of 1921, evidence on the ground suggested that the IRA was proving adaptive and resilient, benefiting from the classic advantages of guerrillas operating in a friendly and supportive population.[56] If such conditions led to a stalemate, with neither side scoring a decisive win, morale would remain high in the IRA. Their smaller numbers holding off the mightier resources of the British Empire would be seen as a kind of victory for the insurgents.[57] The government in fact was finding itself in an invidious position: it could not order martial law for all of Southern Ireland – public opinion at home would not allow it – nor would it be easy to find sufficient military forces to enforce it. On the other hand the government could not bend to the demands for Irish independence. This would be met with certain and unalterable opposition from Conservatives and Unionists, whose numbers remained dominant in the coalition and in Parliament at large.

A conference in early March 1921 between Lloyd George and Irish officials heard Lord Midleton, the moderate leader of southern Irish Unionists, declare that Irish conditions continued to be 'appalling'.[58] Midleton's information was particularly disheartening because of an important upcoming deadline. Under the Government of Ireland Act 1920, parliamentary elections in both Ulster and Southern Ireland were mandated for May 1921. Could elections be held at a time of such violence? This was the question that the Cabinet attempted to address in a series of meetings beginning in April. Discussions centred on the possibility of either cancelling the elections or offering a truce so that elections could proceed peacefully; but inevitably the Cabinet drifted on to other Irish topics, revealing the government's decidedly uncertain path.[59] Lloyd George's role was particularly important in attempting to establish a consensus. The minutes of the meetings reveal a slightly menacing Prime Minister, one whose remarks bore a distinctly anti-Irish tone. He doubted that the Irish could be dealt with reasonably and that any bargain made would not be kept, because there was 'no real leadership there'. He also condemned 'the Irish nature' – 'greedy beyond any other part of the United Kingdom'. Furthermore, he believed that Ireland was 'not ripe for conciliation at this moment'.[60]

A fortnight later, having decided that the elections should go forward, the Cabinet focused on whether a truce ought to be offered. Balfour took a hard line, claiming that a truce offering would be 'a sign of weakness'. He wanted 'no further concessions made, for if made they'll only strengthen the Republicans'.[61] Curzon, admitting that he had formerly been in favour of a truce, had changed his mind. He feared that the truce, once offered, may not hold; and in breaking down, would make matters worse. Other Cabinet members disagreed. Addison denied that offering a truce was a sign of weakness. Fisher thought that it was worth the risk of offering a truce – 'a natural part of a constitutional policy'.[62] Munro, the Secretary for Scotland, believed that the public were 'alienated and disgusted by our present policy' and would welcome a truce.[63] Churchill agreed. The present policy was 'very unpleasant' and was negatively affecting Britain's interests 'all over the world'.[64] Lloyd George and his supporters in the Cabinet remained firm in their belief that a truce was too risky an option. By a vote of nine to five, they turned it down.[65] It was Curzon who perhaps summed up best the growing mood of despair overshadowing the Irish Question. To the Cabinet he confessed: 'I'm sick and weary of this dismal tale of tragedy and squalid catalogue of murder.'[66]

Thus the May elections in both Ulster and Southern Ireland went forward with predictable results: resounding victories for Sinn Féin in the South and equally overwhelming wins by Ulster Unionist candidates in the North. In the South, the Sinn Féin majority MPs (a fair number of whom were IRA officers) simply reconstituted themselves as the second Dáil Éireann with its unalterable republican programme.[67] Consequently, the establishment of two separate parliaments by the Act of 1920 had effectively created the partitioning of Ireland, an action desired by Ulster but abhorred by the South. Still, a thread of hope remained: the Act of 1920 had also mandated a potentially significant instrument of cooperation, a Council of Ireland. Given the outcome of Cabinet debates just prior to the elections, however, little optimism could be found among the various contending parties. Shortly after the April and May Cabinet meetings, Tom Jones wrote to Bonar Law: 'The ghastly tale of horror from Ireland continues.'[68] The military position of British forces in Ireland continued to look bleak: they were 'anything but satisfactory', as the Secretary of State for War, Worthington-Evans, put it in a report on 24 May.[69] Although recent historical examinations of the IRA has shown that the IRA's record was not as mythically successful nor as widespread as had once been thought, there is no doubt that the number of IRA military operations was increasing during the spring of 1921 – 53 in March, 67 in April and 107 in May.[70]

In response, the Cabinet – perhaps motivated by sheer desperation – drifted towards even harsher measures. On 2 June 1921, the Cabinet decided that general martial law should be imposed on Southern Ireland. On 15 June, General Macready presented a draft report to the Cabinet on the consequences of such an act. Martial law would entail severe restrictions: the declaration of the IRA and the Dáil as treasonable organizations; the suppression of hostile newspapers; the closure of ports; and the institution of an extensive system of passports and identification cards. The government should also be prepared for as many executions as a hundred a week to enforce the law. As disconcerting as this report was, the Cabinet was determined, nevertheless, to press forward. Four battalions were sent to Ireland, with another four to be dispatched later that month. As many as needed would follow on later.

At the height of these distinctly discouraging circumstances an unexpected event occurred which dramatically altered the tense standoff between Southern Ireland and the British government. On 22 June, King George V, in a strongly conciliatory speech before the newly elected Ulster Parliament in Belfast, urged cooperation among all Irishmen to work together in ending the conflict, and in addition to work together for common purposes for the good of Ireland as a whole. His greatest wish was that his speech 'may prove to be the first step towards [sic] an end to strife' among the Irish of 'whatever their race or creed'. He then appealed 'to all Irishmen to pause, to stretch out the hand of forbearance and conciliation, to forgive and forget, and to join in making for the land which they love a new era of peace, contentment and good will'.[71] Within 48 hours of the King's speech, Lloyd George summoned a Cabinet meeting where he proposed to send a copy of the speech along with an invitation to both de Valera and Sir James Craig to a conference in London to 'see whether we can arrive at an accommodation'.[72] Churchill was 'delighted' with the proposed arrangement. Birkenhead was 'entirely in favour'. Curzon viewed it 'with the intensest satisfaction'. There was, as Tom Jones observed, 'a general murmur of agreement'.[73] After some preliminary diplomatic skirmishing between Dublin and London, a truce between British and Irish military forces became effective on 11 July. Three days later, Lloyd George and de Valera began the first of four negotiating sessions from 14–21 July 1921.

What had happened? Within a matter of days, it seemed that Lloyd George and the Cabinet had moved from a firmly anti-Irish position to one of accommodation. Churchill himself observed that no British government in modern times 'has ever appeared to make so complete and sudden a reversal of policy'.[74] Later historians have also made mention of Lloyd George's 'suddenly reversed policy', as Morgan terms it.[75] Hopkinson describes it as Lloyd George's 'U-turn in British policy'.[76] Examining the background of Lloyd George's decision, however, reveals that it was neither impulsive nor ill considered. Even during his firmest declarations against Ireland, Lloyd George and various members of the government had been engaged in a full round of secret meetings, diplomatic manoeuvring and back-channelling sources of information in an attempt to establish the groundwork for peace. Lloyd George had no doubt often been exasperated by Irish actions and he was perhaps occasionally flummoxed by their obstinate and (to him) impertinent demands. Yet he remained at heart what he had always been, a determined negotiator and seeker of consensus, even when expressing in public an opinion frequently at odds with his more secretive plans.

The government's moderating actions had in fact begun a year earlier than the King's speech in Belfast. Under Lloyd George's direction, the cadre of British administration in Ireland at Dublin Castle was replaced in May 1920. This served two purposes – to improve an efficient pursuit of the IRA and to establish lines of communication with Sinn Féin.[77] Among the most important new officials were the Joint Under Secretary, Sir John Anderson and the Assistant Under Secretary, Alfred W. Cope, who was to become the main British contact with Sinn Féin and the IRA.[78] The gradual introduction of new blood at Dublin Castle continued a year later when in April 1921, Lord French was replaced as Lord Lieutenant of Ireland by the first Roman Catholic to hold this position, Lord Edmund Talbot, Viscount Fitzalan. Though a Unionist, Fitzalan was solidly against the coercionist inclinations of French.

To reinforce avenues of approach out of the public eye, other contacts were brought into play. These included the engagement of Archbishop Clune of Perth, Western Australia. Clune, born in County Clare, had been visiting England and Ireland when Joseph Devlin, a leader of the Ulster Catholic minority, persuaded him to serve as a secret intermediary between the British government and the Irish. Devlin arranged an interview between Clune and Lloyd George on 1 December 1920. This began an attempt between Dublin and London to strike a deal, concentrating on the possibility of a truce, to be followed by a meeting of the Dáil. By the end of the month, however, negotiations fell apart in an atmosphere of suspicion and bad faith.[79] Other straws were in the wind. Under the auspices of Dublin Castle officials, a meeting between de Valera and Craig took place in early May 1921. From the British point of view, Craig could serve as an instrument for ascertaining at first hand de Valera's position and to determine if there were areas for compromise. Although no breakthrough occurred, the very fact of the meeting suggested the possibility of future contacts between North and South.[80]

More strenuous attempts to bring peaceful closure to the Anglo-Irish conflict occurred during the early months of 1921 at a time of some of the worst outrages of the Anglo-Irish War. From the pages of a diary kept by Mark Sturgis, who was effectively a Joint Assistant Under Secretary at Dublin Castle, comes the most detailed evidence of these efforts. Sturgis summed up Lloyd George's policy as 'cracking the whip with one hand and holding out the carrot in the other'.[81] Although Sturgis did not minimize the depressing rounds of violence and retribution, he also saw hopeful signs of accommodation. These 'peace balloons', as he called them, often directly involved the Prime Minister. He noted how Lloyd George, operating secretly with Dublin Castle, engaged in numerous initiatives and interviews with a wide variety of Irish contacts. These included a direct connection with businessmen, local politicians, imperial statesmen and even members of the Dáil – which Sturgis believed at the time was 'an enormous step towards peace'.[82] Perhaps the climax of Dublin Castle's influence for peace came shortly after the Cabinet's decision to establish martial law. On 18 June, Sir John Anderson, off his own bat, wrote to Hamar Greenwood, the Chief Secretary, requesting that his letter also be circulated to both the Prime Minister and Chamberlain, leader of the House of Commons. In the letter, Anderson deplored the prospects of martial law in Ireland as a 'drastic measure' and urged as a counterpoise some measures of concession.[83]

It is very likely that Anderson's letter fell upon receptive ears. As Mansergh has observed, the letter – bearing a 'note of near-desperation' – may have been a crucial determinant in altering the government's policy.[84] But is also important to remember that for many months, Lloyd George and the government had operated on two separate tracks in dealing with the Irish conflict. The government was plainly willing to continue fighting, as its recent declaration of martial law indicated, yet they were equally willing to continue negotiations if conditions were favourable. Such a strategy had three important potential benefits. First, it indicated that the British government would not tolerate armed insurrection against its authority. Second, by using force in Southern Ireland, the government could also neutralize those diehard coalition British Unionists who perennially suspected Lloyd George of a sell-out over Ireland. Finally, by signalling a willingness to negotiate, the government hoped to separate moderates from what Sturgis called 'the Gun-boys'[85] – the extremists among the Sinn Féin and the IRA. It can reasonably be argued that by May 1921, these objectives had been largely achieved. At about the same time, Sinn Féin and the IRA had also come to believe that their best opportunity for achieving their political aims had arrived. They may have been nudged forward by the prospects of severe hardship that martial law would engender. In short, when the King made his June overtures for peace in Belfast, a tipping point had been reached on all sides: an opportunity for genuine negotiations was at hand. The King's speech was thus only the occasion, not the cause, of a diplomatic opening between Ireland and Britain.

Equally important in the run-up to the face-to-face negotiations between the Prime Minister and the President of Ireland was the evolution of Lloyd George's views on the form of Irish government that Britain would allow in a reconstituted Ireland. To many observers, it was obvious that Home Rule for Ireland was an antiquated concept inapplicable to the new political realities. What form an Irish state should assume was less clear, however. The key to the solution proved to be a concurrent debate among the constituent nations of the British Empire that had begun during the later stages of World War I. The war had spurred national feelings in such Dominions as Canada, Australia, New Zealand and South Africa. Their contributions to the war effort and the peacemaking that followed had also strengthened their inclinations to play a more independent role on the world's stage. The consensus among them was their desire to remain connected to Britain, but in a less subordinate role than had been customary. They demanded more freedom of national decision-making while simultaneously enjoying the benefits of a collective security that the Empire provided. In short, they advocated a Dominion status, rather than a colonial or imperial one.[86]

It would not be surprising, given these developments, if the notion of a Dominion status for Ireland had also been bruited about. In fact, during the Irish Convention of 1917, such plans had been discussed. Once the war was over, Dominion status for Ireland gained wider attention with the establishment of the Irish Dominion Party by the quirky social reformer, Sir Horace Plunkett (who had chaired the Convention). Further fitful murmurings about Dominion status for Ireland were occasionally heard. Lloyd George himself had touched briefly upon the subject with C.P. Scott in early 1919.[87] But it was not until mid-1920 that the idea was officially taken up at a Cabinet meeting and then only briefly and inconclusively. Tom Jones, however, was encouraged enough to believe that Dominion status for Ireland had merit and drew up a proposal for Lloyd George in advocacy of the plan, pointing out that in certain circles (such as Labour) there was 'a widespread sympathy' for an Irish Dominion.[88] Several days later, the Prime Minister and several Cabinet colleagues met a deputation of businessmen from Cork and Dublin. Some members of the delegation were Unionists and some were Nationalists but all were opposed to any imposition of a Home Rule Bill. They did, however, favour some form of Dominion status.[89] Lloyd George at that time was not convinced: in late 1920, he still regarded himself as 'a

Gladstonian Home Ruler', by which he meant that Ireland should remain 'an integral part of the United Kingdom'.[90]

In the following months, there was little change in the Prime Minister's views. As late as 12 May 1921, Lloyd George remained opposed to the idea of Dominion status. He declared in a Cabinet meeting of that day: 'We've been generous in the Home Rule Act. Anything beyond that would contain germs of trouble.'[91] In this, Lloyd George voiced the opinions of a solid body of opponents to the idea of Dominion status for Ireland. Many thought the term itself was ambiguous. Even among the outlying Dominions such as Canada and New Zealand there were varying interpretations of its meaning and how much independence such status would confer. Moreover, Unionist leaders such as Bonar Law and Walter Long – undoubtedly voicing the opinions of many British Conservative Unionists – had strong reservations about Dominion status for Ireland.

Nevertheless, the idea continued to gather strength as all other options for Ireland lost their appeal. A fortuitous London conference of imperial prime ministers in June 1921 brought this and other matters to a head. In attendance was General Smuts of South Africa, who arrived at the very time that King George was preparing his speech before the opening of the Ulster Parliament on 22 June. As a personal friend of Lloyd George since the Paris Peace Conference and a publicly avowed champion of Ireland, Smuts was well positioned to strike a balance of interests.[92] The opportunity came during lunch at Windsor Castle on 13 June 1921 when the King solicited Smuts's advice on his proposed speech. Smuts believed the speech was a unique opportunity for the King to initiate and to 'foreshadow the grant of Dominion status' to Southern Ireland.[93] Smuts drafted a proposed speech, a copy of which he sent to Lloyd George, along with a letter to the Prime Minister in which he urged action on the 'unmeasured calamity' that existed in Ireland.[94] This may have been the catalyst for Lloyd George's change of mind.[95] As we know, Lloyd George – through his advisers – rewrote the Smuts draft. Although they excised any direct reference to Dominion status for Ireland, they nevertheless validated and extended the invitation to Ireland for the purpose of exploring the grounds for a peaceful solution to the Irish question.

Thus serving as an interlocutor between the King, Lloyd George and de Valera, Smuts smoothed the way for an agreement. But further groundwork was necessary to bring all sides together. Again, Smuts played an important role. He was in attendance at the Cabinet meeting two days after the King's speech during which the Cabinet sanctioned the conference between Lloyd George and de Valera to be held in London. Pursuant to the Cabinet meeting, Smuts remained in London for several days, engaging in talks with de Valera's emissaries. In early July, he travelled incognito to the Mansion House in Dublin to begin a direct dialogue with the Irish leader. There, Smuts attempted to dissuade de Valera from his insistence upon an Irish republic. Afterward, Smuts formed the opinion that de Valera was willing to negotiate on the matter, and might be willing to consider the prospects of a Dominion. On 6 July, Smuts reported directly to the Cabinet.[96] The crux of his remarks was a question he had posed to de Valera. When Smuts asked de Valera directly if he would accept Dominion status, the Irish leader responded 'such an offer had never been made to them'.[97] But if such an offer were to be made, de Valera continued, it should not contain limitations, which would show 'distrust of the Irish people'.[98] The Irish leader's tentative remarks on Dominion status was encouragement enough for the two sides to agree on a truce by which the British promised to cease all raids and searches and to lift curfews, while the Irish agreed to cease attacks on both British military and civilians. On 14 July 1921, the week long conference began.

At the first meeting between Lloyd George and de Valera, the Prime Minister famously attempted to impress the grandeur of the British Empire upon the Irish leader by displaying a large map with 'great blotches of red all over it', a 'sisterhood of nations' – the Prime Minister said – with whom Ireland could join.[99] Lloyd George's firm offer was Dominion status concurrent with allegiance to Crown and Empire. Southern Ireland would have its own police and all other government services. The British Navy, however, would maintain control of the seas around Ireland and would operate naval bases on Irish soil. The new Ireland would be prohibited from imposing hostile tariffs against Britain. The Ulster government must be recognized and would enter the constitutional government of Southern Ireland only if it so chose. These restrictions, falling short of the republican vision for Ireland, were not well received by de Valera. Dominion status itself was doubtful. It might well work for far-flung Dominions such as Canada, but Ireland as a Dominion so close to Britain, de Valera believed, would surely be under its thumb. Indeed, the Irish feared that 'geographical propinquity' might lead to continued subordination to British interests.[100] Signs of broad Irish displeasure with the British proposals were evident when de Valera returned to Ireland. The Dáil granted de Valera the title of President of the Irish Republic. In addition, the Dáil declared itself as the government of the Irish Republic. Moreover, it firmly rejected the tentative British proposals.

In a letter to Lloyd George, de Valera declared that Ireland must 'choose for herself the path she shall take to realize her own destiny'. In addition, de Valera made it plain that Britain had no right 'to mutilate our country'.[101] Ireland alone must determine its boundaries. In other words, de Valera not only insisted upon an Irish republic, but it was also to be an all-Ireland republic, inclusive of Ulster. These twin demands of Irish sovereignty and Irish unity remained at the heart of their negotiating position thereafter. A British reply came quickly. Crafted by a Cabinet committee (but shaped primarily by Lloyd George), the official response to de Valera clearly stated that Britain would never acknowledge the right of Ireland to secede from its allegiance to the King.[102] This exchange set the tone for the negotiations that followed throughout the remainder of the summer of 1921. In the meantime Lloyd George prepared a military option should further negotiations fail.

After weeks of intensive long distance debates and hard bargaining, it became obvious that only face-to-face negotiations could resolve a dangerous deadlock. It was agreed that an Irish delegation should meet Lloyd George and members of his government in London for further diplomatic exchanges. The possibility of such talks had emerged from developments during the communications between the two governments over the summer that suggested a possible way forward. This first was that – in acknowledging the immovable objections of the British government to an Irish republic – de Valera had hinted at a constitutional arrangement that would stop short of demanding a republic, yet would go farther than a Dominion status for Ireland. De Valera proposed what he called an 'external association' with Britain and the Empire. On the British side, the offer of a conference was tied to (in a loosely but carefully worded communiqué) the aim of reconciling Ireland's desire for independence with some sort of association with the British Empire. So stated, the British seemed to follow along de Valera's implied retreat from his demands for a republic. Could a compromise be in the offing? Could the Anglo-Irish War be nearing its end? Much depended upon the negotiating skills of both sides, and the prospects of compromise. Most of all, the success or failure of the conference depended upon the Prime Minister, whose life-long reputation for conciliation was put to its supreme test.

The Anglo-Irish peace conference began on 11 October and lasted until 6 December 1921. From the first, de Valera's absence – justified by him as necessary for a head of state to remain at his post in Ireland – was awkward.[103] Nevertheless, the Irish delegation was solid. Led by Arthur Griffith, the founder of Sinn Féin, and Michael Collins, the fabled leader of the IRA and Finance Minister of the Dáil government since 1919, the delegation also included Robert Barton, a Protestant landowner and member of the Dáil Cabinet; the solicitors E.J. Duggan and Gavan Duffy; and the British-born novelist, veteran of the Royal Navy and former clerk of the House of Commons, Erskine Childers. Lloyd George, Churchill, Chamberlain and Birkenhead, among other designated members of the Cabinet, led the British side.

The Irish delegation was initially aggressive. Griffith began for the Irish by condemning British rule. 'We feel', he said in response to Lloyd George's opening remarks, 'that from the days of Pitt onwards it has been the policy of this country to keep Ireland in a subordinate position'.[104] In later sessions, the Irish were equally vocal on the issues. They wanted the right to be neutral in the event of any war declared by Britain. In trade relations, they feared dumping on the part of Britain. They charged Britain with 'standing behind Ulster' thus making it difficult for the southern Irish to strike a deal.[105] The British, for example, by granting an Ulster Parliament, had aided in partitioning Ireland. 'Like all Empires', Griffith claimed, Britain 'divides and conquers'.[106] In reply to Lloyd George's query on what should be done about Ulster, Griffith responded laconically: 'You must stand aside'.[107] In their attempts to discount these charges, Lloyd George and the British delegates were on the defensive. Indeed, they were forced to assert, as a surety of their serious intentions and their desire to right earlier wrongs, that they were endangering their own political futures in negotiating with Ireland. As Lloyd George put it, 'there was a growing sentiment in a powerful section' of the Conservative Party 'who view with great disfavour' the ministry's efforts to produce a settlement with Ireland.[108] 'We are taking great political risks', the Prime Minister informed the Irish: the 'life of the Government' itself is 'put in issue by our proposals'.[109] The implication was unmistakable: should the Lloyd George government fall, it might be replaced by a reactionary diehard Conservative government – a disaster for Irish aspirations.

Once Lloyd George and the delegates had met the opening barrage by the Irish, they began to address the Irish demands in detail. By late October, the British delegation had gained the upper hand in consistently pressing the Irish on three matters. The Irish must give allegiance to the Crown; they must join 'the fraternity of nations known as the British Empire'; and they must grant the necessary naval facilities to prevent any attack upon British shores by sea.[110] The Irish responded by repeating that they could not give allegiance to the King without first securing the unity of Ireland. Lloyd George took this demand seriously. In an attempt to bring Ulster around to some acceptance of their participation within an all-Ireland governing structure, he consulted with James Craig, who had taken up residence in London during the time of the Anglo-Irish talks. But Craig proved obdurate.

Indeed, Lloyd George's increased pressure upon Ulster raised the alarm among many Conservative Unionists. In early November, Miss Stevenson recorded in her diary with some dismay that Bonar Law in particular was 'proving difficult'.[111] Although Bonar Law was no longer a member of the Coalition, he remained an MP and an unreconstructed Ulster supporter, carrying great weight among Conservatives. To head off any overt action on the part of Bonar Law, Lloyd George met with him privately, warning against any attempt to form a diehard ministry in order to wreck the Irish negotiations. The Prime Minister stated that he would personally lead a coalition of Liberal and Labour MPs against such an effort.[112] Lloyd George also vented his displeasure to Tom Jones, complaining of the 'unfriendly part' that Bonar Law had been playing during the sensitive Irish negotiations. He believed that Bonar Law meant 'to make a bid' for the leadership of the Conservatives in order to 'break up the Coalition'. But he would probably fail, thought Lloyd George, because he 'had not the necessary courage for supreme leadership'.[113]

Following heated discussions with Bonar Law, the Prime Minister went forward with a scheme to resolve the impasse over Irish unity. He commissioned Tom Jones to enquire from Griffith and Collins if they would accept Dominion status for the 26 southern counties in return for a Boundary Commission, which would be appointed to demarcate the division between Ulster and Southern Ireland. The implied understanding was that the commission might very well engage in a frontier correction that – by favouring Southern Ireland – would make Ulster even smaller than its existing six counties. Shorn, say, of a third of its size and thus weakened, Ulster would likely capitulate to the all-Ireland constitutional model and would eventually join its larger southern neighbour as an economic necessity. Jones also suggested to the Irish that the mere threat of the commission might force Ulster into a closer accommodation with Southern Ireland. But if such a threat failed, and Ulster was determined to remain outside of an all-Ireland state, what then? Lloyd George wanted an assurance from the southern Irish delegates that they would not 'break' on Irish unity; that they would not scuttle the conference on that issue; and that they would continue the talks in an effort to settle other outstanding questions, especially the still undecided political relationship with Britain. This assurance he received in a written pledge from Arthur Griffith on 13 November 1921.

With the prospect of a Boundary Commission operating in their favour, the Irish delegates could turn to the equally important subject of an Irish republic. By late November, it had become increasingly clear that their hopes for an independent or quasi-independent Ireland were now fading. Indeed, Lloyd George had never wavered from his clear and unyielding refusal to legitimize republican aspirations. It was important for the Irish to bend the knee to the Crown and to take the oath of fealty to it. This was the Prime Minister's firm position during the preliminary talks with de Valera in July, throughout the interim negotiations of that summer and into the peace conference itself.

After many weeks of negotiations, Lloyd George presented a draft treaty on 1 December 1921. It proposed that Ireland would become a self-governing state with the same status as Canada: in short, Ireland was to be a Dominion. In addition, Ireland would be responsible for its own coastal defences, thus replacing the Royal Navy (dependent upon an agreement to that effect to be carried out through separate negotiations). With a draft in hand, the Irish delegation made a quick trip to Dublin for consultations. Deep divisions emerged during all-day discussions in the Dáil on 3 December. Some held firmly to the republican view: others were willing to continue discussing an altered form of association between Ireland and Britain. Griffith, and likely Collins, were ready to sign the treaty as it stood. But de Valera was displeased by the freedoms won by Ulster and insisted that the delegation refuse to sign the treaty upon its return to London. He also reiterated his preference for an oath that pledged allegiance to an 'external association' with Britain and the empire, rather than an oath to the Crown which would imply too close an association with Britain. Under pressure, Griffith promised to renegotiate the treaty. If this were denied, Griffith would refuse to sign.

Back in London on 4 December, the delegates found a hardened Prime Minister determined to wrap up the conference. When Griffith attempted to bring up the question of a united Ireland as a precondition to any agreement, Lloyd George produced Griffith's letter of 13 November promising to support a Boundary Commission if Ulster refused to join an all-Ireland political arrangement. Griffith could not renege on such an important pledge, which he had given voluntarily and in good faith. Lloyd George and the British delegates also rejected the 'external association', once again proposed by the Irish delegates. In the meantime, the wily Lloyd George sought to divide the Irish delegation by meeting separately with Michael Collins. Perhaps sensing that Collins was not only the most influential of the delegates but also a moderate, Lloyd George won his support for accepting British terms by promising that the two Ulster counties with the largest nationalist majorities (Tyrone and Fermanagh) would be assigned to the South under the auspices of the Boundary Commission.[114] The next day, 5 December, with his ducks all in a row, the Prime Minister presented an ultimatum to the Irish delegation. He insisted they accept Dominion status, allegiance to the king and association with the British Commonwealth of Nations. If they refused, the British government would resume full-scale war against Southern Ireland within three days. He gave them until 10:00 that evening for an answer. As a sweetener, he announced that Ireland was to be granted full fiscal autonomy. Thus confronted, the delegates retired for their final conference meeting. Well past midnight, the delegation struggled with their decision, emerging finally to sign the Anglo-Irish Treaty at 2:30 in the morning of 6 December 1921.

For Lloyd George, praise came from all sides within Britain. One would expect approval from his most trusted advisors. Tom Jones, who had played a significant a role during the Irish negotiations, did not disappoint. On the day of the signing of the treaty, he wrote ecstatically to Hankey that Lloyd George's 'patience and alertness have been extraordinary, even for him'.[115] A week later, Jones amplified his remarks to Hankey: throughout the Irish negotiations, the Prime Minister 'was magnificent'. All his 'great qualities', Jones wrote, 'were at their best'.[116] The press also generally approved. Scott of the *Manchester Guardian* believed that Lloyd George had shown 'extraordinary ... skill and foresight in negotiation'.[117] *The Times*, without mentioning the Prime Minister, was nevertheless fulsome in its praise. 'Reason has prevailed', its leader proclaimed the day following the signing.[118] The treaty was 'one of the greatest achievements in our Imperial history'. Now that 'the Irish problem' – a 'perpetual distraction at home and an increasing peril abroad' – had been settled, Ulster and Southern Ireland were free to make their own constitutional arrangements. Beatrice Webb, speaking for at least some of the intellectual class, greeted the news with enthusiasm, complementing Lloyd George's 'amazing skill'. In her diary, she wrote: 'no other leader could have whipped the Tories to heel and compelled them to recognize the inevitability of Irish independence'.[119]

Debate in the House of Commons also reflected favourable sentiment.[120] When the Articles of Agreement were first presented to the House on 14 December 1921, Lt Col. Sir Samuel Hoare (Conservative MP for Chelsea), gave unstinted praise to Lloyd George. 'Dare he say to the Prime Minister what he believed was in the minds of many other Conservatives, that by his resourcefulness, by his energy, by his intuition' (here Hoare was interrupted by the first of a succession of cheers) 'he had succeeded where the greatest names in our political history had failed'. George Barnes (Coalition Labour MP for Glasgow Gorbals) echoed Hoare. This day, said Barnes, 'would become memorable in he annals of the country'. Stanley Baldwin (Conservative MP for Bewdley and President of the Board of Trade) criticized all those who 'turned away from peace', and reminded the House that it was their duty 'to go on in the strength of the Agreement they had made and go on with faith'. Bonar Law, perhaps less enthusiastic than many, nevertheless gave grudging approval during the House of Commons debate the following week. Admitting that he did not like the treaty, he nevertheless asked two rhetorical questions: 'What is the alternative?'; and, was it not 'worth our while' giving the Irish 'the chance' to carry out the terms of the treaty?[121] *The Times* boldly editorialized that: 'With ratification, every cause of friction between Ireland and this country will have been removed.'[122]

The sigh of relief heard in Britain was not echoed in Ireland, however. When the delegates returned to Dublin, they faced not only a divided Irish Cabinet, but also a tumultuous and contentious Dáil. Griffith argued that Ireland had achieved equality with the nations of the Commonwealth. For the first time in 700 years, he claimed, Britain would evacuate the country. Ireland could now govern largely in her own interests. Although they lost the battle over partition, they had won a qualified victory on sovereignty through the achievement of a Dominion status. As Michael Collins put it, if they had not won 'ultimate freedom', they had won 'the freedom to achieve it'. De Valera, who apparently had expected that the negotiations would continue for some time, may have been shocked by their abrupt termination.[123] He insisted that the delegation should have brought the treaty back to Dublin and the Dáil for discussion and debate before it had been signed. On the floor of the Dáil he denounced the treaty as the surrender of Irish independence. Around these poles of opinion swirled contentious and heated debates as the Dáil became a theatre for recriminations between treaty supporters and their opponents. The close vote in the Dáil in approving the treaty (only 64:57) on 7 January 1922 was prophetic. The split decision soon led to civil war that cost the lives of many of Ireland's potential leaders and left an enduring legacy of bitterness and despair.

The role of Lloyd George throughout the Irish crisis must now be examined more closely to ascertain his role in achieving, if not closure, at least a temporary settlement of the Irish question. Historians – as well as his contemporaries – have often praised him. Packer believes that the treaty was one of Lloyd George's 'greatest triumphs'.[124] Rowland goes further, claiming the settlement was 'the greatest triumph of Lloyd George's career'.[125] Boyce also praises Lloyd George's 'success in settling the Irish question'.[126] Pugh hails it as 'a triumph indeed.[127] Morgan essentially agrees, calling Lloyd George 'the great peacemaker'.[128] Mansergh sums up the general relief felt in Britain. With the important exception of diehard Unionists, the treaty 'was acclaimed … as a political triumph without parallel in recent British history'.[129]

But other historians have queried Lloyd George's methods. Mansergh, though he notes the general public approbation of the treaty in Britain, believes that the Prime Minister misled the Irish leaders on the Boundary Commission, one of the most important negotiating ploys used on the British side. It appears that the idea for such a commission was originally advanced by Sir James Craig as early as December 1919 during the negotiations preparatory to the Government of Ireland Act of 1920. The commission would decide the precise delimitation of the borders to be created by the proposed act and thus act as a device for tidying up and clarifying the boundary between the six Ulster counties and the remainder of Ireland to the South. Lloyd George, as we have seen, presented the Commission as a body which might well favour the southern Irish in any future border rectifications.[130] But Foster thinks that 'a certain amount of Lloyd Georgian chicanery' was at work when the Prime Minister persuaded the Irish delegates that a Boundary Commission could serve their own interests.[131] McColgan also deplores the Prime Minister's 'chicanery' in forcing the Irish to sign the treaty.[132] Bew believes that, in another example of the Prime Minister's bad faith, Lloyd George was merely bluffing in his intimations of resuming military action against the Irish if the treaty were not signed.[133] Perhaps harshest of all is Hopkinson, who doubts that Lloyd George 'merited the favourable press he has generally received on the Irish Question'. Indeed, throughout the Prime Minister's peace initiatives, he 'acted deviously and inconsistently'.[134] Jackson, too, implies some doubt about Lloyd George's handling of the Boundary Commission: it was, he writes, 'one of the more startling examples of Lloyd George's ingenuity'.[135] Jackson's overall observations on the Anglo-Irish Treaty negotiations may stand in summary of the critics when he writes that Lloyd George has often been seen as 'duplicitous and histrionic, and altogether too wily a bird for the honest Irish negotiators'.[136]

If this skein of historical discord can be sufficiently unravelled, we may suggest that in fact Lloyd George pursued a reasonably consistent policy towards Ireland. His record was not spotless. It must be borne in mind that he often encountered unexpected twists and turns and he frequently was forced to react to circumstances well beyond his control. So many issues involving so many constituencies meant that an imperfect resolution was inevitable. First of all, there was the division between Ulster and Southern Nationalist Ireland. Political and sectarian issues, centuries in the making, were at the heart of the antagonism between North and South. For Ulster, events of recent years had been especially troubling. The Easter Rising, the conscriptionist controversy and the rise of militancy in the South (especially the IRA) were enough to make them fearful of any formal association with the South. For Southern Ireland, the militaristic actions in Ulster against the pre-war Home Rule movement and the British government's tepid response had sown the seeds of mistrust. Additional complications also exacerbated tensions within each of these two political divisions. In predominantly Protestant Ulster, a significant Catholic minority, sympathetic with southern aspirations, created a substantial sense of unease and danger among Unionists. In the South, a dominant independent, nationalist and Catholic Ireland seemed to threaten the much smaller Protestant minority. How all these conflicting fears and aspirations might be met was the supreme challenge to Lloyd George and the government.

Lloyd George's approach was one that he had employed innumerable times during his career as a deal maker. While holding fast to a core of objectives, he posed publicly as an impartial mediator between differing parties and positions, holding no brief for either Ulster or Southern Ireland. He broke down the contending groups into their constituent parts in order to negotiate separately with each, thus becoming the essential source of information to all sides. He also employed outside sources to exert influence upon the opposing groups. Such sources might be members of the government, putative disinterested parties or influence peddlers such as newspaper proprietors. How each of these was utilized may be briefly outlined below.

We have noted above that Lloyd George met privately with Michael Collins during the final stages of the negotiations in December. Indeed, this had been Lloyd George's tactic throughout the negotiations. In November, Lloyd George (often accompanied with one or more Cabinet members) met frequently with either Arthur Griffith alone or with Griffith and Michael Collins.[137] Tom Jones was an invaluable emissary: he, too, was frequently in direct contact especially with Griffith. This was characteristic of the so-called sub-conference system by which individual topics, such as naval and financial questions, could be discussed more intensively; but it also provided the opportunity for Lloyd George to set Griffith and Collins apart from the rest of the Irish delegation. By such a stratagem, Lloyd George excluded the more extreme republicans from these smaller sessions. The most vehement republican, Childers, attended only one sub-conference meeting; Barton, another republican, attended only a few. Griffith and Collins, on the other hand, attended separately or together all 24 sub-conferences as well as various meetings with other British Cabinet members. They also met with Tom Jones several times.[138]

Lloyd George also attempted to sway the Irish delegates by proxy. This is best illustrated by his recruitment of C.P. Scott as an intercessor with Michael Collins. The Prime Minister engaged Scott, well known for his Irish sympathies, in late October 1921 to impress upon Collins his disappointment with the negotiations. 'He had great difficulty', as Scott reported the Prime Minister's remarks in his diary, 'in bringing them to the point'. Although he found Griffith 'quite reasonable', Lloyd George confided to Scott, he thought Childers 'the villain of the piece', always working against concession. The Prime Minister was nevertheless determined – 'if it were possible' – to see the negotiations through and to secure peace.[139] But if he could not obtain allegiance to the Crown, as well as an acceptable naval agreement, there 'would be nothing for it' but to fight. To that end, he was willing to send thousands of additional troops to Ireland.

Immediately after this conversation with Lloyd George, Scott telephoned for an appointment with Collins. At their meeting, Scott defended Lloyd George as a statesman who was intent upon settling the Irish question. Then he pressed Collins on the question of allegiance to the Crown; but Collins remained noncommittal. The following morning, Scott went to Chequers where he found the Prime Minister still in bed at 10:30 but hard at work reading papers and drafting reports. So little encouragement from Collins only prompted another stern warning from the Prime Minister: 'though he hated the policy of force he would not shrink from it'.[140] A few weeks later, Scott again served as a middleman. Lunching with Lloyd George on 2 December, Scott listened to complaints about Irish intractability. The government had 'made great concessions', but Sinn Féin had made few. 'If there was not settlement', the Prime Minister once again warned, 'there must be coercion'.[141] That evening, Scott again called on Collins, explaining his mission as one designed 'to save the situation'.[142] Childers, who was also present, was not encouraging. He ruled out any Irish allegiance to the King and appeared to dismiss any prospect that Ireland would accept Dominion status. Collins seemed to agree. Thus negotiations appeared to be deadlocked on the eve of the final signing of the treaty itself.

What effect Scott's intercession may have had is unclear. What is clear is Lloyd George's intention – to impress upon the Irish his determination to continue the war unless Ireland agreed to some fundamental demands. It could still be argued that the Prime Minister was bluffing. But his ultimatum on 5 December certainly reinforced his apparent determination to secure an agreement under the threat of force. Both Griffith and Collins (who by then were already leaning towards signing the treaty) were persuaded that the Prime Minister meant business if the treaty talks should fail.

As the Prime Minister worked tirelessly for concessions from the Irish delegates, he was also shoring up support from moderate coalition Conservatives while simultaneously actively combating the more intransigent diehard Unionists. He beat back a vote of censure in the House of Commons and won a vote of confidence at a Conservative Party conference in Liverpool on 17 November. As was common throughout the treaty-making process, he employed surrogates to lobby for the treaty. For example, he commissioned Sir Robert Bruce, editor of the *Glasgow Herald*, to keep both Bonar Law and Carson informed of the negotiations. Although Carson remained antagonistic, Bonar Law seems to have regained some confidence in Lloyd George's managing of the negotiations.[143] And of course he kept the lines of communication and negotiation open with that most obdurate Unionist, Sir James Craig. Thus Lloyd George had been able to ease the minds of many Conservatives who were fearful of the fate of Ulster. Lloyd George understood that the once fierce Conservative Unionist onslaught against pre-war Liberal Home Rule plans had altered completely. Unionists who had previously challenged constitutional procedures and had even threatened an armed insurrection against Home Rule had been chastened by the upheavals of war, the conscription controversy and the Easter Rising. No longer was it possible to bind Southern Ireland to Britain as it had been in the past. The general feeling among many Conservatives was that the question of Ireland must now be settled on the best terms possible. This meant acceptance of some form of Home Rule for both Ulster and Southern Ireland.[144] There was also a substantial political gain for the Conservatives in loosening the bonds of nationalist Ireland, as Lloyd George surely knew. Dominion status for Southern Ireland meant that Irish MPs who had traditionally supported Liberals would now have their own Parliament in Dublin and would no longer be a thorn in Conservative sides at Westminster.[145]

Lloyd George's use of surrogates, private information channels, newspaper leaks, public statements and negotiations all round carried the peace process forward. As a whirling dervish of diplomatic and political activity, Lloyd George seemed to have established a kind of controlled chaos. Not in every case did he enjoy success, however. Perhaps the most significant example, and one that has earned opprobrium from that day to this, was his proposed Boundary Commission. It will be remembered that the commission's task was to settle the boundary between Ulster and Southern Ireland with the aim, as the southern Irish delegates understood it, of transferring some areas of Ulster to the South should Ulster refuse to join an all-Irish unitary state.[146] In spite of repeated efforts by Lloyd George, however, Ulster resisted efforts to force a union with the South. For them, the risks were too great. Protestant Ulster and its Unionist traditions would inevitably become subordinate to an alien Catholic culture and religion. For the southern Irish delegates, this could be a deal-breaker: Irish unity was a preeminent goal. Moreover, Lloyd George reinforced the notion of boundary modification – even if Ulster refused – by his private promise to Michael Collins on 4 December on the eve of the treaty signing.

To break the deadlock and to ensure that both sides would be willing to accept the commission, Lloyd George apparently made contradictory promises: one to Collins as we have seen; but one also to Craig in which he stated that the commission would be even-handed in its allocations. Any Ulster land assigned to the South by the commission would be balanced by placing equal amounts of southern territory in the North.[147] These divergent promises were apparently discovered by Collins and Craig themselves when the two Irish leaders met in conference in February 1922 to discuss the ramifications of the new treaty. At that meeting, as Hopkinson has shown, the two men found out that Lloyd George had 'by dubious methods' given 'completely different impressions to the northern and southern leadership' as to how much territory was to be involved in any border changes.[148] Given the later unfortunate history of the Commission, Ulster's refusal to accept it and its final demise in 1925, it is not surprising that Lloyd George's role in sponsoring it should have come into question. Yet it seems likely that without the inclusion of the commission in the Anglo-Irish negotiations, the treaty as a whole would not have been signed. Perhaps Lloyd George, knowing this, and realizing that the treaty was as good as could be devised, was willing to fudge the issue. In effect, he consigned the resolution of this contentious problem to be solved at a later date by the contesting parties. He simply washed his hands of the matter. If it is not always clear whether or not Lloyd George engaged in sharp practice to gain an end, in this case, the proof seems convincing.

Once the treaty had been signed, it was fervently hoped by the British government that Ireland's problems were now Ireland's to solve. Dublin Castle was packed up and evacuated. A new Civic Guard replaced British troops and police. But peace in Ireland did not follow. The unsettled border between Ulster and nationalist Ireland was the scene of murder, arson and kidnapping as an emboldened IRA raided nearby Protestant loyalist communities. Within Ulster, Protestant paramilitary forces committed murders and outrages against the Catholic minority. In Southern Ireland, the new Provisional Government of Ireland encountered its most severe trial when staunch anti-treaty Republicans proved recalcitrant and were determined to overthrow the Anglo-Irish agreement.[149] The Republican aim was asserted militarily and symbolically on 14 April 1922 when a band of Irish republicans took over the Four Courts (the Dublin courts) – a clear challenge to the pro-treaty Provisional government. Given the strong, though not dominant sentiment against the treaty, Collins and the pro-treaty supporters felt an obligation to take into account these sentiments. Moreover, Collins knew well enough that even some of the pro-treaty votes during the critical Dáil debates on the treaty in December 1921 had been given with reservations.[150] In a pact with the anti-treatyites, therefore, the Provisional government accepted a proposed constitution which pushed to the limits their previous agreement with the British government. Dropping the oath of allegiance to the Crown, they seemed to retract their pledge to remain within the Commonwealth. They also claimed the right of making their own treaties, and refused to recognize Ulster's special position within Ireland. An electoral pact concluded at the same time provided for the establishment of a coalition government, including anti-treatyite members.

These actions were unacceptable to the British government: in late May Collins and Griffith were summoned to London for a conference to resolve this issue.[151] Other matters discussed included a review of IRA activities in Ulster. Under pressure from the British, the Irish delegates agreed that the treaty should take precedence over any Irish constitution. The meeting was not harmonious and signalled a deepening suspicion between Britain and the Irish. Indeed, for several months past the British government had been watching Irish events with mounting alarm. Chamberlain's sense of foreboding about Ireland (in a letter to his sister) was representative: 'I am', he wrote, 'very anxious about Ireland'.[152] There was in fact some confusion in the government over what actions should be taken. Lloyd George's absence may have been critical: he was away at an international conference in Genoa from mid-April for several weeks and had left to Churchill the responsibility for implementing the treaty. Churchill's inclination was to take a hard line in response to any perceived Irish backsliding. As Tom Jones recorded with some alarm in his diary, Churchill was so disappointed with Irish affairs that he wanted 'to pull the whole plant out of the ground'.[153]

Matters worsened when Sir Henry Wilson was assassinated on 22 June as he was approaching his London house in Eaton Square. His killers, two members of a London branch of the IRA, were quickly apprehended and tried: the jury took three minutes to reach a guilty verdict. So convicted, they were hanged within six weeks. Wilson, who had recently resigned his position as Chief of the Imperial General Staff to become an Ulster MP (North Down), was a severe critic of both the Lloyd George policy in Ireland and of the newly formed Irish government. Wilson's strong and public support for Ulster was undoubtedly the reason for his murder. Wilson's death prompted a quick government response. Churchill in particular was spurred to action: he demanded that the Irish Provisional government launch an immediate attack upon the Republican-held Four Courts. On 28 June, military forces of the Provisional government mounted an offensive, and two days later the Republicans surrendered.

These internecine struggles were a reflection of the continuing dialogue between opposing parties wrestling with the conditions imposed by the treaty. How the Irish could reconcile their aspirations with British demands was proving difficult. A resort to arms was perhaps an inevitable consequence. Thereafter, the two opposing sides in Southern Ireland, the Provisional government and the Republicans, were locked into a fratricidal war.[154] As in any civil war, families were divided, and loyalties tested. The toll taken among the leadership was particularly deadly. Among the casualties were the pro-treaty Michael Collins, assassinated while on military tour in West Cork in August 1922; and the Republican and anti-treaty Erskine Childers, executed in November for carrying a concealed weapon. Only gradually did the better armed Provisional troops gain ground; but a truce between warring parties did not emerge until May 1923. After the Four Courts episode the British government remained largely aloof from Irish matters. As one Irish historian has summed it up, the government 'was able to take a comfortable back seat during the Civil War'.[155]

16

'TO STRAIGHTEN RAGGED EDGES'

For Lloyd George, the release of Ireland to its own devices provided an opportunity to play a larger role on a global stage. Under the Prime Minister's guidance, Britain after the war had begun a robust interventionist foreign policy, harnessed to a vigorous concept of dynamic diplomacy through the instrumentality of frequent summit meetings.[1] That Lloyd George's was the active brain and hand behind this policy is generally agreed.[2] In fact, the Prime Minister had, since his accession to power in 1916, gradually been drawing together the reigns of authority in diplomatic affairs by assuming the duties of the Foreign Office. By the end of the war, the Foreign Office came to believe that it had become 'simply a rubber stamp' for the government.[3] Foreign Secretaries in the Cabinet bore the immediate brunt of Lloyd George's minimizing of their functions. Balfour, who was Foreign Secretary from 1916–19, seems to have taken this in his stride. Although he attended numerous sessions of the War Cabinet, he was never a member and was quite willing that Lloyd George take the lead in foreign affairs.

Curzon, however, who succeeded Balfour in 1919, was less happy with the diminution of the power and prestige of the Foreign Secretary's office. Lloyd George's insistence that the Foreign Office remain secondary after the war was especially galling to Curzon, a former Viceroy to India who had a reputation of overweening self regard and prickliness. Curzon also had reservations about the influence of Lloyd George's private secretariat (the 'Garden Suburb') and the Cabinet Secretariat (headed by Hankey), both of which continued in the postwar era as the primary cadre for advice and implementation of foreign policy. As one of Curzon's early biographers has noted, these amateur experts with their devoted loyalty to the Prime Minister had 'a most unsettling effect' upon Curzon's 'sensitive and egocentric' nature.[4] Personal relations between Curzon and Lloyd George were thus often strained. Indeed, it seems that Lloyd George intentionally bullied Curzon in Cabinet meetings and was often publicly rude to him.[5]

In the main, then, Lloyd George's diplomacy by conference simply ignored the Foreign Office. His suspicions of the Foreign Office were likely based upon his belief that it was 'hidebound' and that it reflected the views of the 'reactionary, possessing classes' who hoped for a return to the pre-1914 days.[6] Thus, Lloyd George's pursuit of an independent postwar foreign policy was in part a reaction against the titled and privileged world that he had for so long struggled against. And, in fact, this was how he presented his 'new diplomacy'. It would be a diplomacy shorn of its secretive meetings and elitist participation. It would also be a diplomacy open to public discussion and examination led by freely elected public officials representative of the people. Frequent meetings at the highest levels would set agendas and pursue specific aims, thus ensuring a focused attention and a greater likelihood of success. President Wilson had most famously articulated these ideals during the final years of the war; but their most notable advocate and practitioner in postwar Europe was Lloyd George. The British Prime Minister faced formidable hurdles, however. In spite of his hopes for peace after the Treaty of Versailles, small wars continued along the Polish and Russian borders, in the Middle East and in the Balkans. In addition, some of the significant issues that had been postponed during the peace conference – such as reparations for Germany – continued to nag into the 1920s.

Undaunted by the continued international uncertainties, Lloyd George pursued his personal diplomacy with 'prodigious energy' throughout the 'dizzying round' of summit meetings and conferences that dotted the European landscape from 1919 onward.[7] Morgan testifies to Lloyd George's 'unprecedented' role as a British Prime Minister in promoting so extensively diplomacy by conference.[8] Pugh believes that with his talent for making compromises, Lloyd George 'found his apotheosis' at the various international conferences.[9] But Lloyd George also has his critics in this dynamic and high-profile postwar approach to foreign relations. Gordon A. Craig deplored Lloyd George's 'cavalier treatment' of the British Foreign Office. Lloyd George's 'deficiencies' and 'eccentricities' in his diplomatic practices 'had unfortunate results'.[10] McKercher thinks that the Prime Minister can legitimately be accused of 'meddling' because he 'arrogated' control of foreign policy for himself; appointed 'his friends and political cronies' to important diplomatic posts; and carried out his diplomacy through the agency of 'hand-picked dilettantes'.[11] Dockrill and Goold have also condemned Lloyd George's 'peculiar brand of peripatetic diplomacy'.[12]

An appeal to the numerous conferences and meetings – some two dozen in all – which Lloyd George attended throughout 1919–22 may help in any evaluation of his effectiveness as a world leader in postwar diplomacy. The necessity for so many meetings might at first seem surprising, given the recent lengthy and gruelling Paris Peace Conference. But the conference had raised as many issues as it had settled. New nations and new problems jostled with the old nations and their traditional rivalries. In addition, some Peace Conference problems, such as reparations, had been postponed to a later date and could no longer be delayed. The consequence was that the immediate postwar years were a time of instability rather than the anticipated settled relations among European states.

Sadly enough, the two most significant wartime allies, Britain and France, were unable to bridge their differences sufficiently to forge a unified front in solving these problems. For France, strategic security was paramount and a weak Germany was the key to this aim.[13] Thus French diplomacy focused on a rigidly enforced reparations schedule from Germany. France continued to insist that Germany, in spite of its straightened resources, was perfectly capable of paying reparations. A depleted treasury and a rightful sense of grievance – having borne most of the fighting on its own soil – fuelled French demands. Great Britain, under Lloyd George's leadership, was less interested in burdening the German economy with substantial reparations. Britain preferred to integrate Germany into the European states system as soon as possible by promoting postwar economic reconstruction. Once Germany was on its feet, reparations could then be levied more realistically. This of course ran directly counter to France's attempt to keep Germany economically weak as a means of deterring the revival of Germany's military power. Britain's inability to resolve those fears and to understand the French position added to the alienation between the two powers.

Tensions between France and Britain were apparent in the early postwar conferences. The new French Premier, Alexandre Millerand, the leader of an anti-German Conservative coalition, had displaced Clemenceau during the elections of October 1919. It was soon clear that he was determined not only to force the pace on German reparations, but also to react quickly to any suspected German employment of its military beyond the most limited circumstances. Particularly galling to the French was the German delay in delivering substantial amounts of coal in compensation for mines destroyed by the German army in 1918.[14] At a London meeting of the Allied leadership in February and March 1920 Millerand demanded (but was refused) an occupation of the Ruhr to force Germany to pay scheduled reparations. By then, French anti-German policy had become an irritant to British policy makers. Hankey confessed to his diary in late March 1920 that 'we are at loggerheads with the French. They never seem able to see eye to eye with us anywhere'.[15] An example soon gave point to Hankey's complaint. On 3 April, German troops marched into the Ruhr demilitarized zone to put down communist insurgents. In retaliation, French troops occupied several German cities in a show of force. Most importantly, the French had acted without informing British officials. Caught flat-footed, Lloyd George, meeting with the Cabinet a few days later, roundly condemned the French incursion as 'a very serious departure' from Anglo-French agreements to preserve unity among the Allies in order to solve postwar problems.[16] Curzon was fully supportive of his chief: he thought that the French were 'making difficulties at every turn'.[17] Moreover, he was concerned that the forthcoming Allied meeting at San Remo, Italy, in late April had been placed in jeopardy by France's unilateral action.

Curzon's apprehensions about San Remo were at first fully realized.[18] With the Ruhr incident hanging heavily overhead, the initial talks between Lloyd George and Millerand were, as Hankey put it, 'the reverse of cordial'.[19] There was an immediate conflict between Millerand and Lloyd George over reparations, with the former demanding a payment on account while the latter insisted first upon the need for an established lump sum total. Riddell, who was also present, recorded in his diary that Lloyd George was 'very anti-French' upon his arrival at San Remo, and that a 'terrible hullabaloo' between British and French representatives had ensued.[20] Fortunately for all parties, tempers cooled, but the conference was unable to resolve the reparations issue. Nevertheless, there emerged some constructive agreement from an imperial point of view. The Middle Eastern mandates of Syria, Palestine and Iraq were allocated, and an Anglo-French oil agreement in the region divided further the spoils of war. The French also agreed to withdraw from the German towns they had invested. And perhaps most importantly, Millerand accepted the principle of a fixed sum for reparations payments.[21]

Over the next few months, conferences at Hythe, Boulogne and Spa also discussed reparations. In addition, meetings between French and British financial experts were at work. Proposals and counter proposals flew back and forth. There were some positive results. Reparations were scaled back. Germany's first reparations payment of a billion gold marks was made during the summer of 1921. An agreement on reparations to be paid in kind followed. However, skies darkened later that year when the German government informed the Reparations Committee in December 1921 that it could not pay the required reparations instalments due early in 1922. Given France's predisposition to use force in the face of German intransigence, Lloyd George warned the French that should they invade the Ruhr in retaliation, the Anglo-French alliance would be at an end.[22] Other issues further soured relations between the two allies. Britain was concerned at the support France gave Poland during the Russo-Polish War in 1920. France in turn was miffed at the Anglo-Russian trade talks and the Trade Agreement of April 1921. Tensions between the two countries over their conflicting aims in the Middle East remained high.[23] Diplomatic strains were not immediately eased even when the left-leaning Aristide Briand replaced Millerand as Prime Minister in 1921. By the end of the year, however, both sides had determined to reverse the slide in the entente.[24] In late December 1921, Lloyd George and Briand met for high-level discussions in London in the hope of settling all outstanding issues between the two countries. France was especially interested in a regional security treaty that would essentially restore the entente. These conversations led to further discussions at Cannes the following week.

During the Cannes Conference Lloyd George proved quite willing to act amicably with France on outstanding issues such as establishing a common ground in the Near East. He also advocated cooperation on seeking solutions to economic recovery. But he insisted that economic renewal should be a project in common with all the major world powers. This would also include those pariah nations, Germany and the Soviet Union. Lloyd George was especially intent upon granting a moratorium to Germany, honouring its request for a delay in payments.[25] No less important was the role of the Soviet Union in European reconstruction. In his opening speech to the conference, Lloyd George set out conditions for the Soviets if they wished to participate in the European community and especially if they hoped to receive aid for their flagging economy. These included a guarantee of property rights of investors; an obligation to restore or compensate property owners for any confiscation; and cessation of all subversive propaganda against other nations.

There was an air of suspended animation about the Cannes Conference since no definite agreements emerged; but there was one important result – that a broader

based conference should be held at Genoa in the spring of 1922. Often hailed as
the world's first economic summit, the Genoa Conference hoped for a resolution to
postwar problems relating to international trade. Representatives from 34 nations
whose every move was followed by an enormous press corps assured worldwide
interest in the proceedings.[26] Lloyd George has been called the 'spiritual father' of
the Genoa Conference; but he was also the Chairman of the Board, dominating
the proceedings as the conference wound its complex way towards a turbulent
conclusion.[27] Whatever success or failure the conference might achieve would
inevitably be laid at Lloyd George's door.

The conference began on 10 April 1922. Lloyd George had arrived two days
earlier with his wife and daughter, Megan. His official party included Sir Robert
Horne, Chancellor of the Exchequer; Sir Laming Worthington-Evans, Secretary
for War; Sylvester and Grigg as secretaries; and the indispensable Hankey. The
conference centre was the Palazzo San Giorgio where Lloyd George opened the
proceedings with a speech that pleaded for 'a real peace' in Europe. He deplored
what he called a 'canine clamour' among the European nations. Expanding on this
homely metaphor, he declared that there were too many dogs in too many countries
'who imagine the louder they bark the deeper the impression they make of their
ferocity and determination'. But this only 'rattles the nerves of a nerve-ruined
continent'. This conference, he continued, must 'stop the snarling'. Europe must
find 'rest, quiet, tranquillity – that is, it needs peace'.[28]

Since the ostensible goal of the conference was the economic reconstruction
of postwar Europe, important commissions were quickly established to study
such topics as currency, credit, transport and finance. Soon, however, political and
diplomatic issues became dominant. The simmering Anglo-French discord had
continued to rise near boiling point since Cannes. Lloyd George resisted a security
alliance with France, fearing that it would strengthen French recalcitrance against
Germany. Lloyd George was rather more interested in discussions with the Soviet
delegates. In his mind, Anglo-Soviet talks at Genoa could be the culmination of a
lengthy process of accommodation between the two powers that had begun during
the trade talks, culminating in the Trade Agreement of 1921.

So much hard bargaining and patience expended by the British delegation went
unrewarded, however. Within a week after the Genoa Conference had opened came
the news of a secret treaty between the Soviet Union and Germany signed under the
very noses of the conferees. The treaty – named for the Italian city of Rapallo, near
which the Soviet delegation was housed – established full diplomatic and consular
relations between the two countries.[29] Thus, their treaty went well beyond the more
limited economic agreements of the Anglo-Soviet Trade Agreement of the previous
year. The treaty repudiated all claims for war costs and damages of both countries.
Equally significant was the Soviet Union's renunciation of any claims against
Germany sanctioned by the Treaty of Versailles. Furthermore, Germany waived any
claims that its citizens might make against Soviet expropriation of their property.
The treaty in effect wiped the slate clean of the political consequences of war and
revolution between these two countries.

Conferees were bewildered at the news of the treaty. After all, Genoa was to have been a European effort at addressing postwar reconstruction. Having accepted the aims of Genoa and reinforcing that acceptance by their presence, Germany and the Soviet Union suddenly opted out of the conference, placing their own interests above all others. Yet it was widely known that Germany and the Soviet Union had been drawing closer together since Versailles.[30] After an initial period of nearly a year and a half, during which Germany attempted to reach an agreement with the Allied powers, Germany had turned East. Germany had been a substantial trading partner with Russia in pre-war days and was eager to resume that role. The Soviets, in their mode of reaching out for potential allies, were responsive. By September 1921, military negotiations had also begun. The German General Staff was particularly interested in finding ways of circumventing the restrictions imposed upon the German military by the Treaty of Versailles. In return, Germany would assist in the development of the Soviet armaments industry.

All in all, the Rapallo Treaty can be viewed as the re-establishment of normal relations between the Soviet Union and Germany, fulfilling each country's immediate economic and militarily needs. Viewed in this light, there is a sense of inevitability in the accord between the two countries. This was of little comfort to the Allied powers, especially Britain and France. As the prime mover of the conference, Lloyd George was placed in a particularly difficult position by Rapallo. Indeed, he seems at first to have been, as one historian has noted, 'angry and bewildered' by the treaty.[31] Nevertheless, as another historian has observed, after the initial shock, Lloyd George 'doggedly pressed on' with the conference.[32] Too much was at stake to disband the conference: perhaps a reprimand for such an egregious example of diplomatic discourtesy would suffice. But others were less forgiving. The French had been dubious about the prospects of Genoa even before the conference opened. Poincaré had sent Louis Barthou, Minister of Justice, as the French envoy, with instructions to block any British concessions to either Germany or the Soviet Union. Rapallo only convinced them even more of the danger of a revived German Reich.[33]

As the news spread that a secret mutual security pact was at the heart of Rapallo, Lloyd George acted firmly. A private meeting with members of the German delegation was, as Hankey noted, 'rather stormy' when the Germans refused to withdraw from the treaty as Lloyd George proposed.[34] Nor did the Soviets capitulate. For the remaining five weeks of the conference there was a sense of growing disappointment.[35] Some delegates departed early. The smaller powers in attendance began to lose interest. Among the major parties remaining, attitudes hardened. France made it known that it would leave the conference should there be any further attempts to make concessions to either Germany or the Soviet Union. The French delegation was also suspicious – even fearful – that Britain was contemplating a formal recognition of the Bolshevik government. The Soviet Union, perhaps emboldened by Rapallo, was less inclined to offer concessions to secure de jure recognition. Thus any possibility of a repayment of foreign debts, particularly private ones, and the restoration of private property expropriated by the Bolshevik government were once again put on hold. Lloyd George attempted palliative measures. He negotiated nonstop.[36] He engineered an important memorandum (the 2 May memorandum) by which the Allies would establish relations with the new Soviet state. He recommended a commission, meeting at The Hague within a month's time, which would re-examine the complicated matter of debts and the allocation of private property.[37] He suggested a non-aggression pact of conference members to guarantee peace in the meantime.

But Lloyd George's attempts at conciliation were unsuccessful. The conference itself and Lloyd George's role in it has been criticized in varying degrees by most historians. Some have administered only mild reproofs. A.J.P. Taylor, for example, an admirer of Lloyd George, observed merely that the Prime Minister emerged 'empty-handed' from Genoa.[38] Although Keith Robbins recognizes Genoa as the apotheosis of Lloyd George's personal diplomacy, he wonders whether or not this method of settling disputes was necessary.[39] Stephen White, whose main purpose is to summarize the events of the conference, believes that its direct results were 'distinctly modest'.[40] Other historians have been harsher in their judgement. McDougall blames Lloyd George for the misconstrued idea of Genoa as a means of advancing European reconstruction and condemns outright the 'disastrous result of Lloyd George's personal policy'.[41] Bruce Kent considers Lloyd George's reconstruction plans a 'pipe-dream' and denounces the Genoa Conference as memorable 'chiefly for demonstrating the absurdity of Lloyd George's contention that European reconstruction could precede a provisional resolution of the reparation problem'.[42] G.H. Bennett is succinct: Genoa was a 'dramatic failure'.[43] Furthermore, having 'achieved little' at Genoa, Lloyd George extended his failure to the succeeding conference at The Hague from May to July 1922.[44] P.M.H. Bell echoes Bennett: Genoa ended in 'complete failure'.[45] Andrew Williams charges Lloyd George with arrogance; and, more definitively, Williams believes that the conference revealed him to be a 'wizard with declining powers'.[46] Morgan, usually sympathetic, admits that the conference was 'fruitless' and 'yielded no decision on any major question'. It was, he additionally notes, 'a noble failure, but failure nevertheless'.[47] Tom Jones, a staunch defender of his former chief, only admitted to an 'inconclusive' conference: one could judge its failure or success 'according to the tests applied'.[48] He was more certain that Lloyd George had held the conference together as long as it lasted by 'his undefeatable spirit, his inexhaustible good humour, resilient temperament, [and] amazing patience'.[49]

Fink, who has written widely on Genoa, is more balanced than most in assessing blame. She believes that the important causes for its failure included 'Soviet intransigence, French nervousness, German perfidy' and 'American aloofness'. She nevertheless claims that 'the critical factor' was Lloyd George's methods – such as an 'unrealistically' large agenda and a 'haphazard' organization.[50] Giving full credit to Lloyd George's talents of energy and insight, flexibility and persuasiveness, Fink faults his overconfidence in attempting to master the complexities of such a large and inevitably divided conference. In a later evaluation, Fink extols the conference as a 'daring' enterprise, but one that was also 'improvisational and flawed'. Lloyd George she sees as 'astute and pragmatic', but also at times 'weary and churlish', which had the effect of alienating potential allies to his programme.[51] Cohrs, too, thinks that Lloyd George's 'abortive scheme' for European reconstruction 'foundered' at Genoa; but it had done so in part because of French intransigence over reparations and its insistence upon a mutual defence pact with Britain.[52] In addition, the refusal of the United States – 'the world's new main creditor' – to participate in the conference, hindered Lloyd George's plan for European economic reconstruction.[53] The most recent evaluation, that of Zara Steiner, also lays a heavy burden at Lloyd George's door: he had 'overreached himself; and his 'grand design was far too ambitious and ended in failure'.[54] She, too, believes that the conference 'proved to be a total failure'.[55] But Steiner, like Fink and Cohrs, also alludes to extenuating circumstances. Lloyd George was hindered in some measure by his domestic opposition. He could not, for example, offer outright de jure recognition to the Soviet Union, which might have averted Rapallo. Lloyd George's hopes to ease reparation payments for Germany were torpedoed first by French resistance and then by the impact of Rapallo. In the face of such difficulties, Steiner believes that Lloyd George did his best to salvage the conference: 'he swallowed his own dismay and sought to contain the diplomatic damage'.[56]

In reviewing the most recent accounts of Genoa, there is a sense that historians, while not exonerating Lloyd George's dubious role, have been discovering that he alone was not responsible for its failure. Genoa in fact represents the climax of a process begun in the early days of Lloyd George's wartime government. It was essential for the Prime Minister to assume primary direction of the war. So centralized, the Prime Minister's office could save time by expediting decisions made quickly with a handful of advisers, some of whom (as in the Garden Suburb) were outside the purview of such traditional bodies as the Foreign Office. Once the war had ended, the Paris Peace Conference continued the practice of a strong negotiating role for the Prime Minister in settling the enormous problems of peace. The Treaty of Versailles had to be enforced or adjusted to postwar realities. This was the intent of the postwar conferences.[57] In this sense, Lloyd George was merely continuing the practice of a dominant role for a British Prime Minister who attempted to manage traditional conflicts in a new guise. There were some successes but also significant failures – Genoa being one of them.

In contrast to the postwar conference system designed to thrash out the benefits and international consequences of the Paris Peace Conference, Lloyd George's Middle East policy was more intent upon preserving solely British interests and securing where possible British territorial advantage – most especially at the expense of the Ottoman Empire. The line of his thought was fully demonstrated as early as January 1915, when Lloyd George (then Chancellor of the Exchequer) submitted a memorandum to the CID, which called for a military expedition to protect the Suez Canal from Turkish military incursions. In March of that year he additionally suggested to the War Council that Britain establish territorial claims upon the postwar Ottoman Empire. To that end, he advocated expeditious action to carry out British intentions.[58] Churchill tended to support Lloyd George; but other Cabinet members were less certain – Asquith and Gray, for example, were in opposition.[59]

Unable to decide, Asquith appointed a high level committee in April 1915 to develop a programme of British desiderata in the Middle East. Chaired by Sir Maurice de Bunsen, a former minister in the British embassy at Vienna, the Committee filed its report six weeks later. Arguing in favour of extending British territorial claims, the Committee justified its conclusions by stating that although the British Empire was 'wide enough already', it was necessary 'to consolidate the possessions we already have' and 'to take advantage of the present opportunity ... to straighten ragged edges'.[60] The report explored various options of territorial aggrandizement such as partitioning, spheres of influence and annexation. It ultimately recommended the development of decentralized systems of administration guided by British authorities.[61]

Although the de Bunsen report never received official approval, it nevertheless provided the rationale for a continuation of existing imperial holdings and justified as well an energetic pursuit of new and enlarged areas of British influence. Indeed, as John Darwin has argued, British imperial policy after World War I showed no loss of vigour, though it often operated in subtle ways, maintaining its authority under the guise of a benevolent supervision.[62] Egypt provides an instructive example. Because of its strategic importance, Egypt – which had gradually been brought under informal British control during the late nineteenth century – fell under enhanced British authority once the Ottoman Empire joined the Central Powers in late 1914. Egypt thus became a British protectorate.[63] Other parts of the Ottoman Empire also offered tempting plums to be plucked should the Allies achieve victory in the field. Lloyd George was fully aware of the possibilities. Hankey records a conversation with the Prime Minister in early October 1918, a conversation he described as 'very interesting discussion about the cutting up of Turkey'. Lloyd George took 'a very *intransigeant* [sic] attitude' in hoping for a lion's share of Turkish possessions.[64] Mesopotamia, Syria and Palestine were clearly up for grabs.

But Lloyd George realized that Britain could not act unilaterally in the Middle East. France would certainly have a say.[65] Given historic French cultural and economic connections with Syria, for example, British accommodation was essential in preserving an amicable relationship with its Entente partner. In 1916, therefore, Britain and France devised the (secret) Sykes-Picot Agreement creating separate spheres of influence in the Middle East between Britain and France, with some small concessions to Arab interests. Apart from the need to meet French demands in the Middle East, the British government was also well aware of an emerging nationalist movement during the war among the large indigenous Arab population which made up a significant part of the old Ottoman Empire. Should their allegiance be harnessed against the common Ottoman foe, the war might be shortened in the Eastern theatre. A series of contacts between Arab leaders and British authorities resulted in an apparent bargain: if the Arabs revolted against the Ottomans, Britain would assist. In addition, Britain pledged its support and protection to the establishment of an extensive and independent postwar Arabia, stretching from the Mediterranean Sea to the Persian Gulf. In a series of famous letters, this bargain was implicitly struck between Sir Henry McMahon, successor to Kitchener as the High Commissioner in Egypt, and Hussein ibn Ali, the Sherif and Emir of Mecca.[66]

In June 1916, Hussein's revolt in the Hejaz began. Britain made substantial contributions to the Arab war effort: some £11 million in gold; naval and air support; and a shipment of Muslim troops from the Egyptian army to reinforce Arab operations once the revolt was under way.[67] Although the revolt did not overthrow the Ottoman Empire, it was useful on a limited scale. Not surprisingly, Hussein reminded Britain of its part of the bargain – to sponsor an independent Arab nation. The Arabs were soon shocked to learn, however, that their trust in the European powers was misplaced. In 1917, the secret Sykes-Picot Agreement, which had already divided significant parts of the Middle East between Britain and France with little consideration for Arab aspirations, was made public by the new Bolshevik government. Its publication was clear evidence of Allied perfidy toward the Arabs.

Equally unsettling to Arab leaders was a secret plan to establish a homeland for the Jews in Palestine, an enterprise long advocated by articulate and persistent Zionists. Lloyd George himself was strongly in support of this idea. Some have suggested that the British occupation of the Holy Land appealed to Lloyd George's religious sensibilities. As a member of a dissenting sect, he may have been influenced by the Old Testament belief that the return of the Jews to the Promised Land of Palestine was an ancient and justifiable right of the Jewish people.[68] But as we might suspect, Lloyd George was probably motivated more by geopolitical aims. Indeed, most historians see his desire for a Jewish national presence in the region as primarily a cat's paw for British interests.[69] A Zionist presence in Palestine under British protection would help create a buffer zone between the Suez Canal to the South and French interests in Syria to the North.[70] Lloyd George undoubtedly also understood an equally important advantage of a mandated Palestine: the short route to India through the Canal would be given additional protection.

As we have seen, General Allenby had reinvigorated the Palestinian campaign after replacing General Murray in June 1917, promising to reach Jerusalem by the end of the year. With a watchful eye on Allenby's advances toward Palestine, and with a delicate sense of timing, Lloyd George and his supporters pressed the Zionist issue in Cabinet meetings. Lloyd George's 'brisk and decisive' leadership, assisted by Balfour as an able second in command, brought the matter to a successful conclusion in early November 1917.[71] On 9 November, the famous Balfour Declaration was made public in the form of a brief letter to Lord Rothschild, a prominent British spokesman for Zionism.[72] In it, Balfour declared that the British Cabinet officially viewed 'with favour' the establishment of a national home for the Jewish people in Palestine. In addition, the government would 'use their best endeavours to fulfill the achievement of this object'.[73] The Balfour Declaration thus officially sanctioned Palestine as a Jewish homeland. Allenby's capture of Jerusalem in December 1917, his Christmas gift to the nation, seemed to authenticate Lloyd George's Palestinian policy.

Meanwhile, Lloyd George was also busily orchestrating a press campaign throughout 1917 to drum up public support for a British takeover of Ottoman provinces. C.P. Scott of the *Manchester Guardian* led the way. Other newspapers, including *The Times*, expressed support for a strong postwar British presence in the Middle East. Lloyd George publicly justified his campaign as a policy of self-determination for small nationalities.[74] Such a Wilsonian message was sure to play well in the United States. General Allenby's continued victories further strengthened Lloyd George's hand. In early October 1918, Allenby – aided by anti-Ottoman allies and French naval operations – took Damascus. By the end of that month, Aleppo had fallen, the final link in the chain of Allenby's victories. Success at arms undergirded the government's policy in the Middle East: Britain was now a major force in that part of the world. But this new affront to the Arabs deepened their sense of betrayal. Their anger focused on Palestine. Jewish settlers, an island in an Arabic sea, found themselves unwelcome and at risk. Lloyd George's policy had placed Britain in the awkward position of supporting two different client populations – Arabic and Jewish – who were immediately at odds with their competing cultures, religions and ambitions.[75] How this would ultimately be resolved remains an unanswered question to this day.

It is indisputable that Lloyd George pursued an imperial goal in the postwar Middle East. Buttressed by military success and the employment of nearly a million and a half men on the Eastern front, the Lloyd George government was eager, as Dockrill and Goold have observed, 'to exploit this position of strength'.[76] As Morgan puts it, the war itself 'had reinforced the call of empire'.[77] This was not merely a matter of high-level imperial policies fostered by the political leadership. As Cannadine has observed, there was an 'imperial consciousness' widespread among the British public at large. The empire was accepted almost without question: it seemed to be 'a permanent, indissoluble part of the providential order of things'.[78]

In addition to Lloyd George, self-conscious imperialists like Amery, Milner and Curzon, now members of his coalition government, recognized the opportunity and hoped to make imperialist aims a part of formal government policy.[79] As British imperial advances in the Middle East during World War I suggest, Lloyd George was intent not only upon protecting the Suez Canal but also safeguarding the routes to India. It was this determination, which bumped up against traditional French designs in the Middle East, that partly shaped the postwar Anglo/French antagonism that, as we have seen, was characteristic of the early 1920s.

The breadth of Britain's emerging geopolitical postwar policy in the Middle East was also indicated by its actions in Mesopotamia (later Iraq). As historians have pointed out, this imperial venture was based upon the shadowy premise that 'Iraq' had a territorial integrity.[80] Starting from scratch, Britain deployed substantial military forces after World War I to bring together a congeries of independent chiefdoms and commercial urban centres carved from the three distinct Ottoman provinces of Basra, Baghdad and Mosul. These geographical entities had neither an ideal of national unity nor an allegiance toward one another. Naturally enough the British government was eager to maintain at least the appearance of legitimacy and acceptance among the population. To foster a notion of unity, Britain sought and received a mandate over Iraq at the San Remo Conference of 1920, thus (officially and publicly) binding itself to refrain from annexing Iraq into the Empire and to act in trust for guaranteeing an eventual independence under the auspices of the League of Nations. But as the occupation continued, an Iraqi opposition emerged and eventually hardened into intransigence. Armed rebellion broke out in the summer of 1920. British officials responded harshly: arrests, censorship and air strikes by the Royal Air Force were directed against pockets of resistance throughout 1920 and 1921. Thousands of casualties attested to the seriousness of the outbreak. Post-World War I Mesopotamia was not a peaceful land.

In Iran, too, British imperial designs were at work. Driven by a long-standing competition with Russia for influence, Britain had been closely involved with Iranian affairs since at least the eighteenth century.[81] British intention was to prevent Russia from establishing a dominant role in Iran, which in turn could threaten British northwest India. An Anglo-Russian accord in 1907 had stabilized contending influences in Iran, but World War I had made Iran once again a field of conflict between these two powers, complicated further by the subversive actions of German agents. To forestall any hostile intent from other powers and to prop up the Iranian government, British troops entered Iran in 1916. Thereafter, Britain moved to consolidate its presence in that country. Subsidies and the exertion of political pressure by 1918 had established a compliant Iranian government.

In 1919 Curzon – through secret negotiations with Iranian officials – crafted the Anglo-Persian Agreement. By its terms, British advisors were sent to reorganize Iranian finances and establish and train Persian military forces. Britain also granted Iran a substantial loan.[82] This heightened intrusion into Iranian affairs, however, has been most often understood as an attempt, as Nikki Keddie has put it, at creating 'a British protectorate ensuring administrative and economic control' of Iran.[83] But within two years of the signing of the agreement, Iranian opposition had scotched the treaty.[84] It was never ratified. Most Iranians, as Poulson has pointed out, wanted to be independent after the war. They believed that, had the agreement been enforced, it would have 'reduced Iran to a mandated state under the authority of the British'.[85]

Throughout the Iranian episode, Lloyd George spoke in a muted voice. His attention remained focused on the innumerable postwar international crises, Ireland and continuing domestic turmoil. When Curzon's forward movement in Iran came under heavy criticism during the summer of 1920, however, Lloyd George supported his embattled Foreign Secretary.[86] Lloyd George was in fact very active in pursuing another imperial project in Iran, and in Mesopotamia as well, that complemented Britain's strategic territorial aim in that region of protecting India. Both Iran and Mesopotamia had substantial oil reserves.[87] Even before the war, the Royal Navy, which would benefit most from an unrestricted supply of oil for its ships, had begun to make a case for bringing certain areas in the Middle East under British control.[88] When the war's need for petroleum products to fuel an expanding mechanized military force (tanks, trucks and aeroplanes) increased significantly, Lloyd George was central in taking the lead in satisfying the empire's thirst for oil. In 1917, he appointed the Colonial Secretary, Walter Long, to pursue a vigorous oil strategy.[89]

By December 1917, a new government department, the Petroleum Executive, was created to centralize the gathering of statistical information on petroleum products.

Other influential official spokesmen began to beat the drum for an expansion of British control of oil-producing areas of the Middle East. Even before the war's end, Hankey for example (most surely sanctioned by Lloyd George), wrote Balfour in August 1918 about 'the petroleum situation in the British Empire'.[90] In any future war, he predicted, oil would 'occupy the place of coal in the present war'. It was necessary therefore to make the oil supplies in Persia and Mesopotamia 'a first-class British war aim'. The following year, Hankey directed Tom Jones to gather information from the Anglo-Persian Oil Company as to the feasibility of constructing an oil pipeline from Mosul to the Mediterranean, terminating at the Palestinian port of Haifa.[91] Once Mesopotamia had fallen to the British after the war, their campaign for control of the oilfields accelerated. After a series of lengthy negotiations between Britain and France, an agreement was reached in 1920 granting Britain significant oil concessions in Mesopotamia.[92] Lloyd George knew well enough that accessible oil greased the wheels of empire.

One final example of the British government's postwar imperial posture must be cited here – the most shocking single episode of the use of force against unarmed civilians during Lloyd George's tenure as Prime Minister. On 13 April 1919, a British military force in India, commanded by General Reginald Dyer, opened fire on an unarmed crowd of several thousands at Amritsar in the Punjab. Nearly 400 were killed outright and over 1,200 wounded. A.J.P. Taylor writes that it was 'the worst bloodshed' since the Mutiny of 1857–58 'and the decisive moment when the Indians were alienated from British rule'.[93] Morgan also notes the 'appalling horrors' of that day.[94] Yet, at the time, Dyer neither apologized nor expressed regret, insisting that he was justified in his actions: it was necessary, he said, to teach the demonstrators 'a lesson' and 'to make a wide impression'.[95] In so doing, he believed that he had prevented a second Indian Mutiny.

Viewed more broadly in retrospect, Amritsar can be understood as an inevitable consequence of the increasing tensions between Britain and India. The catalyst of war had raised Indian consciousness of itself as a nation.[96] India's contributions of men and material to the war had included nearly 1.5 million in both combatant and non-combatant roles. Indian revenues directed to the war effort reached £146 million Indians fighting alongside British and colonial troops thousands of miles from home brought a better sense of a wider world. Within India, the British were willing to adapt to some degree to rising sentiments of self rule. In August 1917, Edwin Montagu, Secretary for India, made provisions for increasing Indian participation at many levels of government. Under the Government of India Act two years later, provincial administrations were enlarged and given greater authority especially in education and self-government. Yet a colonial mentality remained: suspicions of public meetings and demonstrations brought added restrictions and emergency powers to deal with suspected subversives. This underlay General Dyer's attitude that he acted appropriately in disbanding by force a banned meeting.

Amritsar thus became an example of what one historian has observed as 'the spectre of revolutionary violence' in India which 'continued to haunt the government'.[97]

Lloyd George and the coalition government were clearly willing and able to protect, strengthen and advance the British Empire during the challenges of the postwar era. Diplomacy, secret treaties, broken promises and the use of military might (in Ireland and India most notably) were among the varied tactics. The government always hoped to avoid military force in its programme of imperial consolidation, but it was fully prepared to sanction such force when necessary. Moreover, the underlying postwar imperial attitude within the Lloyd George government may well have influenced negatively any support that it might have entertained for a League of Nations. Even before the war had ended, President Wilson's dream of an irenic postwar world enshrined in his Fourteen Points did not strike a positive chord. Indeed, Lloyd George thought President Wilson's Fourteen Points were 'dangerous' and 'nebulous', especially the provision that advocated freedom of the seas, which could impinge upon the actions of the Royal Navy.[98] So strongly did he hold these beliefs that he declared to Riddell that he could not accept them.[99] Overall, Lloyd George believed, Wilson had a tendency to talk 'a lot of sentimental platitudes'.[100] Once the war had begun to wind down, his initial reservations solidified. By December 1918 Cabinet reservations concerning the potential impact of the League upon the security of the Empire surfaced. Some Cabinet members thought that a league established for peace already existed in the very fact of the British Empire. This was a popular view, too, among many Conservatives outside the government. Other influential insiders, like Hankey, agreed.[101] By the time of the Paris Peace Conference, Lloyd George was expressing little interest in the league.[102] Morgan seems to have it about right when he states that Lloyd George based his foreign policy not on the 'abstract generalities' of the league, but rather on 'the realities' of great power involvement.[103]

Given the strength of Lloyd George's imperial sentiment and the support this had within the coalition government, it was perhaps ironic that Lloyd George's downfall and final removal from power occurred over an imperial issue – the fate of a postwar Ottoman Empire. For decades prior the war, British policy had upheld the ramshackle Ottoman government as a guardian of the Straits and as one of the protectors of the British route to India.[104] But the Ottoman Empire, by joining Germany and Austria during the war, had forfeited Britain's good will. Once the war ended and the Ottomans had been defeated, British policy toward that country came under review. Curzon, strongly anti-Ottoman, advocated the expulsion of the Sultan from power as a symbol of that Empire's 'corruption in European politics' and of its history of oppression and misrule.[105] Lloyd George, also Turkophobic, agreed in principle with Curzon: he thought the Turks 'a decadent race' and believed that they should pay a heavy price for their wartime perfidy.[106] This point of view certainly lay at the heart of his determination to break up that Empire during and after the war. Montagu, however, as Secretary for India, was concerned that harsh treatment of the Sultan and any undue punishment for Turkey as a whole could alienate the considerable Muslim population in India. Nevertheless, as Cabinet proceedings went forward, anti-Turkish sentiment prevailed.

A broad philhellenism in Britain was in strong contrast to its anti-Turkish sentiment: the Foreign Office and diplomatic corps were notably pro-Greek.[107] Among all Greek supporters, foremost was Lloyd George. He was particularly close to Eleftherios Venizelos, a politically active Greek supporter of Liberal principles, who was to serve several times as Prime Minister of Greece. The two statesmen had first met in 1912 when Venizelos visited London. Thereafter, their friendship ripened and remained firm throughout their lives.[108] At the Paris Peace Conference, Venizelos played an important role in raising his international profile by his astute defence of Greek claims against the Ottoman Empire.[109] Seizing the initiative early on, Venizelos advocated a greater Greece in postwar Asia Minor, including Macedonia, Thrace and islands in the Aegean, among them Cyprus; and most fatefully of all, Smyrna in Asia Minor. To substantiate these claims a Greek flotilla, under the sponsorship of the Allied Council of Four, then making peace terms in Paris, landed at the port city of Smyrna on 15 May 1919. Within hours, clashes between Greeks and minority Turkish citizens had left several hundreds dead.

The Smyrna occupation was one of several joint operations of Allied units from France and Britain. In March 1920, British forces occupied the Turkish capital, Constantinople – a symbolic end to the Ottomans. Allied peace terms, dictated a month later at the San Remo Conference and enshrined in the Treaty of Sevres, parcelled out the remnants of the old Ottoman Empire. Britain would assume the mandates for Mesopotamia and Palestine, while the French were given mandates over Syria and Lebanon. (Thus the Sykes-Picot Agreement was effectively abrogated.) The Straits would thereafter be open to all ships, in both peacetime and war; and would be governed by an international commission. The Turkish army was limited to 50,000 men and its navy severely reduced in size.[110]

Sevres was not, however, the end of Turkish hostilities. The treaty and continuing Allied encroachment on their homeland inflamed Turkish nationalist sentiment. Under the leadership of Mustafa Kemal, Turkish forces began to organize during the summer of 1919. Operating both militarily and politically on interior lines, Kemal reorganized the Turkish army; took command of its civilian government; and carried out extensive diplomatic efforts to counter the Allied offensives. His major goal was to repel the Greek army, the largest force threatening Turkey. Kemal had learned lessons from the static, linear defence warfare so characteristic of 1914–18. Departing from a rigid positional warfare, he used a flexible and rapid deployment of troops, which engulfed and outflanked Greek forces. By mid-1922, he was ready for the final push, not only against Greece but also against all other remaining Allied troops in Turkey.[111]

In September 1922, Turkish troops approached Chanak, a coastal town, strategically important because of its position on the Asiatic side of the Dardenelles, directly across the strait from the ill-fated Gallipoli peninsula. Only a small British military force of some 3,500 men defended British interests from Chanak to Constantinople. Chanak was also important to Kemal and his invigorated Turkish army. As Turkish forces swept the Greeks aside in their eastward march in September 1922, emergency Cabinet meetings in London sought to avert a military debacle. On

15 September, the Cabinet decided to call a peace conference while simultaneously sending reinforcements to Chanak. In addition, an appeal would be made to other nations for assistance: Rumania and Serbia would (it was hoped) help guard the Straits. France it was thought would be diplomatically supportive. That same day Churchill as Colonial Secretary prepared a telegram to the Dominions requesting their direct aid – in no uncertain terms – 'to guard the freedom of the Straits ... against a violent and hostile Turkish aggression'.[112] The following day, Churchill and Lloyd George issued a press release which publicly revealed the government's serious intent to defend British interests in Turkey, by force if necessary.

Unfortunately, given the distances involved and the need for coding and decoding the official government telegram, the contents of the press release reached the Dominions first through their local newspapers. This blunder gave an unintended sense of officiousness to the government's request: there had been no prior private consultations. Moreover, the Dominions were reluctant to engage in any further overseas commitment to wage war. Canada and Australia refused outright. South Africa did not respond. Only New Zealand and Newfoundland were favourable. France, too – ostensibly Britain's closest European ally – was distinctly cool to any hints of war against Turkey. (Although they did agree to a joint cautionary note to Kemal.) Equally damaging to the government was British public opinion, already on edge at the developing crisis in Turkey. In spite of the tide of opposition, the government went forward. Hankey's diary records that those mid-September days were spent 'in innumerable Conferences and Committees' in an attempt to 'scrape up guns, air craft, troops etc.'.[113] Simultaneously, there were frequent communications between the Cabinet and Sir Charles Harington, Commanding Officer of the British army of occupation, stationed in Constantinople. His standing orders were that he could withdraw British forces to that city as his judgement dictated. But he was also directed to resist to the utmost if Kemal and his army attempted to cross the Bosporus and enter European territory. This, in fact, was the crux of British resistance to Kemal's apparent inexorable advance – to contain Turkey within its Asian confines. It was certainly Lloyd George's firm view. Hankey reported the Prime Minister as stating that 'no Kemalist forces must be allowed to cross the salt-water'.[114] The Cabinet was largely behind Lloyd George's belligerent stance. On 20 September, the Cabinet sanctioned a telegram (again drafted by Churchill) which explicitly stated to General Harington that it was 'of the highest importance' to hold Chanak. If it were to fall to Kemal, it would be 'a blow' to Britain, for Chanak had become 'a point of great moral significance to the prestige of the Empire'.[115]

Yet within a few days, the Cabinet came to the realization that it could not reasonably expect to stay Kemal's hand. His military advantage was too great. The Cabinet began to waver. On 23 September, Britain, France, and Italy invited the Turkish leader to negotiate an armistice. As a lure, the allies signalled a return of eastern Thrace to Turkey. To Allied surprise, there was no immediate response. In fact, a more ominous development was apparent: Turkish troops began moving in force towards Chanak. The British government had little choice but to prepare for military engagement. On 29 September, the Cabinet instructed General Harington to issue an ultimatum to the commander of Turkish troops in the neighbourhood of Chanak. If the troops were not withdrawn by an hour to be determined by Harington, he had the authority to open fire with all means at his disposal, including army, naval and air forces.

The Cabinet expected to hear one of two events by the following day – either a Turkish stand down or the sound of gunfire. Neither occurred. Harington had determined to delay the ultimatum. From his perspective – nearer the potential scene of action – tensions had actually eased. In a telegram to London on 30 September, Harington explained that Kemalist authorities were in the process of preparing a formal and favourable reply to the allied note of 23 September. On 1 October, therefore, the Cabinet rescinded their earlier direction of an immediate ultimatum. Two days later, the proposed armistice conference opened in Mudania, on the shores of the Sea of Marmara, nearly 200 miles northeast of Chanak. After some hard bargaining, Turkey gained what it wanted: Eastern Thrace up to the Maritsa River, essentially the pre-war boundary of the old Ottoman Empire.[116] Additional terms of the armistice, after Greece had withdrawn to the left bank of the Maritsa River, included a one month delay before Turkish authorities moved in. Other issues would be discussed at a future peace conference. For the Turks, the Mudania Armistice, concluded on 11 October, was 'a great diplomatic success', as Sonyel has claimed.[117] For Britain, it was a national humiliation.

Harsh criticisms were directed especially against Lloyd George. Riddell, whose relations with the Prime Minister were beginning to cool, believed that the 'Turkish situation' had become 'deplorable'. Kemal, he thought, was 'completely victorious' while Lloyd George's policy was 'disastrous'.[118] C.P. Scott, who had been a consistent critic of Lloyd George's Turkish policy for some time, was in despair. In a letter to L.T. Hobhouse, he declared that British policy towards the Greek and Turkish conflict was 'a nightmare'. Furthermore, he questioned the government's 'competence and their disposition' in settling the issues involved.[119] Among politicians more in the know, there were also numerous expressions of discontent. Hankey was concerned about the bellicosity of the Prime Minister. During a small dinner party at Philip Sassoon's on Park Lane in late September with Lloyd George and Churchill, all the talk 'was of war'. Writing in his diary afterwards, Hankey confessed that he was 'more impressed than they with the intense repugnance that our people feel for war'.[120] Arthur Lee, then First Lord of the Admiralty, was discouraged and angry, as he confessed to his wife, at the conclusion of a late night Cabinet meeting on 30 September. A number of Cabinet members, he believed, 'positively *want* hostilities to break out'.[121] These included Lloyd George, Churchill, as well as Birkenhead (Lord Chancellor) and Sir Robert Horne (who was then Chancellor of the Exchequer) and possibly Austen Chamberlain.

Historians since Chanak have been nearly universal in their criticism of Lloyd George. A.J.P. Taylor thinks that Lloyd George roused such anxiety with his war talk that Britons feared they were 'being recklessly hurried into an unnecessary war'.[122] Jenkins characterizes Chanak as 'the last spurt of Lloyd George adventurism'.[123] Morgan writes that Chanak was only one of a series of foreign policy failures in the postwar period which did his reputation and his government 'great harm'.[124] Moreover, Lloyd George had misunderstood the mood of battle-weary Britons. 'The Chanak affair', Morgan writes, 'conflicted mightily with a national yearning for peaceful isolation'.[125] Dockrill and Goold are particularly condemnatory. The 'militant band' in the Cabinet, led by Lloyd George, Churchill and Birkenhead, was largely responsible for the 'mismanaged, inflexible and irresponsible' policy which led to the 'debacle' at Chanak. But of all the 'personal failures' of British officials, the man most responsible was the Prime Minister, whose 'misjudgments' were exacerbated by his anti-Turkish bias, his refusal to accept expert military advice and his slighting of his own authorities on the spot.[126] Walder takes a different interpretive approach. He maintains that Lloyd George (and his Cabinet supporters) suffered from the 'politician's disease' – the 'delusion' of thinking oneself irreplaceable as a political leader – a development which 'rotted their judgement'.[127]

But these explanations do not wholly account for Lloyd George's persistent drive for dominance over Turkey. Was it merely his dislike of what he considered to be the flawed Turkish national character? Did the Prime Minister operate on such impressionable and over-generalized beliefs? It seems more likely that Lloyd George was – as we have noted above, and as Morgan has observed – heeding once again 'the call of empire'.[128] Lloyd George believed himself the steward of the empire and to that end he strove mightily to maintain, and where possible, to expand it. He clearly believed, too, that the nation would support him. Lloyd George stoutly defended his policy to Riddell: 'The country will willingly support our action regarding the Straits by force of arms if need be.'[129] Indeed, the defeat of Turkey especially would give Britain a unique opportunity to expand its power and influence throughout the Middle East. The Straits were particularly valuable in this regard. Greece could serve as a welcome instrument of British imperial interests in that region. But Turkey, now risen from the dead as it seemed, was an unwelcome deterrent to these plans.

At a critical point during the intensive Cabinet discussions on Chanak, however, Lloyd George began to backpedal. As Arthur Lee observed at the Cabinet meeting on 2 October, 'the fire-eaters were overborne by the more moderate members'.[130] Within a few days, Balcarres, too, had noticed a shift in the Cabinet – 'a rather sudden change of temperament'.[131] A recognizable peace party in the Cabinet was emerging. Curzon, for example, modified his strongly anti-Turkish view: he had become increasingly convinced that Lloyd George's pronounced favouritism toward the Greeks and their army was misplaced. With Cabinet support draining away from him, Lloyd George may also have taken a second glance at other mitigating circumstances. The most important fact was a recognition that General Harington in Constantinople as the man on the spot had a better grasp of military intelligence than did the Cabinet. Harington advised caution.[132]

Equally significant is that Lloyd George's celebrated energy and decisiveness – personal characteristics that had carried him through crisis after crisis throughout his life – had been weakened after years of war and the concurrent stresses of a difficult peace. In early March 1922, Riddell noticed that 'LG evidently [was] very tired'.[133] Edward Grigg, one of Lloyd George's firmest supporters, believed that the Prime

Minister was so worn out that 'he had lost his power of initiative' and should resign to take a well deserved rest.[134] Lloyd George was not unaware of a physical and mental impairment. Throughout the difficult year of 1922, he complained frequently about his health and poor physical disposition, most often to Frances Stevenson. In March, he had mentioned 'racking pains'.[135] Two days later, he confessed how much he 'needed a rest'.[136] In April, from the Genoa Conference, he complained of the workload: it took 'such a lot of life out of my frame'. Moreover, there remained 'a fortnight of nerve racking work'.[137] Three days later, still at the conference, he wrote: 'just now very tired'.[138] Again from the conference, he confessed that he was sometimes 'almost overwhelmed with anxieties'.[139] That summer, Lloyd George confessed wearily to Riddell that he was 'tired': he 'had seventeen years' continuous work'.[140] Additional evidence in letters to his wife confirms Lloyd George's state of mind. As the Turkish military forces gathered strength in September 1922, he wrote to her: 'I really cannot stand this much longer. I don't believe my nerve & spirits can sustain the constant wear & tear'. He felt 'depressed, dejected' and 'worried & unhappy.'[141] The following day, he reported: 'Crisis after crisis.' And the day after that: 'There is no nerve relaxation for me.'[142]

Other apparent errors in foreign affairs, when added together, also indicated a lack of considered judgement of the Lloyd George ministry: overextension in Iraq; diplomatic failure in Iran; trouble in India; as well as military embarrassment in Turkey. On the domestic front, there were also causes for concern. Foremost among them was a growing complaint that Lloyd George was connected in some way to corrupt practices, especially in the granting of honours.[143] That honours – the granting of a title, or an advance in the peerage – were legitimate as a means of reward for party or public service was unquestioned. But the charge against Lloyd George was that he had stretched the system beyond reasonable bounds. The Prime Minister appeared to be offering titles and privileges outright for cash: he was, in short, guilty of illegally seeking personal gain. The record seemed to speak for itself. In 1920, there were seven new peers created. In 1921, there were 20: one of these, a successful shipowner, had been convicted of food hoarding during the war. By 1922, the public at large and many politicians had simply had enough, especially when in that year a South African mine owner who had once been fined a half million pounds for fraudulent practices was offered a baronetcy. Reaction in the press and Parliament was swift and overwhelmingly negative at this fresh evidence of what seemed to be 'a systematic traffic in titles'.[144] The unlucky baronet was eventually forced to decline the proffered title; but the damage had been done. In June of 1922, agitation for some sort of redress and reform of the honours system was gaining ground. Calls for an enquiry originated from all sides of the House – Labour, Asquithian Liberals and coalition Conservatives. Ultimately, Lloyd George himself was forced to announce in the House of Commons in July 1922 the creation of a Royal Commission to look into the matter.

There were other complaints, too, about the tone set by Lloyd George in governing practices. Too many Scotsmen (eight) in a Cabinet of 21 in 1919, and too few from the most elite public schools and Oxford and Cambridge (eight each). Too few in the Cabinet were gentlemen: businessmen had replaced them in both Cabinet and Parliament.[145] Swelling the chorus of complaint against the Prime Minister were criticisms of his associations with louche, crude and unsavoury characters such as J.H. Dalziel, F. Handel Booth, L. Chiozza Money and William Sutherland – a company of cads, as some would have it.[146] There existed, too, a sense that men of this sort were somehow involved in making the government less effective, and perhaps even heedless of governmental efficiency and prudence. In a reaction against perceived extravagant government expenditures, an Anti-Waste League came into being. Established in early 1921 by Lord Rothermere, utilizing his *Sunday Pictorial* as a propaganda tool, the Anti-Waste campaign enjoyed a few electoral successes at by-elections in 1921. Its influence beyond these slight indicators of voter dissent is difficult to ascertain. It may very well be that Lloyd George was forced to jettison Addison from his post as Minister without Portfolio, since that office was regarded as an example of official waste.[147]

The anti-waste slogan may have induced the government to reduce its expenditure.[148] But its main importance seems to have been a flashpoint to members of the political far right, who had never forgotten Lloyd George's role in the Marconi Scandal of 1912–13. In 1917, Henry Page Croft had founded the National Party designed in part to purify British political practices. Abuses in the honours system became one of its rallying cries.[149] More numerous and more critical of the Prime Minister were the Die Hard Conservatives, the ideological heirs of the pre-war Die Hards who had taken their stand against the House of Lords reform. Not an official party, they were a likeminded group of approximately 40 Conservative backbenchers in the House of Commons who were increasingly outraged over the apparent misuse of the honours system.[150] There were also various fringe groups and individuals who saw Lloyd George as being in cahoots with Bolsheviks, Sinn Féiners, or Labour militants. The influence of international Jewry was thought particularly insidious.[151]

These various groupings may be considered as being on the fringes of opposition to the Prime Minister and his leadership of the coalition government. More important to the fate of Lloyd George was the emergence of mainstream Conservative opinion – which had supported the coalition – against his policies and politics. There had long been a hankering among Conservative coalitionists for a government of their own. Conservatives should lead Conservatives became an underground refrain. Evidence of anti-coalition sentiment can be found as early as the summer of 1921. In June of that year, Robert Sanders confided to his diary that the feeling among Conservatives for 'a pure Conservative party' was stronger than 'at any time since the armistice'. Two months later, Sanders reported that Lloyd George must face the fact that in any forthcoming election, many Conservative candidates would stand as Conservatives 'pure and simple'.[152] In October, Sanders was hearing reports about a 'Tory revolt against L.G. … gaining head'.[153] By July 1922, even though a junior member of the coalition, Sanders himself had been converted. Speaking before a meeting of Conservative ministers outside the Cabinet, he stated publicly: 'we wanted a Conservative Prime Minister and Conservative preponderance in the Cabinet'.[154]

The dry tinder heaped around the coalition government leapt into flame in early October 1922 when the House of Commons reassembled after its summer recess. Criticisms against Lloyd George over his evident loss of direction during the Chanak affair combined with the scandals arising from the sale of honours lay in the background. But the flashpoint was likely Lloyd George's decision in mid-September to hold an early election – designed no doubt to reinvigorate coalition prospects. When disenchanted Conservatives heard this news, they rose in opposition.[155] Conservatives needed, however, an authoritative voice to speak for them and to present unequivocally their case against Lloyd George. On 7 October, that voice was heard – if slightly muted and tentative. Bonar Law, from his place of retirement, wrote a public letter to *The Times* in which he summed up the firm opposition to Lloyd George's risky Middle Eastern policy. 'We cannot alone', Bonar Law wrote, 'act as the policeman of the world'.[156] This criticism of the Prime Minister's postwar foreign policy, and its somewhat Olympian tone, has been widely quoted. But the sentence following has not: 'The financial and social condition of this country makes that impossible.'[157] In this second sentence lay a more than implied political criticism of Lloyd George around which the Conservative Party could rally.

Three days later, Conservative leaders met to discuss their options further.[158] In counterpoint, the loyal Austen Chamberlain defended Lloyd George and the coalition. On 13 October, for example, he spoke before the Midland Conservative Club in Birmingham. He declared that he had worked 'in perfect harmony' with the Prime Minister over the years and there had been 'no difference of political principle' on important issues.[159] Furthermore, Lloyd George 'acted with perfect loyalty towards his Unionist allies' throughout. This stout defence did not convince coalition critics. *The Times*, in a leader of the same day, denounced Chamberlain's remarks as neither wise nor fair; and in some parts they were 'directly misleading'. It was also a speech, *The Times* continued, that revealed Chamberlain 'as an uncompromising Lloyd Georgian' and would thus spur the Conservative Party against him, against Lloyd George, and against the coalition government.[160] Probably in a coordinated effort with Chamberlain, Lloyd George spoke two days later at Manchester in defence of the government's Middle Eastern policy in general and most particularly of Chanak. 'We have not been war-mongers', he claimed, 'we have been peace makers'. The government had been intent upon the defence of British interests, especially the control of the Straits – 'the biggest and the most important prize which we won by our victory over Turkey in the Great War'.[161]

Meanwhile, Conservative Party members were hurriedly meeting in large groups and small to discuss the future prospects of their party. Beginning on 16 October, Conservative ministers, under-secretaries, backbenchers and the executive of the National Union of Conservative and Unionist Associations were all in conference.[162] The decisive moment came at a meeting of Conservative MPs at the Carlton Club called by Chamberlain, the party leader, on 19 October. Chamberlain's speech did little to settle troubled waters – 'very rigid and unbending' was Balcarres's view.[163] A resolution declaring that in any future election, Conservatives would fight free of the coalition and would be led by their own leaders and party platform was overwhelmingly passed (187 for; 88 opposed; with one abstention). The implications were clear to all. For Conservatives, their immediate task was to select a party leader to implement their declaration of independence from Lloyd George's coalition government. This was an easy task: Bonar Law, in spite of his recent illness, was the obvious choice. At the Carlton House meeting on 19 October his brief speech was taken as an acceptance of the heavy responsibilities of leading the Party at the next general election. On 23 October he was officially selected as party leader by the Parliamentary Conservative Party (made up of peers, MPs and candidates).[164] Later that day, Bonar Law was designated Prime Minister by the King. Reading the unmistakable signs, Lloyd George had already resigned. As Kinnear has observed, Lloyd George's overthrow was 'abrupt and complete'.[165]

THE LONG GOOD-BYE

There was no reason to think that Lloyd George would not rebound from his defeat and return once again to Downing Street. Not yet 60, he was relatively young. Few political leaders were as experienced as he at governing. A cadre of loyalists remained staunchly behind him, including some influential Conservative coalitionists such as Balfour. Indeed, after his fall from power, Lloyd George proved remarkably resilient. As canny in defeat as he had been crafty in office by balancing contending interests, he remained in the political limelight during the postwar era. Frequently bidding his time or, when circumstances allowed, quietly conspiring, he never lost sight of his goal – to lead the nation once again. But there were also some disadvantages to his position. His home base of Wales had been weakened through significant inroads by the Labour Party.[1] The Liberal Party itself remained divided, with Asquith at the head of one wing and Lloyd George at the other. Perhaps most of all, a widespread weariness with coalition politics weighed down his appeal. These played into the hands of a resurgent Conservative Party.

A test of Lloyd George's future prospects occurred during the general election immediately following Bonar Law's assumption of office. Although large crowds met Lloyd George wherever he spoke on the campaign trail, he failed to rouse them. His speeches were sometimes tedious and defensive. Occasionally he slipped into hackneyed sloganeering. At Leeds, for example, he promised to 'fight for national interests against a mere party game' and to continue 'the old battle for a steady but progressive England'.[2] He occasionally appeared listless and weary. The crowds were often restive, puzzled at his orations.[3] His waffling speeches appeared inconsistent. Privately, too, he seemed indecisive. In a discussion with C.P. Scott, he promised to stand during the election as 'a Liberal pure and simple'.[4] But in his diary of that same day, Scott wrote that Lloyd George 'seems to be pretty closely bound to the Conservatives who have stood by him'.[5] Lloyd George's vacillation was apparent to the public at large. The *Dundee Courier*, in a post-election leader, observed that the former Prime Minister had proved 'a pitiable spectacle … casting wildly about on this side and that for an army' who would follow him.[6] Lloyd George was clearly not at his best. His exhaustion, built up over the wartime and postwar years, was the likeliest cause. Perhaps, too, the election had come so quickly that he had not had time to organize his thoughts and to formulate his campaign strategy.[7] Poignantly enough, Lloyd George himself understood how badly he had failed. To his wife he confessed that it had been a 'difficult & baffling fight'.[8]

With the greatest speaker of the day hobbled by an ineffective campaign, the National Liberals (as the Lloyd George wing of the Liberals was now termed) fared poorly on election day, 15 November 1922.[9] The Conservatives, led by Bonar Law, on the other hand, struck the right note, emphasizing the need for tranquillity and a less active role for government in the life of the country. Their campaign produced a decided victory: 345 Conservative seats out of 615 total. The Labour Party, establishing itself as a viable alternative, won 142. The two Liberal Parties trailed the pack. The Lloyd George National Liberals won 62 and the Asquithian Independent Liberals 54.[10]

Bonar Law was as good as his word in promising to reverse the course and tone of the Lloyd George government.[11] His Cabinet veered rightward: of 16 offices, seven were members of the House of Lords. Each Cabinet member was made more responsible for the working of his department than had been the case under the directorial Lloyd George regime.[12] The large circle of unofficial advisers under Lloyd George, the Garden Suburb, was disbanded. The Cabinet Secretariat, with Hankey at its head, remained but reduced in number. Bonar Law's term as Prime Minister proved to be brief, lasting only seven months. During his short tenure, he naturally had few legislative initiatives. Perhaps the most important was the ratification of the constitutional arrangements of the December 1921 Anglo-Irish Treaty, the terms of which required this action within a year of its signing. Less successful were Bonar Law's forays in foreign affairs. His attempt to moderate French demands on German reparations failed in January 1923, when French troops marched into the Ruhr.[13] Across the Atlantic, the American government began demanding repayment of the British wartime debt. When the Chancellor of the Exchequer, Stanley Baldwin, attempted to settle by accepting a disadvantageous interest rate during his official visit to Washington, Bonar Law thought the terms disastrously high and threatened resignation. He was persuaded against this course only with difficulty by a Cabinet virtually united against him.[14]

These early missteps might well be accounted for by a novice administration, and could have been overcome as Bonar Law gained greater experience as Prime Minister. But it was soon clear that he was seriously ill. For some time, he suffered from what at first appeared to be a succession of sore throats. By 10 April 1923, when Parliament assembled for its regular session, he could scarcely speak. On 1 May, he left on a recuperative Mediterranean cruise. Two weeks later, he was in Paris where his personal doctor met him. Diagnosed with incurable throat cancer, Bonar Law knew his time was short. His primary task now became the selection of his successor. Early indications were that Curzon was favoured, given his long experience in both the imperial sphere and domestic political life. Yet within 48 hours of Bonar Law's resignation from office on 20 May 1923, Stanley Baldwin was the new Prime Minister. Baldwin's solid appearance and personal affability contrasted favourably to Curzon's aristocratic hauteur and public aloofness. Moreover, Baldwin had had a credible record in his short term in office as Chancellor of the Exchequer under Bonar Law. Baldwin also seems to have benefited from an intrigue engineered by his supporters designed to ease his path in the eyes of the King, who would make the final decision. Their concern was that any new Prime Minister must be a member of the House of Commons. In an age of an expanded electorate and increasing democratic sensitivities, they argued that a Conservative Prime Minister sitting in the House of Lords would send the wrong signal.[15]

Baldwin's first domestic priority as Prime Minister was to deal with the continuing postwar problem of unemployment. To protect domestic manufacturing and to reduce unemployment in that sector, he decided to introduce a tariff on selected manufactured goods. This attempt at reviving a protectionist tariff seemed to many at the time and to some historians since an irresponsible attempt to reintroduce a contentious and now defunct policy. But in fact Baldwin was acting within recent precedent. During Lloyd George's postwar administration, selected items had been singled out for protectionist duties, as in the case of the Dyestuffs Act (1920) which restricted the importation of that commodity. The following year the Safeguarding of Industries Act set duties of 33 per cent on such articles as optical glass, certain electrical instruments and chemicals. With these examples in mind, Baldwin doubtless believed that he had a sound economic policy and a winning electoral ploy.

Baldwin's decision to adopt protectionism was also influenced by his determination to undercut any potential move on Lloyd George's part to steal a protectionist march on the Conservative government. Rumours had reached Baldwin that the former Prime Minister had begun to think along protectionist lines. As Baldwin told Tom Jones many years later, he had information that Lloyd George 'was going protectionist, and I had to get in quick'.[16] To Canadian Prime Minister William Mackenzie King, Baldwin also revealed his apprehension about Lloyd George's intentions. If he, Baldwin, came out for protection, Lloyd George would probably declare for free trade; but if Baldwin declared for free trade, Lloyd George would advocate protection. Baldwin thought that Lloyd George lacked convictions: 'he was a pure opportunist'.[17] Whether or not that was true, Baldwin was clearly acting under the shadow of Lloyd George.

That shadow fell across Baldwin's early essays into foreign policy as well.[18] In his only significant foreign policy initiative during this, his first term as Prime Minister, Baldwin attempted to heal the mistrust between Britain and France that had arisen during the postwar era by engaging in official talks with French President Raymond Poincaré in September 1923. In contrast to the strains put upon the alliance by Lloyd George's insistence upon a moderate policy on German reparations, Baldwin – a Francophile in sentiment and policy – hoped to soothe French sensibilities by contrasting his views with Lloyd George's. Indeed, as the transcript of Baldwin's meeting with Poincaré reveals, Baldwin made explicit his belief that Lloyd George was the source of France's loss of confidence in Britain.[19] As a surety of his own good intentions, Baldwin declared that he would never 'serve under Mr Lloyd George in any capacity whatever …'.[20] Apart from his strictures on Lloyd George, Baldwin did make his main point – that Britain was opposed to the occupation of the Ruhr.

Furthermore, he hoped to return to the days of Lord Grey's policy when relations between the two countries were more amicable than at present.

During these months when Baldwin was settling in as Prime Minister, Lloyd George was attempting to find his voice as an opposition leader. But throughout 1923 he seemed unsure – as Michael Bentley puts it – 'which way to turn'.[21] In March of that year Lloyd George began a sustained campaign to reunite the two wings of the Liberal Party. Speaking before the Liberal Club in Edinburgh, he called for binding up of old wounds, and moving forward with an active social policy.[22] The following month he was in Manchester, outlining in more specific detail his plans for a united Liberal Party. He claimed 'fair play for the underdog' not only as a theme for Liberal unification: it could also be an effective election cry for the Party. In practical terms, his proposal meant redressing low pay and unemployment, which would not only advance economic needs but social justice as well. It had the added benefit of undercutting the appeal of socialism. To pacify Liberal imperialists (and to negate the programme of imperial Conservatives), he advocated a more comprehensive development of a Liberal empire. Above all, he unequivocally advocated the hoary touchstone of Liberalism – free trade. On foreign affairs, too, Lloyd George spoke up. In the pages of the friendly *Daily Chronicle* he was particularly critical of French actions against Germany, including its invasion of the Ruhr and continuing intransigence over German reparations.

In September 1923, Lloyd George began a lengthy trip to the United States and Canada.[23] The trip had been carefully planned months beforehand and was no doubt orchestrated for maximum publicity to keep his name before the public. A strong secondary motive was the hope of financial reward. As he jocularly put it to John W. Davis, who had extended the invitation nearly a year earlier: 'I am now engaged in the almost forgotten tasks of earning a living and improving my golf.'[24] The trip did in fact raise his international visibility. He received a hero's welcome in his extensive journey throughout North America, and the favourable press reports there resonated in Britain.[25] The trip also had a solid impact upon domestic politics. Baldwin's concern about the continuing favourable (and substantial) news reports of Lloyd George abroad led him to a substantial error in judgement. In late October, Baldwin called for a general election to be held on 6 December. In part the election was to be a mandate on protection, but it was also designed to preempt any action on the part of Lloyd George who at the time of the announcement was on his way home from his triumphant tour of North America.[26] With Lloyd George still on the high seas, Baldwin could gain valuable time to prepare the electorate for a protectionist policy.[27]

The prospect of protective tariffs, however, galvanized Liberals of all stripes. Asquithians and supporters of Lloyd George joined forces in the defence of free trade and opposition to Baldwin's government. Shortly after Lloyd George's return from North America, a tentative Liberal reunion was formalized. Lloyd George brought to the election campaign a significant fighting fund built up over his years as Prime Minister and Liberal Party leader. Asquith, who had no such financial backing, nevertheless had retained over the years the affection and respect of many

Liberals. These Liberal advantages, combined with Baldwin's sudden introduction of protection as a Conservative rallying cry, reversed to a fair extent the general election results of the previous year. Conservatives fell to 258 seats, while Labour increased to 191. The combined Liberal forces rose significantly to 158 seats, placing them in a position to hold the balance of power. The prospect of a governing partnership between Labour and Liberal drew the two parties together. Thus a Lib–Lab alliance brought to office for the first time a Labour government. The pact was symbolized by the Liberal Party's decision to seat its MPs on the Labour government's side in the House of Commons.[28]

This was a shocking and dismaying event to the political right. That socialists should now have become the governing party was abhorrent. Would they govern constitutionally? Or would they subvert the established order of things? And moreover, could the inexperienced and (to their minds) doctrinaire Labour MPs do the job? The new Prime Minister, Ramsay MacDonald, had been – as everyone knew – an early activist in the Labour movement and a supporter of socialist ideals from the 1890s onward. One of the founders of the Labour Party, he had long advocated radical social and political changes against the privileged elites. Resilient and spirited in advancing Labour's cause, MacDonald had nevertheless proved adaptable in the Labour Party's early years by allying with the dominant Liberals.[29] Now, with the election of 1923, Labour replaced the Liberal Party as the foremost partner in the progressive alliance. Aware of these potential threats to their rightful claim as the legitimate government of Britain, Labour leaders approached royal officials and the King himself to ease their reservations to a Labour government, assuring both Stamfordham and King George V that they would neither introduce extreme legislation nor engage in violent administrative changes.[30]

But this did not ease the alarm among many who opposed the notion of Labour in power. Balcarres, for example, had strong doubts. Once a member of the Lloyd George coalition, he had since retired from active political life but had kept his eye open on political developments. Commenting in his diary on the rise of Labour, he doubted that 'these great spouters' would succeed.[31] The 'chief men' in the Labour party, he believed, were 'doctrinaires, intellectuals and cranks'. Those Labourites whom he knew during his coalition days were 'among the slowest-witted folk' he had ever encountered. One particular Labour member of the coalition he thought 'had the brain as well as the appearance of a lizard'. Other Conservatives were more openly desirous of undermining the Liberal/Labour alliance. A senior minister of the fallen Baldwin government wrote to J.C.C. Davidson, recommending a plan of action; that is, to 'force Lloyd George on Labour'. Because Lloyd George was 'the most detested scoundrel in the country', this would weaken the Labour government.[32] Even ostensibly friendly Labour supporters had reservations about the new government. Beatrice Webb – in spite of the fact that her husband Sidney had become MacDonald's President of the Board of Trade – wondered whether or not the new Labour team could govern properly. She questioned MacDonald's capacity for leadership. She feared that his ministry might linger on in 'legislative impotence' while 'trying to govern in spite of having no mandate for carrying out its distinctive policy'. She also thought that the election results – 'the clearly expressed will of the people' – dictated a Liberal/Conservative coalition.[33]

In the earliest days of the new Labour Ministry, some Liberal members also had doubts about MacDonald's trial run (as many Liberals thought it to be) at governing. They were uncertain about the expertise of their legislative partners. Patronizing Labour as their junior partners and often assuming the role of a wiser older sibling in matters political, Liberal leaders frequently offered unwanted advice.[34] In their turn, Labourites tended to view Liberals not only as antediluvian and irrelevant to the issues of the day, but also increasingly right wing in political orientation. In addition, MacDonald had little affection for Asquith. As for Lloyd George, MacDonald's opinion was even lower.[35] The most divisive issue was not personal, however, but the fact that Liberals and Labour were contending rivals for the progressive electorate and rivals, too, as the legitimate opponent to the Conservative Party.

In spite of these contentious and divisive issues between Liberals and Labour, MacDonald was able initially to prove himself and his party skilful in addressing common problems. His foremost aim was to convince the public that Labour was not bound to follow the impractical notions of irresponsible revolutionaries, and that it had policies well within the moderate limits of the British political tradition. MacDonald was determined to demonstrate furthermore that his Labour government had a wider mandate than adhering to narrow class interests and could be trusted to operate even-handedly among workers, businessmen and industrialists alike. As his chief biographer has summed up MacDonald's broader intention, the new Prime Minister intended to govern 'in a severely pragmatic spirit'.[36] At the opening session of Parliament in February 1924, MacDonald set the tone of his ministry by giving 'a dignified and forceful exposition' of his policy, emphasizing the responsible nature of the new government and its intention to be loyal and careful 'custodians of the nation's welfare'.[37] Actions on the domestic front bore this out. There were no radical shifts in policy – no nationalization of mines or railways for example. Major legislation was within the mainstream. Chancellor of the Exchequer Philip Snowden presented a popular budget in April, which reduced both indirect and direct taxes by substantial amounts. In an attempt to ease the housing shortage, Minister of Health John Wheatley's successful housing act provided state subsidies for local authorities to construct dwellings for rental usage.[38]

MacDonald enjoyed even more success in his brief intervention into foreign affairs. Determined to resolve postwar Anglo-French differences, MacDonald invited the new Premier Edouard Herriot to Chequers. During high-level diplomatic talks in July 1924, MacDonald took charge of the negotiations. Over a period of many weeks, a compromise agreement was reached. France would withdraw from the Ruhr and accept the American Dawes Plan by which German reparations to France would be rescheduled on a more realistic basis.[39] To set a broader seal on the agreement, MacDonald arranged a joint appearance with Herriot at the League of Nations in September where they sponsored a resolution calling for a disarmament conference. The League responded favourably, passing the Geneva Protocol in October, a scheme of arbitration between nations designed to prevent future wars.

Thus was the Anglo-French rift settled amicably, contributing to a broader scheme of collective security and easing French fears of a German revanchism.[40]

While the Labour government under MacDonald was establishing its credentials for effective governing, their Liberal partners engaged in a series of internecine struggles. Chief among them was the question of party control which threatened the 'shotgun reconciliation'[41] between its Asquithian and Lloyd Georgeite wings. Although Asquith had retained leadership of the official party machinery – as he had throughout the days of the Lloyd George coalition government – he had little access to campaign funds. Lloyd George, on the other hand, was flush with party contributions because of his long years as Liberal Prime Minister and then coalition leader. The sale of honours had also freshened the coffers. Refusing to surrender any control over these funds, he was nevertheless willing from time to time to contribute substantially to Liberal campaigns: the Lloyd George fund, for example, gave £160,000 to the 1923 election battle.[42]

In addition to his alienation from the Asquithian wing of the Liberal Party, Lloyd George was finding it difficult to establish a viable political posture toward the new Labour government. Early on, he sought the advice of C.P. Scott, whose firm Liberalism was always a useful sounding board. Scott summarized Lloyd George's concerns as primarily political and tactical. After a lengthy discussion on 1 February 1924, Scott recorded in his diary that Lloyd George 'kept coming back' to the difficulties between Liberal and Labour 'from the party point of view'.[43] Lloyd George put the political conundrum thus: if Labour succeeded, they would get all the credit. But if MacDonald should fail, Liberals would get the blame for putting him in power. Scott responded by admitting that the existing alignment of parties was 'obviously unreal' but that in time there would be natural adjustments. Perhaps eased by Scott's emollient words, Lloyd George confided encouragingly a few days afterwards to his daughter, Megan, that the new Labour government had 'come in like a lamb'. It seemed tame and respectable. Labour was, he thought, 'out to soothe ruffled nerves'. After all, this had been part of the Liberal plan. 'The Liberals were bound to turn Baldwin out & the King was bound to call Ramsay in & we are all bound to give him a chance.'[44]

Ex post facto reasoning to Megan could not disguise Lloyd George's continued flailing. During the early months of 1924 he adopted a number of positions, only to abandon them in short order. As one historian has noted, he was 'like a caged animal unused to its loss of freedom'.[45] At first he seemed to think that a Liberal/Labour partnership could foster an era of reforming measures satisfactory to both parties. As the prospects of this potential partnership faded, however, he became openly more hostile to MacDonald.[46] By March 1924, Lloyd George was criticizing MacDonald's hesitancy in failing to curb continuing French diplomatic hostility towards Germany – a premature judgement on his part, as it happened. On Labour's domestic programmes, he denounced the Labour government's inability to address the continuing high rate of unemployment.

Perhaps Lloyd George's most hypocritical act against MacDonald was his response to a heated issue emerging late in the life of the brief Labour government.

MacDonald sought an agreement with the Soviet Union in which Britain guaranteed loans to the Soviet Union in turn for a settlement of British claims for property compensation owed from pre-revolutionary days. This initiated considerable controversy – not only among political Conservatives, who remained wary of a Bolshevist threat. Operating through his puppet newspaper, the *Daily Chronicle*, Lloyd George also criticized the treaties in a series of articles.[47] On 16 August, for example, he wrote that the Labour government had surreptitiously shown only its moderate face to the public. In reality, it was waiting for the opportune moment to tear off 'the mask of sweet reason and moderation': only then 'will appear the stern face of the relentless enemy which has pursued private enterprise and individual property'. Socialism, he warned further, was 'approaching skilfully under cover to the grand attack on the existing order of society'.[48] Apparently forgetting his own trade negotiations with Soviet Russia when he was Prime Minister, Lloyd George condemned the idea of making a substantial loan to Soviet Russia, a country, he said, that was openly dedicated to the destruction of the British Empire.[49]

Earlier that summer, a second series of events began which precipitated additional criticisms of the Labour government. In late July 1924, an article appeared in the *Workers' Weekly*, the official organ of the Communist Party, calling upon soldiers in the British Army to refrain from turning their guns upon British workers during any future strikes or demonstrations. The article, written by the paper's Editor, John Campbell, seemed an incitement to mutiny. But opinion among legal officials was divided. When the matter came before the House of Commons and later the Cabinet, Campbell was recognized as a World War I war hero. The decision was then made to drop the prosecution. Meanwhile, the matter had become public. Opinion now consolidated among anti-Bolshevik elements, especially on the Conservative right. They claimed that the ministry, by refusing to prosecute Campbell, was kowtowing to its left wing – just as it had in formulating the prospective Soviet treaties.[50] In early October, the Conservatives tabled a censure motion: this was followed by a Liberal amendment calling for a committee of inquiry. Lloyd George confided to his daughter, Megan, that events were likely leading to a general election. 'I have done my best', he added, 'to precipitate it'.[51]

On 8 October, both Conservatives and Liberals joined in calling for a select committee on the Campbell case: the vote was carried 364:198. The next morning, MacDonald saw the King and asked for a dissolution of Parliament. Bad luck and poor judgement continued to dog the Labourites during the campaign. Anti-Soviet sentiment, with its trailing effect upon MacDonald, was further stoked by the public revelation of an ostensible secret communiqué sent by Grigori Zinoviev (who was President of the Communist International) to the British Communist Party instructing it to agitate for the Anglo-Russian treaties.[52] In addition, Zinoviev encouraged the CPGB to establish cells in military units, military store depots and in munitions factories to take advantage of any civilian unrest. This letter, published in the *Daily Mail* only a few days before the election, was sensational news. The red menace was now fully exposed.[53] Damaging though the letter was, even more so was MacDonald's response – at first silence, and then temporizing about the facts on the floor of the House of Commons. The effect upon MacDonald's government and the Labour parliamentary campaign during the upcoming election 'was little short of catastrophic' as Marquand notes.[54] On election day, 29 October, Conservatives won a decisive victory, gaining 155 seats, returning to office with 413 MPs. Labour lost 40 seats, but retained a respectable 151 MPs. The Liberals suffered most of all, losing 118 seats, returning only 40 to the House of Commons. Baldwin was back in office and the Conservatives indisputably in command.

Still, Labour in defeat was in far better shape than the Liberal Party. Liberal leaders – among them Lloyd George – had mistaken the temper of the electorate. Lloyd George had thought that, given the loss of confidence in MacDonald, Liberals might well lose some seats as a by-product of the Liberal/Labour alliance. But he also believed that in a general election, Labour would fare far worse. Liberals could then become the alternative progressive party in future periods of normal rotation with the Conservatives. The shattering reduction of Liberal MPs ended this delusion. There was at least one sign of comfort for Lloyd George: Asquith lost his seat at Paisley and was soon to be elevated to the House of Lords as the Earl of Oxford and Asquith. The way was now clear for Lloyd George to claim sole leadership of a revived Liberal Party.

But another straw in the wind told against any hope of a Liberal resurrection: Churchill joined the new Baldwin government.[55] Ejected from his Dundee seat (which he had held since 1908) during the general election of 1922, Churchill had been out of office since then. In the months following, Labour's surging electoral strength and then the formation of MacDonald's government presented a political crisis for him. Perhaps influenced by his pronounced anti-Bolshevist views developed during the war, Churchill became fully convinced that any Labour ministry would not only be unfit to govern, but that it would be positively dangerous. His centre-left political position shifted rightward. In a public letter to *The Times* in early 1924, he predicted that a Labour government would cast 'a dark and blighting shadow on every form of national life'.[56] Churchill's move towards the Conservative Party, however, was not easy: Conservatives remembered with chagrin his earlier defection to the Liberals two decades earlier. After two unsuccessful attempts to regain a seat in the House of Commons, he finally succeeded at Epping during the general election of 1924, which had brought Baldwin back to power for his second term of office.

Lloyd George lost not only a former colleague in arms. Churchill, by embracing Baldwin, seemed to be a straw in the wind and represented an additional hurdle for any early Liberal return to office. Indeed, Baldwin's second Cabinet proved noticeably stronger than his first, in part due to its inclusion of several former Lloyd George coalition Conservatives. In addition to Churchill – who somewhat surprisingly became Chancellor of the Exchequer – Austen Chamberlain went to the Foreign Office and Worthington-Evans to the War Office. Curzon, denied the Foreign Office, reluctantly accepted the Lord Presidency of the council. The erratic and bibulous Lord Birkenhead (F.E. Smith) – whose brilliance was widely recognized but self-proclaimed adherence to 'Tory democracy' was a matter of suspicion among many Conservatives – became Secretary of State for India. Thus Baldwin, realizing that the Conservatives had won re-election in part based upon working-class and former Liberal voters, constructed his Cabinet to reflect a more centrist approach to the persistent economic and social problems facing the nation.

Certainly, Baldwin was philosophically Conservative, as Williamson has amply demonstrated.[57] But during his second term of office, Baldwin demonstrated aspects of a 'new conservatism' – an emphasis upon the role of government in promoting social betterment.[58] He supported Neville Chamberlain's initiatives in housing, health and local government, including extensions of national insurance and widows' pensions. Although allowing some carefully regulated tariff impositions, he abandoned a comprehensive tariff reform. He avoided previous hard-line Conservative shibboleths such as restoring the House of Lords to its once lofty parliamentary status. He discouraged any attempt to enact punitive measures against the trade unions. With regard to Ireland, Baldwin was determined to moderate tension between Ulster and the Irish Free State over their disputed common boundary. In foreign relations, he was a strong supporter of Austen Chamberlain's Locarno Pact by which the major European powers renounced their right to change national boundaries by force. Ramsden sums up Baldwin's aim as the making of peace – peace abroad in Ireland and Europe, and peace at home in industrial relations.[59]

Industrial relations, however, proved to be the thorniest, and ultimately the most critical, of the issues facing Baldwin. As coal prices continued to fall on the world market throughout the 1920s, tensions rose sharply between mine owners and workers. Owners sought to reduce costs by lowering miners' wages while simultaneously increasing their hours of work. Miners naturally enough rejected these proposals. Their position was succinctly put: 'Not a penny off the pay, not a minute on the day.' To break the deadlock, the ministry under Baldwin's leadership agreed in July 1925 to extend a government subsidy to the industry with the hope that the delay would somehow resolve the dispute peacefully. But in the months that followed, positions hardened.

Out of office and undercut by Baldwin's social programmes and moderate political tone, Lloyd George for a time lost his voice. He was nevertheless alert to any possible opening – should opportunities present themselves, he began sounding the alarm. In a letter to J.L. Garvin, he used an extended metaphor to describe Baldwin's dilemma as attempting to navigate heavy seas. The ship of State, he wrote, was like 'a barque which has had a rough shaking in a prolonged typhoon. Water is gradually seeping through the loosened timbers at every joint, and in spite of much pumping is rising in the hold'. What was needed, he suggested, was 'that the ship should turn in at the first available port for a complete overhaul'.[60]

Indeed, Baldwin was eventually forced to bring out all hands on deck. Once the coal subsidy had expired, the likelihood of a general strike in support of the miners increased. Should that happen, the maintenance of public order would be the first priority. In anticipation, the government had made preparations by reorganizing the Supply and Transport Committee (originally established under Lloyd George's coalition government) and by placing local authorities and volunteers on alert. On 3 May 1926, the anticipated general strike began when, in support of the miners, the

Trades Union Congress called out workers in other industries, including railways, the docks, iron and steel, printing, heavy chemicals and gas and electric. Lasting nine days, the strike involved 2.5 million workers. Although the strike did not close down national economic life entirely – essential services, transport and food supply were maintained – it revealed a remarkable unity of spirit and organization among the unions and their sympathizers.[61] Equally remarkable was the relative lack of violence. Some destruction of property and injuries resulting from numerous overly overzealous demonstrations and overturned vehicles was inevitable. But there was not a single loss of life. It was soon evident, however, that the government would hold firm. No negotiations were planned: no concessions were offered. Better prepared and financed to meet the emergency, Baldwin and the emergency services, aided by well-organized teams of volunteers, kept the country running.

Reaction to the General Strike and its sudden collapse was a mixture of relief and disappointment: relief in the public at large at its brevity; and disappointment among Labour at its lack of success. The most vehement response, however, was anger felt by many on the Conservative right. Appalled at the threat to public order posed by the trade unions in sponsoring a general strike, they were determined to exact punitive measures. Their hand was strengthened by the refusal of the miners to cease their industrial actions after the strike had officially ended: miners held out for several months' longer before capitulating. Anti-Labour sentiment was clearly evident during the October 1926 Conservative Party conference at Scarborough, where delegates were seen 'baying for blood' as they pressured the Party leadership for punitive trade union legislation.[62]

Baldwin's role throughout the strike was curiously detached. Tom Jones paints a picture of Baldwin as often hesitant and frequently a silent participant in negotiations both prior and during the strike. [63] Whether or not Baldwin was temperamentally disinclined to intervene, or whether he was pursuing a calculated policy, his role in the aftermath of the strike was to find and hold a neutral corner. His detachment and absence thus gave the intransigent right a clear field of play. In March 1927, they brought forward the Trades Disputes Bill. The bill – 'entirely negative', as Ramsden describes it[64] – essentially reversed or altered the legal immunities won by trade unions since the pre-war era. For example, the law of picketing was tightened. In addition, Labour's political fighting fund (the political levy) was reduced by new rules of union members' payments towards the levy. Previously, payment was made automatically to the levy, unless one contracted out. Under the new regulations, payment would only be made by contracting in. Thus it was much easier for a recalcitrant or indifferent union member to refuse or neglect to contribute. This led to a significant decline in Labour's funds and weakened its position politically.

Throughout the strike and the events that followed, the Labour Party tended to support its vigorous working-class allies in the unions, though not always enthusiastically. Ramsay MacDonald thought the Baldwin government was largely at fault, but he was nevertheless opposed in principal to a general strike, believing it a clumsy and unpredictable tactic. Better was a Labour victory at the ballot box.[65] The effect of the General Strike upon the Liberal Party was more profound. Asquith

– still formally head of the party – spoke from the House of Lords as the Earl of Oxford and Asquith, condemning the strike 'unreservedly'.[66] Lloyd George, however, took a more conciliatory line. Although he opposed the strike, he criticized Baldwin's government for its inflexible approach and advocated a negotiated settlement.[67] He never regarded the strike as a revolutionary threat to established order. Indeed, he regarded the confrontation as a natural outcome of a trade dispute. In general, he supported the miners in their objections to wage cuts. Alone among Liberal leaders, he spoke critically of the Baldwin government's decision to break off negotiations with strike leaders. This difference of opinion on the strike led Asquith to denounce Lloyd George publicly, in effect expelling him from the Liberal Party.[68] But as historians have generally agreed, Asquith overreached himself. Among party members in the country at large, as well as within the parliamentary membership, Lloyd George's popularity remained high. Within a month of the strike's conclusion in May 1926, moreover, Asquith suffered the first of a series of strokes. His leadership of the party was at an end. In October 1926, Asquith retired from active politics. The mantle of party leader now fell wholly on Lloyd George.

For Lloyd George, the removal of the dead hand of Asquith freed him from the old leader's more Conservative brand of Liberalism: he could now lead the Liberal Party leftward. He believed that it was essential to tap into the growing Labour sentiment of the electorate that had led the Labour Party to its recent successes. He did not fear the advance of Labour, understanding that the Labour Party and its followers were determined to work within the political system. If he could re-establish the Liberal Party's progressive tradition and tendencies yet remain essentially centrist in its policies, Lloyd George could position the Liberals as a viable alternative to Labourites. Ever the politician of ideas as well as of manoeuvre and stratagem, he believed that Liberals must first be seen as a party preparing for office. Well before the General Strike, he had begun devising plans that would clarify Liberal and progressive intentions to the electorate. To that end, he drew upon the Liberal Summer School, a group of experts made up of progressive thinkers who had initially organized in 1921. Meeting alternately in Oxford and Cambridge, the Summer School participants hoped to lend intellectual and organizational heft to public policy.[69] Based upon their research, Lloyd George published *Coal and Power* in July 1924. The report examined the continuing economic problems of the coal mining industry. It advocated the nationalization of mining royalties and recommended the establishment of Royalty Commissioners with the authority to close pits and amalgamate collieries. The Commissioners would additionally create a welfare fund designed to improve housing and pit facilities for miners.[70]

Lloyd George's next attempt to establish a broader and more progressive Liberal Party platform focused on the agricultural life of the country.[71] First, he appointed a committee of Liberal politicians and agricultural experts to examine rural conditions and make recommendations. Then he presented the committee's findings at a meeting of the shadow Cabinet in August 1925. At the heart of the proposal was the nationalization of agricultural land, with suitable compensation to the landlords. Farmers would have security of tenure under a new County Agricultural Authority, which would also determine whether or not farmers adhered to practices of good cultivation. The Authority would contribute to farmers' productivity by assisting in capital costs such as drainage and reclamation. It was a radical scheme; indeed, to one historian, it was an attempt to establish a working synthesis of socialist ideals with capitalist practices.[72] Lloyd George publicly launched his land reform programme on 17 September 1925. Speaking to a crowd of 25,000 on the estate of Sir Francis Dyke Acland at Killerton Park, Devon, near Exeter, Lloyd George had prepared carefully. Sir Francis, the Liberal son of a Liberal father, had warned Lloyd George that fully half of his audience would be Tories, 'and it would be well not to tread too hard on their toes – though a little chaff of Baldwin would be distinctly well taken'.[73]

The theme of Lloyd George's Killerton Park speech was the need for greater regulation of agriculture: 'the time had come', he declared in his opening remarks, 'when the state should resume its legal authority over the land'.[74] The national problem of unemployment must be addressed by settling more men on the land. The new farmers under his plan would be given training. In addition, the State would sponsor programmes of land reclamation, drainage and afforestation. The role of the state was crucial: landlords could no longer play their traditional roles as improvers of the land. The landlord was in fact 'no longer a real working partner'. Lloyd George did not advocate state ownership of the land, for 'that would be nationalization'. But, he continued, the state must give 'the necessary security to the cultivator' of the soil. Agriculture was, in short, 'undercapitalized'. By regulating cultivation and production, the state guaranteed better agricultural practices. Ineffective farmers would be weeded out: 'indolent, inefficient and careless cultivators' must be removed. He also promoted the idea of relief for farm labourers by increasing the number of smallholdings. 'Every labourer should have half an acre as a right.' In conclusion, Lloyd George summed up his programme in ringing terms: 'a living wage for the worker and an adequate return to a good cultivator'.

Three weeks after Killerton Park, details of the plan were published as *The Land and the Nation*, popularly known as the Green Book (from the colour of its cover). Criticism of the plan emerged quickly, however. The idea of a host of intrusive rural civil servants working at will among the thousands of small and middling farmers to improve their agricultural practices was completely unacceptable. Conservative critics criticized the policy by characterizing it as both socialistic and bureaucratic. Even some in the Liberal Party were opposed to what they considered the collectivist aspects of the scheme.[75] All ten of the agricultural constituencies in Cornwall and Devon – usually strongholds of Liberal politics – rejected the imposition of public regulation and official supervision of farmers' agricultural practices.[76] In the face of this criticism, Lloyd George was forced to retract the notion of a powerful state presence on the land. He quickly turned his attention to a more tempting target for reform, urban land. This less controversial scheme, published as *Towns and the Land* (the Brown Book), advocated the extension of the powers of urban local authorities to acquire land for housing and open spaces with an eye to reduce overcrowding and alleviate slum conditions. It also proposed the reform of the leasehold system.

It was clear, then, that by early 1926, Lloyd George's proposed policies were trending leftward. When possible, he allied openly with the Labour Party. On the occasion of a parliamentary debate on Churchill's Economy Bill – which reduced the government's contribution to health and unemployment insurance during the spring of 1926 – Lloyd George and members of the Labour Party led the attack. In her précis of the debate, Frances Stevenson marvelled at the change that had come about in the relations between Lloyd George and Labour. 'The most amazing thing about D. since he went out of office', she wrote in her diary, has been 'his gradual conquest of Labour'.[77] A few weeks later, after the General Strike, Stevenson reported that Lloyd George's friendly relations with Labour remained firm. 'The Labour people are pleased with him.'[78] When he spoke out in the House during the strike, 'the Labour people cheered him'. His idea, Stevenson wrote in her diary, 'is to go definitely towards the *Left*, and gradually to co-ordinate and consolidate all he progressive forces of the country, against the Conservative and reactionary forces'. Substantiating Stevenson, who was doubtless recounting Lloyd George's own words, is Rowland's judgement: 'It is undeniably the case that Lloyd George wanted a closer relationship with the Labour Party at this time.'[79] Rowland made it additionally clear, however, that Lloyd George had no intention of actually joining the Labour Party. For Lloyd George the goal was to establish a radical but non-socialist alternative to the Conservatives.[80]

The most significant and far-reaching commission that Lloyd George established in pursuit of his goal of uniting progressive forces was the Liberal Industrial Inquiry.[81] Spurred perhaps by the lessons of the General Strike, he invited economic experts to his home at Churt in September 1926.[82] Their task was to begin the development of policies on such critical issues as state and industry; Labour and trade unions; unemployment; pay and status; and industrial and financial organization. These experts were largely members of the Liberal Summer School. Chief among them was John Maynard Keynes. It may seem surprising that any cooperation between Lloyd George and Keynes would be possible after Keynes's denunciation of Lloyd George's policies and actions at the Paris Peace Conference. But Keynes had become disillusioned with Asquith for his harsh opposition to the General Strike and the strikers: he much preferred Lloyd George's more conciliatory approach. Keynes believed in finding a middle ground to mitigate the periodical bouts of capitalist excesses during which severe unemployment and social unrest were prevalent. By steering between the protectionism of the right and the redistributionism of the left and utilizing an effective monetary policy and sufficient capital spending, Keynes believed that a managerial state could control the worst downturns of the business cycle.[83] In this, he was broadly in agreement with Lloyd George, who described his own brand of social and economic policy as one that upheld private enterprise and individual incentive. But 'when private enterprise has conspicuously broken down or proved itself to be inadequate to the public needs', he would then embrace 'public ownership'.[84]

The completed report of the Liberal Industrial Inquiry, published as *Britain's Industrial Future* in February 1928, was 500 pages long.[85] Widely known as the Yellow

Book, it recommended strong government action to address comprehensively the unresolved domestic problems of the day. It advocated, for example, the nationalization of the mineral royalties from coalmines. In agriculture, it proposed substantial change, primarily by promoting a secure tenurial system. The most important theme of the Yellow Book – and its major recommendation – was a sweeping programme to address unemployment. Only a massive infusion of government assistance to provide the funds for road building, housing, slum clearance, electrification, afforestation and the improvement of docks, harbours and canals could reverse the stagnation of national unemployment.[86] The Yellow Book was also sharply critical of the Baldwin government and its record on unemployment. Likely enough it was Lloyd George himself who wrote the most denunciatory passages. Condemning the government for its 'timid, unimaginative, unenterprising' policy, the Yellow Book claimed that the Conservative government must bear a major responsibility for 'damming up in the stagnant pool of unemployment so much of the available forces of willing labour'.[87] This became a theme in the months that followed as the Liberal Party sought to establish itself under Lloyd George's leadership as the most plausible alternative to the Conservatives.

In addition to sharpening the Liberal Party platform and refining its progressive goals, Lloyd George was also actively re-organizing and streamlining the Party organization. A new Liberal Campaign Department as well as a new Organization Committee came into being. Herbert Samuel, a former member of Asquith's pre-war reforming Liberal government and more recently the High Commissioner for Palestine, became Chairman of the party. Lloyd George also 'poured money unstintingly' into the Liberal Party treasury.[88] Formerly dormant local associations sprang to life; paid speakers to boost Liberal electoral prospects were hired; and printed material – pamphlets, leaflets, newspapers – carried out Liberal Party propaganda. Even the Asquithian Lord Grey put aside (temporarily) his dislike of Lloyd George to share a platform at the National Liberal Club in July 1927 to denounce Conservative right wing proposals such as the Trades Disputes Bill.

Throughout 1928 and into early 1929, Lloyd George also stepped up his own speaking engagements in anticipation of the general election to be held in 1929.[89] Emphasizing the poor economic record of the Baldwin government, Lloyd George recaptured some of the oratorical flair that had once established him as the firebrand of British politics. At Aberystwyth in August 1928, he assured his audience that the Liberals were 'a great army carrying on behind the pillar of fire that leads the nation to the Promised Land'.[90] Nor was the Labour Party spared. At the Liberal Party Conference in Yarmouth in October 1928, he declared that Liberals should support neither Conservatives nor Labour. There was little to chose 'between the strangling rope of tariff and the drawing and quartering of Socialism'.[91] Speaking before the House of Commons on 9 November 1928, Lloyd George castigated the government's return to the gold standard: it was a 'grave blunder' because it was 'handicapping our exports'. He cited specifically the increased price of British coal in foreign markets, which had 'calamitous' affects upon the trade.[92]

Into the new year, Lloyd George continued his election initiative. On 1 March 1929, he spoke at the Connaught Rooms in London to more than 400 prospective Liberal candidates for the House of Commons.[93] There he extolled the Liberal Party's 'systematic and thorough' inquiries into national problems. He emphasized, too, the Party's broad objectives for regenerating the economy and the need for more action by the state to accomplish greater ends. 'When a man's condition is subnormal', he declared, 'the doctor gives him a stimulant'. Lloyd George also set out in significant detail the specific benefits of his stimulus plan. Road traffic, he said, had increased dramatically over the past few years. It was time to widen and straighten roads, and where possible to build ring roads around the towns. Within the cities were too many slums, 'hideous, grey, dusty – no place to bring up children of a great Empire'. Better housing was critical. Money for these programmes could be found by reducing expenditures elsewhere, such as in counterproductive armaments and defence spending. government borrowing would also be substantially increased. So certain was Lloyd George of these measures that he predicted 'in the course of a single year', the unemployment rate would be reduced 'to normal proportions'.

A few days later, the last of the programmatic 'colour' publications appeared – the Orange Book, whose title was *We Can Conquer Unemployment: Mr Lloyd George's Pledge*. In pamphlet form and costing only sixpence, it was essentially a boiled down version of the Yellow Book. It laid out in simpler language plans for road building, housing and reclamation projects. Added to these was a proposed extension of the telephone system and London transport.[94] That Lloyd George's campaign was beginning to have an impact was evident in the spring by-elections. Between 19 and 21 March 1929, by-elections were held in five Conservative constituencies. Of these, the Conservatives carried only a single seat; Labour gained one; and the Liberals won the other three. To heighten the sense that Liberals were riding the crest of an electoral wave, Lloyd George addressed a triumphant meeting at the Royal Albert Hall on 26 March. His speech was carried by broadcast to 12 other cities across the country. On 12 April at the Manchester Free Trade Hall, he directly attacked Baldwin. Comparing Baldwin to an irresponsible driver of a meandering vehicle, Lloyd George declared that whereas Baldwin may be a clever passenger, he was 'casual as a driver. He dozes for long stretches, turns round and talks to the passengers, and recharges his pipe. Easy going is all right if circumstances are easy, but they are not'.[95] This speech was relayed to 28 other cities.

Favourable press accounts applauding the Liberal campaign began to appear. Beaverbrook, always sensitive to public opinion, believed that neither Baldwin nor MacDonald was pursuing an attractive or convincing campaign. Lloyd George, on the other hand, was 'making the running of the election, and he alone has persuaded the electors that he has a definite scheme for the cure of unemployment, which is the one and only issue'.[96] Indeed, it appeared that the Conservatives had lost momentum. As Ramsden has observed, the Conservatives were 'an unhappy party' approaching the general election.[97] The earlier Baldwinian promise of conciliation had been broken by the General Strike and the government's punitive attitude afterward with its Trades Disputes Bill. Baldwin himself seemed out of touch with the Conservative lurch toward the right and did not enter heartily into the campaign.[98] Nor was there a convenient episode analogous to the Red scare of 1924 that could redound to the advantage of the Conservatives. Most of all, there was no evident plan in prospect for addressing the crisis of unemployment.[99] Emboldened by Conservative disarray, and fielding more than 500 candidates generously supported by the Lloyd George Fund, Liberal hopes rose correspondingly.

Nevertheless Lloyd George, an old and experienced campaigner, was cautious. In January 1929, he confessed to Frances that: 'As to politics, I am fuddled about them still.' What was essential was that his own plan of campaign 'must be strenuous[ly] energetic'.[100] Two weeks before election day, he seemed more confident, reporting to Frances that the campaign was going well: 'Immense meetings & great enthusiasm.' But he also remained tentative: 'with this amorphous electorate the issue is too obscure for a premature crow'. He could not as yet 'hazard a prediction'. The major problem was, as he accurately realized, that a three-cornered fight 'muddles everything up'.[101]

Lloyd George's doubts were borne out. As expected, Conservatives lost heavily – more than 100 seats – for a total of 260. Labour did well at 289, becoming the largest parliamentary party, but not enough for a majority in the House of Commons. The Liberal outcome was the surprise of the election. They gained only a handful of seats, to raise their total to 59 MPs. They had lost heavily in the largest cities of the kingdom. Their gains were largely confined to the agricultural districts, primarily in Wales, Scotland and a few agricultural districts in East Anglia.[102] A large section of the electorate seemed to have drawn the logical conclusion from Lloyd George's energetic plans for dealing with the economy – that the goals of the working class and of progressive legislation as a whole could best be accomplished not by the Liberals, but by the Labour Party. For Lloyd George, there were at least family consolations: apart from his own victory, his son Gwilym won at Pembroke and his daughter Megan won Anglesey.

Baldwin's resignation was followed by MacDonald's formation of his second government – without, it seems, making any overtures to Lloyd George and his band of Liberals. The new Prime Minister simply assumed that the small Liberal contingent would serve as Labour allies. Lloyd George publicly confirmed several days later that the Liberal Party would support the Labour government, provided that MacDonald's government policy did not stray from acceptable Liberal ideals. This was at best a tentative and lukewarm endorsement; but for Lloyd George it was important to have an avenue open for progressive measures in the House of Commons. Beatrice Webb, in musing over the election, believed, however, that the election result meant 'the final collapse of the Liberal Party'. As for Lloyd George, the future was 'blank'.[103]

Historians since have tended to agree. Rowland believes that the 1929 election was a 'traumatic experience' for Lloyd George and the Liberal Party.[104] Wilson concurs: 'it was the end of the line for the old Liberal party'.[105] It was true enough that in spite of the expenditure of considerable campaign cash and the exertion of 513 Liberal candidates, the party had improved their parliamentary representation only slightly. Yet their vote total throughout the country was quite respectable – 5.3 million. This was nearly a quarter of the total vote, but it won only a tenth of all parliamentary seats. The Conservative Party also felt this electoral anomaly. They had actually won the most votes in the election: 8.6 million to Labour's 8.3 million, but had gained fewer seats. In reviewing the election results, Lloyd George drew the conclusion that a system of proportional representation at general elections would not only be a fairer expression of voter preference, but that it would also redound to Liberal advantage.[106] Indeed, Packer makes the case that because Liberals held the balance of power in the House of Commons – in spite of their disappointing electoral showing – 'they were still in a powerful position'. In addition, Lloyd George retained 'his customary political dexterity', which he was to prove in the months that followed.[107]

As had been true in his first administration, MacDonald was off to a fast start in pursuing Britain's international goals. To ease deteriorating relationships between Britain and the United States occasioned by an increasing naval rivalry, MacDonald paid an official visit to that country, the first British Prime Minister to do so.[108] Early negotiations there prompted a second round of talks in London, with an expansion to include France, Italy and Japan. Naval ratios were argued and adjusted among these powers to general satisfaction in concluding the London Naval Treaty of 1930. The terms of the treaty dictated that Britain agreed to a rough naval parity with the United States. Japan's right to an enlarged navy was also recognized, with France, Italy and Germany additionally gaining a certain status – although Germany was at the tail end of allowable ships.[109]

Less successful, however, was MacDonald's attempt to solve the major domestic challenges, chief among them the intractable unemployment rate. In 1929, the year that MacDonald assumed office, the total unemployed was slightly more than 1.2 million. Two years later, it had more than doubled to 2.6 million. As historians have pointed out, not all sections of the economy suffered equally. The older industrial areas were hardest hit. Unemployment in the coal industry, for example, rose from 18.2 per cent in 1929 to 41.2 per cent in 1932; cotton from 14.5 per cent to 31.1 per cent; shipbuilding from 23.2 per cent to 59.5 per cent; and iron and steel from 19.9 per cent to 48.5 per cent. By the winter of 1932–33, the number of unemployed was near three million. It quickly became apparent that among the diverse political and economic interests, there was little agreement on remedies. It was not a simple division of opinion between socialists and capitalists, but rather, as Skidelsky reminds us, a division between economic Conservatives and economic radicals.[110] In sum, it was a contest between laissez-faire capitalism and interventionist capitalism.[111] On one side were the orthodox bankers and financiers, who doubted the efficacy of any governmental action; and on the other was the Trades Union Congress, whose membership represented those who suffered the most severe effects of the depression. The Labour government itself, with Ramsay MacDonald as Prime Minister, was torn between the two.

Though unemployment became the dominant issue of political life from 1929 onward, other matters also threatened the life of the ministry. Chief among these were the continuous machinations of Lloyd George, who, as leader of the Liberal Party, held the balance of power in the House of Commons. It was not long before he attempted to take advantage of Labour's somewhat perilous position by opening private conversations with his old comrade Churchill, out of office since the 1929 election. This *tête-à-tête* was bound to become known, and to be a cause for comment and speculation. Leo Amery, for example, confided to his diary in June 1929 that Churchill had recently 'been colloguing vigorously with Lloyd George since the election and is heading straight for a coalition'.[112] Amery was undoubtedly referring to Churchill's meeting that day with Lloyd George to discuss a possible Conservative-Liberal compact. A fortnight later, Churchill openly advocated such a pact – this time, during a meeting of the Conservative shadow Cabinet.[113] Months later, towards the end of that year, Tom Jones, in commenting on Lloyd George's active participation in the House of Commons ('he has made a series of speeches which rank with the most effective of his career'), observed that Churchill remained 'restive' and 'would much prefer to be running in double harness with L.G. than with the cautious S.B.'.[114]

Not long afterward, however, Lloyd George and Churchill seemed to have drifted apart and the projected alliance never bore fruit. Altering his political tactics, Lloyd George was soon devoting his energy directly to Labour's legislative efforts. In December 1929, the Labour government introduced a Coal Bill, an important initiative designed to rationalize the coal industry. The bill gave even-handed assistance to both miners and owners by reducing hours of work and protecting wages on the one hand, and guaranteeing price maintenance and export subsidies on the other. But the bill's compromise left itself open to criticism. Conservatives were wholly opposed, as one might expect. More seriously, Lloyd George was also vehemently against it, condemning it as an 'incredibly bad' bill.[115] He argued instead for the compulsory amalgamation of mines to enhance broader efficiency in the industry and better protection for the consumer. Because the Liberals held the balance of power between the two larger political parties, Lloyd George's opinions were critical.

The bill eventually passed but hard feelings remained. MacDonald was furious. Lloyd George, he wrote in his diary, was 'a colleague who was ever disloyal; he never used a partner but for his own ends & sacrificed everyone who ever trusted him'.[116] Indeed, it seems that Lloyd George overreached himself. Apart from the undying enmity of MacDonald and other Labour members who were resentful of Lloyd George's threat to overturn the government, some Liberal MPs rebelled against their leader in disagreement over the tactical manoeuvring on the bill. On the first reading, two Liberal MPs actually voted for it and six abstained. On an amendment to the bill in February 1930, four Liberals voted with the government, and eight abstained. Facing reality and the likelihood of additional division within Liberal ranks, Lloyd George called off any further attempts to delay its passage. There is some evidence that Lloyd George's opposition to the Coal Bill was based less on the specifics of the bill than on a tactical deployment to wring concessions from MacDonald's government on electoral reform, dearer to the heart and ambitions of the Liberal leader. A commission on the topic had in fact been appointed in early December 1929, but had made little progress. Indeed, MacDonald was opposed to proportional representation for purely political reasons: it could strengthen the parliamentary representation of third parties – most particularly the Liberal Party and its current leader.[117]

Given MacDonald's staunch opposition to electoral reform, Lloyd George turned to the Conservatives in an attempt to further that cause. In November 1930, he opened a line to the Conservatives through his former aide Edward Grigg. He proposed a limited form of proportional representation by which both Conservatives and Liberals could benefit. His plan reached the ears of Neville Chamberlain, but no deal was ever struck. Lloyd George then turned once again to the Labour leadership. As before, his words fell flat. Rebuffed, Lloyd George demonstrated his resilience and determination a few months later by returning to the Conservatives. This time he offered a compromise by which a limited electoral reform would buy his (and the Liberal Party's) pledge to help the Conservatives turn out the Labour government.[118]

Lloyd George's reputation for inconstancy and double-dealing was only enhanced by these actions. His gyrations from right to left to right again and his apparent inconstancy puzzled and infuriated his political opponents – and historians as well. Even Campbell's extended apologia for Lloyd George falters slightly when he asks: 'what is to be made of this? Whenever Lloyd George appears to be on a leftward tack, there are always contrary indications of him exploring to the right'. Campbell attributes Lloyd George's apparent deceitful behaviour to 'the dialectical nature of his mind – his liking for a balance of forces'.[119] Setting aside any questions about the nature of Lloyd George's fidelity, political or personal, there is something to be said for Campbell's point of view. It is true that Lloyd George always had a penchant for coalitions in political life. Thus, when he seemed to move rightward, it was not an attempt to become Tory, but rather an appeal to the more flexible and accommodating wing of that party represented by Churchill and Austen Chamberlain. He disliked intensely ideological Toryism. But he also disapproved of the ideological socialism of the left. In the particular case of electoral reform, Lloyd George saw the issue as one of life and death for the Liberal Party. Without some change in the voting system, the future of the Liberal Party seemed dim indeed. It was no surprise that he sought some political arrangement – wherever it might be found – to gain that end.[120]

On one particular issue, however, Lloyd George was absolutely consistent – his concern about unemployment. As economic conditions worsened throughout 1930, he intensified his efforts at finding a solution. During the summer and early autumn, he entered into two-party talks with MacDonald (Baldwin and the Conservatives declined to participate.). Lloyd George continued to insist upon extensive government spending as a corrective stimulus to job losses. He especially pressed hard for an expansive road programme. But MacDonald's Cabinet 'jibbed at the notion of spending money in order to create work' as Rowland has characterized it.[121] Marquand seconds this view of the Labour government, adding that MacDonald's own reluctance to accept the notion of borrowing money to spend it on public works was 'glib and unconvincing'.[122] As the talks appeared to be ending fruitlessly in September 1930, however, Lloyd George took the initiative in proposing a scheme directed at agricultural unemployment. MacDonald seemed intrigued at the idea, and brought it forward to his Cabinet for discussion.[123]

Meanwhile, Lloyd George kept up the pressure on the government by utilizing his usual approach to political deadlock – direct appeals to the countryside. No doubt designed to influence Parliament soon to meet for its autumn session, Lloyd George spoke at Torquay on 17 October 1930 before a meeting of the National Liberal Federation Conference.[124] De-emphasizing partisan rhetoric, he proposed familiar solutions and added new ones in appealing to all 'patriotic members' of the British nation. No serious proposal should be ruled out. He called for an all-party conference to consider 'exceptional measures'. For his own part, Lloyd George seemed to suggest that he would even consider re-examining the question of tariffs. He also advocated a reduction in military spending. He argued at length for a more active role of the state in revitalizing agricultural production and marketing, and for a scheme of massive road construction. But the mistrust between the Labour leader and his Liberal counterpart resurfaced and ultimately brought an end to any possibility of fruitful discussions. MacDonald thought that Lloyd George was 'the most consummate cheat & wirepuller of the time'.[125] For his part, Lloyd George neither liked nor respected the Labour leader: 'Ramsay is just a fussy Baldwin – and no more', he had once confided to his daughter Megan.[126] Nor did Lloyd George believe that MacDonald would ever seriously cooperate with the Liberals because of his 'vanity and vindictiveness'. Macdonald's 'snobbish instincts' would always 'incline him to association with Tories'.[127]

Lloyd George's message nevertheless had resonance beyond members of his own Liberal Party. Some Conservatives – those who believed that the leaders of all parties had failed to address the economic and social problems engendered by the Depression – were willing to listen to the Liberal leader. Tom Jones recounts a discussion in late October 1930 among a group of 'young disgruntled Tories', houseguests of the Astors at Cliveden, who praised the Liberal leader's proposals. Among those present were Robert Boothby and Harold Macmillan, both of whom were attracted to Lloyd George's calls for action.[128] The consensus among the group was that Lloyd George could be the most effective political leader in addressing the economic crisis. As Jones put it in his diary afterwards: 'The tide has tuned very much in favour of L.G. because of his incomparable executive power, and I think most of this group would follow him if he could be got into the saddle again.'[129]

As unemployment continued to rise throughout 1931, no consensual political agreement on solutions emerged. This left the field open to influential financial circles. Most especially concerned were leading British bankers who continued to insist that severe economies, such as restricting expenditure and balancing the budget, should be enacted as soon as possible. Their hand was strengthened by the Economy Committee's report issued in late July 1931. Appointed by MacDonald to propose reductions in national expenditure, the Committee projected a deficit of £120m the following year. Such devastating news dictated severe reductions in government spending, including education, the police and the armed forces. But above all, the committee believed that social programmes, such as unemployment benefits, must bear the brunt of deficit reductions. Their estimate was that more than half the deficit, £67m, could be met by this admittedly drastic measure. The trade unions, given voice by the General Council of the Trades Union Congress, were naturally dead against any reduction in unemployment benefits. Such a programme, if implemented, would, as Marquand observes, strike 'savagely at the deepest instinct of the Labour movement'.[130] The unemployed had already been victimized by losing their jobs: to victimize them again could not be tolerated.

MacDonald's Cabinet mirrored these diverse opinions. Deadlocked at the end of August 1931 by conflicting interests and advice, the Cabinet split almost evenly, half favouring unemployment reductions, half opposed.[131] MacDonald could not govern with a divided Cabinet on the most pressing problem before the nation. For some time he had been thinking of a coalition ministry structured on all-party lines which could deal more effectively with the economic crisis. It would operate only temporarily until a viable solution was found, after which the parties would once again return to their traditional roles. Consulting with the leaders of all political parties, MacDonald formed a National Government which took office on 24 August. The stripped-down Cabinet, apart from MacDonald, retained three other Labour ministers – J.H. Thomas, Philip Snowden and Lord Sankey Added to them were four Conservatives: Sir Samuel Hoare, Sir Philip Cunliffe-Lister and the two prominent veterans, Baldwin and Neville Chamberlain. Two Liberals, Herbert Samuel and Rufus Isaacs, the Marquis of Reading, filled out the remaining offices.

This small Cabinet with its interparty composition was reminiscent of the emergency wartime Cabinets under Lloyd George.[132] Lloyd George himself was not included in the National Government. Nor did he in take part in the intensive consultations and negotiations that led to the new government. This was not because of any diminished interest on his part in addressing the financial and political crisis facing the country. He had continued his campaign to devise a strategy for recovery throughout the latter months of 1930 and into 1931. When it seemed that by the summer of 1931 MacDonald was moving towards some sort of collaborative government, Lloyd George was determined to form a counter force, which would be ready to oppose any undesirable (from his point of view) legislation. On 21 July 1931, he chaired a meeting held at Archibald Sinclair's home at Coombe, near Kingston-on-Thames. Motoring down to the meeting with him were Harold Nicolson and Oswald Mosley of the New Party. Churchill, attended by Brendan Bracken, was also present. Lloyd George informed the group that he believed Baldwin and MacDonald would soon form a coalition. Should that prove true, he advocated a National Opposition. Having introduced the topic, he then, as Nicolson records it, entered into a long conversation 'throwing out little sparks of compliments to right and left', drawing from each of those present their ideas. The Liberal leader seemed at his best, weaving together a disparate group with the intention of taking political advantage of the economic crisis. Nicolson was reminded – in characterizing Lloyd George's performance – 'of a master-at-drawing sketching in a fig-leaf, not in outline, but by means of the shadows around it'.[133]

Within a few days, however, Lloyd George was taken seriously ill: on 29 July his prostate gland was removed. His recuperation was slow and for many weeks following he was bedridden. This 'cruel timing'[134] ended the likelihood that Lloyd George could actively exercise any influence on the events of August. What role he may have played in shaping the National Government will never be known.[135] Sidelined by his illness, he lost valuable influence at a crucial time during a fluctuating political drama. But his political position was surely better than MacDonald's. The shock of MacDonald's treachery in joining hands with the Conservatives to form a National Government alienated Labourites. Seizing their advantage, Conservatives forced MacDonald to legitimate the new coalition by calling a general election in late October.

Hobbled by his illness, Lloyd George did not play an active role in the electioneering. In any case, it is unlikely that he could have stemmed the tide of the Conservatives, who won 473 seats. Labour returned only 52. The Liberal total was surprisingly large at 72, but it was divided among three separate groups: Liberals; National Liberals; and the miniscule family group of Lloyd George (which included his daughter, Megan; his son, Gwilym; and Gwilym's brother-in-law Goronwy Owen – all of whom represented Welsh seats). Thereafter, the two larger wings of the triadic Liberal Party began to go their separate ways. Herbert Samuel as Home Secretary represented the traditional free trade Liberal wing in MacDonald's Cabinet. Growing protectionist sentiment there forced his resignation in July 1932. Over the next few years, the Samuelites faded entirely from view. On the other hand, the National Liberals, headed by Sir John Simon, Foreign Secretary in the new Cabinet, became increasingly enamoured of protectionism and survived for a time until many of them joined the Conservative Party.[136] Lloyd George had by then already recognized the obvious. In a letter to one of his oldest friends, Sir Herbert Lewis, in late December 1931, he wrote 'for all practical purposes' the Liberal Party was 'annihilated'.[137]

With the Liberal Party's splintering, his own Liberal base of support steadily declining and the Conservatives dominant, Lloyd George found the political scene sharply tilted against any likelihood of his resumption of office during the early 1930s. His enforced political sabbatical found him active in other spheres, however. Always a keen traveller, Lloyd George was often abroad during the years from late 1931 to 1934. He was also very fully engaged in writing his *War Memoirs* and to some degree reliving the dangerous yet triumphant years of World War I.[138] As Frances Stevenson observed in her diary: 'He is wrapped up in the work, and considers he is doing more important work by writing his memoirs than anything he could be doing at the moment in politics.'[139] Only rarely did he appear in the House of Commons. During the 1933–34 session, he did not make a single speech.[140]

By late 1934, however, there were signs of Lloyd George's stirring.[141] Reviews of volume IV of his *War Memoirs* were largely positive and kept his name before the public. He had begun to form study groups to advise him on domestic and foreign policy matters. As Frances Stevenson noted in November: 'D. getting keener on politics as the election draws nearer.'[142] Later that month, he gave a major speech in the House of Commons. The occasion was Churchill's latest warning about Adolf Hitler's rise to power in Germany and the consequent threat to peace in Europe. Churchill, who was also at that time in the political wilderness, had been sounding the alarm for more than a year. His speech painted a gloomy picture of the deficiencies of the Royal Air Force as compared to the Luftwaffe. An enemy attack upon London alone, he warned, could kill or maim tens of thousands. Birmingham or Sheffield could face the same danger. The only answer was to increase rapidly the size of a defending air force.[143] Rising in rebuttal, Lloyd George spoke in reaction against Churchill's alarmist statements. He advocated a cautious response to German rearmament. It was doubtless important, he said, 'to organize a defence which was adequate to our reasonable needs and to practical probabilities'. He believed, however, that Germany at that moment was fit only for defensive warfare, not offensive. Admitting that Germany 'was not normal for the time being', having 'offended every kind of sentiment' – from Jew and Gentile, Catholic and Protestant, to Communist and trade unionist – Lloyd George nevertheless reminded the House that Germany was in the midst of a revolution and 'a revolutionary country was a dangerous country to treat as a pariah'. Germany, he believed further, must be given 'fair, impartial, and judicial consideration' to its grievances.[144]

Lloyd George's comments could be interpreted as supportive of MacDonald's National Government – however tepid. The general sense that Lloyd George was raising his political profile and beginning a campaign, perhaps for inclusion in the government, became evident when he delivered a major speech at Bangor on 17 January 1935. This was his 72nd birthday, and he seemed as hearty as ever in speaking to a crowd of several thousand in outlining a plan for dealing with the lingering domestic economic crisis. The country remained 'in a critical situation', he declared. Those who believed in the notion that the normal trade cycle would remedy the unacceptably high rates of poverty and unemployment were wrong. It was time to stop 'piffling with distress'. Wait and see was 'a hopeless policy'. Action was imperative. Referring to President Franklin Roosevelt's 'New Deal', Lloyd George promised a like-minded scheme for Britain. In remarks reminiscent of his 1929 scheme, 'We can Conquer Unemployment', he declared that the State should use its financial resources to begin developments in both town and country to 'bring into fruitful activity our underutilized labour, our idle capital and our undeveloped resources and opportunities'. More specifically, he advocated a housing programme 'of considerable dimensions'; rebuilding and expanding the road system; aiding agriculture; improving railways, canals and the telephone system – all of which would drive down unemployment while modernizing the national infrastructure. To implement such a programme, he advocated the establishment of an administrative body not unlike the old War Cabinet – which was, as Lloyd George told the assembled crowd, 'the most effective committee of action on a great scale which this country has ever seen'. Such a National Development Council would be no larger than five members, who would sit continuously, free from all departmental work.[145]

That Lloyd George's ideas were gaining some traction in the highest rank of political circles is clearly evident from MacDonald's diary. As Marquand observes, MacDonald 'was at least half-attracted' by the idea of bringing Lloyd George into the Cabinet.[146] Indeed, in noting what he called Lloyd George's 'come-back', MacDonald gave some thought to reshuffling the Cabinet to make room for Lloyd George. As he put it in his diary: 'Ll.G. has had a rest & ought to be fresh'[147] That MacDonald was willing to consider the inclusion of Lloyd George in the government was a recognition of his own ministry's failure to solve the problem of unemployment, which remained high at slightly more than two million at the end of 1935. In the staple industries, unemployment had actually increased: coal now had 25 per cent unemployed; and iron and steel 29.5 per cent.[148]

An additional reason for MacDonald's initially favourable reaction towards the notion of inviting Lloyd George into the government was his own weariness as Prime Minister. Aging rapidly and prone to poor health, MacDonald was also beginning to experience some mental confusion and an inability to perform capably in the House of Commons. His rambling and diffuse speeches, which even he recognized, made him loath to appear at the dispatch box.[149] Moreover, as a Labour Prime Minister, he had not adjusted well to the overwhelmingly Conservative make-up of his National Government.[150] The Labourite reaction against his alliance with the Conservatives was perhaps hardest to bear. Condemning him to his face as a traitor during Commons debates and elsewhere, his former comrades drove him further into spasms of loneliness and depression, as his diary indicates. Perhaps, to MacDonald's way of thinking, Lloyd George could provide not only a source of progressive ideas within the Cabinet, but also act as an effective apologist for the government both in and out of Parliament.

But MacDonald's enquiries among his colleagues to find a place for Lloyd George in the government drew only mixed responses. Party scouts discovered some support, especially among younger Tories; but two thirds of the polled members were opposed.[151] Baldwin himself was at first intrigued, but soon pulled back. Lloyd George, he confided to Tom Jones, 'is not a cohesive but a disintegrating force'.[152] By far the most resolute opponent was Neville Chamberlain. He condemned Lloyd George's Bangor speech and the prospects of a New Deal as 'the poorest stuff imaginable, vague, rhetorical and containing not a single new idea'.[153] Policy differences aside, it is also likely that Chamberlain had never forgotten the slights suffered under Lloyd George when he served as Director-General of National Service during World War I. He refused to invite Lloyd George to serve in any governmental capacity and certainly he would 'in no circumstances sit in a Cabinet with him'.[154] As Chancellor of the Exchequer and the rising star among Conservative leaders, Chamberlain's influence was determinative.

In spite of the absence of any overtly positive sign from the government, Lloyd George was nevertheless encouraged by some influential support for his New Deal. The day following the Bangor speech, for example, *The Times* declared: 'Some of Mr Lloyd George's proposals are in full harmony with the sort of policy which a reconstituted National Government might well pursue.' Furthermore, *The Times* believed that a 'recasting of the Government is not inconceivable and would not be unwelcome'. Most specifically, *The Times* praised Lloyd George's 'energy and versatility … if he is given a definite job to do, he will do it with all his considerable might'.[155] Frances Stevenson confirmed the generally favourable press reports on the Bangor proposals. 'Much fluttering of the political dovecotes as to D.'s position, now & in the future. The Press is full of it, the Lobbies also. There is, they say, no other topic of conversation in the House.'[156] When the Conservatives lost a by-election to Labour at Liverpool Wavertree in early February, there was additional talk of Lloyd George's 'coming in'. By 15 February, however, Stevenson recorded that there were 'no messages from the political front'.[157] She drew the correct inference: 'the Govt. have … made up their minds not to have him in'. That meant, she thought, 'Neville Chamberlain has won the day'.[158]

But Lloyd George, ever resourceful, was undiscouraged. In a manoeuvre designed to complement his New Deal economic initiative, he simultaneously initiated a pressure group drawn from his oldest allies, the nonconformist churchmen who had worked shoulder to shoulder with the young parliamentarian years before to gain religious and educational freedoms. Nonconformists, organized loosely under the National Council of Evangelical Free Churches, worshipped at an estimated 10,000 chapels throughout the country. This potentially influential pressure group was associated with the National Free Church Women's Council, one of whose previous presidents was Dame Margaret Lloyd George.[159] Concerned with social questions in the past, the National Council had begun to consider expanding their mission to include actions for peace during the troubled 1930s. Such a programme would naturally appeal to Lloyd George, and in his revived state of political visibility, he reached out to the nonconformists. In June 1935, he published a manifesto, *A Call to Action*, signed by numerous Free Church leaders, which advocated more active policies in the cause of international peace. Lloyd George also linked the peace cry to the economic crisis, advancing once again what he saw as a better programme for solving the lingering unemployment. Thus was born the Council of Action with its dual slogan of 'Peace and Reconstruction'.[160]

The council received some early support. Philip Snowden hailed the council as the beginning of 'a crusade' which could revive industry and 'rescue the mass of our population from the hardship and suffering of unnecessary poverty'.[161] Philip Kerr (Lord Lothian since 1930, when he succeeded as brother as the 11th Marquis) also believed that the Council of Action could help move the country toward public works and thus alleviate unemployment. But his main concern was the maintenance of peace. He was fearful that there was a drift 'back towards the sort of situation which existed in 1914 in which it was possible for a fool or a knave or an accident to start a movement towards war'.[162] The council's platform of peace could serve as a bulwark against international incidents that could lead to war. Not surprisingly, the pro-Lloyd George newspaper, the *News Chronicle*, under the editorship of Walter Layton, also strongly promoted the aims of the council.[163] From its pages, readers also found support for the League of Nations on the international scene and for Lloyd George's New Deal as a guide for domestic policy.

That the new council was designed not merely as an altruistic pressure group for the prevention of war and the alleviation of unemployed workers was soon apparent. As Jones has observed, Lloyd George's 'primary aim' in establishing the council was political – to exert influence on the next election.[164] The critical test of the council came during the general election of November 1935.[165] Attempting to influence voters along Lloyd Georgian lines, the council published two pamphlets – one called *Peace* and the other *Reconstruction*. In addition, it sent out questionnaires to all candidates, enquiring as to their position on these important issues. But in spite of spending £400,000 on council business in the months prior to the election, Lloyd George had scarcely any return for his investment. In part, this was due to the council's curiously muted response to the election. There were, for example, no specific council candidates. There were also signs of internal dissention within the council that may have detracted from a unified and more forceful message.[166] Perhaps the Council of Action was from the outset a 'non-starter'.[167] But it did reveal Lloyd George's fertile imagination in his enduring attempts at gaining ground among the voters and to be once again in the political limelight.[168]

Baldwin, who had replaced the failing MacDonald as Prime Minister in the last stages of the first National Government, won handily, with an overall majority of nearly 250 seats. Squeezed between the Conservative and Labour Parties, Liberal MPs numbered only 21, including Lloyd George's family group of four. Liberals fared best in Wales, winning seven of their 21 parliamentary seats. The remainder were scattered randomly throughout Scotland and England.[169] Lacking in campaign cash, unable to distinguish itself adequately from the Labour Party in its policies and with little support from the mass media, Liberals sank to their lowest point. It appeared to be the end of a once dominant progressive party in Britain. The nonconformist presence in the election campaign had proven a weak reed. Once solidly Liberal nonconformists now leaned towards Labour.

With the failure of the Council of Action as an electoral springboard and the virtual collapse of the Liberal Party at the general election in November 1935, Lloyd George, now isolated, faced gloomy political prospects. Rebuffed by Conservatives and ostracized by suspicious Labourites, he could no longer rely upon even the fractured Liberals, increasingly fissiparous since 1930. By the mid-1930s, then, it would seem that the ever-resourceful politician, national leader and imaginatively programmatic Lloyd George had at last reached a dead end in public life. There were for him, however, attractive personal options which tempered his enforced absence from the pursuit of political power. His estate at Churt, with its hilly land covered with pine, bracken and heather and fine views from the top of a knoll where he built his house, became increasingly an important refuge from the political wars. Frances Stevenson had undertaken much of the supervision of the building of the residence in 1922. She was also in charge of furnishing as the house neared completion. In assuming responsibility for these projects, Frances developed a greater sense of security than during her earlier years with Lloyd George. Writing to him (then away at the Genoa Conference), she confessed that she felt 'as if I were already Mrs Ll.G'.[170] Not for many years did Frances indeed become Lloyd George's second wife, but Churt was to become her primary residence, largely off limits to Lloyd George's family.

In the immediate years after his fall from office, Lloyd George used his earnings as a highly paid syndicated columnist to purchase additional parcels of land adjacent to his Churt estate.[171] From the original 60 acres, Lloyd George expanded it to 750 acres. His extensive farm eventually became a commercial operation, with Lloyd George actively serving as his own estate manager. He grew apples and other fruit as well as vegetables: he also kept bees and poultry. In season, he hired several hundred temporary harvesters. Chemical sprays using the newest pesticides were in regular use, as were fertilizers for most of the crops. Lloyd George also built a number of cottages for farm workers. Several buildings on the property attested to Lloyd George's serious preoccupation with agriculture. Some were for storage. Others had specialized uses. In one barn, he began raising pedigree pigs – later bringing in a trained pig manager to look after them. Another served as a large fruit store outfitted with an electrically cooled storage shed to preserve the fruit once picked.[172] Lloyd George had in fact become an English gentleman farmer – an ironic turn of events for the former Welsh cottage boy.

Churt (called Bron-y-de, 'Breast of the South', in Welsh), with its thriving agricultural pursuits, was not only a diversion from politics. It was also a comforting environment for recharging depleted energy. Riddell discovered this on his visit only a few days after the disastrous 1922 election. Lloyd George, he reported, 'seemed remarkably well'; and was already 'working like a little dynamo' to recapture the government from the Conservative victory.[173] Nevertheless, politics could never be excluded from Lloyd George's concerns, even at Churt. It was to become the political nerve centre for his various political schemes. Its proximity to London made it convenient for summoning advisers and confidants in the planning of future political forays. During the mid-1920s, when Lloyd George was busily devising his social agenda with the aid of the Liberal Summer Schools, he erected accommodations and offices on the grounds at Churt for the numerous sub-committees – a latter day Garden Suburb.[174] It was at Churt that he largely wrote his *War Memoirs*. His love of Churt, as Thomas Jones reminds us, was representative of his love of the land and of country things.[175] Churt was for Lloyd George a balm in Gilead.

If Churt provided a sanctuary and place of peace for Lloyd George, other aspects of his private life continued to disturb his domestic tranquillity – especially his relationship with Frances Stevenson and the attendant strains upon his wife and children. Lloyd George's *de facto* bigamous relationship with Frances, and his simultaneous attempts to remain on good terms with his family, stretched even his fabled talents of conciliation to the limit. In addition, rumours of his other liaisons with younger women threatened to complicate his life to an unbearable degree. The most recent account by Ffion Hague examines in detail Lloyd George's 'casual flings' as well as his 'dalliance' with one or other of his female acquaintances.[176] But Hague is properly careful. In one instance, she prefaces her comment about an alleged affair between Lloyd George and a 'Mrs J' with a cautionary: 'If this is true … .'[177] In mentioning another episode linking Lloyd George with Roberta Lloyd George, the wife of his son Richard, Hague claims that it was 'the least forgivable of all his dalliances' – 'if true'.[178] Putative evidence of this affair Hague also qualifies: 'if such it is'.[179]

It may be, however, that Lloyd George – who was undoubtedly attracted to women, and they to him – simply sought their attentions. His so-called affairs, in the absence of convincing evidence, may have been merely flirtatious behaviour. Skirting the edge of seduction could have been sufficiently satisfying. As Hague has observed, Lloyd George's 'self-belief and mental buoyancy needed to be constantly fuelled by the devotion of his women'. [180] Explicit approbation from women, as well as from men, was essential to his sense of well being, a fact also recognized by Hague when she notes that a primary need for Lloyd George was to be 'the centre of attention'.[181] Indeed, as we have noticed in earlier chapters, Lloyd George craved (and actively sought) praise from a wide circle of family, friends and political associates. Examples abound from his early life onwards in his letters to and from Margaret, Uncle Lloyd and his brother William among others. His speeches throughout the countryside, his rise to the pinnacle of power and his leadership within his party and the country at large were points of reference to which he openly demanded recognition of a job well done. The primary task of bolstering, however, fell to Frances Stevenson. He depended upon her flattery from their earliest years together. Unless a fulsome note from Frances followed his major parliamentary speeches in the House of Commons, for example, he was downcast. And yet, it was Frances who dangerously veered from her devotion to him, behaviour that could have led to the greatest scandal of his career.

Perhaps because of her desire for marriage and security and perhaps because she and Lloyd George had begun to drift apart emotionally once they had lost the tang of office and greater responsibility, Frances was emotionally drawn towards another suitor in the late 1920s. Thomas Tweed, a World War I hero who rose from Lieutenant to Colonel during the course of the war and had earned the Military Cross, cut a dashing figure. After the war, he became a political adviser and campaign manager for Lloyd George. Sometime in late 1927 or early 1928, he and Frances became lovers: the affair was to last six years.[182] In spite of her new relationship, she continued her life with Lloyd George. This triadic complication deepened in January 1929 when Frances became pregnant and was uncertain who the father was. Jennifer's birth in October 1929 pleased both mother and Lloyd George, who thought himself the father. A.J.P. Taylor has unequivocally endorsed Lloyd George's paternity.[183] Nevertheless doubts have arisen. John Campbell entertains the possibility that Tweed was Jennifer's father.[184] Yet through these undoubtedly trying events Lloyd George and Frances remained attached, if with understandably varying moods.

Witnessing at first hand these distressing emotional events, and often censorious of them, but fully collaborative in all the intrigues and artful schemes at deception was A.J. Sylvester. His diary portrays – within the framework of a testy master and obedient servant relationship – an irresponsible and dishonourable side of Lloyd George.[185] Throughout the often strained relationship between Lloyd George and

Frances, Sylvester worked elaborate schemes to keep the secretive lovers in touch, especially during Lloyd George's often lengthy holidays abroad during the winter months when members of his family would sometimes accompany him. During his recuperative tour to Ceylon, along with Margaret, Megan and Gwilym after his prostate operation in late 1931, Sylvester was charged with buying gifts for Frances and surreptitiously receiving mail from her to pass along to Lloyd George.[186] On other trips abroad, Frances would often accompany Lloyd George, either before or after the family arrived or departed. On occasion, there is a flavour of theatrical farce, with Frances going out one door and Margaret entering another. Sometimes, the lovers took their chances and were simply reckless. In January 1936, they stayed on holiday at the same hotel as Churchill in Marrakech, Morocco. Lloyd George busied himself with his *War Memoirs*, while Churchill found (in Jenkins's telling) enough sunshine to provide 'wonderful colours for painting', as well as time to work on his biography of Marlborough.[187] Just prior to the arrival of Margaret and Megan, Frances returned home.[188]

Lloyd George's boldness in travelling with his mistress had not gone unnoticed. Indeed, he seemed occasionally foolhardy in his public appearances with Frances and Jennifer, most remarkably during the summer of 1936. In August of that year, he took both Frances and Jennifer on a tour of south Wales. This prompted an anguished response from Sylvester. 'He is an extraordinary man. He is trying to get the Council of Action going by drawing Nonconformity to him and yet he hawks about his mistress and what he, at any rate, believes is his own illegitimate child all round his native land.'[189] A few months later, in November 1936, Lloyd George and Frances – accompanied by Sylvester and his wife, Evelyn – went on an extended holiday in Jamaica, where Lloyd George spent much time on the golf course, as well as beginning work on a sequel to his *War Memoirs*.[190]

But Lloyd George's leisurely holiday was soon interrupted by an extraordinary constitutional crisis developing at home. King Edward VIII, who had succeeded his father George V to the throne in January 1936, had determined to marry his mistress, Mrs Wallis Simpson, who was once (and soon twice) divorced. The proposed marriage was an affront to the Church of England as well as to many in elite political circles. Lloyd George took the King's side. Although he was not fond of Mrs Simpson, he believed that the King should have the right to marry whom he wished. Moreover, his relations with Edward had always been positive. Many years earlier, he had coached the young Edward in a few Welsh phrases when he was invested as Prince of Wales at Caernarfon Castle. After World War I, Lloyd George had sent the young prince on a series of tours throughout the empire to show the flag and to promote a spirit of imperial unity. Since that earlier time, Edward had expressed sympathy during the depression years for the working class, including an outright declaration after meeting with unemployed South Wales steelworkers that 'something must be done to find them work'.[191] In addition, Lloyd George believed that opposition to the King had political overtones: Edward was 'too progressive' for Baldwin and the Conservatives.[192] Lloyd George was on the verge of leaving Jamaica and returning to Britain to support the King when news of his abdication ended the matter. Not long after the King's abdication, in early January 1937, Frances and Evelyn sailed for home. Within a week of their departure, Margaret and Megan arrived at Port Royal for a fortnight's stay with Lloyd George and Sylvester.

The following year, Lloyd George, again accompanied by Frances, went to Antibes in southern France where he continued work on the peace treaties. And again, Frances began her journey home just as Margaret and the children left London to be with Lloyd George on their golden wedding anniversary, celebrated on 24 January 1938. Their secretive holidays, however, were taken under a lengthening shadow of mistrust between Lloyd George and Frances. As early as December 1932, Lloyd George discovered the facts about Frances and Tweed. In a striking example of the dysfunctional unit that the Lloyd Georges had become, members of his family also learned of the Tweed-Stevenson liaison and used their knowledge as a weapon in an attempt to break Lloyd George's affection for Frances: they told him outright what they knew.[193] These sordid events took another turn when Tweed apparently threatened blackmail if Lloyd George should attempt any retribution.[194] Perhaps this was effective: it is certain that Tweed remained a part of Lloyd George's staff. Lloyd George had his own reasons for treading softly about the Tweed affair. He had become very found of Jennifer, his belief unshaken that she was his own child. He realized, too, that the infirmities of old age, which had begun gradually to make their mark after his prostate operation in 1931, made him increasingly dependent upon Frances. Thus he responded with some equanimity to the oddly triangular relationship that had developed.

18

RETURN TO WALES

Perhaps his own personal disappointments and the inevitable pain they caused spurred Lloyd George to participate more vigorously in politics from the mid-1930s onward.[1] Once again an active political figure, he directed his energies principally to international events. From the time of the general election of 1935, Britain was drawn irrevocably into the increasingly troubling developments on the Continent. The legacies of World War I – especially the new national boundaries and the consequent divided populations – combined with economic distress and the decline of democracy all foreshadowed the rise of European dictatorships. Stalin had shown the way in the Soviet Union with its mass purges and show trials but Italy and Germany had soon followed. Adventurism abroad on the part of Italy, especially in Africa, revealed the dangers of fascist expansionism. The greater threat was in Germany, where Adolf Hitler had brought about a revolutionary and military tyranny founded on national pride, racial hatred and a determination to rewrite the Treaty of Versailles.

In the face of these threatening developments, the primary issue in Britain was how to strike a balance between diplomacy and rearmament in preparation for any eventual military action. With the rapid build up of German military might under the Nazis, accompanied by their increasingly belligerent diplomatic position, British rearmament would seem (especially in hindsight) to have been a natural response. But the production of arms faced significant difficulties. The victory fleet of 1918 and the air arm were now much diminished. Moreover, even the faintest shadow of preparations for a possible armed conflict was anathema to a generation vividly mindful of the horrors of the Great War. In addition, there were significant manpower restraints hindering a comprehensive and accelerated rearmament programme. A quick shift of skilled labour from peacetime industry to war materiel, for example, would force a significant dislocation of the domestic workforce.[2] The Labour Party was consequently particularly suspicious of any rearmament programme proposed by the Conservative dominated National Government.[3]

Thus successive British governments from the mid-1930s engaged in active diplomacy, following in rough outline a policy of appeasement in an attempt to placate the European dictators. This has been a controversial topic. Historical judgement since has often faulted the practice of appeasement as weak-minded and counterproductive. But appeasement has had a long history in British diplomacy, extending at least from the time of Gladstone in the nineteenth century.[4] The basic assumption was that both sides in any diplomatic bargaining had clear interests in mind and would act reasonably in their defence, but would also be receptive to any diplomatic quid pro quo. It followed that sensible concessions made from a position of strength for the removal of international conflicts and the preservation of peace was a desirable goal.[5] Indeed, during the 1930s there was a broad consensus in Britain favouring appeasement. It was not limited to any particular political party. In addition to Neville Chamberlain were his predecessors as prime ministers (Bonar Law, Baldwin and MacDonald), all of whom have been claimed as appeasers.[6] The most rabid appeasers, often driven by a fierce anti-Communism, especially among the right wing of the Conservative Party,[7] favoured appeasement towards Germany in the belief that Hitler would be a reliable bulwark against the Soviet Union.

The press also inclined towards appeasement. The most authoritative British newspaper of the day, *The Times*, and its editor, Geoffrey Dawson, advocated appeasement.[8] Harold Harmsworth, Viscount Rothermere, owner of the *Daily Mail*, was an energetic appeaser.[9] Beaverbrook's *Daily Express*, *Sunday Express* and *Evening Standard*; the Liberal papers *News Chronicle* and the *Manchester Guardian*; and the Labour Party paper, the *Daily Herald* favoured appeasement. Other newspapers, such as *The Observer* and the *Sunday Times*, followed suit.[10] So, too, did the important British weeklies – *The Spectator*, *The Economist* and the *New Statesman*.[11] Beyond the politicians and opinion makers, there was a general sense in Britain at large that the Treaty of Versailles was nothing less than a punitive instrument directed specifically at Germany. Such an injustice had led to a lenient and forgiving attitude towards the early transgressions of the Hitler regime.[12] When, therefore, in March 1936 elements of the German army marched into the Rhineland, the western area of Germany which stretched from the Netherlands in the North to the Swiss border in the South, British opinion was not much alarmed. It was considered a minor territorial adjustment and, moreover, justified as a reaction against the Versailles Treaty.[13]

It is true, of course, that some well-informed Britons watched with concern the Nazification within Germany. The purging of the professions and the removal of all potential opponents even in such voluntary organizations as sports associations, women's organizations and agricultural pressure groups were signs that the Nazi government was determined, through force and government initiated intimidation, to turn the nation into a *Volksgemeinschaft* – a common community united against both internal foes and external enemies.[14] Nevertheless, such actions could be either dismissed or excused by outsiders as the growing pains of a new and dynamic process necessary for the repudiation of the flaws of Versailles, the failures of the Weimar Republic and the successful regeneration of Germany.

To shore up its own legitimacy and to calm fears about the intentions of the Nazi revolution, the Third Reich initiated a substantial public relations campaign, directed especially towards Britain. The Dienststelle (Bureau) Ribbentrop was created in 1934 as an umbrella organization to foster closer Anglo-German relations.[15] Under its auspices, an Anglo-German Fellowship was designed to promote closer commercial ties with Germany and to arrange visits to Berlin for British businessmen. The Dienststelle also supported visiting British war veterans' associations, journalists and Members of Parliament. Special treatment was given to important individuals such as British Cabinet members, newspaper magnates like Beaverbrook and Rothermere and other public figures. Some were invited to audiences given by Hitler at the Reich Chancellery. The privileged few were granted the rare opportunity of speaking directly with the Führer at the Berghof, Berchtesgaden, Hitler's mountain retreat in Bavaria.

These public relations efforts were largely successful. Lord Lothian, for example, after engaging in unofficial talks with Hitler in January 1935, came away with the belief that Hitler's aggressive policy in Europe was designed to redress wrongs inflicted upon Germany by the Treaty of Versailles. Hitler convinced Lothian that he had no larger ambitions in mind. Lothian reported to both MacDonald (then Prime Minister) and to Baldwin that the German leader also sought direct discussions with leading British ministers in the hope of settling outstanding issues.[16] Two months later, Sir John Simon, then Foreign Secretary, accompanied by a rising young star among the Conservatives, Anthony Eden, made a more official trip at Hitler's court. Though this visit proved inconclusive, the stream of British visitors continued. When Leo Amery visited Hitler in August 1935, he was favourably impressed, admiring Hitler's 'directness' and his grip on important economic and political matters.[17] That Hitler sought to draw in politicians from all sides was evident from the trip taken by George Lansbury in April 1937. Lansbury, a pacifist and Labour MP, came away from his interview believing that Hitler would be willing to participate in a world conference on armament and peace. 'It seemed to me', Lansbury reported afterwards, 'that he could listen to reason'.[18] By such means Hitler – avoiding established diplomatic channels – allayed British fears of German intentions and tamped down any reservations arising from internal developments within Germany.

In 1935, the year following the establishment of the Dienststelle, another apparent milestone in the path towards appeasement was reached. The Anglo-German Naval Agreement, eagerly sought by Hitler, established a production ratio between the navies of the two countries. Germany was prepared to limit the size of her navy to only 35 per cent of the tonnage of all Royal Navy surface vessels. Submarine tonnage was to be equal, but Germany pledged to give notice if they intended to expand beyond 45 per cent of Britain's tonnage. Somewhat startling was the fact that these ratios – which seemed to favour the British Navy heavily – were advocated by Germany. A number of reasons have been advanced for Germany's decision to initiate such a pact which at first sight seemed disadvantageous to their own interests. Hitler's reaching out to Britain could have been an implied threat to France. Or it could have masked his real intention: by establishing a tentative friendship with Britain he could thus cover his Western Front, freeing his hand for armed intervention in the East. Britain's decision to sign the agreement was complementary to possible German intentions. It could channel Hitlerian aggressive tendencies towards Bolshevik Russia. Moreover, by openly laying down numerical ratios, Britain established benchmarks for estimating German naval strength. The agreement was thus designed 'to put a lid on covert German rearmament'.[19] Should Germany flout the designated ratios, Britain could act accordingly. Perhaps above all, because the agreement breached the Treaty of Versailles' restrictions upon the German navy, it represented a tangible sign of appeasement and reconciliation between Britain and Germany.[20]

In the movement forward of appeasement in the mid-1930s, symbolized by the Dienststelle and the Anglo-German Naval Agreement, Lloyd George played a role not dissimilar from other leading public and political figures. He had been, from early on, inclined towards appeasement. Although initially punitive in his response to Germany at the close of the war in 1918, he had changed his mind during the course of the Paris Peace Conference. His Fontainebleau Memorandum, emphasizing postwar reconstruction for the defeated enemy, particularly supported the idea that the German-speaking populations in such territories as Danzig, the Polish Corridor, the Sudetenland and Saarland be free of foreign rule. In the immediate postwar period, Lloyd George maintained a moderate position with regard to reparations.[21] He was among those appeasers who believed that the entire German nation should not be held accountable for the transgressions of a ruling few. Moreover he, like many others, was willing to tolerate even some extreme measures of the Hitlerian regime in the belief that they were understandable reactions against the injustice of Versailles. So long as the harsh Versailles Treaty was a bone in the throat of German national sentiment, the leadership of Germany could be forgiven much. In time, Lloyd George believed, Germany would feel more secure and enter amiably into the family of nations.

Lloyd George's most dramatic public act in promoting better relations with Germany was his celebrated visit to Hitler in September 1936 at the Berghof. He was not the first British public figure to see the Nazi leader directly; but he was the first who had held prime ministerial office. Lloyd George had more than one reason for accepting Hitler's invitation. He had been from the earliest days of his political career an admirer of German efficiency and their pioneering ideas of economic and social reform which he had experienced at first hand during his trip to Germany in 1908. He was therefore keen to observe at first hand Hitler's public works programmes, such as his extensive road building schemes. Perhaps foremost, Lloyd George needed high visibility to keep his name before the British public in his continuous campaign to remain relevant politically. Hitler had his own reasons for inviting Lloyd George. The former Prime Minister's reputation was still high in Germany because of his irenic postwar policies. In February 1936, Lloyd George had given ample proof of positive sentiments towards Germany when he publicly advocated the return of former German colonies which had become mandated territories under the terms of the Treaty of Versailles.[22] Hitler also needed to reassure a jittery Europe that his remilitarization of the Rhineland in March 1936 was not a prelude to greater aggression, but merely righting an old wrong. Lloyd George might well serve as a source of reassurance to Britain and other countries of his peaceful intentions.

Tom Jones and T.P. Conwell-Evans, a Welsh academic and Germanophile who lectured in German universities, made the arrangements for Lloyd George's trip to Berchtesgaden, Hitler's mountain retreat in Bavaria.

In addition to these two, Lloyd George's entourage included his daughter Megan and his son Gwilym; Lord Dawson (Lord George's physician); and A.J. Sylvester. The first meeting with the Führer occurred on 4 September 1936. Discussion began in general terms. Lloyd George assured the German leader that he had always been sincere in hoping for good relations between Germany and Britain. Hitler responded that good relations between the two countries was his wish as well, adding that the recent Anglo-German Naval Treaty was a sound example of shared mutual interests. In referring obliquely to the German incursion into the Rhineland, Hitler also defended the occasional necessity of being 'compelled to take steps to establish the security of his own country'.[23] Hitler's major topic of discussion, however, was the threat of Russian Bolshevism. His special concern was the alliance of Russia with Czechoslovakia, which brought a potential enemy close to German borders. He feared that Germany could become 'an island in a sea of Bolshevism'.[24] In answer to this, Lloyd George advocated mutual cooperation at the forthcoming (second) Locarno Conference which would address such matters of general European concern. There followed an extended discussion on Germany's reconstruction programme, especially the building of motorways.

The following day was less content oriented as the two leaders reminisced about the Great War and traded compliments. Hitler praised Lloyd George's leadership in that great conflict. 'It was you', he addressed Lloyd George directly, 'who galvanized the people into a will to victory'. He then justified some of his dictatorial actions as Führer, admitting 'on certain points' because Germany had 'fallen so low' after the war, that he 'had to insist a little more stubbornly' on certain acts than would have been necessary 'for a country enjoying normal conditions'. Lloyd George responded with equal flattery, calling him 'the greatest German of the age'.[25]

The meeting between Hitler and Lloyd George was likely beneficial to both men. Hitler once again could be seen as taking a conciliatory line with a prominent member of the British governing establishment.[26] This served two purposes. First, Hitler could be seen as a man of peace, as important to the German population as it was to Hitler's near neighbours. Secondly, it was consistent with his aim of securing an alliance with Britain, thus negating any threat from the West and freeing his hand for a more adventurist policy towards Soviet Russia.[27] For Lloyd George, it was an opportunity – even though he was out of office – to stake a claim as a high profile diplomat. Upon his return to Britain, he publicized his visit through an adroit newspaper campaign. In an interview with the *Daily Express*, he reiterated his favourable impression of Hitler and the new Germany.[28] A few days later, he arranged another interview, this time with A.J. Cummings, editor of the pro-Lloyd George *News Chronicle*. Given full attention from a friendly source, Lloyd George once again set out his impressions of the German leader. Admitting that he was a dictator; that he had established concentration camps for his opponents; and that he had persecuted the Jews in Germany, Lloyd George nevertheless believed that Hitler had 'done great things for his country'. He was 'unquestionably a great leader'.[29] Within the context of a widespread sentiment of appeasement in Britain as a whole, Lloyd George's comments probably resonated well enough.

Yet it must be said that Lloyd George went beyond his public praise for Hitler in his private correspondence where he revealed a more fulsome admiration for the German leader. In a letter of appreciation upon his return, Lloyd George thanked von Ribbentrop for the opportunity of meeting 'your wonderful Führer'. Hitler was, he continued, 'the greatest piece of luck that has come to your country since Bismarck, and personally, I would say since Frederick the Great'. Furthermore, Lloyd George believed that in time Hitler's 'great achievements' would 'win the approbation, and I hope, the emulation of our own country'. Perhaps sensing that he had gone too far, Lloyd George closed his letter on a more measured note. Britain's way of improving the conditions of the people would, he wrote, 'naturally be in accordance with our own traditions. Each country has to consider the system that is best adapted to its own temperament and history'.[30] As late as December 1937 in a letter to Conwell-Evans, Lloyd George reiterated his admiration for the German leader. Admitting that sometimes he had 'moments of profound disagreement' with Hitler's policy, he nonetheless reaffirmed his belief in the 'fundamental greatness of Herr Hitler as a man'. He only wished that Britain 'had a man of his supreme quality at the head of affairs in our country today'.[31]

In retrospect, Lloyd George's comments may seem shocking. Even Morgan finds them hard to explain. Perhaps 'simple vanity', he once wrote, led Lloyd George to a state of 'near hero-worship' of Hitler. Lloyd George's comments in the newspaper press Morgan thought 'astonishing', marking the 'rhetorical climax of inter-war appeasement'.[32] But it must be recognized that Lloyd George's views, allowing for some exaggeration, were not uncommon at the time. The acceptance of Nazism by the mass of the German population was thought by many British observers to be temporary. Nazism as a form of protest would soon pass away once the background conditions that had fuelled its rise – economic weakness, social dislocation and political failure – were addressed. In the meantime, Hitler would be, it was hoped, a unifying, consolidating, even moderating force in Germany.

In the months following Lloyd George's visit to Germany, however, there was little advance in Anglo-German relations. Indeed, tensions rose steadily as a result of a series of German aggressive actions. In late 1936, Germany's demands heightened for a return of the colonies lost after World War I. Additionally, Germany began reaching out to other like-minded nations, especially Mussolini's Italy, to further its own aggressive intentions. The following year Germany, allied with General Franco's rightist military forces against the socialist republican government, became increasingly involved in the Spanish Civil War. Even more threatening were Hitler's aggressive designs against Germany's neighbours. In March 1938, Germany annexed Austria, designating that country as the *Ostmark* (Eastern March) of a greater Germany. With this action, and the justification for it, further annexations in central Europe seemed likely. A natural target would be the Sudetenland, an enclave of three million Germans within the borders of Czechoslovakia.

In the face of continued German interventions, both diplomatic and military, the British government took the initiative to dissuade Hitler from future military operations. The lead in these tactical efforts fell to Neville Chamberlain, the strong man in the British Cabinet and, since May 1937, Prime Minister. Flying to Germany on three separate missions in September 1938, Chamberlain ironed out an agreement with Hitler by which the Sudeten would be surrendered to German demands. Additional Czech territories were ceded to both Poland and Hungary. What remained was a rump Czech republic with its capital in Prague. Chamberlain believed that he had won – as he publicly proclaimed – 'peace for our time'. In early October 1938, the German army marched into the Sudeten under the terms of the agreement. A weakened and diminished Czechoslovakia was now nearly surrounded by hostile forces.

With Hitler's expansionist aims increasingly obvious, the critics of Chamberlain's brand of appeasement gained ground, Lloyd George among them. For many months after his meeting with Hitler, Lloyd George had retained his favourable opinion of Hitler. He had expected the annexation of Austria and it gave him little pause: the Austrians were Germanic and enthusiastic for the union.[33] When the Germans forced Czechoslovakia to cede the Sudetenland to Germany, however, he condemned Chamberlain's failure to stand firmly against this act of aggression. By late 1938 Lloyd George was privately sounding the alarm. Writing to Leo Amery, he warned: 'The whole of our defensive preparation is not merely inadequate, but utterly irrelevant to the demand which the situation may, at any moment, make imperative'.[34] On 26 October, Lloyd George made public his concerns, condemning Britain's betrayal of the Czechs. Speaking at a luncheon meeting of the London Free Church Federation Ministers' Club at the City Temple, he deplored Hitler's 'wiping out … that small democratic state'. He blamed the Chamberlain government for its role in abandoning Czechoslovakia: peace had been purchased, no doubt, but at a price – 'the price of conscience and honour'. Recalling Abyssinia and Spain, Lloyd George cited Czechoslovakia as only the latest victim of fascist aggression. Britain had begun to descend 'a ladder of dishonour rung by rung'.[35]

Two months later, Lloyd George launched a wide-ranging attack upon Chamberlain in the House of Commons. Denouncing the Prime Minister as too easily gulled by the fascist dictators, Lloyd George claimed that Chamberlain did not recognize that Britain was being treated 'with contempt' by them. 'It was a mistake', he added, 'in dealing with men of this kind to surrender to every demand they made'.[36] Lloyd George continued his criticism of the Chamberlain government into the new year. He was especially concerned with Britain's lack of any allies who could serve as a deterrent to German ambitions. Speaking at Llandudno in January 1939, he deplored generally the 'rapidly growing deterioration in the international situation'. He especially condemned the government's passive diplomatic policy: it had 'failed to mobilize powerful outside aid which was available'. Why, he asked, 'was Russia never approached?'[37] The following month, at a meeting of the Council of Action at Caxton Hall, Westminster, he reiterated the need for powerful allies. Once again, he charged that the government 'had alienated Russia, the greatest military power in the world'.[38] Lloyd George's prophetic words were realized a few weeks later when a German expeditionary force of seven army corps marched into Prague on 13 March 1939. Within 48 hours, Hitler entered the city to signify the German annexation of the much-diminished Czech state.[39]

The German occupation of Czechoslovakia was clearly a potential threat to the Soviet Union. A unique opportunity to draw the Soviet Union into an anti-Nazi pact thus came to pass. But Lloyd George's pleas for an Anglo-Soviet treaty were ignored. Chamberlain continued to hold 'the most profound distrust of Russia' and strongly opposed any opening to the Soviet Union.[40] He also condemned 'the almost hysterical passion of the Opposition egged on by Ll.G. who have a pathetic belief that Russia is the key to our salvation'.[41] Delaying too long any serious nod to the East, the opportunity for an Anglo-Soviet agreement slipped away. As one of Chamberlain's most sympathetic biographers described the consequences of Chamberlain's failed Soviet policy: 'Chamberlain's historical reputation has paid a high price for resisting the clamour for a Soviet alliance'.[42] Chamberlain did not entirely ignore the possibility of an opening to the East. But he backed the wrong horse. He chose instead to make guarantees upholding Polish independence. The prospect of direct British military assistance to Poland did not sit well with the Soviet Union. Thus the way was open for a German bid to the Soviets. On 23 August 1939, the Nazi-Soviet Non-Aggression Pact was signed. Within a week, on 1 September 1939, Germany invaded Poland. Two days later, Britain and France declared war on Germany. On 17 September, the Soviet Union attacked Poland from the East.

As the likelihood of war increased in late summer 1939 and British involvement seemed ever more likely, Lloyd George became the centre of attention from a variety of sources. Information flowed to and from Lloyd George and the Soviet embassy in London.[43] On the other side of the political spectrum, Leo Amery, realizing that the Russo-German pact was a sure sign of an imminent armed conflict, pleaded with Lloyd George to 'take an opportunity in the next few days, to urge the necessity of a War Cabinet'.[44] Robert Boothby complained bitterly to Lloyd George of the Conservative leadership's failure to engage positively with the Soviet Union. 'I cannot believe', he wrote Lloyd George, 'that the men who have landed us in this mess are capable of getting us out'. He, too, hoped that Lloyd George would speak 'to the nation during the next few days', explaining clearly the options before them.[45] From Lord Davies, a Welshman and a strong Lloyd George supporter, came more zealous support. 'Here we are in the soup again', he wrote, 'thanks to the insane policy of the Chamberlain crowd, against which you have so nobly protested during the last three years'.[46]

With war now at hand, however, Lloyd George adopted what initially seems to have been a curiously ambivalent position. At first, he was firm in Poland's defence. Once Poland had been quickly defeated, however, there is some evidence that he momentarily panicked. Harold Nicolson recorded in his diary that, during a visit with him on 20 September, Lloyd George confessed that he was 'frankly terrified and does not see how we can possibly win the war'.[47] Within the next fortnight, Lloyd George seems to have steadied, although his message was muted by a certain hesitancy of purpose. In a speech before the House of Commons on 3 October he indicated his support for a negotiated peace. The government, he declared, ought to be prepared to consider seriously any peace proposals 'which were specific, detailed, broad' and which 'reviewed all the subjects that had been the cause of all the troubles of the past few years'.[48] Lloyd George was promptly chastised by the Conservative Alfred Duff Cooper, a former First Lord of the Admiralty, who thought that Lloyd George's choice of words unfortunate, and had 'a suggestion of surrender'. Lloyd George countered emphatically that he was 'the last man' to propose a surrender; but it was important at least to consider the prospect of summoning a council of nations to review the possibility of seeking a peaceful means to avoid all-out war. In the debate that followed, Duff Cooper retracted his accusation. Several speakers followed, some opposing Lloyd George's plan while others favoured it. Among the latter was Sir Charles Cayzer, Conservative MP for Chester, who praised Lloyd George for his 'gallant and courageous speech'. As a reserve officer himself, he was certainly prepared to fight; but, he said, he 'would like to know what we are fighting for'. He suggested 'a real, sincere offer put forward to secure peace at the present time should not be turned down out of hand'.

Upon reflection, Lloyd George soon altered his tone in a speech to his constituents at Caernarfon. Declaring that his earlier parliamentary remarks 'had been grossly and, he feared, viciously misinterpreted', he emphasized the importance of determining if there were any opportunities 'of achieving our aims by peaceful means now'.[49] Should any proposed conference seeking peaceful measures fail, and if Hitler showed no intention of acting justly and if 'he meant to cling with greedy tenacity to his conquest, we could quit the conference and resume the struggle with a clear conscience'. There would be no doubt of the outcome: 'With the immense resources at our command, and wide and skilful leadership', Britain in the end would 'achieve our aims of checking the aggressor'. [50] In short, Lloyd George proposed a dual strategy: diplomacy first to gain time for a build up of men and arms; and then if forced into it, actively pursuing war with Hitler. In the following months, throughout the remainder of 1939 and early 1940 (the period of the 'Phoney War'), Lloyd George kept his name before the public through various newspaper articles, speeches both in and out of Parliament and private personal contacts with leading politicians and newsmen. His message was consistent. As he put it to Robert Boothby in late September 1939: 'They may say it was defeatism, but it might be necessary to play for time. This is a struggle for world power, in which aeroplanes are one weapon and diplomacy is another. If you haven't got the aeroplanes, you may have to resort to other methods.'[51] There is no doubt that he remained a realist about any prospects of victory in the short term. In early 1940, he confessed to High Cudlipp, editor of the *Sunday Pictorial*: 'People call me a defeatist ... but what I say to them is this: Tell me how we can win!' Nor, he thought, could Hitler win. 'The war will drag wearily on.'[52]

Historians have been divided in their views of Lloyd George's 'defeatism' in the early days of the war. Toye writes that Lloyd George's actions 'sadly' seemed to confirm a 'stereotypical image of him as irresponsible and opportunistic'.[53]

Paul Addison, however, presents a more nuanced explanation. During extended talks with Hitler, Britain could determine with greater accuracy Hitler's intentions: in the meantime, Britain would continue building its military defences to enable negotiation from a position of strength.[54] It is important to remember, too, that at the time it was impossible to know the direction and intensity of the war. In spite of the rapid successes of the German military on the European continent, an attack upon an island nation defended by a strong navy and air force might well give even Hitler pause. It was entirely possible, too, that a stalemate might ensue. In that case, Germany would likely turn its attention towards the East in spite of its recent pact with the Soviet Union.

Although he favoured a flexible approach in the early days of the war, Lloyd George was, when the occasion demanded, firm in his denunciation of Nazi aggression. He was also quick to denounce British failures. Perhaps his most famous wartime speech was in response to the British attempt to counter the German invasion of Norway in early 1940. Condemning the British military operation as a 'half prepared, half-baked expeditionary force', Lloyd George pointed out to the House of Commons that the Norway debacle placed Britain strategically 'in a much worse position than before' with the Germans now having advanced 200 miles closer to British shores. Lloyd George's specific excoriation of Chamberlain's ultimate responsibility was a striking reminder of his oratorical powers. There was, he hinted, no further point in placing Chamberlain in a position of responsibility in the prosecution of the war: 'The Prime Minister must remember he has met this formidable foe of ours in peace and in war, and he has always been worsted.' To loud cheers echoing in the chamber, Lloyd George appealed to the nation to remain firm in the face of this latest military disaster: 'Let us face it ... face it like men of British blood.'[55]

Friends and supporters of Lloyd George naturally praised the speech. Tom Jones noted in his diary that Lloyd George had spoken 'with great effect'.[56] Sylvester, too, thought it 'a great speech'.[57] Frances Stevenson believed that his speech 'was a supreme example of a speech resulting in action'.[58] Even political opponents of Lloyd George recognized its power. Chips Channon – a firm Chamberlainite – while criticizing the content of the speech, acknowledged the authority and greatness of the former wartime Prime Minister: he still projected undeniable authority. 'Lloyd George', he wrote in his diary, was 'full of fire and beans, and his bronzed skin, white locks and bight blue suits, make him a doughty figure'.[59] John Colville, then an assistant private secretary to Chamberlain, observed that: 'Lloyd George made probably the most forceful speech he has made for years.' His fiery speech 'held the House spellbound as he flung his arms about and denounced the incapacity of the P.M. and the Government'.[60] Even more surprising was the comment of Violet Bonham Carter. As the daughter of H.H. Asquith, she had never forgiven Lloyd George for what she believed was his treachery against her father in 1916. Yet her diary reveals not only a strong emotional response to 'the most dramatic debate I have almost ever heard in my whole Parliamentary memory', but also her admiration for Lloyd George's remarks. 'He made the best & most deadly speech I have ever heard from him – voice – gesture – everything was brought into play to drive home his indictment. Material was not lacking. The House was profoundly shaken.'[61] The following day, Chamberlain resigned office. Winston Churchill became the new Prime Minister.

Churchill was immediately plunged into fateful decisions about British policy in response to its worsening military position. During the darkest days of Dunkirk in late May 1940, he led Cabinet discussions on possible options. His first meetings were with the five-member War Cabinet. Conflict quickly emerged about the possibility of negotiating peace terms with Hitler. Halifax, then Foreign Secretary, was strongly in favour: Chamberlain initially supported him.[62] Nor was Churchill at first opposed to the possibility of talks with Hitler. He could not, as Lukacs has observed, answer Halifax 'with a categorical no'.[63] But the two Labour members, Attlee and Greenwood, were opposed, as eventually was Churchill himself. Reporting afterward to the full Cabinet, Churchill told them that it had been his duty at least to consider the option of negotiations with Hitler but that he had rejected that course. Churchill was then freed to make his famous rallying speeches about the dangers of a German invasion during the coming months. The fact that negotiations with the enemy were at least contemplated at such a high level demonstrably indicates that Lloyd George was certainly not alone in considering it as a viable option in the early days of the war.

With Lloyd George's rising profile in early 1940 reaching a climax with his speech during the Norway debate, his supporters began to beat the drum for his return to office. The Liberal politician Harcourt Johnstone, in a letter to the editor of the *Daily Mail*, strongly endorsed Lloyd George as Prime Minister of a new government, with Churchill serving as Minister for Co-ordination of Defence.[64] Boothby once again was willing to advance Lloyd George's name, condemning the 'elderly and fatigued mediocrities' who currently held office.[65] He recommended a form of War Cabinet ('a dictatorial triumvirate') composed of Lloyd George, Churchill and a Labour representative, perhaps Attlee. Addressing himself directly to Lloyd George, Boothby wrote: 'I feel most strongly that your wisdom, your resource, and your experience, should be at the disposal of this country.'[66] Of far more potential significance than Boothby's support was that of Basil Liddell Hart. An eminent military writer and a veteran of World War I, Liddell Hart had assisted Lloyd George in the research for his *Memoirs*. He now believed, as he informed Lloyd George, that 'public opinion throughout the country' was turning towards him 'as the man to deal with the problem of the war'.[67]

In fact, within a few days after assuming office, Churchill offered Lloyd George a position in his government. But it was conditional on Chamberlain's approval. Given these terms, Lloyd George refused on the grounds that the offer was 'tentative and qualified'.[68] Indeed, there was no doubt that Chamberlain would veto such an offer. Although no longer Prime Minister, Chamberlain still retained significant influence and loyalty among his many Conservative supporters. Churchill, as the neophyte premier, could not afford to alienate them.[69] Lloyd George thereafter had strong doubts about Churchill's government. In a confidential memorandum drawn up in September 1940, he wrote that Britain could win the war only by thoroughly recasting the Cabinet.[70] Present Cabinet members were either 'yes men' or were liabilities for various reasons. He reserved special condemnations for Chamberlain and Halifax, who were 'responsible singly and together for the calamitous blunders of the last few years'. Churchill did not escape Lloyd George's wrath. Admitting that Churchill had 'brilliant powers' and 'inexhaustible energy', Lloyd George nevertheless believed that he was also 'impetuous, self-willed and obstinate'. The Cabinet he had chosen was 'worthless' as an effective advisory body. Its members must be removed and replaced by 'independent men of experience, wisdom and judgment chosen without reference to Party considerations'. Otherwise Britain would 'march into a quagmire of calamity'. The model for a wartime Cabinet that Lloyd George had in mind was clearly based upon his own during World War I. A final opportunity for a ministerial post did occur later in 1940 upon Chamberlain's death from cancer in November 1940. When Lord Lothian, then serving as ambassadorship to the United States, died the following month, Churchill hoped to appoint Lloyd George to the vacant position.[71] But Lloyd George turned down the offer on the grounds that at the age of 77, the task of travel and relocation would be too difficult. It proved his last opportunity to serve in any official governmental capacity.

Historians differ in their accounts of Lloyd George's exclusion from Churchill's ministry. Jenkins, in his biography of Churchill, claims that Lloyd George refused to join Churchill's government because he was 'afraid of Hitler'. Believing that Britain's prospects were hopeless, he did not wish to be associated with a failed enterprise.[72] Jenkins's views may have been based on Sylvester's diary entry of 15 May 1940, which recorded Lloyd George's comments about 'giving in without fighting' because 'we are beaten'.[73] Robert C. Self, in his biography of Chamberlain, follows this line of thinking when he notes that Lloyd George's 'well-known defeatism' inclined him to stay out of office so that he would be ready to negotiate peace terms with the Germans should Churchill's government collapse under the stress of war.[74] Perhaps Lloyd George had a momentary sense of despair in May 1940 induced by the recent news that Germany had invaded the Netherlands and France. But it is incorrect to conclude that he refused any offer to join the Churchill government, as his letter of May 1940 indicated.

In short, Lloyd George's 'defeatist' reputation is undeserved. He, no less than Churchill, realized that there was a German invasion plan in being. And, given the crushing defeat through its *Blitzkrieg* tactics over Norway, Denmark, Belgium and France, there was a distinct possibility that Britain would soon face the deadly danger of a German invasion. As Addison notes, Lloyd George wanted the war to be 'fought toughly' to convince Hitler that – if it should come to pass – a negotiated peace was worthwhile, thus saving both countries a lengthy and bloody war of attrition.[75] Toye agrees. The notions that Lloyd George was defeatist in 1940 'are doubtful, even in spite of the apparently damning evidence that came from Lloyd George's own mouth'.[76] Like Addison, Toye believes that Lloyd George neither wanted a British surrender nor 'simply to give up fighting'; but, given Churchill's erratic record in the past, he did have some doubts about his war leadership. A.J.P. Taylor, from his experience in editing the correspondence of both Lloyd George and Frances

Stevenson, had previously come to the same conclusions – that Lloyd George was neither a pacifist nor a defeatist. Rather, Lloyd George believed that Britain would fight Germany to a standstill and in the ensuing deadlock should be prepared to negotiate a peace settlement.[77]

During the final months of 1940, Lloyd George continued writing patriotic pieces for the press in which he urged courage and endurance for the struggle to come. Intermixed with these rallying cries, he expressed his belief that Britain's 'supreme navy and an air force of an unequalled skill and audacity' would convince Hitler of British invincibility: at that point a negotiated peace might become possible.[78] To Frances Stevenson, he explained his approach to the conduct of the war and his role in it. The public, he thought, cherished illusions of complete victory. The nation 'must have a sense of failure of the existing leadership & of the existing order' before they could realistically face the difficulties that lay ahead. That meant 'a long struggle' – but he was confident of its successful outcome. During that intervening period, however, he would not serve in any government. 'I do not possess', he wrote, 'the necessary store of physical strength to do so'.[79]

The trials of warfare and Lloyd George's unsuccessful attempt to find an active role to play were compounded by a great personal loss. Dame Margaret, who was then in Wales, suffered a bad fall in late December 1940. Her condition steadily worsened over the next two weeks. On 19 January 1941, Lloyd George set out by car to Criccieth (leaving the accompanying Frances Stevenson in Shrewsbury) to be at her side. But a severe snowstorm hindered travel westward, forcing an overnight stay in the village of Cerrig-y-Drudion. It was there that he learned that Margaret had died only hours earlier. To Sylvester, who had also travelled westward by train, Lloyd George spoke tearfully: 'She was a great old pal.'[80] His grief over the next few days was genuine – perhaps heightened by some sense of guilt for the many years of his own relationship with Frances.

In the months following, he played a diminishing role in parliamentary affairs, his declining interest in public life prompted in part not only by Margaret's death but also by the deterioration of his health.[81] From the beginning of 1941, he steadily lost weight. He also seemed to lose a vital spark: his famous optimism in the face of difficulty was waning. Even the German invasion of the Soviet Union in June 1941, which at last forced that country into the arms of Britain as an ally thus validating Lloyd George's own preferred policy, did not lighten his spirits. In September 1941, Sylvester, who still believed that Lloyd George should take a more positive active role in the war effort, observed: 'L.G. looked terribly old today. He has lost all his bloom.'[82] From time to time, Lloyd George slipped into pessimism about the course of the war. It is certain that he became increasingly sceptical of Churchill's leadership during the succession of British losses in the early phases of the war. Sylvester noted that in early 1942, he had 'been talking defeatist stuff' to a good number of MPs.[83] Tom Jones recalled that in August of that year Lloyd George was declaring that he had no faith in Churchill's capacity for achieving victory and that 'the odds were in favour of Germany and Japan'. Jones further believed, however, that if Lloyd George had some official responsibility, some avenue for action, 'his pessimism would have vanished'; but 'it was in fact too late'.[84]

How much Lloyd George's views were now occluded by the vulnerabilities of advancing age is difficult to say. Likely enough, his pessimistic views were less a sign of defeatism than an indication of his own declining powers There were, however, occasional rallies of his once ebullient and optimistic self. On 17 January 1943, he celebrated his 80th birthday. A few days later, his birthday was publicly recognized in the House of Commons. Already Father of the House, Lloyd George was gratified by this additional honour, which he had not expected. A month later, in one of his few appearances in the House of Commons, he rose briefly in protest at the government's refusal to endorse further social legislation as set out by the Beveridge Report. Although he thereafter made occasional appearances in the House, this was his last speech to that body.[85] Thereafter, physical and mental disabilities were increasingly noticeable. When Harold Nicolson met Lloyd George in the lobby of the House of Commons in 1943, he was struck by the change in the former dynamic leader: 'for an instant the old charm and vigour reappeared, but then once again there fell on his face that mask of extreme and inarticulate old age. He is now a yellow old man with a mane of dead-white hair, and uncertain movements of his feet and hands'.[86]

Still, he managed an occasional rally. In October 1943, he and Frances at last married. Though this was unwelcome news to his family and especially to his daughter Megan, it was for Frances a long anticipated event and a suitable reward for her personal sacrifices over many years. On occasion Lloyd George reached out in a valedictory mood to friends and acquaintances. In early 1944, for example, he wrote fondly to Baldwin. 'For years we crossed swords on the floor of the House of Commons and in the country', he reminded his former antagonist, 'but now we are lookers-on at the conflict, and heaven knows what will be the end of it and the shape things will take afterwards'.[87] Over the next several months Lloyd George's health palpably declined. In late 1944, Sylvester reported after a visit that Lloyd George was 'just a shrunken old man, looking very delicate and feeble'.[88] Frances saw at first hand Lloyd George's failing health in his final years, and realized that he 'did not feel equal to any sustained job of work'.[89] Twelve years older than Churchill, Lloyd George 'was, in fact, now an old man, and he was aware of it'. Loath to travel to London and attend to his parliamentary duties, he preferred to remain at Churt, often resting before a large picture window, reflective and sombre, as was the case when Hitler attacked Russia and seemed to be winning overwhelmingly. He would sit 'in this window silent', Frances remembered, 'and what was going on in his mind I could not fathom'.

Increasingly withdrawn, he decided to leave Churt and return to Wales in late 1944. A few years earlier he had purchased Ty Newydd, a small farm in the village of Llanystumdwy, his childhood home. There he and Frances stayed for the remaining months of his life. Shortly after his arrival at Ty Newydd, he was diagnosed with inoperable cancer. His famous energy now expended, he found comfort in being close to the land that had given shape and direction to his life. On occasion, he would make small excursions – visiting the village school which he himself had attended; or putting in an appearance at a children's tea party sponsored by the Baptist Chapel in Criccieth. Gradually fading, he slept long hours and spoke little.

No longer able easily to attend the House of Commons, and with the war coming to an end, he faced the prospect of a general election with some trepidation. Yet he wished to participate in the forthcoming peace process. To be in the centre of things once more, and to complete his political life with a second great peace conference was a grand hope. It was surely a reasonable expectation: after all, he had consistently represented Caernarfon Boroughs since 1890 – more than half a century. But his re-election was uncertain. His declining health, preventing an appearance at Westminster, meant that his constituency had been unattended for two long years. Moreover, the local electorate had altered: it was younger, eager for change and with little loyalty to the Liberal Party.[90] A solution was found, much to his delight. On 18 December 1944, a letter from Churchill arrived by special messenger, asking if Lloyd George would consider an earldom. This device had been managed by A.J. Sylvester, who had written to Sir Archibald Sinclair – leader of the Liberal Party, Secretary of State for Air and longstanding friend of Churchill – to recommend such an honour for his old comrade in arms. Thus the former radical, the stalwart spokesman for the commoners of the nation for so many years and the scourge of the aristocracy, became Earl Lloyd-George of Dwyfor in the New Year's Honours List of 1 January 1945. He believed that he now had the opportunity once again to play some role in participating in peace negotiations after a great war.

Lloyd George's 82nd birthday on 17 January 1945 found him in relatively good spirits. The morning of that day was taken up with reading the flood of birthday wishes. Later that afternoon, he walked with Frances. On their return, he enjoyed a birthday tea. After this excursion he remained largely indoors for the next several weeks, his time often spent re-reading Dickens, or gazing out the windows towards the mountains of Merioneth and Cardigan, or sleeping peacefully.[91] Lloyd George's fondest wish of his final days – to sit once again in Parliament, now made possible by his elevation to the Lords – was increasingly improbable. He was too weak to travel. Once this became public news, and as subsequent medical reports confirmed his rapidly declining health, representatives of the press began to arrive in force. Visitors and kindly messages also enlivened his final days. By 20 March he was visibly failing. On the following Monday evening, 26 March, with his daughter Megan on one side of his bed, and Frances on the other, Lloyd George died peacefully in his sleep. He was buried on a bank of the River Dwyfor where he now lies beneath a sturdy boulder taken from the nearby landscape within an enclosure bordered by a stout wall of Welsh slate.

In death as in life, Lloyd George has remained contentious. Since Lloyd George's time, historians, biographers and public figures have also weighed in against him. We have noted samples of these throughout our text. These include Trevor Wilson's condemnation of Lloyd George for destroying the Liberal Party; Donald McCormick's belief in a megalomaniacal Lloyd George; the claims of sexual adventurism by his own son; and a general onslaught of his character by

A.J. Sylvester. More recent historians have also voiced their strongly negative views on Lloyd George. George H. Cassar believes that Lloyd George 'was essentially an opportunist with no fixed principles'. He was additionally 'cunning, vengeful and mean spirited'; and a man whose 'nimble mind and verbal dexterity masked a lack of culture, formal education, and general knowledge'.[92] His latest biographer, Roy Hattersley – although recognizing Lloyd George's contribution to victory in World War I and his contributions to social justice and the welfare state – nevertheless demonstrates a palpable dislike and mistrust of his subject. Hattersley condemns Lloyd George's 'breathtaking hypocrisy' and his too frequent 'bogus public spirit'. Hattersley is also critical of Lloyd George's famous rallying speeches in the countryside, terming them 'destructive' and often full of 'bombast'. He suggests, too, that Lloyd George's famous fiery speeches in Parliament often had a negative impact because 'all he wanted was conflict and confrontation'.[93]

There are of course undeniable reservations that one may entertain about Lloyd George. His treatment of his wife and his relations with Frances Stevenson have raised legitimate questions about his moral character. His insistence upon praise and adulation may raise questions about his steadiness of purpose. His apparent disloyalty to political colleagues, his frequent changes of opinion on party affiliation and his ruthless determination to retain office at seemingly any cost have cast an unflattering light upon his political ambitions. His imperialism during and after World War I has diminished his stature in an increasingly anti-imperial age. His ideas and actions during his final years have further clouded his reputation. His initial appeasement of Hitler, and (it must be said) his fawning over the German leader in the late 1930s have tarnished his stature. His public and private statements during World War II, with its hints of 'defeatism', and the decline of his physical powers have led even his foremost apologist to declare his last years as 'somewhat pathetic'.[94]

Yet in Lloyd George's life there remains a substantial record of achievement and success. His rise to national and international prominence from humble origins was remarkable. His powerful oratory expressed the submerged hopes of Welsh nonconformists, of the socially disadvantaged, and of those other disenfranchised citizens denied the right to express political preference. Though he often spoke as an ideologue, he proved practical and thoroughgoing in securing substantial legislative goals. He was in times of peace a reforming President of the Board of Trade and Chancellor of the Exchequer. In war, he was a dynamic leader, rising from a Minister of Munitions to Minister of War to Prime Minister. As Prime Minister, he organized the productive power of the nation against a determined enemy. In helping to secure peace in Europe after World War I, he attempted to moderate the demands for punitive measures on the part of the victorious allies and in so doing hoped to heal the raw wounds of war. In peace at home, he sought to square the circle of the aspirations of labouring men and women within the confines of a severe postwar economic downturn. Overall, he had an unparalleled ability to bring together diverse, even antagonistic, opposing forces to achieve sensible solutions to political, social and economic problems. He met challenges directly and with dispatch. His administrative practices were perhaps novel; but he had the capacity to recognize talent wherever he found it and to employ it with great effectiveness. This was best shown during World War I when he was particularly skilful in matching men to appropriate tasks. A.J.P. Taylor's evaluation of Lloyd George during that war – 'the response of genius to the challenge of events' – could be said as well of many of his peacetime programmes.[95]

There are recent signs that Lloyd George's larger achievements, once overshadowed by his personal foibles, have begun to assume greater salience. In part, this is due to an intriguing comparison that two biographers – Robert Lloyd George and Richard Toye – have drawn between Lloyd George and his friend, spirited comrade and occasional enemy, Winston Churchill.[96] In some senses, it is easier to account for Churchill's summons to greatness. As a child of privilege, Churchill had every advantage from a young age. His father, Lord Randolph Churchill, the third son of the Duke of Marlborough, was an active politician and public figure. Born into an aristocratic family, educated at elite institutions and almost assured of some high place in his adult life, Winston was certain of success in his chosen field of endeavour. Lloyd George, if not as poor as he sometimes liked to portray, was nevertheless born in far humbler circumstances. A visit to the cramped cobbler's cottage in Llanystumdwy compared to the ducal grandiloquence of Blenheim Palace is dramatically emblematic of the differences in wealth and status between these two giants of British public life.

Robert Lloyd George, a great-grandson of his subject, portrays Lloyd George in proper filial style.[97] In his rendering, Churchill saw Lloyd George as his political mentor. The personal friendship between the two men was also very close, with only an occasional cooling when differences of opinion arose – especially over policy matters when Lloyd George saw too much belligerence and impulsiveness in his younger colleague. But these were, as Robert Lloyd George recounts them, the stray clouds of normally sunny days. Richard Toye, however, sees a more fraught relationship between the two men. Occasionally their relationship broke down. Even during the best of times, both Lloyd George and Churchill tended to manipulate the closeness of their friendship for emotional satisfaction and political gain.[98] Overall, Toye believes that each statesman has had his day of greatness. From the earliest years of the twentieth century until the fall of the wartime coalition of 1922, Lloyd George 'consistently outclassed' Churchill.[99] In the immediate postwar years, Lloyd George retained his ascendancy by his 'genuinely dynamic' proposals, such as his innovative unemployment schemes, whereas Churchill offered only 'economic orthodoxy' and 'lurid denunciations of socialism'. Thereafter, however, Churchill 'undoubtedly comes out on top'. His understanding of the Hitler menace, his rallying of the nation in wartime and his steadfastness in the face of apparent defeat, gave him 'a much greater claim to subsequent vindication than Lloyd George' during the fateful years of World War II.

There is much to be said for following Toye's stages of greatness. Each man had his day as the various eras dictated; and each man had unique qualities and strengths upon which he could draw. If the subtleties of the Welsh Wizard were to have been brought into play during World War II against the brutal and implacable horrors of the Third Reich, would the outcome have been the same? And if the occasional blustering impulsiveness of Churchill had been used against the domestic opponents of reform during the Liberal ministry before World War I, would he have been able to prevail against the entrenched interests of the status quo? The fact seems to be that both Lloyd George and Churchill served their country well in their respective roles. If a recent poll among British academics is any guide, it may be that there is a growing consensus that confirms that each man and his accomplishments are to be evaluated not competitively, but in terms of their respective records.[100] They both served the nation superbly well, according to their characters and talents.

For a student in biography, the enduring question has been how to explain Lloyd George's ability to overcome the disadvantages of birth and background that were absent from almost all of his prime ministerial predecessors. What lies in Lloyd George's heritage and early life that can account for his success and dominant role in the politics of the twentieth century? Fatherless from the age of one, his family far from ducal grandeur, his economic resources and educational opportunities at first uncertain, Lloyd George nevertheless had some advantages. A closely knit and supportive family were not the least of these. To them throughout much of his early life, Lloyd George owed much. His mother, although supportive, was somewhat retiring within his family circle. His Uncle Lloyd has rightly been seen as the primary influence and moulder of Lloyd George's character and ambitions. Secure in the affections and care of his family of origin, Lloyd George was equally rooted in the closely-knit religious circle of family and friends. Although his religious beliefs may not have held true for long, they offered him a grounding and a framework for action that sustained him throughout his life.

It is the ambitious quality in the young Lloyd George that is starkly visible throughout his early life and into young manhood. Combined with a shrewd native intelligence and questing personality, the young Lloyd George, as we have seen, made his indelible mark in the local world of Welsh politics. Yet such was his need for approval, he was also bound to seek signs of it from his family and friends. This does not suggest that he was psychologically dependent upon them: but it does suggest that at the heart of his outgoing, ambitious and forthright manner was a need for assurance in his actions. With this in hand, he felt strengthened to continue onward in an often contentious and difficult public life. It lent him a sense of imperviousness and fearlessness that doubtless overlapped onto his relationships with men in public life, and women in his private life.

In alliance with his native intelligence, his family support and his determination to advance beyond his origins was a firm self-discipline. This tends to fly in the face of much criticism of Lloyd George's work habits, a topic of criticism even among his friends and supporters. It is important to realize, however, the direction and use of his self-discipline. His way of work was not characterized by personally slogging through memos and written agendas. This would slow his ability to make decisions quickly, especially during emergencies. Rather, he took short cuts, delegated authority and sought advice through his extensive network of friends and public officials. Once he had determined a reasonable solution to a problem, he arranged the contingencies to assure a speedy outcome by forcing decisions upon recalcitrant opponents. Less an ideologue than a fixer, he proved time after time to be a practically minded contriver of the possible.

But, as is true of any proposed grand political solution, the test of time was not always kind. If the struggle for the rights of Wales, for nonconformity, for the economic disadvantaged and for victory in war brought him the accolades that he cherished, the solutions for a united Ireland or domestic unrest or peace in the Middle East were less successful. Because of his mixed record, perhaps Lloyd George's historical reputation will always be debatable. It is the useful nature of historians continually to re-examine the past. In such revisions, it is sensible to take into account weaknesses as well as strengths, defeat as well as victory. Only then can a life in the round be understood. Lloyd George accomplished much. But he also failed at times. Even in failure, however, he retained an ability to return to the fray, to gather his resources, to find another way forward. He was, in this sense, indomitable and courageous, unafraid to encounter the inevitable conflict that his actions would generate. For this alone, Lloyd George earns our respect if not always our admiration.

NOTES

Chapter 1. Introduction

1 See the following for historical analyses of Edwardian Britain: Paul Thompson, *The Edwardians: The Remaking of British Society* (Bloomington, Indiana, 1975), esp. ch. 16 'The Edwardian Crisis'; Donald Read (ed.), *Edwardian England* (New Brunswick, NJ, 1982); David Brooks, *The Age of Upheaval: Edwardian Politics, 1899–1914* (Manchester, 1995); and David Powell, *The Edwardian Crisis: Britain 1901–14* (Houndmills, Hants, 1996).

2 Bentley Brinkerhoff Gilbert, *David Lloyd George: A Political Life*, vol. II: *Organizer of Victory 1912–16* (Columbus, OH, 1992), p. 199.

3 Kenneth O. Morgan, *Lloyd George* (London, 1974), p. 10.

4 John Grigg, *The Young Lloyd George* (Berkeley CA, 1973), p. 14.

Chapter 2. The Education of a Statesman

1 As David Cannadine has put it: 'with Lloyd George, the democratic attack on the traditional titled and territorial classes reached its climax. Quite simply, he refused to accept them at their own comfortable and superior self-evaluation, and he persuaded a large number of his fellow countrymen to agree with him. Instead of touching his forelock, he blew them raspberries. He taunted them, threatened them, taxed them, tormented them. He took away their hereditary power, and seemed set fair to take away their hereditary acres as well. No wonder, by 1914, they hated him as much as he hated them' (Cannadine, *The Decline and Fall of the British Aristocracy* (New Haven, 1990), p. 86).

2 Bentley Brinkerhoff Gilbert, *David Lloyd George. A Political Life*, vol. I: *The Architect of Change, 1863–1912* (Columbus, Ohio), 1987, pp. 11–12.

3 John Grigg, *The Young Lloyd George* (Berkeley CA, 1973), ch. 1; Kenneth Morgan, *Lloyd George* (London, 1974), p. 22. For details of William George's early life, see also W.R.P. George, *The Making of Lloyd George* (London, 1976), ch. 3; and Emyr Price, *David Lloyd George* (Cardiff, 2006), ch. 1.

4 The move may have been prompted by disagreeable circumstances in Newchurch, described by W. Watkin Davies, *Lloyd George 1863–1914* (London, 1939), p. 10, as 'a cold and damp Lancashire village, whose people he [William] did not like, and who did not like him'. Davies' book is praised by Grigg, *Young Lloyd George*, p. 304, as the 'best all-round account' of Lloyd George before World War I.

5 William George, *My Brother and I* (London, 1958), p. 7. The author is another memorialist of this prolifically literate family. The posthumous son of his namesake father, William

was David Lloyd George's younger brother. William was the father of W.R.P. George, David Lloyd George's nephew.

6   Grigg believes that the family was probably the best-off in Llanystumdwy, a village of about 1,000 inhabitants (Grigg, *Young Lloyd George*, p. 31). But Emyr Price takes strong exception to this statement: he believes that the family may have been better off than some workers, especially farm labourers, but they were less prosperous than local business men or the major employees of the near by Gwynfryn estate (Price, *Lloyd George*, p. 4).

7   George, *Making of Lloyd George*, p. 69.

8   Ibid., p. 69.

9   Ibid., esp. ch. 2 .

10 Price, *Lloyd George*, p. 4.

11 As Davies remembers him: 'his extraordinary mental powers, his gift of eloquent and ready speech, his essential fairness, and his unfailing urbanity, made him, in fact, the uncrowned king of every assembly in which he found himself' (Davies, *Lloyd George*, p. 32). More recent biographers have been equally impressed with Uncle Lloyd: Grigg thinks him 'the Hans Sachs of Llanystumdwy' (Grigg, *Young Lloyd George*, p. 31). But Price debunks this Wagnerian referencing as 'surely nonsense' (Price, *Lloyd George*, p. 4).

12 George, *My Brother and I*, p. 23.

13 Ibid., entry of 12 December 1880, 22. Grigg, however, is cautious about the influence of Richard Lloyd upon his nephew, both as a child and later ('almost negligible' as a grown man: Grigg, *Young Lloyd George*, p. 29).

14 Davies, *Lloyd George*, p. 32.

15 George, *My Brother and I*, p. 33.

16 Gilbert, *Lloyd George: Architect of Change*, p. 27.

17 Both quotations are from Martin Pugh, *Lloyd George*, paperback edn (London, 1988), p. 2.

18 Grigg, *Young Lloyd George*, p. 27.

19 Grigg implicitly understands this. He observes that the young Lloyd George rewarded his uncle's 'ceaseless adulation' by pretending to value the old man's opinion when in reality 'all that he wanted from Uncle Lloyd was what he unfailingly got – praise, more praise and still more praise' (Grigg, *Young Lloyd George*, p. 29). Lloyd George had sufficient self-knowledge to realize this characteristic about himself. Many decades later, he confessed to Frances Stevenson his lack of self-confidence and his love of approbation. 'He said that Uncle Lloyd realized this failing in him, and for that reason sought to encourage him whenever he did well' (A.J.P. Taylor, *Lloyd George, A Diary by Frances Stevenson* (London, 1971), 19 March 1934, p. 261).

20 See George, *My Brother and I*, ch. 3; George, *Making of Lloyd George*, pp. 72–7; and Davies, *Lloyd George*, pp. 18–26.

21 As Herbert Du Parcq recounts in his *Life of David Lloyd George* (London, 1912), vol. 1, p. 18.

22 National Library of Wales (hereafter NLW), William George Papers 6, 1886, Collins Handy Diary for 1886: diary entries for 17 January 1886, folio 9 verso; 18 January 1886, folio 10 recto; 11 February 1886, folio 20 verso; 11 March 1886, folio 32 verso; 19 August 1886, folio 101 verso. There are detailed entries for some days only: a few entries are in shorthand.

23 George, *My Brother and I*, p. 49; and George, *Making of Lloyd George*, p. 73. This tale likely had a special relevance for two fatherless boys.

24 Davies, *Lloyd George*, p. 19.

25 As Morgan puts it: 'nonconformity was responsible for almost every significant and worthwhile aspect of social and cultural activity in late nineteenth-century Wales'

(Kenneth O. Morgan, *Rebirth of a Nation: A History of Modern Wales*, paperback edn (Oxford, 1982), p. 18. The phrase 'citadels of dissent' appears on p. 14. In general, see also chs 1–4.

26 In this book, 'Conservative Party' includes those Liberal Party Unionists who formed an alliance with the Conservatives in 1886 and who formally merged to form the Conservative and Unionist Party in 1912. Contemporaries sometimes used Conservative Party and Unionist Party interchangeably – as David Dutton notes in *'His Majesty's Loyal Opposition': The Unionist Party in Opposition 1905–1915* (Liverpool, 1992), p. 5 n. 1. Dutton himself, as his title indicates, opts for 'Unionist Party'. John Ramsden, *An Appetite for Power: A History of the Conservative Party since 1830*, paperback edn (London, 1999) uses 'Unionist alliance' or 'Unionist parties' (pp. 163, 168, 171, 177). Unionism refers of course to those who were pledged to preserve a close union with Ireland.

27 Matthew Cragoe has attempted to soften the image of nineteenth-century Welsh landlords. He notes that most landlords were not exploitative parasites: they rather upheld a paternalistic ethos of mutual responsibility and obligation which benefited landlord and tenant. Moreover, as the era of deference slid into an age of dissidence, landlords themselves had legitimate complaints about nonconformist preachers bullying their flocks with threats of everlasting damnation if they did not vote Liberal (Cragoe, *Culture, Politics, and National Identity in Wales, 1832–1886* (Oxford, 2004), p. 174). See also Cragoe, *An Anglican Aristocracy: The Moral Economy of the Landed Estate in Carmarthenshire, 1832–1895* (Oxford, 1996).

28 Grigg (*Young Lloyd George*, p. 34) thinks that Lloyd George thereafter held with a kind of deism and wonders how a man 'whose spiritual luggage was so light' was able to hold for a time so effectively the allegiance of a powerful nonconformist political bloc. On the other hand, Lloyd George's brother William claims that all of Lloyd George's 'professions of faith were sincere and deep-seated' (*My Brother and I*, p. 75). What William means by this, however, is somewhat unclear as he presents evidence from Lloyd George's own diary entries of 1883 and 1884 of distinctly critical thinking directed against his co-religionists. In one 'momentous (for me) disputation', Lloyd George wrote in his diary, he asserted his latitudinarianism and rationalism 'in the society of my religious friends'. He went so far as to doubt 'the essentiality or even expediency of stickling for baptism' (ibid., p. 78). After reading Frederic Harrison's addresses to the Positivist Society, he notes that Harrison's views were 'wonderfully in accord with my own' (ibid., p. 78). Lloyd George also recounts a disputation, this time in a Sunday school, where he denies the 'immutability of the Xtian ordinances' (ibid., p. 78). In another Sunday school discussion, he made his fellow congregants 'mute' when he pointed out a 'glaring inconsistency' between Paul and James on faith and works (ibid., p. 79). One has the sense that Lloyd George may very well have maintained some broad Christian ideals, but that he had drifted far from his fundamentalist origins.

29 Apparently, Uncle Lloyd privately coached his nephew both in improving his speaking voice and in directing the hymns. See, for example, Richard Lloyd's brief diary entries quoted in Davies, *Lloyd George*, pp. 39–40.

30 As Jonathan Rose has pointed out: 'all Nonconformist sects encouraged the habits of close reading, interpretive analysis, and intellectual self-improvement' (Rose, *The Intellectual Life of the British Working Classes*, paperback edn (New Haven, 2002), p. 34).

31 Morgan, *Rebirth of a Nation*, p. 13.

32 Articles of clerkship did not come cheaply: Uncle Lloyd and his family scraped together £180 to secure them.

33 Gilbert, *Lloyd George: Architect of Change*, p. 33.

34 George, *Making of Lloyd George*, p. 82.

35 See Davies, *Lloyd George*, pp. 36–39. Davies compares that preaching tradition with Lloyd George's own political speeches thus: 'there is the same modulation of a naturally beautiful voice, the same lavish use of gesture, the same passion, with its intermingling of humour and pathos, the same love of telling illustration, and the same skill in exploiting to the full the dramatic possibilities of the theme' (ibid., p. 36). Gilbert thinks that Lloyd George never overtly rejected religious belief; but that it 'had quietly slipped away as he had grown older' (Gilbert, *Lloyd George: Architect of Change*, p. 37).

36 When he passed his final law examination in 1884, he earned only third-class honours; whereas William passed his with first-class honours three years later. This was not, as Grigg notes, a measure of their relative abilities, but of David's declining interest in the law (Grigg, *Young Lloyd George*, p. 41).

37 George, *Making of Lloyd George*, pp. 92–93.

38 Ibid., p. 94.

39 To Lloyd George's indignation: see ibid., p. 95.

40 Ibid., p. 98.

41 Grigg believes that Lloyd George's lofty ambitions were in place as early as November 1881 when he first went to London for his intermediate law exam and paid a visit to the House of Commons. Though only 18 at the time, 'he was already dreaming of supreme power' (Grigg, *Young Lloyd George*, p. 44). Gilbert believes, without a precise date in mind, that after 1880, Lloyd George 'was continually campaigning, not entirely unconsciously' to become a Member of Parliament (Gilbert, *Lloyd George: Architect of Change*, p. 43).

42 *North Wales Express*, 3 February 1882, Parliamentary Archives, LG/A/6/1/1.

43 *North Wales Express*, 24 November 1882, Parliamentary Archives, LG/A/6/1/2.

44 George, *Making of Lloyd George*, pp. 124–25.

45 At which he was not very agile: see his own comments where at one drill, his braces broke and his trousers 'were continuously coming down', hindering his running at drill. Altogether, he felt 'most miserable'. At another drill, he confessed that the other Volunteers 'rather pass me as they attend drills more regularly' (ibid., p. 104).

46 Ibid., p. 104. He also admitted that signing the pledge gave him the opportunity to speak at temperance rallies, thus displaying his oratorical prowess – the power of which he was becoming fully aware. But Lloyd George may have realized that his career as a budding politician would be harmed if it were known that he broke the pledge so freely. It appears that he kept the pledge after 1882 (ibid., p. 112).

47 George, *My Brother and I*, p. 83.

48 NLW, Lloyd George Papers, Diary of 1885, 2 February 1885, p. 28.

49 Ibid., 13 March 1885, p. 39.

50 Ibid., 28 March 1885, p. 43.

51 Ibid., 28 February, 1885, p. 35.

52 Ibid., 25 February 1885, p. 35 addendum.

53 The son of an evicted tenant farmer from County Mayo who had emigrated to Lancashire, Davitt, as a child labourer, had lost his right arm in a mill accident. He was successively a Fenian, a member of the Irish Republican Brotherhood (IRB), an ex-prisoner, a founder of the Land League of Mayo and a year later in 1879, the National Land League. He was elected MP for County Meath in 1882.

54 For these quotations and Lloyd George's detailed account of the meeting, see his diary at NLW, William George Papers 6, Collins Handy Diary for 1886, 12 February 1886. See also Gilbert, *Lloyd George: Architect of Change*), pp. 53–4; and the *Cambrian News*, as reprinted in du Parcq, *Life of Lloyd George*, vol. 1, pp. 76–7.

55 See Davies, *Lloyd George*, p. 47–51.

56 Kenneth O. Morgan's phrase in 'The Welsh in English Politics, 1868–1982' included in the volume edited by R.R. Davies et al., *Welsh Society and Nationhood: Historical Essays Presented to Glanmor Williams* (Cardiff, 1984), p. 234. See also Morgan's *Wales in British Politics, 1868–1922* (Cardiff, 1980), ch. 1, 'Wales and British Politics before 1868'.

57 Morgan, *Rebirth of a Nation*, pp. 27–9.

58 Grigg, *Young Lloyd George*, p. 17.

59 Grigg among others believes that from an early age, Lloyd George had set his sights on becoming a Member of Parliament. At the age of 18, Gregg claims, Lloyd George 'was already dreaming of supreme power' (ibid., p. 44). But Price thinks that Lloyd George's primary purpose was to 'create a vibrant, more progressive and a more equal society' in a self-governing Wales, and that he had little intention early on of using his Welsh-centred activities to boost his own prospects on a wider stage (Price, *Lloyd George*, p. x).

60 For this paragraph, see the discussion in Gilbert, *Lloyd George: Architect of Change*, pp. 49–52; and Price, *Lloyd George*, ch. 1.

61 For the anti-tithe campaign, see Price, *Lloyd George*, pp. 32–6.

62 W.R. Lambert, *Drink and Sobriety in Victorian Wales c. 1820–c. 1895* (Cardiff, 1983), p. 4. For England, Brian Harrison, *Drink and the Victorians: The Temperance Question in England 1815–1872* (Pittsburg, 1971) remains essential reading.

63 In their early days of fostering Welsh nationalism, Ellis and Lloyd George initially worked together. Later on their differences tended to divide them. Ellis's view of Wales was cultural and literary whereas Lloyd George was interested in political and social issues. To achieve his ends, Lloyd George was the more ruthless and determined. See Kenneth O. Morgan, 'Tom Ellis versus Lloyd George, the Fractured Consciousness of Fin-de-Siecle Wales', in Geraint H. Jenkins and J. Beverley Smith (eds), *Politics and Society in Wales, 1840–1922: Essays in Honour of Ieuan Gwynedd Jones* (Cardiff, 1988), pp. 93–112.

64 These were also the main objectives of the famous Irish Land Act passed by the second Gladstone administration in 1881. For a discussion of the new men and new issues of Wales in the 1880s and 1890s, see Morgan, *Rebirth of a Nation*, pp. 33–43.

65 George, *Making of Lloyd George*, p. 129.

66 Details of the case may be found in Price, *Lloyd George*, pp. 56–7, 61–4.

67 George, *My Brother and I*, p. 143. William had also made significant contributions to the verdict on appeal, including several trips to the Law Society Library in London to review a number of abstruse points in ecclesiastical law. See his account ibid., pp. 141–3.

68 For Lloyd George's activities in 1889, see George, *Making of Lloyd George*, pp. 160–2. Price, *Lloyd George*, p. 59 notes that Lloyd George was not above conducting a 'ruthless' and 'highly manipulated' press campaign to advance his candidacy.

69 NLW, Lloyd George Papers, 20403C, 2 September 1886, p. 12.

70 Ibid., 11 December, 1886, p. 29.

71 Ibid., 29 July 1886, p. 8.

72 Ibid., 3 October 1886, p. 14.

73 George, *Making of Lloyd George*, p. 149.

74 Gilbert, *Lloyd George: Architect of Change*, pp. 64–5.

75 Kenneth O. Morgan (ed.), *Lloyd George, Family Letters, 1885–1936* (Cardiff and London, 1973), undated (but probably 1885), p. 14.

Chapter 3. To England to Parliament

1 For the election, see Emyr Price, *David Lloyd George* (Cardiff, 2006), ch. 7.

2 Bentley Brinkerhoff Gilbert, *David Lloyd George: A Political Life*, vol. 1: *The Architect of Change, 1863–1912* (Columbus, Ohio, 1987), p. 81, quoting from the *North Wales Observer*, 16 May 1890.

3 Herbert du Parcq, *Life of David Lloyd George*, 4 vols (London, 1912), vol. 1, p. 104.

4 *Hansard*, 3rd Series, vol. 345, 13 June 1890, pp. 871–74.

5 David M. Fahey, 'The Politics of Drink: Pressure Groups and the British Liberal Party, 1883–1908', *Social Science* 54/2 (Spring 1979), pp. 76–85, 80. See also Peter Mathias, 'The Brewing Industry, Temperance and Politics', *Historical Journal* 1/2 (1958), pp. 97–114.

6 The government had some cause for alarm. Meetings and demonstrations against the tithe were frequent and often disorderly from 1886 onward. In the spring of 1887 at Meifod in Montgomeryshire, for example, an attempted distraint brought out a crowd of 800 in opposition. See J.P.D. Dunbabin, *Rural Discontent in Nineteenth-Century Britain* (New York, 1974), ch. 10, 'The Welsh Tithe War'; and Kenneth O. Morgan, *Wales in British Politics, 1868–1922* (Cardiff, 1980), pp. 84–94. Lloyd George had served as secretary of the South Caernarfonshire Anti-Tithe League.

7 To Thomas Gee, Lloyd George wrote: 'we manage to keep the pot boiling and the Liberal Party thereby is awakening to the fact that Welsh questions are very useful – quite as useful as Irish ones – to hurl at the government' (cited in Gilbert, *Lloyd George: Architect of Change*, 2 February 1891, p. 92).

8 *Hansard*, 3rd Series, vol. 349, 2 February 1891, p. 1574.

9 Ibid., vol. 356, 29 July 1891, pp. 694–703.

10 *Hansard*, 4th Series, vol. 3, 28 April 1892, p. 1601. This time, Lloyd George was answered by Gladstone (then Leader of the Opposition Liberal Party) who – in supporting the bill – gently insisted that this was an inappropriate time to pass such an amendment.

11 NLW, William George Papers, 165 (1891). *The Trumpet*, as Price has noted, played a 'vital' part in 'fostering Lloyd George's ambitions' (Price, *Lloyd George*, p. 47; and more generally ch. 4).

12 J. Graham Jones, *David Lloyd George and Welsh Liberalism* (Aberystwyth, 2010), ch. 2, 'Lloyd George and the Caernarfon Boroughs Election of 1892'. Jones is essential reading for Lloyd George's political career in Wales.

13 See Morgan, *Wales in British Politics*, pp. 120–21. Two years later, Ellis was promoted to Chief Whip.

14 Acland was MP for Rotherham, but lived in Caernarfonshire and had introduced Lloyd George on his first day in the House of Commons on 17 April 1890. Known as a friend to Wales.

15 One of his daughters had married one of Gladstone's sons.

16 See the appreciation of Rendel's role in D.A. Hamer, *Liberal Politics in the Age of Gladstone and Rosebery: A Study in Leadership and Policy* (Oxford, 1972), pp. 29–33.

17 Gilbert, *Lloyd George: Architect of Change*, p. 103. For a review of the contretemps between Lloyd George and Gladstone over Welsh disestablishment, see Chris Wrigley, 'Lloyd George and Gladstone', *The Historian* 85 (Spring 2005), pp. 8–17.

18 *The Times*, 13 and 14 September 1892.

19 H.C.G. Matthew (ed.), *The Gladstone Diaries* (Oxford, 1994), vol. 13 (1892–96), Gladstone to Rendel, 3 September 1892, p. 72.

20 Matthew, *The Gladstone Diaries*, a holograph entitled 'Session of 1893' intended for the Cabinet and marked 'Secret', 31 October 1892, p. 128.

21 NLW, William George Papers, 3318, 1 December 1892, f. 35.

22 Apparently Rendel had been working behind the scenes to convince both Gladstone and Asquith that a suspensory bill had a tactical value – as opposed to a wider ranging

disestablishment bill – because it could be limited to 'almost a single clause and give the minimum room for obstruction and division'. It could also, if rejected by the Lords, 'easily be sent up again and again' (W.R.P. George, *Backbencher* (Llandysul, 1983), p. 138). Quoted from a letter to Herbert Lewis, MP for Flint Boroughs, and a close ally of Lloyd George.

23 George, *Backbencher*, 19 February 1894, p. 132.

24 Ibid., 5 March 1894, p. 142.

25 After its passage in the Commons, this bill – renamed the Tenant's Arbitration (Ireland) Bill – met the same fate as the Home Rule Bill of 1893, losing by a vote of 249:30 in the House of Lords.

26 Even though he campaigned for Humphreys-Owen, he pulled no punches in lambasting his favourite targets. As he put it in a letter to his wife, 'I roasted landlords and parsons' (Kenneth O. Morgan (ed.), *Lloyd George: Family Letters, 1885–1936* (Cardiff and London, 1973), 21 March 1894, p. 67).

27 Ibid., 2 April 1894, p. 68.

28 Ibid., 4 April 1894, p. 68. He was paraphrasing a comment made to him – by a Conservative MP no less – which he obviously accepted as true.

29 As Grigg believes, see John Grigg, *The Young Lloyd George* (Berkeley CA, 1973)p. 147.

30 Ellis, as Chief Whip for the Liberals, was not happy with the prospect of a party division and least happy of all with the role of Lloyd George. As he wrote to a close friend: 'George is very threatening. He means to be on the warpath. His whole attitude is to upset the apple cart' (George, *Backbencher*, 20 April 1894, p. 147). The letter was written to D.R. Daniel, also a firm friend of Lloyd George.

31 As Morgan notes in *Wales in British Politics*, p. 146.

32 Morgan, *Lloyd George: Family Letters*, 3–7 June 1894, pp. 74–5.

33 Morgan, *Wales in British Politics*, 162. For Cymru Fydd generally, see ibid., pp. 104–6 and 160–5. Price also has much to say about the Cymru Fydd League: see Price, *David Lloyd George*, especially chs 9 and 10.

34 There is some controversy about Lloyd George's responsibility in bringing down his erstwhile Liberal allies. Morgan believes Lloyd George's actions materially weakened his own government, which led to their resignation and thus retarded disestablishment – a central aim of the Welsh party (Morgan, *Wales in British Politics*, p. 158). Even some of Lloyd George's contemporaries thought so, and regarded him as a traitor to Liberalism for aiding and abetting the Conservative cause. Gilbert, however, emphasizes that wider issues were at work and that Lloyd George's part in the Liberal collapse was 'not great' (Gilbert, *Lloyd George: Architect of Change*, p. 136).

35 Information in this paragraph is from John Ramsden, *An Appetite for Power: A History of the Conservative Party since 1830*, paperback edn (London, 1999), p. 179 and Appendix 3.

36 'They were quite stunned' by his remarks, as he reported the incident to his wife (Morgan, *Family Letters*, p. 87, 16 July 1895).

37 He boasted to his wife about his obstructive tactics in a letter of 22 August 1895 (ibid., p. 88). Additional targets of his remarks may be found in Grigg, *Young Lloyd George*, p. 200.

38 Kenneth O. Morgan, *Rebirth of a Nation: A History of Modern Wales*, paperback edn (Oxford, 1982), p. 59 and in general ch. 3.

39 As a staunch Liberal, Abraham saw no inherent conflict of interest between capital and labour and was known to distrust industrial action. Not surprisingly, he was on excellent terms with leading Welsh coal owners. Later he drifted slightly leftward, becoming a Lib./Lab. MP for Rhondda and for Rhondda West, 1918–22. See E.W. Evans and John Saville's entry, 'Abraham, William (Mabon)', in Joyce M. Bellamy and John Saville (eds),

Dictionary of Labour Biography (Clifton, NJ, 1972), pp. 1–4; and Kenneth O. Morgan, *Labour People: Leaders and Lieutenants, Hardie to Kinnock* (Oxford, 1987), 'Mabon and Noah Ablett', pp. 69–77.

40 'My lecture tour is a decided success', he wrote to Margaret (Jones, *Lloyd George and Welsh Liberalism*, p. 69, 7 November 1895). For Lloyd George's Cymru Fydd League campaign as a whole, see ibid., ch. 4, 'Lloyd George, Cymru Fydd and the Newport meeting of January 1896'.

41 Morgan, *Lloyd George: Family Letters*, 16 January 1896, p. 94.

42 As Morgan has noted in his *Wales in British Politics*, p. 166.

43 Peter Rowland, *David Lloyd George* (London, 1975), p. 116. It seemed to Rowland that almost every week during the parliamentary session of 1896 Lloyd George's voice was heard in the Chamber (p. 115).

44 As Graham Jones puts it, Cymru Fydd had proved to be 'simply the temporary vessel for his ambitions' (Jones, *Lloyd George and Welsh Liberalism*, p. 81).

45 *Hansard*, 4th Series, vol. 40, 30 April 1896, pp. 238, 242.

46 Ibid., 20 May 1896, pp. 38–9.

47 Historians have given Lloyd George high marks for his campaign against the bill. Morgan thinks that he gave the Liberals 'new heart' in his unrelenting attacks against the Conservative government (Morgan, *Lloyd George: Family Letters*, p. 96). Grigg claims that Lloyd George's line of attack 'was excellent politically' (Grigg, *Young Lloyd George*, p. 204). Packer believes that he 'had particular success' in scoring points against the bill (Ian Packer, *Lloyd George*, paperback edn (Houndmills, 1998), p. 14.

48 Quoted in J. Hugh Edwards, *The Life of David Lloyd George* (London, n.d. [1913], p. 145.)

49 Lloyd George, ever the politician, spent the week off from parliamentary duties by campaigning for J.E. Barlow, the Liberal candidate in the Frome by-election. Barlow won and held the seat until 1918.

50 Morgan, *Lloyd George: Family Letters*, 4 June 1896, p. 104. See Grigg, *Young Lloyd George*, pp. 203–5 and Gilbert, *Lloyd George: Architect of Change*, pp. 151–4 for accounts of Lloyd George's parliamentary devices against the bill.

51 Gilbert believes that Lloyd George's experiences with Irish MPs during the 1890s taught him that 'the Irish were a political exasperation' (Gilbert, *Lloyd George: Architect of Change*, pp. 157–8).

52 The most complete analysis is R. Merfyn Jones, *The North Wales Quarrymen, 1874–1922* (Cardiff, 1982), esp. ch. 7.

53 Gilbert, *Lloyd George: Architect of Change*, p. 174.

54 Chris Wrigley, *David Lloyd George and the British Labour Movement: Peace and War* (Hassocks, 1976), p. 15, quoting from Welsh newspaper reports.

55 *Hansard*, 4th Series, vol. XLV, 28 January 1897, 741–2, 746. Afterwards, he wrote to Margaret that he had 'roasted' Penrhyn on the floor of the House (Morgan, *Lloyd George: Family Letters*, 29 January 1897, p. 109). In the same letter he claimed that he 'never made a more effective debating speech in the House of Commons'.

56 Gilbert, *Lloyd George: Architect of Change*, pp. 174–5.

57 Indeed, Grigg says it (*Young Lloyd George*, p. 176). Gilbert is particularly critical of Lloyd George's treatment of his brother, noting that he was 'quite willing to allow the fire of his own ambition to consume others' (Gilbert, *Lloyd George: Architect of Change*, p. 47).

58 Printed extracts are in George, *Backbencher*.

59 Ibid., p. 20.

60 Ibid., 10 December 1890, p. 49.

61 Ibid., 4 September 1891, p. 72.

62   Ibid., 27 August 1891, p. 63. Perhaps it was all a matter of Lloyd George's aversion to legal detail. Decades later, William's son explained his uncle's behaviour thus: he 'couldn't stomach doing the humdrum work of a legal practice' (ibid., p. 72).

63   NLW, William George Papers, March 1890, p. 24.

64   A lengthy discussion of this episode may be found in Grigg, *Young Lloyd George*, pp. 178–95. See also George, *Backbencher*, pp. 108–17, 123–36, and 201–6.

65   Ibid., 21 October 1892, p. 116. William nevertheless held about 600 shares, Lloyd George more than 1,000.

66   Morgan, *Lloyd George: Family Letters*, 16 August 1893, p. 61, marked 'Confidential'.

67   Cited in Grigg, *Young Lloyd George*, 26 December 1893, p. 183 n. 2.

68   NLW, William George Papers, 3 March 1894, p. 245. The Patagonia scheme had already distracted Lloyd George from his parliamentary ambitions. As he confided to William a few months earlier: 'I am so full of this business just now that even if there were any Welsh issues knocking about I couldn't apply myself to them' (ibid., 20 December 1893, p. 217).

69   As two letters to William suggest. 'Patagonia looks promising', he wrote in July 1896 (ibid., 13 July 1896, p. 397). The following month he was more specific: 'The gold deposits are no doubt exceedingly rich' (ibid., 18 August 1896, p. 403).

70   Grigg, *Young Lloyd George*, p. 186.

71   Ibid., p. 188.

72   See Jones, *Lloyd George and Welsh Liberalism*, pp. 50–4 and 83–4.

73   Gilbert, *Lloyd George: Architect of Change*, p. 165.

74   See Grigg's account in *Young Lloyd George*, pp. 228–39.

75   Morgan: *Lloyd George*, p. 201.

76   Ffion Hague, *The Pain and the Privilege: The Women in Lloyd George's Life* (London, 2008), p. 133.

77   Morgan, in his introduction to *Lloyd George: Family Letters*, pp. 1–10.

78   Ibid., 7 May 1890, p. 25.

79   Ibid., 5 June 1890, p. 27.

80   Ibid., 14 June 1890, p. 29.

81   George, *Backbencher*, p. 30.

82   Morgan, *Lloyd George: Family Letters*, 16 June 1890, pp. 29–30.

83   Ibid., 3 February 1891, p. 42.

84   George, *Backbencher*, 54. The *Speaker* was the official organ of the Gladstonian Liberals.

85   Morgan, *Lloyd George: Family Letters*, 31 July 1891, p. 44.

86   Ibid., 25 September 1891, p. 44.

87   Ibid.

88   Ibid., 29 April 1892, p. 48.

89   George, *Backbencher*, undated, p. 93.

90   Morgan, *Lloyd George: Family Letters*, 28 January 1893, p. 59.

91   Quotations above are from ibid., 17 May 1894, p. 71; 18 May 1894, p. 71; 17 January 1895, p. 78; 14 February 1895, p. 80; 3 June 1895, p. 84; 12 November 1895, p. 90; 28 February 1896, p. 100; 30 June 1896, p. 105.

92   See Lloyd George's relatively short intervention in *Hansard*, 4th Series, vol. 53, 17 February 1898, pp. 974–9.

93   Morgan omits this revealing aspect of Lloyd George's correspondence, which is clearly evident in the archives. This may be explained by Morgan's intention to omit all letters or parts of letters he considered 'banal' or trivial (Morgan, *Lloyd George: Family Letters*, p. 9.)

94 NLW, Lloyd George Papers, 20406C, 7 July 1890, p. 96.

95 Ibid., 20407C, 28 July 1890, p. 116.

96 Ibid., 5 December 1890, p. 148i.

97 Ibid., 20408C, 21 January 1891, p. 154.

98 Ibid., 31 January 1891, p. 160.

99 Ibid., 20410C, 8 August 1892, p. 272.

100 Ibid., 20409C, 17 February 1892, p. 200.

101 Ibid., 13 February 1892, p. 197.

102 Ibid., 20410C, 29 October 1892, p. 283.

103 Ibid., 20411C, 25 July 1893, p. 345.

104 Ibid., 20413C, 3 August 1894, p. 468.

105 Ibid., 20422C, 24 August 1899, p. 989.

106 Ibid., 25 August 1899, p. 992.

107 Morgan, *Lloyd George: Family Letters*, p. 5.

108 Grigg, *Young Lloyd George*, p. 28.

109 As demonstrated, for example, by his career-long courting of the newspaper press: see S. Koss, 'Asquith versus Lloyd George: the Last Phase and Beyond', in Alan Sked and Chris Cook (eds), *Crisis and Controversy: Essays in Honour of A.J.P. Taylor* (New York, 1976), p. 71; and Stephen Koss, *The Rise and Fall of the Political Press in Britain: The Twentieth Century* (London, 1984), p. 302.

110 Many years earlier, in a rare moment of self-knowledge, Lloyd George confessed to Frances Stevenson that 'he lacks self-confidence, but possesses the quality of love of approbation, which to a certain extent supplies the stimulus which lack of self-confidence needs. He said that Uncle Lloyd realized this failing in him, and for that reason sought to encourage him whenever he did well' (A.J.P. Taylor, *Lloyd George: A Diary by Frances Stevenson* (London, 1971), 19 March 1934).

111 Biographers with an interest in the psychological disposition of their subjects may find theories of narcissism useful in explaining Lloyd George's behaviour.

112 NLW, Lloyd George Papers, 22518E, dated 10 February 1890, but probably 1891, pp. 7–8.

113 NLW, William George Papers, 26 June 1891, p. 139.

114 William George, *My Brother and I* (London, 1958), undated letter, p. 29.

115 Ibid., 20 April 1895, p. 84.

116 Ibid., 3 June 1895, pp. 84–5. Roberts was a Liberal member for South Caernarfonshire from 1885–1906. He and Lloyd George were frequently at odds on Welsh issues.

117 Ibid., 11 February 1896, p. 98.

118 See Morgan, *Wales in British Politics*, p. 142 and Gilbert, *Lloyd George: Architect of Change*, p. 100.

119 George, *Backbencher*, letter dated 24 May 1892, p. 78.

120 Ibid., dated 25 May 1894, p. 146. In 1889, when Humphreys-Owen heard that Lloyd George would be the Liberal candidate for the Caernarfon Boroughs, he denigrated his qualifications as merely 'a second-rate County Court attorney' (ibid., undated, p. 77). Perhaps it should be borne in mind that Humphreys-Owen was well-Anglicized – a barrister, and a product of Harrow and Trinity College, Cambridge.

121 George, *Backbencher*, 30 April 1894, p. 147.

122 Written by 'M' for the Conservative *Daily Mail*, 3 October 1901, quoted in Du Parcq, *Life of Lloyd George*, vol. 2, pp. 261–3.

123 Morgan, *Lloyd George: Family Letters*, undated (but probably 1887), p. 19.

124 Ibid., 28 May 1897, p. 111.

125 NLW, Lloyd George Papers, 20412C, 21 March 1894, p. 409.

126 Morgan, *Lloyd George: Family Letters*, undated, May 1890, p. 26.

127 Ibid., 12 June 1890, pp. 28–9.

128 Ibid., 29 July 1890, p. 31.

129 NLW, Lloyd George Papers, 20408C, 25 May 1891, p. 170.

130 Ibid., 22 July 1891, p. 172.

131 Ibid., 20411C, 18 September 1893, p. 374.

132 Ibid., 20415C, 9 November 1895, p. 595.

133 Ibid., 20414C, 25 April 1895, p. 548.

134 Ibid., 20418C, 26 May 1897, pp. 798i–ii.

135 Ibid., 20423C, 1 September 1900, p. 1025.

136 Martin Pugh, *Lloyd George*, paperback edn (London, 1988), p. 15.

137 Grigg, *Young Lloyd George*, p. 58.

138 Don M. Cregier, *Bounder from Wales: Lloyd George's Career before the First World War* (Columbia, 1976), p. 60.

139 Gilbert, *Lloyd George: Architect of Change*, p. 166.

140 Ian Packer, *Lloyd George*, paperback edn (Houndmills, Hants, 1998), pp. 32–3.

141 Donald McCormick, *The Mask of Merlin: A Critical Biography of David Lloyd George* (New York, 1964), pp. 15, 17. McCormick in his conclusion remarks that Lloyd George 'pursued sexual pleasures with the single-mindedness which another man might devote to chess, to cricket or to painting' (ibid., p. 309).

142 Davies later became Mayor of Fulham and served as Liberal MP for Fulham from 1906–10.

143 As Morgan notes in refutation to those who claim that Mrs Tim was something more than a gracious hostess (Morgan, *Lloyd George*, p. 203). Pugh tends to agree with Morgan that Mrs Tim was a mother figure to Lloyd George (Pugh, *Lloyd George*, p. 16). Peter Rowland, however, insinuates that Lloyd George went beyond the bounds of amiable flirtation on these visits: he bases his comments on Richard Lloyd's *My Father Lloyd George*. See Rowland, *Lloyd George*, p. 129. It should be noted that Richard's sister, Olwen, also believed that Mrs Tim became her father's mistress (Olwen Carey Evans, *Lloyd George was My Father* (Llandysul, Dyfed, 1985), p. 63). John Campbell thinks that '"Mrs Tim" gave LG for several years exactly the sort of womanly pampering he always craved'. Furthermore: 'sex was certainly a part of it, since Lloyd George was a highly sexed man …' (*If Love Were All … The Story of Frances Stevenson and David Lloyd George*, paperback edn (London, 2007), p. 22). Hague's more recent account agrees: 'Mrs Tim embarked on an affair with Lloyd George that was to last many years' (Hague, *Pain and the Privilege*, p. 136). It was certainly true that Lloyd George was friendly to Mrs Tim for quite some time. As late as 1916, Frances Stevenson records in her diary that Lloyd George was taking Mrs Tim to tea (Taylor, *A Diary by Frances Stevenson*, 9 February 1916, p. 96). Stevenson seemed unperturbed at the prospect and accepted Lloyd George's explanation: 'she has been a good friend to him, and he does not wish to appear to neglect her' (ibid., 9 February 1916, p. 96).

144 NLW, William George Papers, 4824, 1890, ff. 13–4. It is a matter of keen regret to historians that so few of Margaret Lloyd George's letters have survived.

145 Rowland, *Lloyd George*, 27 May 1897, p. 129. Morgan's version of this letter is curtailed, omitting the first paragraph (Morgan, *Family Letters*, 27 May 1897, p. 110).

146 Grigg, *Young Lloyd George*, p. 241.

147 See Rowland, *Lloyd George*, for the letter, dated 21 August 1897, p. 131.

148 Morgan, *Lloyd George: Family Letters*, 21 August 1897, p. 112.

149 NLW, Lloyd George Papers, 20419C, 21 August 1897, p. 823ii.

150 Rowland thus describes Lloyd George's household habits in *Lloyd George*, p. 94.

151 As A.J.P. Taylor notes in his Preface to *A Diary by Frances Stevenson*, p. ix.

Chapter 4. With Radical Intent?

1   For what follows, see H.V. Emy, *Liberals, Radicals and Social Politics, 1892–1914* (Cambridge, 1973), chs 1–4; Paul Adelman's *Victorian Radicalism: The Middle-Class Experience, 1830–1914* (London, 1984); and G.R. Searle, *The Liberal Party: Triumph and Disintegration, 1886–1929* (New York, 1992), chs 1–4.

2   See Howard Reinroth, 'Left-Wing Opposition to Naval Armaments in Britain before 1914', *Journal of Contemporary History* 6:4 (1971), pp. 93–120; and Gerald H.S. Jordan, 'Pensions not Dreadnoughts: The Radical and Naval Retrenchment', in A.J.A. Morris (ed.), *Edwardian Radicalism 1900–1914: Some Aspects of British Radicalism* (London, 1974), ch. 10.

3   Kenneth O. Morgan, *Rebirth of a Nation: A History of Modern Wales*, paperback edn (Oxford, 1982), p. 27 and ch. 2 more generally for what follows.

4   As Morgan observes, the Reform Act of 1884 had 'a massive effect' on Welsh politics, making Wales 'something resembling a political democracy' (ibid., p. 27). Searle echoes this view, noting that the Reform Act was a 'massive stride' toward democracy throughout all of Britain (G.R. Searle, *A New England? Peace and War, 1886–1918* (Oxford, 2004), p. 134.

5   Ibid., p. 212.

6   Leo McKinstry describes Rosebery thus: 'there was within him a perpetual conflict between a powerful, aristocratic sense of duty, and an attachment to sensual idleness' (*Rosebery: Statesman in Turmoil*, paperback edn (London, 2006), p. 51).

7   Michael Bentley, *The Climax of Liberal Politics: British Liberalism in Theory and Practice 1868–1918* (London, 1987), p. 106.

8   In a speech at Caernarfon on 5 July 1895, he declared himself strongly in favour of old age pensions, suggesting that diverting the tithe away from parsons and towards the poor could raise the £5 million necessary to fund them. Additional funds could be found by increasing inheritance taxes and taxing ground rents and royalties (see John Grigg, *The Young Lloyd George* (Berkeley CA, 1973), p. 169).

9   See an excerpt of the speech in Peter Rowland, *David Lloyd George* (London, 1975)., pp. 134–35.

10 Kenneth O. Morgan (ed.), *Lloyd George: Family Letters, 1885–1936* (Cardiff and London, 1973), 27 July 1899, p. 118.

11 Ibid., 27 July 1899, p. 118.

12 For the most recent evaluation of Chamberlain's life and career, see Travis L. Crosby, *Joseph Chamberlain: A Most Radical Imperialist* (London, 2011).

13 A concise contemporary account of working-class conditions and the need for a national plan of old age pensions is J.A. Spender, *The State and Pensions in Old Age* (London, 1894).

14 NLW, William George Papers, 450, 25 April 1897.

15 To William he wrote his own reason for going: 'I felt it was a great chance to get a holiday on the cheap' (ibid., 804, 17 August 1899).

16 Letters quoted in Grigg, *Young Lloyd George*, dated 7 and 14 September 1899, pp. 251–3.

17 NLW, William George Papers, 812, 7 September 1899.

18 William George, *Backbencher* (Llandysul, 1983), 18 September 1899, p. 286, writing from Glacier, British Columbia.

19 For these letters, see Morgan, *Lloyd George: Family Letters*, 24, 25, 27 September 1899, p. 122.

20 This is the theme of Morgan's *Lloyd George: Welsh Radical as World Statesman*.

21 Wrigley, however, cites these as examples of Lloyd George's genuinely patriotic feelings at the time: see Chris Wrigley, *David Lloyd George and the British Labour Movement: Peace and War* (Hassocks, 1976), pp. 58–9.

22 Even the hypercritical Donald McCormick has words of praise for Lloyd George during the war: 'he showed immense moral courage' in acting 'as a highly necessary antidote to the unthinking jingoism of a majority of the British people …'. It was, as McCormick sums up in Churchillian fashion, Lloyd George's 'finest hour' (Donald McCormick, *The Mask of Merlin: A Critical Biography of David Lloyd George* (New York, 1964), pp. 47–8).

23 See John Grigg, 'Lloyd George and the Boer War', in A.J.A. Morris (ed.), *Edwardian Radicals 1900–1914: Some Aspects of British Radicalism* (London, 1974), ch. 1. Grigg points out that Lloyd George was not opposed to imperialism 'as such'; nor was he a pacifist (ibid., p. 13). But he was opposed to Chamberlain's provocations against South Africa which led to war (ibid., p. 14).

24 *Hansard*, 4th Series, vol. 77, 27 October 1899, pp. 782–4.

25 NLW, William George Papers, 3347, 5 November 1899.

26 His boasts to Margaret: see Morgan, *Lloyd George: Family Letters*, 27 October 1899, p. 124.

27 NLW, William George Papers, 831, 3 November 1899.

28 *The Welshman*, 1 December 1899, Parliamentary Archives, LG/A/9/1/25.

29 George, *Backbencher*, pp. 303–5.

30 *Hansard*, 4th Series, vol. 78, 6 February 1900, pp. 758–9.

31 George, *Backbencher*, pp. 308–9.

32 Cited from the Herbert Lewis Papers in Rowland, *David Lloyd George*, p. 143, n. 2.

33 *Hansard*, 4th Series, vol. 85, 29 June 1900, p. 167.

34 Ibid., vol. 86, 25 July 1900, pp. 1199–211. Lloyd George's choice of Chamberlain as his primary target during the South African War was not an idle one. Chamberlain, as Colonial Secretary, bore primary responsibility for the diplomacy preceding the war; and, as the war continued, his authority over it grew to such an extent that, as Marsh has noted, he came close to becoming the Prime Minister for the war (Peter Marsh, *Joseph Chamberlain: Entrepreneur in Politics* (New Haven, 1994), p. 504).

35 *Hansard*, 4th Series, vol. 87, 8 August 1900, pp. 1008–14. For this parliamentary episode, see also Marsh, *Chamberlain*, pp. 493–4.

36 NLW, William George Papers, 979, 8 August 1900.

37 *Carnarvon Herald*, 21 September 1900, Parliamentary Archives, LG/A/9/2/27.

38 NLW, William George Papers, 1022, 20 December 1900.

39 Ibid., 1023, 21 December 1900.

40 Cited in Grigg, *Young Lloyd George*, 7 November 1900, p. 277.

41 *Hansard*, 4th Series, vol. 88, 10 December 1900, pp. 397–417.

42 Marsh, *Chamberlain*, pp. 502–4.

43 For a detailed analysis of these allegations, see G.R. Searle, *Corruption in British Politics, 1895–1930* (Oxford, 1987), pp. 52–65.

44 Morgan, *Lloyd George: Family Letters*, 31 August 1900, p. 127.

45 NLW, William George Papers, 1031 [1900]. Gilbert calls it 'an astonishing coup' (Bentley Brinkerhoff Gilbert, *David Lloyd George: A Political Life*, vol. 1: *The Architect of Change, 1863–1912* (Columbus, Ohio, 1987), p. 198).

46 The leading anti-war newspaper, the *Manchester Guardian*, was of course not London based.

47 NLW, William George Papers, 1063, 12 March 1901.

48 George, *Backbencher*, 21 April 1901, p. 328.

49 Cited in Rowland, *David Lloyd George*, p. 152.

50 *Hansard*, 4th Series, vol. 95, 11 June 1901, pp. 51–2.

51 Ibid., vol. 95, 17 June, pp. 573–83.

52 Ibid., vol. 95, 27 June, pp. 153–4.

53 Ibid., vol. 95, 4 July 1901, p. 902.

54 *Carnarvon Herald*, 25 October 1901, Parliamentary Archives, LG/A/10/1/26.

55 *Cambrian News*, 25 October 1901, Parliamentary Archives, LG/A/10/1/27.

56 Martin Pugh, *Lloyd George*, paperback edn (London, 1988), p. 31. Ideas for his speeches seem to have come to him at inspired moments. He then jotted down topics on any scrap of available paper: old envelopes; House of Commons stationery; letterheads from country houses where he stayed; and on one occasion, on the back of a printed menu from a complimentary supper given him by the Liberal Club of Glasgow.

57 *Daily Mail*, 3 October 1901, cited in Rowland, *David Lloyd George*, pp. 154–5.

58 Accounts of the Birmingham riot may be found in Grigg, *Young Lloyd George*, pp. 286–8; Rowland, *David Lloyd George*, pp. 158–61; Gilbert, *Lloyd George: Architect of Change*, pp. 210–4.

59 George, *Backbencher*, p. 343.

60 Ibid., pp. 344–5.

61 *Hansard*, 4th Series, 20 March 1902, pp. 638–58. To his wife, he wrote: 'Several have told me that it was the best I ever delivered in this House … Dilke just tells me this morning he thought I was like Shelley's *Adonais*. I had at last through toil & trouble got to fame' (Morgan, *Lloyd George: Family Letters*, 21 March 1902, p. 131). In an aside, he reiterated Dilke's compliment by informing Margaret that: 'I haven't got the quotation but you can see it in Shelley's *Adonais*' (ibid., 21 March 1902, p. 131).

62 The authoritative work on Liberal imperialism remains H.C.G. Matthew, *The Liberal Imperialists: The Ideas and Politics of a Post-Gladstonian Elite* (Oxford, 1973).

63 For Campbell-Bannerman, see John Wilson, *CB: A Life of Sir Henry Campbell-Bannerman* (London, 1973). Both Campbell-Bannerman and the Earl of Kimberley (Liberal leader in the House of Lords from 1896–1902) were often in despair at the prospects of the Party, especially during the war years. At the very beginning of hostilities, Kimberley deplored 'a party split', and regretted that 'differences amongst ourselves most seriously weaken us' (Angus Hawkins and John Powell (eds), *The Journal of John Wodehouse, First Earl of Kimberley for 1862–1902*, Camden Fifth Series, vol. 9 (London, 1997), 17 October 1899, p. 471. Several months later, Kimberley bemoaned 'our discordant & disorganized party' (ibid., 30 January 1900, p. 473). The summer brought no respite when he asked a rhetorical question: 'Can anyone have succeeded in leading such a broken & distracted party' (ibid., 25 July 1900, p. 477)? Matters had not changed in the following summer: 'The prospects of the Liberal party worse than ever' (ibid., 25 June 1901, p. 483). And in one of the last entries before his death the following year: 'Still squabbling' (ibid., 17 July 1901, p. 484).

64 NLW, William George Papers, 1120, 7 November 1901.

65 Eric Eaglesham makes the case that the main impetus behind the bill was to preserve the voluntary schools for the Church of England: see his 'Planning the Education Bill of 1902', *British Journal of Educational Studies* 9:1 (November 1960), pp. 3–24. Other educational specialists tend to agree that religious reasons rather than educational improvement lay behind the bill. See Alan Rogers, 'Churches and Children – A Study in the Controversy over the 1902 Education Act', *British Journal of Educational Studies* 8:1 (November 1959), pp. 29–51 and N.J. Richards, 'Religious Controversy and the School Boards 1870–1902',

398 THE UNKNOWN LLOYD GEORGE

British Journal of Educational Studies 18:2 (1970), pp. 180–96. J.E.B. Munson discusses the complexities of ministerial compromises in piloting the bill to his final form in 'The Unionist Coalition and Education, 1895–1902', *Historical Journal* 20:3 (September 1977), pp. 607–45. The most comprehensive work on the bill and the subsequent Educational Act of 1902 is Benjamin Sacks, *The Religious Issue in the State Schools of England and Wales: 1902–1914: A Nation's Quest for Human Dignity* (Albuquerque, 1960).

66 Morgan, *Lloyd George: Family Letters*, 24 March 1902, pp. 131–2.

67 D.W. Bebbington, *The Nonconformist Conscience: Chapel and Politics, 1870–1914* (London, 1982), p. 35.

68 See Stephen Koss, *Nonconformity in British Politics* (London, 1975), chs 2–3; Bebbington, *Nonconformist Conscience*, chs 1–2, 7; R.J. Helmstadter, 'The Nonconformist Conscience', in Peter Marsh (ed.), *The Conscience of the Victorian State* (Hassocks, Sussex, 1979); and R.J. Helmstadter, 'The Nonconformist Conscience' in Gerald Parsons (ed.), *Religion in Victorian Britain: Interpretations*, vol. 4 (Manchester, 1988), ch. 4.

69 Local Free Church Councils had proliferated throughout the kingdom during the 1890s as a consequence of the continuing revitalization of nonconformity in the late Victorian era. Each council consisted of representatives from the chapels of all the denominations in a town or village. See Bebbington, *Nonconformist Conscience*, ch. 4.

70 Koss, *Nonconformity in Modern British Politics*, p. 48. Nicoll remained an important link between Lloyd George and the nonconformist community for many years afterwards, as we shall see.

71 George, *Backbencher*, pp. 357–8.

72 Ibid., p. 359.

73 Ibid., p. 362. Lloyd George wrote in characteristic fashion to Margaret after the meeting, declaring it 'an immense success': it was also hailed by those present as 'magnificent'. He concluded: 'I have hardly ever seen an audience so completely in my hands' (Morgan, *Lloyd George: Family Letters*, 21 May 1902, p. 135).

74 *South Wales Daily News*, 1 October 1902, Parliamentary Archives, LG/A/10/2/35.

75 *Lincoln Leader*, 13 December 1902, Parliamentary Archives, LG/A/10/2/41.

76 W.R.P. George claims that during the committee stage of the bill – in two separate sessions (2 June to 7 August and 16 October to 3 December 1902) – Lloyd George had either spoken in debate or intervened in some fashion 150 times (George, *Backbencher*, p. 364). Grigg essentially agrees, claiming 160 (Grigg, *Young Lloyd George*, p. 33).

77 *Hansard*, 4th Series, vol. 110, 9 July 1902, p. 1212.

78 As Grigg puts it: see his discussion in *Lloyd George: The People's Champion, 1902–1911* (Berkeley, 1978), pp. 34–40. Other useful sources are Morgan: *Wales in British Politics*, ch. 5; Gilbert, *Lloyd George: Architect of Change*, ch. 4; and George, *Backbencher*, ch. 9.

79 As Lloyd George explained it to William: 'Control is all we want – the crux of that is the appointment of teachers' (NLW, William George Papers, 1176, 12 February 1903).

80 In a telegram to William, Lloyd George stated plainly his determination: 'Asaph clergy break off negotiations. Relentless war now' (ibid., 1208, 28 April 1903).

81 George, *Backbencher*, p. 379. In a letter to William after the meeting, Lloyd George was characteristically immodest: 'Made the greatest speech I have ever made on a South Wales platform last night' (NLW, William George Papers, 1233, 4 June 1903).

82 The conflict between Welsh local authorities and the Conservative Board of Education over the Default Act has been thoroughly examined by Gareth Elwyn Jones, 'The "Welsh Revolt" Revisited: Merioneth and Montgomeryshire in Default', *Welsh History Review* 14:3 (June 1989), pp. 417–38.

83 Chamberlain's motives have been a mystery in that his tariff reform scheme proved dysfunctional by both energizing the Liberals whilst simultaneously weakening the Conservatives. Was he prophet, party maverick, or an opportunistic schemer (options suggested by Michael Bentley, *Politics Without Democracy* (London, 1984), p. 219)?

84 See the debate in *Hansard*, 4th Series, vol. 122, 22 May 1903, pp. 1541–9 and 1553. Lloyd George's version of the debate followed quickly to his family. To William he wrote: 'Just gave Joe the worst quarter of an hour he ever had – so everybody says ... It was a great & almost a dramatic scene. I pounded him. He turned green. He sprang up when I sat down – but he made a miserable exhibition of himself' (NLW, William George Papers, 1223, 22 May 1903).

85 *South Wales Daily News*, 6 June 1903, Parliamentary Archives, LG/A/11/1/45.

86 Excerpts from these speeches are in Grigg, *The People's Champion*, pp. 62–3.

87 *Oxford Chronicle*, 27 November 1903, Parliamentary Archives, LG/A/11/2/45. To Margaret he wrote afterwards that he had made 'a very deep impression' and achieved 'a great triumph' in carrying a free trade motion by twenty votes' (Morgan, *Lloyd George: Family Letters*, 27 November 1903, pp. 139–40).

88 See Ramsden's aptly titled chapter 'Drifting, 1900–1914' in his *An Appetite for Power: A History of the Conservative Party since 1830*, paperback edn (London, 1999), ch. 8.

89 Bebbington, *Nonconformist Conscience*, p. 111. But, as Jon Lawrence has pointed out, moral considerations were not always uppermost in the Liberal criticisms of Chinese 'slavery'. Some Liberals condemned the importation of Chinese labour into a British colony as a Conservative scheme designed to replace honest (and higher paid) British workers with cheaper labour. And in some Liberal tracts an implicit racism was also evident. See Lawrence, *Speaking for the People: Party, Language and Popular Politics in England, 1867–1914* (Cambridge, 1998), ch. 8, 'The Fall and Rise of Popular Liberalism, 1886–1906', esp. pp. 223–4.

90 See Grigg, *The People's Champion*, p. 71; Rowland, *David Lloyd George*, pp. 177–8; and Bebbington, *Nonconformist Conscience*, pp. 46–51.

91 *The Times*, 11 May 1904.

92 W.R. Lambert, *Drink and Sobriety in Victorian Wales c. 1820–c. 1895* (Cardiff, 1983), p. 175.

93 To William: see NLW, William George Papers, 1389, 12 April 1904.

94 *Hansard*, 4th Series, vol. 135, 7 June 1904, pp. 955–62. Later that day, Lloyd George commented on his performance to William: 'Gave it hot & strong & full of pepper for them' (NLW, William George Papers, 1416, 7 June 1904).

95 Michael Craton and H.W. McCready, *The Great Liberal Revival, 1903–6* (London, 1966). See Appendix A for a useful list of by-election results from 1903–5, including total votes, percent of poll and comparisons between the general elections of 1900 and 1906.

96 NLW, William George Papers, 1458, 19 September 1904.

97 Named Relugas after Grey's fishing lodge in Scotland where he received Asquith and Haldane. Grey's fondness for fishing was legendary.

98 Asquith would be Chancellor of the Exchequer; Grey, Foreign Secretary; and Haldane, Lord Chancellor.

99 As he reported it to Margaret on 11 January 1904 in Morgan, *Lloyd George: Family Letters*, p. 140.

100 Recounted in a letter to William, 24 November 1904: see George, *Backbencher*, p. 400.

101 As Morgan observes in his *Lloyd George*, p. 52. Indeed, Lloyd George may have taken the initiative in arranging the November 1904 meeting with Rosebery. Several months earlier, he had confided to R.W. Perks, a leading Roseberyite, that Rosebery was 'the only possible man' to be Liberal leader. Perks, MP for Louth from 1892–1910 and known as 'Imperial

Perks', sent this information along to Rosebery (cited from the Rosebery Papers, dated 25 July 1904 by D.A.Hamer, *Liberal Politics in the Age of Gladstone and Rosebery: A Study in Leadership and Policy* (Oxford, 1972), p. 287).

102 Lloyd George of course told William about his triumph there – 'a glorious success' and 'a very pleasant day with C.B.'. Although Rosebery wanted him to return to Dalmeny, Lloyd George confided further, he had to return to London to prepare for upcoming speeches (George, *Backbencher*, p. 400).

103 *The Times*, 17 January 1905.

104 Ibid., 24 January 1905.

105 NLW, William George Papers, 1529, 7 February 1905. Afterwards, he claimed the dinner as a 'great success' (ibid., 1530, 8 February 1905).

106 From the *South Wales Daily News*, 4 March 1905, cited in George, *Backbencher*, pp. 420–1.

107 *The Times*, 17 March 1905.

108 Ibid., 29 April 1905.

109 Ibid., 8 May 1905.

110 Ibid., 13 May 1905.

111 Ibid., 29 July 1905.

112 Ibid., 16 September 1905. Charles Vane-Tempest-Steward, 6th Marquess of Londonderry, was President of the Board of Education from 1902–5. Lloyd George was probably delighted to have the amiable but dim Londonderry as a target at the Board of Education. Even the Tory diarist, Lord Crawford, thought Londonderry one of the two stupidest men in Britain. The other was Earl Bathurst (John Vincent (ed.), *The Crawford Papers: The Journals of David Lindsay, Twenty-Seventh Earl of Crawford and Tenth Earl of Balcarres during the years 1892 to 1940* (Manchester, 1984), 8 July 1912, p. 277).

113 *The Times*, 21 September 1905.

114 Ibid., 20 October 1905.

115 Ibid., 28 October 1905. The Kirkcaldy meeting was crowded, 'with a large overflow;' but it was 'a great triumph', Lloyd George reported to William. Furthermore he claimed: 'I don't believe I ever spoke better' (NLW, William George Papers, 1698, 28 October 1905).

116 Ibid., 1698, 2 November 1905.

117 British Library, Campbell-Bannerman Papers, Add Mss 41238, ff 92–3, 29 November 1905.

118 Lewis Harcourt reported to Campbell-Bannerman in a letter full of political gossip that, following the negative reactions to his Bodmin speech, Rosebery 'has gone down to Brighton a complete wreck morally and physically' (British Library, Campbell-Bannerman Papers, Add. Mss 52518, ff 25–33, 30 November 1905). Harcourt, a Liberal politician and son of Sir William Harcourt, served as Colonial Secretary from 1910–5 and briefly as First Commissioner of Works, 1915–6. He was widely known as 'Loulou'.

119 This was not easily accomplished, however. See T. Boyle, 'The Formation of Campbell-Bannerman's Government in December 1905: A Memorandum by J.A. Spender', *Bulletin of the Institute of Historical Research* 105:112 (November 1972), pp. 283–302; and Wilson: *CB*, chs 29–30.

120 Precisely how influential the Liberal Imperialists were is difficult to say with precision. Boyle's analysis is somewhat unclear. Although he divides the party into Gladstonians and Liberal Imperialists, he admits there were shades of grey in these categories. See T. Boyle, 'The Liberal Imperialists, 1892–1906', *Bulletin of the Institute of Historical Research* 52 (1979), pp. 48–82.

121 As we might expect, Lloyd George's letters home were filled with the news of this, his greatest achievement to date. With pardonable pride, he wrote to his brother: 'Board

of Trade with a seat in the Cabinet … I am delighted.' His ministry would be housed in 'that grand new building by the House of Commons' (William George, *My Brother and I* (London, 1958), 8 December 1905, p. 206). To make sure that William understood the importance of his new position, Lloyd George mentioned a few days later that: 'I have under me in all 1,000 men' (ibid., 12 December 1905, p. 207). As Pugh notes, he actually had a staff of 750 (Pugh, *Lloyd George*, p. 32).

122 In remarks to Reginald McKenna (who became President of the Board of Education in CB's Cabinet in January 1907), who told it to George Riddell several years later. See Lord Riddell, *More Pages from My Diary, 1908–1914* (London, 1934), 30 September 1913, p. 177). Riddell's famous diary has been re-edited by J.M. McEwen in *The Riddell Diaries, 1908–1923* (London, 1986). Errors of transcription and dating in the original published diaries have there been corrected. Where accurate, however, the original edition of the diary is used throughout this book. McEwen also has a useful short biography of Riddell which comprises the Introduction. What is striking about the friendship between Lloyd George and Riddell is the similarity of their backgrounds. Both had been born into a lower-middle-class environment – Riddell in Brixton. Both lost their fathers in infancy. Both were unusually able in school. Both began in the law, although Riddell was more successful in the business sense, eventually becoming the wealthy proprietor of the *News of the World*. The bond between the two men held until their later years. For a very long time, however, each could provide something the other needed: Lloyd George fed Riddell inside secrets, and Riddell aided Lloyd George financially.

123 For the following, A.K. Russell's *Liberal Landslide: The General Election of 1906* (Newton Abbot, 1973) remains essential.

124 See the complaint by the Conservative journalist Iwan-Muller: 'I hate demagogues and tub-oratory and all the rest of it but I recognise that we must have "samples" of it at an election time, and we had none at all' (cited in Russell, *Liberal Landslide*, p. 132, from the British Library, Balfour Papers, Add MS 49797, ff 115–59).

125 For these two meetings, see *The Times*, 3 January 1906.

126 This seems to have been a campaign charge given to Lloyd George, perhaps by CB himself. When Lloyd George informed his brother William of his appointment to the Board of Trade, he put it thus: 'They want me there as that is the Department most directly associated with the great fight to defend Free Trade, in the House and in the country against Joe's attacks' (George, *Backbencher*, 8 December 1905, p. 453).

127 *The Times*, 15 January 1906.

128 Ibid., 17 January 1906.

129 Ibid., 18 January 1906.

130 For these Liberal rallies, see ibid., 4 January 1906; 6 January 1906; 12 January 1906; and 24 January 1906.

131 For this paragraph, see the following: Henry Pelling, *Social Geography of British Elections, 1885–1910* (New York, 1967), 434; George L. Bernstein, 'Liberalism and the Progressive Alliance in the Constituencies, 1900–1914: Three Case Studies', *Historical Journal* 26:3 (1983), pp. 617–40; Pat Thane, 'Labour and Local Politics: Radicalism, Democracy and Social Reform, 1880–1914', in Eugenio F. Biagini and Alastair J. Reid (eds), *Currents of Radicalism: Popular Radicalism, Organised Labour and Party Politics in Britain, 1850–1914* (Cambridge, 1991); Andrew Thorpe, *A History of the British Labour Party* (New York, 1997), ch. 1; Duncan Tanner, Pat Thane, and Nick Tiratsoo (eds), *Labour's First Century* (Cambridge, 2000), Appendix I.

132 See John Shepherd, 'Labour and Parliament: the Lib–Labs as the First Working-Class MPs, 1885–1906', ch. 9 in. Biagini and Reid: *Currents of Radicalism*.

Chapter 5. In the Cabinet

1   Peter Rowland, *The Last Liberal Governments: The Promised Land, 1905–1910* (New York, 1969), p. 30.

2   G.R. Searle, *The Liberal Party: Triumph and Disintegration, 1886–1929* (New York, 1992), pp. 79–81.

3   H.V. Emy, *Liberals, Radicals and Social Politics, 1892–1914* (Cambridge, 1973), p. 146.

4   Martin Pugh, *Lloyd George*, paperback edn (London, 1988)., p. 32.

5   This is the heading for Chapter 5 in George L. Bernstein's *Liberalism and Liberal Politics in Edwardian England* (Boston, 1986).

6   Bentley Brinkerhoff Gilbert, *David Lloyd George: A Political Life*, vol. 1: *The Architect of Change, 1863–1912* (Columbus, Ohio, 1987), p. 292.

7   Herbert Lewis's lament to his diary entry of 24 April 1907, NLW, Lewis Papers, cited in Cameron Hazlehurst and Christine Woodland (eds), *A Liberal Chronicle: Journals and Papers of J.A. Pease, 1st Lord Gainford, 1908–1910* (London, 1994), p. 14. Lewis was one of Lloyd George's oldest and firmest comrades in arms. He was MP for Flint Borough 1892–1918 and for the University of Wales 1918–22 and served in minor government positions through 1922.

8   Congregationalists were the largest sect with Wesleyans next, followed by Unitarians and a variety of Methodists and a few smaller sects. See D.W. Bebbington, 'The Free Church MPs of the 1906 Parliament', in Stephen Taylor and David L. Wykes (eds), *Parliament and Dissent* (Edinburgh, 2005), pp. 136–50.

9   Chris Cook, *A Short History of the Liberal Party, 1900–2001*, 6th edn (Houndmills, 2002), pp. 42–3.

10   As has been true of his earlier leadership of the Liberal Party, CB as a prime minister has not fared well at the hands of historians. Although personally pleasant with an ability to coin an occasional striking phrase, he was an indifferent speaker, seldom exercised his authority and was fitful in his Cabinet responsibilities. See Jose F. Harris and Cameron Hazlehurst, 'Campbell-Bannerman as Prime Minister', *History* 55:185 (October 1970), pp. 360–83. Even the friendlier John Wilson, who believes CB's easy-going nature helped maintain some Cabinet unity, admits that CB was 'an idle man' and lacked panache as a party leader – all in all, a rather pedestrian character (John Wilson, *CB: A Life of Sir Henry Campbell-Bannerman* (London, 1973), passim, but especially ch. 40).

11   For a useful thumbnail sketch of each Cabinet member in the House of Commons, see Rowland, *Last Liberal Governments*, pp. 34–43; for Cabinet members in the House of Lords, see p. 64.

12   Gilbert, *Lloyd George: Architect of Change*, p. 286.

13   John Grigg, *Lloyd George: The People's Champion, 1902–1911* (Berkeley, 1978), p. 98.

14   Gilbert, *Lloyd George: Architect of Change*, p. 323.

15   Kenneth O. Morgan, *Lloyd George* (London, 1974), p. 60.

16   Ian Packer, *Lloyd George*, paperback edn (Houndmills, Hants, 1998), p. 20.

17   Diary entry of 21 December 1906 in John Vincent (ed.), *The Crawford Papers: The Journals of David Lindsay, Twenty-Seventh Earl of Crawford and Tenth Earl of Balcarres during the years 1892 to 1940* (Manchester, 1984), p. 99.

18   As Gillian Sutherland notes in her introduction to *Studies in the Growth of Nineteenth-Century Government* (Totowa: 1972).

19   Where he met another Booth collaborator, Beatrice Potter (as she then was before her marriage to Sidney Webb). Potter described Smith as 'a clever, ambitious young Oxford graduate' and a good friend and working comrade (Norman and Jeanne MacKenzie (eds),

The Diary of Beatrice Webb, vol. 1, *1873–1892* (Cambridge, MA, 1982), 16 December 1888, p. 268).

20 During a period of significant social legislation, as Roger Davidson has noted, the Board of Trade 'alone possessed the statistical data and expertise that could provide the basis for informed debate and the formulation of policy' (see Roger Davidson, 'Llewellyn Smith, the Labour Department and Government Growth 1886–1909', in Sutherland, *Growth of Nineteenth-Century Government*, p. 260).

21 Discussions of the bill may be found in Grigg, *The People's Champion*, pp. 103–8 and Gilbert, *Lloyd George: Architect of Change*, pp. 324–6. Lloyd George continued to keep his brother abreast of his accomplishments as a Cabinet member. In the shaping of the Merchant Shipping Bill, he reported that he had received 'congratulations on all hands on tact & knowledge displayed' (NLW, William George Papers, 1822, 18 June 1906).

22 For these examples, see *The Times*, 17 February 1906; 8 March 1906; 14 December 1906.

23 *Hansard*, 4th Series, vol. 157, 16 May 1906, pp. 500–2.

24 *The Times*, 24 July 1906. For a brief discussion of the Census of Production Act, see Grigg, *The People's Champion*, pp. 107–8 and Chris Wrigley, *David Lloyd George and the British Labour Movement: Peace and War* (Hassocks, 1976), p. 48. Wrigley believes that the census was 'a considerable innovation' (ibid., p. 48). Lloyd George could not restrain his own sense of achievement in the passage of the bill through the House of Commons. 'Nobody thought I could do so', he wrote William, 'whips & everybody trying to persuade me it was any use. But I insisted & now it is through' (NLW, William George Papers, 1862, 14 December 1906).

25 This argument has not, however, convinced even so firm a supporter of Lloyd George as Kenneth Morgan who writes that the Patents Act – as well as the Merchant Shipping Act – 'showed a remarkably free-and-easy attitude to free trade' (Morgan, *Lloyd George*, p. 60). Indeed, in the framing of his legislation as a whole during his tenure at the Board of Trade, Morgan finds that Lloyd George displayed a distinct 'casualness towards Liberal dogma' (ibid., p. 60).

26 See *The Times*, 21 November 1906 for these citations.

27 Ibid., 25 May 1907.

28 See Grigg, *The People's Champion*, pp. 119–22.

29 NLW, William George Papers, 1933, 28 August 1907.

30 A general discussion of union activity in this era may be found in A. Clegg, Alan Fox and A.F. Thompson, *A History of British Trade Unions since 1889*, vol. 1: *1889–1910* (Oxford, 1964), chs 8–10. For a concise account of the railway dispute, see Wrigley, *Lloyd George and the British Labour Movement*, pp. 50–8. See also Grigg, *The People's Champion*, pp. 112–8 and Gilbert, *Lloyd George: Architect of Change*, pp. 313–20.

31 Wrigley describes Bell as 'a paragon of moderation' (Wrigley, *Lloyd George and the British Labour Movement*, p. 51).

32 As he put it to his brother William: 'Conciliation at first but, failing that, the steam roller. The Companies must give way ...' (William George, *My Brother and I* (London, 1958), 21 October 1907, p. 212).

33 Kearley's reminiscences, taken from his privately printed *The Travelled Road* (1930), are cited in Grigg, *The People's Champion*, pp. 113–4.

34 George, *My Brother and I*, 25 October 1907, p. 212.

35 Ibid., 29 October 1907, p. 212.

36 This appears to be the first example of what Iain McLean has called 'the sudden ultimatum' – a tactical device Lloyd George commonly used thereafter in his negotiations. See McLean, *Rational Choice and British Politics: An Analysis of Rhetoric and Manipulation from*

Peel to Blair (Oxford, 2001), p. 164 and more generally ch. 6, 'Lloyd George: Supreme Tactician and Ambitious Strategist'.

37 George, *My Brother and I*, undated, but probably 7 November 1907, p. 213.

38 As Wrigley points out in *Lloyd George and the British Labour Movement*, p. 57.

39 J.A. Spender, who served directly under Lloyd George as a member of a Departmental Committee of the Board of Trade on the railway question, saw him at first hand as a negotiator. Lloyd George was extraordinarily skilful at managing opposing camps, Spender observed: he had 'an almost uncanny way of persuading men in opposite camps that they really meant the same thing' and before long irreconcilable opponents 'were dissolving into an incredible unity' (Spender, *Life, Journalism and Politics*, vol. 1 (New York, n.d.), p. 157). Spender became one of the most influential journalists of his time as Editor of the *Westminster Gazette*. Later in life he was best known as an author of and an activist for the Liberal cause.

40 Rowland, *Lloyd George*, p. 195.

41 As *The Times* observed: 'The two parties did not sit together. The President of the Board of Trade interviewed first one side and then the other ...' (*The Times*, 25 November 1907). See also *The Times*, 23 November 1907 and 6 December 1907.

42 *The Times*, 29 January 1907.

43 Ibid., 18 March 1907.

44 He was speaking at the annual meeting of the Chamber of Shipping of the United Kingdom (ibid., 16 February 1907).

45 Ibid., 27 March 1907.

46 For the work of the committee, see Neil D. Daglish, 'Lloyd George's Education Bill? Planning the 1906 Education Bill', *History of Education* 23:4 (1994), pp. 375–84. Other useful accounts of the bill include Gilbert, *Lloyd George: Architect of Change*, pp. 292–303; and Noel J. Richards, 'The Education Bill of 1906 and the Decline of Political Nonconformity', *Journal of Ecclesiastical History* 23:1 (January 1972), pp. 49–63. Benjamin Sacks's *Religious Issue in the State Schools of England & Wales* is a mine of information, especially on the variety of contemporary opinions concerning the bill.

47 Daglish makes this claim based upon his examination of the records of the committee, held at the National Archives, Kew: see Daglish, 'Lloyd George's Education Bill?', p. 380.

48 Leading Gilbert to characterize the bill as 'a warped and misshapen monster' (Gilbert, *Lloyd George: Architect of Change*, p. 296).

49 Birrell told this to the author, publisher and editor Wilfred Meynell, who relayed it to his friend, Wilfred Scawen Blunt: see Blunt's diary entry for 9 May 1906 (Blunt, *My Diaries: Being a Personal Narrative of Events, 1888–1914* (New York, 1923), p. 143). As Daglish puts it, the failure of the bill cannot be wholly laid at the door of the House of Lords. As a result of Cabinet disunity and Lloyd George's strength in the Cabinet committee, 'Birrell was faced with the task of having to try to secure the passage of an educational measure which was not really of his making' (Daglish, 'Lord George's Education Bill?', p. 384).

50 Among these was the moderate Archbishop of Canterbury, who made numerous attempts behind the scenes at compromise: see G.K.A. Bell, *Randall Davidson, Archbishop of Canterbury*, vol. 1 (New York, 1935), ch. 29, 'The Education Controversy'.

51 *The Times*, 27 April 1906.

52 Ibid., 22 June 1906.

53 Ibid., 17 July 1906.

54 Ibid., 9 August 1906.

55 Ibid., 1 October 1906.

56 *Spaulding Guardian*, 3 November 1906, Parliamentary Archives, LG/B/4/2/32. In this speech, he denounced the Anglican catechism, describing it as 'the old teaching that you are to be humble and lowly to your betters (laughter). There's one thing that the House of Lords have forgotten; the people have outgrown that (loud cheers). I was taught that myself, and was told that my better was the squire. Later, that squire was my political opponent, and there was a majority of the people in that district who said I was the better (laughter and cheers). Well, now it's his business to be humble and lowly to me (renewed laughter).'

57 *Citizen* (Gloucester), 26 November 1906, Parliamentary Archives, Lloyd George Papers, B/4/2/37.

58 *The Times*, 3 December 1906.

59 Wilson, *CB*, p. 555.

60 McKenna was MP for North Monmouthshire since 1895, and served in various Cabinet positions under Campbell-Bannerman and Asquith. He was in time to prove a combative foe to Lloyd George.

61 Gilbert, *Lloyd George: Architect of Change*, pp. 301–2.

62 *Hansard*, 4th Series, vol. 227, 26 June 1907, p. 1429.

63 *The Times*, 18 January 1907.

64 Ibid., 24 January 1907.

65 Ibid., 9 March 1907.

66 Ibid., 25 March 1907. The 5th Marquess of Lansdowne began his political life as a Liberal. But under Salisbury he was Secretary of State for War, 1895–1900, and for the next five years served under both Salisbury and Balfour as Secretary of State for Foreign Affairs. He was also leader of the Conservative peers from 1903–16. Details of his life may be found in Lord Newton, *Lord Lansdowne: A Biography* (London, 1929).

67 *The Times*, 21 June 1907.

68 *Sheffield Independent*, 30 August 1907, Parliamentary Archives, LG/B/5/1/36.

69 W. Watkin Davies, *Lloyd George 1863–1914* (London, 1939), pp. 263–4.

70 Grigg, *The People's Champion*, pp. 98–9.

71 *The Times*, 5 November 1907. F.E. Smith, soon a rising star for the Conservatives, was MP for Liverpool (Walton) 1906–18 and Liverpool (West Derby) 1918–9. He served later under Lloyd George's wartime coalition ministry as Attorney General, 1915–9, and Lord Chancellor, 1919–22. Created first Baron, then Viscount and finally Earl of Birkenhead in 1922.

72 For Lloyd George and Welsh disestablishment, see Gilbert, *Lloyd George: Architect of Change*, pp. 303–13.

73 *The Times*, 2 May 1907.

74 Ibid., 2 July 1907.

75 Ibid., 22 July 1907.

76 For the following, see Herbert du Parcq, *Life of David Lloyd George*, 4 vols (London, 1912), vol. 3, pp. 461–74.

77 For Lloyd George's speech, see *The Times*, 11 October 1907. Gilbert believes that Lloyd George saved the government from a serious public defeat by giving this, one of the greatest speeches of his life (Gilbert, *Lloyd George: Architect of Change*, pp. 311–2).

78 See Bell, *Randal Davidson*, pp. 504–5 for these negotiations.

79 As Morgan notes, the conduct of the commission itself, divided as it was between Anglican and Nonconformist members, was proof of the 'atmosphere of religious civil war' between Christian sects: three of the nonconformist members resigned at what they considered obstructive tactics of the Anglican chairman of the commission. The

commission did not issue a report until 1910 (Kenneth O. Morgan, *Rebirth of a Nation: A History of Modern Wales*, paperback edn (Oxford, 1982), p. 136).

80 For the following, see J. Graham Jones, *David Lloyd George and Welsh Liberalism* (Aberystwyth, 2010), ch. 7, 'Mair Eluned Lloyd George 1890–1907'.

81 See respectively, Gilbert, *Lloyd George: Architect of Change*, p. 320; Peter Rowland, *David Lloyd George* (London, 1975), p. 198; and Grigg, *The People's Champion*, p. 125.

82 George, *My Brother and I*, p. 215.

83 NLW, William George Papers, 1970, 7 December 1907; 1974, 23 December 1907; 1979, 5 January 1908.

84 Kenneth O. Morgan (ed.), *Lloyd George: Family Letters, 1885–1936* (Cardiff and London, 1973), p. 149.

85 Jones, *Lloyd George and Welsh Liberalism*, p. 122.

86 There is evidence that Lloyd George badly wanted the office and indeed campaigned for it, basing his claim upon his work at the Board of Trade and his services to the Liberal Party (Grigg, *The People's Champion*, p. 133). Murray believes that Lloyd George inspired the *Manchester Guardian* to make the case that a radical Chancellor (i.e. Lloyd George) was in the best interest of the Liberal Party (Bruce K. Murray, *The People's Budget 1909/10: Lloyd George and Liberal Politics* (Oxford, 1980), pp. 64–65). However, the evidence cited by Murray, taken from the published diaries of C.P. Scott, editor of the *Manchester Guardian,* is not wholly conclusive (see Trevor Wilson (ed.), *The Political Diaries of C.P. Scott, 1911– 1928* (Ithaca, 1970), pp. 30–1). A more significant intervention was a series of newspaper articles on potential Cabinet members published by the *Daily Chronicle*. Lloyd George was specifically mentioned as having an 'undeniable' claim as Chancellor of the Exchequer. This would have the effect – in lieu of any official statement about the composition of the new Cabinet – of pressuring Asquith, should he have lingering doubts of promoting Lloyd George. Although admitting that there was 'no clear evidence', Gilbert believes that Lloyd George was leaking information to the *Daily Chronicle* (Gilbert, *Lloyd George: Architect of Change*, pp. 330–4).

87 For these quotations, see NLW, William George Papers, 2048, 11 April 1908; 2049, 13 April, 1908; 2050, 14 April 1908.

88 An analysis of Asquith and his new ministry may be found in Stephen Koss, *Asquith*, paperback edn (New York, 1985), pp. 87–90. Rowland discusses the Cabinet changes in his *Last Liberal Governments: 1905–1910*: pp. 149–54.

89 Martin Pugh, *Lloyd George*, paperback edn (London, 1988), p. 39.

90 Responsibility for the bill fell to Lloyd George and the Treasury because pensions were designated as a part of the financial arrangements for the coming year. See a discussion of the bill in Rowland, *Last Liberal Governments: 1905–1910*, pp. 156–8; Grigg, *The People's Champion*, pp. 158–62; and Gilbert, *Lloyd George: Architect of Change*, pp. 336–43.

91 *The Times*, 12 October 1906. Lloyd George reiterated to William his political reasons for promoting old age pensions. 'It was time', he wrote, to do something 'that appealed straight to the people'. Otherwise, electoral dissatisfaction among the electorate 'might react in the House & bring us down prematurely' (NLW, William George Papers, 2059, 6 May 1908).

92 For an analysis of the background to the old age pensions plan, see Bentley Brinkerhoff Gilbert, *The Evolution of National Insurance in Great Britain: The Origins of the Welfare State* (London, 1966), ch. 4.

93 NLW, William George Papers, 2078, 18 June 1908 and 2084, 2 July 1908.

94 Grigg calls the sums 'very modest'; and Gilbert terms them 'stingy'. For a discussion of the act, see Grigg, *The People's Champion*, pp. 158–62 and Gilbert, *Lloyd George: Architect of Change*, pp. 337–43.

95 Margaret Jones, 'The 1908 Old Age Pensions Act: The Poor Law in New Disguise?', in Keith Laybourn (ed.), *Social Conditions, Status and Community 1860–c. 1920* (Stroud, 1997), ch. 5. Sydney Checkland, however, believes that these various eligibility requirements were necessary to meet any potential political resistance to the act (Checkland, *British Public Policy, 1776–1939: An Economic, Social and Political Perspective* (Cambridge, 1983), p. 249.

96 This was Lloyd George's view. See his speech in the House of Commons on the second reading of the bill, when he acknowledged that it was an incomplete bill, but a good beginning. He also admitted that it was 'a great experiment' (*Hansard*, 4th Series, vol. 190, 15 June 1908, p. 585).

97 For the progress of the bill, see John Greenaway, *Drink and British Politics since 1830: A Study in Policy-making* (Basingstoke, 2003), pp. 81–6.

98 Hazlehurst and Woodland, *Liberal Chronicle*, p. 40.

99 *The Times*, 16 October 1907.

100 Ibid., 27 March 1908.

101 Ibid. 10 April 1908.

102 Ibid., 25 May 1908.

103 Ibid., 27 March 1908.

104 Gilbert believes that these two acts 'marked the beginning of the construction of the welfare state' (Bentley Brinkerhoff Gilbert, *The Evolution of National Insurance in Great Britain: The Origins of the Welfare State* (London, 1966), p. 102, and more generally ch. 3, 'The Children of the Nation').

105 For this paragraph, see P.F. Clarke, *Lancashire and the New Liberalism* (Cambridge, 1971); Michael Freeden, *The New Liberalism: An Ideology of Social Reform* (Oxford, 1978); and Peter Weiler, *The New Liberalism: Liberal Social Theory in Great Britain, 1889–1914* (New York, 1982).

106 Bernstein, *Liberalism and Liberal Politics*, p. 97. For an evaluation of the roles of both Liberals and Labour in creating a reformist culture, see also Martin D. Pugh, 'Yorkshire and the New Liberalism?', *Journal of Modern History* 50:3 (September 1978), D1169 [On Demand Supplement]; A.W. Purdue, 'The Liberal and Labour Parties in North-East Politics 1900–14: The Struggle for Supremacy', *International Review of Social History* 26 (1981), Part 1, pp. 1–24; A.W. Purdue, 'Jarrow Politics, 1885–1914: The Challenge to Liberal Hegemony', *Northern History* 18 (1982), pp. 182–98; Bernstein, 'Liberalism and the Progressive Alliance'; and David Powell, 'The New Liberalism and the Rise of Labour, 1886–1906', *Historical Journal* 29:2 (1986), p. 384.

107 See Harris, 'Political Thought and the Welfare State 1870–1940: An Intellectual Framework for British Social Policy', *Past & Present*, no. 135 (May 1992), 116–41.

Chapter 6. Robbing the Hen Roost

1 For this journey and the influence of German welfare plans impact upon Lloyd George, see Kenneth O. Morgan, 'Lloyd George and Germany', *Historical Journal* 39:3 (September 1996), pp. 755–8.

2 *The Times*, 27 August 1908.

3 *The Daily News*, 27 August 1908, cited by E.P. Hennock, 'The Origins of British National Insurance and the German Precedent', in W.J. Mommsen and Wolgang Mock (eds), *The*

Emergence of the Welfare State in Britain and Germany, 1850–1950 (London, 1981), pp. 84–106.

4   For this account, see *The Times*, 2 October 1908. To William, Lloyd George wrote of the 'immense success' of the meeting. 'Never had such a reception in my life' (NLW, William George Papers, 2107, 2 October 1908). In a letter the following day, he reiterated his success: the Swansea visit 'from the point of view of enthusiasm was the greatest personal tribute I have ever received from the crowd' (ibid., 2108, 3 October 1908).

5   Two recent accounts of their lengthy political and personal friendship are Robert Lloyd George, *David and Winston: How a Friendship Changed History*, paperback edn (London, 2005); and Richard Toye, *Lloyd George and Churchill: Rivals for Greatness*, paperback edn (London, 2007). Robert Lloyd George, a great-grandson of David, believes the two men formed a genuine and lasting friendship. Toye is less convinced and takes issue with any romanticized version of the relationship between them. A concise analysis of Churchill's interest in social issues is Paul Addison, 'Churchill and Social Reform', ch. 4 in Robert Blake and William Roger Louis (eds), *Churchill* (New York, 1993).

6   The Hussars were, as one biographer has put it, 'a very smart, exclusive and expensive cavalry regiment' (Geoffrey Best, *Churchill: A Study in Greatness* (London, 2001), p. 9. See also his ch. 2 for Churchill's early military adventures. Best's *Churchill and War* (Hambledon, 2005) is an extensive analysis of Churchill's military thinking and active career in the British Army.

7   Best, *Churchill: A Study in Greatness*, p. 11.

8   Roy Jenkins, *Churchill: A Biography*, paperback edn (London, 2002), p. 81; and generally, ch. 4, 'Tory into Liberal'.

9   See Bentley Brinkerhoff Gilbert, 'Winston Churchill versus the Webbs: The Origins of British Unemployment Insurance', *American Historical Review* 74 (April 1966), pp. 846–62. Later Churchill broke with the Webbs over the form that unemployment relief should take.

10 Born in Bengal where his father was a member of the Indian Civil Service, Beveridge was educated at Charterhouse and Balliol College, Oxford. Thereafter, he had a varied career as sub-warden at Toynbee Hall, a leader writer for the *Morning Post* and as a civil servant at the Board of Trade under Churchill. He served as Minister of Food during World War I in Lloyd George's coalition government. During his time as Master of University College, Oxford, from 1937–45, he made his name most significantly as one of the architects of the post-1945 British welfare state.

11 Balfour's Conservative government during its waning days had also realized this issue as a potential vote getter and had passed in 1905 the Unemployed Workmen's Act. But its temporary nature and reliance upon make-work projects consigned it to failure. See Kenneth D. Brown, 'Conflict in Early British Welfare Policy: The Case of the Unemployed Workmen's Bill of 1905', *Journal of Modern History* 43 (1971), pp. 615–29; and Bentley Brinkerhoff Gilbert, *The Evolution of National Insurance in Great Britain: The Origins of the Welfare State* (London, 1966), pp. 238–46.

12 For Churchill's policies as President of the Board of Trade, see Paul Addison, *Churchill on the Home Front, 1900–1955*, Pimlico edn (London, 1993), ch. 2. Addison informs much of the following discussion on Churchill's early career.

13 The strengthened Labour representation in the 1906 Parliament had aggressively pushed for an active Liberal response to unemployment, but had been repeatedly rebuffed by the government, especially (and surprisingly) by John Burns, the working class Head of the Local Government Board. Burns, in fact, was proving an ineffective Cabinet member: Asquith therefore shifted the unemployment question from Burns to Churchill. See

Kenneth D. Brown, 'The Labour Party and the Unemployment Question, 1906–1910', *Historical Journal* 14:3 (1971), pp. 599–616, esp. 606–7.

14 See Gilbert, *Evolution of National Insurance*, pp. 261–5 for a clear explication of the act. Just as Lloyd George had discovered at the Board of Trade, Churchill found Hubert Llewellyn Smith an important legislative facilitator in offering crucial statistical evidence on social questions.

15 The costs of a new naval construction programme, as we shall see, were also included in the Budget.

16 Lloyd George's famous remark was in response to a parliamentary question during the ongoing debate over the Old Age Pensions Bill. The question posed was: did the Chancellor of the Exchequer have a nest egg to pay for the bill? Lloyd George responded with some candour. 'I have no nest eggs at all. I have got to rob somebody's hen roost next year. I am on the look-out ... where I shall get the most eggs' (*Hansard*, 4th Series, vol. 191, 29 June 1908, p. 395).

17 For discussions of the evolution of a new taxation policy among Liberals, see Martin Pugh, *State and Society: British Political and Social History, 1870–1992* (London: 1994), pp. 134–36 and Robert Self, *The Evolution of the British Party System, 1885–1940* (Harlow, 2000), pp. 74–7. For details of Asquith's budgets as Chancellor of the Exchequer, see Roy Jenkins, *Asquith* (London, 1964), pp. 165–7.

18 Discussions of the Budget must begin with Murray's indispensable *The People's Budget*. See also Bentley Brinkerhoff Gilbert, *David Lloyd George: A Political Life*, vol. 1: *The Architect of Change, 1863–1912* (Columbus, Ohio, 1987), pp. 368–76.

19 NLW, William George Papers, 2176, 12 February 1909 and 2181, 22 February 1909.

20 Edward David (ed.), *Inside Asquith's Cabinet: From the Diaries of Charles Hobhouse* (New York, 1977), 12 April 1909, p. 77. The previous month Hobhouse had noted that instead of working at the details of his budget, Lloyd George had gone to Cannes to play golf. After the parliamentary session had been adjourned and the Budget sent to the Lords in November, Hobhouse summed up Lloyd George's performance as 'idleness and ignorance personified' (21 November 1909, p. 82). But as Rowland points out, Lloyd George had voted in 462 divisions in the House relating to the Budget, more than twice as many as either Asquith or Churchill, though not so many – not surprisingly – as the Chief Whip, J.A. Pease, who clocked in 518 divisions (Rowland: *Last Liberal Governments: 1905–1910*, p. 235n.) Hobhouse had never been fond of Lloyd George: he had written in his diary on 5 August 1908 that Lloyd George's contempt for details made him 'a bad official' (David, *Inside Asquith's Cabinet*, p. 73).

21 Indeed, as Murray points out, historians have not appreciated the extent to which Lloyd George accepted modification of his budget in these crucial meetings (Bruce K. Murray, *The People's Budget 1909/10: Lloyd George and Liberal Politics* (Oxford, 1980), p. 150). This is in contrast to Peter Rowland's claim that the Cabinet allowed Lloyd George 'a free hand to do what he thought best' (Peter Rowland, *The Last Liberal Governments: The Promised Land, 1905–1910* (New York, 1969), pp. 220–1).

22 *The Times*, 30 April 1909.

23 This may be attributed to the physical toll that working up the Budget had taken. As he related to William, he had been working anxiously 14 hours a day, which had left him 'somewhat exhausted' (NLW, William George Papers, 2214, 18 April 1909).

24 As Neal Blewett describes it in *The Peers, the Parties and the People: The British General Elections of 1910* (London, 1972), p. 72.

25 Blewett: *Peers, Parties and People*, p. 70.

26 Sir Austen Chamberlain, *Politics from Inside: An Epistolary Chronicle, 1906–1914* (New Haven, 1937), p. 10. Austen had been a previous Chancellor of the Exchequer under the Balfour ministry.

27 Thomas Wodehouse Legh Newton, 2nd Baron, *Lord Lansdowne: A Biography* (London, 1929), p. 378.

28 Often thought of as the quintessential English country gentleman, Long was MP for a number of constituencies: he sat for South Dublin during the time of the Budget debates. He served in the Conservative ministries of 1895–1905 and later in Lloyd George's wartime coalition government.

29 *The Times*, 4 November 1909.

30 Lloyd George told a different story to William. 'Budget going strong' he wrote the day after its presentation (NLW, William George Papers, 2219, 1 May 1909). A few days later: 'debate going well' (ibid., 2221, 4 May 1909). This was followed by his reporting of an 'immense success' and 'a real triumph' in the House (ibid., 2222, 7 May 1909 and 2227, 13 May 1909).

31 John Vincent (ed.), *The Crawford Papers: The Journals of David Lindsay, Twenty-Seventh Earl of Crawford and Tenth Earl of Balcarres during the years 1892 to 1940* (Manchester, 1984), 21 May 1909, p. 128; and 12 June 1909, p. 128.

32 Ibid., 15 July 1909, p. 129.

33 Ibid., 11 September 1909, p. 133. Balcarres thought Lloyd George was kept fresh primarily by playing rounds of golf during parliamentary sessions. For the Conservative response to the Budget, there are numerous sources. See especially David Dutton, *'His Majesty's Loyal Opposition': The Unionist Party in Opposition 1905–1915* (Liverpool, 1992), ch. 5; and Bruce K. Murray, 'The Politics of the "People's Budget"', *Historical Journal* 14:3 (1973), pp. 555–70.

34 There is evidence that Lloyd George, in association with Churchill at the Budget League, promised honours to those who donated to the League. These sums could be considerable. J.C. Horsfall, a Yorkshire textile manufacturer apparently contributed £15,000 to the League and received a baronetcy not long afterward. Jack Pease, the Liberal Chief Whip took a dim view of this practice and denounced Lloyd George to his face for 'buying funds for the Budget League by selling honours' (Cameron Hazlehurst and and Christine Woodland (eds), *A Liberal Chronicle: Journals and Papers of J.A. Pease, 1st Lord Gainford, 1908–1910* (London, 1994), diary entry of 3 December 1909, p. 145). Hazlehurst and Woodland also believe that the Budget League became 'the creature' of Churchill and Lloyd George (ibid., p. 121). Pease sat as Liberal MP for Tyneside (1892–1900); Saffron Walden (1901–10); and Rotherham (1910–17). He was Chief Whip from 1908–10 and served in the Cabinet as Chancellor of the Duchy of Lancaster, 1910–1 and President of the Board of Education, 1911–5. He was created Baron Gainford in 1917. In later years, he was Chairman and then Vice-Chairman of the BBC from 1922–32.

35 *The Times*, 31 July 1909.

36 'Limehouse was great', Lloyd George reported to William – this time with some justification. 'The people are at last thoroughly aroused' (NLW, William George Papers, 2271, 31 July 1909). A few days later, Lloyd George noted again his success: the Tories were 'raging over Limehouse but our fellows most enthusiastic' (ibid., 2273, 3 August 1909).

37 *The Times*, 2 August 1909.

38 Ibid. Carson was Conservative MP for Dublin University, a distinguished lawyer and a leading spokesman for the Ulster Unionist cause. He later served in Lloyd George's wartime coalition ministry.

39   Ibid., 3 August 1909.

40   Born in Canada, Bonar Law emigrated to Scotland, becoming a successful iron merchant. Elected to a Glasgow seat during the Khaki Election of 1900; defeated during the Liberal landslide of 1906; returned at a by-election at Dulwich in 1910; defeated at North West Manchester at the general election of December 1910; returned once again at the Bootle by-election in February 1911. He was leader of the Conservative Party from 1911–21, and the following year became Prime Minister. He also had served in Lloyd George's wartime government as a member of the War Cabinet.

41   *The Times*, 9 August 1909. Bonar Law was speaking at the West of Scotland Women's Unionist Association at Fullerton, Ayrshire.

42   For these samples of Conservative aristocratic response to Limehouse and the Budget, see *The Times*, 5 August 1909; 25 August 1909; and 3 September 1909. The second Duke of Westminster would likely have been the type of aloof and irresponsible aristocrat that Lloyd George had in mind. The much-married Westminster, who enjoyed 'colossal riches', had the reputation of a self-indulgent and irritable skinflint. The fifth Earl Lonsdale fell into the same category. He was, as Cannadine notes, a 'full-time sportsman, playboy, and adventurer' (for thumbnail sketches of Westminster and Lonsdale, see David Cannadine, *The Decline and Fall of the British Aristocracy* (New Haven, 1990), pp. 360, 386–7). Cannadine notes, however, that Lloyd George's comments on aristocrats and the House of Lords were not entirely fair. A prime example was the Liberal Earl Carrington (who became the Marquis of Lincolnshire in 1912), owner of 26,000 acres, a responsible and generous landlord, a land reformer and President of the Board of Agriculture in both the Campbell-Bannerman and Asquith governments. He hailed the Lloyd George's People's Budget as 'bold, Liberal, and humane'. See Andrew Adonis, 'Aristocracy, Agriculture and Liberalism: The Politics, Finances and Estates of the Third Lord Carrington', *Historical Journal* 31:4 (1988), pp. 871–97, esp. 877 for the quotation.

43   NLW, William George Papers, 2278, 17 August 1909.

44   See *The Times*, 11 October 1909, for the following extracts from the Newcastle-on-Tyne speech.

45   Ibid., 12 October 1909.

46   Ibid., 14 October 1909.

47   George Nathaniel Curzon was Conservative MP for Southport from 1886–98. Created an Irish peer in 1898 and later given an earldom and eventually a marquisate. He was Viceroy of India 1899–1905. He, too, was one of the many Conservatives who later served in Lloyd George's wartime Cabinet.

48   *The Times*, 16 October 1909.

49   Ibid., 30 October 1909.

50   As Murray notes in his *People's Budget*, p. 190.

51   Bentley Brinkerhoff Gilbert, *David Lloyd George: A Political Life*, vol. 1: *The Architect of Change, 1863–1912* (Columbus, Ohio, 1987), pp. 364, 370, 380–1, 394.

52   Ian Packer, *Lloyd George*, paperback edn (Houndmills, Hants, 1998), p. 26.

53   John Grigg, *Lloyd George: The People's Champion, 1902–1911* (Berkeley, 1978), pp. 170–1, 203, 214, 226–7.

54   Martin Pugh, *Lloyd George*, paperback edn (London, 1988), pp. 48–9.

55   William George, *My Brother and I* (London, 1958), 3 August 1909, p. 230.

56   Ibid., 4 August 1909, p. 230. Northcliffe was the leading newspaperman of his day. He owned or held a controlling interest in such papers as *The Times*, the *Evening News*, and the *Daily Mail* (in which he initiated a literary supplement as well as a Braille edition).

Subsidiary publications included *Horner's Penny Stories*, *Home Chat*, the *Harmsworth Magazine* and at least a dozen other such journals.

57   George, *My Brother and I*, 17 August 1909, p. 230.

58   Jenkins, *Asquith*, p. 200.

59   George, *My Brother and I*, 19 October 1909, 232.

60   Ibid., 25 November 1909, 233.

61   As Murray puts it, there is 'no substantial evidence that Lloyd George contrived the Budget as a trap for the Lords' (Murray, 'The Politics of the "People's Budget"', p. 555).

62   At first, some Conservatives (including Lansdowne) favoured amending the bill, purging it of the most offensive clauses, but sentiment within the party overwhelmingly favoured rejection (Murray, *People's Budget*, pp. 209–23).

63   As Blewett notes in *Peers, Parties and People*, p. 103.

64   See *The Times*, 4 December 1909.

65   Ibid., 10 December 1909.

66   Ibid., 22 December 1909.

67   Ibid., 23 December 1909. William St John Brodrick, 1st Earl Midleton, who was Conservative MP for West Surrey and later for Guildford, served as War Secretary from 1900–3 and India Secretary from 1903–5.

68   W. Watkin Davies, *Lloyd George 1863–1914* (London, 1939), pp. 341–2.

69   *The Times*, 1 January 1910.

70   Hamilton was Conservative MP for Middlesex and later Ealing. He had been First Lord of the Admiralty under Salisbury and Secretary of State for India under both Salisbury and Balfour.

71   *The Times*, 10 January 1910. Lord George's comments came during a campaign speech at Uxbridge: see ibid., 6 January 1910.

72   Ibid., 13 January 1910.

73   For this paragraph, see Alan Sykes, *Tariff Reform in British Politics, 1903–1013* (Oxford, 1979), ch. 6 'Socialism' and pp. 203–9.

74   *The Times*, 29 December 1909.

75   *The Times*. Wyndham was Conservative MP for Dover and Chief Secretary for Ireland 1900–5.

76   Chamberlain, *Politics from Inside*, 20 September 1909, p. 182.

77   Quoted from the Asquith Papers by Jenkins, *Asquith*, p. 205, n. 1.

78   For these comments, see Murray, *People's Budget*, p. 246. Some historians have tended to agree that Lloyd George's contribution to the Liberal effort during the election campaign was mixed. Grigg, for example, thinks that Lloyd George was indeed a morale builder for Liberal candidates; but he nevertheless 'must have' contributed to the alienation of some portion of the voters in the countryside (Grigg, *People's Champion*, pp. 241–2).

79   A concise analysis of the election may be found in Michael Kinnear, *The British Voter: An Atlas and Survey since 1885* (Ithaca, 1968), pp. 31–2.

80   Denis Gwynn, *The Life of John Redmond* (London, 1932) remains the standard biography. A brief appreciation of Redmond by Nicholas Mansergh may be found in Conor Cruise O'Brien (ed.), *The Shaping of Modern Ireland* (London, 1960), pp. 38–49.

81   For this paragraph, there are numerous Irish sources; but see especially H.W. McCready, 'Home Rule and the Liberal Party, 1899–1906', *Irish Historical Studies* 13 (1963), pp. 316–48; Patricia Jalland, 'A Liberal Chief Secretary and the Irish Question: Augustine Birrell, 1907–1914', *Historical Journal* 19:2 (1976), pp. 421–51; and Alvin Jackson, *Home Rule: An Irish History 1800–2000* (Oxford, 2003), chs 6 and 7.

82 In the meantime, the Cabinet had been shuffled, with Churchill replacing Herbert Gladstone as Home Secretary: Gladstone had resigned to take Governor-Generalship of South Africa. Sydney Buxton replaced Churchill at the Board of Trade. Herbert Samuel took Buxton's former office as Postmaster-General. J.A. Pease replaced Samuel as Chancellor of the Duchy of Lancaster.

83 Balcarres exulted in the change of temperament in the new House of Commons. Before the election, he noted in his diary, Conservatives had often been disheartened in the House of Commons at their 'terrible paucity of numbers'; but now all was changed: 'We attack a glum and dejected government' (Vincent, *Crawford Papers*, 24 February 1910, p. 146). Austen Chamberlain wrote in like vein to his stricken father on the first day of the parliamentary session: 'Our men are keen and full of fight and spirits. The Government side is chastened' (quoted in Rowland, *Last Liberal Governments: 1905–1910*, p. 287n.). Lloyd George confirmed the loss of morale among Liberals in his correspondence with William during late February 1910. 'Things are for the moment looking very gloomy', he wrote on 24 February 1910. The following day, he thought that during a long Cabinet meeting, Asquith's nerves seemed 'shattered'; and later that same day: 'Situation still very critical' (see NLW, William George Papers, 2349, 24 February 1910; 2350, 25 February 1910; 2351, 25 February 1910).

84 Jenkins notes other examples of a troubled Asquith who had begun to exhibit a weakening 'sureness of touch' (Jenkins, *Asquith*, p. 204). See also Koss's *Asquith*, which hints at early signs of prime ministerial inertia (p. 115).

85 Vincent, *Crawford Papers*, 7 November 1910, pp. 165–6.

86 Parliamentary Archives, LG/C/6/5/1, 17 August 1910.

87 The sceptical Asquith seems, however, to have been among the least favourable. See Jenkins, *Asquith*, p. 217.

88 Earl of Birkenhead, *The Life of F.E. Smith, First Earl of Birkenhead* (London, 1960), 20 October 1910, pp. 156–7. This work by FE's son is essentially a second edition of an earlier two-volume biography published in the 1930s. FE, a renegade not unlike Lloyd George and Churchill, had become a fast friend of the two in spite of political differences.

89 Chamberlain, *Politics from Inside*, 21 October 1910, pp. 283–5. So striking were the concessions to Conservatives that, Chamberlain still recalled two years later his surprise that Lloyd George could face his party in surrendering such important Liberal principles (in a letter to Lansdowne, ibid., 26 August 1912, pp. 292–3).

90 Ibid., pp. 286–87. It is important to note here that both of these proposals referred not to the August memo, but to the October memo. See below for the distinction between the two memos.

91 *The Times*, 18 October 1910.

92 Gilbert, *Lloyd George: Architect of Change*, pp. 413–4.

93 Rowland, *Last Liberal Governments: 1905–1910*, p. 308.

94 Kenneth O. Morgan, *Lloyd George* (London, 1974), pp. 71–2.

95 Addison, *Churchill on the Home Front*, p. 100.

96 Grigg, *People's Champion*, 273, 272.

97 Dutton, *'His Majesty's Loyal Opposition'*, pp. 83–84.

98 For Searle's analysis, see his *The Quest for National Efficiency: A Study in British Politics and Political Thought, 1899–1914*, paperback edn (London, 1990), ch. 6, 'Lloyd George's Attempted National Settlement of 1910'. See also Searle's 'A.J. Balfour's Secret Coalition Talks Memorandum', *Historical Research* 66:160 (June 1993), pp. 222–9.

99 Searle, *Quest for National Efficiency*, p. 195.

100 Ibid., p. 189.

101 Robert J. Scally, *The Origins of the Lloyd George Coalition: The Politics of Social-Imperialism, 1900–1918* (Princeton, 1975), pp. 199, 206 and generally ch. 7, 'The Lloyd George Plan'. See also Appendix B, which prints both the August and October memoranda (pp. 371–86).

102 Gilbert, *Lloyd George: Architect of Change*, p. 416.

103 Gilbert suggests that Lloyd George drafted it as a response to Conservatives who desired more specific proposals than those outlined in the August memo (ibid., p. 415). A few pages later Gilbert writes that it was 'very likely' Balfour who asked Lloyd George to draft the October memo (ibid., p. 425).

104 Blewett, *Peers, Parties, and People*, pp. 164–5.

105 Corinne Comstock Weston does not agree and in fact blames Lloyd George for the failure of the conference. However, she does not mention his coalition plan and concentrates narrowly on the single issue of the Lord's veto as it was discussed during the conference. It is also possible that she was influenced by her primary sources, both Conservative in origin. Although the conference proceedings were secret, two members of the eight participants – the Conservatives Chamberlain and Lansdowne – took extensive notes. These notes are held in the Chamberlain Papers at the University of Birmingham [Chamberlain's notes are Ac 10/2/35–Ac 10/2/64 and Lansdowne's are Ac 10/2/65]. Weston draws extensively from them. See her 'The Liberal Leadership and the Lords' Veto, 1907–1910', *Historical Journal* 11:3 (1968), pp. 508–37.

106 For Lloyd George's version of events see his *War Memoirs*, new edn, vol. 1 (London, n.d. [1939?]), pp. 20–4. Written under the long shadow of World War I, Lloyd George's account of this episode emphasizes the diplomatic and strategic necessities of that time and transposes them to the 1910 era. Thus Lloyd George implies that Conservatives under Balfour bore a significant responsibility for the British lack of preparation in the early days of World War I by rejecting the coalition plan with its provisions for strengthening the military. For an analysis of Lloyd George's tendency to vindicate his political career in the *War Memoirs*, see George W. Egerton, 'The Lloyd George *War Memoirs*: A Study in the Politics of Memory', *Journal of Modern History* 60 (1988), pp. 55–90.

107 See Chamberlain, *Politics from Inside*, p. 190.

108 See Alfred M. Gollin, The Observer *and J.L. Garvin, 1908–1914: A Study in a Great Editorship* (London, 1960), pp. 213–5 for Garvin's letter and pp. 215–9 for Balfour's, dated 22 October 1910. Garvin, a Conservative Unionist, was Editor of the influential *Observer* newspaper with strong ties to such men as Balfour, R.S. Sandars (Balfour's confidential secretary), and to Austen Chamberlain. An acolyte of Joseph Chamberlain, Garvin wrote the earlier volumes of the six-volume biography of Chamberlain ultimately completed by Julian Amery.

109 Ibid., p. 215.

110 R.J.Q. Adams confirms that Balfour, then a firm supporter of union with Ireland, was never enthusiastic about the coalition because it was predicated on some form of Irish devolution (*Balfour: The Last Grandee* (London, 2007), p. 246.

111 See E.H.H. Green's comprehensive work, *The Crisis of Conservatism: The Politics, Economics and Ideology of the British Conservative Party, 1880–1914*, paperback edn (London, 1996). Green believes that the Edwardian Conservative Party was 'anything but sagacious and disciplined' (p. 3); that there were 'deep fissures' in its ranks (p. 271); and that, in short, the Party 'was in a mess' (p. 304). Dutton, in *'His Majesty's Opposition'* agrees. The Conservative Party in this era bore 'little more' than a passing resemblance to 'a viable alternative government' (p. 4). Balfour as a leader often appeared 'defensive, lugubrious and vulnerable' (p. 37). The Party sometimes breached 'accepted conventions of

constitutional propriety' (p. 69) and it lacked 'a sufficient identity of purpose and sense of direction to meet the challenges of the new age' (p. 295). Every party had difficulty in facing the complicated social and political issues of Edwardian Britain, as Martin Pugh observes, but the Conservatives 'were the most deeply troubled' (Martin Pugh, *State and Society: A Social and Political History of Britain, 1870–1997*, 2nd edn (London, 1999), p. 145.

112 Indeed, as Fanning has observed, 'a certain uneasiness' was stirring among Conservatives at large when they realized that the Irish question was coming to the fore at the conference (in spite of the secrecy of its proceedings) and that decisions made there could sow dissension among their ranks (J.R. Fanning, 'The Unionist Party and Ireland, 1906–10', *Irish Historical Studies* 15 (1966), pp. 147–71, p. 164). John Fair agrees that Lloyd George sensed an opportunity in appealing to the Federalists within the Conservative Party which led him to strengthen the Irish provisions to that end in his October memorandum (see Fair, *British Interparty Conferences: A Study of the Procedure of Conciliation in British Politics, 1867–1921* (Oxford, 1980), p. 96 and more generally ch. 4, 'The Constitutional Conference of 1910').

113 Reviewing Lloyd George's coalition proposal and his actions in attempting to implement it, Alan Sykes succinctly states that Lloyd George flew his coalition kite 'to exploit the divisions of the Unionists over policy, and to deepen their indecision' (in Sykes, *Tariff Reform in British Politics*, pp. 231–2).

114 Anticipating an electoral battle over outstanding issues, Lloyd George was eager for the contest. To William he wrote: 'Combat is joy if the cause be good' (NLW, William George Papers, 2423, 3 November 1910).

115 For a discussion of the referendum initiative, see Dutton, '*His Majesty's Loyal Opposition*', pp. 83 and 87–94; and Blewett, *Peers, Parties, and People*, pp. 178–91. Conservative adoption of a referendum was not unprecedented. Corinne Comstock Weston sees it originating in the 1840s when Tory agricultural protectionists attempted to halt Sir Robert Peel's drift toward free trade by demanding that Peel consult the electorate before repealing the Corn Laws. See Weston's *The House of Lords and Ideological Politics: Lord Salisbury's Referendal Theory and the Conservative Party, 1846–1922* (Philadelphia, 1995) and her earlier article 'Salisbury and the Lords, 1868–1895', *Historical Journal* 25:1(1982), pp. 103–29.

116 Chamberlain, *Politics from Inside*, 16 November 1910, p. 300, see also pp. 302–11.

117 Vincent, *Crawford Papers*, 16 November 1910, p. 167.

118 See *The Times*, 22 November 1910.

119 *The Times*, no friend of Lloyd George, put it thus: the crowd was 'restless and unenthusiastic' during the Budget part of the speech, but it became 'keenly attentive and fiercely demonstrative' when he began his 'violent attack' upon the aristocracy (22 November 1910).

120 As Balcarres well understood. Admitting his own feelings of 'nauseous impotence' at Lloyd George's Mile End speech and condemning its 'scurrility', Balcarres knew that Lloyd George had calculated some minor electoral losses caused by his scathing speeches would likely be compensated for by attracting to the Liberals a greater number of those voters who had a 'sullen vindictiveness' against both the House of Lords and the 'Tories' (Vincent, *Crawford Papers*, 20 November 1910 and 22 November 1910, pp. 169–70).

121 For the campaign in Scotland, see *The Times*, 28 November 1910.

122 Ibid., 30 November 1910.

123 Ibid.

124 Ibid., 3 December 1910.

125 Ibid., 6 December 1910.

126 Ibid., 1 December 1910 and 8–10 December 1910.

127 For Bonar Law's speech, see ibid., 15 November 1910. A number of Conservative MPs and military officers were present as well as the Duke of Marlborough and the Lords Stradbroke, Colchester, Ashbourne, Malmsebury, Hardinge and Hindslip. Rudyard Kipling spoke briefly at the end of the meeting, expressing 'a distinct feeling of hopefulness in regard to the coming fight'.

128 Ibid. 19 November 1910.

129 Ibid., 24 November 1910.

130 For a detailed analysis, chs 9, 10 and 18 in Blewett, *Peers, Parties, and People* are essential. P.F. Clarke emphasizes the very high voter turnout as evidence of voter engagement with the issues: the two elections of 1910, he writes, were expressions of 'an unparalleled level of popular participation' (P.F. Clarke, 'The Electoral Position of the Liberal and Labour Parties, 1910–1914, *English Historical Review* 90 (October 1975), pp. 828–36. The quotation may be found on p. 828). Other useful discussions of the December 1910 election are in Rowland, *Last Liberal Governments: 1905–1910*, ch. 17; and Kinnear, *The British Voter*, pp. 31–7 and 82–3.

131 Vincent, *Crawford Papers*, 21 December 1910, p. 171. Historians have generally agreed. Sykes believes that the Conservatives were probably foredoomed to failure because the election found them 'completely unprepared' and they were forced 'into the hurried announcement of policies they had hoped to avoid' (Sykes, *Tariff Reform in British Politics*, p. 232). Ramsden thinks the December 1910 election confirmed the previous January outcome and was in effect 'a clear mandate to end the Lords' veto' (John Ramsden, *An Appetite for Power: A History of the Conservative Party since 1830*, paperback edn (London, 1999), p. 211).

Chapter 7. Triumph

1 For the course of the Parliament Bill through the Lords, see Peter Rowland, *The Last Liberal Governments: Unfinished Business, 1911–1914* (London, 1971), ch. 2, 'Domestic Affairs, January–July 1911', passim.

2 See Dutton's analysis in ch. 5, 'Policy: The Constitution 1906–1911' in David Dutton, *'His Majesty's Loyal Opposition': The Unionist Party in Opposition 1905–1915* (Liverpool, 1992). As he puts it, the Conservative Party came close to breaching and at times almost certainly 'did breach accepted conventions of constitutional propriety' during its opposition to Liberal initiatives after 1906 (p. 69). Gregory D. Phillips, however, defends the Diehard position in his *The Diehards: Aristocratic Society and Politics in Edwardian England* (Cambridge, 1979), passim. Phillips works hard to lend a note of historical empathy to the plight of the Diehards, claiming that they were far from being 'blind reactionaries' or 'simple reactionaries' (*The Diehards*, p. 141). But in candidly noting their 'extremism' as well as their tendency in public announcements and private letters to advocate violence against the state and their determination to go so far as to contemplate fomenting civil war and anarchy in England and Ireland (p. 152), Phillips reveals them in a dangerous and unconstitutional light. See also Phillips, 'The "Diehards" and the Myth of the "Backwoodsmen"', *Journal of British Studies* 16 (1977), pp. 107–20; and 'Lord Willoughby de Broke and the Politics of Radical Toryism, 1909–1914', *Journal of British Studies* 20:1 (Fall 1980), pp. 205–24. See also Geoffrey Searle, 'The "Revolt from the Right" in Edwardian Britain', in Paul Kennedy and Anthony Nicholls (eds), *Nationalist and Racialist Movements in Britain and Germany before 1914* (London, 1981), ch. 2.

3 Lansdowne's remarks were met with 'a dignified if frigid silence' in the House of Lords, according to Lord Newton (Thomas Wodehouse Legh Newton, 2nd Baron, *Lord Lansdowne: A Biography* (London, 1929), pp. 414–5).

4 Asquith officially informed Balfour on 20 July 1911 about the King's pledge to increase as needed the peerage in the House of Lords.

5 See John Vincent (ed.), *The Crawford Papers: The Journals of David Lindsay, Twenty-Seventh Earl of Crawford and Tenth Earl of Balcarres during the years 1892 to 1940* (Manchester, 1984), ch. 6, 'The Parliament Act 1911', passim.

6 Ibid., 1 February 1911, 173 and 3 February 1911, p. 175.

7 Ibid., 24 July 1911, p. 199.

8 Balfour confided to Lady Elcho the reason for his departure: 'Politics have been to me quite unusually odious' (quoted in Max Egremont, *Balfour: A Life of Arthur James Balfour*, paperback edn (London, 1998), 19 August 1911, p. 238. Balcarres thought Balfour's fleeing the scene was unfortunately timed: 'most embarrassing', he wrote in his diary (ibid., 4 August 1911, p. 212); and a few days later more accusingly: 'he means to let things slide' (ibid., 7 August 1911, p. 213).

9 The Conservative votes had been very well orchestrated. Lord Lansdowne and the Conservative front bench were opposed to the Diehard position of resistance to the Parliament Bill. On the other hand, they did not, as potential office holders in some later Conservative governments, wish to be known as supporters of a bill that restricted the power of the Lords. To cover their tracks, they devised a covert scheme by which enough Conservative peers would vote for the bill in alliance with the Liberal peers thus thwarting the Diehards and avoiding the problems that a rejection of the bill would surely engender. David Southern has described the dilemma of the Conservative leadership thus: they were 'unable to conquer, unwilling to perish, wanting to retreat, but unwilling to give the order ...' ('Lord Newton, the Conservative Peers and the Parliament Act of 1911', *English Historical Review* 96:381 (October 1981), p. 837). See also Corinne Comstock Weston and Patricia Kelvin, 'The "Judas Group" and the Parliament Bill of 1911', *English Historical Review* 99 (July 1984), pp. 551–65. As Balcarres wrote to Balfour the day after the bill succeeded in the Lords: 'We are uncomfortable, irritable, and apprehensive of the immediate future' (Vincent, *Crawford Papers*, p. 217).

10 Balcarres observed that the club differed on a number of issues but were 'united in disapproval of their leader's advice' (ibid., 15 October 1911, p. 231). An analysis of the campaign against Balfour may be found in Peter Fraser, 'The Unionist Debacle of 1911 and Balfour's Retirement', *Journal of Modern History* 35:4 (December 1963), pp. 354–65. Summing up, Fraser believes that the Conservatives wanted a leader who could help reformulate basic policies especially in domestic affairs and provide a dynamic leadership in order to compete more effectively with a reforming Liberalism and a growing socialist sentiment. See also Dutton, *'His Majesty's Loyal Opposition'*, pp. 149–62.

11 Vincent, *Crawford Papers*, 2 June 1911, p. 186.

12 Ibid., 30 September 1911–2 October 1911, pp. 224–9. Others found him 'low and depressed', such as W.A.S. Hewins, in a conversation with Balfour, as reported to Balcarres on 1 October 1911, ibid., p. 227. Hewins was the first Director of the London School of Economics, 1895–1903. An ardent Chamberlainite and supporter of tariff reform, he became a Conservative MP for Hereford, 1912–8. He also served in Lloyd George's coalition government from 1917–9 as Undersecretary of State for the Colonies.

13 The idea here, as Pugh points out, was to aid some of the most skilled labouring professions who might otherwise be forced onto the Poor Law. These professions, too, could more easily afford the required contributions mandated by the new legislation

(Martin Pugh, *State and Society: A Social and Political History of Britain, 1870–1997*, 2nd edn (London, 1999), p. 129).

14 Gilbert notes that the legislative history of unemployment insurance is thus 'almost without interest' (Bentley Brinkerhoff Gilbert, *The Evolution of National Insurance in Great Britain: The Origins of the Welfare State* (London, 1966), p. 283, and more generally, ch. 5).

15 Sidney Buxton had guided unemployment insurance through the House of Commons. The radical Buxton, MP for Poplar, was Postmaster General in the Asquith government until 1910. In that year, he became President of the Board of Trade, replacing Churchill, who was appointed Home Secretary. Buxton was at the Board of Trade until 1914 when he became Governor-General of South Africa, a position he held until 1920.

16 See Chaper 5 above. Gilbert notes that government intervention in both illness and unemployment insurance was far more dangerously competitive to Friendly Societies than old age pensions had been (Gilbert, *Evolution of National Insurance*, p. 293).

17 Ibid., pp. 318–43 examines the industrial insurance companies in detail.

18 When widows' pensions were dropped from the scheme, the cost of projected benefits fell by 50 per cent (Bentley Brinkerhoff Gilbert, *David Lloyd George: A Political Life*, vol. 1: *The Architect of Change, 1863–1912* (Columbus, Ohio, 1987), p. 432).

19 For this meeting, see *The Times*, 3 November 1910.

20 A convenient summary of the benefits of the bill and its administration is in Rowland, *Last Liberal Governments, 1911–1914*, pp. 32–33.

21 NLW, William George Papers, 2472, 4 May 1911.

22 Gilbert, *Evolution of National Insurance*, p. 354.

23 *The Times* leader of 5 May 1911 also praised Lloyd George's 'lengthy and clear' exposition in the House of Commons. Of the bill, *The Times* admitted that: 'It is a great object and it imposes a corresponding task on the Legislature.' Nevertheless, there was some reservation: numerous points were doubtful or obscure; and some worry, too, about the 'enormous burden' on taxpayers.

24 Sir Austen Chamberlain, *Politics from Inside: An Epistolary Chronicle, 1906–1914* (New Haven, 1937), 5 May 1911, p. 336. Two days of further reflection led Chamberlain to a more nuanced response as he considered the political consequences of the bill: 'Confound Ll. George. He has strengthened the Government again. His Sickness scheme *is* a good one and he is on right lines this time. I must say I envy him the opportunity and I must admit that he has made good use of it' (ibid., 7 May 1911, p. 338).

25 As Derek Fraser points out in *The Evolution of the British Welfare State: A History of Social Policy since the Industrial Revolution* (London, 1973), p. 156. See also G.C. Peden, *British Economic and Social Policy: Lloyd George to Margaret Thatcher* (Oxford, 1985), p. 28.

26 Pugh claims that in order to insure Labour support for the bill, the government 'gave a firm promise' to enact payment of salaries for MPs (Martin Pugh, *Lloyd George*, paperback edn (London, 1988), p. 57). Gilbert (*Lloyd George: Architect of Change*, pp. 441–2) discounts the idea that there was a formal *quid pro quo*.

27 See Peden, *British Economic and Social Policy*, p. 31.

28 See the lengthy report in *The Times*, 2 June 1911. Braithwaite reported that the meeting consisted of 200 to 300 delegates from all over the country who represented the 'scores of furious meetings of doctors breathing blood and fury' (Sir Henry N. Bunbury (ed.), *Lloyd George's Ambulance Wagon: Being the Memoirs of William J. Braithwaite, 1911–1912* (London, 1957), p. 175).

29 For the speech and the following quotations, see *The Times*, 12 June 1911.

30 There may have been a political context for the BMA's decision: its President was Sir James Barr, an Ulsterman and a strong Conservative Unionist at a time when, as we shall

see, Home Rule for Ireland was rapidly emerging as the next great constitutional crisis (Bentley Brinkerhoff Gilbert, *David Lloyd George: A Political Life*, vol. 2: *Organizer of Victory 1912–16* (Columbus, 1992), pp. 28–9).

31 This turn of events was, in Gilbert's words, a 'dazzling victory' for Lloyd George: see ibid., p. 30.

32 NLW, William George Papers, 2536, 4 December 1911.

33 Ibid., 2541, 11 December 1911.

34 Ibid., 2543, 16 December 1911.

35 Gilbert claims that Braithwaite was the 'chief architect of national insurance' (*Evolution of National Insurance*, p. 339). At this time, Braithwaite was Assistant Secretary of the Board of Inland Revenue. He had been educated at Winchester and Oxford and was a resident at Toynbee Hall from 1898–1903. His residence in the East End of London made him a radical for life.

36 Bunbury, *Memoirs of Braithwaite*, p. 63. Well into the drafting process of the Health Insurance Bill, Braithwaite's opinion of Lloyd George had not changed. On 5 April 1911, he wrote: 'It will be an enormous misfortune if this man by any accident should be lost to politics' (ibid., p., 143).

37 As Braithwaite notes, Lloyd George's breakfasts were famous in their day: the Chancellor 'did much of his work at them; getting people together and picking their brains' (ibid., p., 92).

38 See Rowland, *Last Liberal Governments, 1911–1914*, p. 86; Kenneth O. Morgan, *Lloyd George* (London, 1974), p. 74; Ian Packer, *Lloyd George*, paperback edn (Houndmills, Hants, 1998), p. 31; and G.R. Searle, *A New England? Peace and War, 1886–1918* (Oxford, 2004), p. 386.

39 The work of James E. Cronin is useful here. See, for example, his *Industrial Conflict in Modern Britain* (London, 1979) and 'Strikes and Power in Britain, 1870–1920', in Leopold H. Haimson and Charles Tilly (eds), *Strikes, Wars, and Revolutions in an International Perspective: Strike Waves in the late Nineteenth and Early Twentieth Centuries* (Cambridge, 1989), ch. 5. A brief summary of the various strikes may be found in Hugh Armstrong Clegg, *A History of British Trade Unions since 1889*, vol. 2, *1911–1933* (Oxford, 1985), ch. 2. More recent but far briefer is W. Hamish Fraser, *A History of British Trade Unionism 1700–1998* (London, 1999), ch. 5. Lord Askwith's autobiographical *Industrial Problems and Disputes* (London, 1920) has a unique perspective on the strikes of that era. Serving in the railway department at the Board of Trade, George Askwith was the chief government conciliator and had first-hand knowledge of the labour unrest from his experience in negotiating almost every major dispute before 1914. Arthur J. McIvor reviews more recent work on unions and industrial unrest in his 'Industrial Relations in Britain, 1900–1939', in Chris Wrigley (ed.), *A Companion to Early Twentieth Century Britain* (London, 2003), ch. 20.

40 For these managerial strategies, see Joe White, '1910–1914 Reconsidered', in James E. Cronin and Jonathan Schneer (eds), *Social Conflict and the Political Order in Modern Britain* (New Brunswick, 1982), ch. 4, esp. pp. 75–8.

41 The importance of economic factors in contributing to Edwardian labour unrest is a matter of debate. Standish Meacham believes that a new class consciousness was at work, whereas Roy Church emphasizes that at least in the coal industry, 'solidarity issues' such as alleged victimization or the use of non-union labour by management were most important. See Meacham, '"The Sense of an Impending Clash": English Working-Class Unrest before the First World War', *American Historical Review* 77 (1972), pp. 1343–64 and Church, 'Edwardian Labour Unrest and Coalfield Militancy, 1890–1914', *Historical Journal* 30:4 (1987), pp. 841–57. In addition, some workers may have been influenced by syndicalism, which advocated direct workers' control of production, in contrast to state

socialism, which was based upon the utilization of state power to nationalize industry. See Bob Holton, *British Syndicalism, 1900–1914: Myths and Realities*, paperback edn (London, 1976). In short, no one doubts the fact of labour insurgency, but its causes remain in dispute.

42 Eric Wigham, *Strikes and the Government, 1893–1974* (London, 1976) examines the development of government intervention during industrial disputes: see ch. 2.

43 Philip S. Bagwell, *The Railwaymen: The History of the National Union of Railwaymen* (London, 1963), p. 292. See also ch. 12, '1911 – The First National Railway Strike' for what follows.

44 Geoffrey Alderman agrees that some railway companies in particular had adopted a 'rigid attitude' against recognizing unions. These companies feared that any negotiation could legitimize union wage demands, thus further reducing profits (Alderman, 'The Railway Companies and the Growth of Trade Unionism in the Late Nineteenth and Early Twentieth Centuries', *Historical Journal* 14:1 (1971), p. 147).

45 Kenneth O. Morgan (ed.), *Lloyd George: Family Letters, 1885–1936* (Cardiff and London, 1973), 19 August 1911, p. 158.

46 As recounted by Haldane a year later to Austen Chamberlain: see Chamberlain's *Politics from Inside*, p. 437. Confirmation of Lloyd George's crucial role in settling the railway strike also comes from Herbert Samuel, then serving as Postmaster General in the Cabinet, who informed his wife that Lloyd George had 'managed to keep a door open' thus providing 'the glimmer of hope in settling the strike' (HLRO, Samuel Papers, SAM/7/157/621, 18 August 1911). In the meantime, the dock strike had been settled under the leadership of John Burns.

47 For the following discussion, see Chris Wrigley, *David Lloyd George and the British Labour Movement: Peace and War* (Hassocks, 1976), pp. 68–73; and Rowland, *Last Liberal Governments, 1911–1914*, pp. 146–54.

48 Askwith made his remarks at an informal lunchtime meeting with the Archbishop of Canterbury and George Riddell: see George Allardice Riddell, Baron, *More Pages from My Diary, 1908–1914* (London, 1934), 27 February 1912, p. 40.

49 Ibid., 27 February 1912, p. 42.

50 NLW, William George Papers, 2561, 1 March 1912.

51 Riddell, *More Pages from My Diary*, 14 March 1912, p. 43.

52 As Hobhouse notes: see his diary entry of 27 March 1912 (Edward David (ed.), *Inside Asquith's Cabinet: From the Diaries of Charles Hobhouse* (New York, 1977), pp. 112–3). The date of the entry clearly indicates a retrospective view of several recent Cabinet meetings.

53 David, *Inside Asquith's Cabinet*, p. 113.

54 Both Roy Jenkins and Stephen Koss applaud Asquith's dexterity in settling the strike (Roy Jenkins, *Asquith* (London, 1964), pp. 237–8; Stephen Koss, *Asquith*, paperback edn (New York, 1985), pp. 132–4).

55 W. Hamish Fraser, *A History of British Trade Unionism 1700–1998* (London, 1999), p. 118.

56 Wrigley praises Lloyd George for his 'pre-eminence' in coping with the labour unrest, noting that he was 'usually foremost' among the ministers in settling the more difficult issues (Wrigley, *Lloyd George and the British Labour Movement*, p. 76). On the other hand, Cronin believes that both men and managers frequently distrusted Lloyd George in his attempts to negotiate (James E. Cronin, 'Strikes, 1870–1914', in Chris Wrigley (ed.), *A History of British Industrial Relations, 1875–1914* (Amherst, 1982), ch. 4.

57 The German government at the time was under pressure from business interests to strengthen its ties with Morocco: see Joanne Stafford Mortimer, 'Commercial Interests and German Diplomacy in the Agadir Crisis', *Historical Journal* 10:4 (1967), pp. 440–56.

58 The Algeciras Conference of 1906, called to settle the tensions between Germany and France had left Germany's Moroccan ambitions unfulfilled: see S.L. Mayer, 'Anglo-German Rivalry at the Algeciras Conference', in Prosser Gifford and William Roger Louis (eds), *Britain and Germany in Africa: Imperial Rivalry and Colonial Rule* (New Haven, 1967).

59 For details of the Anglo-German naval arms race and its implications for both foreign and domestic policies, as well as Lloyd George's role in them, see Chapter 9 below.

60 *The Times*, 22 July 1911.

61 Thus Jacques Willequet's statement that Lloyd George's speech had 'declared his support for France' is somewhat misleading (Willequet, 'Anglo-German Rivalry in Belgian and Portuguese Africa?', in Gifford and Louis, *Britain and Germany in Africa*, p. 258).

62 See Howard S. Weinroth, 'The British Radicals and the Balance of Power, 1902–1914', *Historical Journal* 13:4 (December 1970), pp. 653–82.

63 Lloyd George was not, of course, the only member of the government to manage the press. As Stephen Koss jibed, it would be wrong to suppose that the Liberals 'practiced *laissez-faire* in their dealings with the press'. But it was certainly Lloyd George's job to see to it that Scott's pacifist conscience 'did not get the better of him' (Stephen Koss, *The Rise and Fall of the Political Press in Britain: The Twentieth Century*, 2 vols (London, 1984), vol. 2, pp. 173–4).

64 For the following, see Trevor Wilson (ed.), *The Political Diaries of C.P. Scott, 1911–1928* (Ithaca, 1970), pp. 45–9. The direct quotation is on p. 46. Scott was not above flattery; but his diary entries betray some scepticism and bemusement at the obvious attempts to influence his public response to the Mansion House speech.

65 Gilbert, *Lloyd George: Architect of Change*, p. 526, n. 203. Gilbert also notes that Lloyd George had 'silenced' his friend Robertson Nicoll of the *British Weekly*, just as he had 'mollified' Scott of the *Guardian* (ibid., p. 460).

66 K.G. Robbins, 'The Foreign Secretary, the Cabinet, Parliament and the Parties', in F.H. Hinsley (ed.), *British Foreign Policy under Sir Edward Grey* (Cambridge, 1977), p. 14.

67 John Grigg, *Lloyd George: The People's Champion, 1902–1911* (Berkeley, 1978), p. 305.

68 M.L. Dockrill, 'David Lloyd George and Foreign Policy Before 1914', in A.J.P. Taylor (ed.), *Lloyd George: Twelve Essays* (New York, 1971), p. 17. See also Dockrill's later 'British Policy during the Agadir Crisis', in Hinsley: *British Foreign Policy under Grey*.

69 Michael G. Fry, *Lloyd George and Foreign Policy*, vol. i, *The Education of a Statesman: 1890–1916* (Montreal, 1977), p. 138.

70 Keith Wilson, 'The Agadir Crisis, the Mansion House Speech, and the Double-Edgedness of Agreements', *Historical Journal* 15:3 (1972), pp. 513–32. The crisis ended with the signing on 4 November of a German and French accord giving the Germans compensation in the French Congo. Additional information on the Agadir crisis may be found in Gilbert's analysis (*Lloyd George: Architect of Change*, pp. 447–61).

71 As Searle puts it, Lloyd George managed to head off a national rail strike by 'pleading patriotic necessity' (Searle, *A New England?*, p. 451).

72 Paul M. Kennedy, *The Rise of the Anglo-German Antagonism, 1860–1914* (London, 1980), p. 449.

73 Rowland, *Last Liberal Governments, 1911–1914*, p. 121.

74 Searle, *A New England?*, p. 496.

75 Gilbert, *Lloyd George: Architect of Change*, p. 453.

76 Eyre Crowe, the senior clerk in the Western department of the Foreign Office, minuted to Grey on 18 August 1908 that it was 'somewhat alarming to see Cabinet Members with obvious imperfect understanding of foreign affairs plunge into public discussion abroad

of an "entente" with Germany' (quoted in Dockrill, 'Lloyd George and Foreign Policy', p. 8). Grey agreed and wrote to Asquith four days later, warning that it was 'very risky for Cabinet Ministers to go abroad and make utterances about international affairs, when they are out of touch with the FO' (ibid., p. 9).

77 Grey complained to Francis Bertie, British Ambassador in Paris, that the newspaper interviews caused 'far more annoyance at home' even than in France (Dockrill, 'Lloyd George and Foreign Policy', p. 11).

78 Cited ibid., p. 12, from the Murray Papers.

79 Ibid., p. 18, quoting from the Nicolson Papers, 27 July 1911. A distinguished and seasoned diplomat, Nicolson (1st Baron Carnock) held a variety of posts throughout his career, including Ambassador to Russia in 1906–1910. He was Permanent Under-Secretary at the Foreign Office from 1910–1916. Hardinge (1st Baron Harding of Penshurst) also served with distinction in several diplomatic positions, including Constantinpole, Berlin and Washington, DC. He, too, was Permanent Under-Secretary at the FO (1906–10) until he was appointed Viceroy of India.

80 Stephen Gwynn (ed.), *The Letters and Friendships of Sir Cecil Spring-Rice: A Record* (London, 1929), 1 August 1911, p. 163. Tyrell was also to have a distinguished career at the Foreign Office, serving nearly 40 years before he became Ambassador to France from 1928–34. He was created Baron Tyrrell in 1929. Spring-Rice served in a variety of diplomatic posts, including Cairo and St Petersburg, before he became Ambassador to the United States from 1912–8.

81 Balfour had established the CID in 1904 as the principal advisory body for the Cabinet on all matters concerned with home and imperial defence. Born of the organizational difficulties revealed during the second South African War, it developed as its special task military planning. Although a secretary and assistant secretary provided its organizational structure, the CID was largely a creature of the Prime Minister. It was he who could order up various reports as well as call meetings to address specific military issues. The most thorough and lengthy account of the CID is Franklyn Arthur Johnson, *Defence by Committee: The British Committee of Imperial Defence, 1885–1959* (New York, 1960). John P. Mackintosh's 'The Role of the Committee of Imperial Defence before 1914', *English Historical Review* 77 (July 1962), pp. 490–503, however, thinks that Johnson has overstated its importance because of the infrequency of its meetings and its lack of authority. John F. Naylor believes that Johnson's book is now obsolete: see Naylor, *A Man and an Institution: Sir Maurice Hankey, the Cabinet Secretariat and the Custody of Cabinet Secrecy* (Cambridge, 1984), p. 325, n. 94. See also Stephen Roskill, *Hankey: Man of Secrets*, vol. I (London, 1970), ch. 4, 'Assistant Secretary, Committee of Imperial Defence, 1908–1912'. As will become clear, however, the CID under Hankey later assumed a greater importance than in its earlier years.

82 Wilson had spent much of his spare time cycling along the Franco-German border to perfect his knowledge of the French countryside from the standpoint of military advantage. His observations on the intricacies of political and military relationships during World War I are of particular interest, as we shall see from Major-General Sir Charles E. Callwell's *Field-Marshall Sir Henry Wilson: His Life and Diaries* (London, 1927). A recent biography of Wilson is Keith Jeffery, *Field Marshal Sir Henry Wilson: A Political Soldier* (Oxford, 2006).

83 As Samuel R. Williamson Jr puts it in *The Politics of Grand Strategy: Britain and France Prepare for War, 1904–1914* (Cambridge, 1969), p. 193. See also chs 6 and 7 for his analysis and background of the Agadir crisis.

84 And from Churchill as well: see Callwell, *Sir Henry Wilson*, vol. 1, p. 99.

85 For this letter and the following quotations, see Parliamentary Archives, LG/C/3/15/6, 25 Aug. 1911.

86 Callwell, *Sir Henry Wilson*, vol. 1, p. 103.

87 From Harold Nicolson's biography of his father, *Sir Arthur Nicolson, Bart., First Lord Carnock: A Study in the Old Diplomacy* (London, 1930), p. 347.

88 Chamberlain, *Politics from Inside*, p. 363, letter dated 23 October 1911.

89 Lucy Masterman, *C.F.G. Masterman: A Biography* (London, 1939), p. 213.

90 See Fry, *Lord George and Foreign Policy*, vol. 1, chs 1 and 7.

91 Certainly Grey believed that the speech had discouraged Germany from going too far in its Moroccan claims: see Dockrill, 'British Policy during the Agadir Crisis', p. 285.

92 Dockrill thinks that there was in fact a 'considerable' improvement between Britain and Germany; and by 1913 there were 'cordial' relations between the two countries ('Lloyd George and Foreign Policy', p. 23).

Chapter 8. Scandal and Failure

1 As early as January 1912, he confided to William that he was 'instigating a move to dish Tories over Ulster' (NLW, William George Papers, 2551, 31 January 1912).

2 Historians are widely in agreement on this change in his fortunes. Gilbert suggests that Lloyd George's greatest parliamentary achievements, especially his reform programmes, were behind him by 1912. Thereafter, for a time his political life was characterized by failure and near disaster (Bentley Brinkerhoff Gilbert, *David Lloyd George: A Political Life*, vol. 2: *Organizer of Victory 1912–16* (Columbus, 1992), p. 13). Even the most favourably disposed toward Lloyd George believe that he entered a 'darker period' and that he was comparatively 'in the shadows' for the duration of the pre-war era (Kenneth O. Morgan, *Lloyd George* (London, 1974), pp. 77, 80).

3 Gilbert's 'David Lloyd George and the Great Marconi Scandal', *Historical Research* 62:149 (October 1989), pp. 295–317 is essentially recapitulated in his *Lloyd George: Organizer of Victory*, pp. 32–52. The most complete analysis is Frances Donaldson, *The Marconi Scandal* (New York, 1962), with substantial quotations from journalists' articles, parliamentary debates, and testimonies before a parliamentary select committee.

4 See Denis Judd, *Lord Reading, Rufus Issacs, First Marquess of Reading, Lord Chief Justice and Viceroy of India, 1860–1935* (London, 1982), ch. 8, 'The Marconi Scandal, 1912–13'.

5 Murray, eldest son of the 10th Lord Elibank, was styled The Master of Elibank until he was raised to the peerage as Baron Murray of Elibank in August 1912. He had previously served as Under Secretary of State for India and Parliamentary Secretary to the Treasury.

6 So vitriolic was their criticism with its anti-Semitic overtones that some historians have seen it as a forerunner of the Fascist movements of the 1920s and 1930s. See, for example, Kenneth Lunn, 'Political Anti-Semitism before 1914: Fascism's Heritage?', in Kenneth Lunn and Richard C. Thurlow (eds), *British Fascism: Essays on the Radical Right in Inter-War Britain* (New York, 1980), ch. 1; and Tom Villis, *Reaction and the Avant-Garde: The Revolt Against Liberal Democracy in Early Twentieth-Century Britain* (London, 2006), pp. 80–2. Searle, though noting the anti-Semitic overtone of some Marconi critics, does not comment on it as a precursor of Fascism (G.R. Searle, *Corruption in British Politics, 1895–1930* (Oxford, 1987), ch. 8, 'Marconi'.

7 *The Times*, 12 October 1912.

8 For Samuel's role in the Marconi affair, see John Bowle, *Viscount Samuel: A Biography* (London, 1957), ch. 7, 'Marconi'. In general, Bowle makes a sharp contrast between Samuel – who 'always insisted on the moral basis of politics' in following fundamental

Liberal principles – and the 'opportunist improvisations' of Lloyd George (ibid., pp. 38–9).

9   See John Ambrose Hutcheson Jr, 'Leopold Maxse and the *National Review*, 1893–1914: A Study in Unionist Journalism and Politics', PhD dissertation (Chapel Hill, 1974), ch. 9. Maxse continued his attacks upon Lloyd George and the government well into 1914, although as Hutcheson points out, his continuing attempt to tar Lloyd George's reputation and to derail Lloyd George's land campaign were 'not particularly successful' (ibid., p. 490).

10 Weetman Pearson, 1st Viscount Cowdray, was one of the new breed of 'plutocratic peers' characteristic of the Edwardian era (David Cannadine, *The Decline and Fall of the British Aristocracy* (New Haven, 1990), p. 200). In a brief letter to Lloyd George – marked 'Secret' and 'Burn' – Murray suggested that it would be best for both Lloyd George and himself to avoid being seen together while the Marconi inquiry was under way. See Parliamentary Archives, LG/6/5/8, 13 November 1913 (probable date).

11 Searle, *Corruption in British Politics*, pp. 181–7.

12 Trevor Wilson (ed.), *The Political Diaries of C.P. Scott, 1911–1928* (Ithaca, 1970), 7 June 1913, p. 70.

13 The Cabinet was motivated by general political considerations of course, but they were also determined to thwart any serious threat against Lloyd George. As Reginald McKenna, then Home Secretary, put it: Lloyd George was 'the greatest platform asset' the Liberal Party had. But McKenna also admitted that his value 'as a public statesman' among 'serious people' was 'gone for ever'. This was said to Charles Hobhouse, who recently had become Chancellor of the Duchy of Lancaster, succeeding J.A. Pease. See Edward David (ed.), *Inside Asquith's Cabinet: From the Diaries of Charles Hobhouse* (New York, 1977), 13 June 1913, p. 138.

14 After a round of golf at Walton (George Allardice Riddell, Baron, *More Pages from My Diary, 1908–1914* (London, 1934), p. 161).

15 Peter Rowland, *The Last Liberal Governments: Unfinished Business, 1911–1914* (London, 1971), p. 208.

16 From an account in the *Daily Telegraph* of 2 July 1913, Parliamentary Archives, LG/C/36/1/9.

17 Frances Donaldson, *The Marconi Scandal* (New York, 1962), pp. 249, 52.

18 John Grigg, *Lloyd George: From Peace to War, 1912–1916* (London, 1985), pp. 56, 60–1.

19 Cannadine, *Decline and Fall of the British Aristocracy*, p. 333.

20 Gilbert, *Lloyd George: Organizer of Victory*, p. 51.

21 G.R. Searle, *A New England? Peace and War, 1886–1918* (Oxford, 2004), p. 436.

22 Ian Packer, *Lloyd George*, paperback edn (Houndmills, Hants, 1998), p. 35.

23 William George, *My Brother and I* (London, 1958), p. 203.

24 Gilbert, *Lloyd George: Organizer of Victory*, p. 56.

25 For this paragraph, see Emy's discussion, 'The Debate upon the Land', in his *Liberals, Radicals and Social Politics*, pp. 203–11.

26 See Bruce K. Murray's discussion, 'Lloyd George and the Land: The Issue of Site-Value Rating', in J.A. Benyon, C.W. Cook, T.R.H. Davenport and K.S. Hunt (eds.), *Studies in Local History: Essays in Honour of Professor Winifrid Maxwell* (Cape Town, 1976), pp. 37–47 for this paragraph.

27 Such a scheme of land evaluation would be, as Offer observes, 'a veritable Domesday' (Avner Offer, *Property and Politics, 1870–1914: Landownership, Law, Ideology and Urban Development in England* (Cambridge, 1981), 363).

28 The most recent examination of the land question is Ian Packer's *Lloyd George, Liberalism and the Land: The Land Issue and Party Politics in England 1906–1914* (Woodbridge, Suffolk, 2001).

29 See Patricia Lynch, *The Liberal Party in Rural England, 1885–1910: Radicalism and Community* (Oxford, 2003) esp. ch. 5.

30 Smallholdings were generally defined as small farms for agricultural labourers.

31 There were also other groups advocating reform of the land, the most famous of whom were the advocates of the American Henry George, whose doctrine of replacing all taxation by a tax on the capital value of land had achieved some popularity. Although Packer denies that George had any influence on the Liberal leadership (Packer, *Lloyd George, Liberalism, and the Land*, p. 30), Gilbert has discovered that Lloyd George had read and taken notes on George's *Progress and Poverty* as early as 1884 (Gilbert, *Lloyd George: Organizer of Victory*, p. 55).

32 Regulating agricultural wages was, as Packer notes, an 'astonishing departure' from previous policies, but Packer also explains it as a natural corollary to the government's recently passed Coal Mines (Minimum Wage) Act (Packer, *Lloyd George, Liberalism and the Land*, p. 77).

33 For this conversation, see Riddell, *More Pages from My Diary*, 27 May 1912, pp. 63–66.

34 NLW, William George Papers, 2600, 30 May 1912.

35 For the establishment of the committee, see Packer, *Lloyd George, Liberalism and the Land*, pp. 83–7.

36 Rowntree was a member of a famous Quaker family whose wealth (derived from cocoa manufacturing) and philanthropic work made them one of the leading Liberal lights of provincial England. Rowntree's father was the founder of the Liberal Association in York. See Asa Briggs, *Social Thought and Social Action: A Study of the Work of Seebohm Rowntree, 1871–1954* (London, 1961).

37 Parliamentary Archives, LG /C/2/1/7, 15 August 1912.

38 NLW, William George Papers, 2693, 10 February 1913.

39 Parliamentary Archives, LG/C/2/3/3, 2 September 1913.

40 Parliamentary Archives, LG/C/2/3/16a, 9 October 1913. Cadbury was another of the philanthropic 'cocoa Liberals' who supported Lloyd George.

41 Packer, *Lloyd George, Liberalism and the Land*, p. 87. Nevertheless, Offer believes that the information when eventually published was a valuable record of economic and social conditions (Offer, *Property and Politics*, 372).

42 Packer, *Lloyd George, Liberalism and the Land*, p. 99.

43 Conservatives were in full cry against the measure, in part because only four days earlier the unfortunate Marconi debate of 11 October 1912 had taken place in the House: they scented another opportunity to strike a blow against the ministry.

44 Kenneth O. Morgan (ed.), *Lloyd George: Family Letters, 1885–1936* (Cardiff and London, 1973), 16 October 1912, 164. He could not refrain from adding how delighted 'our fellows' were at his part in the debate: 'they rose & cheered as I left the House.' *The Times*, however, expressed its doubts, believing that Lloyd George's land agitation had 'suffered a serious setback' because his 'backstairs' investigation had been revealed as 'a mass of one-sided figures' (15 October 1912).

45 After a Cabinet meeting in February 1913, Hobhouse noticed that Lloyd George stayed behind for several minutes 'evidently deep in thought' – probably, Hobhouse surmised, because he had wanted to bring forward the land question, but did not wish 'to incur a rebuff' from the Cabinet (David, *Inside Asquith's Cabinet*, pp. 132–3). Indeed, as Lloyd George confessed to Riddell, he was determined to make no definite proposals until

he had carefully discussed them with his Cabinet colleagues (Riddell, *More Pages from My Diary*, 9 July 1913, p. 169).

46 In July 1913, for example, Robertson Nicoll, Masterman and Lloyd George met for dinner at George Riddell's house to discuss the best method of presenting the Land Inquiry Committee's report (Riddell, *More Pages from My Diary*, p. 168).

47 See Packer, *Lloyd George, Liberalism and the Land*, ch. 6 for the discussion that follows.

48 Packer describes the resulting memo as 'masterly' in its primary object of soothing the nerves of any 'timorous spirits' in the Cabinet who might be uneasy about land reform (ibid., pp. 118–9).

49 Parliamentary Archives, LG/C/2/2/44, LG to Rowntree, 23 August 1913, cited in Gilbert, *Lloyd George: Organizer of Victory*, 62.

50 Parliamentary Archives, LG/C/8/1/9, 4 September 1913.

51 Apparently both Masterman and John Burns thought that the speech was designed 'to stampede' a divided Cabinet into agreement (Gilbert, *Lloyd George: Organizer of Victory*, p. 63, citing the Masterman Papers and Burns's diary).

52 For the speeches, see *The Times*, 13 October 1913.

53 Gilbert believes that the speech largely failed, claiming that Lloyd George 'said very little and outlined no programme' (*Lloyd George: Organizer of Victory*, p. 63). Grigg agrees: 'Neither the tone nor the balance of his oratory was right for the occasion' (*Lloyd George: From Peace to War*, p. 94).

54 He could not resist a few words of self-congratulation about the Bedford gatherings. 'The meetings were great', he wrote William. 'Enthusiasm, determination – all present. We shall win. Landlordism is doomed' (NLW, William George Papers, 2773, 13 October 1913).

55 See Riddell, *More Pages from My Diary*, 13 October 1913, p. 180.

56 David, *Inside Asquith's Cabinet*, 17 October 1913, pp. 146–8.

57 NLW, William George Papers, 2776, 16 October 1913.

58 See *The Times*, 23 October 1913 for the following account of the Swindon meeting.

59 Lloyd George's inevitable boast to William followed Swindon: 'Letters pouring in today approving of Swindon. It has gone like hot cakes' (NLW, William George Papers, 2777, 24 October 1913).

60 Alun Howkins sees this as a sign that agricultural workers were abandoning the 'Gladstonian synthesis' – whereby Liberals represented workers' interests – and were moving toward a position of labour independence (Howkins, 'Edwardian Liberalism and Industrial Unrest: A Class View of the Decline of Liberalism', *History Workshop Journal* 4 (1977), pp. 143–61).

61 As Michael Tichlear argues in his 'Socialists, Labour and the Land: the Response of the Labour Party to the Land Campaign of Lloyd George before the First World War', *Twentieth Century British History* 8:2 (1997), pp, 127–44.

62 *Glasgow Forward*, 20 July 1912, cited in Tichlear, 'Socialists, Labour and the Land', p. 133.

63 Packer's phrase in his *Lloyd George, Liberalism and the Land*, p. 165. See generally ch. 9 'Labour and the Land Issue, 1912–1914'.

64 H.V. Emy, 'The Land Campaign: Lloyd George as a Social Reformer, 1909–14', in A.J.P. Taylor (ed.), *Lloyd George: Twelve Essays* (New York, 1971), p. 66.

65 Offer, *Property and Politics*, p. 373.

66 Martin Pugh, *Lloyd George*, paperback edn (London, 1988), p. 65.

67 Only two proposals received ministerial support. The first would have guaranteed legal protection for urban leaseholders and business tenants from unfair evictions, rent rises, and restrictive covenants. The second would have enabled local authorities to purchase

land at its market value in advance of any immediate need for such land (Packer, *Lloyd George, Liberalism and the Land*, p. 139 and ch. 7, 'The Urban Land Campaign, 1913–1914').

68 Brian Harrison, *Separate Spheres: The Opposition to Women's Suffrage in Britain* (New York, 1978), esp. ch. 4, 'The Heart of the Matter'.

69 See Susan Kingsley Kent, *Sex and Suffrage in Britain, 1860–1914*, paperback edn (Princeton, 1990).

70 Hereafter 'suffragist' will be used primarily in a general sense for the more moderate women's suffrage movement and specifically in reference to the National Union, while 'suffragette' will refer to the WSPU.

71 The depth and scope of suffragist sentiment is well documented by Elizabeth Crawford, *The Women's Suffrage Movement in Britain and Ireland: A Regional Survey* (London, 2006).

72 David, *Inside Asquith's Cabinet*, p. 8. Hobhouse made these remarks at Bristol on 16 February 1912, where he claimed that there been no significant signs of public support for women's suffrage such as had been witnessed in 1867 with the smashing of the Hyde Park railings in support of the Reform Bill of that year. Some women's groups took him at his word and began more action-oriented protests. They also plagued Hobhouse, widely known as a hay fever sufferer, by sending him grass seed and pepper through the post.

73 Roy Jenkins, *Churchill: A Biography*, paperback edn (London, 2002), p. 109.

74 E. Sylvia Pankhurst, *The Suffragette Movement: An Intimate Account of Persons and Ideals* (London, 1931), p. 295.

75 *The Times*, 29 February 1908.

76 Ibid., 25 May 1908.

77 Ibid., 30 July 1908.

78 NLW, Lloyd George Papers, 22521E, 5 October 1908, pp. 175–6. Pethick-Lawrence began as a militant and a member of the WSPU, but later became disenchanted with their violent tactics and moderated her views.

79 See the complete account in *The Times*, 7 December 1908.

80 H.M. Swanwick, *I Have Been Young* (London, 1935), p. 198. Swanwick was at the meeting as a freelance journalist for the *Manchester Guardian*. She was later a member of the executive of the National Union of Women's Suffrage Societies. In 1909, she became the founding editor of the National Union's journal, *The Common Cause*.

81 *The Times*, 14 December 1908.

82 Quotations describing the Liverpool meeting are from *Ibid.*, 22 December 1908.

83 As *The Times* noted in reporting a speech by Lloyd George at Newcastle-on-Tyne in October 1909 (ibid., 11 October 1909).

84 Ibid., 24 March 1910.

85 Ibid., 17 December 1909.

86 Ibid., 18 December 1911. At the hearing the following day at Bow Street Police Court, the assailant was charged with common assault (ibid., 19 December 1911). Lloyd George downplayed the incident. In a letter to William, he called it 'trivial' and 'grossly exaggerated'. The 'satchel' struck his cheek, 'but did not leave even a scratch' (NLW, William George Papers, 2544, 17 December 1911).

87 As Sandra Stanley Holton points out, the National Union, founded in 1897, and the WSPU, founded in 1903, initially worked in harmony, but were later divided over the issue of tactics: see Holton, *Feminism and Democracy: Women's Suffrage and Reform Politics in Britain, 1900–1918* (Cambridge, 1986), esp. ch. 2, 'Militants and Constitutionalists'.

88 *The Times*, 13 July 1910.

89 Ibid., 13 July 1910.

90 See Sandra Stanley Holton, 'The Making of Suffrage History', in Jane Purvis and Sandra Stanley Holton (eds), *Votes for Women* (London, 2000), p. 25.

91 Claire Hirshfield, 'Fractured Faith: Liberal Party Women and the Suffrage Issue in Britain, 1892–1914', *Gender and History* 2:2 (Summer 1990), pp. 172–97, p. 183.

92 John Grigg, *Lloyd George: The People's Champion, 1902–1911* (Berkeley, 1978), pp. 169, 295.

93 Asquith was intractably opposed to votes for women and impervious to the suffragist campaign. Pease recorded that suffragist tactics, especially interruptions during Asquith's addresses in the countryside, 'nettled' and 'upset' the Prime Minister (see, for example, Cameron Hazlehurst and and Christine Woodland (eds), *A Liberal Chronicle: Journals and Papers of J.A. Pease, 1st Lord Gainford, 1908–1910* (London, 1994), 28 October 1908, p. 81). It does appear that the more forward of the suffragettes made Asquith a special target. Even at such a hallowed place as the Lympne Golf Course, he was assaulted by several women in late 1909. Later at dinner, a stone was thrown through the window of the room at the Golf Club that he was sharing with his wife, Margot, who was also a firm anti-suffragist. On another occasion, this time at Lossiemouth Golf Club, Asquith's daughter, Violet, used a golf club to fend off attacks upon her father (Colin Clifford, *The Asquiths*, paperback edn (London, 2003), p. 191. To a Cabinet meeting discussing women's suffrage in June 1910, Asquith confessed his displeasure with this 'most repulsive subject' (Hazlehurst and Woodland, *Journals and Papers of Pease*, 15 June 1910, p. 185). Jenkins, who notes that Asquith was often hectored and hustled by suffragists, suggests that such militant tactics merely reinforced Asquith's intransigency (Roy Jenkins, *Asquith* (London, 1964), pp. 246–7).

94 As Martin Pugh notes in his *Lloyd George*, pp. 61–3.

95 As he put it to the Chief Whip: Elibank, cited in David Morgan, *Suffragists and Liberals: The Politics of Woman Suffrage in England* (Totowa, 1975), 5 September 1911, p. 82. Some in the Conservative Party also held that women could be a conservative force in the electorate. Lord Selbourne, in a letter to Bonar Law, wrote that 'the addition of the wives as voters will lead to increase the general conservatism of the classes of manual workers, not its Radicalism' (David Jarvis, 'British Conservatism and Class Politics in the 1920s', *English Historical Review* 111:440 (February 1996), pp. 59–84, p. 67, quoting from the Bonar Law Papers, Parliamentary Archives, 13 March 1912.

96 In this, he had been consistent since 1892, when he wrote to his wife during the House of Common's consideration of an early franchise bill of his opposition on the grounds that enfranchising widows and spinsters must be balanced by also granting the vote to married women (Morgan, *Lloyd George: Family Letters*, 27 April 1892, p. 48).

97 Martin Pugh, *Electoral Reform in War and Peace, 1906–18* (London, 1978), p. 26.

98 The complicated arrangements involved, on the one hand, attempts by the Conciliation Committee to pursue its limited Franchise Bill, and on the other hand, the government's attempts to delay the measure are carefully set out by Sophia A. van Wingerden, *The Women's Suffrage Movement in Britain, 1866–1928* (London, 1999), ch. 7, 'Conciliation'.

99 See Constance Rover, *Women's Suffrage and Party Politics in Britain 1866–1914* (London, 1967), pp. 129–30.

100 The background and formulation of the bill within the Cabinet may be found in Martin Pugh, *Electoral Reform in War and Peace, 1906–18* (London, 1978), ch. 3, passim.

101 As Rover rightly notes, this 'perpetual postponement' was likely more difficult for suffragists to accept than an outright refusal to grant votes for women (Constance Rover, *Women's Suffrage and Party Politics in Britain 1866–1914* (London, 1967), p. 135).

102 *The Times*, 25 November 1911.

103 Sylvia Pankhurst remembered of that meeting: 'Men hecklers were present in force' (Pankhurst, *Suffragette Movement*, p. 361).

104 Lloyd George had in fact been warned away from the use of that term by no less a personage than Helena Swanwick, to whom he had given in private a full dress rehearsal of his Bath speech. Swanwick remembers telling him to expunge his boast of torpedoing the Conciliation Bill on the grounds that it would alienate '*all* suffragists' (that is, both moderate and militant) who had campaigned for the bill (see Swanwick: *I Have Been Young*, p. 216). Lloyd George ignored her suggestion, to his cost. As Sylvia Pankhurst has observed, Lloyd George's use of the word 'torpedoed' became 'a slogan in the attack on him' (Pankhurst, *Suffragette Movement*, p. 361) The offensive term 'torpedoed' has also inclined some historians to convict Lloyd George of 'trickery' (Andrew Rosen, *Rise Up, Women! The Militant Campaign of the Women's Social and Political Union, 1903–1914* (London, 1974), pp. 154–5; see also Rover, *Women's Suffrage and Party Politics*, pp. 130–1. Martin Pugh writes that, indeed, Lloyd George's reputation as a suffragist has often been considered suspect because of his actions against the Conciliation Bill; but, Pugh concludes, 'this seems unjustified' (Pugh, *Electoral Reform*, p. 33).

105 Parliamentary Archives, LG/C/8/1/1, 30 November 1911.

106 NLW, William George Papers, 2561, 1 March 1912; and 2563, 4 March 1912.

107 See Martin Pugh, 'Labour and Women's Suffrage', in K.D. Brown (ed.), *The First Labour Party, 1906–1914* (London, 1985), ch. 10.

108 See Crawford, *Women's Suffrage Movement*, passim for details of suffragist incidents.

109 There is some controversy about the Speaker's actions. It has been put about that the Speaker, James Lowther, who was a Conservative and personally opposed to women's suffrage, had consorted with Lord Rothschild, a leading contributor to the anti-suffragist movement, a few days prior to his ruling. See Harold L. Smith, *The British Women's Suffrage Campaign 1866–1928* (Harlow, 1998), p. 45. Holton thinks that the Liberal ministers knew beforehand that the Speaker would rule against the bill and were not at all surprised by his actions (Holton, *Feminism and Democracy*, p. 92). And in fact Asquith privately expressed 'great relief' at the Speaker's 'coup d'etat' which 'bowled over the Women for this Session …' (Michael and Eleanor Brock (eds), *H.H. Asquith Letters to Venetia Stanley*, paperback edn (Oxford, 1985), 27 January 1913, p. 27).

110 van Wingerden's term in her *Women's Suffrage Movement in Britain*, p. 136.

111 How this cycle of violence between prisoners and the authorities was repeated has been well documented in the case of Lady Constance Lytton, the sister of Lord Lytton. See Marie Mulvey-Roberts, 'Militancy, Masochism or Martyrdom? The Public and Private Prisons of Constance Lytton', in Jane Purvis and Sandra Stanley Holton (eds), *Votes for Women* (London, 2000), ch. 7.

112 See Brian Harrison, *Peaceable Kingdom: Stability and Change in Modern Britain* (Oxford, 1982), ch. 1, 'The Act of Militancy. Violence and the Suffragettes, 1904–1914', passim.

113 In a letter to C.P. Scott in Wilson, *Diaries of Scott*, 21 July 1909, p. 34. Scott led the *Manchester Guardian* in support of women's suffrage, but he had his doubts about the efficacy of militancy in gaining that end.

114 See for example Laura E. Nym Mayhall, *The Militant Suffrage Movement: Citizenship and Resistance in Britain, 1860–1930* (Oxford, 2003).

115 See Martin Pugh, *The March of the Women: A Revisionist Analysis of the Campaign for Women's Suffrage, 1866–1914* (Oxford, 2000, ch. 8, 'The Anatomy of Militancy', passim.

116 Smith, *British Women's Suffrage Campaign*, p. 36.

117 Rover, *Women's Suffrage and Party Politics in Britain*, p. 96.

118 Rosen, *Rise Up, Women!*, p. 155.

119 Harrison, *Peaceable Kingdom*, passim. See also Harrison, *Separate Spheres*, ch. 9, 'Scoring Off the Suffragettes'.

120 John Vincent (ed.), *The Crawford Papers: The Journals of David Lindsay, Twenty-Seventh Earl of Crawford and Tenth Earl of Balcarres during the years 1892 to 1940* (Manchester, 1984), 2 March 1912, p. 265.

121 Sir Austen Chamberlain, *Politics from Inside: An Epistolary Chronicle, 1906–1914* (New Haven, 1937), 5 March 1912, pp. 438–39.

122 Wilson, *Diaries of Scott*, 15–16 January 1913, pp. 64–65. It was also true that John Redmond, leader of the Irish Nationalists, was himself an anti-suffragist: furthermore, he had no intention of alienating Asquith, who was spearheading the fight for Irish Home Rule. In addition, Irish Nationalists had always given Home Rule a far greater priority than women's suffrage. For the Irish women's suffrage movement, see Margaret Ward, '"Suffrage First – Above all Else!" An Account of the Irish Suffrage Movement', *Feminist Review* 10 (February 1982), pp. 21–36; and Ward's longer work, *Unmanageable Revolutionaries: Women and Irish Nationalism*, paperback edn (London, 1989). See also Rosemary Cullen Owens, *Smashing Times: A History of the Irish Women's Suffrage Movement, 1889–1922* (Dublin, 1984); and Cliona Murphy, *The Women's Suffrage Movement and Irish Society in the Early Twentieth Century* (Philadelphia, 1989).

123 NLW, Lloyd George Papers, 22524E, 2 August 1912, pp. 53–6. Brailsford was a well-known journalist, pro-suffragette and member of the ILP.

124 Holton, *Feminism and Democracy*, pp. 129–30.

125 See Sylvia's account in her autobiography, *Suffragette Movement*, pp. 564–77.

126 Asquith was apparently forced to receive the deputation under the threat of a hunger strike to the point of death by Sylvia Pankhurst. She had been eight days without food or water in prison. As Asquith wrote to Miss Stanley, Pankhurst's threat put him in a bind: 'I don't want, if I can help, to secure her the martyr's crown, but *que faire?*' (Michael and Eleanor Brock (eds), *H.H. Asquith Letters to Venetia Stanley*, paperback edn (Oxford, 1985), 18 June 1914, p. 89).

127 Pankhurst, *Suffragette Movement*, p. 575.

128 Les Garner, 'Suffragism and Socialism: Sylvia Pankhurst 1903–1914', in Ian Bullock and Richard Pankhurst (eds), *Sylvia Pankhurst: From Artist to Anti-Fascist* (New York, 1992), pp. 77–9.

129 Martin Pugh, *The Pankhursts*, paperback edn (London, 2002), pp. 294–95. Pugh believes that Asquith was motivated largely by political reasons – the concern that both Labour and the Conservative Parties could strike a bargain with the suffragists before the general election of 1915, thus outflanking the Liberal Party.

130 Asquith's remarks to the delegation as recorded in Sylvia's autobiography, *Suffragette Movement*, p. 575.

131 Patricia W. Romero, for one, is not convinced of Asquith's conversion to women's suffrage. She claims that he was unmoved by the deputation and that 'nothing ultimately came of this meeting' (see Patricia W. Romero, *E. Sylvia Pankhurst: Portrait of a Radical* (New Haven, 1987), p. 85).

132 See John M. McEwen, *The Riddell Diaries, 1908–1923* (London, 1986) *Riddell Diaries*, 27 July 1912, p. 48.

133 NLW, William George Papers, 2674, 16 January 1913.

134 Leslie Parker Hume, *The National Union of Women's Suffrage Societies, 1897–1914* (New York, 1982), pp. 122–3, quoting from the Parliamentary Archives, LG/C 8/1/1, 30 November 1911.

135 See Jo Vellacott, *From Liberal to Labour with Women's Suffrage: The Story of Catherine Marshall* (Montreal, 1993), esp. ch. 13, passim.

136 See Smith, *British Women's Suffrage Campaign*, pp. 53–4; Holton, *Feminism and Democracy*, pp. 124–30; and Holton, 'The Making of Suffrage History'.

137 Frances Lloyd George, *The Years That Are Past* (London, 1967), p. 49, and ch. 4 generally for her account of the origins of their affair. See also Ruth Longford, *Frances, Countess Lloyd-George: More than a Mistress* (Leominster, 1996), chs 1–2. Longford is the granddaughter of Frances.

138 For this paragraph, see Ffion Hague, *The Pain and the Privilege: The Women in Lloyd George's Life* (London, 2008), ch. 10, 'Frances'.

139 Susan Pedersen, 'The Story of Frances Stevenson and David Lloyd George', in Wm Roger Louis (ed.), *Penultimate Adventures with Britannia: Personalities, Politics and Culture in Britain* (London, 2008), ch. 2.

140 Frances Lloyd George, *The Years That Are Past* (London, 1967), p. 55.

Chapter 9. Imperial Matters and Foreign Affairs

1 In a letter to William, to whom he suggested that they 'must get up' a golf club in Criccieth (William George, *Backbencher* (Llandysul, 1983), 14 September 1895, p. 183).

2 Parliamentary Archives, LG/A/1/2/2, 14 February 1905. Crosfield was returned as Liberal MP for Warrington in the January 1906 election.

3 Information on golfing in this paragraph may be found in Roland Quinault, 'Golf and Edwardian Politics', in Negley Harte and Roland Quinault (eds), *Land and Society in Britain, 1700–1914: Essays in Honour of F.M.L. Thompson* (Manchester, 1996), ch. 9.

4 Michael Bentley claims that the club had almost become 'a surrogate Parliament' in the pre-war years (Michael Bentley, *Politics without Democracy, 1815–1914*, 2nd edn (Oxford, 1996), p. 245).

5 As remembered by the second Marquess of Reading, whose father, the first Marquess, played with Lloyd George and his friends (recounted in the second Marquess's biography of his father: Gerald Rufus Isaacs, *Rufus Isaacs: First Marquess of Reading* (New York, 1940), p. 239).

6 Ibid.

7 Histories of the Home Rule controversy are numerous. Most useful for our account are Alan O'Day, *Irish Home Rule, 1867–1921* (Manchester, 1998) and Alvin Jackson, *Home Rule: An Irish History 1800–2000* (Oxford, 2003).

8 There are numerous works which examine Ulster's opposition to the Home Rule Bill. F.S.L. Lyons provides an authoritative summary of the Ulster crisis in *Ireland since the Famine*, paperback edn (London, 1989), Part II, ch. 9, 'Ulster Blocks the Way' and Part III, ch. 1, 'Phoenix Resurgent'. See also Patricia Jalland, *The Liberals and Ireland: The Ulster Question in British Politics to 1914* (Aldershot, 1993). A.T.Q. Stewart, an Ulster sympathizer, looks at the popular movement behind the Ulster resistance in *The Ulster Crisis* (London, 1967). Paul Bew's reconstruction of the Home Rule debate and his analysis of the conflicting assumptions that lay behind the antagonisms of Unionists and Nationalists is essential reading: see his *Ideology and the Irish Question: Ulster Unionism and Irish Nationalism, 1912–1916* (Oxford, 1994). D. George Boyce and Alan O'Day (eds), *The Ulster Crisis* (Houndmills, Hants, 2006) contains a variety of scholarly articles ranging from the Ulster Volunteer Force and the Irish Volunteers to examinations of local opinion on the controversy both North and South of the Ulster-Southern Irish border.

9   Craig, a veteran of the Boer War, had been MP for East Down and was later Northern Ireland MP for County Down from 1921–7. A wealthy businessman, he was also active in the Orange Order. He became the first Prime Minister of Northern Ireland from 1921 to his death in 1940. Created Viscount Craigavon in 1927.

10 As the Conservative constitutional scholar A.V. Dicey had argued in his *England's Case Against Home Rule* published in 1886 (quoted by Alan O'Day, 'Home Rule and the Historians', in D. George Boyce and Alan O'Day (eds), *The Making of Modern Irish History* (London, 1996), ch. 8).

11 See Richard Murphy, 'Faction in the Conservative Party and the Home Rule Crisis, 1912–14', *History* 71:232 (1986), pp. 222–34.

12 The two major biographies of Law are somewhat similar, although R.J.Q. Adams, *Bonar Law* (London, 1999) has the advantage of newly opened archives since the publication of Robert Blake's *The Unknown Prime Minister: The Life and Times of Andrew Bonar Law, 1858–1923* (London, 1955).

13 See extracts of the speech in Adams, *Bonar Law*, pp. 108–9.

14 See P.J. Buckland, 'The Southern Irish Unionists, the Irish Question, and British Politics 1906–14', *Irish Historical Studies* 15:59 (March 1967), pp. 228–53; Gregory D. Phillips, 'Lord Willoughby de Broke and the Politics of Radical Toryism, 1909–1914', *Journal of British Studies* 20:1 (Fall 1980), pp. 205–24; and John Kendle, *Walter Long, Ireland, and the Union, 1905–1920* (Montreal, 1992), esp. chs 1–3.

15 Jeremy Smith, 'Bluff, Bluster and Brinksmanship: Andrew Bonar Law and the Third Home Rule Bill', *Historical Journal* 36:1 (March 1993), pp. 161–78. Not all historians agree. Koss, for example, condemns Bonar Law as a politician who gave 'a new definition to viciousness and who sedulously exploited the sectarian hatreds' in Ulster (Stephen Koss, *Asquith*, paperback edn (New York, 1985), pp. 134–5).

16 A celebrated and learned legal advocate, Carson was an Irish Protestant who served as Unionist MP for Dublin University from 1892–18 and for Belfast Duncairn from 1918–21. He was briefly in Lloyd George's War Cabinet as first Lord of the Admiralty.

17 D.M. Jackson and D.M. MacRaild, 'The Conserving Crowd: Mass Unionist Demonstrations in Liverpool and Tyneside, 1912–13', in Boyce and O'Day, *Ulster Crisis*, ch. 12.

18 See Daniel M. Jackson, *Popular Opposition to Irish Home Rule in Edwardian Britain* (Liverpool, 2009).

19 Of particular note is that the UVF was not necessarily led by traditional elites nor by the Unionist Party apparatus: it was rather a popular movement. As Timothy Bowman has put it, the UVG was 'a bottom up rather than top down force' ('The Ulster Volunteer Force, 1910–1920: New Perspectives', ch. 13 in Boyce and O'Day, *Ulster Crisis*).

20 Patricia Jalland, 'A Liberal Chief Secretary and the Irish Question: Augustine Birrell, 1907–1914', *Historical Journal* 19:2 (1976), pp. 421–51, p. 441.

21 Matthew Kelley, 'The Irish Volunteers: A Machiavellian Moment?', in Boyce and O'Day, *Ulster Crisis*, p. 64. See also Charles Townshend, *Political Violence in Ireland: Government and Resistance since 1848* (Oxford, 1983), ch. 5, 'Political Armies'.

22 See Patricia Townshend, 'United Kingdom Devolution 1910–14: Political Panacea or Tactical Diversion?', *English Historical Review* 94:373 (October 1979), pp. 757–85.

23 Edward David (ed.), *Inside Asquith's Cabinet: From the Diaries of Charles Hobhouse* (New York, 1977), 11 February 1912, p. 111.

24 For Birrell see Jalland, 'A Liberal Chief Secretary'. Privately, Birrell was more favourable to Ulster exclusion: see Jalland, *The Liberals and Ireland*, pp. 59–60.

25 To Gilbert, this was 'one of the most disastrous mistakes of modern British, not to mention Irish, history' (Gilbert, *David Lloyd George: A Political Life*, vol. 2: *Organizer of*

Victory 1912–16 (Columbus, 1992), p. 94). Jalland is equally critical, claiming that if the Ulster issue had been brought forward early on in the parliamentary struggle over the Home Rule controversy, much of the ensuing difficulties could have been avoided.

26 Riddell's diaries contain several references to Lloyd George's continuing worries about the scandal. On 24 March 1913, Riddell observed that Lloyd George was 'very anxious' and 'very dark and gloomy' (John M. McEwen, *The Riddell Diaries, 1908–1923* (London, 1986), 24 March 1913, p. 60). Additional references include 19–22 March 1913, pp. 57–60; 20 March 1913, p. 58; 30 March 1913, p. 60; 1 April, 4 April and 12 April 1913, p. 61.

27 Jalland, *Liberals and Ireland*, p. 143. Jalland notes that Lloyd George 'assumed real control of Home Rule policy' (p. 174).

28 Martin Pugh believes that this was an 'ingenious compromise' (*The Making of Modern British Politics, 1867–1945*, 3rd paperback edn (Oxford, 2002), p. 104).

29 Gilbert, *Lloyd George: Organizer of Victory*, pp. 96–7). To this point, many Conservatives had played the Orange card not because they wanted Ulster exclusion, but rather as a device for scuttling Home Rule entirely (Blake, *Unknown Prime Minister*, pp. 149–50 and more generally, ch. 9, 'The Irish Problem – Attempts at Compromise'). See also Adams, *Bonar Law*, pp. 125–44, for another account of Bonar Law's evolving acceptance of an Ulster exclusion policy.

30 Redmond's summaries of these meetings may be found in Denis Gwynn, *The Life of John Redmond* (London, 1932), pp. 234–38. At one point, Lloyd George intimated that should Redmond reject county option, he (Lloyd George) might resign and this would likely mean the collapse of the Liberal ministry and thus the loss of a Home Rule Bill. Redmond sensibly countered that should Lloyd George do so, such a debacle would possibly mean the end of the Liberal Party for a generation and the end of Lloyd George's career as well.

31 For these quotations, see NLW, William George Papers, 2819, 16 February 1914; 2823, 27 February 1914; 2824, 28 February 1914.

32 Stewart's sympathy for Ulster leads him to think so: 'there can no longer be any doubt', he writes, that a government operation was planned 'for the coercion of Ulster' (A.T.Q. Stewart, *The Ulster Crisis* (London, 1967), p. 175).

33 The *Clydevalley* had been renamed the *Mountjoy* after the British ship that broke the siege at Derry on 1 August 1689 for the Protestant cause. Historians have variously estimated the quantity of arms. Blake thinks that the number was 35,000 rifles (Blake, *Unknown Prime Minister*, p. 203) and three million rounds of ammunition. Adams agrees (*Bonar Law*, p. 160) as does David Dutton (*'His Majesty's Loyal Opposition': The Unionist Party in Opposition 1905–1915* (Liverpool, 1992), p. 231) Jackson agrees on the quantity of ammunition, but lowers the rifle estimate to 25,000 (Jackson, *Home Rule*, p. 132). Quite a large number of weapons, in any case.

34 How involved the Conservative leaders were in the Larne episode remains a debatable question. If prior knowledge and direct encouragement could be proved, some Conservatives might be considered as engaging in treasonous acts. Overall, there seems to be a consensus that Bonar Law was not informed of the operation, but that Carson was. How many other Conservative leaders were informed is unclear. Kendle states that, for example, one of the most vigorous supporters of Ulster, Walter Long, had not been apprised beforehand of the plot (Kendle, *Walter Long*, p. 85). But Jackson thinks it 'probable' that Long and other Conservative leaders knew from the start about the operation (Jackson, *Home Rule*, p. 132).

35 For this letter, see NLW, William George Papers, 2865, 17 July 1914.

36 The cache was, however, less impressive than at Larne – only 1,500 obsolete Mausers and 25,000 rounds of ammunition (Roy Foster, *Modern Ireland, 1600–1972* (London, 1988), pp. 468–9).

37 Jalland, *Liberals and Ireland*, pp. 254–5 and Jackson, *Home Rule*, pp. 140–1.

38 See Gilbert, *Lloyd George: Organizer of Victory*, pp. 104–6 for a brief account of the conference.

39 For this paragraph and those that immediately follow, see Arthur J. Marder, *From the Dreadnought to Scapa Flow: The Royal Navy in the Fisher Era, 1904–1919*, vol. 1, *The Road to War, 1904–1914* (London, 1961); A.J. Anthony Morris, *Radicalism Against War, 1906–1914: The Advocacy of Peace and Retrenchment* (Totowa, 1972); Paul M. Kennedy, *The Rise and Fall of British Naval Mastery* (Malabar, 1982), ch. 8, 'The End of Pax Britannica (1897–1914)'; Tetsuro Sumida, *In Defence of Naval Supremacy: Finance, Technology and British Naval Policy, 1889–1914* (Boston, 1989); and D.W. Sweet, 'Great Britain and Germany, 1905–1911', in F.H. Hinsley (ed.), *British Foreign Policy under Sir Edward Grey* (Cambridge, 1977), ch. 11.

40 For a concise review of the German side of the Anglo-German naval rivalry, see Jonathan Steinberg, 'The German Background to Anglo-German Relations, 1905–1914', in Hinsley: *Foreign Policy under Sir Edward Grey*, ch. 10.

41 Marder, Dreadnought *to Scapa Flow*, vol. 1, pp. 135–50.

42 Ibid., p. 56.

43 See Gilbert's account in his *David Lloyd George: A Political Life*, vol. 1: *The Architect of Change, 1863–1912* (Columbus, Ohio, 1987), pp. 347–52. Gilbert describes the trip as a 'courageous, if inept, campaign to slow the disastrous naval race with Germany' (ibid., p. 351).

44 Quoted in Morris, *Radicalism Against War*, p. 144.

45 Randolph S. Churchill, *Winston S. Churchill*, vol. 2, *1901–1914: Young Statesman* (Boston, 1967), 21 December 1908, p. 497 and Randolph S. Churchill, *Winston S. Churchill, Companion vol. 2, Part 2, 1907–1911* (Boston, 1969), 3 January 1909, p. 938.

46 Parliamentary Archives, LG/C/6/11/2 (2 February 1909).

47 Ibid.

48 Ibid., LG/C/6/11/4 (8 February 1909).

49 For a summary of Lloyd George's role in this celebrated 'naval scare', see Gilbert, *Lloyd George: Architect of Change*, pp. 364–68. Phillips Payson O'Brien, *British and American Naval Power: Politics and Policy, 1900–1936* (Westport, 1998), ch. 4, 'The 1909 Naval Estimates Crisis', attributes Lloyd George's change of mind to official reports circulating about the rapid capacity of Krupp, the great German industrial firm, having recently developed its capacity for constructing naval armaments at a rate equal to or greater than comparable British firms.

50 *The Times*, 3 April 1909. Lloyd George had been apprehensive of a negative reaction from Liberals in the country at large, who might oppose the £38 million navy budget; but he no doubt hoped that their opposition would be offset by the dramatically increased social programmes also included in the Budget. See the discussion in Bruce K. Murray, *The People's Budget 1909/10: Lloyd George and Liberal Politics* (Oxford, 1980), pp. 125–30.

51 See Howard Weinroth, 'Left-Wing Opposition to Naval Armaments', *Journal of Contemporary History* 6:4 (October 1971), pp. 93–120, 111 ff. Lloyd George was surely aware of the popularity of the Royal Navy: its history, traditions, and victories were often commemorated in fleet reviews and public launchings. Civic pride was fostered by the Navy's occasional naming of ships after British cities. Lloyd George knew this at first hand from the HMS *Carnarvon*, an armoured cruiser of nearly 11,000 tons, launched in 1903. As a free trade Liberal, too, he supported a strong navy as a guarantor of

unhindered free trade in the sea lanes of the world. See Michael Lewis, *The History of the British Navy* (London, 1959), chs 14–15; Gerald S. Graham, *The Politics of Naval Supremacy: Studies in British Maritime Ascendancy* (Cambridge, 1965); Bernard Semmel, *Liberalism and Naval Strategy: Ideology, Interest, and Sea Power during the Pax Britannica* (Boston, 1986); and Jan Ruger, *The Great Naval Game: Britain and Germany in the Age of Empire* (Cambridge, 2007).

52   Roy Jenkins, *Churchill: A Biography*, paperback edn (London, 2002), p. 204. His duties as First Lord, Jenkins notes further, became 'almost an obsession' (ibid., p. 204). Randolph Churchill's biography of his father agrees in the importance of Morocco: it was the 'decisive event' that altered Churchill's long held belief that Germany posed no threat to Britain (Churchill, *Winston S. Churchill*, vol. 2, p. 503). McKenna took Churchill's previous office as Home Secretary.

53   But as Marder has pointed out, Churchill's frequent forays into the naval yards and to the fleet were not always welcomed. His demanding behaviour and his strictly held opinions on some matters not fully within his competence sometimes raised official eyebrows (Marder, Dreadnought *to Scapa Flow*, pp. 254–5.

54   The *Enchantress* was no small craft. At 4,000 tons and a crew of nearly 200 with lavishly furnished interiors, it was an attractive perk for a young First Lord of the Admiralty. During his 35 months as peacetime First Lord, Churchill spent eight of those months on the *Enchantress* (Jenkins, *Churchill*, p. 207).

55   See John H. Maurer, 'Churchill's Naval Holiday: Arms Control and the Anglo-German Naval Race, 1912–1914', *Journal of Strategic Studies* 15:1 (March 1992), pp. 102–27. As Morris puts it, Churchill's proposal was an exercise in public relations by which he hoped 'to placate the sensibilities of the Radicals while offering encouragement to the Jingoes' (Morris, *Radicalism Against War*, p. 332).

56   NLW, William George Papers, 2621, 4 July 1912.

57   Lloyd George wrote William that Winston was entertaining doubts about the land campaign, but that he would not 'give trouble provided I give him money for his navy. If he keeps quiet he is worth a million or two' (NLW, William George Papers, 2623, 8 July 1912). Lloyd George mentioned this bargain to Riddell the following year. See McEwen's edition of *The Riddell Diaries, 1908–1923*, 31 October and 1 November 1913, p. 71 which gives a more complete account of Lloyd George's comments on this matter than the earlier version by George Allardice Riddell, Baron, *More Pages from My Diary, 1908–1914* (London, 1934), p. 182.

58   Richard Toye suggests that the contretemps between Lloyd George and Churchill can be attributed to 'unresolved tensions' which led to Churchill's misunderstanding of Lloyd George's 'shadow-boxing'. That is, Lloyd George abused Churchill openly in order to disguise his own willingness to accept high naval estimates. In that way, he could placate the radical Liberals, while winning Churchill's support for land reform. But Churchill did not grasp this subtlety, and was genuinely angered by Lloyd George's tactics. See Richard Toye, *Lloyd George and Churchill: Rivals for Greatness*, paperback edn (London, 2007), pp. 102–12.

59   McEwen, *Riddell Diaries*, 14 December 1913, p. 73.

60   Ibid., 18 December 1913, p. 73.

61   Parliamentary Archives, LG/C/3/16/8, 26 January 1914.

62   McEwen, *Riddell Diaries*, 17 January 1914, p. 77.

63   Parliamentary Archives, LG/C/8/1/14, 23 January 1914. Whether or not Lloyd George's resignation threat was genuine is moot. A series of meetings between him and Scott in January 1914 suggests that Lloyd George was using Scott as a conduit to the radical Liberal faithful to communicate his reluctance to capitulate to Churchill's naval demands.

Should the Cabinet override Lloyd George and agree to an enhanced naval programme, Lloyd George would thus have been spared radical criticism. See Scott's diary entries from 15 January to 25 January 1914 in Trevor Wilson (ed.), *The Political Diaries of C.P. Scott, 1911–1928* (Ithaca, 1970), pp. 73–80.

64 See John Grigg, *Lloyd George: From Peace to War, 1912–1916* (London, 1985), p. 102 for an account of this meeting, held on 13 November 1913. For this paragraph in general, see Emy, 'The 1914 Budget', in H.V. Emy, *Liberals, Radicals and Social Politics, 1892–1914* (Cambridge, 1973), pp. 224–34. Additional sources for the paragraphs that follow include Murray, *People's Budget*, pp. 302–10; and Peter Rowland, *The Last Liberal Governments: The Promised Land, 1905–1910* (New York, 1969), pp. 323–7.

65 See Gilbert, 'David Lloyd George: Land, the Budget, and Social Reform', esp. pp. 1062–3; and his 'David Lloyd George: The Reform of British Landholding and the Budget of 1914', *Historical Journal* 21:1 (1978), pp. 117–41.

66 John Vincent (ed.), *The Crawford Papers: The Journals of David Lindsay, Twenty-Seventh Earl of Crawford and Tenth Earl of Balcarres during the years 1892 to 1940* (Manchester, 1984), 5 May 1914, pp. 333–4.

67 John Ramsden (ed.), *Real Old Tory Politics: The Political Diaries of Sir Robert Sanders, Lord Bayford, 1910–35* (London, 1984), 6 May 1914, p. 77. At first blush, Sanders may seem an old school Tory country gentleman; he was after all Master of the Devon and Somerset Staghounds at an early age. But he also earned a First in Jurisprudence at Oxford and was often surprising in his political opinions. He was Conservative MP for Bridgwater (1910–23) and Wells (1924–9) and served several years in the Whip's office. During World War I, he was an officer on active duty in Gallipoli and other theatres. He also held minor positions in Lloyd George's wartime coalition government.

68 Ian Packer tends to discount their influence, but it was undoubtedly a sign of Liberal dissatisfaction with the direction that Lloyd George was taking as Chancellor of the Exchequer: see Packer, 'The Liberal Cave and the 1914 Budget', *English Historical Review* 111:442 (June, 1996), pp. 620–35.

69 McEwen, *Riddell Diaries*, 23 June 1914, p. 83.

70 In a letter to Venetia Stanley: Michael and Eleanor Brock (eds), *H.H. Asquith Letters to Venetia Stanley*, paperback edn (Oxford, 1985), 5 May 1914, p. 70.

71 Sir Bernard Mallet and C. Oswald George, *British Budgets: Second Series, 1913–14 to 1920–21* (London, 1929), p. 29.

72 Bruce Murray, '"Battered and Shattered": Lloyd George and the 1914 Budget Fiasco', *Albion* 23:3 (Fall 1991), pp. 483–507, pp. 493, 496.

73 Kenneth O. Morgan, *Lloyd George* (London, 1974), p. 78.

74 Gilbert, *Lloyd George: Organizer of Victory*, p. 84.

75 Ibid., p. 88.

76 Brock, *Asquith Letters to Stanley*, 18 June 1914, p. 89.

77 As Gilbert observes, the failure of Lloyd George's budget of 1914 was a clear demonstration that 'the government was tired and losing control of the party' (Gilbert, *Lloyd George: Organizer of Victory*, p. 91).

Chapter 10. A Nightmare World

1 Most useful have been the following: David E. Kaiser, 'Germany and the Origins of the First World War', *Journal of Modern History* 55 (September 1983), pp. 442–74; Geoff Eley, *From Unification to Nazism: Reinterpreting the German Past* (Boston, 1986), 'Introduction' recounts the author's personal journey into the thickets of German historiography;

Konrad H. Jarausch, 'Revising German History: Bethmann Hollweg Revisited', *Central European History* 21:3 (September, 1988), pp. 224–43; Roger Chickering (ed.), *Imperial Germany: A Historiographical Companion* (Westport, 1996); James Retallack, *Germany in the Age of Kaiser Wilhelm II* (London, 1996); David Stevenson, *Armaments and the Coming of War: Europe, 1904–1914* (Oxford, 1996); Volker R. Berghahn, 'The German Empire, 1871–1914: Reflections on the Direction of Recent Research', *Central European History* 35:1 (2002), pp. 75–81 and Margaret Lavinia Anderson, 'Reply to Volker Berghahn', *Central European History* 35:1 (2002), pp. 83–90; Gordon Martel, *The Origins of the First World War*), 3rd edn (Harlow, 2003). Other important reviews include two by Niall Ferguson. In the first, 'Germany and the Origins of the First World War: New Perspectives', *Historical Journal* 35:3 (1992), pp. 725–52, Ferguson argues that Germany went to war in part because German military leaders felt weak, not strong. In both economic support and military manpower, the German army was falling behind the other powers. Thus, they were inclined to act preemptively in 1914. In his 'Public Finance and National Security: The Domestic Origins of the First World War Revisited', *Past and Present* 142 (1994), pp. 141–68, Ferguson recapitulates his earlier argument, with a special emphasis on Germany's fiscal policy which shortchanged defence spending, limiting the size of the German military *vis-à-vis* other European powers. Had Germany spent more, it would have felt 'less strategically insecure' and hence less willing to initiate war (p. 143). The most recent review of historians' treatment of the causes of World War I makes the plea for an integrated treatment of both 'decision-makers' and structural (or environmental) causes of the war: see Talbot C. Imlay, 'The Origins of the First World War', *Historical Journal* 49:4 (2006), pp. 1253–71.

2   Volker Berghahn's *Germany and the Approach of War in 1914*, 2nd edn (New York, 1993), passim, informs the following discussion.

3   Ibid., p. 41.

4   Ibid., p. 52.

5   Ibid., p. 76.

6   See Michael Eckstein, 'Great Britain and the Triple Entente on the Eve of the Sarajevo Crisis', in Hinsley: *British Foreign Policy under Sir Edward Grey*, p. 342.

7   John M. MacKenzie, *Propaganda and Empire: The Manipulation of British Public Opinion, 1880–1960* (Manchester, 1984). See also Anne Summers, 'Militarism in Britain before the Great War', *History Workshop* 2 (Autumn 1976), pp. 104–23. Summers notes 'the tremendous upsurge of interest in things military in Edwardian Britain' (p. 111). Summers's chapter, 'The Character of Edwardian Nationalism: Three Popular Leagues', in Paul Kennedy and Anthony Nicholls (eds), *Nationalist and Racialist Movements in Britain and Germany before 1914* ((London, 1981), examines particularly the Navy League and the National Service League: the Tariff Reform League rounds out the trio. Frans Coetzee, *For Party or Country: Nationalism and the Dilemmas of Popular Conservatism in Edwardian England* (New York, 1990) traces the rise of right-wing patriotic leagues and their influence, especially upon the Conservative Party. Michael Blanch characterizes the years from the Boer War to World War I as 'the heyday of popular nationalism and imperialism' (Blanch, 'Imperialism, Nationalism and Organized Youth', in J. Clarke, C. Critcher and R. Johnson (eds), *Working Class Culture: Studies in History and Theory* (New York, 1979), p. 104). Blanch examines particularly the diffusion of imperialist and nationalist ideas in Birmingham and Manchester through such organizations as Boys' Brigades, Girls' Life Brigades, and scouting.

8   G.R. Searle, *The Quest for National Efficiency: A Study in British Politics and Political Thought, 1899–1914*, paperback edn (London, 1990), esp. chs 2 and 3.

9   As Searle notes, Germany served in the 'dual role of model and enemy: a state whose threat to vital British interests could be fended off only through an adoption of her own methods and institutions' (ibid., p. 57). Searle rightly points out, however, that there were significant opponents of the national efficiency movement and of the German model: chief among these was the radical wing of the Liberal Party: see ibid., pp. 101–6.

10 Colin Nicolson, 'Edwardian England and the Coming of the First World War', in Alan O'Day (ed.), *The Edwardian Age: Conflict and Stability 1900–1914* (Hamden, 1979), pp. 162, 155.

11 Samuel R. Williamson Jr, *The Politics of Grand Strategy: Britain and France Prepare for War, 1904–1914* (Cambridge, 1969), p. 352.

12 Nicolson, 'Edwardian England and the Coming of the First World War', p. 153.

13 Williamson, 'The Origins of World War I', *Journal of Interdisciplinary History* 18:4 (Spring 1988), pp. 795–818, p. 814.

14 Keith Wilson, 'Grey', in Keith Wilson (ed.), *British Foreign Secretaries and Foreign Policy: From Crimean War to First World War* (London, 1987), ch. 7.

15 Zara S. Steiner, *Britain and the Origins of the First World War* (New York, 1977), p. 227 and ch. 9, 'The July Crisis', passim.

16 Michael G. Fry, *Lloyd George and Foreign Policy*, vol. 1, *The Education of a Statesman: 1890–1916* (Montreal, 1977), p. 188.

17 Stephen J. Valone, '"There Must Be Some Misunderstanding": Sir Edward Grey's Diplomacy of August 1, 1914', *Journal of British Studies* 27 (October 1988), pp. 405–24.

18 Keith Robbins, *Sir Edward Grey: A Biography of Lord Grey of Fallodon* (London, 1971), pp. 287–95.

19 Randolph S. Churchill, *Winston S. Churchill*, Companion vol. 2, *Part 3, 1911–1914* (Boston, 1969), 28 July 1914, p. 1989.

20 The following discussion of Cabinet proceedings owes much to Cameron Hazlehurst's detailed analysis in his *Politicians at War: July 1914 to May 1915: A Prologue to the Triumph of Lloyd George* (New York, 1971), Part I, chs 2–9; and to K.M. Wilson, 'The Cabinet Diary of J.A. Pease, 24 July–5 August 1914', *Proceedings of the Leeds Philosophical and Literary Society, Literary and Historical Section* 19, part 3 (March 1983), pp. 39–51. Pease was then the President of the Board of Education, a leading Quaker spokesman, and an active member of the National Peace Society.

21 Parliamentary Archives, SAM/7/157/691, 29 July 1914. Samuel was then President of the Local Government Board.

22 Keith Wilson, 'The Cabinet Diary of J.A. Pease, 24 July–5 August 1914', *Proceedings of the Leeds Philosophical and Literary Society, Literary and Historical Section* 19, part 3 (March 1983), pp. 39–51, p. 43.

23 See Michael and Eleanor Brock (eds), *H.H. Asquith Letters to Venetia Stanley*, paperback edn (Oxford, 1985), 29 July 1914, p. 132.

24 Wilson, 'Diary of Pease', p. 44.

25 As recounted by Arthur J. Marder, *From the* Dreadnought *to Scapa Flow: The Royal Navy in the Fisher Era, 1904–1919*, vol. 1, *The Road to War, 1904–1914* (London, 1961), p. 433.

26 Brock, *Asquith Letters to Stanley*, 30 July 1914, p. 136.

27 Pease tersely noted in his diary: 'Policy we agreed to: British opinion would not now enable us to support France …' (Wilson, 'Diary of Pease', 31 July 1914, p. 45).

28 As Hazlehurst has termed the peace party: see ch. 5 in his *Politicians at War*, esp. pp. 54–5.

29 Wilson, 'Diary of Pease', 2 August 1914, p. 46.

30 Ibid., p. 47.

31 Confiding to Miss Stanley later that day, Asquith wrote that the Cabinet had been 'on the brink of a split' (Brock, *Asquith Letters to Stanley*, 2 August 1914, p. 146).

32 Parliamentary Archives, SAM/7/157/697, 2 August 1914.

33 Hazlehurst, *Politicians at War*, pp. 93–4, quoting from the Runciman Papers.

34 Major-General Sir Charles E. Callwell, *Field-Marshall Sir Henry Wilson: His Life and Diaries*, 2 vols (London, 1927), excerpt from Wilson's diary entry of 31 July 1914, vol. 1, p. 152.

35 A detailed account of the Conservative letter may be found in Sir Austen Chamberlain, *Down the Years* (London, 1935), ch. 5, 'When War Came'. Chamberlain remembers himself as taking an important role in spurring the Conservative leadership to action. However, Blake believes that the letter 'did little beyond recording the Conservative attitude' and was not instrumental in the decision by the government to declare war two days later. See Robert Blake, *The Unknown Prime Minister: The Life and Times of Andrew Bonar Law, 1858–1923* (London, 1955), p. 223. Adams is in general agreement, although he allows that 'in some small way' the letter may have eased the minds of both Conservative and Liberal interventionists (Adams: *Bonar Law*, p. 171). K.M. Wilson, however, believes that the Conservative letter was an additional argument that Grey could use to drum up support for France in his pursuit of an interventionist policy. See Wilson, 'The British Cabinet's Decision for War, 2 August 1914', *British Journal for International Studies* I (1975), pp. 148–59, p. 151. This article also appears in a somewhat revised version in Wilson's *The Policy of the Entente: Essays on the Determinants of British Foreign Policy, 1904–1914* (Cambridge, 1985) as ch. 8, 'The Cabinet's Decision for War, 1914'.

36 Brock, *Asquith Letters to Stanley*, 3 August 1914, p. 148.

37 This summary is taken from the reprint of the speech from *Hansard*, to be found in Sir Edward Grey, *Speeches on Foreign Affairs, 1904–1914*, selected by Paul Knaplund (London, 1931), pp. 297–315.

38 Ibid., p. 302.

39 Ibid., p. 303.

40 Ibid., p. 304.

41 Ibid., p. 309.

42 Ibid., p. 311.

43 Ibid., p. 313.

44 As G.M. Trevelyan notes in his biography, *Grey of Fallodon* (London, 1948), p. 266.

45 Herbert Samuel remembered, more than three decades later, that 'Lloyd George's attitude had been doubtful throughout' (Rt Hon. Viscount Samuel, *Memoirs* (London, 1945), p. 103).

46 Edward David (ed.), *Inside Asquith's Cabinet: From the Diaries of Charles Hobhouse* (New York, 1977), undated August entry, p. 179.

47 Frances Lloyd George, *The Years That Are Past* (London, 1967), p. 73.

48 John Grigg, *Lloyd George: From Peace to War, 1912–1916* (London, 1985), p. 140.

49 Jenkins notes that Asquith's major objective was to keep the Cabinet united and that Lloyd George was 'the key to this objective' (Roy Jenkins, *Asquith* (London, 1964), p. 326). Koss agrees: Lloyd George was 'the crucial figure' to Cabinet coherence (Stephen Koss, *Asquith*, paperback edn (New York, 1985), p. 156).

50 A.J. Anthony Morris, *Radicalism Against War, 1906–1914: The Advocacy of Peace and Retrenchment* (Totowa, 1972), ch. 10, passim. See also Howard S. Weinroth, 'The British Radicals and the Balance of Power, 1902–1914', *Historical Journal* 13:4 (December 1970), pp. 653–82 and Morris, *Radicalism against War*, pp. 191–3.

51 Trevor Wilson (ed.), *The Political Diaries of C.P. Scott, 1911–1928* (Ithaca, 1970), 27 July 1914, p. 93.

52 Marvin Swartz, 'A Study in Futility: The British Radicals at the Outbreak of the First World War', in A.J.A. Morris (ed.), *Edwardian Radicalism, 1900–1914: Some Aspects of British Radicalism* (Manchester, 1974), ch. 15. Ponsonby's views on Lloyd George had long been ambivalent. In a characterization dating from 1907, he observed that although Lloyd George's instincts were true, 'he would not be above scheming to keep his position'. There was also in Lloyd George 'a breathless eagerness to keep up the crescendo of fame'. Yet he was 'a real democrat, full of humanity, with great charm and originality' (Raymond A. Jones, *Arthur Ponsonby: The Politics of Life* (London, 1989), pp. 80–1).

53 Sources confirming the military briefing include Callwell, *Sir Henry Wilson*, vol. 1, p. 154; Nicolson, 'Edwardian England and the Coming of the First World War', p. 158; and Fry, *Lloyd George and Foreign Policy*, vol. 1, pp. 210–1.

54 Churchill, *Churchill*, Companion Vol. 2, *Part 3, 1911–1914*, 1 August 1914, pp. 1996–7.

55 John Viscount Morley, *Memorandum on Resignation, August 1914* (New York, 1928), p. 24.

56 Morris, *Radicalism Against the War*, pp. 390–1.

57 Wilson, 'Diary of Pease', 2 Aug. 1914, p. 46.

58 Viscount John Morley, *Memorandum on Resignation, August 1914* (New York, 1928), pp. 15, 16.

59 Ibid., p. 16.

60 Ibid., p. 20.

61 Brock, *Asquith Letters to Stanley*, 1 August 1914, p. 140. The following day – also in a letter to Venetia – Asquith estimated that 'a good ¾ of our own party in the H. of Commons are for absolute non-interference at any price' (ibid., 2 August 1914, p. 146).

62 John McEwen, *The Riddell Diaries, 1908–1923* (London, 1986), 2 August 1914, p. 87. Also present were Simon, Masterman and Ramsay MacDonald. Riddell's diary entry claims MacDonald agreed with Lloyd George that Germany's violation of Belgium neutrality would be a legitimate reason for a British declaration of war (ibid., 2 August 1914, p. 87). David Marquand, however, thinks it 'highly unlikely' that MacDonald ever made such a statement, given his anti-war position (Marquand, *Ramsay MacDonald* (London, 1977), p. 820, n. 2). MacDonald's diary had only a laconic reference to the meeting: 'Masterman jingo, George ruffled, Simon broken' (cited ibid., p. 164).

63 Wilson, 'Diary of Pease', 3 August 1914, p. 48.

64 Ibid., 3 August 1914, p. 88. Apparently, on 1 August Lloyd George had received a letter from Nicoll that stated that he and the Free Churches 'would strongly oppose any war'. After Riddell's conversation with Nicoll, however, the *British Weekly* printed an article by Nicoll supporting the war (see ibid., 9 August 1914, pp. 88–9).

65 Ibid., 12 July 1914, p. 84.

66 Morley's reflections may be found in his *Memorandum on Resignation*, p. 20.

67 Wilson, 'British Cabinet's Decision for War', 154–5 and *Policy of the Entente*, pp. 140–2.

68 Keith Wilson, 'Britain', in Keith Wilson (ed.), *Decisions for War 1914* (New York, 1995), esp. pp. 181–2.

69 Bentley Brinkerhoff Gilbert, 'Pacifist to Interventionist: David Lloyd George in 1911 and 1914. Was Belgium an Issue?' *Historical Journal* 28:4 (December 1985), pp. 863–85, pp. 885 and 882. Gilbert softens 'double game' to 'game' in his *David Lloyd George: A Political Life*, vol. 2: *Organizer of Victory 1912–16* (Columbus, 1992), p. 110.

70 Hazlehurst, *Politicians at War*, pp. 66, 68.

71 J. Paul Harris, 'Great Britain', in Richard F. Hamilton and Holger H. Herwig (eds), *The Origins of World War I* (Cambridge, 2003), pp. 294, 299.

72 Fry, *Lloyd George and Foreign Policy*, vol. 1, p. 203.

73 Kenneth O. Morgan, *Lloyd George* (London, 1974), p. 81.

74 For these comments, see John Vincent (ed.), *The Crawford Papers: The Journals of David Lindsay, Twenty-Seventh Earl of Crawford and Tenth Earl of Balcarres during the years 1892 to 1940* (Manchester, 1984), 3 and 4 August 1914, p. 340.

Chapter 11. 'The Righteousness That Exalteth a Nation'

1 Teresa Seabourne, 'The Summer of 1914', in Forest Capie and Geoffrey E. Wood (eds), *Financial Crises and the World Banking System* (New York, 1986), ch. 3 passim. See also Bentley Brinkerhoff Gilbert, *David Lloyd George: A Political Life*, vol. 2: *Organizer of Victory 1912–16* (Columbus, 1992), pp. 113–6.

2 See A.W. Kirkaldy, *British Finance During and After the War, 1914–21* (London, 1921), chs 1–3; and R.S. Sayers, *The Bank of England, 1891–1944*, vol. 1 (Cambridge, 1976), pp. 66–78.

3 One canny contemporary observer criticized those joint stock bank managers who acted selfishly and short-sightedly by hoarding money they had called in from the City: see John Maynard Keynes, 'War and the Financial System, August, 1914', *Economic Journal* 24 (September 1914), pp. 460–86, esp. pp. 471–6.

4 E. Victor Morgan, *Studies in British Financial Policy, 1914–25* (London, 1952), p. 11; and more generally, ch. 1, 'The Crisis of 1914'.

5 The extension of the Bank Holiday had two aims: to allow time for the preparation of the emergency paper currency and to provide an opportunity for consultation among the financial experts.

6 John Vincent (ed.), *The Crawford Papers: The Journals of David Lindsay, Twenty-Seventh Earl of Crawford and Tenth Earl of Balcarres during the years 1892 to 1940* (Manchester, 1984), 11 August 1914, p. 342.

7 Edward David (ed.), *Inside Asquith's Cabinet: From the Diaries of Charles Hobhouse* (New York, 1977), 21 August 1914, p. 182. Runciman had recently been moved from his position as President of the Board of Agriculture to the Board of Trade upon the resignation of John Burns. Hobhouse by then had become Postmaster-General in the Cabinet.

8 Hartley Withers, *War and Lombard Street* (London, 1916), p. 36. For Lloyd George's role during the August crisis, see also Kathleen Burk, 'The Treasury: from Impotence to Power', in Kathleen Burk (ed.), *War and the State: The Transformation of British Government 1914–1919* (London, 1982), ch. 4, passim.

9 William George, *My Brother and I* (London, 1958), 13 August 1914, pp. 248–9.

10 Kenneth O. Morgan (ed.), *Lloyd George: Family Letters, 1885–1936* (Cardiff and London, 1973), 7 August 1914, p. 168.

11 For the background and technical aspects of the war risk insurance plan, see Sir Norman Hill, 'State Insurance Against War Risks at Sea', pp. 11–53 in *War and Insurance* (London, 1927) – one of the volumes in the estimable *Economic and Social History of the World War, British Series* published by the Carnegie Endowment for International Peace.

12 Cameron Hazlehurst, *Politicians at War: July 1914 to May 1915: A Prologue to the Triumph of Lloyd George* (New York, 1971), p. 173.

13 Christopher Addison, *Four and a Half Years: A Personal Diary from June 1914 to January 1919*, vol. 1 (London, 1934), 4 August 1914, p. 33. Addison was a medical doctor and a prominent social reformer who was to serve in Lloyd George's government as Minister of Munitions, 1916–17; Minister of Reconstruction, 1917–19; Minister of Health, 1919–21; and Minister without Portfolio, 1921. He later joined the Labour Party, and became Leader of the House of Lords. He was created Baron (1937) and Viscount (1945). See his

biography by Kenneth Morgan and Jane Morgan, *Portrait of a Progressive: The Political Career of Christopher, Viscount Addison* (Oxford, 1980).

14 The budget summary may be found in John Grigg, *Lloyd George: From Peace to War, 1912–1916* (London, 1985), pp. 187–9: he finds the budget was 'on the whole well received' (ibid., p. 189). Gilbert (*Lloyd George: Organizer of Victory*, p. 139) thinks the budget 'an unadventurous affair', even 'remarkably pedestrian'. Hew Strachan, however, believes that the taxation provisions of the budget were significant in financing the war; and that none of the other belligerents had such an effective form of wartime income tax. See Hew Strachan, *Financing the First World War* (Oxford, 2004), pp. 63–71.

15 Sir Bernard Mallet and George, C. Oswald, *British Budgets: Second Series, 1913–14 to 1920–21* (London, 1929), p. 44.

16 Robert B. Asprey, *The First Battle of the Marne* (Philadelphia, 1962), p. 99. A more recent account of the battle, briefly told, may be found in Hunt Tooley, *The Western Front: Battle Ground and Home Front in the First World War* (Houndmills, Hants, 2003), pp. 65–73.

17 So Grigg suggests in *Lloyd George: From Peace to War*, p. 169.

18 In a letter to Margaret: see Morgan, *Lloyd George: Family Letters*, 10 September 1914, p. 172.

19 See *The Times*, 20 September 1914 for the quotations that follow.

20 Martin Pugh, *Lloyd George*, paperback edn (London, 1988), p. 79.

21 As Kenneth O. Morgan, *Lloyd George* (London, 1974), pp. 82–83 and Grigg, *Lloyd George: From Peace to War*, pp. 167–8 have noted. Frances Stevenson reported that Lloyd George was at first depressed about the speech, but the overwhelmingly favourable newspaper response buoyed him up. See A.J.P. Taylor, *Lloyd George: A Diary by Frances Stevenson* (London, 1971), 21 September 1914, p. 2. This is the first entry of Stevenson's famous diary.

22 For Griggs's analysis, see *Lloyd George: From Peace to War*, pp. 169–74.

23 John McEwen, *The Riddell Diaries, 1908–1923* (London, 1986), 25 August 1914, p. 89.

24 *The Times*, 20 September 1914.

25 Gilbert, *Lloyd George: Organizer of Victory 1912–16*, p. 123. Gilbert goes further: by appointing Kitchener, he writes, Asquith had created 'a glittering political monster who neither could be controlled nor killed' (ibid., p. 123).

26 Grigg, *Lloyd George: From Peace to War*, p. 157.

27 Pugh, *Lloyd George*, p. 78.

28 George H. Cassar, *Kitchener's War: British Strategy from 1914 to 1916* (Washington, 2004), ch. 2, passim.

29 It was said that the Cabinet 'burst into laughter' when Churchill's telegram was read out to them (Geoffrey Best, *Churchill and War* (Hambledon, 2005), p. 53). Asquith thought the request for military rank and command 'a real bit of tragic-comedy' (Michael and Eleanor Brock (eds), *H.H. Asquith Letters to Venetia Stanley*, paperback edn (Oxford, 1985), 5 October 1914, p. 262). Sir Almeric Fitzroy condemned Churchill's 'characteristic impetuosity' (Sir Almeric William Fitzroy, *Memoirs*, vol. 2 (London, 1928), 9 October 1914, p. 573). Historians generally agree with these criticisms. Roy Jenkins seems amused that Churchill was simply 'enjoying himself' as he was 'swept along' by the opportunity to conduct 'a little war of his own' (Roy Jenkins, *Churchill: A Biography*, paperback edn (New York, 2002), p. 250). Martin Gilbert notes that Churchill's 'Antwerp blunder' became 'a butt of Conservative derision' (Martin Gilbert, *Churchill: A Life*, paperback edn (New York, 1991), p. 286). But Gilbert also believes that Churchill's mission, by engaging the Germans for an additional few days, gave added time for British forces to regroup in Flanders.

30 These quotations are from Hobhouse's diary (David, *Inside Asquith's Cabinet*, 28 October 1914, p. 204). Hobhouse noted additionally that everyone in the Cabinet sided with Lloyd George and the General 'got a great rebuff'. Hobhouse concluded his account with a terse comment – that the Prime Minister throughout the contentious meeting was 'very silent'. Perhaps Asquith was distracted, possibly framing his letter to Miss Stanley, to whom he confided that the Cabinet had witnessed 'a royal row' between Kitchener and Lloyd George. Asquith believed that Kitchener was 'much the most to blame: he was clumsy & noisy …' (Brock, *Asquith Letters to Stanley*, 28 Oct. 1914, p. 291).

31 As Simkins observes, Kitchener's 'reluctance to accept alternative administrative machinery for the direction and supervision of munitions production … limited the ability of industry to respond in full to the demands of war' (Peter Simkins, *Kitchener's Army: The Raising of the New Armies, 1914–1916* (Manchester, 1988), p. 128).

32 Vincent, *Crawford Papers*, 11 October 1914, pp. 343–4.

33 McEwen, *Riddell Diaries*, 19 November 1914, p. 95. Riddell's informant was Reginald Herbert Brade, Permanent Secretary at the War Office.

34 Hazlehurst, *Politicians at War*, p. 15.

35 These guns, as R.J.Q. Adams notes, were the backbone of the British artillery (R.J.Q. Adams, *Arms and the Wizard: Lloyd George and the Ministry of Munitions, 1915–1916* (College Station, 1978), pp. 18–9).

36 David, *Inside Asquith's Cabinet*, 8 October 1914, p. 196.

37 Ibid., 9 October 1914, p. 197.

38 Adams, *Arms and the Wizard*, p. 19.

39 Morgan, *Lloyd George: Family Letters*, 20 October 1914, p. 173.

40 Lloyd George's actions considerably vexed von Donop, who suggested through an intermediary that the Chancellor of the Exchequer would be well advised to stick to financial matters. For an account of this episode, see Gilbert, *Lloyd George: Organizer of Victory*, pp. 126–7.

41 Lloyd George was quite pleased at the appointment. To his brother, William, he wrote: 'P.M. has appointed a *secret* War Council to consider all questions bearing on the War. I am on it. Glad of that' (NLW, William George Papers, 2882, 24 November 1914).

42 Parliamentary Archives, LG/C/4/5/5, 9 March 1915. Within a few months, Derby was to become Director General of Recruiting.

43 See Gilbert's account in his *Lloyd George: Organizer of Victory*, pp. 151–71.

44 Trade unions were naturally offended by the implications of Lloyd George's remarks. Indeed, John Greenaway thinks that Lloyd George's anti-drink campaign went too far in casting blame upon workers. The effect was to create a classic example of moral panic, stirring up a kind 'public hysteria' on the drink question (John Greenaway, *Drink and British Politics since 1830: A Study in Policy-making* (Basingstoke, 2003), pp. 92, 97). But Lloyd George never wavered in his attempts to justify his anti-drink campaign. In his *War Memoirs*, published more than two decades later, he claimed that the 'first effect of the War' was 'to increase the habit of excessive drinking … a real menace to the nation'. He cited as evidence a report from the Shipbuilding Employers' Federation which was 'unanimous' in urging that the sale of liquor 'should be totally prohibited'. The Federation illustrated its case by citing the example of a battleship entering port in need of immediate repair, but having those repairs 'delayed a whole day by the absence of the riveters though drink and conviviality'. The Federation claimed that this case was illustrative of 'hundreds' of others. See David Lloyd George, *War Memoirs*, new edn, vol. 1 (London, n.d. [1939?]), pp. 193–4.

45 George, *My Brother and I*, p. 250.

46 See Hazlehurst, *Politicians at War*, Part II, ch. 12, 'Another Little Drink'.

47 For these comments to Miss Stanley, see Brock, *Asquith Letters to Stanley*, 25 March 1915, p. 508; and 31 March 1915, p. 525.

48 Ibid., 8 April 1915, p. 536.

49 See John Turner, 'State Purchase of the Liquor Trade in the First World War', *Historical Journal* 23:3 (September 1980), pp. 589–615, p. 591. Turner notes further that over-investment in licensed property, obsolescent brewing facilities and the steady decline of beer drinking all played a role in the brewers' receptivity to such a scheme.

50 Morgan, *Lloyd George: Family Letters*, 16 April 1915, p. 176.

51 Under the terms of the Act, the Central Control Board (Liquor Traffic) was created with the powers of control over the sale and consumption of alcohol. Members were appointed by the newly created Minister of Munitions, who by then was Lloyd George himself. For the work of this Board in discouraging alcohol consumption during the war, see Michael E. Rose, 'The Success of Social Reform: The Central Control Board (Liquor Traffic) 1915–21', in M.F.D. Foot (ed.), *War and Society: Historical Essays in Honour and Memory of J.R. Western, 1928–1971* (London, 1973), ch. 5.

52 See the account of the budget debate in Sir Josiah Stamp, *Taxation During the War* (London, 1932), esp. pp. 35–6.

53 F.W. Hirst and J.E. Allen, *British War Budgets* (London, 1926), p. 47. Hirst and Allen note additionally that the alcohol taxes 'were coldly received' (p. 37).

54 Ibid., p. 48.

55 Mallet and George, *British Budgets, Second Series*, p. 67.

56 Grigg, *Lloyd George: From Peace to War*, p. 238.

57 Gilbert, *Lloyd George: Organizer of Victory*, p. 171.

58 Martin Daunton, *Just Taxes: The Politics of Taxation in Britain, 1914–1979* (Cambridge, 2002), pp. 38–40.

59 Adrian Gregory believes that Lloyd George was 'playing to the nonconformist gallery' on the drink question (*The Last Great War: British Society and the First World War*, paperback edn (Cambridge, 2008), p. 96).

60 Lord Beaverbrook, *Politicians and the War, 1914–1916*, one-volume edn (London, 1960), pp. 65, 78 and more generally ch. 6, 'Drink and the Devil'.

61 For a critique of the historical accuracy of *Politicians and the War*, see John O. Stubbs, 'Beaverbrook as Historian: 'Politicians and the War, 1914–1916' Reconsidered', *Albion* 14 (1982), pp. 235–53. Even more critical is Peter Fraser, 'Lord Beaverbrook's Fabrications in *Politicians and the War, 1914–1916*', *Historical Journal* 25:1 (1982), pp. 147–66.

62 Frank Owen, *Tempestuous Journey: Lloyd George and his Times* (London, 1954), p. 284.

63 Grigg, *Lloyd George: From Peace to War*, p. 231.

64 Morgan, *Lloyd George*, p. 84.

65 Robert Blake, *The Unknown Prime Minister: The Life and Times of Andrew Bonar Law, 1858–1923* (London, 1955), pp. 239–40.

66 R.J.Q. Adams, *Bonar Law* (London, 1999), p. 179.

67 Gilbert, *Lloyd George: Organizer of Victory*, p. 164.

68 Turner, 'State Purchase of the Liquor Trade', p. 595. Turner reiterates this point in his *British Politics and the Great War: Conciliation and Conflict, 1915–1918* (New Haven, 1992), where he notes that the purpose of the drink campaign was 'to soften up traditional Liberal supporters for the extension of state control by creating a sense of emergency' (p. 60).

69 David French, *British Economic and Strategic Planning, 1905–1915* (London, 1982), p. 159.

70 Ibid., p. 160.

71 Given at Bangor in his own constituency: see *The Times*, 1 March 1915.

72 With his open confession that the necessities of war could trump perhaps even civil liberties, Lloyd George's speech may well have been unsettling to some Liberals. But other Liberals, such as C.P. Scott of the *Manchester Guardian*, applauded its tone. Scott believed that the nation must be 'marshalled and regimented for service'. As a part of that regimentation, Scott thought that the country was 'perfectly prepared for a little compulsory temperance'. For these two quotations, see Trevor Wilson (ed.), *The Political Diaries of C.P. Scott, 1911–1928* (Ithaca, 1970), pp. 121–2.

73 Chris Wrigley, *David Lloyd George and the British Labour Movement: Peace and War* (Hassocks, 1976), p. 109.

74 Reginald Pound and Geoffrey Harmsworth, *Northcliffe* (New York, 1960), pp. 472–81.

75 As Jenkins puts it, Churchill's 'strategic restlessness' drove him forward (Jenkins, *Churchill*, p. 254).

76 David French, 'The Origins of the Dardanelles Campaign Reconsidered', *History* 68 (June 1983), p. 210.

77 See Trevor Wilson, *The Myriad Faces of War: Britain and the Great War 1914–1918* (London, 1986), chs 11 and 13.

78 The most recent accounts are Edward J. Erickson, 'Strength Against Weakness: Ottoman Military Effectiveness at Gallipoli, 1915' *Journal of Military History* 65:4 (October 2001), pp. 981–1011; Tim Travers, *Gallipoli 1915*, paperback edn (Stroud, 2004); and Erickson's, *Ottoman Army Effectiveness in World War I: A Comparative Study* (London, 2007), ch. 2, 'Gallipoli'. Both Travers and Erickson use Turkish sources.

79 For the fundamental errors of the naval operation, see Arthur J. Marder, *From the Dardanelles to Oran: Studies of the Royal Navy in War and Peace, 1915–1940* (London, 1974), ch. 1.

80 Eilot A. Cohen and John Gooch, *Military Misfortunes: The Anatomy of Failure in War* (New York, 1990), pp. 137–8.

81 Wilson (*Myriad Faces of War*, p. 132) notes that the Gallipoli peninsula was 'a defender's dream' with its steep hills above the short and shallow beaches onto which the invasion troops crowded.

82 McEwen, *Riddell Diaries*, 13 March 1915, p. 102.

83 Ibid., 24 April 1915, p. 109. The press had also been quick to compare Lloyd George's Bangor speech with Asquith's at Newcastle – to the latter's disadvantage (Stephen Koss, *Asquith*, paperback edn (New York, 1985), p. 181).

84 Taylor, *Stevenson Diary*, 15 May 1915, pp. 49–50.

85 As Adams notes in his *Bonar Law*, p. 180.

86 Hazlehurst believes that the evidence is inconclusive as to whether Lloyd George or Bonar Law was the first to propose coalition (Hazlehurst, *Politicians at War*, p. 233). For Hazlehurst's account of the formation of the coalition, see ibid., Part III, 'A National Government', pp. 227–82.

87 Asquith would have been the logical choice for Bonar Law's expostulation; but the two were not on such friendly terms as Law and Lloyd George. The following accounts of the construction of the coalition government follow mainly Adams, *Bonar Law*, pp. 184–8; Gilbert, *Lloyd George: Organizer of Victory*, 192–207; Grigg, *Lloyd George: From Peace to War*, pp. 248–55; and Peter Fraser, 'British War Policy and the Crisis of Liberalism in May 1915', *Journal of Modern History* 54:1 (March 1982), pp. 1–26.

88 A copy may be found in the Parliamentary Archives, LG/C/17/5/1, 17 May 1915.

89 Addison, *Four and a Half Years*, 17 May 1915, p. 78.

90 NLW, William George Papers, 2936, 17 May 1915.

91 Churchill survived removal from the Cabinet entirely only 'by the skin of his teeth', according to Fitzroy, *Memoirs*, vol. 2, 26 May 1915, p. 595.

92 See Koss's discussion of the restructuring of the Cabinet in his *Asquith*, pp. 189–92.

93 For Hobhouse's views, see David, *Inside Aquith's Cabinet*, 17–27 May 1915, pp. 243–7.

94 Addison, *Four and a Half Years*, 19 May 1915, p. 80.

95 NLW, William George Papers, 2938, 19 May 1915.

96 Roy Jenkins, *Asquith* (London, 1964), p. 360.

97 Brock, *Asquith Letters to Stanley*, p. 599. Brock notes further that it was just as well his relationship with Stanley ended: it had become an 'obsession'. Peter Clarke believes, however, that both Asquith and Lloyd George had relations 'with women half their age' as 'a release from political tension' (Peter Clarke, 'Asquith and Lloyd George Revisited', in J.M.W. Bean (ed.), *The Political Culture of Modern Britain: Studies in Memory of Stephen Koss* (London, 1987), ch. 8).

98 Quoted from MacCallum Scott's diary by Martin Pugh, 'Asquith, Bonar Law, and the First Coalition', *The Historical Journal* 17:4 (December 1974), pp. 813–36 p. 818. MacCallum Scott was Liberal MP for Bridgeton, Glasgow, from 1910–22. He served later as Parliamentary Private Secretary to Churchill from 1917–9. In 1924 he joined the Labour Party.

99 For his analysis, see Koss, *Asquith*, pp. 185–7. It is, of course, entirely possible that Asquith presented different faces to different audiences during the May crisis. In any case, as Koss notes, Asquith soon enough found new feminine confidantes to whom he wrote with equal 'frequency, ardour, and indiscretion' (Koss, *Asquith*, p. 187).

100 For these quotations, see W.A.S. Hewins, *The Apologia of an Imperialist: Forty Years of Empire Policy*, vol. 2 (London, 1929), 15 October 1914, 5 and 6 May 1915, p. 29.

101 Blake, *Unknown Prime Minister*, p. 243.

102 David Dutton, *'His Majesty's Loyal Opposition': The Unionist Party in Opposition 1905–1915* (Liverpool, 1992), p. 290.

103 In a letter to his mistress, Mrs Winifred Bennett, 21 September 1915 (cited in George H. Cassar, *The Tragedy of Sir John French* (Cranbury, 1985), p. 261).

104 Cited in Robin Prior and Trevor Wilson, *Command on the Western Front: The Military Career of Sir Henry Rawlinson, 1914–18*, paperback edn (Barnsley, 2004), diary entry of 20 August 1915, p. 105.

105 Gary Sheffield and John Bourne (eds), *Douglas Haig War Diaries and Letters, 1914–1918* (London, 2005), 19 August 1915, p. 137.

106 Elements of the French Army had used gas against the Germans as early as 1914. See Ulrich Trumpener, 'The Road to Ypres: The Beginnings of Gas Warfare in World War I', *Journal of Modern History* 47:3 (September 1975), pp. 460–80, esp. pp. 461–3. This seems to belie Donald Richter's claim that the Germans 'did it first' (Richter, *Chemical Soldiers: British Gas Warfare in World War I* (Lawrence, 1992), ch. 1.

107 Historical opinion of the British command since the battle has been largely unfavourable. Wilson thinks that Loos was at best a 'military curate's egg' – good in parts by gaining some ground – but overall it had achieved little (Wilson, *Myriad Faces of War*, ch. 23, 'Loos and After': the quotation at p. 256). J.P. Harris blames General Haig for the losses: his principal planning and execution of the offensive proved 'much bloodier and more self–destructive than was really necessary' (J.P. Harris, *Douglas Haig and the First World War* (Cambridge, 2008), ch. 7, 'The Battle of Loos', quotation at p. 177).

108 NLW, William George Papers, 2983, 30 September 1915.

109 Ibid., 2986, 9 October 1915.

110 Lloyd George, *War Memoirs*, vol. 1, p. 362.

111 As Robert Rhodes James has it in his *Gallipoli* (New York, 1965), p. 350.

112 Travers, *Gallipoli*, p. 305.

113 'To his discredit', thinks Koss (*Asquith*, p. 173). In addition, Jenkins observes that Asquith 'never thought it his duty to impose strategic decisions upon the service chiefs' (*Asquith*, p. 350). Nor did Asquith act upon his own knowledge when promoting to high command doubtful candidates. Once describing General Hamilton as having 'too much feather in his brain' (Brock, *Asquith Letters to Stanley*, 30 September 1914, p. 257), Asquith nevertheless appointed him as commander of the military expedition to Gallipoli. Violet Asquith relayed the news of Hamilton's appointment to Rupert Brooke, who was in the Royal Naval Division bound for Gallipoli (Mark Pottle, *Champion Redoubtable: The Diaries and Letters of Violet Bonham Carter, 1914–1945*, paperback edn (London, 1999), 12 March 1915, p. 32). Brooke died six weeks later of septicemia aboard a French hospital ship while en route.

114 Best, *Churchill and War*, p. 56.

115 Martin Gilbert, *Churchill: A Life*, paperback edn (New York, 1991), p. 320.

116 Grigg, *Lloyd George: From Peace to War*, p. 200.

117 David R. Woodward, *Lloyd George and the Generals* (Newark, 1983), p. 41, quoting from the War Council minutes of 24 February 1915, CAB 42/1/42.

118 Lloyd George, *War Memoirs*, vol. 1, p. 235.

119 Ibid., pp. 235–6.

120 For the following, see A.J. Barker's colourful account, *The Neglected War: Mesopotamia, 1914–1918* (London, 1967), chs 1–13; and John S. Galbraith, 'No Man's Child: The Campaign in Mesopotamia, 1914–1916', *The International History Review* 6:3 (August 1984), pp. 358–85. Paul K. Davis, *Ends and Means: The British Mesopotamian Campaign and Commission* (Cranbury, 1994), is highly critical not only of the 'almost hopeless turmoil' (p. 112) in the British chain of command, but also of the 'ignorance' (p. 138) of the political leadership behind the campaign.

121 Barker, *Neglected War*, p. 266.

122 For Lloyd George's role in the War Council deliberations and his campaign to launch a Balkan offensive, see Paul Guinn, *British Strategy and Politics, 1914–1918* (Oxford, 1965), ch. 2 and passim; Woodward, *Lloyd George and the Generals*, ch. 2, passim; David Dutton, 'The "Robertson Dictatorship" and the Balkan Campaign in 1916', *Journal of Strategic Studies* 9:1 (March 1986), pp. 64–78; Wilson, *Myriad Faces of War*, pp. 103–7 and pp. 271–4.

123 Woodward, *Lloyd George and the Generals*, p. 32.

124 Ibid., p. 37.

125 Ibid., p. 38.

126 Ibid., p. 39.

127 See Glenn E. Torrey, 'Rumania and the Belligerents, 1914–1916' *Journal of Contemporary History* 1:3 (July 1966), pp. 171–91.

128 See Peter Fraser, 'The British "Shells Scandal" of 1915', *Canadian Journal of History* 18:1 (1983), pp. 69–86, esp. p. 83.

129 Brock, *Asquith Letters to Stanley*, 18 March 1915, p. 488.

130 Gilbert discusses this committee in his *Lloyd George: Organizer of Victory*, pp. 172–8.

131 See David French, 'Munitions and the Edwardian Army', in his *British Economic and Strategic Planning, 1905–1915* (London, 1982), ch. 3: an earlier version appeared as 'The Military Background to the "Shell Crisis" of May 1915', *Journal of Strategic Studies* 2 (1979), pp. 192–205.

132 Cassar, *Kitchener's War*, pp. 169–70. Cassar admits that the War Office was slow to react to the danger of a diminished munitions supply, in part because of Kitchener's inability to delegate responsibility.

133 Pointed out particularly well by Chris Wrigley, 'The Ministry of Munitions: an Innovatory Department', in Burk, *War and the State*.

134 NLW, William George Papers, 2945, 9 June 1915.

135 For this discussion of Lloyd George's work at the Ministry of Munitions, see Adams, *Arms and the Wizard*, especially chs 4, 5, and 6.

136 Of course, it would be too much to claim that Lloyd George was the only official who understood the need to harness the nation's creative and productive forces in winning the war. Guy Hartcup reviews the work of numerous scientists and engineers whose contributions were essential to the war effort (see *The War of Invention: Scientific Developments, 1914–18* (London, 1988).

137 More than 20 per cent of the workers in the following industries had joined the forces by mid-1915: mining, electrical engineering, chemical and explosive works. The iron and steel industries, shipbuilding and small arms manufacturing had lost 18.8 per cent, 16.5 per cent and 16 per cent respectively (Adams, *Arms and the Wizard*, p. 72).

138 As Adams points out: *Arms and the Wizard*, p. 77.

139 For this meeting, see *The Times*, 4 June 1915.

140 A special correspondent for *The Times* described this group as smartly turned out with an obvious pride in themselves. This surprised the reporter, who was pleasantly startled at their appearance and demeanour, given the fact that they had been 'formed out of he most unpromising material possible ... Liverpool dockers ... a rougher set of men' one could not imagine (*The Times*, 5 June 1915). *The Times*' leader of the same day applauded Lloyd George's speech, praising him for his 'manly frankness' and for his giving the kind of official statement that the nation had long been waiting. Here was a minister, it added, 'who rises to the greatness of the crisis upon us ...'. Praise indeed from *The Times*, not then noted for its friendliness either to Liberal or Labour causes or to Lloyd George.

141 *The Times*, 12 June 1915.

142 Ibid., 14 June 1915.

143 Hobhouse had received information (at third hand) that Lloyd George 'had practically dictated' the article to Robertson Nicoll, who 'took notes' and then 'reproduced the harangue almost verbatim' (David, *Inside Asquith's Cabinet*, 22 June 1915, p. 249). Corroborating evidence comes from Riddell, to whom Robertson Nicoll confessed that Lloyd George had 'inspired' the article at a private meeting between the two men. Riddell thought the article 'injudicious' and hastened to call upon Lloyd George to tell him so, and to ask him if he really intended to desert his country at such a time by resigning simply because he would not get his own way. Riddell recorded that Lloyd George 'coloured slightly' and 'made no reply' (see the diary entries of 9 and 10 June 1915 in McEwen, *Riddell Diaries*, pp. 121–22). The apparent hope of Lloyd George was that other newspapers would reprint the article: as indeed *The Times* did on 11 June 1915, from which the quotations above are taken.

144 Grigg, *Lloyd George: From Peace to War*, p. 256.

145 Parliamentary Archives, LG/D/3/3/5, 22 June 1915.

146 Ibid., LG/D/3/2/40, 7 February 1916.

147 Ibid., LG/D/3/2/49, 22 February 1916.

148 Ibid., LG/D/3/2/73, 17 May 1916.

149 To his brother, William (NLW, William George Papers, 2959, 26 July 1915).

150 For this, see Wrigley, 'The South Wales Miners' Strike, July 1915', in *Lloyd George and the British Labour Movement*, ch. 7.

151 For the following discussion, see especially James Hinton, 'The Clyde Workers' Committee and the Dilution Struggle', in Asa Briggs and John Saville (eds), *Essays in Labour History, 1886–1923* (Hamden, 1971), ch. 7; Wrigley, *Lloyd George and the British Labour Movement*, ch. 9, 'Enforcing Dilution on the Clyde'; and John Foster, 'Strike Acton and Working-Class Politics on Clydeside 1914–1919', *International Review of Social History* 35 (1990), pp. 33–70.

152 *The Times*, 27 December 1915, quoting from what it called the 'authorized report'.

153 Gilbert, *Lloyd George: Organizer of Victory*, p. 248.

154 Gilbert believes that his response to questions was neither 'a credible nor an honest performance' (ibid., p. 249). Frances Stevenson seems to have been unintentionally revealing in recounting this event. Observing in her diary that the suppression of the *Forward* 'caused trouble', she also noted that 'D. had to work up a case afterwards to justify himself' (Taylor, *Stevenson Diary*, 21 January 1916, p. 88).

155 Wrigley (*Lloyd George and the British Labour Movement*, p. 162) characterizes the ministry's action as 'firm'; but Hinton, more sympathetic to the Clydesiders, condemns it as ruthless: see his 'Clyde Workers' Committee', p. 184. Alastair Reid, however, believes that this characterization of a repressive governmental regime in league with employers to reduce workers' rights is somewhat overblown: see his 'Dilution, Trade Unionism and the State in Britain during the First World War', in Steven Tolliday and Jonathan Zeitlin (eds), *Shop Floor Bargaining and the State: Historical and Comparative Perspectives* (Cambridge, 1985).

156 McEwen, *Riddell Diaries*, 26 October 1912, pp. 49–50.

157 Martin Gilbert, *Churchill Companion*, vol. 3, Part 2, May 1915–December 1916, F.S. Oliver to Milner, 11 August 1915, p. 1124. Oliver was a businessman, head of Debenham and Freebody, a Chamberlainite and an ardent conscriptionist. He was reporting what Carson, then Attorney General in the Asquith coalition Cabinet, had told him at lunch that day. Milner was at that time out of office, though soon to become a member of the War Cabinet in Lloyd George's government.

158 Gilbert, *Churchill Companion*, vol. 3, Part 2, 18 August 1915, p. 1138.

159 For the Cabinet division over conscription, see Asquith's report to King George V, Gilbert, *Churchill Companion*, vol. 3, Part 2, 12 October 1915, p. 1216.

160 See Taylor, *Stevenson Diary*, 11 October 1915 to 23 October 1915, pp. 65–71, passim.

161 R.J.Q. Adams, 'Asquith's Choice: The May Coalition and the Coming of Conscription, 1915–1916', *Journal of British Studies* 25 (July 1986), pp. 244–6; and John Turner, 'Cabinets, Committees and Secretariats: the Higher Direction of War', ch. 3 in Burk, *War and the State*, p. 61. See also R.J.Q. Adams and Philip P. Poirier, *The Conscription Controversy in Great Britain, 1900–18* (London, 1987). A concise analysis of the conscriptionist campaign may also be found in Simkins, *Kitchener's Army*, ch. 5

162 Taylor, *Stevenson Diary*, 30 November 1915, p. 81.

163 NLW, William George Papers, 3013, 29 November 1915.

164 Addison, *Four and a Half Years*, 23 February 1916, p. 177.

165 McEwen, *Riddell Diaries*, 17 February 1916, p. 147.

166 Wilson, *Diaries of Scott*, 18 February 1916, p. 182.

167 Taylor, *Stevenson Diary*, 8 February to 23 February 1916, pp. 96–102 passim.

168 McEwen, *Riddell Diaries*, 1 April 1916, 1 p. 50.

169 Wilson, *Diaries of Scott*, 13 April 1916, p. 197.

170 NLW, William George Papers, 3075, 15 April 1916.

171 As Koss sums it up: the Prime Minister, without 'conciliating his enemies', had 'progressively forfeited the sympathy of many of his friends' (*Asquith*, p. 209).

172 Stephen Roskill, *Hankey: Man of Secrets*, 3 vols (London, 1970), 25 March 1916, p. 258.

173 McEwen, *Riddell Diaries*, 28 April 1916, p. 154.

174 As Trevor Wilson believes: see *The Downfall of the Liberal Party, 1914–1935* (London, 1966), p. 66.

175 Turner, *British Politics and the Great War*, p. 88.

Chapter 12. Prime Minister in War

1 The historiography of the Rising has been as fraught as the event itself. See D. George Boyce, '1916, Interpreting the Rising', in the essential D. George Boyce and Alan O'Day (eds), *The Making of Modern Irish History: Revisionism and the Revisionist Controversy* (London, 1996), ch. 9. The most recent account, thorough and convincing, is Charles Townshend, *Easter 1916: The Irish Rebellion* (Chicago, 2006).

2 Roy Foster, *Modern Ireland, 1600–1972* (London, 1988), p. 484.

3 John M. McEwen, 'The Liberal Party and the Irish Question During the First World War', *Journal of British Studies* 12:1 (1972), pp. 114–5.

4 John O. Stubbs, 'The Unionists and Ireland, 1914–18', *Historical Journal* 33:4 (1990), pp. 879–80.

5 Roy Jenkins, *Asquith* (London, 1964), pp. 397–8.

6 Reporting to William, Lloyd George wrote: 'So I shall for the next few weeks be immersed in an Irish bog' (NLW, William George Papers, 3092, 24 May 1916).

7 John Turner, *British Politics and the Great War: Conciliation and Conflict, 1915–1918* (New Haven, 1992), p. 92. 'Getting on well', he wrote William of his negotiations, 'still many barbed wire entanglements to get through. Though I have already captured many formidable positions' (NLW, William George Papers, 3098, 31 May 1916).

8 Brian Bond and Simon Robbins (eds), *Staff Officer: The Diaries of Walter Guinness (First Lord Moyne), 1914–1918* (London, 1987), p. 98. Guinness, Dublin born, the third son of the Earl of Iveagh, was Conservative MP for Bury St Edmunds from 1907 to 1931. He also served in the war, first at Gallipoli and later on the Western Front, rising to the rank of Lieutenant.

9 For Carson, see John Kendle, *Walter Long, Ireland, and the Union, 1905–1920* (Montreal, 1992), p. 112 and for Curzon, p. 221, n. 58.

10 *The Times*, 28 June 1916.

11 John Vincent (ed.), *The Crawford Papers: The Journals of David Lindsay, Twenty-Seventh Earl of Crawford and Tenth Earl of Balcarres during the years 1892 to 1940* (Manchester, 1984), 8 July 1916, p. 355. Balcarres had been serving for more than a year on the Western Front, having volunteered at the age of 43 for the Royal Army Medical Corps.

12 Long was President of the Local Government Board. Lansdowne served as Minister Without Portfolio.

13 Kendle, *Walter Long, Ireland, and the Union*, p. 113.

14 In Kendle's words, Long and Lansdowne 'were ceaseless in their plotting and in their determination' to defeat Lloyd George's Irish plan (ibid., p. 126 and ch. 4, 'Countering Lloyd George', passim).

15 NLW, William George Papers, 3112, 20 June 1916.

16 As Lloyd George explained it to Scott, both he and Asquith were prepared to resign 'if it would have been any good … but the Unionists were united and the government would have been broken up' (Trevor Wilson (ed.), *The Political Diaries of C.P. Scott, 1911–1928* (Ithaca, 1970), 27 July 1916, p. 223). Boyce seconds this reasoning, adding that the consequences of a fallen government at that time could have 'irreparably' damaged the

war effort (David G. Boyce, 'British Opinion, Ireland, and the War, 1916–1918', *Historical Journal* 17:3 (September 1974), p. 582).

17 Duke had been a successful advocate, becoming a PC in 1915, and was Conservative MP for Plymouth at the time of his appointment. But his performance as Chief Secretary is a matter of some dispute. Boyce and Hazlehurst believe him to have been conscientious, reasonably tolerant, and moderate in his actions (D.G. Boyce and Cameron Hazlehurst, 'The Unknown Chief Secretary: H.E. Duke and Ireland, 1916–18', *Irish Historical Studies* 20:79 (March 1977), pp. 286–311. Eunan O'Halpin, however, thinks that Duke was a political lightweight, ignorant of the country and its problems, erratic, weak and somewhat prone to panic. O'Halpin does admit, though, that Duke 'did little harm in Ireland' (Eunan O'Halpin, 'Historical Revision XX: H.E. Duke and the Irish Administration, 1916–18', *Irish Historical Studies* 22:88 (September 1981), pp. 362–76: for this quotation, see p. 376.

18 He expressed some sense of his failure to William: 'Irish settlement is off. Cannot be helped. Sorry' (NLW, William George Papers, 3140, 22 July 1916).

19 As even the sympathetic Morgan observes: see his *Lloyd George*, p. 92. Other historians have been more critical. Townshend, for example, terms Lloyd George's attempted negotiations 'a fudge' (Charles Townshend, *Ireland: The 20th Century* (London, 1999), p. 81). Loughlin damns Lloyd George's 'rather duplicitous attempt' to craft a Home Rule measure (James Loughlin, *The British Monarchy and Ireland: 1800 to the Present* (Cambridge, 2007), p. 302).

20 To Riddell, Lloyd George indicated there were those who hoped he would 'come a cropper over Ireland', perhaps Asquith among them (John McEwen, *The Riddell Diaries, 1908–1923* (London, 1986), 27 May 1916, pp. 156–7 and 402, n. 31).

21 David W. Savage suggests this in his 'The Attempted Home Rule Settlement of 1916', *Eire-Ireland* 2:3 (1967), pp. 132–45, p. 135.

22 Ian Colvin, *The Life of Lord Carson*, vol. 3 (New York, 1937), p. 167.

23 See Trevor Royle, *The Kitchener Enigma* (London, 1985), ch. 14, for an account of the sinking of the *Hampshire*. Lloyd George's private comment on Kitchener's death was succinct and slightly patronizing: 'Poor K. Died at best moment & best way for him' (NLW, William George Papers, 3103, 6 June 1916).

24 Aitken was a native Canadian millionaire businessman and newspaper magnate, author and MP for Ashton-under-Lyne (1910–6). Granted a peerage as Baron Beaverbrook in 1917. He became Minister of Information (1918) in Lloyd George's coalition government. He was a supreme influence peddler and the confidant of politicians both Left and Right.

25 R.J.Q. Adams, *Bonar Law* (London, 1999), p. 214.

26 McEwen, *Riddell Diaries*, 11 June 1916, p. 159. General Douglas Haig had replaced Field Marshall Sir John French as Commander in Chief of the BEF in December 1915.

27 Ian F.W. Beckett, *The Great War 1914–1918* (Harlow, 2001), p. 114. Woodward claims that Robertson became 'the virtual dictator of British strategy' (David R. Woodward, 'Britain in a Continental War: The Civil-Military Debate over the Strategic Direction of the Great War of 1914–1918', *Albion* 12:1 (Spring 1980), p. 41).

28 See the account in Robin Prior and Trevor Wilson, *The Somme*, paperback edn (New Haven and London, 2006).

29 German losses have been estimated at 'a relatively trivial 8,000' (Trevor Wilson, *The Myriad Faces of War: Britain and the Great War 1914–1918* (London, 1986), p. 326).

30 For a discussion of the evolving strategy of attrition, see David French, 'The Meaning of Attrition, 1914–1916', *English Historical Review* 103 (April, 1988), pp. 385–405.

31 Margot Asquith, the Prime Minister's wife, asked a question which must have been asked by many: 'Can it be right to lose nine to ten thousand in casualties every two or three days?' (Colin Clifford, *The Asquiths*, paperback edn (London, 2003), p. 379).

32 Robert Blake, *The Unknown Prime Minister: The Life and Times of Andrew Bonar Law, 1858–1923* (London, 1955), pp. 278–9.

33 Gary Sheffield and John Bourne (eds), *Douglas Haig War Diaries and Letters, 1914–1918* (London, 2005), diary entry of 6 September 1916, p. 227.

34 When word of this reached Haig, he dismissed Lloyd George's behaviour as 'ungentlemanly' (ibid., 17 September 1916, p. 232). Philip Sassoon, Haig's military secretary from December 1915 until March 1919, also reported his chief's opinion: Haig had been 'terribly disappointed' in Lloyd George. Lord Derby, then Under-Secretary of State for War, attempting to explain Lloyd George to Sassoon, pointed out that Lloyd George 'was not a soldier', and that 'his antecedents' were unlikely to make him 'view things as we view them': in other words, 'with all his cleverness – it won't make up for his not being a gentleman' (Peter Stansky, *Sassoon: The Worlds of Philip and Sybil* (New Haven, 2003), p. 64). Haig, a product of Oxford and Sandhurst, had made similar comments about General Robertson, the son of a Lincolnshire village tailor, who had run away from home at the age of 17 to join the army.

35 Denis Winter, *Haig's Command: A Reassessment*, paperback edn (London, 2001), pp. 13, 14, 20. Winter has been among the harshest of Haig's critics. But there is some evidence that Winter has misused evidence. See Mark Connelly's review in the *Journal of Modern History* 82:3 (September 2010), pp. 694–5. Tim Travers believes that Haig's aloof personality discouraged senior officers and staff from entering into a dialogue with their chief, which inhibited a free interchange of ideas during planning stages of various operations. See Travers, 'A Particular Style of Command: Haig and GHQ, 1916–18', *Journal of Strategic Studies* 10:3 (September 1987), pp. 364–5 and passim.

36 Dan Todman thinks that particularly by the end of 1917, British High Command had 'allowed themselves to lose touch with the experiences and emotions of the units at the sharp end' ('The Grand Lamasery Revisited: General Headquarters on the Western Front, 1914–1918', in Garry Sheffield and Dan Todman (eds), *Command and Control on the Western Front: The British Army's Experience 1914–1918*, paperback edn (Stroud, 2007), p. 65.

37 Tim Travers, *The Killing Ground: The British Army, the Western Front and the Emergence of Modern Warfare, 1900–1918*, paperback edn (Barnsley, 2003), p. 131.

38 Prior and Wilson, *The Somme*, pp. 306–7.

39 J. Paul Harris, *Douglas Haig and the First World War* (Cambridge, 2008), pp. 230, 234, 221.

40 Ibid., p. 249.

41 Ibid., p. 255.

42 Ibid., p. 257.

43 Ibid., p. 267.

44 'Bite and hold' was the favoured tactical operation of General Sir Henry Rawlinson, who was General Officer Commanding of the BEF 4th Division in 1914; GOC of IV Corps 1914–5; and GOC Fourth Army 1916–9. For the origins of Rawlinson's 'bite and hold' operations, see Robin Prior and Trevor Wilson, *Command on the Western Front: The Military Career of Sir Henry Rawlinson, 1914–18*, paperback edn (Barnsley, 2004), pp. 77–80.

45 Harris, *Haig and the First World War*, p. 272.

46 John Terraine, *Douglas Haig: The Educated Soldier*, paperback edn (London, 2005), pp. 206, 214.

47 Ibid., p. 230. See also Gary Sheffield's qualified praise of Haig in *The Somme*, paperback edn (London, 2004) where he admitted that during the battle of the Somme, Haig 'lacked

consistency and "grip'" (p. 58); but by keeping his nerve, 'delivered a series of body blows' to the German forces, thus ensuring that the campaign as a whole was 'a success' (ibid., pp. 160, 162).

48 For a brief account of these actions, see Bryan Ranft, 'The Royal Navy and the War at Sea', in John Turner (ed.), *Britain and the First World War* (London, 1988), ch. 3.

49 For the battle, see Arthur J. Marder's *From the* Dreadnought *to Scapa Flow*, vol. 3, *Jutland and After* (London, 1966).

50 Ibid., p. 198. For Marder's evaluation of the battle, see *From the* Dreadnought *to Scapa Flow*, vol. 3, ch. 6. He believes that in the long run Jutland made two important contributions to the war effort: ensuring British naval reforms which enhanced the Navy's battle worthiness; and a 'moral ascendancy' over the German fleet. After all, the German fleet remained in port thereafter and never challenged the Royal Navy again. A recent evaluation claims that Jutland was 'an unequivocal British victory' because British vessels lost 'were tactically insignificant' – that is, older vessels went down, compared to the sinking of newer, more valuable ships of the German navy (Nick Hewitt, 'Writing about Jutland: Historiography and Hysteria', in Michael Howard (ed.), *A Part of History: Aspects of the British Experience of the First World War* (London, 2008), p. 45).

51 Vincent, *Crawford Papers*, 8 Oct. 1916, 361. A week later, he seemed even more alarmed: 'There is every indication that the amount of wheat necessary for our sustenance is lamentably short' (ibid., 14 October 1916, p. 362).

52 Ibid., 3 November 1916, p. 362.

53 Ibid., 4 November 1916, p. 363.

54 For the following, see Kathleen Burk, *Britain, America and the Sinews of War, 1914–1918* (Boston, 1985).

55 A.J.P. Taylor, *Lloyd George: A Diary by Frances Stevenson* (London, 1971), 31 October 1916, p. 120.

56 Ibid., 10 November 1916, p. 121.

57 Ibid., 13 November 1916, p. 122.

58 McEwen, *Riddell Diaries*, 29 October 1916, p. 171.

59 Ibid., 19 November 1916, p. 173.

60 Stephen Roskill, *Hankey: Man of Secrets*, 3 vols (London, 1970), diary entry of 28 October 1916, p. 311. Hankey noted privately in his diary that he agreed with Lloyd George 'to a great extent' (ibid., p. 312).

61 J.A. Turner, *British Politics and the Great War: Conciliation and Conflict, 1915–1918* (New Haven, 1992), p. 130.

62 McEwen, *Riddell Diaries*, 30 July 1916, p. 167.

63 Vincent, *Crawford Papers*, 18 November 1916, 365. Balcarres also observed that 'Asquith's somnolence is heart-rending' (ibid.).

64 Ibid., 22 November 1916, p. 366. The phrase 'knock-out blow' was a reference to a public statement two months earlier by Lloyd George in which he declared in a newspaper interview that this was his preferred strategy for carrying on the war: see John Grigg, *Lloyd George: From Peace to War, 1912–1916* (London, 1985), ch. 16, 'The Howard Interview'.

65 Vincent, *Crawford Papers*, 24 November 1916, p. 368.

66 Ibid., 25 November 1916, p. 368.

67 For Asquith's responses to the triumvirs' initiative, see Jenkins, *Asquith*, ch. 26, 'A Palace Revolution I', passim.

68 Quoted ibid., p. 452.

69 Sydney H. Zebel, *Balfour: A Political Biography* (Cambridge, 1973), p. 224, quoting from the Balfour Papers, British Library, Add Mss 49692, ff 180–8.

70 Ibid., p. 225, from the Balfour Papers, Add Mss 49692, ff 189–95. Thus began the close cooperation between Balfour and Lloyd George for the duration of the war – and afterwards (R.J.Q. Adams, *Balfour: The Last Grandee* (London, 2007), p. 323).

71 Balfour's doubts about Asquith had been growing for some time. As early as March 1915, he had confided to his sister, Lady Evelyn Rayleigh, that it was 'not in Asquith's nature to speed up things' and that Lloyd George was 'the only member of the government with any drive in him' (Max Egremont, *Balfour: A Life of Arthur James Balfour*, paperback edn (London, 1998), p. 268).

72 For these events of late 5 December–early 6 December, see Adams, *Bonar Law*, pp. 237–8. The idea of a conference seems to have been widely mooted. In addition to Balfour, others such as Bonar Law, Henderson, Montagu and Derby have all been mentioned as originators of a royal conference (Jenkins, *Asquith*, pp. 455–6). Hankey, tiring of 'these muddy politics in the midst of a great war', also claims some credit. On the evening of 5 December, he went to Buckingham Palace to see the venerable Stamfordham, Private Secretary to King George, recommending mediation by the King (Roskill, *Hankey*, diary entries of 4 Dec. and 10 Dec. 1916, pp. 326–9). John D. Fair observes that it is impossible to know specifically who originally devised the conference scheme, but it seems likely that there were several important individuals to whom the idea may have occurred simultaneously (*British Interparty Conferences: A Study of the Procedure of Conciliation in British Politics, 1867–1921* (Oxford, 1980), ch. 7, 'The Political Crisis of 1916').

73 Both Stephen Koss, *Asquith*, paperback edn (New York, 1985), p. 222 and Adams, *Bonar Law*, p. 238 call the conference 'fruitless'.

74 Donald McCormick, *The Mask of Merlin: A Critical Biography of David Lloyd George* (New York, 1964), pp. 112–3.

75 Clifford, *The Asquiths*, p. 381.

76 Mark Pottle, *Champion Redoubtable: The Diaries and Letters of Violet Bonham Carter, 1914–1945*, paperback edn (London, 1999), 26 December 1916, p. 98.

77 Fair, *British Interparty Conferences*, p. 58.

78 Martin Pugh, *Lloyd George*, paperback edn (London, 1988), p. 95; Ian Packer, *Lloyd George*, paperback edn (Houndmills, Hants, 1998), p. 54.

79 Kenneth O. Morgan, *Lloyd George* (London, 1974), p. 93. Elsewhere, Morgan rejects 'the traditional picture of venial intrigue by Lloyd George on the one hand and of unsullied honour by Asquith on the other' as a 'gross over-simplification' (Kenneth O. Morgan, *Lloyd George: Welsh Radical as World Statesman* (Cardiff, 1963), p. 55).

80 For the following, see J.M. McEwen, 'The Press and the Fall of Asquith', *Historical Journal* 21:4 (1978), pp. 863–83, p. 864.

81 Ibid., p. 872.

82 Ibid., p. 874.

83 Ibid., p. 869. The *Morning Post* was edited by H.A. Gwynne, who had come to his pro-Lloyd George point of view somewhat reluctantly, given his political views. To Philip Sassoon, Gwynne had written in October: 'Whatever L.G'.s faults are one must … concede that he is out to beat the Boche' (Keith Wilson (ed.), *The Rasp of War: The Letters of H.A. Gwynne to The Countess of Bathurst 1914–1918* (London, 1988), p. 196. Gwynne's political views in general may be judged from a letter to his proprietress, Lady Bathurst, to whom he once wrote: 'when we handed over the pistol to our masters in 1832 we let ourselves in for all the evils that have pursued us' (ibid., 11 April 1917, p. 215). This was music to the Countess's ears. She was anti-Irish, anti-suffragette and a strong imperialist. She inherited ownership of the *Morning Post* in 1908 from her father, Algeron Borthwick, Lord Glenesk.

84 For Lloyd George and Aitken during the crisis, see A.J.P. Taylor's *Beaverbrook* (London, 1972), ch. 6, 'The Kingmaker, 1916'. Lloyd George's meetings with Riddell, Burnham and Donald may be found in McEwen, *Riddell Diaries*, 26 November–6 December 1916, pp. 173–7.

85 Wilson, *Diaries of Scott*, 3 December 1916, p. 243. See ibid., 2 December–5 December 1916, pp. 242–8 for more extensive diary entries.

86 For the following see J.M. McEwen, 'Northcliffe and Lloyd George at War, 1914–1918', *Historical Journal* 24:3 (1981), pp. 651–72.

87 As Riddell once observed of Lloyd George: 'He never misses an opportunity with the Press' (McEwen, *Riddell Diaries*, 12 April 1913, p. 61). At times, this was apparently a source of jealousy on Riddell's part: he liked to think of himself as the chief repository of Lloyd George's state secrets.

88 As Frances Stevenson (never fond of Northcliffe) observed, Northcliffe had been 'grovelling, and trying to be friends with D. again', surmising that if there were 'anything big happening Northcliffe would hate to be out of the know' (Taylor, *Stevenson Diary*, 1 December 1916, p. 130).

89 Reginald Pound and Geoffrey Harmsworth, *Northcliffe* (New York, 1960), p. 513.

90 McEwen concludes that the Northcliffe press 'indisputably' aided Lloyd George 'enormously' during that fateful first week of December 1916 (McEwen, 'Northcliffe and Lloyd George', p. 664). Lloyd George's use of the press had been no doubt effective; but to some observers, like Hankey, it had been offensive. In his diary for 2 December 1916, Hankey wrote that the morning papers of that day contained a great deal of information 'obviously inspired by Ll. George'. Hankey condemned such 'publicity and press methods' as 'intolerable' (Roskill, *Hankey*, pp. 323–4).

91 Grigg believes that support for Lloyd George among Liberal backbenchers was 'substantial' (*Lloyd George: From Peace to War*, p. 476). Pugh agrees, stating that such strong support for Lloyd George was a sign of the 'disillusionment with Asquith' among the majority of Liberal MPs (*Lloyd George*, p. 98). These assertions are based on a poll taken by Addison on 4–6 December which reported that there were 49 'out-and-out' Liberal supporters of Lloyd George, with an additional 126 supporters if he could form a government. Addison declared that, given these numbers, there would soon be 'a stampede' towards Lloyd George (Christopher Addison, *Four and a Half Years: A Personal Diary from June 1914 to January 1919*, vol. 1 (London, 1934), p. 274). But J.M. McEwen, after analyzing the original lists in the Addison Papers at the Bodleian and the Lloyd George papers in the Parliamentary Archives, shows that Addison's tally was 'a generously inflated estimate of Liberal backing' for the proposed Lloyd George government (McEwen, 'Lloyd George's Liberal Supporters in December 1916: A Note', *Bulletin of the Institute of Historical Research* 53 (1980), pp. 265–72, p. 272). These inflated numbers, which Addison reported to Lloyd George, Bonar Law, Carson and Lord Edmond Talbot (Unionist Chief Whip) during a meeting at the War Office on the evening of 6 December, may very well have been decisive, McEwen believes, in the decision that Lloyd George, rather than Bonar Law, should be Prime Minister (ibid., pp. 265–6).

92 Richard Murphy argues for the importance of Long to the new government's success: he was 'the pivot on which Unionist support for the new government was balanced' ('Walter Long, the Unionist Members, and the Formation of Lloyd George's Government in December 1916', *Historical Journal* 29:3 (1986), pp. 735–45, p. 744).

93 An opinion perhaps only expressed in private to Miss Stevenson: see Taylor, *Stevenson Diary*, 22 November 1915, p. 76.

94 McEwen, *Riddell Diaries*, 1 October 1916, p. 170. Balcarres had noticed this same quality, commenting once how favourably impressed he was 'by the readiness with which Curzon seizes and diagnoses an argument' (Vincent, *Crawford Papers*, 8 June 1914, p. 336).

95 As Searle observes in his *A New England? Peace and War, 1886–1918* (Oxford, 2004), pp. 703–4. See also Alfred M. Gollin's discussion in *Proconsul in Politics* (London, 1964), ch. 14, 'The Threshold of Power'.

96 P.A. Lockwood, 'Milner's Entry into the War Cabinet, December 1916', *Historical Journal* 7:1 (1964), pp. 120–34.

97 These included Cecil, Chamberlain and Long: see Sir Austen Chamberlain, *Down the Years* (London, 1935), p. 128.

98 Taylor, *Stevenson Diary*, 7 December 1916, p. 134. Lloyd George agreed with his secretary, characteristically telling Riddell that he gave the deputation 'the best speech I have ever made' (McEwen, *Riddell Diaries*, 10 December 1916, p. 177).

99 David Lloyd George, *War Memoirs*, new edn, vol. 1 (London, n.d. [1939?]), vol. 1, p. 641. H. Montgomery Hyde accepts this rationale: see his *Carson: The Life of Sir Edward Carson, Lord Carson of Duncairn* (London, 1974), pp. 414–5.

100 Pugh, *Lloyd George*, p. 101.

101 Grigg, *Lloyd George: From Peace to War*, p. 485.

102 John F. Naylor, 'The Establishment of the Cabinet Secretariat', *Historical Journal* 14:4 (December 1971), pp. 783–803. The extent of Hankey's work in the early days of the War Cabinet may also be gauged in Roskill, *Hankey*, ch. 12, 'The War Cabinet in Action. December 1916–March 1917', passim.

103 To which J.A. Turner takes exception: see his 'The Formation of Lloyd George's "Garden Suburb": "Fabian-like Milnerite Penetration"?', *Historical Journal* 20:1 (March 1977), pp. 165–84, where he argues that the Garden Suburb was established for 'genuine administrative reasons', as well as providing jobs for 'an assortment' of Lloyd George supporters who could not be easily accommodated elsewhere. See also Turner's much expanded analysis on the Garden Suburb in his *Lloyd George's Secretariat* (Cambridge, 1980).

104 Roskill, *Hankey*, pp. 353–4.

105 Philip Kerr, perhaps the most notable member of the Garden Suburb, 'raked and harrowed the ground which Lloyd George might plough' as Turner describes it in *Lloyd George's Secretariat*, p. 169. After reading history under H.A.L. Fisher at New College, Oxford, Kerr became a distinguished member of the Milner set during the reconstruction of South Africa after the second South African War. Upon his return, he participated in the Round Table movement. He became the 11th Marquess of Lothian in 1930. He was Ambassador to the USA from 1939–40, a term cut short by his early death. See J.R.M. Butler, *Philip Kerr (Lord Lothian) 1882–1940* (London, 1960).

106 For the committee structure, see John Turner, 'Cabinets, Committees and Secretariats: The Higher Direction of War', in Kathleen Burk (ed.), *War and the State: The Transformation of British Government 1914–1919* (London, 1982), passim, esp. pp. 66–9.

107 This pact has been widely reported. See Robert Rhodes James (ed.), *Memoirs of a Conservative: J.C.C. Davidson's Memoirs and Papers 1910–37* (London, 1969), p. 48, which quotes from the memoir by J.C.C. Davidson, who was soon to become Private Secretary to Bonar Law in the new government. Additionally, in the Curzon papers is a corroborative memorandum dated 7 December 1916 (quoted by David R. Woodward, *Lloyd George and the Generals* (Newark, 1983), p. 133 and Turner, *British Politics and the Great War*, p. 154).

108 Woodward, *Lloyd George and the Generals*, pp. 138–41.

109 See Wilson, *Myriad Faces of War*, p. 440. Or, as David French describes Lloyd George's strategy – 'to achieve spectacular results at a minimal cost to the British army' (*The Strategy of the Lloyd George Coalition, 1916–1918* (Oxford, 1995), p. 53).

110 In their demands, the generals enjoyed continued support from the patriotic press, especially from Northcliffe's papers.

111 Derby, in frequent and friendly contact with both Robertson and Haig, served as a reliable mouthpiece within the government for the generals: see Randolph S. Churchill, *Lord Derby, 'King of Lancashire': The Official Life of Edward, Seventeenth Earl of Derby, 1865–1948* (London, 1959), chs 11–12.

112 Woodward, *Lloyd George and the Generals*, p. 153, quoting from Cabinet papers.

113 Ibid., pp. 148, 153.

114 French, *Strategy of the Lloyd George Coalition*, p. 56.

115 Wilson, *Myriad Faces of War*, pp. 442–3.

116 John Grigg, *Lloyd George: War Leader 1916–1918* (London, 2002), p. 43. For a comprehensive criticism of Lloyd George as war leader, see George H. Cassar, *Lloyd George at War, 1916–1918* (London and New York, 2009). Cassar believes that Lloyd George's 'impulsive nature' (p. 17) and 'reckless behaviour' (p. 90) led to 'fatal flaws' (p. 78) in his strategic thinking. However, Cassar also praises Lloyd George as 'imperturbable and at his best in a crisis' (p. 249). Moreover, the Prime Minister's 'vitality and buoyancy' imbued the public 'with determination and confidence in ultimate victory' (p. 171). All in all, Lloyd George 'did advance' the cause of the Allies 'significantly in some ways' (p. 351).

117 Holger H. Herwig, *The First World War: Germany and Austria-Hungary, 1914–1918* (London, 1997), pp. 250–2. Herwig calls operation Alberich 'the war's greatest feat of engineering' (p. 250).

118 Roger Chickering, *Imperial Germany and the Great War, 1914–1918*, paperback edn (Cambridge, 2003), pp. 173–4.

119 Grigg, *Lloyd George: War Leader*, p. 44. Wilson speaks of the 'calamity' of Nivelle's failed offensive which left the Prime Minister 'at the Commander's mercy' (*Myriad Faces of War*, p. 457). French is more circumspect, observing that in any future quarrel between the generals and the Prime Minister, Lloyd George's views 'would be at a discount' (*Strategy of the Lloyd George Coalition*, p. 61). Miss Stevenson, doubtless echoing Lloyd George's private sentiments, confided to her diary that 'D. will have to be very careful in future as to his backings [sic] of the French against the English' (Taylor, *Stevenson Diary*, 12 May 1917, p. 157).

120 Woodward, *Lloyd George and the Generals*, p. 160.

121 Sheffield and Bourne, *Haig*, 4 May 1917, p. 292.

122 Brigadier-General John Charteris, *At G.H.Q.* (London, 1931), 7 May 1917, p. 223.

123 Sheffield and Bourne, *Haig*, 19 June 1914, p. 300. As his diary indicates, Haig confused the War Policy Committee, before which he testified, with the War Cabinet.

124 Ibid., 2 June 1917, p. 297.

125 See David French, 'Who Knew What and When? The French Army Mutinies and the British Decision to Launch the Third Battle of Ypres', in Lawrence Freedman, Paul Hayes, and Robert O'Neill (eds), *War, Strategy, and International Politics* (Oxford, 1992), ch. 8. See also Jean-Jacques Becker, *The Great War and the French People* (New York, 1986), ch. 15.

126 Indeed, during the continuous strategic debate throughout the war between military and civilian authorities, secrecy was the most effective means used by the high command to manage decisions in their favour (Woodward, 'Britain in a Continental War', p. 42).

127 French, *Strategy of the Lloyd George Coalition*, pp. 122–3.

128 Grigg's description of the third meeting of the WPC on 21 June reveals that Lloyd George tried a last ditch alternative to Haig's more grandiose battle plans for Flanders: 'a punch here and there, and a process of wearing down the enemy' was his recommendation. In short, Lloyd George recommended a tactical 'bite and hold' approach. Grigg believes it 'a great pity' that he did not advocate his view more strongly. See Grigg, *Lloyd George: War Leader*, pp. 167, 172.

129 Searle, *A New England?*, p. 715.

130 There is evidence of some confusion about the objectives of the campaign – a confusion beginning at the top command level – as to whether or not the attack was to be a measured stage by stage advance or another attempt at a breakthrough. Haig apparently gave mixed signals to the impetuous General Gough, GOC Fifth Army, who led the attack. See Tim Travers, *How the War was Won: Command and Technology in the British Army on the Western Front, 1917–1918* (London, 1992), ch. 1, 'Paralysis of Command: From Passchendaele to Cambrai'; and Andrew A. Wiest, 'Haig, Gough and Passchendaele', in G.D. Sheffield (ed.), *Leadership and Command: The Anglo-American Military Experience since 1861* (London, 1997), ch. 5.

131 Wilson, *Myriad Faces of War*, p. 483. Wilson believes that the toll of casualties left the British army 'dangerously short' of fighting men (ibid., p. 482). For a detailed account of the campaign, see ibid., chs 42–3; and Robin Prior and Trevor Wilson, *Passchendaele: The Untold Story*, paperback edn (New Haven, 2002).

132 For a summary of the Battle of Cambrai, see Wilson, *Myriad Faces of War*, ch. 44.

133 Gerard J. de Groot, *Douglas Haig, 1861–1928* (London, 1988), p. 336; Travers, *Killing Ground*, p. 216; Beckett, *The Great War*, pp. 163–4; Harris, *Haig and the First World War*, pp. 381–2. Even Haig's supporters have found it difficult to defend him. Terraine – admitting that Cambrai was 'the lowest ebb of Haig's career' – believes that he must bear at least 'part of the blame' for the 'unclarity of intention' and 'imprecision of execution' of the battle plans (Terraine, *Haig: The Educated Soldier*, p. 379). Prior and Wilson in *Passchendaele*, sum up the operation as a succession of attacks 'often delivered in abysmal conditions' using a sizeable proportion of the British Army's 'alarmingly dwindling reserves of manpower' to hold positions 'it could not hope to retain if confronted by an enemy riposte' (Prior and Wilson, *Passchendaele*, p. 181).

134 Woodward, *Lloyd George and the Generals*, p. 185.

135 Prior and Wilson, *Passchendaele*, p. 155.

136 Ibid., p. 38.

137 Grigg, *Lloyd George: War Leader*, pp. 279–80. Perhaps in a belated realization of his own complicity in allowing Passchendaele to go forward (and in his desire to exculpate himself publicly), Lloyd George made the military leadership and Haig a special target in his *War Memoirs*. If all the facts had been known, he wrote, the ministry would not have allowed the battle to go forward. 'Ministers were misled on several critical points', he claimed (Lloyd George, *War Memoirs*, vol. 2, p. 1294). As it was, he himself was reluctant to overrule the military: 'I had no expert military counsel which I could weigh against theirs' (ibid., p. 1304). So absolved, Lloyd George could then condemn the campaign as 'this bath of mud and blood' (ibid., p. 1308). Haig he also castigated, descrying his 'fatuous orders' and his 'unrivalled facility for covering up failure with complacent beliefs' (ibid., pp. 1312, 2029). Overall, Haig was 'a second-rate Commander' who was throughout the long Passchendaele campaign 'wasting his own fighting men' (ibid., pp. 2014, 1421).

138 French, *Strategy of the Lloyd George Coalition*, p. 123.

139 See the discussion in Wilson, *Myriad Faces of War*, ch. 46, 'A Land No Longer Merry'.

140 William Philpott, 'Squaring the Circle: The Higher Co-ordination of the Entente in the Winter of 1915–16', *English Historical Review* 114:458 (September 1999), pp. 875–98.

141 As Woodward puts it, Lloyd George used 'the artichoke method', stripping away leaf by leaf the authority of the general staff's authority (Woodward, *Lloyd George and the Generals*, p. 221). For what follows, see ibid., chs 9 and 10.

142 Keith Grieves, 'Haig and the Government, 1916–1918', in Brian Bond and Nigel Cave (eds), *Haig: A Reappraisal 80 Years On* (Barnsley, 2009), p. 116.

143 Taylor, *Stevenson Diary*, 5 November 1917, p. 163.

144 Sheffield and Bourne, *Haig*, 4 November 1917, p. 338.

145 For Lloyd George's autumn 1917 whirlwind tour in France and Italy, see Woodward, *Lloyd George and the Generals*, ch. 10.

146 For the address and the following quotations, see *The Times*, 13 Novemer 1917.

147 Ibid., 13 and 14 November 1917.

148 As Smuts put it to Scott, SAWC was designed to counter 'national particularism' among the various military commands (Wilson, *Diaries of Scott*, 12–13 November 1917, p. 311).

149 As Elizabeth Greenhalgh has observed, Lloyd George was 'the prime mover' in replacing the unproductive Allied summit meetings with a centralized organization that eventually evolved into a unified military command – crucial to victory in 1918 (*Victory through Coalition: Britain and France during the First World War* (Cambridge, 2005), pp. 183, 261).

150 Information on the Executive War Board may be found in French, *Strategy of the Lloyd George Coalition*, pp. 214–7.

151 It was 'a thorough sweep' – indeed, a 'purge', according to Terraine (*Haig: The Educated Soldier*, p. 388).

152 See David R. Woodward, *Field Marshall Sir William Robertson: Chief of the Imperial General Staff in the Great War* (Westport, 1998), ch. 11, 'Robertson's Downfall'.

153 Randolph S. Churchill, *Lord Derby, 'King of Lancashire': The Official Life of Edward, Seventeenth Earl of Derby, 1865–1948* (London, 1959), ch. 15.

154 Carson was thought too subservient to the naval establishment. He was to the admirals, as Grigg observes, 'what Derby was to the generals' (*Lloyd George: War Leader*, p. 175).

155 Jellicoe, like Kitchener, had difficulties in decentralizing responsibility. He also suffered from poor health, brought on perhaps by a 'worrying temperament' (See S.W. Roskill, 'The Dismissal of Admiral Jellicoe', *Journal of Contemporary History* 1 (1966), pp. 69–93; p. 69 for the quotation).

156 As Matthew Hughes puts it: see his *Allenby and British Strategy in the Middle East, 1917–1919* (London, 1999), p. 23.

157 Lloyd George quickly made his wishes known soon after becoming Prime Minister. As Freddie Maurice, the Director of Military Operations in the War Office, informed Major General A.L. Lynden-Bell, Chief of Staff of the Egyptian Expeditionary Force, on 13 December 1916: 'The Prime Minister is very anxious … for some success to enliven the winter gloom which has settled upon England …' (David R. Woodward, *Hell in the Holy Land: World War I in the Middle East* (Lexington, 2006), p. 55).

158 The energetic and charismatic Allenby was publicly likened in Britain to the crusading King Richard the Lionheart in his march through Ottoman territory. Sources for the Palestine campaign include Woodward's *Hell in the Holy Land* which is based in large part upon letters from officers and men of the EEF; and Edward K/ Erickson, *Ottoman Army Effectiveness in World War I: A Comparative Study* (London, 2007), chs 4 and 5. Erickson draws heavily upon Turkish sources in his analysis of the campaign.

159 See Lloyd George's brief account of the interview in his *War Memoirs*, vol. 2, pp. 1089–90.

160 Yigal Sheffy, 'The Origins of the British Breakthrough into South Palestine: The ANZAC Raid on the Ottoman Railway, 1917', *Journal of Strategic Studies* 22:1 (March 1999), pp. 124–47, p. 125.

161 For analyses of the German spring offensive, see Wilson, *Myriad Faces of War*, chs 50–53; Rod Paschall, *The Defeat of Imperial Germany, 1917–1918* (Chapel Hill, 1989), ch. 6; Herwig: *First World War: Germany and Austria-Hungary*, chs 10–11; and Martin Kitchen, *The German Offensives of 1918*, paperback edn (Stroud, 2005).

162 Sheffield and Bourne, *Haig*, 21 March 1918, p. 389.

163 Ibid., 22 March 1918, p. 390.

164 As Terraine argues in his *Haig: The Educated Soldier*, pp. 424–5.

165 Travers, *How the War was Won*, p. 68. Winter also believes that Haig was in a state of panic at Doullens (*Haig's Command*, p. 188). Kitchen agrees (*German Offensives of 1918*, pp. 88–9). Elizabeth Greenhalgh has a more extensive analysis in which she charges that Haig essentially altered his diary after the fact (a 'posthoc amendment') to enhance his reputation and to disguise his panicky frame of mind: see Elizabeth Greenhalgh, 'Myth and Memory: Sir Douglas Haig and the Imposition of Allied Unified Command in March 1918', *Journal of Military History* 68:3 (July 2004), pp. 771–820. Sheffield and Bourne acknowledge Greenhalgh's interpretation and are judicious in their response, admitting that Haig had not only been misled by the German deceptive operations prior to their attack on 21 March, but that he also miscalculated both 'the weight and axes' of that attack (Sheffield and Bourne, *Haig*, p. 9).

166 Greenhalgh's conclusions in her 'Myth and Memory'.

167 Major-General Sir Charles E. Callwell, *Field-Marshall Sir Henry Wilson: His Life and Diaries*, 2 vols (London, 1927), pp. 73–4.

168 Ibid., p. 74.

169 Ibid.

170 Roskill, *Hankey*, vol. 1, p. 511.

171 Callwell, *Sir Henry Wilson*, vol. 2, p. 76.

172 Roskill, *Hankey*, vol. i, 29 March 1918, p. 514.

173 McEwen, *Riddell Diaries*, 23 March 1918, p. 223.

174 Trevor Wilson sums up what seems to be a consensus: Lloyd George 'by common consent, rose heroically to the occasion' (*Myriad Faces of War*, p. 565). Woodward is even more laudatory: 'Lloyd George was magnificent' (*Lloyd George and the Generals*, p. 286).

175 Wilson, *Myriad Faces of War*, pp. 565–6.

176 Rod Paschall, *The Defeat of Imperial Germany, 1917–1918* (Chapel Hill, 1989), p. 147. The Germans fired from nearly 1,000 guns, opposed by only 200 British artillery (see Wilson, *Myriad Faces of War*, pp. 569–72).

177 Roskill, *Hankey*, vol. 1, 8 April 1918, p. 521.

178 Sheffield and Bourne, *Haig*, 3 April 1918, p. 397.

179 For the account which follows, see especially Grigg, *Lloyd George: War Leader*, ch. 27; John Gooch, 'The Maurice Debate 1918', *Journal of Contemporary History* 3:4 (October 1968), pp. 211–28; and David R. Woodward, 'Did Lloyd George Starve the British Army of Men Prior to the German Offensive of 21 March 1918?', *Historical Journal* 27:1 (March 1984), pp. 241–52.

180 See Woodward, *Robertson*, 'Epilogue'.

181 McEwen, *Riddell Diaries*, 11 May 1918, p. 226.

182 Addison, *Four and a Half Years*, 9 May 1918, p. 523.

183 Roskill, *Hankey*, vol. 1, 9 May 1918, p. 545.

184 Vincent, *Crawford Papers*, 9 May 1918, p. 389.

185 See Rhodes James, *Memoirs of a Conservative*, pp. 73–4.

186 Wilson, *Diaries of Scott*, Scott to Courtney, 10 May 1918, p. 344.

187 Woodward, 'Did Lloyd George Starve the British Army?', p. 242 n. 5.

188 Roskill notes that Hankey's published memoir, *The Supreme Command*, omits the incriminating diary entry of 9 May 1918. Roskill, however, includes it in his *Hankey*, vol. 1, pp. 544–5.

189 At that stage of the war, Terraine writes, 'verbal victories over British generals were agreeable to the Prime Minister, perhaps in default of the victories over the Germans which his policy had made so difficult' (*Haig: The Educated Soldier*, p. 392).

190 Roskill, *Hankey*, vol. 1, p. 544.

191 Woodward, 'Did Lloyd George Starve the British Army?', p. 244.

192 Cassar, *Lloyd George at War*, p. 270.

193 Grigg, *Lloyd George: War Leader*, pp. 507 and 511. More generally, see ibid., ch. 27 'The Maurice Affair'.

194 Pugh, *Lloyd George*, p. 116.

195 May 1918 was a month, as Turner has observed, in which Lloyd George's parliamentary position was 'critical' (*British Politics and the Great War*, p. 294).

196 McEwen, *Riddell Diaries*, 11 May 1918, p. 226 and May [n.d.], p. 227. Fitzroy confirmed Lloyd George's view of the political effect of the debate: it was 'a nasty knock for Asquith' (Sir Almeric William Fitzroy, *Memoirs*, vol. 2 (London, n.d.), 10 May 1918). Furthermore, Fitzroy added: 'No one is likely to kill Lloyd George in order to make Asquith PM' (ibid., 10 May 1918).

197 Thomas Jones, *Lloyd George* (Cambridge, 1951), p. 149.

198 David Stevenson, *Cataclysm: The First World War as Political Tragedy* (New York, 2004), p. 340.

199 Roskill, *Hankey*, vol. 1, 27 May 1918, p. 555.

200 Ibid., 28 May 1918, p. 555.

201 Ibid., 30 May 1918, p. 555.

202 Amery described the work of the committee as 'discursive', but often 'momentous'. He characterized Lloyd George's role in the committee's meetings as 'at once' always suggesting some solution, 'shrewd or fanciful' to set off discussion. See Leo Amery, *My Political Life*, vol. 2, *War and Peace, 1914–1929* (London, 1963), pp. 157–8.

203 As Turner notes in his 'Cabinet, Committees and Secretariats: Higher Direction of War', pp. 66–7.

204 Paschall, *Defeat of Imperial Germany*, p. 146.

205 Trevor Wilson makes much of what he calls 'Ludendorf's dilemma' – the deeper the offensive penetration, the more exposed his position (*Myriad Faces of War*, p. 563). Herwig emphasizes a more fundamental flaw – that Ludendorf, the architect of victory on the Eastern Front, lacked a strategic vision in the West. Ludendorf's plan was simply to push forward against Allied forces, driving them before him, without wider objectives. The plan obviously achieved some success, but soon gave the appearance of lurching from one tactical objective to another without a clear idea of how to bring about a decisive victory (Herwig, *First World War*, pp. 406–7, 415).

206 For what follows, see David R. Woodward, *Trial by Friendship: Anglo-American Relations, 1917–1918* (Lexington, 1993).

207 The Earl of Derby, newly appointed ambassador to France, thought Pershing 'pig-headed' (David Dutton (ed.), *Paris 1918: The War Diary of the British Ambassador, the 17th Earl of Derby* (Liverpool, 2001), 18 October 1918, p. 274. Haig believed Pershing to be 'very obstinate, and stupid' (Sheffield and Bourne, *Haig*, 28 September 1918, p. 467).

Lloyd George was in agreement. He confessed to Lord Reading, British ambassador to the United States, that Pershing was 'a most difficult, conceited man' (McEwen, *Riddell Diaries*, 12 October 1918, p. 241).

208 Travers considers Amiens the turning point in 1918. It was especially important in demonstrating, he believes, the crucial role of tanks in keeping the offensive rolling forward (Tim Travers, 'The Evolution of British Strategy and Tactics on the Western Front in 1918: GHQ, Manpower, and Technology', *Journal of Military History* 54:2 (April 1990), pp. 173–200). Wilson agrees that Amiens was significant and that tanks had clearly improved since their introduction to the battlefield; but he also thinks that artillery and aerial observation were more important. See Wilson, *Myriad Faces of War*, ch. 52.

209 Ibid., p. 593, puts the number of attack tanks on the first day of the offensive at 430.

210 David Stevenson, *Cataclysm: The First World War as Political Tragedy* (New York, 2004), pp. 347–8.

211 Gregory Blaxland, *Amiens 1918* (London, 1968), pp. 162, 168.

212 Simon Robbins, *British Generalship on the Western Front 1914–18* (London, 2005). Robbins believes that the Somme marked the beginning 'of a steep learning curve' (p. 142). He makes the case that by 1918, 'the cherished stereotype of a futile and blundering BEF' must be replaced by a more accurate picture of a British Army which at all levels had learned from its mistakes (Simon Robbins, *British Generalship on the Western Front 1914–18* (London, 2005), p. 2). Brian Bond summarizes the effect of the learning curve thus: 'after a sluggish start and many slips, the 'learning curve' had risen sharply from late 1917 to produce a war machine to which the enemy had no answer' (*The Unquiet Western Front: Britain's Role in Literature and History* (Cambridge, 2002), p. 99).

213 Harris, *Haig and the First World War*, p. 516. For a contrary view, see Jay Winter and Antoine Prost, *The Great War in History: Debates and Controversies, 1914 to the Present*, paperback edn (Cambridge, 2005), p. 75; and Winter, *Haig's Command*, p. 204.

214 Harris, *Haig and the First World War*, p. 516.

215 Ibid., pp. 516–7.

216 For this paragraph, see Prior and Wilson, *Command on the Western Front*, esp. Part 6, 'Victory'.

217 Ibid., p. 374.

218 Ibid., chs 31–3. See also Jackson Hughes, 'The Battle for the Hindenburg Line', *War and Society* 17:2 (October 1999), pp. 55–7.

219 See Avner Offer, *The First World War: An Agrarian Interpretation* (Oxford, 1989), ch. 1 and passim.

220 Some units reported that one quarter of their men fought in bare feet. See Richard C. Hall, '"The Enemy is Behind Us": The Morale Crisis in the Bulgarian Army during the Summer of 1918', *War in History* 11:2 (April 2002), pp. 209–19.

221 Titles of chapters 10 and 11 in Rowland's biography of Lloyd George.

222 The subtitle of Gilbert's second volume of his biography of Lloyd George.

223 Trevor Wilson, *The Downfall of the Liberal Party, 1914–1935* (London, 1966), p. 44.

224 Thomas Jones, *Lloyd George* (Cambridge, 1951), pp. 89–90. A fuller flavour of Jones's views on his hero will be found ibid., ch. 5, 'Prime Minister in War, 1916–18', passim.

225 Ibid., p. 90.

226 Roger Chickering, 'World War I and the Theory of Total War: Reflections on the British and German Cases, 1914–1915', in Roger Chickering and Stig Förster (eds), *Great War, Total War: Combat and Mobilization on the Western Front, 1914–1918* (Cambridge, 2000), p. 45.

227 See Keith Grieves, 'Improvising the War Effort: Eric Geddes and Lloyd George, 1915–18', *War and Society* 7:2 (September 1989), pp. 40–55. Grieves cites Geddes as the best known example, but Lloyd George's tenure at the Minister of Munitions in 1915 had already demonstrated this practice.

Chapter 13. Prime Minister in Peace

1 See David French's account of the armistice proceedings '"Had We Known How Bad Things Were in Germany, We Might Have Got Stiffer Terms": Great Britain and the German Armistice', in Manfred R. Boemeke, Gerald D. Feldman and Elisabeth Glaser (eds), *The Treaty of Versailles: A Reassessment after 75 Years*, (Cambridge, 1998), ch. 2.

2 Douglas Newton, *British Policy and the Weimar Republic, 1918–1919* (Oxford, 1997), ch. 1. Newton terms this alliance the 'Knock-Out Blow' Coalition. See also Bruce Kent, *The Spoils of War: The Politics, Economics, and Diplomacy of Reparations 1918–1932* (Oxford, 1989), ch. 1.

3 The act was a remarkable piece of progressive legislation for its day. In expanding the electorate from eight million to 21 million, the Act essentially granted universal manhood suffrage and gave the vote to most women over 30. See Pugh's *Electoral Reform in War and Peace, 1906–18* (London, 1978) for a detailed discussion of the framing and passage of the bill.

4 Trevor Wilson (ed.), *The Political Diaries of C.P. Scott, 1911–1928* (Ithaca, 1970), 8 August 1918, p. 353. In any event, an election was required by the necessities of the electoral law: the last election had been in 1910 and a general election was long over due.

5 See Barry McGill, 'Lloyd George's Timing of the 1918 Election', *Journal of British Studies* 14:1 (November 1974), pp. 109–24.

6 See R.J.Q. Adams, *Bonar Law* (London, 1999), pp. 275–9.

7 Trevor Wilson, 'The Coupon and the British General Election of 1918', *Journal of Modern History* 36:1 (March 1964), pp. 28–42, pp. 30, 39; and Trevor Wilson, *The Downfall of the Liberal Party, 1914–1935* (London, 1966), p. 149. In all, 229 Liberal candidates were deprived of the coupon.

8 For these and the following quotations, see *The Times*, 13 November 1918.

9 Wilson, *Downfall of the Liberal Party*, pp. 140, 150.

10 Newton, *British Policy and the Weimar Republic*, p. 261, quoting from the Scott Papers, 335/54, 15 November 1918.

11 For Sanders's remarks, see John Ramsden (ed.), *Real Old Tory Politics: The Political Diaries of Sir Robert Sanders, Lord Bayford, 1910–35* (London, 1984), 16 November 1918, p. 113.

12 David Dutton, *A History of the Liberal Party in the Twentieth Century* (Houndmills, 2004), p. 74.

13 As Morgan has observed in his *Consensus and Disunity: The Lloyd George Coalition Government 1918–1922*, paperback edn (Oxford, 1986), p. 27. See more generally ibid., ch. 2, 'Coupon and Coalition'. Morgan takes issue with Trevor Wilson's suggestion that Lloyd George was a kind of demonic force in cooperating with the Conservatives to destroy the Liberal Party through the instrumentality of the coupon. The coupon was, Morgan believes, a 'realistic outcome of the politics of war' (ibid., p. 32).

14 Ibid., pp. 28–30.

15 John McEwen, *The Riddell Diaries, 1908–1923* (London, 1986), 27 January 1918, p. 214.

16 It was a campaign, as Morgan has observed, 'for building a specifically Lloyd George brand of Liberalism' (*Consensus and Disunity*, p. 28).

17 For this meeting, see Wilson, *Diaries of Scott*, 25–26 October 1918, pp. 358–60.

18 Dalziel's support for Lloyd George, as we have noted, remained loyal through thick and thin. He was one of the companions who had accompanied the young Welsh MP on his ill-fated Patagonian adventure in 1896.

19 The sale of an important newspaper to the agents of a Prime Minister, as J.M. McEwen observes, 'went far beyond custom or precedent'. See McEwen, 'Lloyd George's Acquisition of the *Daily Chronicle* in 1918', *Journal of British Studies* 22:1 (Fall 1982), pp. 127–44, p. 127. The purchase, a complicated series of manoeuvres, was completed by 1 October 1918. For details, see Stephen Koss, *The Rise and Fall of the Political Press in Britain: The Twentieth Century*, 2 vols (London, 1984), pp. 333–8. Riddell seems to have had some reservations about the take-over. His understated comment was that Lloyd George's full control of the editorial policy of the paper through Dalziel – 'who will in effect be his agent' – would be an 'interesting experiment' (McEwen, *Riddell Diaries*, 1 October 1918, p. 240).

20 Wilson, *Diaries of Scott*, letter to J.L. Hammond, 4 December 1918, p. 362. Scott had also become increasingly critical of the coalition government during the course of the campaign.

21 John Barnes and David Nicholson (eds), *The Leo Amery Diaries*, vol. 1, *1896–1929* (London, 1980), 26 November 1918, p. 246.

22 John Vincent (ed.), *The Crawford Papers: The Journals of David Lindsay, Twenty-Seventh Earl of Crawford and Tenth Earl of Balcarres during the years 1892 to 1940* (Manchester, 1984), 28 December 1918, p. 399.

23 Stephen Koss, *Asquith*, paperback edn (New York, 1985), p. 237.

24 Wilson, *Downfall of the Liberal Party*, p. 173.

25 Kenneth O. Morgan, *Lloyd George* (London, 1974), p. 124; and Morgan, *Consensus and Disunity*, pp. 40–1.

26 John Turner, *British Politics and the Great War: Conciliation and Conflict, 1915–1918* (New Haven, 1992), p. 328.

27 Ibid., p. 329.

28 See *The Times*, 18 November 1918.

29 Ibid., 25 November 1918.

30 Ibid., 30 November 1918.

31 Ibid., 12 December 1918.

32 Ibid., 14 December 1918.

33 Ibid., 18 November 1918.

34 Different sources give different numbers, but all roughly agree upon the totals. Although the official election day was 18 December, service votes were not finally tabulated until 28 December when the final result was announced. The National Democratic Party had been formed by Milner to promote patriotism and imperialism among the working class. Its short life was significant only in demonstrating the drift to the Right at the 1918 election. Two of its members beat Ramsay MacDonald and Arthur Henderson at the polls. See J.O. Stubbs, 'Lord Milner and Patriotic Labour, 1914–1918', *English Historical Review* 87 (October 1972), pp. 717–54.

35 Asquith's defeat can easily enough be attributed to his record as a wartime Prime Minister; but Stuart Ball makes the case that a major reason was Asquith's poor relations with his constituency. Asquith was an infrequent visitor and seldom cultivated the electors whom he neglected 'to the point of contempt' (Stuart Ball, 'Asquith's Decline and the General Election of 1918', *Scottish Historical Review* 62:171 (April 1982), pp. 44–61, p. 50. He was defeated by Colonel Sir Alexander Sprott, who stood as an independent supporter of the Lloyd George coalition. Sprott, a landowner near St Andrews and former Master of

the Fife Foxhounds, was also a war hero, serving gallantly on the Western Front at an advanced age for which he received several medals and his baronetcy.

36 Wilson, *Downfall of the Liberal Party*, 175; Koss, *Asquith*, 239; Jenkins, *Asquith*, p. 479.

37 Grigg describes Hughes as one whose 'natural acerbity was aggravated by chronic dyspepsia and deafness' (John Grigg, *Lloyd George: War Leader 1916–1918* (London, 2002), p. 538).

38 Sally Marks suggests as much in 'Behind the Scenes at the Paris Peace Conference of 1919', *Journal of British Studies* 9:2 (1970), pp. 154–80, pp. 162, 169.

39 McEwen, *Riddell Diaries*, 12 October 1918, p. 241.

40 Ibid., 9 December 1917, p. 210.

41 Margaret MacMillan, *Peacemakers: The Paris Conference of 1919 and its Attempt to End War*, paperback edn (London, 2002), p. 39.

42 Martin Pugh, *Lloyd George*, paperback edn (London, 1988), p. 132.

43 Ffion Hague, *The Pain and the Privilege: The Women in Lloyd George's Life* (London, 2008), p. 343.

44 A.J.P. Taylor, *Lloyd George: A Diary by Frances Stevenson* (London, 1971), 1 April 1919, p. 177.

45 For concise analyses of the Peace Conference and the Treaty of Versailles, see Michael L. Dockrill and J. Douglas Goold, *Peace Without Promise: Britain and the Peace Conferences, 1919–23* (Hamden, 1981), chs 2–4; and Alan Sharp's *The Versailles Settlement: Peacemaking After the First World War, 1919–1923* (Houndmills, 2008).

46 As Zara Steiner puts it: 'Neither the conditions in Europe nor in Paris were conducive to rational peacemaking' (*The Lights that Failed: European International History, 1919–1933* (Oxford, 2005), p. 16).

47 For the following discussion, see David Stevenson, *French War Aims Against Germany, 1914–1919* (Oxford, 1982); and his 'French War Aims and Peace Planning', in Manfred R. Boemeke, Gerald D. Feldman and Elisabeth Glaser (eds), *The Treaty of Versailles: A Reassessment after 75 Years*, (Cambridge, 1998), ch. 3.

48 McEwen, *Riddell Diaries*, 8 March 1919, p. 259.

49 Territorial demands from other countries at the expense of Germany were substantially less. Belgium gained Moresnet, Malmedy and Eupen. Through a plebiscite, Denmark – though neutral during the war – gained northern Schleswig.

50 MacMillan, *Peacemakers*, pp. 206–8.

51 A copy of the memorandum may be found in William R. Keylor (ed.), *The Legacy of the Great War: Peacemaking, 1919* (Boston, 1998), pp. 32–8. It should be noted that from the day of the presentation of the Fontainebleau Memorandum, the Council of Ten effectively ceased to exist as the premier Allied decision-making body and was replaced by the smaller Council of Four.

52 Paul Mantoux, *The Deliberations of the Council of Four (March 24–June 28, 1919) Notes of the Official Interpreter*, vol. 1, trans. and ed. Arthur S. Link (Princeton, 1992), 27 March 1919, p. 37.

53 Ibid.

54 Ibid.

55 Sharp, *Versailles Settlement*, p. 119.

56 Polish representatives at the peace conference were understandably less than appreciative of Lloyd George's role in reducing their territorial demands. Some Polish historians have agreed. Titus Komarnicki, for example, soundly criticizes Lloyd George as 'haughty and overbearing', 'tainted by many prejudices', lacking 'a sound knowledge of history, geography, economics or politics' and thus unqualified to be involved in European

peacemaking (see Titus Komarnicki, *Rebirth of the Polish Republic: A Study in the Diplomatic History of Europe 1914–1920* (London, 1957), pp. 319–20. For the complexity of the Polish question, see Carole Fink, 'The Minorities Question at the Paris Peace Conference: The Polish Minority Treaty, June 28, 1919', in Boemeke, Feldman and Glaser: *The Treaty of Versailles*, ch. 11; and Piotr S. Wandycz, 'The Polish Question', in Boemeke, Feldman and Glaser: *Treaty of Versailles*, ch. 13. The most recent account of Lloyd George's role in the Polish question is Roger Moorhouse, '"The Sore That Would Never Heal": The Genesis of the Polish Corridor', in Conan Fischer and Alan Sharp (eds), *After the Versailles Treaty: Enforcement, Compliance, Contested Identities*, paperback edn (London, 2009), ch. 12. For a defence of Lloyd George, see MacMillan, *Peacemakers*, ch. 17. MacMillan's book is chockfull of anecdotal asides about the personalities at the Conference and has much to say concerning the deeply rooted rivalries of the countries involved. As the great granddaughter of Lloyd George, MacMillan may tend to favour her famous ancestor to some degree. But she also recognizes his shortcomings, such as his 'disregard of geography' (ibid., p. 183), which she sees as a symptom of his occasional ignorance of the complexities of national cultures and their historical context.

57 As noted, among others, by Michael Graham Fry, 'British Revisionism', in Boemeke, Feldman, and Glaser: *Treaty of Versailles*, p. 598.

58 David Lloyd George, *War Memoirs*, new edn, vol. 2 (London, n.d. [1939?]), p. 1513.

59 See Robert E. Bunselmeyer, *The Cost of the War, 1914–1919: British Economic War Aims and the Origins of Reparation* (Hamden, 1975), p. 191 n. 2; and Erik Goldstein, *The First World War Peace Settlements, 1919–1925* (Harlow, 2002), pp. 14–7.

60 See Mantoux, *Deliberations of the Council of Four*, vol. 1, 24 March 1919, p. 3; 27 March 1919, p. 37.

61 In Lloyd George's *The Truth about Reparations and War-Debts* [1932] (New York, 1970), p. 17, he accurately defined indemnity as 'a penal fine which the victors exact from their defeated foe': reparations were 'simply a bill for civil damages suffered' by the victors.

62 Newton, *British Policy and the Weimar Republic*, pp. 281–317.

63 The report did not italicize this phrase. Furthermore, the Report, containing only five brief paragraphs, specifically mentioned the term 'indemnity' three times (Philip Mason Burnett, *Reparation at the Paris Peace Conference from the Standpoint of the American Delegation*, vol. 1 (New York, 1965), p. 430).

64 He claimed in later years that the report 'repelled and shocked' him, and was 'an absurdity' (David Lloyd George, *Memoirs of the Peace Conference*, vol. 1 (New Haven, 1939), pp. 305–6).

65 *The Times*, 12 December 1918.

66 See Robert E. Bunselmeyer, *The Cost of the War, 1914–1919: British Economic War Aims and the Origins of Reparation* (Hamden, 1975), ch. 6, 'Britain, Hughes, and Indemnity'; and Sharp, *Versailles Settlement*, ch. 4, 'Reparations'.

67 Mantoux, *Deliberations of the Council of Four*, vol. 1, 5 April 1919, p. 151.

68 See Burnett, *Reparation at the Paris Peace Conference*, ch. 8, 'The Inclusion of Pensions'.

69 As Pugh describes it, the Germans were forced to accept an 'unlimited liability' (Pugh, *Lloyd George*, p. 134).

70 For these quotations, see Newton, *British Policy and the Weimar Republic*, 350, 355, and more generally, pp. 349–60.

71 McEwen, *Riddell Diaries*, 28 March 1919, p. 262. Lloyd George ordered Riddell to use his influence to bring the press into line: 'You really must try', he said, 'to get the papers to be more reasonable' (ibid., 28 March 1919, p. 262).

72 Taylor, *Stevenson Diary*, 14 April 1919, pp. 179–80.

73 For the speech, see *The Times*, 17 April 1919.

74 In this, he was at odds with Churchill, then at the War Office, who was pressing for a more aggressive posture against the Bolshevik government. Only a few days before his April speech in the House of Commons, Lloyd George was critical of Churchill's Russian proposals: 'He is a dangerous man. He has Bolshevism on the brain ... and was 'mad for operations in Russia'. Bonar Law agreed. Churchill, he said, was 'a dangerous fellow. His judgment is bad. He is too impulsive' (McEwen, *Riddell Diaries*, 11 April 1919, p. 267). Jenkins also agrees. Churchill's 'anti-Bolshevik campaign' and 'Russian adventurism', which 'vastly over-estimated' the possibility of overthrowing the regime, was 'horribly reminiscent of Churchill's Dardanelles illusions' (Roy Jenkins, *Churchill: A Biography*, paperback edn (London, 2002), pp. 350–1).

75 Peter Rowland, *David Lloyd George* (London, 1975), pp. 490–1.

76 Taylor, *Stevenson Diary*, 17 April 1919, p. 180. She also reported that Lloyd George 'was very sick' that she had not been with him, and that 'he missed my note which I always send him directly after a speech' (ibid.).

77 David Dutton, *Austen Chamberlain: Gentleman in Politics* (Bolton, 1985), p. 160.

78 Robert C. Self (ed.), *The Austen Chamberlain Diary Letters: The Correspondence of Sir Austen Chamberlain with his Sisters Hilda and Ida, 1916–1937*, vol. 5 (Cambridge, 1995), 18 April 1919, p. 112. Chamberlain's view then was in stark contrast to his opinion a year earlier when he had complained of Lloyd George's 'folly and crookedness' (ibid., 2 March 1918, p. 77).

79 Newton, *British Policy and the Weimar Coalition*, p. 398.

80 As Morgan notes, for the next three years Lloyd George's policy of appeasement for both Russia and Germany – the need to bring them 'fully into the comity of nations' – was his 'overwhelming preoccupation' (Morgan, *Consensus and Disunity*, pp. 133–4).

81 See Kent, *Spoils of War*, 80–82; Burnett, *Reparation at the Paris Peace Conference*, ch. 16.

82 For the German point of view, see Arno J. Mayer, *Politics and Diplomacy of Peacemaking: Containment and Counterrevolution at Versailles, 1918–1919*, paperback edn (New York, 1969), ch. 22, 'The Versailles Treaty'.

83 For these quotations, see Major-General Sir Charles E. Callwell, *Field-Marshall Sir Henry Wilson: His Life and Diaries*, 2 vols (London, 1927), vol. 2, p. 195.

84 Ibid., p. 196. Wilson himself thought that those clauses which mandated occupation of the Rhine for as long as 15 years were too harsh. Two years was sufficient, he believed.

85 Howard Elcock, *Portrait of a Decision: The Council of Four and the Treaty of Versailles* (London, 1972), p. 273. For a summary of the events in June concerning the revision of the draft treaty, see ibid., ch. 12.

86 For Lloyd George's comments, see Mantoux, *Deliberations of the Council of Four*, vol. 2, 2 June 1919, pp. 268–72.

87 See Georges-Henri Soutou, 'The French Peacemakers and Their Home Front', in Boemeke, Feldman and Glaser: *Treaty of Versailles*.

88 Quoted in Elcock, *Portrait of a Decision*, p. 276.

89 See Manfred F. Boemeke, 'Woodrow Wilson's Image of Germany, the War-Guilt Question, and the Treaty of Versailles', in Boemeke, Feldman and Glaser, *Treaty of Versailles*.

90 Mantoux, *Deliberations of the Council of Four*, vol. 2, 3 June 1919, p. 287.

91 Ibid., 7 June 1918, p. 339. The reasons for delay Lloyd George justified differently two days later: 'The figure we set would terrify the Germans, or it would be impossible for M. Clemenceau and me to get public opinion to accept it' (ibid., 9 June 1919, p. 355).

92 Ibid., 10 June 1919, p. 363.

93 Ibid., 13 June 1919, p. 426.

94 Ibid., 13 June 1919, p. 427.

95 Ibid.,, 16 June 1919, p. 462.

96 Ibid., 16 June 1919, p. 468.

97 Ibid., 17 June 1919, p. 479.

98 Seventy-four ships were sunk, including ten battleships, six battle cruisers, eight light cruisers, and 50 destroyers. More than 50 went to the bottom; others were beached or saved by armed British naval parties. Salvage operations later raised 45 of the ships. A few remain below the waves as objects of interest for scuba enthusiasts on diving holidays.

99 Mantoux, *Deliberations of the Council of Four*, vol. 2, 22 June 1919, p. 514. Elcock observes that Lloyd George, who 'had always been the most ardent advocate of moderation in the Council of Four', now hardened his attitude toward the Germans (Elcock, *Portrait of a Decision*, p. 289).

100 Mantoux, *Deliberations of the Council of Four*, vol. 2, 22 June 1919, p. 512.

101 Ibid., 23 June 1919, p. 528.

102 For a detailed account of Scapa Flow, see Arthur J. Marder, *From the* Dreadnought *to Scapa Flow: The Royal Navy in the Fisher Era, 1904–1919*, vol. 5, *Victory and Aftermath* (London, 1970), ch. 11.

103 As reported by Frances Stevenson in Taylor, *Stevenson Diary*, 28 June 1919, p. 187; and McEwen, *Riddell Diaries*, 28 June 1919, p. 281.

104 John Maynard Keynes, *The Economic Consequences of the Peace* (New York, 1920), ch. 5, 'Reparation'. Direct quotations are on pp. 126, 132, 138, 142, 144, 147.

105 More personal attacks on Lloyd George may be found in John Maynard Keynes, *Essays in Biography* (New York, 1951), ch. 2. There he characterizes Lloyd George – in an often-quoted phrase – as 'this syren, this goat-footed bard' (p. 35). The Prime Minister was, in addition, a 'Welsh witch' whose broomstick 'sped through the twilit air of Paris (p. 34)'. Furthermore, he was 'rooted in nothing … void and without content …' a being who 'lives and feeds on his immediate surroundings'; 'a vampire and a medium in one' (p. 36). Lest it be forgotten, Keynes dipped his pen in malice toward others as well. Of the French President, he wrote that Clemenceau was 'silent and aloof … dry in soul and empty of hope, very old and tired, but surveying the scene with a cynical and almost impish air' (p. 13). Nor did Woodrow Wilson escape. He was a man who 'had thought out nothing' and whose ideas 'were nebulous and incomplete'. In fact, Wilson 'had no plan, no scheme, no constructive ideas whatever for clothing with the flesh of life the commandments which he had thundered from the White House' (pp. 21–2).

106 Marc Trachtenberg, *Reparation in World Politics: France and European Economic Diplomacy, 1916–1923* (New York, 1980), p. 61.

107 For this and the following quotation, see Marc Trachtenberg, 'Reparation at the Paris Peace Conference', *Journal of Modern History* 51 (March 1979), pp. 24–55, pp. 26, 52.

108 Sharp, *Versailles Settlement*, p. 103.

109 Antony Lentin, *Lloyd George, Woodrow Wilson and the Guilt of Germany: An Essay in the Pre-History of Appeasement* (Baton Rouge, 1985), pp. 99,107, 120,135, 154.

110 Morgan, *Lloyd George*, p. 132.

111 Dockrill and Goold, *Peace without Promise*, pp. 45–56.

112 Pugh, *Lloyd George*, p. 133.

113 Ian Packer, *Lloyd George*, paperback edn (Houndmills, Hants, 1998), pp. 68–9.

114 Antony Lentin, *Lloyd George and the Lost Peace: From Versailles to Hitler, 1919–1940* (Houndmills, 2001). Direct quotations are on pp. 4, 6–10, 12, 14, 16–17, 20. xvii. Lentin notes in the Preface to this work (p. xi) that the essays therein had been crafted since his earlier book of 1984. He admits further that he has 'obsessively' reworked them over

time 'to reconsider the facts' and '[more] than once' he has changed his mind. In an admirable cautionary aside, he writes of 'the attraction and the despair of the chronicler of Lloyd George that in grappling with the evidence, fragmentary and inadequate or superabundant and contradictory, he can seldom let bygones be bygones or achieve a satisfactory finality' (p. xi).

115 Maurice Pascal Alers Hankey, Baron, *The Supreme Control at the Paris Peace Conference 1919: A Commentary* (London, 1963), p. 113.

116 Mantoux, *Deliberations of the Council of Four*, vol. 1, 29 March 1919, p. 77.

117 Ibid., 5 April 1919, pp. 152–3. This position would not only satisfy domestic hard liners on reparations, but it could also be used diplomatically against the Germans should they prove recalcitrant to any provisions of the treaty. As Lloyd George put it on 1 April: 'We can tell the Germans that, if they refuse to accept one of our categories, for instance pensions, we will resume our unlimited right of claims for all damages suffered, whatever they may be' (ibid., 1 April 1919, pp. 105–6).

118 MacMillan, *Peacemakers*, pp. 198–200.

119 Robert Skidelsky, *John Maynard Keynes*, vol. 1, *Hopes Betrayed, 1883–1920*, paperback edn (New York, 1994), p. 356. For a brief and balanced account of Hughes at the Peace Conference, see W.J. Hudson, *Billy Hughes in Paris: The Birth of Australian Diplomacy* (West Melbourne, 1978).

120 Arthur Link in his 'Editor's Introduction' to Mantoux, *Deliberations of the Council of Four*, vol. 1, p. xxix.

121 Keynes, *Essays in Biography*, p. 38.

Chapter 14. Reconstruction and Resistance

1 Paul Barton Johnson, *Land Fit for Heroes: The Planning of British Reconstruction, 1916–1919* (Chicago, 1968) is the essential source for this topic.

2 For Addison's contribution to reconstruction, see Kenneth O. Morgan and Jane Morgan, *Portrait of a Progressive: The Political Career of Christopher, Viscount Addison* (Oxford, 1980), chs 3 and 4.

3 Sources for this paragraph include D.W. Dean, 'H.A.L. Fisher, Reconstruction and the Development of the 1918 Education Act', *British Journal of Educational Studies* 18 (1970), pp. 259–76; Lawrence Andrews, *The Education Act, 1918* (London, 1976); Geoffrey Sherington, *English Education, Social Change and War* (Manchester, 1981), ch. V; and Dennis Dean, 'The Dilemmas of an Academic Liberal Historian in Lloyd George's Government: H.A.L. Fisher at the Board of Education, 1916–1922', *History* 79 (February 1994), pp. 57–81.

4 Kenneth O. Morgan, *Consensus and Disunity: The Lloyd George Coalition Government 1918–1922*, paperback edn (Oxford, 1986), p. 84.

5 Kenneth O. Morgan, *Lloyd George* (London, 1974), pp. 135–6.

6 Praise for the Whitley Councils seems unanimous among historians: these include Johnson, *Land Fit for Heroes*, pp. 158–62; Clegg, *History of British Trade Unions*, vol. 2, pp. 204–7; W. Hamish Fraser, *A History of British Trade Unionism 1700–1998* (London, 1999), pp. 141–2; and Chris Howell, *Trade Unions and the State: The Construction of Industrial Institutions in Britain, 1890–2000* (Princeton, 2005), esp. ch. 3.

7 For the following discussion, see Morgan, *Consensus and Disunity*, ch. 3; Chris Wrigley, *Lloyd George and the Challenge of Labour: The Post War Coalition, 1918–1922* (Hemel Hempstead, 1990); Fraser, *History of British Trade Unionism*, ch. 6; A. Clegg, Alan Fox and A.F.

Thompson, *A History of British Trade Unions since 1889*, vol. 1: *1889–1910* (Oxford, 1964), vol. 2, chs 5 and 7.

8   Chris Wrigley, 'The Trade Unions between the Wars', in Chris Wrigley (ed.), *A History of British Industrial Relations*, vol. 2, *1914–1939* (Brighton, 1987), p. 74.

9   See James E. Cronin, 'Coping with Labour, 1918–1926', in James E. Cronin and Jonathan Schneer (eds), *Social Conflict and the Political Order in Modern Britain* (New Brunswick, 1982); and Cronin: 'Strikes and Power in Britain, 1870–1920', pp. 98–9.

10 Wrigley, *Lloyd George and the Challenge of Labour*, p. 56; and see generally ch. 4 'Unrest in the Police Force'.

11 Ibid., p. 66.

12 Cited ibid., 4 June 1919, p. 72.

13 Ibid., chs 5 and 6 for the following discussion.

14 See Barry Supple's indispensable *The History of the British Coal Industry*, vol. 4, *1913–1946: The Political Economy of Decline* (Oxford, 1987), esp. chs 3–4. Supple notes that postwar conditions provided the opportunity for 'a spectacular enhancement' of the bargaining power of miners and the MFGB (p. 78).

15 This hint at nationalization may seem surprising; but during the war, public control of all rail services had been, in effect, a nationalization programme. Several ministers of state, Churchill among them, favoured continuing public control.

16 Philip S. Bagwell, 'The Triple Industrial Alliance, 1913–1922', in Asa Briggs and John Saville (eds), *Essays in Labour History, 1886–1923* (Hamden, 1971).

17 Rodney Lowe, 'The Failure of Consensus in Britain: The National Industrial Conference, 1919–1921', *Historical Journal* 21:3 (1978), pp. 649–75.

18 Wrigley, *Lloyd George and the Challenge of Labour*, p. 138.

19 Lowe, 'Failure of Consensus in Britain', p. 671.

20 *The Times*, 12 February 1919.

21 Morgan, *Consensus and Disunity*, p. 49.

22 Ibid., p. 50.

23 Ralph Desmarais, 'Lloyd George and the Development of the British Government's Strikebreaking Organization', *International Review of Social History* 20, part 1 (1975), pp. 1–15: the quotations are at pp. 2 and 3.

24 Ibid., footnote 1.

25 W.S. Adams, 'Lloyd George and the Labour Movement', *Past & Present* 3 (1953), pp. 55–64: the quotation is from p. 62.

26 Martin Pugh, *Lloyd George*, paperback edn (London, 1988), p. 144.

27 Morgan, *Consensus and Disunity*, p. 50.

28 Wrigley, *Lloyd George and the Challenge of Labour*, p. 143.

29 *The Times*, 12 February 1919.

30 See Supple's discussion in *History of the British Coal Industry*, vol. 4, pp. 126–40.

31 In a letter to Thomas Jones, 17 March 1919, Parliamentary Archives, Lloyd George Papers, cited by Barry Supple in his '"No Bloody Revolutions but for Obstinate Reactions"? British Coalowners in their Context, 1919–20', in D.C. Coleman and Peter Mathias (eds), *Enterprise and History: Essays in Honour of Charles Wilson* (Cambridge, 1984), p. 219.

32 For the discussion that follows, see Supple, *British Coal Industry*, vol. 4, pp. 136–40.

33 It may be that nationalization was never an important issue among rank and file miners and that higher wages and shorter hours satisfied their immediate needs, thus negating any broader reformist notions.

34 See Wrigley, *Lloyd George and the Challenge of Labour*, pp. 197–200.

35 Mined coal was the private property of owners of the surface land, to whom royalties were paid for its extraction.

36 Supple, *History of the British Coal Industry*, vol. 4, p. 138.

37 Philip S. Bagwell, *The Railwaymen: The History of the National Union of Railwaymen* (London, 1963), p. 388.

38 Norman and Jeanne MacKenzie (eds), *The Diary of Beatrice Webb*, vol. 3, *'The Power to Alter Things'* (Cambridge, 1984), 28 September 1919, p. 349.

39 Stephen Roskill, *Hankey: Man of Secrets*, 3 vols (London, 1970), vol. 2, 29 September 1919, p. 122.

40 *The Times*, 29 September 1919.

41 Susan Armitage, *The Politics of Decontrol of Industry: Britain and the United States* (London, 1969), p. 79.

42 John Ramsden (ed.), *Real Old Tory Politics: The Political Diaries of Sir Robert Sanders, Lord Bayford, 1910–35* (London, 1984), 9 October 1919, p. 129. Sanders was well informed on Conservative opinion: he was then Deputy Chairman of the Conservative Party Organization and a party whip. He was also serving as Treasurer of the Household.

43 Thus Roskill could claim that the railway strike of 1919 ended 'in an atmosphere not far removed from *opera bouffe*' (Roskill, *Hankey*, vol. 2, p. 124).

44 With both government and union members in a cooperative mood, as Morgan puts it, the strike 'had genuinely constructive results' (*Consensus and Disunity*, p. 62).

45 Wrigley, *Lloyd George and the Challenge of Labour*, pp. 222–3; see also Morgan, *Consensus and Disunity*, pp. 60–2.

46 Bagwell, *Railwaymen*, ch. 15, and p. 398 for the quotation.

47 Bagwell blames the Conservative coalition in Commons and Cabinet which had captured the Prime Minister and made him 'a prisoner on his own government benches' (Philip S. Bagwell, *The Transport Revolution from 1770* (London, 1974), p. 245),

48 Keith Grieves, 'Sir Eric Geddes, Lloyd George and the Transport Problem, 1918–21', *Journal of Transport History* 13:1 (1991), pp. 26–7.

49 For these conversations, see John McEwen, *The Riddell Diaries, 1908–1923* (London, 1986), 28 September–11 October 1919, pp. 292–3.

50 Wrigley observes that Lloyd George was 'usually very skilful in the postwar period in dividing moderate trade unionists from the more militant' (Wrigley, *History of British Industrial Relations*, vol. 2, p. 83).

51 Norman and Jeanne MacKenzie (eds), *The Diary of Beatrice Webb*, vol. 3, *'The Power to Alter Things'* (Cambridge, 1984), 28 September 1919, p. 349.

52 Ibid., 11 October 1919, p. 293. Lloyd George's reference to guild socialism and syndicalism was overwrought. Guild socialism enjoyed some popularity in the immediate postwar era in its advocacy of workers' management through unions (or guilds): it rejected revolutionary activity to gain its ends. See Frank Matthews, 'The Building Guilds', in Asa Briggs and John Saville (eds), *Essays in Labour History, 1886–1923* (Hamden, 1971); and Geoffrey Foote, *The Labour Party's Political Thought: A History* (New York, 1997), ch. 6. Syndicalism, revolutionary in intent, opposed collective bargaining and was committed to disrupting the ruling capitalist oligarchy through constant strike activity. Eventually a culminating revolutionary general strike would then establish a workers' society. Joseph White doubts syndicalist influence among British workers: see his 'Syndicalism in a Mature Industrial Setting: the Case of Britain', in Marcel van der Linden and Wayne Thorpe (eds), *Revolutionary Syndicalism: An International Perspective* (Aldershot, Hants, 1990).

53 Hodges was secretary of the Miners' Federation; Smillie, one of the founders of the Independent Labour Party, was Vice-President of the Miners' Federation of Britain; and Thomas was Parliamentary Secretary of the NUR and MP for Derby.

54 James Hinton, *Labour and Socialism: A History of the British Labour Movement, 1867–1974* (Amherst, 1983), p. 115.

55 Keith Middlemas, *Politics in Industrial Society: The Experience of the British System since 1911* (London, 1979), pp. 131–2 and more generally chs 5 and 6. Lloyd George was directly involved in the creation of the agency, as were William Sutherland, the coalition chief whips, and the newspaper magnate and Lloyd George confidant, George Riddell. A fund of £100,000, contributed by private industrial sources, was to be used for such items as anti-Labourite posters, leaflets, press advertisements and speakers (ibid., p. 473, n. 24). Middlemas claims, however, that such action was counter-productive. By creating a machine for surveillance, he believes that the government 'highlighted the things they feared' (ibid., p. 133).

56 Major-General Sir Charles E. Callwell, *Field-Marshall Sir Henry Wilson: His Life and Diaries*, 2 vols (London, 1927), vol. 2, 31 December 1919, p. 219.

57 Ibid., 1 January 1920, p. 221.

58 Keith Jefferey, *Field Marshal Sir Henry Wilson: A Political Soldier* (Oxford, 2006), p. 245.

59 Keith Middlemas (ed.), *Thomas Jones: Whitehall Diary* (Oxford, 1969), vol. 1, 2 February 1920, pp. 99–103. The following quotations are taken from this source.

60 In an aside to this comment, Jones wryly observed that Bonar Law's frequent referral to loyal stockbrokers made one think 'that potential battalions of stockbrokers were to be found in every town' (ibid., p. 101).

61 Callwell, *Sir Henry Wilson*, vol. 2, 2 April 1920, pp. 231–2.

62 For this paragraph, see Keith Jeffery and Peter Hennessy, *States of Emergency: British Governments and Strikebreaking since 1919* (London, 1983), chs 1–3.

63 The origins of the Corps began in 1914 when Czech workers on the job in Russia joined with their brother Slavs to fight against the German led Central Powers. By the time of the Bolshevik Revolution, they numbered 40,000. Why they turned against the Bolsheviks is, as one historian has noted, 'a much debated question' (Evan Mawdsley, *The Russian Civil War* (Boston, 1987), p. 477).

64 For what is almost a blow by blow account, see Edgar Anderson, 'An Undeclared Naval War: The British-Soviet Naval Struggle in the Baltic, 1918–1920', *Journal of Central European Affairs* 22:1 (1962/63), pp. 43–78. Lloyd George admitted to senior naval officers in July 1919 that 'we were at war with the Bolsheviks, but had decided not to make war'. By which he meant that although British land forces would not carry on the fight, naval operations must continue. See Clifford Kinvig, *Churchill's Crusade: The British Invasion of Russia, 1918–1920* (London, 2006), p. 147, quoting from War Cabinet minutes.

65 For the following discussion, see Arno J. Mayer, *Politics and Diplomacy of Peacemaking: Containment and Counterrevolution at Versailles, 1918–1919*, paperback edn (New York, 1969), chs 10, 13–14, 18; Richard H. Ullman, *Anglo-Soviet Relations, 1917–1921*, vol. 2, *Britain and the Russian Civil War, November 1918–February 1920* (Princeton, 1968); and Ullman, *Anglo-Soviet Relations, 1917–1921*, vol. 3, *The Anglo-Soviet Accord* (Princeton, 1972).

66 Curzon's anti-Russian views had been shaped by his own experiences as Indian Viceroy where he encountered at first hand Russian imperial ambitions in central Asia (see G.H. Bennett, *British Foreign Policy During the Curzon Period, 1919–24* (New York, 1995), ch. 4).

67 Ullman, *Anglo-Soviet Relations*, vol. 2, p. 90.

68 Ibid., pp. 91–2.

69 Ibid., p. 96.

70 Ibid., p. 97.

71 Ibid. This disagreement between Lloyd George and Churchill was, as Richard Toye has observed, 'one of their most prolonged and substantive disputes' (*Lloyd George and Churchill: Rivals for Greatness*, paperback edn (London, 2007), p. 195.

72 For the following, see Ullman, *Anglo-Soviet Relations*, vol. 2, ch. 3; and Kinvig, *Churchill's Crusade*, passim. As Jenkins notes, the 'dominant theme' of Churchill's War Secretaryship was 'his dedicated attempt at strangling near to birth the Bolshevik regime in Russia'. His 'Russian adventurism' was, Jenkins further believes, 'horribly reminiscent of Churchill's Dardanelles illusions' (Roy Jenkins, *Churchill: A Biography*, paperback edn (London, 2002), pp. 350–2). Markku Ruotsila provides a specific example of Churchill's employment of 'extensive and prolonged secret contacts' to create a war coalition 'that would be alternative to, and partly independent' of both the War Office and the Paris Peace Conference. The initial aim was the capture of St Petersburg, using Finnish White troops under the command of General Carl Mannerheim. See, 'The Churchill-Mannerheim Collaboration in the Russian Intervention, 1919–1920', *The Slavonic and East European Review* 80:1 (January 2002), pp. 1–20.

73 Kinvig, *Churchill's Crusade*, p. 152.

74 Ibid., p. 181. General Wilson seems to have changed his mind. Several weeks earlier, having lost confidence in both generals Denikin and Kolchak, he had counselled a withdrawal of British troops from Russia during a meeting of the War Cabinet (Callwell, *Sir Henry Wilson*, vol. 2, p. 169).

75 See for example the map in John Bradley, *Allied Intervention in Russia* (London, 1968), pp. 60–1.

76 Mark von Hagen, *Soldiers in the Proletarian Dictatorship: The Red Army and the Soviet Socialist State* (Ithaca, 1990), pp. 124–6.

77 Morgan, *Consensus and Disunity*, p. 134.

78 For this speech, see *The Times*, 10 November 1919.

79 Ibid., 10 November 1919.

80 Ibid., 18 November 1919.

81 Ibid., 18 November 1919.

82 Richard K. Debo, 'Prelude to Negotiations: The Problem of British Prisoners in Soviet Russia, November 1918–July 1919', *Slavonic and East European Review* 58:1 (January 1980), pp. 58–75.

83 Richard K. Debo, 'Lloyd George and the Copenhagen Conference of 1919–1920: The Initiation of Anglo-Soviet Negotiations', *Historical Journal* 24:2 (1981), pp. 429–41.

84 In doing so, Lloyd George operated outside the usual diplomatic channels of Curzon and the Foreign Office. These actions prompted Ullman to characterize Lloyd George's behaviour as 'devious' (*Anglo-Soviet Relations*, vol. 2, p. 329).

85 For Lloyd George's remarks, see *The Times*, 11 February 1920.

86 For these negotiations, see Ullman, *Anglo-Soviet Relations*, vol. 3, ch. 3; M.V. Glenny, 'The Anglo-Soviet Trade Agreement, March 1921', *Journal of Contemporary History* 5:2 (1970), pp. 63–82; and Andrew J. Williams, *Trading with the Bolsheviks: The Politics of East-West Trade, 1920–39* (Manchester, 1992), ch. 2, passim.

87 Hankey records that Churchill was 'quite barmy' in his detestation of the Bolsheviks. During one Cabinet meeting in late 1920, Churchill made a 'frantic appeal' against the emerging trade agreement. Voted down, he turned 'quite pale' and that very night went to the Oxford Union to deliver 'a violently anti-Bolshevist speech'. See Roskill, *Hankey*, vol. 2, 18 November 1920, pp. 172–3.

88 Bennett, *British Foreign Policy During the Curzon Period, 1919–24*, pp. 64–9.

89　From decrypted messages by British Secret Services: see Christopher Andrew, *Defend the Realm: The Authorized History of MI5* (New York, 2009), p. 144.

90　Horne, Conservative MP for Glasgow Hillhead, was Minister of Labour, 1919–20, for which service he was knighted. He was President of the Board of Trade from 1920–1.

91　Self, *Chamberlain Diary Letters*, 28 February 1920, pp. 129–30.

92　Ullman, *Anglo-Soviet Relations*, vol. 3, p. 435.

93　*The Times*, 23 March 1921. Britain did not formally recognize the Bolshevik government as *de jure* until 1924.

94　Printed in full in Ullman, *Anglo-Soviet Relations*, vol. 3, pp. 479–82.

95　Christopher Andrew, 'The British Secret Service and Anglo-Soviet Relations in the 1920s. Part I: From the Trade Negotiations to the Zinoviev Letter', *Historical Journal* 20:3 (1977), pp. 673–706.

96　Ibid., p. 684.

97　This was the premise outlined in Cabinet discussions on 29 July 1920: see L.J. MacFarlane, 'Hands Off Russia: British Labour and the Russo-Polish War, 1920', *Past & Present* 38 (December 1967), pp. 126–52, p. 133, citing Cabinet minutes.

98　Norman Davies, 'Sir Maurice Hankey and the Inter-Allied Mission to Poland, July-August 1920', *Historical Journal* 15:3 (1972), pp. 553–61.

99　For the conference, see Ullman, *Anglo-Soviet Relations*, vol. 3, ch. 4 'Spa'.

100　*The Times*, 22 July 1920.

101　Ibid., 11 August 1920. *The Times* leader of that day found much to praise in Lloyd George's remarks. The Prime Minister was 'so frank and clear, so convincing, moderate, and firm that we are all satisfied it will command the confidence and the approbation he demands' (*The Times*, 11 August 1920).

102　Norman Davies, 'Lloyd George and Poland, 1919–20', *Journal of Contemporary History* 6:3 (1971), pp. 132–54, p. 146.

103　Elcock argues that Lloyd George's Eastern European policy was broadly consistent throughout. He was pledged to uphold Polish independence and to contain Bolshevism within the borders of Russia (Howard Elcock, 'Britain and the Russo-Polish Frontier, 1919–1921', *Historical Journal* 12:1 (1969), pp. 137–54).

104　Cited in Ullman, *Anglo-Soviet Relations*, vol. 3, 15 January 1920, p. 275, from the Wilson MSS diary. Callwell, in his published edition of Wilson's diary, omits this quotation. See Callwell, *Sir Henry Wilson*, vol. 2, p. 225.

105　Ullman, *Anglo-Soviet Relations*, vol. 3, 27 May 1920, p. 275. Callwell also omits this quotation.

106　Ibid., 27 May 1920, p. 275. Callwell remains silent on Wilson's opinions of the Prime Minister.

107　See Walter Kendall, *The Revolutionary Movement in Britain, 1900–21* (London, 1969), ch. 13; and Andrew Thorpe, *The British Communist Party and Moscow, 1920–43* (Manchester, 2000), ch. 3.

108　Ullman, *Anglo-Soviet Relations*, vol. 3, 18 August 1920, 278. Ullman notes that Callwell's published version of the diary relating to this event 'bears virtually no relationship to the original' (ibid., 18 August 1920, p. 278, footnote 31).

109　Ibid., 18 August 1920, p. 280.

110　Ibid., citing Wilson's MSS diary of 31 December 1920, p. 308. Callwell here allows some of Wilson's criticism of Lloyd George to stand. 'No matter where we look,' Wilson wrote, 'we find Lloyd George totally unfit to govern'. Especially noteworthy in Wilson's mind was that the Prime Minister had tried – 'luckily with little success' – 'to make love to Kameneff [sic] and Krassin and the Bolsheviks' (Callwell, *Sir Henry Wilson*, vol. 2, 31

December 1920, p. 275). When Wilson's diaries were published in 1927, Lloyd George's supporters came swiftly to his defence. Sir Robert Borden, prime minister of Canada during World War I, responded to Wilson's diatribes in lawyerly fashion. Those passages of Wilson's diary of which he, Borden, had personal knowledge were 'by no means reliable' and conveyed impressions that were 'quite misleading' (Parliamentary Archives, LG/G/8/18/7, Borden to Hankey, 22 November 1927). Others were more offended. Hankey wrote a lengthy letter to Lloyd George, deploring in the strongest terms Wilson's diatribe. 'It is really sickening that petulant extracts from his diary, written no doubt in moments of disappointment or irritability, should be published' (ibid., LG/G/8/18/3, 9 October 1927). Eric Geddes also forcefully condemned Wilson's diary as not only 'terribly vain and foolish', but also 'hopelessly incorrect' (ibid., LG/G/8/7/10, 10 October 1927). Lloyd George responded tersely to Geddes that 'Wilson was always a queer fellow and very mercurial' (ibid., LG/G/8/7/11, 13 October 1927).

111 These quotations are from Ullman, *Anglo-Soviet Relations*, vol. 3, pp. 293, 294.

112 For the terms of the Kamenev note, see Richard K. Debo, *Survival and Consolidation: The Foreign Policy of Soviet Russia, 1918–1921* (Montreal, 1992), p. 233. For the Lloyd George-Kamenev interview, see Ullman, *Anglo-Soviet Relations*, vol. 3, pp. 300–10.

113 As stated in a public declaration issued by the Council of Action on 10 August 1920. Quoted in Macfarlane, 'Hands Off Russia', p. 138.

114 Riddell understood immediately the significance of the Council: 'A very important movement', he acknowledged in his diary entry of 14 August 1920 (McEwen, *Riddell Diaries*, p. 322).

115 A brief history of the Council may be found in Stephen White, 'Labour's Council of Action, 1920', *Journal of Contemporary History* 9 (1974), pp. 99–122.

116 One may easily guess General Wilson's opinion of the Councils of Action. In a communication with Churchill, he condemned the councils as collaborators with the Russian Soviets 'for the downfall and ruin of England' (Ullman, *Anglo-Soviet Relations*, vol. 3, p. 279). In this instance, Callwell documents Wilson's candid views: see Callwell, *Sir Henry Wilson*, vol. 2, 19 August 1918, p. 259.

117 See an account of this meeting in Stephen Richards Graubard, *British Labour and the Russian Revolution, 1917–1924* (Cambridge, 1956), pp. 106–8. Ernest Bevin, who had once worked as a van boy, a waiter and a conductor on horse trams in London, became a paid official for the Dockers' Union in 1911. A centrist and a pragmatic leader of the Labour movement, he is best known as Labour Secretary under Winston Churchill's coalition government during World War II and as Foreign Secretary in Clement Atlee's postwar Labour government.

118 For the following, see G.C. Peden, 'The Road to and from Gairloch: Lloyd George, Unemployment, Inflation, and the "Treasury View" in 1921', *Twentieth Century British History* 4:3 (1993), pp. 224–49.

119 As Garside has pointed out, the Treasury believed its main responsibility lay in budgetary control and debt management, not in determining the level of employment (W.R. Garside, *British Unemployment, 1919–1939: A Study in Public Policy* (Cambridge, 1990), p. 320).

120 Rodney Lowe, 'The Erosion of State Intervention in Britain, 1917–24', *Economic History Review*, 2nd Series, 31 (May 1978), pp. 270–86, p. 278.

121 It is interesting to note that at this point in his economic thinking, Keynes agreed with the Treasury – a view he held until 1925. See Robert Skidelsky, 'Keynes and the Treasury View: The Case for and Against an Active Unemployment Policy 1920–1939', in W.J. Mommsen (ed.), *The Emergence of the Welfare State in Britain and Germany, 1850–1950* (London, 1981).

122 These statistics are from C.H. Feinstein, *National Income, Expenditure, and Output of the UK 1855–1965* (Cambridge, 1972) as reprinted in Jim Tomlinson, *Public Policy and the Economy since 1900* (Oxford, 1990), p. 46.

123 See Peter K. Cline, 'Eric Geddes and the 'Experiment' with Businessmen in Government, 1915–22', esp. pp. 99–103 in Kenneth D. Brown (ed.), *Essays in Anti-Labour History: Responses to the Rise of Labour in Britain* (Hamden, 1974); and Andrew McDonald, 'The Geddes Committee and the Formulation of Public Expenditure Policy, 1921–1922', *Historical Journal* 32:2 (1989), pp. 643–74.

124 There is some evidence, too, that Addison's failures as an administrator contributed to the disappointing reconstruction scheme. See William Bridgeman's opinion in his diary for February 1918 where he is severely critical of Addison's management of the Ministry of Reconstruction: 'having no experience of the civil service, and not enough capacity to realise [sic] his ignorance', Addison 'embarked on all sort of works which were already being done by one dept. or another' (Philip Williamson (ed.), *The Modernisation of Conservative Politics: The Diaries and Letters of William Bridgeman, 1904–1935* (London, 1988), p. 125). Bridgeman also thought that Addison was 'not trusted' (ibid., p. 127). Bridgeman was a Conservative member for Oswestry and held minor positions on both the Asquith and Lloyd George coalitions. He later served as Home Secretary in the brief Bonar Law and first Baldwin ministries (1922–24). Another critic of Addison was Robert Sanders, who often had words of praise for Lloyd George. He thought, for example, the Prime Minister's handling of the miners' strike 'a model of tact and dexterity' (Ramsden, *Real Old Tory Politics*, 5 March 1919, p. 123). But he, too, was critical of Addison. He claimed that Addison was 'a hopeless failure at Munitions' and had been given the Ministry of Reconstruction to pension him off (ibid., 29 July 1917, p. 88). However, the Morgans take exception to theses charges and firmly defend Addison's ministerial career: see their *Portrait of a Progressive*, chs 3–5.

125 Riddell was more explicit a few months later when he noted in his diary that Lloyd George, 'at heart opposed to the claims of Labour', was 'steadily veering over to the Tory point of view' (McEwen, *Riddell Diaries*, 27 March 1920, p. 309). See also Wrigley, *Lloyd George and the Challenge of Labour*, pp. 255–58).

126 He may have believed, as the Morgans observe, that the time was ripe 'to translate his semi-presidential ascendancy of the wartime years into something more permanent' (*Portrait of a Progressive*, p. 116).

127 Riddell, who was also present, records that Lloyd George and Winston had 'evidently' decided on some joint action regarding the formation 'of a Central Party, so called' (McEwen, *Riddell Diaries*, 12 to 15 July, p. 285).

128 *The Times*, 16 July 1919.

129 Trevor Wilson (ed.), *The Political Diaries of C.P. Scott, 1911–1928* (Ithaca, 1970), 30 November 1919, p. 379.

130 As Trevor Wilson calls it in his *The Downfall of the Liberal Party, 1914–1935* (London, 1966), p. 193.

131 For the speech, see *The Times*, 8 December 1919.

132 Ramsden, *Real Old Tory Politics*, 8 January 1920, p. 134.

133 Ibid. Gilbert also believes that Lloyd George hoped to use fusion to create a broadly based government against any future Labour Party upsurge. In addition, fusion would strengthen the Prime Minister's tenuous position within the coalition by pruning out the malcontents. See Bentley Brinkerhoff Gilbert, *British Social Policy, 1914–1939* (Ithaca, 1970), pp. 33–48.

134 McEwen, *Riddell Diaries*, 1 February 1920, p. 304.

135 John Vincent (ed.), *The Crawford Papers: The Journals of David Lindsay, Twenty-Seventh Earl of Crawford and Tenth Earl of Balcarres during the years 1892 to 1940* (Manchester, 1984), 15 March 1920, p. 406.

136 Ibid., 19 March 1920, p. 406.

137 Wilson, *Downfall of the Liberal Party*, p. 196.

138 Morgan, *Consensus and Disunity*, p. 185.

139 Ibid. Wrigley believes that the Prime Minister was genuinely undergoing a sea change, a final shift away from his radical origins (Wrigley, *Lloyd George and the Challenge of Labour*, pp. 255–58).

140 For these settlements, see Wrigley, *Lloyd George and the Challenge of Labour*, pp. 258–60; and Eric Taplin, *The Dockers' Union: A Study of the National Union of Dock Labourers, 1889–1922* (Leicester, 1986), ch. 10.

141 This was part of the government's general policy of postwar decontrol. For other examples, see Derek H. Aldcroft, *Studies in British Transport History, 1870–1970* (Newton Abbot, 1974), ch. 5, 'The Decontrol of Shipping and Railways after the First World War'.

142 Middlemas, *Jones: Whitehall Diary*, vol. 1, 4 April 1921, p. 134.

143 For this concise summary, see Supple, *History of the British Coal Industry*, vol. 4, pp. 154–61.

144 Middlemas, *Jones: Whitehall Diary*, vol. 1, 12 April 1921, p. 146.

145 Ibid., 13 April 1921, p. 146. Said to Jones after he relayed the call from Thomas.

146 Ibid., p. 148.

147 Ibid., 24 April 1921, p. 153.

148 Ibid., 27 June 1921, p. 162.

149 For what follows, see Morgan, *Consensus and Disunity*, p. 77.

Chapter 15. The Irish Revolution

1 For a discussion of the 'profoundly inward-looking nature of provincial Irish politics' before the Rising, see Michael Wheatley, *Nationalism and the Irish Party: Provincial Ireland, 1910–1916* (Oxford, 2005). The quotation is from ibid., p. 40.

2 See Michael Laffan, *The Resurrection of Ireland: The Sinn Fein Party, 1916–1923* (Cambridge, 1999). The whole of Laffan's admirable work informs the following analysis.

3 The internment camps served, as Jackson notes, 'as revolutionary academies for a thrusting generation of young radicals' (Alvin Jackson, *Home Rule: An Irish History 1800–2000* (Oxford, 2003), p. 176).

4 Two other sons took part in the Rising but were spared execution and suffered only imprisonment. Plunkett's title was neither English nor Irish: he was a papal count and had been known to display at his house in Kimmage the banner of the Holy Sepulchre. His sympathies with Irish separatism were unmistakable, however. Prior to the Rising, his house had served as an arsenal for the insurgents (Laffan, *Resurrection of Ireland*, p. 79).

5 As Laffan notes: 'Sinn Féin was the fad or the craze of 1917' (ibid., p. 94).

6 Ibid., p. 102.

7 The standard account is R.B. McDowell, *The Irish Convention, 1917–18* (London, 1970). For a detailed analysis of the work of Lloyd George's Garden Suburb in formulating Irish policy and specifically the plan for the convention, see J.A. Turner, *Lloyd George's Secretariat*, ch. 5. Turner writes that the Garden Suburb took more responsibility for the substance of Irish policy than it did on 'any other subject' (ibid., 85).

8 John Grigg, *Lloyd George: War Leader 1916–1918* (London, 2002), p. 407.

9 Parliamentary Archives, LG/F/37/4/8, 26 January 1917, LG to Duke.

10 Ibid., LG/F/30/2/8, 30 January 1917, Duke to LG in a memo marked 'Confidential'.

11 PIbid., LG/F/48/1/3, 17 February 1917. See also Pauric Travers, 'The Priest in Politics: the Case of Conscription', in Oliver MacDonagh, W.F. Mandle and Pauric Travers (eds), *Irish Culture and Nationalism, 1750–1950* (New York, 1983); Tom Garvin, *Nationalist Revolutionaries in Ireland, 1858–1928* (Oxford, 1987), 57–66; and Theodore Hoppen, *Ireland since 1800: Conflict and Conformity* (London, 1999), pp. 173–84.

12 Parliamentary Archives, LG/F/48/1/6, 23 February 1918. Cattle driving might include – as a warning – the removal of cattle from graziers' lands at night, releasing them to wander at will. David S. Jones analyzes the 'land-acquisitive tendencies' of graziers and their negative impact upon smaller farmers ('The Cleavage between Graziers and Peasants in the Land Struggle, 1890–1910', in Samuel Clark and James S. Donnelly Jr (eds), *Irish Peasants: Violence and Political Unrest, 1780–1914* (Madison, 1983).

13 Cited in Fergus Campbell, *Land and Revolution: Nationalist Politics in the West of Ireland, 1891–1921* (Oxford, 2005), p. 242.

14 For the following analysis, see Alan J. Ward, 'Lloyd George and the 1918 Irish Conscription Crisis', *Historical Journal* 17:1 (March 1974), pp. 107–29.

15 Parliamentary Archives, LG/F/48/6/7, 18 April 1918. French, it will be remembered, had been General Officer Commanding-in-Chief of the BEF from 1914–5 when he was recalled and replaced by Haig. For the next three years, French served as GOC-in-C Home Forces until his appointment to Ireland in May 1918.

16 Ibid., LG/F/48/6/8, 19 April 1918.

17 For this account of the conscriptionist controversy, see Laffan, *Resurrection of Ireland*, pp. 133–42.

18 Stephen Roskill, *Hankey: Man of Secrets*, vol. 1 (London, 1970), p. 554, 21 May 1918.

19 See the account by Eunan O'Halpin, 'British Intelligence in Ireland, 1914–1921', in Christopher Andrew and David Dilks (eds), *The Missing Dimension: Governments and Intelligence Communities in the Twentieth Century* (Urbana, 1984).

20 For the partnership of French and Long over Ireland, see Eunan O'Halpin, *The Decline of the Union: British Government in Ireland, 1892–1920* (Dublin, 1987), ch. 6; and John Kendle, *Walter Long, Ireland, and the Union, 1905–1920* (Montreal, 1992), pp. 164–5. As Kendle notes, Long 'remained forever convinced that the Irish, like an unruly hound, would respond only to a firm hand' (ibid., p. 200).

21 F.S.L. Lyons, *Ireland since the Famine*, paperback edn (London, 1989), p. 396.

22 Charles Townshend, *Easter 1916: The Irish Rebellion* (Chicago, 2006), p. 340.

23 Ward, 'Lloyd George and Irish Conscription', p. 107.

24 Morgan, *Lloyd George*, p. 113.

25 Martin Pugh, *Lloyd George*, paperback edn (London, 1988), p. 121. On the other hand, as Pugh observes, the Prime Minister's governing style appeared to be distinctly presidential, if not dictatorial, during the war. This of course had to be the case: only a centralized war effort from the top, as Lloyd George knew, could win the war. It seems likely that Lloyd George considered Ireland as a war zone and acted accordingly.

26 Ward, 'Lloyd George and Irish Conscription', p. 112.

27 For the Sinn Féin campaign and the election that followed, see Laffan, *Resurrection of Ireland*, pp. 151–68.

28 For a succinct review of these developments, see F.S.L. Lyons, 'The War of Independence, 1919–21', in W.E. Vaughan (ed.), *A New History of Ireland*, vol. 6, *Ireland under the Union, II, 1870–1921* (Oxford, 1996), pp. 243–4.

29 David Fitzpatrick, *Politics and Irish Life 1913–21: Provincial Experiences of War and Revolution* (Cork, 1977), p. 284 and passim, esp. ch. 5 'Revolutionary Administrators'.

30 Roy Foster, *Modern Ireland, 1600–1972* (London, 1988), p. 492. Foster notes further that it was a revolution that had already taken place 'in the hearts and minds of the people' (Foster, *Modern Ireland*).

31 Charles Townshend, 'Historiography: Telling the Irish Revolution', in Joost Augusteijn (ed.), *The Irish Revolution, 1913–1923*, paperback edn (Houndmills, 2002), p. 8.

32 In a letter to Lord French, 21 January 1919, quoted in O'Halpin, *Decline of the Union*, p. 181.

33 John Butler, 'Select Documents XLV: Lord Oranmore's Journal, 1913–27', *Irish Historical Studies* 29:116 (November 1995), pp. 553–93, 16 April 1920, p. 580. The Browne family had settled in Ireland in the thirteenth century. By the nineteenth century, they owned enormous tracts of land in Counties Mayo, Roscommon, and Galway. A Conservative and southern Unionist, Oranmore and Browne was elected an Irish representative peer in 1902.

34 Parliamentary Archives, LG/F/15/6/3, 23 February 1919. O'Halpin: *Decline of the Union*, p. 30 describes Dunraven describes as a moderate unionist landowner.

35 Ibid., 193. See also Charles Townshend, *The British Campaign in Ireland, 1919–1921: The Development of Political and Military Policies* (Oxford, 1975), pp. 20–32.

36 Keith Middlemas (ed.), *Thomas Jones: Whitehall Diary*, vol. 1 (Oxford, 1969), Jones to J.T. Davies, 23 May 1919, p. 87.

37 In a letter to Ian Macpherson, who had succeeded Edward Shortt as Irish Chief Secretary in January 1919; cited in O'Halpin, *Decline of the Union*, 18 February, 1920, p. 200. It may be noted here that O'Halpin holds French largely, if not primarily, accountable for the decline of British civil government in Ireland, so evident by early 1920. As Lord Lieutenant, French – 'little more than a mendacious blusterer' – was responsible for the concentration of power at Dublin Castle into the hands 'of incompetent die-hards' (ibid., 18 February, 1920, pp. 206–7).

38 Meda Ryan argues that the Kilmichael ambush marked a turning point because its tactical sophistication finally convinced the British government that the Irish were in fact engaging in warfare and that the IRA was indeed an army (Ryan, 'The Kilmichael Ambush, 1920: Exploring the "Provocative Chapters"', *History* 92:306 (April, 2007), pp. 235–49, pp. 237–8).

39 For this paragraph, see Charles Townshend's *The British Campaign in Ireland, 1919–1921: The Development of Political and Military Policies* (Oxford, 1975); and for a recent analysis, Paul Bew, *Ireland: The Politics of Enmity, 1789–2006* (Oxford, 2007), ch. 9.

40 Richard Murphy, 'Walter Long and the Making of the Government of Ireland Act, 1919–20', *Irish Historical Studies* 25 (1986–7), pp. 82–96, p. 83 and passim. Additionally useful is Kendle, *Walter Long, Ireland, and the Union*, esp. pp. 180–96.

41 Nicholas Mansergh, *The Unresolved Question. The Anglo-Irish Settlement and its Undoing, 1912–72* (New Haven/London, 1991), ch. 5; and Jackson, *Home Rule*, 204–8.

42 As J.J. Lee has observed, this proposed border was chosen explicitly to provide unionists only 'with as much territory as they could safely control' (*Ireland, 1912–1985: Politics and Society* (Cambridge, 1989), p. 45.

43 D.G. Boyce, *Englishmen and Irish Troubles: British Public Opinion and the Making of Irish Policy, 1918–22* (London, 1972) analyzes this debate authoritatively. Boyce's title is, however, somewhat misleading. Women were also interested in Ireland. Boyce himself recounts, for example, the activities of Lady Mark Sykes, Lady Bonham Carter, Margaret Bondfield, Ishbel Lady Aberdeen and Edith Stopford (p. 69).

44 For this paragraph, see David Fitzpatrick, 'The Irish in Britain, 1871–1921' in Vaughan: *New History of Ireland*, pp. 684–5; and Maurice Walsh, *The News from Ireland: Foreign Correspondents and the Irish Revolution* (London, 2008).

45 Walsh, *News from Ireland*, p. 72.

46 *Manchester Guardian*, 29 October 1920, cited ibid., p. 79.

47 *Daily News*, 29 October 1920, cited ibid., p. 80.

48 R.J.Q. Adams, *Bonar Law* (London, 1999), p. 286.

49 Major-General Sir Charles E. Callwell, *Field-Marshall Sir Henry Wilson: His Life and Diaries*, 2 vols (London, 1927), vol. 2, 28 May 1920, p. 241; and 28 June 1920, p. 246.

50 Ibid., 11 July 1920, p. 252.

51 Ibid., 29 September 1920, pp. 263–4.

52 Contrast Hankey's diary entry of 22 April 1918 (Roskill, *Hankey*, vol. 1, p. 517) when he pled to Lloyd George in person during the conscription crisis for a conciliatory policy towards Ireland. Two years later, he wrote in his diary that: 'terror must be met by greater terror' (ibid., vol. 2, 23 May 1920, p. 153).

53 This and the following quotations may be found in letters to his sisters, Ida and Hilda, reprinted in Robert C. Self (ed.), *The Austen Chamberlain Diary Letters: The Correspondence of Sir Austen Chamberlain with his Sisters Hilda and Ida, 1916–1937*, vol. 5 (Cambridge, 1995). See 10 June 1918, p. 90; 29 July 1918, p. 92; 24 July 1920, pp. 138–9; 31 October 1920, 142; 3 April 1921, p. 157. Self describes Chamberlain's attitude towards Ireland as 'both complex and ambivalent' (152). Chamberlain served as Chancellor of the Exchequer in Lloyd George's coalition government until March 1921 when he became Lord Privy Seal and leader of the Conservative Party.

54 John M. McEwen, *The Riddell Diaries, 1908–1923* (London, 1986), 20 November 1919, p. 296.

55 *The Times*, 11 October 1920.

56 They also were constantly on the alert for any weapons advantage to use against British forces, and proved nimble in their acquisition. For example, they were able to purchase and have shipped in May 1921 a substantial number of a new American weapon, the Thompson sub-machine-gun (Townshend, *British Campaign in Ireland*, p. 180).

57 For this analysis, see ibid., ch. 6, 'Deadlock'.

58 Keith Middlemas (ed.), *Thomas Jones: Whitehall Diary*, vol. 3, *Ireland 1918–1925* (London, 1971), 8 March 1921, p. 54.

59 For these important discussions, see ibid., 27 April 1921, pp. 55–63; and 12 May 1921, pp. 63–70.

60 These three quotations are from ibid., pp. 60 and 61. Lloyd George's negative views of Ireland were not new. In remarks to Riddell in late 1919, he had stated his belief that Ireland was 'a most unfortunate country. Something awkward always occurs at critical moments in her history' (McEwen, *Riddell Diaries*, 21 December 1919, p. 297).

61 For Balfour's comments, see Middlemas, *Jones: Whitehall Diary*, vol. 3, 12 May 1921, pp. 64 and 65.

62 Ibid., p. 66.

63 Ibid., p. 67.

64 Ibid., p. 69.

65 Lloyd George had confessed to Riddell the previous month: 'I see no alternative but to fight it out. A republic at our doors is unthinkable' (McEwen, *Riddell Diaries*, 2 April 1921, p. 340).

66 Middlemas, *Jones: Whitehall Diary*, vol. 3, 12 May 1921, p. 69.

67 Lyons, *Ireland since the Famine*, pp. 424–46.

68 Middlemas, *Jones: Whitehall Diary*, vol. 3, 19 May 1921, p. 71.

69 Ibid., 24 May 1921, p. 71: see also Townshend, *British Campaign in Ireland*, 189–91.

70 The accomplishments, composition, and membership of the IRA has found no general agreement among historians. See the following: Charles Townshend, 'The Irish Republican Army and the Development of Guerrilla Warfare, 1916–1921', *English Historical Review* 94:371 (April 1979), pp. 318–45; David Fitzpatrick, 'The Geography of Irish Nationalism, 1910–1921', in C.H.E. Philpin (ed.), *Nationalism and Popular Protest in Ireland* (Cambridge, 1987); Peter Hart, *The IRA at War 1916–1923* (Oxford, 2003), esp. ch. 2: and Joost Augusteijn, 'Accounting for the Emergence of Violent Activism among Irish Revolutionaries, 1916–21', *Irish Historical Studies* 35:139 (May 2007), pp. 327–44.

71 *The Times*, 23 June 1921.

72 Middlemas, *Jones: Whitehall Diary*, vol. 3, 24 June 1921, p. 80. Craig became leader of the Ulster Unionist Party a few months earlier and then the first Prime Minister of Northern Ireland in June 1921.

73 Ibid., pp. 80–1.

74 Winston S. Churchill, *The Aftermath* (New York, 1929), p. 303.

75 Kenneth O. Morgan, *Consensus and Disunity: The Lloyd George Coalition Government 1918–1922*, paperback edn (Oxford, 1986), p. 130.

76 Michael Hopkinson, *Irish War of Independence* (Montreal, 2002), p. 194.

77 So Boyce states in *Englishmen and Irish Troubles*, p. 129. It may be argued that the changes were also necessary to reinvigorate an antiquated system of governance at the Castle, which had been fully revealed under the strains and tensions of the Irish uprising. Responsible for the proper functioning of the RIC, the Castle's 'inflexibility of system, incapacity of personnel, inadequacy of equipment' simply could not cope, as Richard Hawkins has observed ('Dublin Castle and the Royal Irish Constabulary (1916–1922)', in Desmond Williams (ed.), *The Irish Struggle, 1916–1926* (London, 1966), p. 167).

78 Michael Hopkinson (ed.), *The Last Days of Dublin Castle: The Mark Sturgis Diaries* (Dublin, 1999), Introduction. Hopkinson believes that Cope was 'probably' commissioned by Lloyd George to establish these contacts and was made additionally responsible for setting up 'a host of peace initiatives' (ibid., p. 5).

79 For this episode, see Hopkinson, *Irish War of Independence*, pp. 182–5. According to Hopkinson, negotiations failed largely due to Lloyd George's imposition of terms: before a truce could be proclaimed, Lloyd George insisted upon IRA disarmament (p. 184).

80 As Hopkinson describes the meeting, it had great 'potential' significance (ibid., p. 161). See also Mansergh's account of the meeting in his *Unresolved Question*, p. 158. Elsewhere, however, Hopkinson strongly condemns Lloyd George's 'undoubted deviousness' in his attempts to negotiate with the Irish. He claims further that Lloyd George 'does not merit the favourable historical press he has generally received on the Irish Question' (see Hopkinson, 'Negotiation: The Anglo-Irish War and the Revolution', in Joost Augusteijn (ed.), *The Irish Revolution, 1913–23* (London, 2002), pp. 125, 126.

81 Hopkinson, *Mark Sturgis Diaries*, 12 December 1920, p. 89.

82 Ibid., 9 November 1920, p. 68.

83 Mansergh, *Unresolved Question*, p. 160.

84 To quote Mansergh here: Anderson's 'courageous departure from the Civil Service convention' in writing his letter 'must have had its influence on the Prime Minister and the Leader of the House and through them the Cabinet, where opinion was nicely balanced between those in favour of concession and those in favour of persevering for months or years of guerilla warfare' (ibid., pp. 160–1).

85 Hopkinson, *Mark Sturgis Diaries*, 7 December 1920, p. 87.

86 For the following discussion on Dominion status for Ireland, see D.G. Boyce, 'How to Settle the Irish Question: Lloyd George and Ireland, 1916–21', in A.J.P. Taylor (ed.), *Lloyd George: Twelve Essays* (New York, 1971), 137–64; Boyce: *Englishmen and Irish Troubles*, chs 6 and 7, passim; David Harkness, 'Britain and the Independence of the Dominions: the 1921 Crossroads', in T.W. Moody (ed.), *Nationality and the Pursuit of National Independence: Historical Studies* XI (Belfast, 1978), pp. 141–59; Mansergh, *Unresolved Question*, chs 6 and 7, passim.

87 Only to dismiss it: he told Scott that he could 'take no action while the condition of Ireland remained as at present' (Trevor Wilson (ed.), *The Political Diaries of C.P. Scott, 1911–1928* (Ithaca, 1970), 22 February 1919, p. 372).

88 Middlemas, *Jones: Whitehall Diary*, vol. 3, 24 July 1920, p. 32.

89 Ibid., 4 August 1920, pp. 34–6.

90 Ibid., 13 October 1920, p. 40.

91 Ibid., 14 May 1921, p. 68. Lloyd George's mastery of the Cabinet was firm at this time. Arthur Lee reported that the Prime Minister's 'domination of the Cabinet' was 'complete and wonderful' – in fact, 'tremendous' (Alan Clark (ed.), *'A Good Innings': The Private Papers of Viscount Lee of Fareham* (London, 1974), 13 May 1921, p. 209). Lee had recently replaced Walter Long as First Lord of the Admiralty.

92 See W.K. Hancock, *Smuts: The Fields of Force 1919–1950* (Cambridge, 1968), pp. 49–61.

93 Ibid., p. 54

94 Middlemas, *Jones: Whitehall Diary*, vol. 3, 14 June 1921, p. 75.

95 Roy Foster, however, rejects the 'sentimentally assumed' notion that King George's conciliatory speech had any bearing upon events and argues that the primary reason for the government's willingness to negotiate was based upon Ulster's unilateral removal from any union with Southern Ireland on the one hand and on the other hand, the unhappy prospect of governing Southern Ireland under martial law (Foster, *Modern Ireland*, p. 504).

96 Middlemas, *Jones: Whitehall Diary*, vol. 3, 6 July 1921, pp. 82–5.

97 Ibid., p. 83.

98 Ibid.

99 A.J.P. Taylor, *Lloyd George: A Diary by Frances Stevenson* (London, 1971), 14 July 1921, pp. 227–8. De Valera was reportedly unimpressed by this geography lesson.

100 Nicholas Mansergh, 'Ireland and the British Commonwealth of Nations: The Dominion Settlement', in Desmond Williams (ed.), *The Irish Struggle, 1916–1926* (London, 1966), p. 131.

101 Middlemas, *Jones: Whitehall Diary*, vol. 3, 10 August 1921, pp. 93, 95.

102 As both British and Irish negotiators well knew, fealty to the King was no light matter. Loughlin notes that the monarch was the primary 'hegemonic signifier of British national identity' (James Loughlin, *The British Monarchy and Ireland: 1800 to the Present* (Cambridge,2007), p. 317).

103 This decision has been a matter of some debate among historians. Lyons tends to think that de Valera hoped to emphasize his position as head of state by remaining in Dublin (Lyons, *Ireland Since the Famine*, p. 429). Coogan argues that de Valera had become convinced that Lloyd George would refuse Irish demands for a republic and therefore did not wish to be associated with a compromised conference (Tim Pat Coogan, *De Valera: Long Fellow, Long Shadow*, paperback edn (London, 1995), p. 244). Costello on the other hand believes that de Valera, bearing in mind the unhappy experience of Woodrow Wilson at the Paris Peace Conference, could best serve as a 'neutral broker' by remaining above the negotiating fray (Francis Costello, *The Irish Revolution and its Aftermath, 1916–1923: Years of Revolt* (Dublin, 2003), pp. 242–4.

104 Middlemas, *Jones: Whitehall Diary*, vol. 3, 11 October 1921, pp. 119–20.

105 Ibid., 14 October 1921, p. 128.

106 Ibid., p. 131.

107 Ibid., 17 October 1921, p. 134.

108 Ibid., 133. This was a chief worry for Austen Chamberlain, who was then Lord Privy Seal and Leader of the House of Commons in Lloyd George's coalition government. To his sister, he wrote: 'Opposition to the Conference & to our action is growing among our own people …' (Self, *Chamberlain Diary Letters*, 13 October 1921, p. 170).

109 Middlemas, *Jones: Whitehall Diary*, vol. 3, 21 October 1921, p. 139.

110 As succinctly stated by Lloyd George on 21 October 1921 (Ibid., pp. 140–1).

111 Taylor: *Stevenson Diary*, 6 November 1921, 234. Bonar Law was, as Maurice Cowling points out, 'in continuous contact' with Lloyd George throughout the negotiations. (*The Impact of Labour, 1920–1924: The Beginning of Modern British Politics* (Cambridge, 1971) p. 126.

112 According to Stevenson, Lloyd George painted 'a lurid picture' to Bonar Law of what could happen should the Conservative leader go too far (Taylor, *Stevenson Diary*, 6 November 1921).

113 Middlemas, *Jones: Whitehall Diary*, vol. 3, 17 November 1921, p. 167.

114 However, as Costello notes, there is some question as to what was promised in this meeting. Costello does believe that 'at this juncture in the Conference' Collins broke with orthodox republican sentiment (Costello, *Irish Revolution and its Aftermath*, p. 268).

115 Middlemas, *Jones: Whitehall Diary*, vol. 3, 6 December 1921, p. 184.

116 Ibid., 13 December 1921, p. 187. Over the years, Jones's opinion was only strengthened. In his biography of Lloyd George, he wrote of his Chief's qualities during the Irish negotiations: 'Tenacity, foresight, vigilance, fairness to opponents, patience with opponents and colleagues alike, a mind of the most extraordinary intuitive swiftness, the most unfailing good temper day and night, in hours of intense strain no less than in times of comparative smoothness – these were the shining qualities that brought to an end the deadlock which had baffled all the great statesmen of England' (Thomas Jones, *Lloyd George* (Cambridge, 1951), p. 193).

117 Wilson, *Diaries of Scott*, 6 December 1921, p. 412.

118 *The Times*, 7 December 1921.

119 MacKenzie: *Diary of Beatrice Webb*, vol. 3, 7 December 1921, p. 390.

120 Quotations below are from *The Times*, 15 December 1921.

121 Quoted in Adams, *Bonar Law*, p. 305.

122 *The Times*, 15 December 1921.

123 Sheila Lawlor, *Britain and Ireland, 1914–23* (Dublin, 1983), p. 146.

124 Ian Packer, *Lloyd George*, paperback edn (Houndmills, Hants, 1998), p. 83.

125 Peter Rowland *David Lloyd George* (London, 1975), p. 555.

126 Boyce, 'How to Settle the Irish Question', p. 163. But Boyce also thinks this was accomplished by somewhat devious means: 'Not only did Lloyd George browbeat the Irish: he also hoodwinked the English' (ibid.).

127 Pugh, *Lloyd George*, p. 148.

128 Morgan, *Consensus and Disunity*, p. 132.

129 Mansergh, *Unresolved Question*, p. 196.

130 Ibid., pp. 130–31, 198–200, 219–25.

131 Foster, *Modern Ireland*, p. 505.

132 John McColgan, *British Policy and the Irish Administration, 1920–22* (London, 1983), p. 67.

133 Bew, *Ireland: The Politics of Enmity, 1789–2006*, p. 421.

134 Hopkinson, *Irish War of Independence*, p. 179.

135 Alvin Jackson, *Ireland 1798–1998* (Oxford, 1999), p. 259.

136 Jackson, *Home Rule*, p. 324.

137 See Middlemas, *Jones: Whitehall Diary*, vol. 3, 1 November 1921–22 December 1921, pp. 152–79.

138 Tim Pat Coogan, *The Man Who Made Ireland: The Life and Death of Michael Collins* (Niwot, 1992), p. 244. See also Coogan, *De Valera*, p. 262 and Costello, *Irish Revolution and its Aftermath*, pp. 256–57.

139 These quotations are from Wilson, *Diaries of Scott*, 28–29 October 1921, p. 402.

140 Ibid., p. 406.

141 Ibid., 2 December, 1921, p. 407.

142 Ibid., p. 408.

143 Jones, *Lloyd George*, pp. 191–2.

144 As Laffan notes, the events of 1921 were especially ironical for Ulster – 'the only part of Ireland which had not sought Home Rule was the only part to obtain it' (Michael Laffan, *The Partition of Ireland, 1911–25* (Dundalk, 1983), p. 70.

145 Not all Conservatives were mollified. During the parliamentary debates on the treaty, there were some denunciations of 'astonishing virulence' (Mansergh, *Unresolved Question*, pp. 197–98) against the British delegates, but Bonar Law's support helped mollify the critics.

146 Information on the Boundary Commission is scattered: see Lyons, *Ireland since the Famine*, pp. 433–8; Laffan, *Partition of Ireland*, ch. 6; Mansergh, *Unresolved Question*, ch. 10; Costello, *Irish Revolution and its Aftermath*, ch. 9; Jackson, *Home Rule*, pp. 209–13.

147 Dennis Kennedy, *The Widening Gulf: Northern Attitudes to the Independent Irish State, 1919–49* (Belfast, 1988), p. 69.

148 Michael Hopkinson, 'The Craig-Collins Pacts of 1922: Two Attempted Reforms of the Northern Ireland Government', *Irish Historical Studies* 27:106 (November 1990), pp. 145–58, pp. 145 and 149.

149 For a general analysis of the events during the early months of 1922, see Paul Canning, *British Policy Towards Ireland, 1921–1941* (Oxford, 1985), ch. 3. 'Defending the Treaty'.

150 The difficulties encountered by Collins and the Treatyites and the ambiguities forced upon them, is discussed in John M. Regan, 'The Politics of Reaction: the Dynamics of Treatyite Government and Policy, 1922–33', *Irish Historical Studies* 30:120 (November 1997), pp. 542–63.

151 For an account of the conference, see T. Ryle Dwyer, *Big Fellow, Long Fellow: A Joint Biography of Collins and De Valera* (New York, 1998), pp. 299–304.

152 In a letter to his sister: Self, *Chamberlain Diary Letters*, 22 April 1922, p. 188.

153 Middlemas, *Jones: Whitehall Diary* vol. 3, 15 May 1922, p. 200. Churchill's tendency to undisciplined action during these delicate times brought a rebuke from Lloyd George, though in private. To Jones he confided that Churchill reminded him of a perfectly sane and responsible driver who on occasion suddenly 'takes you over a precipice'. He thought 'there was a strain of lunacy' in Winston (ibid., 8 June 1922, p. 212).

154 For a recent analysis of the Irish Civil War and its treatment by historians, see Bill Kissane, *The Politics of the Irish Civil War* (Oxford, 2005).

155 Michael Hopkinson, *Green Against Green: The Irish Civil War* (New York, 1988), p. 116.

Chapter 16. 'To Straighten Ragged Edges'

1 Morgan's apt summary: see his *Consensus and Disunity: The Lloyd George Coalition Government 1918–1922*, paperback edn (Oxford, 1986), p. 327.

2 As Lowe and Dockrill rightly claim, British foreign policy from the Paris Peace Conference into the early months of 1922 was 'largely determined' by Lloyd George (C.J. Lowe and M.L. Dockrill, *The Mirage of Power*, vol. 2, *British Foreign Policy 1914–22* (London, 1972), p. 335).

3 Roberta M. Warman, 'The Erosion of Foreign Office Influence in the Making of Foreign Policy, 1916–1918', *Historical Journal* 15:1 (March 1972), pp. 133–59, p. 159.

4 Harold Nicolson, *Curzon: The Last Phase, 1919–1925. A Study in Postwar Diplomacy* (New York, 1939), p. 60.

5 David Gilmour, *Curzon: Imperial Statesman, 1859–1925* (London, 1994), pp. 534–6; Alan J. Sharp, 'The Foreign Office in Eclipse, 1919–22', *History* 61 (1976), pp. 198–218. Gaynor Johnson, however, takes issue with the generally accepted animus between Lloyd George and Curzon (Johnson, 'Curzon, Lloyd George and the Control of British Foreign Policy, 1919–22: A Reassessment', *Diplomacy and Statecraft* 11:3 (November 2000), pp. 49–71). Johnson believes that there were 'substantial areas' of agreement' (p. 50); that Curzon 'respected Lloyd George's skill at political persuasion' (52); that they 'worked closely together and shared similar views' (p. 56); and that overall, 'the differences between the two men have been exaggerated' (p. 58).

6 Morgan, *Consensus and Disunity*, pp. 111, 115. See also Zara Steiner's analysis of the privileged elite who traditionally had made up the Foreign Office and the diplomatic service, 'Elitism and Foreign Policy: The Foreign Office before the Great War', in B.J.C. McKercher and D.J. Moss (eds), *Shadow and Substance in British Foreign Policy, 1895–1939: Memorial Essays Honouring C.J. Lowe* (Edmonton, Canada, 1984), pp. 19–55.

7 As the doyenne of diplomatic history, Zara Steiner, has put it in her *The Lights that Failed: European International History, 1919–1933* (Oxford, 2005), p. 611.

8 Morgan, *Consensus and Disunity*, 111.

9 Martin Pugh, *Lloyd George*, paperback edn (London, 1988), p. 136.

10 Craig, 'The British Foreign Office from Grey to Austen Chamberlain', ch. 1 in Gordon A. Craig and Felix Gilbert (eds), *The Diplomats, 1919–1939* (Princeton, 1953), pp. 21, 35.

11 Brian McKercher, 'Old Diplomacy and New: the Foreign Office and Foreign Policy, 1919–1939', ch. 5 in Michael Dockrill and Brian McKercher (eds), *Diplomacy and World Power: Studies in British Foreign Policy, 1890–1950* (Cambridge, 1996), pp. 94, 92.

12 Michael L. Dockrill and J. Douglas Goold, *Peace without Promise: Britain and the Peace Conferences, 1919–23* (London, 1981), pp. 81–2.

13 For French postwar policy, see Walter A. McDougall, *France's Rhineland Diplomacy, 1914–1924: The Last Bid for a Balance of Power in Europe* (Princeton, 1978).

14 Marc Trachtenberg, *Reparation in World Politics: France and European Economic Diplomacy, 1916–1923* (New York, 1980), pp. 122–5.

15 Stephen Roskill, *Hankey: Man of Secrets*, 3 vols (London, 1970), vol. 2, 27 March 1920, p. 149.

16 Keith Middlemas (ed.), *Thomas Jones: Whitehall Diary* (London, 1971), vol. 1, 8 April 1920, p. 108.

17 Ibid.

18 For a discussion of the San Remo Conference, see Jukka Nevakivi, *Britain, France and the Arab Middle East 1914–1920* (London, 1969), ch. 12, 'San Remo and After'.

19 Roskill, *Hankey*, vol. 2, 18 April 1920, p. 159.

20 John M. McEwen, *The Riddell Diaries, 1908–1923* (London, 1986), 24 April 1920, p. 311; and 23–24 April 1920, p. 310.
21 Trachtenberg, *Reparation in World Politics*, p. 132. Trachtenberg attributes this success to Lloyd George's persistent approach to the French position. By a tactical series of careful and incremental steps, he moved the French gradually towards moderating their demands over reparations (ibid., p. 130).
22 This warning occurred on 5 December 1921 at Chequers during a conversation between the Prime Minister and Louis Loucheur, a close friend of Briand and a member of his government. For this incident, see Carole Fink, *The Genoa Conference: European Diplomacy, 1921–1922* (Chapel Hill, 1984), pp. 22–3. Fink's book informs the following discussion.
23 See Nevakivi, *Britain, France and the Arab Middle East*, passim.
24 For the following, see Hines Hall III, 'Lloyd George, Briand and the Failure of the Anglo-French *Entente*', *Journal of Modern History* 50:2 (December 1978), D1121–38.
25 Lloyd George emphasized, as he had in the past, that Germany 'must pay to the utmost of her capacity'; but he also mentioned an important caveat. In determining that capacity, prudence and restraint must be employed (*The Times*, 7 January 1922).
26 The only major power absent was the United States, which had recently sponsored the Washington Naval Conference (November 1921–February 1922). After the Naval Conference had set naval limitations for the USA, Britain and Japan, the Americans showed little interest in participating in any further diplomatic entanglement on continental Europe.
27 Carole Fink uses the quoted phrase in 'Beyond Revisionism: The Genoa Conference of 1922', in Fink, Alex Frohn and Jurgen Heideking (eds), *Genoa, Rapallo, and European Reconstruction in 1922* (Cambridge, 1991), p. 13. In her larger work, Fink makes abundantly clear the supremacy of Lloyd George at Genoa (see Fink, *Genoa Conference*, passim).
28 *The Times*, 11 April 1922. Carole Fink characterizes Lloyd George's speech as 'dramatic, vigorous, clear, practical, and idealistic' (Fink, *Genoa Conference*, pp. 152, 153).
29 Much has been written on the background to Rapallo and its consequences. Most useful are Fink, *Genoa Conference*, pp. 162–76 and ch. 6; and the edited collection in Fink, Frohn, and Heideking, *Genoa, Rapallo, and European Reconstruction in 1922*. See also Hartmut Pogge von Strandmann, 'Rapallo – Strategy in Preventive Diplomacy: New Sources and New Interpretations', in Volker Berghahn and Martin Kitchen (eds), *Germany in the Age of Total War* (London, 1981), ch. 6; and Stephen White, *The Origins of Détente: The Genoa Conference and Soviet-Western Relations, 1921–1922* (Cambridge, 1985), chs 7 and 8.
30 For the complex negotiations between the Soviet Union and Germany that led to Rapallo, see Robert Himmer, 'Rathenau, Russia, and Rapallo', *Central European History* 9: 2 (June 1976), pp. 146–83.
31 Stephanie Salzmann, *Great Britain, Germany and the Soviet Union: Rapallo and After, 1922–1934* (Woodbridge, Suffolk, 2003), p. 7.
32 Carole Fink, 'European Politics and Security at the Genoa Conference of 1922', in Carole Fink, Isabel V. Hull, and MacGregor Knox (eds), *German Nationalism and the European Response, 1890–1945* (Norman, OK, 1985), p. 147.
33 McDougall, *France's Rhineland Diplomacy*, pp. 188–9.
34 Roskill, *Hankey*, vol. 2, p. 160. Privately, Lloyd George expressed his concerns to Frances Stevenson. On 19 April, he wrote that the Conference was 'in serious peril'. A few days later, the Conference was 'still laboring heavily'; and later, it was 'trembling on the edge of a precipice, though he claimed that he was 'still sanguine' (see A.J.P. Taylor, *My Darling Pussy: The Letters of Lloyd George and Frances* (London, 1975), 19 April 1922, p. 44; 23 April 1922, p. 44; and 26 April 1922, p. 45).

35 For the following discussion, see Fink, *Genoa Conference*, chs 6–10; and Stephen White, *The Origins of Détente: The Genoa Conference and Soviet-Western Relations, 1921–1922* (Cambridge, 1985), ch. 8.

36 Morgan, *Consensus and Disunity*, 313.

37 This is White's view in his *Origins of Détente*, p. 189. Roskill, however, relying on Hankey's diary, reports that the Commissions of Enquiry were a Soviet initiative, which Lloyd George accepted (*Hankey*, vol. 2, p. 275).

38 A.J.P. Taylor, *English History, 1914–1945* (New York, 1965), p. 190.

39 Keith Robbins, '"Experiencing the Foreign": British Foreign Policy Makers and the Delights of Travel', in Dockrill and McKercher, *Diplomacy and World Power*, pp. 19–42, pp. 30–1.

40 White, *Origins of Détente*, p. 192.

41 McDougall, *France's Rhineland Policy*, p. 189.

42 Bruce Kent, *The Spoils of War: The Politics, Economic, and Diplomacy of Reparations 1918–1932* (Oxford, 1989), pp. 169, 177.

43 Bennett, *British Foreign Policy during the Curzon Period*, p. 71.

44 Ibid., p. 72.

45 P.M.H. Bell, *France and Britain 1900–1940: Entente and Estrangement* (London, 1996), p. 130.

46 Andrew Williams, 'The Genoa Conference of 1922: Lloyd George and the Politics of Recognition', in Fink, Frohn, and Heideking, *Genoa, Rapallo, and European Reconstruction*, pp. 29–47.

47 Morgan, *Consensus and Disunity*, pp. 315–6.

48 Jones, *Lloyd George*, p. 184.

49 Ibid., p. 186.

50 Quotations are from Fink, *Genoa Conference*, p. 276.

51 Carole Fink, 'The NEP in Foreign Policy: The Genoa Conference and the Treaty of Rapallo', in Gabriel Gorodetsky (ed.), *Soviet Foreign Policy, 1917–1991: A Retrospective* (London, 1994), pp. 11–20, pp. 16, 19.

52 See Patrick O. Cohrs, *The Unfinished Peace after World War I: America, Britain and the Stabilisation of Europe, 1919–1932* (Cambridge, 2006), p. 72.

53 Ibid., p. 73.

54 Steiner, *Lights that Failed*, p. 213.

55 Ibid., p. 211.

56 Ibid., p. 212.

57 Of course, there was a likely secondary (some would say primary) reason for Lloyd George's numerous conferences – to enhance his own visibility and popularity among the British electorate and to maintain his dominance in the coalition government.

58 See Aaron S. Klieman, 'Britain's War Aims in the Middle East in 1915', *Journal of Contemporary History* 3 (July 1968), pp. 237–52, pp. 240–2.

59 Elizabeth Monroe, *Britain's Moment in the Middle East, 1914–1971*, rev. edn (Baltimore, 1981), p. 29.

60 Ibid., pp. 243–4.

61 David Fromkin, *A Peace to End All Peace: The Fall of the Ottoman Empire and the Creation of the Modern Middle East*, paperback edn (New York, 1989), pp. 146–8; Marian Kent, 'Asiatic Turkey, 1914–1916', in F.H. Hinsley (ed.), *British Foreign Policy under Sir Edward Grey* (Cambridge, 1977), pp. 436–51; and Dockrill and Goold, *Peace without Promise*, pp. 133–4.

62 John Darwin, 'Imperialism in Decline? Tendencies in British Policy between the Wars', *Historical Journal* 23:3 (1980), pp. 657–79.

63   Brief accounts of the British occupation of Egypt may be found in P.J. Vatikiotis, *The History of Egypt*, 3rd edn (Baltimore, 1985), ch. 8, 'The British in Egypt'; and M.W. Daly, 'The British Occupation, 1882–1922', in M.W. Daly (ed.), *The Cambridge History of Egypt*, vol. 2, *Modern Egypt, from 1517 to the End of the Twentieth Century* (Cambridge, 1998).

64   For this conversation, see Roskill, *Hankey*, vol. 1, 6 October 1918, p. 609.

65   See Nevakivi, *Britain, France and the Arab Middle East*, passim.

66   Isaiah Friedman, 'The McMahon-Hussein Correspondence and the Question of Palestine', *Journal of Contemporary History* 5 (1970), pp. 83–122.

67   For a concise discussion of the revolt, see Fromkin, *A Peace to End all Peace*, ch. 28. 'Hussein's Revolt'. It was in this military action that T.E. Lawrence, then a young junior intelligence officer with the Arab Bureau in Cairo, first became intimately involved with the Arab cause.

68   Fromkin, *A Peace to End All Peace*, p. 268.

69   See, for example, Keith Wilson, *The Myriad Faces of War: Britain and the Great War 1914–1918* (London, 1986), pp. 623–4; Matthew Hughes, *Allenby and British Strategy in the Middle East, 1917–1919* (London, 1999), ch. 6; and John Grigg, *Lloyd George: War Leader 1916–1918* (London, 2002), ch. 19. John Darwin calls the British plan for a Jewish homeland 'strategic Zionism' (Darwin, *The Empire Project: The Rise and Fall of the British World System, 1830–1970* (Cambridge, 2009), p. 316). But Malcolm Yapp sees no guiding principle in Lloyd George's actions in the Middle East: 'it is impossible to discover whether he really cared about the Bible or Palestine or Zionism' because he 'had no principles' (Yapp, 'The Making of the Palestine Mandate', *Middle Eastern Lectures*, no. 1 (Tel Aviv, 1995), p. 15).

70   As Mayir Verete observes, Lloyd George's support of the Zionist cause in Palestine was also 'the neatest, most convenient and becoming way' of pressuring France to abandon any Palestinian ambitions (Verete, 'The Balfour Declaration and Its Makers', in Elie Kedourie and Sylvia G. Haim (eds), *Palestine and Israel in the 19th and 20th Centuries* (London, 1982), pp. 60–88, esp. p.72.

71   Isaiah Friedman, *The Question of Palestine: British-Jewish-Arab Relations: 1914–1918*, 2nd expanded edn (New Brunswick, NJ, 1992), p. 265.

72   Balfour was then Foreign Secretary and an acquaintance of the Zionist leader, Dr Chaim Weizmann. Balfour had become convinced that Zionism, as the guardian of ancient traditions, would act as a conservative and constructive force in Palestine. See Max Egremont, *Balfour: A Life of Arthur James Balfour*, paperback edn (London, 1998), pp. 204–5, 263–4; and Jason Tomes, *Balfour and Foreign Policy: The International Thought of a Conservative Statesman* (Cambridge, 1997), ch. 8, 'The Balfour Declaration'. For the persuasive power of Wiezmann upon the British government, see Jehuda Reinharz, *Chaim Weizmann: The Making of a Statesman* (New York, 1993). Leonard Stein's *The Balfour Declaration* (New York, 1961) is now largely superseded by Jonathan Schneer's detailed and engrossing account (*The Balfour Declaration: The Origins of the Arab-Israeli Conflict* (New York, 2010). See also James Edward Renton, 'The Historiography of the Balfour Declaration: Toward a Multicausal Framework, *Journal of Israeli History* 19:2 (Summer 1998), pp. 109–28; and Renton's *The Zionist Mandate: The Birth of the Anglo-Zionist Alliance, 1914–1918* (Houndmills, Hants, 2007).

73   From the facsimile in Stein, *Balfour Declaration*, frontispiece.

74   Thus, as Friedman points out, the government 'provided a cloak under which Britain could appear free from any annexationist taint' (Friedman, *Question of Palestine*, p. 175). For details of the anti-Ottoman propaganda campaign and Lloyd George's role in it, see James Renton, 'Changing Languages of Empire and the Orient: Britain and the Invention of the Middle East, 1917–1918', *Historical Journal* 50:3 (2007), pp. 645–67, esp. 647–50.

75 See Friedman, 'The McMahon-Hussein'; and Dockrill and Goold, *Peace Without Promise*, ch. 4, 'The Dissolution of the Ottoman Empire: the Middle East, 1919–1920', passim.

76 Dockrill and Goold, *Peace Without Promise*, p. 144. Fromkin, concurring, writes that Lloyd George 'sought hegemony' in the Middle East (*A Peace to End all Peace*, p. 235).

77 Morgan, *Consensus and Disunity*, p. 116.

78 David Cannadine, *Ornamentalism: How the British Saw Their Empire* (New York, 2001), pp. 181, 182.

79 Paul Guinn, *British Strategy and Politics, 1914–1918* (Oxford, 1965), ch. 7, 'The New Imperialism'.

80 Tony Dodge, *Inventing Iraq: The Failure of Nation Building and a History Denied* (New York, 2003), passim. Dodge characterizes Iraq as a 'quasi-state' (p. 31); Peter Sluglett, *Britain in Iraq: Contriving King and Country*, 2nd edn (New York, 2007), Introduction and chs 1–2; Charles Tripp, *A History of Iraq*, 3rd edn (Cambridge, 2007), Introduction and chs 1–2; and Darwin, *Britain, Egypt and the Middle East*, esp. ch. 7.

81 See Rose Greaves, 'Iranian Relations with Great Britain and British India, 1798–1921', in Peter Avery, G.R.G. Hambly and C. Melville (eds), *The Cambridge History of Iran*, vol. 7, *From Nadir Sha to the Islamic Republic* (Cambridge, 1991), pp. 350–73.

82 See William J. Olson, 'The Genesis of the Anglo-Persian Agreement of 1919', in Elie Kedourie and Slvia G. Haim (eds), *Towards a Modern Iran: Studies in Thought, Politics and Society* (London, 1980), pp. 185–216; and Shaul Bakhash, 'The Origins of the Anglo-Persian Agreement of 1919', *Asian and African Studies* 25 (March 1991), pp. 1–29.

83 Nikki R. Keddie, *Modern Iran: Roots and Results of Revolution*, updated edn (New Haven, 2006), p. 76.

84 See Homa Katouzian, *Iranian History and Politics: The Dialectic of State and Society* (London, 2003), ch. 9, 'The Campaign against the Anglo-Iranian Agreement of 1919'.

85 Stephen C. Poulson, *Social Movements in Twentieth Century Iran: Culture, Ideology, and Mobilizing Frameworks* (Lanham, MD, 2005), p. 139.

86 Houshang Sabahi, *British Policy in Persia, 1918–1925* (London, 1990), p. 49.

87 See Stephen Hemsley Longrigg, *Oil in the Middle East: Its Discovery and Development*, 3rd edn (London, 1968), chs. 1–4; and V.H. Rothwell, 'Mesopotamia in British War Aims, 1914–1918', *Historical Journal* 13:2 (1970), pp. 273–94, p. 277.

88 Marian Jack, 'The Purchase of the British Government's Shares in the British Petroleum Company 1912–1914', *Past and Present* 39 (1968), pp. 139–68. Some oil companies, such as the Anglo-Persian Oil Company, solicited government purchase of their shares, realizing the potential of the Admiralty market. See G. Gareth Jones, 'The British Government and the Oil Companies 1912–1924: The Search for an Oil Policy', *Historical Journal* 20:3 (1977), pp. 647–72.

89 See the account in Viscount Long of Wraxall (Walter Long), *Memories* (New York, n.d.), pp. 257–62.

90 For this and the following quotations, see Rothwell, 'Mesopotamia in British War Aims', p. 289.

91 Middlemas, *Jones Whitehall Diary*, vol. 1, 9 September 1919, p. 93. Hankey cautioned Jones that he should treat the matter as 'very confidential'.

92 The San Remo Agreement, concluded at the conference of the same name in April 1920. For the background to this agreement and Lloyd George's importance in its fashioning, see Marian Kent, *Oil and Empire: British Policy and Mesopotamian Oil, 1900–1920* (London, 1976), passim, and esp. ch. 8; and Helmut Mejcher, *Imperial Quest for Oil: Iraq, 1910–1928* (London, 1976), ch. 3.

93 Taylor, *English History, 1914–1945*, pp. 152–3.

94 Morgan, *Consensus and Disunity*, p. 123.

95 Tim Coates (ed.), *The Amritsar Massacre: General Dyer in the Punjab, 1919* (London, 2000), p. 67. This publication contains excerpts from the Hunter Committee, appointed to investigate the Amritsar atrocity.

96 For the following, see Judith M. Brown, *Modern India: The Origins of an Asian Democracy*, 2nd edn (New York, 1994), pp. 194–231.

97 Ibid., p. 203. For a concise and critical analysis of Amritsar, see Derek Sayer, 'British Reaction to the Amritsar Massacre 1919–1920', *Past and Present* 131 (May 1991), pp. 130–64.

98 McEwen, *Riddell Diaries*, 10 October 1918, p. 240; 13 October 1918, p. 242.

99 Ibid., 19 October 1918, p. 243.

100 Ibid., 11 April 1919, p. 268.

101 Ultimately Hankey's view would undergo a change, inclining him toward a small, centralized body fashioned after the Imperial War Cabinet or the Supreme War Council which could direct global policies toward the path of peace (Roskill, *Hankey*, vol. 1, 21 November 1917, p. 462; 5 December 1917, pp. 469 and 482).

102 See George W. Egerton, *Great Britain and the Creation of the League of Nations: Strategy, Politics, and International Organization, 1914–1919* (Chapel Hill, NC, 1978); and Peter Yearwood, '"On the Safe and Right Lines": The Lloyd George Government and the Origins of the League of Nations, 1916–1918', *Historical Journal* 32:1 (March 1989), pp. 131–55, p. 23.

103 Morgan, *Consensus and Disunity*, p. 148.

104 David McLean argues that the Ottoman Empire was among the better examples of the British system of 'informal empire' by which Britain exercised control through commercial and financial means without formal annexation. The primary instrument was the National Bank of Turkey, which loaned British capital to the government. Propping up the Ottoman Empire was particularly designed to counter Russian influence in the Straits. See McLean, 'Finance and "Informal Empire" before the First World War', *Economic History Review*, 30 (1976), pp. 291–305.

105 Quoted in A.L. Macfie, 'The British Decision Regarding the Future of Constantinople, November 1918–January 1920', *Historical Journal* 18:2 (1975), pp. 391–400, p. 391.

106 In a conversation with Riddell: see McEwen, *Riddell Diaries*, 26 June 1920, p. 315.

107 For the following, see Erik Goldstein, 'Great Britain and Greater Greece 1917–1920', *Historical Journal* 32:2 (1989), pp. 339–56.

108 Frances Stevenson reported that the two statesmen 'took to each other from the first, by reason of their Liberal outlook, and by the fact that Venizelos recognized L.G.'s Gladstonian-cum-Byronic attitude to Greek problems' (Francis Lloyd George, *The Years That Are Past* (London, 1967), p. 176). Sylvester recorded in his diary as late as 1940 that on a visit to Churt, he observed in Lloyd George's library, 'a gallery of the famous' including photos of Clemenceau, Smuts, Woodrow Wilson; and a painting of Venzielos (Albert James Sylvester, *Life with Lloyd George: The Diary of A.J. Sylvester*, ed. Colin Cross (London, 1975), p. 273). Thomas Jones suggests that each man saw himself in the other, having much in common--'eloquence, energy, negotiating skill, astuteness' (Jones, *Lloyd George*, p. 197).

109 Erik Goldstein makes the case that Venizelos, because of his 'superb ... diplomatic craftsmanship' was 'one of the giants of the conference' ('Great Britain and Greater Greece 1917–1920', *Historical Journal* 32:2 (1989), pp. 339–56, p. 344).

110 A comprehensive analysis of the Treaty of Sevres is Paul Helmreich, *From Paris to Sevres: The Partition of the Ottoman Empire at the Peace Conference of 1919–1920* (Columbus, Ohio,

1974). Lowe and Dockrill believe that Sèvres was 'a far more punitive peace than that of Versailles' (*Mirage of Power*, vol. 2, p. 365).

111 For a succinct analysis of Kemal's achievements, see George W. Gawrych, 'Kemal Ataturk's Politico-Military Strategy in the Turkish War of Independence, 1919–1922: From Guerrilla Warfare to the Decisive Battle', *Journal of Strategic Studies* 22:3 (September 1988), pp. 318–41. Discussions of Kemal's parallel diplomatic strategy may be found in Roderic H. Davison, 'Turkish Diplomacy from Mudros to Lausanne', in Craig and Gilbert, *The Diplomats*, pp. 172–209; and Salahi Ramsdan Sonyel, *Turkish Diplomacy, 1918–1923: Mustafa Kemal and the Turkish National Movement* (London, 1975).

112 Nicolson, *Curzon: The Last Phase*, p. 272, n. 1.

113 Roskill, *Hankey*, vol. 2, 16–22 September 1922, p. 285.

114 Ibid., p. 287.

115 Cited in A.L. Macfie, 'The Chanak Affair (September–October 1922)', *Balkan Studies* 20:2 (1979), pp. 309–41, p. 323.

116 Sonyel describes the negotiations as 'very tough' (*Turkish Diplomacy*, p. 178).

117 Ibid., p. 182.

118 McEwen, *Riddell Diaries*, 15 September 1922, p. 375.

119 Wilson, *Diaries of Scott*, 4 October 1922, p. 427.

120 Roskill, *Hankey*, vol. 2, 23–27 September 1922, p. 289.

121 Alan Clark (ed.), *'A Good Innings': The Private Papers of Viscount Lee of Fareham* (London, 1974), 1 October 1922, p. 229.

122 Taylor, *English History 1914–1945*, p. 191.

123 Roy Jenkins, *Churchill: A Biography*, paperback edn (London, 2002), p. 368.

124 Morgan, *Consensus and Disunity*, p. 326.

125 Ibid., p. 323.

126 Dockrill and Goold, *Peace Without Promise*, pp. 229, 235, 247–8.

127 David Walder, *The Chanak Affair* (London, 1969), p. 321.

128 Morgan, *Consensus and Disunity*, p. 116.

129 McEwen, *Riddell Diaries*, 24 September 1922, p. 376.

130 As recounted by his wife, Ruth, in her diary (Clark, *Papers of Viscount Lee of Fareham*, 2 October 1922, p. 230).

131 John Vincent (ed.), *The Crawford Papers: The Journals of David Lindsay, Twenty-Seventh Earl of Crawford and Tenth Earl of Balcarres during the years 1892 to 1940* (Manchester, 1984), 6 October 1922, p. 445.

132 See John Ferris, '"Far Too Dangerous a Gamble?" British Intelligence and Policy during the Chanak Crisis, September–October 1922', *Diplomacy and Statecraft* 14 (2003), pp. 139–84.

133 McEwen, *Riddell Diaries*, 2 March 1922, p. 365.

134 Ibid., 4 September 1922, p. 374. Grigg served as a private secretary to Lloyd George in 1921–2; for his services he was created Baron Altrincham. He was the father of John Grigg, biographer of Lloyd George.

135 Taylor, *Darling Pussy*, 15 March 1922, p. 35.

136 Ibid., 17 March 1922, p. 37.

137 Ibid., 23 April 1922, p. 44.

138 Ibid., 26 April, 1922, p. 45.

139 Ibid., 9 May 1922, p. 50.

140 McEwen, *Riddell Diaries*, 22 July 1922, pp. 371–2.

141 Morgan, *Lloyd George: Family Letters*, 6 September 1922, p. 196.

142 Ibid., 7 September 1922 and 8 September 1922, p. 196.

143 For the following discussion, see G.R. Searle, *Corruption in British Politics, 1895–1930* (Oxford, 1987), chs 13–15.

144 Ibid., p. 362.

145 As McKibbin has pointed out, much of the criticism against Lloyd George's bestowal of honours was the belief in certain quarters that he was selecting peers from the wrong classes, thus 'breaking the proper relationship between land and honour'. Peers should not be chosen among such candidates as car manufacturers (Lord Nuffield), or oil magnates (Lords Bearsted and Cowdray). See Ross McKibbin, *Classes and Cultures: England 1918–1951* (Oxford, 1998), p. 17.

146 Searle, *Corruption in British Politics*, p. 323.

147 Maurice Cowling, *The Impact of Labour, 1920–1924: The Beginning of Modern British Politics* (Cambridge, 1971), pp. 120–1. For the Anti-Waste movement, see Morgan, *Consensus and Disunity*, passim, esp. pp. 244–6.

148 Kinnear believes the Anti-Waste campaign reduced government spending 'dramatically' (Michael Kinnear, *The Fall of Lloyd George: The Political Crisis of 1922* (Toronto, 1973), p. 24).

149 Page Croft was Unionist MP for Christchurch from 1910. At the outset of World War I, he volunteered, serving 22 months at the front, longer than any other MP. He became a Brigadier General at the age of 34. See William D. Rubinstein, 'Henry Page Croft and the National Party 1917–22', *Journal of Contemporary History* 14 (1979), pp. 129–48. There were ultimately seven MPs and 18 peers who became members of the National Party.

150 The Die Hards have been thoroughly examined: see Cowling, *Impact of Labour*, passim; Kinnear, *The Fall of Lloyd George*, passim; esp. ch. 4; Morgan, *Consensus and Disunity*, ch. 10; and Searle, *Corruption in British Politics*, chs 13–15, passim.

151 As Searle observes, the radical right 'almost to a man' was disturbed at having a Jew (Lord Reading of Marconi fame) in charge of the Indian government (he was appointed Viceroy in January 1921) at the same time that a Jew (Montagu) was Secretary for India (ibid., p. 333).

152 For these quotations from Sanders, see John Ramsden, (ed.), *Real Old Tory Politics: The Political Diaries of Sir Robert Sanders, Lord Bayford, 1910–35* (London, 1984), 24 June 1921, p. 158; and 21 August 1921, p. 160.

153 Ibid., 3 October 1921, p. 161.

154 Ibid., 21 July 1922, p. 179.

155 Cowling, *Impact of Labour*, p. 192.

156 *The Times*, 7 October 1922.

157 Ibid.

158 See R.J.Q. Adams, *Bonar Law* (London, 1999), pp. 320–9, for Conservative manoeuvres during the final days of the Lloyd George coalition.

159 For this speech, see *The Times*, 14 October 1922.

160 Ibid.

161 Ibid., 16 October 1922.

162 See Kinnear, *Fall of Lloyd George*, ch. 6. The National Union comprised delegates from constituent Conservative parties and thus broadly represented Conservative opinion in the countryside. Balcarres reported that the meeting of Conservative coalition ministers pivoted around Lloyd George's 'mercurial personality' (Vincent, *Crawford Papers*, 16 October 1922, p. 452).

163 Ibid., 19 October 1922, p. 453.

164 See Robert Blake, *The Unknown Prime Minister: The Life and Times of Andrew Bonar Law, 1858–1923* (London, 1955), pp. 447–58; and Adams, *Bonar Law*, pp. 317–29.

165 Kinnear, *Fall of Lloyd George*, p. 1.

Chapter 17. The Long Good-Bye

1 Kenneth O. Morgan, *Rebirth of a Nation: A History of Modern Wales*, paperback edn (Oxford, 1982), pp. 272–3.
2 *The Times*, 21 October 1922.
3 Peter Rowland, *David Lloyd George* (London, 1975), p. 590.
4 Trevor Wilson, (ed.), *The Political Diaries of C.P. Scott, 1911–1928* (Ithaca, 1970), 23 October 1922, p. 429.
5 Ibid., p. 430.
6 John Campbell, *Lloyd George: The Goat in the Wilderness, 1922–1931* (London, 1977), p. 37.
7 Martin Pugh, *Lloyd George*, paperback edn (London, 1988), p. 160.
8 Kenneth O. Morgan (ed.), *Lloyd George: Family Letters, 1885–1936* (Cardiff and London, 1973), probably late November 1922, p. 200.
9 As Morgan notes, the National Liberal campaign as a whole was 'somewhat pathetic … with their leader adopting a variety of erratic positions from constituency to constituency' (Kenneth O. Morgan, *Consensus and Disunity: The Lloyd George Coalition Government 1918–1922*, paperback edn (Oxford, 1986), p. 358).
10 This count is from R.J.Q. Adams, *Bonar Law* (London, 1999), p. 337. G.R. Searle (*The Liberal Party: Triumph and Disintegration, 1886–1929* (New York, 1992), p. 216) and David Dutton (*A History of the Liberal Party in the Twentieth Century* (Houndmills, 2004), pp. 88–9) both agree with this number. Other historians have different Liberal tallies. Perhaps these various accounts attest to the fluidity of Liberal allegiances at this critical time in their history.
11 For the following, see Robert Blake, *The Unknown Prime Minister: The Life and Times of Andrew Bonar Law, 1858–1923* (London, 1955), chs 29–32; and Adams, *Bonar Law*, ch. 15.
12 As Adams puts it, the Cabinet was now more a committee of governors with the Prime Minister serving only as *primus inter pares*, rather than being the dominant force as had been true under Lloyd George (ibid., p. 333).
13 See John F.V. Keiger, 'Raymond Poincaré and the Ruhr Crisis', in Robert Boyce, *French Foreign and Defence Policy, 1918–1940: The Decline and Fall of a Great Power* (London, 1998), pp. 49–70.
14 For the dispute over the Anglo-American debt, see Keith Middlemas and John Barnes, *Baldwin: A Biography* (New York, 1970), pp. 128–48.
15 See Cameron Hazlehurst, 'The Baldwinite Conspiracy', *Historical Studies* 16:63 (1974–75), pp. 167–91, esp. p. 186. Other accounts are: Middlemas and Barnes, *Baldwin*, pp. 158–69; and Philip Williamson, *Stanley Baldwin: Conservative Leadership and National Values* (Cambridge, 1999), pp. 26–7.
16 Middlemas and Barnes, *Baldwin*, p. 212.
17 Philip Williamson and Edward Baldwin (eds), *Baldwin Papers: A Conservative Statesman, 1908–1947* (Cambridge, 2004), p. 119, quoting from Mackenize King's Diary of 20 October 1923.
18 As John Campbell puts it, Baldwin was 'obsessed' (*Goat in the Wilderness*, p. 3) by the fear of Lloyd George after 1922; or as Campbell suggests more colorfully: 'Lloyd George's spectre haunted the Cabinet Room of his successors like Banquo's ghost' (ibid.).
19 Williamson and Baldwin, *Baldwin Papers*, p. 104, quoting from the transcript of the meeting of 23 September 1923 held at the British Embassy in Paris.
20 Ibid.

21 Michael Bentley, 'The Liberal Response to Socialism, 1918–29', in Kenneth D. Brown (ed.), *Essays in Anti-Labour History: Responses to the Rise of Labour in Britain* (Hamden, 1974), p. 53.

22 For this important campaign, see Campbell, *Goat in the Wilderness*, pp. 61–74.

23 For the details of Lloyd George's North American visit, see Rowland, *Lloyd George*, pp. 598–601.

24 Parliamentary Archives, LG/G/6/3/2, 7 December 1922. Davis had met Lloyd George when he had been the American Ambassador to the Court of St James from 1918–21. In 1924 Davis became the Democratic nominee for the presidency: he lost to the Republican Calvin Coolidge. For the scant details of his contacts with Lloyd George, see William H. Harbaugh, *Lawyer's Lawyer: The Life of John W. Davis* (New York, 1973), passim.

25 Rowland claims that Lloyd George returned to Britain 'as a giant refreshed' and his reputation as a world statesman 'greatly enhanced' (*Lloyd George*, p. 601).

26 Writing from Indianapolis on 22 October to Frances, Lloyd George reported that he had been enthusiastically received everywhere. He had so far spoken 40 times – once addressing a crowd of 75,000 'through a microphone' (A.J.P. Taylor, *My Darling Pussy: The Letters of Lloyd George and Frances* (London, 1975), 22 October 1923, p. 72).

27 Middlemas and Barnes believe that Baldwin, who had at first been hesitant in calling for an election, was influenced by Lloyd George's absence from the political scene: 'there is no other plausible reason' (*Baldwin*, p. 234). Nick Smart, however, thinks that Baldwin played a more subtle hand in calling the election: it was primarily to unify and strengthen the Conservative Party rather than commit it to a protectionist policy (Smart, 'Debate: Baldwin's Blunder? The General Election of 1923', *Twentieth Century British History* 7:1(1996), pp. 110–39).

28 Trevor Wilson, *The Downfall of the Liberal Party, 1914–1935* (London, 1966), p. 267.

29 It will be remembered that MacDonald had engineered with Herbert Gladstone an electoral pact between Labour and Liberals bringing about the great reformist Liberal government led by Asquith in 1906.

30 Maurice Cowling, *The Impact of Labour, 1920–1924: The Beginning of Modern British Politics* (Cambridge, 1971), pp. 366–7. As Cowling notes further, relations between MacDonald and the King 'developed cordially' over the life of the Labour government (ibid., p. 367).

31 See John Vincent (ed.), *The Crawford Papers: The Journals of David Lindsay, Twenty-Seventh Earl of Crawford and Tenth Earl of Balcarres during the years 1892 to 1940* (Manchester, 1984), 13 December 1923, p. 489 for this and the following quotations.

32 Robert Rhodes James (ed.), *Memoirs of a Conservative: J.C.C. Davidson's Memoirs and Papers 1910–37* (London, 1969), 9 December 1923, p. 190. Davidson had been Parliamentary Private Secretary to both Bonar Law and Baldwin.

33 Norman and Jeanne MacKenzie (eds), *The Diary of Beatrice Webb*, vol. 3, *'The Power to Alter Things'* (Cambridge, 1984), 12 and 18 December 1924, pp. 432–3.

34 For a perceptive analysis of the strained Liberal/Labour alliance, and the declining fortunes of the Liberal Party, see G.R. Searle, *The Liberal Party: Triumph and Disintegration, 1886–1929* (New York, 1992), ch. 8, 'The 1920s'.

35 MacDonald thought him cynical and unprincipled (David Marquand, *Ramsay MacDonald* (London, 1977), p. 320).

36 Ibid., p. 303.

37 Ibid., 311.

38 Richard W. Lyman, *The First Labour government, 1924* (London, [1957]), ch. 8, 'Housing'. Lyman remains a valuable source for MacDonald's first ministry.

39 For MacDonald's foreign policy, see Marquand, *Ramsay MacDonald*, ch. 15; and P.M.H. Bell, *France and Britain 1900–1940: Entente and Estrangement* (London, 1996), pp. 142–9.

40 For Marquand, the 'brilliant compromise' between Britain and France represented for MacDonald a 'spectacular success' in foreign affairs (*Ramsay MacDonald*, pp. 355 and 329).

41 David Dutton's phrase in his *History of the Liberal Party*, p. 93.

42 Alan Sykes, *The Rise and Fall of British Liberalism, 1776–1988* (London, 1997), p. 234.

43 For this and the following quotation, see Wilson, *Diaries of Scott*, 2–3 February 1924, p. 455.

44 For this letter see Morgan, *Lloyd George: Family Letters*, 4 February 1924, p. 202.

45 Chris Cook, *The Age of Alignment: Electoral Politics in Britain 1922–1929* (London, 1975), p. 216. See ibid., ch. 3, for Cook's general analysis of Lloyd George's attempt to find a critical platform against Labour. See also Campbell, *Goat in the Wilderness*, ch. 3.

46 This was reciprocated by MacDonald, who once complained to Scott (only a few days after the 1923 election) that Lloyd George's behavior during the recent election campaign – 'in its gross demagogic vulgarity' – was one of the reasons that Labour would have nothing to do with him (Wilson, *Diaries of Scott*, 11 December 1923, p. 449). A month later, MacDonald reiterated and expended his complaint, claiming that the Labour Party as a whole had a 'strong feeling of hostility' toward Lloyd George. 'They felt they could not trust him' (ibid., 6 January 1924, p. 453). Hankey, who was on good terms with MacDonald, once called him down for 'his unconcealed hatred' of Lloyd George (Stephen Roskill, *Hankey: Man of Secrets*, 3 vols (London, 1970), vol. 2, 5 August 1924, p. 371).

47 Marquand, *Ramsay MacDonald*, p. 363.

48 Campbell, *Goat in the Wilderness*, p. 104.

49 Ibid., p. 103. Lloyd George may have believed that if the principle of the loan was agreeable, the timing of it was wrong. To Churchill, he wrote in September 1924 that: 'We had no right to lend British money in such circumstances and on such security, when domestic and imperial needs were so pressing' (as reported by Churchill to Balfour: see National Archives of Scotland, Whittingehame Papers, GD 433/2/19, frame 123, 1 September 1924).

50 A detailed discussion of the Campbell case may be found in Marquand, *Ramsay MacDonald*, pp. 364–77.

51 Morgan, *Lloyd George: Family Letters*, 2 October 1924, p. 204.

52 See the account in Marquand, *Ramsay MacDonald*, pp. 381–9.

53 Christopher Andrew, *Secret Service: The Making of the British Intelligence Community* (London, 1985), ch. 10, 'Zinoviev Letter and the Breach with Russia'. The letter was likely a forgery, designed to prejudice voters against the Labour Party.

54 Ibid., p. 383.

55 For the following see Roy Jenkins, *Churchill: A Biography*, paperback edn (London, 2002), pp. 353, 382–92.

56 Quoted by Martin Gilbert, *Churchill: A Life*, paperback edn (New York, 1991), p. 460.

57 Williamson, *Baldwin*, passim.

58 For an appreciation of Baldwin's 'new conservatism', see John Ramsden, *The Age of Balfour and Baldwin 1902–1940* (London, 1978), pp. 207–15.

59 Ibid., p. 271.

60 Parliamentary Archives, LG/G/8/5/1, 19 August 1925.

61 The strike has attracted considerable scholarly attention. See for example A. Mason, 'The Government and the General Strike, 1926', *International Review of Social History* 14 (1969), pp. 1–21; Patrick Renshaw, *The General Strike* (London, 1975); Geoffrey McDonald,

'The Defeat of the General Strike', in Gillian Peele and Chris Cook (eds), *The Politics of Reappraisal, 1918–1939* (New York, 1975), pp. 64–87; G.A. Phillips, *The General Strike: The Politics of Industrial Conflict* (London, 1976); M.W. Kirby, *The British Coalmining Industry, 1870–1946: A Political and Economic History* (London, 1977), ch. 5; R.A. Florey, *The General Strike of 1926: The Economic, Political and Social Causes of that Class War* (London, 1980); Hugh Armstrong Clegg, *A History of British Trade Unions since 1889*, vol. 2, *1911–1933* (Oxford, 1985), ch. 10; and Keith Laybourn, *The General Strike Day by Day* (Phoenix Mill, Gloucestershire, 1999).

62   Middlemas and Barnes, *Baldwin*, p. 446.

63   Keith Middlemas (ed.), *Thomas Jones: Whitehall Diary*, vol. 2, *1926–1930* (Oxford, 1969), 23 April 1926, p. 19.

64   Ramsden, *Age of Balfour and Baldwin*, p. 285.

65   Phillips, *General Strike*, p. 272; Marquand, *Ramsay MacDonald*, pp. 434–40.

66   Roy Jenkins, *Asquith* (London, 1964), p. 514. Asquith wrote to Mrs Harrison of his pride at seeing his family engaging in strikebreaking activity. His niece drove East End shop girls and typists to their City jobs. His younger son, Puffin, plied 'his little car' in ferrying out-patients to and from hospitals, as well as picking up 'stray people' who were 'stranded in the streets' of London (Stephen Koss, *Asquith*, paperback edn (New York, 1985), p. 276).

67   Campbell, *Goat in the Wilderness*, pp. 136–8.

68   The details of Asquith's attempts to remove Lloyd George from the Liberal Party may be found in A.J. Sylvester, *The Real Lloyd George* (London, 1947), ch. 12. See also Roy Jenkins, *Asquith* (London, 1964), pp. 512–6; and Koss, *Asquith*, pp. 276–81.

69   See Michael Freeden, *Liberalism Divided: A Study in British Liberal Thought, 1914–1939* (Oxford, 1986), ch. 4.

70   For Lloyd George's sustained efforts at publicizing Liberal solutions to the economic and social questions of the 1920s, see Pugh, *Lloyd George*, pp. 166–74. As Pugh describes Lloyd George's aims: 'he intended to make a bid for radicalism by contrasting his constructive approach to the economy with the common conservatism and passivity of his rivals' (ibid., p. 166).

71   For the following, see Michael Dawson, 'The Liberal Land Policy, 1924–1929: Electoral Strategy and Internal Division', *Twentieth Century British History* 2:3 (1991), pp. 272–90; Campbell, *Goat in the Wilderness*, pp. 119–28; Pugh, *Lloyd George*, p. 167.

72   Campbell, *Goat in the Wilderness*, p. 123.

73   Parliamentary Archives, LG/G/1/2/1, 2 September [1925]. Acland had also thoughtfully included a train schedule from Waterloo Station to Exeter in his letter to Lloyd George. After the speech, Lloyd George graciously praised his host: 'The meeting itself was a perfect piece of organization, and owed its success chiefly to you' (ibid., LG/G/1/2/3, undated draft).

74   For the following, see *The Times*, 18 September 1925.

75   Michael Bentley, 'The Liberal Response to Socialism, 1918–29', esp. pp. 63–4.

76   Dawson, 'Liberal Land Policy, 1924–1929', pp. 282–3.

77   A.J.P. Taylor, *Lloyd George: A Diary by Frances Stevenson* (London, 1971), 1 April 1926, p. 244. Perhaps in an even more exaggerated comment, she wrote later that day: 'Now he speaks almost as the Leader of the Opposition, with the Labour & Liberal benches around him' (ibid.). It is not beyond imagining, however, that this was precisely the position he hoped to attain.

78   For this and the following quotations, see ibid., 15 May 1926, pp. 245–6.

79   Rowland, *Lloyd George*, p. 629.

80 So Campbell, *Goat in the Wilderness*, p. 131, suggests.

81 For the origins of the Inquiry, see Robert Skidelsky, *John Maynard Keynes*, vol. 2, *The Economist as Saviour, 1920–1937* (New York, 1994), pp. 257–69.

82 As he wrote excitedly to Margaret: 'This weekend I have *14* professors at Churt' (Morgan, *Lloyd George: Family Letters*, 22 September 1926, p. 207).

83 Skidelsky, *Keynes*, vol. 2, p. 222.

84 As he put it in a letter to Sir Robert Hutchinson, Liberal MP for Montrose District of Burghs and chief whip of the Liberal Party (Parliamentary Archives, LG/G/10/9/2, 3 June 1926).

85 For a discussion of the Liberal Industrial Inquiry and its famous report, see Campbell, *Goat in the Wilderness*, ch. 7, 'The Liberal "Yellow Book"' .

86 Ibid., p. 199.

87 Ibid. As Campbell points out, Lloyd George with a few exceptions did not contribute directly to the Yellow Book: he did, however, supply 'the essential political drive' and organizing skills to see it through (ibid., p. 204). Because of its modernity and openness to new ideas, the Yellow Book – to Campbell's way of thinking – was 'the outstanding achievement' of Lloyd George's later years (ibid., p. 205). Even Conservative commentators have recognized the Yellow Book and its predecessors as 'impressive political contributions by any standard' (Rhodes James, *Memoirs of a Conservative*, p. 302). For a more critical analysis of the Yellow Book, see Sykes, *Rise and Fall of British Liberalism*, pp. 247–52. Sykes believes that there was 'an air of unreality' about its recommendations, offering only 'sweet reasonableness', far removed from the reality of industrial confrontation that characterized the inter-war era (p. 248).

88 Rowland, *Lloyd George*, p. 644: and see more generally ibid., pp. 644–8 for this paragraph. See also Wilson, *Downfall of the Liberal Party*, ch. 18, 'Fighting to Win'.

89 The discussion which follows relies heavily on Campbell's *Goat in the Wilderness*, ch. 8.

90 Quoted from ibid., p. 214.

91 Ibid., p. 217.

92 *The Times*, 10 November 1928.

93 Ibid. 2 March 1929.

94 Campbell, *Goat in the Wilderness*, p. 225.

95 *The Times*, 13 April 1929.

96 A.J.P. Taylor, *Beaverbrook* (London, 1972), p. 260: in a letter to Sir Robert Borden, dated 30 April 1929. Even historians unfriendly to Lloyd George have words of praise. Wilson, for example, writes that the election campaign of 1929 was for Lloyd George 'a mighty personal triumph' (*Downfall of the Liberal Party*, p. 346).

97 Ramsden, *Age of Balfour and Baldwin*, p. 290.

98 John Ramsden, *An Appetite for Power: A History of the Conservative Party since 1830*, paperback edn (London, 1999), p. 268.

99 Philip Williamson, reliably an apologist for Baldwin, admits that by early 1927, the Baldwin government 'was losing its sense of purpose' (Williamson, '"Safety First": Baldwin, the Conservative Party, and the 1929 General Election', *Historical Journal* 25:2 (1982), pp. 385–409, p. 392); and that two years later, there was 'a serious decline in the confidence of the Conservative rank-and-file' (p. 404). Williamson also points out that Baldwin himself had doubts about a Conservative victory and thought that Lloyd George might somehow attain a parliamentary balance of power against the Conservatives (p. 403).

100 Taylor, *My Darling Pussy*, 29 January 1929, p. 121.

101 Ibid., 15 May 1929, p. 128.

102 As Michael Kinnear's *The British Voter: An Atlas and Survey since 1885* (Ithaca, 1968), p. 49 graphically illustrates. See also Dutton, *History of the Liberal Party*, pp. 112–4.

103 Norman and Jeanne MacKenzie, *The Diary of Beatrice Webb*, vol. 4, *1924–1943: The Wheel of Life* (Cambridge, 1985), 1 June 1929, p. 172. Sydney Webb, elevated to the House of Lords as Baron Passfield, became Colonial and Dominions Secretary in the new Labour Cabinet.

104 Rowland, *Lloyd George*, p. 656.

105 Wilson, *Downfall of the Liberal Party*, p. 351.

106 See Jenifer Hart, *Proportional Representation: Critics of the British Electoral System, 1820–1945* (Oxford, 1992), ch. 10, 'The Labour Government and the Alternative Vote, 1929–1931'.

107 Ian Packer, *Lloyd George*, paperback edn (Houndmills, Hants, 1998), pp. 101–2.

108 For MacDonald's foreign policy, see Marquand, *MacDonald*, pp. 501–17.

109 See Raymond G. O'Connor, *Perilous Equilibrium: The United States and the London Naval Conference of 1930*, reprint edn (New York, 1969); and Zara S. Steiner, *The Lights that Failed: European International History, 1919–1933* (Oxford, 2005), pp. 588–92.

110 Robert Skidelsky, *Politicians and the Slump: The Labour government of 1929–1931* (London, 1967), p. xi. Skidelsky, along with John Stevenson and Chris Cook, *The Slump: Society and Politics during the Depression* (London, 1977), inform the following discussion.

111 Skidelsky, *Politicians and The Slump*, p. xii.

112 See John Barnes and David Nicholson, *The Empire at Bay: The Leo Amery Diaries, 1929–1945* (London, 1988), 27 June 1929, p. 41.

113 Gilbert, *Churchill*, p. 491.

114 For these quotations, see Middlemas, *Jones Whitehall Diary*, vol. 2, 23 December 1929, p. 229.

115 Rowland, *Lloyd George*, p. 665. See also Skidelsky, *Politicians and the Slump*, pp. 112–3 and 131–4.

116 Marquand, *Ramsay MacDonald*, 19 December 1929, p. 527

117 Marquand believes that MacDonald's strong personal animus against Lloyd George – 'an unprincipled adventurer, who would do or say anything to get back to power' – was buttressed by his belief that Lloyd George was his chief rival for the leadership of the British Left (ibid., p. 528).

118 For the details of Lloyd George's efforts to strike bargains with the Conservatives and Labour on electoral reform, see John D. Fair, 'The Second Labour government and the Politics of Electoral Reform, 1929–1931', *Albion* 13 (1981), pp. 276–301.

119 For these quotations, see Campbell, *Goat in the Wilderness*, p. 251.

120 Years before, two of Lloyd George's Conservative associates, Balfour and Bonar Law, attempted to understand Lloyd George's occasional abrupt and changeable opinions. In a memo of a conversation between the two, they agreed that Lloyd George – when faced with difficulties 'with which there was no precedent' – tended to suggest 'any expedient, however impossible'. But these suggestions were often 'more in the nature of the transitory mental experiments of a man thinking aloud than of plans which had reached any sort of maturity' (National Archives of Scotland, Whittingehame Papers, GD 433/2/19, 22 December 1922).

121 Rowland, *Lloyd George*, p. 671.

122 Marquand, *Ramsay MacDonald*, p. 538.

123 See ibid., pp. 564–7.

124 For the following, see *The Times*, 18 October 1930. A *Times* leader this day took issue with some of Lloyd George's specific proposals, but thought overall there was 'much to applaud in principle' (ibid.).

125 Marquand, *Ramsay MacDonald*, p. 547.

126 Morgan, *Lloyd George: Family Letters*, 4 February 1924, p. 202.

127 Parliamentary Archives, LG/G/17/11/25, 19 October 1927, in a letter to C.P. Scott.

128 Macmillan had long been favourably impressed by Lloyd George. As early as 1913, he had heard Lloyd George speak at the Oxford Union. 'It was as if', Macmillan later remembered, 'a Cleon or a Danton had suddenly invaded our quiet academic groves' (Alastair Horne, *Harold Macmillan*, vol. 1, *1894–1956* (New York, 1988), 22.

129 Middlemas, *Jones Whitehall Diary*, vol. 2, 26 October 1930, p. 275.

130 Marquand, *Ramsay MacDonald*, p. 623.

131 See Skidelsky, *Politicians and The Slump*, ch. 13, 'The Fall of the Labour government'.

132 The formation of this brief ministry has been a controversial issue among historians. John D. Fair believes that whereas MacDonald must share much of the responsibility for betraying the Labour Party, it was Neville Chamberlain 'who seduced MacDonald' (Fair, 'The Conservative Basis for the Formation of the National Government of 1931', *Journal of British Studies* 19 (1980), pp. 142–64). Stuart Ball, however, exonerates Chamberlain and comes to the conclusion that all the major players were hesitant, not to say reluctant, to form a national government – mainly because no one was enthusiastic about the notion of a forced coalition. The lessons of Lloyd George's coalition in its final stages were too fresh in most minds (Ball, 'The Conservative Party and the Formation of the National Government: August 1931', *Historical Journal* 29:1 (1986), pp. 159–82).

133 Nigel Nicolson (ed.), *Harold Nicolson, Diaries and Letters 1930–1939* (New York, 1966), 21 July 1931, pp. 81–2.

134 Campbell, *Goat in the Wilderness*, p. 297.

135 The conspiratorial meeting at Archie Sinclair's could hardly have been called a summoning of the mighty. Indeed, Jenkins calls them 'a strange gathering of political plotters' (Jenkins, *Churchill*, p. 440). But Campbell believes that Lloyd George may have been near forcing MacDonald to take a coterie of Liberals (including himself) into a new coalition thus forming a progressive bloc. Indeed in July 1931, according to Campbell, Lloyd George 'stood closer to regaining office than at any other time between 1922 and 1940' (Campbell, *Goat in the Wilderness*, pp. 293–4).

136 For the misfortunes of the Liberal Party during the 1930s, see Dutton, *History of the Liberal Party*, pp. 122–33.

137 Quoted in Rowland, *Lloyd George*, 31 December 1931, p. 695. See J. Graham Jones, *David Lloyd George and Welsh Liberalism* (Aberystwyth, 2010), ch. 19, 'Lloyd George and Welsh Liberalism and the Political Crisis of 1931' for an analysis of that disappointing year in the life of Lloyd George.

138 This was labour well rewarded: he earned approximately £65,000 in sales over the next few years (Packer, *Lloyd George*, p. 105).

139 Taylor, *Stevenson Diary*, 29 March 1934, p. 264.

140 Rowland, *Lloyd George*, pp. 697–711.

141 For the following, see Jones, *Lloyd George and Welsh Liberalism*, ch. 21, 'Lloyd George, the New Deal, and the Council of Action for Peace and Reconstruction'.

142 Taylor, *Stevenson Diary*, 6 November 1934, p. 288.

143 Quoted in Jenkins, *Churchill*, p. 476.

144 See *The Times*, 29 November 1934 for this speech.

145 For the Bangor speech, see *The Times*, 18 January 1935.

146 Marquand, *MacDonald*, p. 764.

147 Ibid., p. 765.

148 Stevenson and Cook, *The Slump*, p. 286. Averages for the staple industries are as of 1936.

149 Marquand, *Macdonald*, p. 698.

150 As Marquand has observed, MacDonald 'could not help but view the massed Conservative battalions on the benches behind him' in the House of Commons 'with a mixture of alarm and distaste' (ibid., p. 671).

151 Middlemas and Barnes, *Baldwin*, pp. 808–10.

152 Thomas Jones, *A Diary with Letters, 1931–1950*, reprint edn (London, 1969), 17 November 1934, pp. 138–9.

153 In a letter to his sister Ida: Robert Self (ed.), *The Austen Chamberlain Diary Letters: The Correspondence of Sir Austen Chamberlain with his Sisters Hilda and Ida, 1916–1937* (Cambridge, 1995), 20 January 1935, p. 112.

154 Ibid., 6 January 1935, p. 110, in a communication to Baldwin, repeated several months later (ibid., 4 May 1935, p. 131). Other comments during 1935 further reflect Neville's negative views of Lloyd George. He condemned 'all the wiles of that most artful little mischief maker' (ibid., 2 February 1935, p. 115); found him 'offensive' (ibid., 23 February 1935, p. 117); 'impudent' (ibid., 3 March 1935, p. 118); guilty of 'sheer impertinence' (ibid., 9 March 1935, p. 120); and full of 'canting humbug' (ibid., 22 September 1935, p. 152). His half-brother Austen, however, whose experience with Lloyd George was wholly different, cautiously favoured bringing in Lloyd George, 'a man for a crisis when heroic remedies must be tried' (ibid., 19 January 1935, 473).

155 *The Times*, 18 January 1935.

156 Taylor, *Stevenson Diary*, 29 January 1935, p. 299.

157 Ibid., 15 February 1935, p. 301.

158 Ibid.

159 She had been created Dame of the Grand Cross of the British Empire in 1920 in recognition of her work in wartime charities.

160 See Stephen Koss, 'Lloyd George and Nonconformity: the Last Rally', *English Historical Review* 89 (1974), pp. 77–108.

161 Parliamentary Archives, LG/G/18/7/11, 14 January 1935, Snowden to Lloyd George. Snowden was a noted pacifist and the Labour Party's first Chancellor for the Exchequer in 1924 and again in 1929–31. MP for Blackburn 1906–1918 and Colne Valley 1922–31.

162 Ibid., LG/G/141/28/15, 18 July 1935, Lothian to Lloyd George.

163 Maurice Cowling, *The Impact of Hitler: British Politics and British Policy 1933–1940* (Cambridge, 1975), pp, 233–4.

164 Jones, *Lloyd George and Welsh Liberalism*, p. 409.

165 Tom Stannage, *Baldwin Thwarts the Opposition: The British General Election of 1935* (London, 1980), p. 11.

166 Tom Jones thought so in his election post mortem: 'L. G. has been captious and bad-mannered and his Councils of Action have justified the quip Councils of Faction' (Jones, *Diary with Letters*, 17 November 1935, p. 157).

167 As Koss characterizes it in 'Lloyd George and Nonconformity', p. 78.

168 Tom Jones summarized the Council accurately enough as 'a fresh attempt by Lloyd George to get his hand on the levers of power at the next election by means of an organization under his own control' (Jones, *Lloyd George*, p. 243).

169 Trevor Wilson, *The Downfall of the Liberal Party, 1914–1935* (London, 1966), p. 381.

170 John Campbell, *If Love Were All … The Story of Frances Stevenson and David Lloyd George*, paperback edn (London, 2007), 17 May 1922, p. 237.

171 He also purchased residences in London to keep a high profile in the capital city (Rowland, *Lloyd George*, p. 593).

172 For this description of the farm at Churt, see Jones, *Lloyd George*, p. 274; and Frances Lloyd George, *The Years That Are Past*, ch. 17, passim.

173 John M. McEwen, *The Riddell Diaries, 1908–1923* (London, 1986), 18 November 1922, p. 382.

174 Rowland, *Lloyd George*, p. 645.

175 Jones, *Lloyd George*, p. 215.

176 Ffion Hague, *The Pain and the Privilege: The Women in Lloyd George's Life* (London, 2008), pp. 228, 232.

177 Ibid., p. 104.

178 Ibid., p. 464.

179 Ibid., p. 465.

180 Ibid., p. 327.

181 Ibid., p. 310.

182 For details of the Stevenson-Tweed romance, see Campbell, *If Love Were All*, ch. 26.

183 Taylor *My Darling Pussy*, pp. 110–1.

184 Campbell, *If Love Were All*, p. 336.

185 Two published versions of Sylvester's extensive private diary give some flavour of his censorious, yet often forgiving, portrait. Both abound in anecdotal evidence – not only of Lloyd George's public life where Sylvester thought him 'a great man' – but also in his private personal foibles and his sexual adventures, especially with Frances. J. Graham Jones has given an authoritative analysis of these sources in his 'The Real Lloyd George', *Journal of Liberal History* 51 (Summer 2006), pp. 4–12; and 'Life with Lloyd George', *Journal of Liberal History* 55 (Summer 2007), pp. 28–36.

186 Sylvester, *Life with Lloyd George*, 8 December–16 December1931, pp. 64–6.

187 Jenkins, *Churchill*, p. 486. Campbell believes that Lloyd George and Churchill spent their mornings competitively writing (*If Love Were All*, p. 443).

188 Sylvester, *Life with Lloyd George*, 10 January 1936, p. 138.

189 Ibid., 8 August 1936, pp. 443–4.

190 Published in 1938 as *The Truth about the Peace Treaties*. For the Jamaica holiday, see Rowland, *Lloyd George*, pp. 738–41.

191 Roy Hattersley, *David Lloyd George: The Great Outsider* (London, 2012), p. 625.

192 J. Graham Jones, 'Lloyd George and the Abdication of Edward VIII', in J. Graham Jones, *David Lloyd George and Welsh Liberalism* (Aberystwyth, 2010), p. 431. See also Philip Ziegler, *King Edward VIII: A Biography* (New York, 1991), passim; and Frances Donaldson, *Edward VIII* (Philadelphia, 1975), ch. 6 'The First Tours'.

193 For this paragraph, see Campbell, *If Love Were All*, ch. 32, 'Tweed Again'.

194 Ibid., pp. 422–3.

Chapter 18. Return to Wales

1 He hints as much in a letter to Frances in 1937. 'We have', he wrote, 'trodden the cinders of hell these past few years … Often my heart has been chilled with despair & despondency & I saw nothing but a gloomy future with no ray of consolation. Work is only a distraction & I have worked like a maniac to divert my thoughts from poignant memories that sting' (John Campbell, *If Love Were All … The Story of Frances Stevenson and David Lloyd George*, paperback edn (London, 2007), 24 January 1937, p. 452).

2 R.A.C. Parker, 'British Rearmament 1936–39: Treasury, Trade Unions and Skilled Labour', *English Historical Review* 96 (1981), pp. 306–43.

3   Richard Toye, 'The Labour Party and the Economics of Rearmament, 1935–39', *Twentieth Century British History* 12:3 (2001), pp. 303–26.

4   Paul M. Kennedy, 'The Tradition of Appeasement in British Foreign Policy, 1865–1939', *British Journal of International Relations* 2 (1976), pp. 195–215.

5   William R. Rock, *British Appeasement in the 1930s* (New York, 1977), p. 99.

6   Appeasers in the sense that, as William Rock explains it, they sought to mediate differences between France and Germany and to foster negotiations for peaceful change (ibid., p. 35).

7   Many of these came from an aristocratic, gentry, or military background. Perhaps the most notorious example was Charles Stewart Henry Vane-Tempest-Stewart, 7th Marquess of Londonderry, who served as Air Minister in Baldwin's National Government. See Ian Kershaw's *Making Friends with Hitler: Lord Londonderry, the Nazis and the Road to World War II* (New York, 2004).

8   John Evelyn Wrench, *Geoffrey Dawson and Our Times* (London, 1955), p. 373; and Gordon Martel (ed.), The Times *and Appeasement: The Journals of A.L. Kennedy, 1931–1939* (London, 2000). Kennedy was a foreign correspondent who sometimes worked hand in glove with the Foreign Office in shaping the news as reported by *The Times*: see especially ibid., pp. 9–15.

9   Paul Addison, 'Patriotism under Pressure: Lord Rothermere and British Foreign Policy', in Gillian Peele and Chris Cook (eds), *The Politics of Reappraisal, 1918–1939* (New York, 1975), pp. 189–208. The journals of Collin Brooks, a writer for Rothermere's newspapers who became a protégé closely involved with Rothermere's campaign for appeasement, are especially valuable in revealing the mind of the hard right appeasers. See N.J. Crowson (ed.), *Fleet Street, Press Barons and Politics: The Journals of Collin Brooks, 1931–1940* (London, 1998).

10 For a general review of the press and its position on appeasement, see Franklin Reid Gannon, *The British Press and Germany, 1936–1939* (Oxford, 1971), esp. ch. 2.

11 Benny Morris, *The Roots of Appeasement: The British Weekly Press and Nazi Germany during the 1930s* (London, 1991).

12 For all these reasons, as R.A.C. Parker has put it, 'almost everyone favoured the policy of 'appeasement' ' (Parker, *Chamberlain and Appeasement: British Policy and the Coming of the Second World War* (New York, 1993), p. 1. Parker presents on the whole a reasoned and balanced view of appeasement, but here he nevertheless overstates his case. There were in fact influential and outspoken anti-appeasers. Among them were such prominent public men as Conservatives Duff Cooper and Winston Churchill in Parliament; the Labourite Hugh Dalton; and Sir Robert Vansittart at the Foreign Office. See Neville Thompson's *The Anti-Appeasers: Conservative Opposition to Appeasement in the 1930s* (Oxford, 1971); and Donald Cameron Watt, 'Churchill and Appeasement', in Robert Blake and Wm Roger Louis (eds), *Churchill* (New York, 1993). For a recent concise and thoughtful review of the historical controversy surrounding appeasement, see Sidney Aster, 'Appeasement: Before and After Revisionism', *Diplomacy and Statecraft* 19 (2008), pp. 443–80.

13 Thompson, *The Anti-Appeasers*, ch. 5; Richard J. Evans, *The Third Reich in Power*, paperback edn (London, 2006), pp. 635–7.

14 As Evans has described in riveting detail throughout *The Third Reich in Power*.

15 See G.T. Waddington, '"An Idyllic and Unruffled Atmosphere of Complete Anglo-German Misunderstanding": Aspects of the Operations of the Dienststelle Ribbentrop in Great Britain, 1934–1938', *History* 82:2654 (January 1997), pp. 44–72. Joachim von Ribbentrop, head of the Dienststelle, was an aristocratic *arriviste* and Hitler lackey who became ambassador to Britain in 1936 and later Minister of Foreign Affairs. He was

executed for war crimes in 1946 following the Nuremberg Trials. For details of his curious life, see Michael Bloch, *Ribbentrop*, paperback edn (London, 2003).

16 J.R.M. Butler, *Lord Lothian (Philip Kerr) 1882–1940* (London, 1960), pp. 202–4, 217–8, 330–7. At a second interview with Hitler in May 1937, however, Lothian found the German leader in a testier mood. Hitler believed that relations between the two countries had deteriorated and suggested that a 'colonial adjustment' could help repair the widening gap between Germany and Britain (ibid., pp. 337–45). Philip Kerr had succeeded to the title of 11th Marquess of Lothian in March 1930.

17 John Barnes and David Nicholson (eds), *The Empire at Bay: The Leo Amery Diaries, 1929–1945* (London, 1988), 13 August 1935, p. 397. 'A bigger man, on the whole, than I had expected', was Amery's considered judgement (ibid.).

18 John Shepherd, *George Lansbury: At the Heart of Old Labour* (Oxford 2002), p. 341.

19 Joseph A. Maiolo, *The Royal Navy and Nazi Germany, 1933–39: A Study in Appeasement and the Origins of the Second World War* (Houndmills, Hants, 1998), p. 20.

20 In addition to ibid, ch. 1, see the following: D.C. Watt, 'The Anglo-German Naval Agreement of 1935: An Interim Judgment', *Journal of Modern History* 28:2 (June 1956), pp. 155–75; Hines H. Hall III, 'The Foreign Policy-Making Process in Britain, 1934–1935, and the Origins of the Anglo-German Naval Agreement', *Historical Journal* 19:2 (1976), pp. 477–99; and Thomas Hoerber, 'Psychology and Reasoning in the Anglo-German Naval Agreement, 1935–1939', *Historical Journal* 52:1 (2009), pp. 153–74. As Martin Gilbert observes, the agreement at the time 'promised to inaugurate a period of positive appeasement' (*The Roots of Appeasement* (London, 1966), p. 150. Gerhard L. Weinberg, however, believes that the Agreement was merely a smokescreen behind which Germany was determined to build a blue water navy of big battleships and aircraft carriers (Weinberg, 'Hitler and England, 1933–1945: Pretense and Reality', *German Studies Review* 8 (1985), pp. 299–309).

21 See Kenneth O. Morgan, 'Lloyd George and Germany', *Historical Journal* 39:3 (1996), pp. 755–66.

22 This was within the context of a parliamentary debate on the most productive ways of reducing the possibility of an arms race around the globe and the most effective ways of promoting peace. Lloyd George had spoken in the House of Commons in favour of reducing German fears of encirclement by hostile powers. German suspicions, he believed, could not come about until 'the British Empire was prepared to reconsider the question of mandates' (*The Times*, 6 February 1936).

23 This quotation is from notes taken by Conwell-Evans and reprinted as Appendix 2 in Gilbert, *Roots of Appeasement*, p. 202.

24 Ibid., 203. A more extensive account of Lloyd George's German visit is in Thomas Jones, *A Diary with Letters, 1931–1950*, reprint edn (London, 1969)., pp. 240–59. An abbreviated version of the trip may be found in Albert James Sylvester, *Life with Lloyd George: The Diary of A.J. Sylvester*, ed. Colin Cross (London, 1975), pp. 144–54.

25 Anthony Lentin, *Lloyd George and the Lost Peace: From Versailles to Hitler, 1919–1940* (Houndmills, Hants, 2001), pp. 209–10.

26 He certainly convinced Tom Jones, to whom Hitler came across as 'an idealist', one who was 'neither fierce nor savage' and who genuinely sought friendship with Britain. Jones was additionally persuaded that Hitler 'does not seek war with us' (Jones, *Diary with Letters*, p. 252).

27 For Hitler's foreign policy, see Ian Kershaw, *The Nazi Dictatorship: Problems and Perspectives of Interpretation*, 4th (paperback) edn (London, 2000), ch. 6.

28   The Germans, he claimed, 'have no longer the desire themselves to invade any other land' (quoted in Peter Rowland, *David Lloyd George* (London, 1975), p. 735).

29   Rowland, *Lloyd George*, p. 736.

30   Parliamentary Archives, LG//19/16/8, 21 September 1936.

31   Ibid., LG/G/6/14/3, 17 December 1937. Lloyd George's views on Hitler and National Socialism were consistent over time. As early as 1933, in a letter to Morris Wartski, he had professed himself 'profoundly shocked at the outrages' perpetrated especially against the Jews. But he also claimed that there would have been neither Hitler nor Nazi movement had not the powers 'constantly broken faith' with Germany and had unfairly treated that country since World War I. He concluded: 'Injustice breeds injustice' (ibid., LG/G/34/2/27, 3 October 1933). Lloyd George's correspondent was likely Morris Wartski, proprietor of Wartski, the London jewellers, which had first begun business in Bangor, North Wales. Lloyd George had been the firm's lawyer.

32   For these quotations, see Morgan, 'Lloyd George and Germany', p. 764.

33   Sylvester records him saying that Hitler's move into Austria 'was a natural sequence of events' (Sylvester, *Life with Lloyd George*, 13 March 1938, p. 201).

34   Parliamentary Archives, LG/1/6/5, 21 October 1938.

35   *The Times*, 27 October 1938.

36   Ibid., 20 December 1938.

37   Ibid., 20 January 1939.

38   Ibid., 4 February 1939.

39   See Donald Cameron Watt, *How War Came: The Immediate Origins of the Second World War, 1938–1939* (New York, 1989), ch. 9, 'Hitler Enters Prague'.

40   Robert Self (ed.), *The Neville Chamberlain Diary Letters*, 2 vols (Burlington, 2000), to his sister Ida, 26 March 1939, p. 396. Chamberlain frequently reiterated his negative views of the Soviet Union into the spring and summer of 1939. To his sister Hilda, he repeated that he was 'deeply suspicious' of the Soviet Union (ibid., 29 April 1939, p. 412). To Ida, a few weeks later: 'I cannot rid myself of the suspicion that they are chiefly concerned to see the "capitalist" Powers tear each other to pieces' (ibid., 21 May 1939, p. 417). Again to Hilda, several weeks later: 'I am so sceptical of the value of Russian help that I should not feel that our position was greatly worsened if we had to do without them' (ibid., 2 July 1939, pp. 425–6).

41   Ibid., to Ida, 9 April 1939, p. 404.

42   Self, *Neville Chamberlain*, p. 366. Chamberlain was not alone in his suspicions of the Soviets; the Cabinet was also unwilling to take risks with what they considered to be a thoroughly unprincipled and opportunistic regime. See Robert Manne, 'Some British Light on the Nazi-Soviet Pact', *European Studies Review* 11:1 (January 1981), pp. 83–102).

43   See Sidney Aster, 'Ivan Maisky and Parliamentary Anti-Appeasement, 1938–39', in A.J.P. Taylor (ed.), *Lloyd George: Twelve Essays* (London, 1971), pp. 31–57, p. 354. Lloyd George had established friendly relations with Maisky, the Soviet Ambassador, as early as 1932.

44   Parliamentary Archives, LG/1/6/7, 25 August 1939.

45   Ibid., LG/G/3/13/13, 29 September 1939. This was necessary, Boothby suggested in an earlier letter, because the man in the street was 'deeply suspicious of the motives of the present government' (ibid., LG/G/3/13/10, 10 September 1939).

46   Ibid., LG/G/5/13/12, 5 September 1939. David Davies, lst Baron Llandinam, served as a Parliamentary Secretary to Lloyd George during World War I. He was MP for Montgomeryshire from 1906–29.

47   Nigel Nicolson (ed.), *Harold Nicolson: Diaries and Letters, 1939–1945* (London, 1967), p. 35.

48   For this and the following quotations, see *The Times*, 4 October 1939.

49 *The Times*, 23 October 1939.

50 Sylvester records that the speech and its effect among the thousands present (an estimated 6,000 to 9,000) 'was superb'. At one moment, Sylvester observed, Lloyd George 'was playing up the blue-blooded Tories – and many were present – talking about our superb air force and the greatest navy in the world'; and the next moment, 'he was playing up to the peacemongers, by advocating a conference and peace' (Sylvester, *Life with Lloyd George*, 21 October 1939, p. 242).

51 Robert Boothby, *I Fight to Live* (London, 1947), p. 197. This conversation was held on 28 September 1939.

52 William Armstrong (ed.), *With Malice Toward None: A War Diary by Cecil H. King* (Cranbury, NJ, 1971), p. 3 January 1940, p. 13. Cudlipp reported this conversation to King, who was a director of both the *Daily Mirror* and the *Sunday Pictorial*. Several months later, both Cudlipp and King visited Lloyd George at Churt. In the ensuing conversation, Lloyd George once again advocated playing for time. Although King disagreed with this tactic, he nevertheless respected Lloyd George's opinion. 'Of all the political figures I have talked politics with', he wrote later in his diary, 'Lloyd George seemed to me the most realistic' (ibid., 6 June 1940, p. 46). A few months afterward, Lloyd George showed a firm sense of timing for any discussions with Hitler. In response to an entreaty from the Duke of Bedford for negotiations with the Reich, he declined. 'Were we to make peace overtures now whilst the threat of invasion was impending over our heads', he wrote, 'it would be stigmatised as a Petain move inspired by fear of utter defeat'. In any case, he doubted that a German invasion would succeed: 'I have only the old rooted tradition which comes from a long series of failures which have befallen all these ventures, that it cannot succeed' (Parliamentary Archives, LG/G/3/4/9, 14 September 1940).

53 Richard Toye, *Lloyd George and Churchill: Rivals for Greatness*, paperback edn (London, 2007), pp. 340–1.

54 Paul Addison, 'Lloyd George and Compromise Peace in the Second World War', in Taylor, *Lloyd George: Twelve Essays*, pp. 361–84.

55 For the 'Norway Debate', see *Hansard*, 5th Series, vol. CCCLX, 8 May 1940, pp. 1277–83.

56 Jones, *Diary with Letters*, 8 May 1940, p. 458.

57 Sylvester, *Life with Lloyd George*, 8 May 1940, p. 260.

58 Frances Lloyd George, *The Years That Are Past* (London, 1967), p. 262.

59 Robert Rhodes James (ed.), *Chips: The Diaries of Sir Henry Channon*, paperback edn (London, 1970), 9 May 1940, p. 304. Channon, an American transplant and society figure, was Conservative MP for Southend-on-Sea for many years from 1935.

60 John Colville, *The Fringes of Power: 10 Downing Street Diaries, 1939–1955* (New York, 1985), 8 May 1940, p. 119.

61 Mark Pottle (ed.), *Champion Redoubtable: The Diaries and Letters of Violet Bonham Carter, 1914–1945*, paperback edn (London, 1999), 14 May 1940, p. 210.

62 Self, *Neville Chamberlain*, pp. 437–8. Chamberlain remained in the War Cabinet as Lord President.

63 John Lukacs, *Five Days in London: May 1940* (New Haven, CT, 1999), p. 113. Lukacs repeats this information twice more: 'Churchill felt that he could not oppose Halifax unconditionally' (p. 117); and 'he felt that he should not, because he could not, oppose Halifax's proposals entirely' (p. 128). Other historians substantiate Churchill's seriously considered peace negotiations. Andrew Roberts, in his biography of Halifax, writes that Halifax's peace offer was an attempt to obtain 'a breathing space' (*'The Holy Fox': A Biography of Lord Halifax* (London, 1991), p. 214). Roberts notes further that Churchill 'expressed his willingness to examine peace along those lines' (ibid.). See also David

Reynolds, 'Churchill and the British 'Decision' to fight on in 1940: Right Policy, Wrong Reasons', in Richard Langhorne (ed.), *Diplomacy and Intelligence During the Second World War: Essays in Honor of F.H. Hinsley* (Cambridge, 1985). Reynolds sums up Churchill's thinking thus: he 'expressed acceptance, in principle, of the idea of an eventual negotiated peace, on terms guaranteeing the independence of the British Isles, even if that meant sacrificing parts of the empire and leaving Germany in command of Central Europe' (pp. 165–6). Bernd Martin agrees, pointing out that Churchill was initially doubtful which path to pursue – diplomacy or continued war against Germany. Churchill certainly 'did not completely exclude' the possibility of peace negotiations. As Martin explains it: 'Churchill considered taking up these proposals at least to achieve an armistice in order to gain time for the still insufficiently prepared British military'. See Martin, 'Churchill and Hitler, 1940: Peace or War?', in R.A.C. Parker (ed.), *Winston Churchill: Studies in Statesmanship* (London, 1995), pp. 87, 90–1. But some historians deny such claims: see Martin Gilbert, *Churchill: A Life*, paperback edn (New York, 1991), p. 651. Jenkins has a more tempered judgement, suggesting that Churchill was in fact hesitant about his decision on negotiations. 'Any apparent waverings on Churchill's part' during the War Cabinet meetings can be explained by 'the harsh reality that Churchill … was by no means certain of an adequate majority within his own recently chosen War Cabinet' (Roy Jenkins, *Churchill: A Biography*, paperback edn (London, 2002), p. 601).

64 Parliamentary Archives, LG/G/10/11/7, 7, May 1940.
65 Ibid., LG/G/3/13/22, 10 June 1940.
66 Ibid., LG/G/3/12/33, 15 June 1940. Boothby wrote in like manner to Churchill. After a discussion with Lloyd George – whose general views 'were very robust' – Boothby stressed Lloyd George's reluctance to enter a Cabinet containing both Chamberlain and Halifax, whose policies 'were a liability to the country' (quoted in Robert Rhodes James, *Robert Boothby: A Portrait of Churchill's Ally* (New York, 1991), 262.
67 Parliamentary Archives, LG/G/9/3/18, 20 April 1940. But as Brian Bond has pointed out, Liddell Hart was 'very much an outsider' at this time in his career and operated 'only on the fringe of politics' (Bond, *Liddell Hart: A Study of his Military Thought* (London, 1977), 119–20). Liddell Hart was sceptical of waging total war against Germany, given the hard lessons of World War I. He believed that conciliation and negotiation with Hitler would be the most appropriate path to peace. Hitler, he thought, would respond favourably to such an approach if Britain combined it with a military firmness that would convince the German leader he could not win a war with force of arms only. Bond sums up Liddell Hart thus: 'He was a pessimist but not a defeatist; he was always in favour of negotiations, but the terms must be honourable from a British viewpoint' (ibid., p. 158).
68 From Lloyd George's 'Secret and Personal' letter to Churchill, Parliamentary Archives, LG/G/4/5/47, 29 May 1940. See also Martin Gilbert, *Winston S. Churchill*, vol. 6, *Finest Hour 1939–1941* (Boston, 1985), pp. 425–6.
69 As John Charmley has phrased it: 'It was a Government with Churchill as Prime Minister, but it was not Churchill's Government' (*Churchill: The End of Glory, A Political Biography* (London, 1993), p. 397.
70 The memo may be found at Parliamentary Archives, LG/G/9/3/34, 12 September 1940.
71 Gilbert, *Finest Hour*, pp. 942–3.
72 Jenkins, *Churchill*, p. 588, note.
73 Sylvester, *Life with Lloyd George*, p. 262. Jenkins clearly had an animus against Lloyd George. As he once confessed to Roy Hattersley, he could never write a biography of Lloyd George, because he 'disliked' him 'so heartily' (*David Lloyd George: The Great Outsider* (London, 2012), p. ix).

74 Robert Self, *Neville Chamberlain: A Biography* (Aldershot, 2006), p. 442.

75 Addison, 'Lloyd George and Compromise Peace', pp. 378–9.

76 Toye, *Lloyd George and Churchill*, p. 372.

77 A.J.P. Taylor, *My Darling Pussy: The Letters of Lloyd George and Frances* (London, 1975), 228–9.

78 Rowland, *Lloyd George*, p. 777.

79 For these quotations, see Lloyd George's letter to Frances in Taylor, *My Darling Pussy*, 4 October 1940, p. 239. It would appear, then, that during the intervening months between May and October 1940, Lloyd George had second thoughts about his ability to withstand the rigours of a wartime office.

80 Sylvester, *Life with Lloyd George*, 20 January 1941, p. 285.

81 As Rowland, *Lloyd George*, p. 787, believes.

82 Sylvester, *Life with Lloyd George* 9 September 1941, p. 294.

83 Ibid., 7 May 1941, p. 290.

84 Jones, *Lloyd George*, pp. 257–8.

85 Rowland, *Lloyd George*, p. 789.

86 Nicolson, *Harold Nicolson: Diaries and Letters, 1939–1945*, 23 June 1943, p. 302. Lloyd George had come to hear his son Gwilym give a major speech.

87 Parliamentary Archives, LG/G/9/1/14, 23 January 1944.

88 Sylvester, *Life with Lloyd George*, 21 September 1944, pp. 328–9.

89 For Frances's comments, see her *The Years That Are Past*, p. 268.

90 See J. Graham Jones, *David Lloyd George and Welsh Liberalism* (Aberystwyth, 2010), ch. 25.

91 See Rowland, *Lloyd George*, p. 797. This account of Lloyd George's final months follows closely Rowland's: see ibid., pp. 790–8.

92 George H. Cassar, *Kitchener's War: British Strategy from 1914–1916* (Washington, 2004), p. 30.

93 For these quotations, see Hattersley, *Lloyd George*, pp. 124, 131, 222, 83, 154.

94 Kenneth O. Morgan, *Lloyd George* (London, 1974), p. 192.

95 For the quotation, see A.J.P. Taylor, *English History 1914–1945* (New York, 1965), p. 34.

96 Previously noted in ch. 6 above.

97 Robert Lloyd George, *David and Winston: How a Friendship Changed History*, paperback edn (London, 2005), passim.

98 Toye, *Lloyd George & Churchill*, p. 5.

99 For this and the following quotations, see ibid., p. 406.

100 Kevin Theakston and Mark Gill, 'Rating 20th-Century British Prime Ministers', *British Journal of Politics and International Relations* 8:2 (May, 2006), pp. 193–213. Those surveyed were academics specializing in British politics and/or modern British history. In every survey, Lloyd George and Churchill ranked at least in fifth place (and usually higher) of the 20 prime ministers from Balfour through to Blair. Most often they were ranked either in first, second or third place, with Churchill usually leading Lloyd George by a place or two.

BIBLIOGRAPHY

Adams, R.J.Q., *Arms and the Wizard: Lloyd George and the Ministry of Munitions, 1915–1916* (College Station, 1978).

——, 'Asquith's Choice: The May Coalition and the Coming of Conscription, 1915–1916', *Journal of British Studies* 25 (July 1986), pp. 244–46.

——, *Bonar Law* (London, 1999).

——, *Balfour: The Last Grandee* (London, 2007).

Adams, R.J.Q. and Poirier, Philip P., *The Conscription Controversy in Great Britain, 1900–18* (London, 1987).

Adams, W.S., 'Lloyd George and the Labour Movement', *Past & Present* 3 (1953), pp. 55–64.

Addison, Christopher, *Four and a Half Years: A Personal Diary from June 1914 to January 1919*, vol. 1 (London, 1934).

Addison, Paul, 'Lloyd George and Compromise Peace in the Second World War', in A.J.P. Taylor (ed.), *Lloyd George: Twelve Essays* (New York, 1971).

——, 'Patriotism under Pressure: Lord Rothermere and British Foreign Policy', in Gillian Peele and Chris Cook (eds), *The Politics of Reappraisal, 1918–1939* (New York, 1975).

——, *Churchill on the Home Front, 1900–1955*, Pimlico edn (London, 1993).

Adelman, Paul, *Victorian Radicalism: The Middle-Class Experience, 1830–1914* (London, 1984).

Adonis, Andrew, 'Aristocracy, Agriculture and Liberalism: The Politics, Finances and Estates of the Third Lord Carrington', *Historical Journal* 31:4 (1988), pp. 871–97.

Aldcroft, Derek H., *Studies in British Transport History, 1870–1970* (Newton Abbot, 1974).

Alderman, Geoffrey, 'The Railway Companies and the Growth of Trade Unionism in the Late Nineteenth and Early Twentieth Centuries', *Historical Journal* 14:1 (1971), pp. 129–52.

Amery, Leo, *My Political Life*, vol. 2, *War and Peace, 1914–1929* (London, 1963).

Anderson, Edgar, 'An Undeclared Naval War: The British-Soviet Naval Struggle in the Baltic, 1918–1920', *Journal of Central European Affairs* 22:1 (1962/63), pp. 43–78.

Anderson, Margaret Lavinia, 'Reply to Volker Berghahn', *Central European History* 35:1 (2002), pp. 83–90.

Andrew, Christopher, 'The British Secret Service and Anglo-Soviet Relations in the 1920s. Part I: From the Trade Negotiations to the Zinoviev Letter', *Historical Journal* 20:3 (1977), pp. 673–706.

——, *Secret Service: The Making of the British Intelligence Community* (London, 1985).

——, *Defend the Realm: The Authorized History of MI5* (New York, 2009).

Andrews, Lawrence, *The Education Act, 1918* (London, 1976).

Armitage, Susan, *The Politics of Decontrol of Industry: Britain and the United States* (London, 1969).

Armstrong, William (ed.), *With Malice Toward None: A War Diary by Cecil H. King* (Cranbury, NJ, 1971).

Askwith, George Rankin, Baron, *Industrial Problems and Disputes* (London, 1920).

Asprey, Robert B., *The First Battle of the Marne* (Philadelphia, 1962).

Aster, Sidney, 'Ivan Maisky and Parliamentary Anti-Appeasement, 1938–39', in A.J.P. Taylor (ed.), *Lloyd George: Twelve Essays* (New York, 1971).

——, 'Appeasement: Before and After Revisionism', *Diplomacy and Statecraft* 19 (2008), pp. 443–80.

Augusteijn, Joost, 'Accounting for the Emergence of Violent Activism among Irish Revolutionaries, 1916–21', *Irish Historical Studies* 35:139 (May 2007), pp. 327–44.

Bagwell, Philip S., *The Railwaymen: The History of the National Union of Railwaymen* (London, 1963).

——, 'The Triple Industrial Alliance, 1913–1922', in Asa Briggs and John Saville (eds), *Essays in Labour History, 1886–1923* (Hamden, 1971).

——, *The Transport Revolution from 1770* (London, 1974).

Bakhash, Shaul, 'The Origins of the Anglo-Persian Agreement of 1919', *Asian and African Studies* 25 (March 1991), pp. 1–29.

Ball, Stuart, 'Asquith's Decline and the General Election of 1918', *Scottish Historical Review* 62:171 (April 1982), pp. 44–61.

——, 'The Conservative Party and the Formation of the National Government: August 1931', *Historical Journal* 29:1 (1986), pp. 159–82.

Barker, A.J., *The Neglected War: Mesopotamia, 1914–1918* (London, 1967).

Barnes, John and Nicholson, David (eds), *The Leo Amery Diaries*, vol. 1, *1896–1929* (London, 1980).

——, *The Empire at Bay: The Leo Amery Diaries, 1929–1944* (London, 1988).

Beaverbrook, Lord (William Maxwell Aitken), *Politicians and the War, 1914–1916*, one-volume edn (London, 1960).

Bebbington, D.W., *The Nonconformist Conscience: Chapel and Politics, 1870–1914* (London, 1982).

——, 'The Free Church MPs of the 1906 Parliament', in Stephen Taylor and David L. Wykes (eds), *Parliament and Dissent* (Edinburgh, 2005).

Becker, Jean-Jacques, *The Great War and the French People* (New York, 1986).

Beckett, Ian F.W., *The Great War 1914–1918* (Harlow, 2001).

Bell, G.K.A., *Randall Davidson, Archbishop of Canterbury*, vol. 1 (New York, 1935).

Bell, P.M.H., *France and Britain 1900–1940: Entente and Estrangement* (London, 1996).

Bennett, G.H., *British Foreign Policy During the Curzon Period, 1919–24* (New York, 1995).

Bentley, Michael 'The Liberal Response to Socialism, 1918–29', in Kenneth D. Brown (ed.), *Essays in Anti-Labour History: Responses to the Rise of Labour in Britain* (Hamden, 1974).

——, *Politics Without Democracy* (London, 1984).

——, *The Climax of Liberal Politics: British Liberalism in Theory and Practice 1868–1918* (London, 1987)

——, *Politics without Democracy, 1815–1914*, 2nd edn (Oxford, 1996).

Benyon, J.A., Cook, C.W., Davenport, T.R.H. and Hunt, K.S. (eds), *Studies in Local History: Essays in Honour of Professor Winifrid Maxwell* (Cape Town, 1976).

Berghahn, Volker R., *Germany and the Approach of War in 1914*, 2nd edn (New York, 1993).

——, 'The German Empire, 1871–1914: Reflections on the Direction of Recent Research', *Central European History* 35:1 (2002), pp. 75–81.

Bernstein, George L., 'Liberalism and the Progressive Alliance in the Constituencies, 1900–1914: Three Case Studies', *Historical Journal* 26:3 (1983), pp. 617–40.

——, *Liberalism and Liberal Politics in Edwardian England* (Boston, 1986).

Best, Geoffrey, *Churchill: A Study in Greatness* (London, 2001).

——, *Churchill and War* (Hambledon, 2005).

Bew, Paul, *Ideology and the Irish Question: Ulster Unionism and Irish Nationalism, 1912–1916* (Oxford, 1994).

——, *Ireland: The Politics of Enmity, 1789–2006* (Oxford, 2007).

Biagini, Eugenio F. and Reid, Alastair J. (eds), *Currents of Radicalism: Popular Radicalism, Organised Labour and Party Politics in Britain, 1850–1914* (Cambridge, 1991).

Blake, Robert, *The Unknown Prime Minister: The Life and Times of Andrew Bonar Law, 1858–1923* (London, 1955).

—— and Louis, William Roger (eds), *Churchill* (New York, 1993).

Blanch, Michael, 'Imperialism, Nationalism and Organized Youth', in J. Clarke, C. Critcher and R. Johnson (eds), *Working Class Culture: Studies in History and Theory* (New York, 1979).

Blaxland, Gregory, *Amiens 1918* (London, 1968).

Blewett, Neal, *The Peers, the Parties and the People: The British General Elections of 1910* (London, 1972).

Bloch, Michael, *Ribbentrop*, paperback edn (London, 2003).

Blunt, Wilfred Scawen, *My Diaries: Being a Personal Narrative of Events, 1888–1914* (New York, 1923).

Boemeke, Manfred F., 'Woodrow Wilson's Image of Germany, the War-Guilt Question, and the Treaty of Versailles', in Manfred R. Boemeke, Gerald D. Feldman and Elisabeth Glaser (eds), *The Treaty of Versailles: A Reassessment after 75 Years* (Cambridge, 1998).

Bond, Brian, *Liddell Hart: A Study of his Military Thought* (London, 1977).

——, *The Unquiet Western Front: Britain's Role in Literature and History* (Cambridge, 2002).

—— and Robbins, Simon (eds), *Staff Officer: The Diaries of Walter Guinness (First Lord Moyne), 1914–1918* (London, 1987).

Boothby, Robert, *I Fight to Live* (London, 1947).

Bowle, John, *Viscount Samuel: A Biography* (London, 1957).

Bowman, Timothy, 'The Ulster Volunteer Force, 1910–1920: New Perspectives', in D. George Boyce and Alan O'Day (eds), *The Making of Modern Irish History* (London, 1996).

Boyce, D. George, 'How to Settle the Irish Question: Lloyd George and Ireland, 1916–21', in A.J.P. Taylor (ed.), *Lloyd George: Twelve Essays* (New York, 1971).

——, *Englishmen and Irish Troubles: British Public Opinion and the Making of Irish Policy, 1918–22* (London, 1972).

——, 'British Opinion, Ireland, and the War, 1916–1918', *Historical Journal* 17:3 (September 1974), pp. 575–93.

——, '1916, Interpreting the Rising', D. George Boyce and Alan O'Day (eds), *The Making of Modern Irish History: Revisionism and the Revisionist Controversy* (London, 1996).

—— and Hazlehurst, Cameron, 'The Unknown Chief Secretary: H.E. Duke and Ireland, 1916–18', *Irish Historical Studies* 20:79 (March 1977), pp. 286–311.

—— and O'Day, Alan (eds), *The Making of Modern Irish History: Revisionism and the Revisionist Controversy* (London, 1996).

——, *The Ulster Crisis* (Houndmills, 2006).

Boyle, T., 'The Formation of Campbell-Bannerman's Government in December 1905: A Memorandum by J.A. Spender', *Bulletin of the Institute of Historical Research* 105:112 (November 1972), pp. 283–302.

——, 'The Liberal Imperialists, 1892–1906', *Bulletin of the Institute of Historical Research* 52 (1979), pp. 48–82.

Bradley, John, *Allied Intervention in Russia* (London, 1968).

Briggs, Asa *Social Thought and Social Action: A Study of the Work of Seebohm Rowntree, 1871–1954* (London, 1961).

Briggs, Asa and Saville, John (eds), *Essays in Labour History, 1886–1923* (Hamden, 1971).

Brock, Michael and Eleanor (eds), *H.H. Asquith Letters to Venetia Stanley*, paperback edn (Oxford, 1985).

Brooks, David, *The Age of Upheaval: Edwardian Politics, 1899–1914* (Manchester, 1995).

Brown, Judith M., *Modern India: The Origins of an Asian Democracy*, 2nd edn (New York, 1994).

Brown, Kenneth D., 'Conflict in Early British Welfare Policy: The Case of the Unemployed Workmen's Bill of 1905', *Journal of Modern History* 43 (1971), pp. 615–29.

——, 'The Labour Party and the Unemployment Question, 1906–1910', *Historical Journal* 14:3 (1971), pp. 599–616.

Buckland, P.J., 'The Southern Irish Unionists, the Irish Question, and British Politics 1906–14', *Irish Historical Studies* 15:59 (March 1967), pp. 228–53.

Bunbury, Sir Henry N. (ed.), *Lloyd George's Ambulance Wagon: Being the Memoirs of William J. Braithwaite, 1911–1912* (London, 1957).

Bunselmeyer, Robert E., *The Cost of the War, 1914–1919: British Economic War Aims and the Origins of Reparation* (Hamden, 1975).

Burk, Kathleen (ed.), *War and the State: The Transformation of British Government 1914–1919* (London, 1982).

———, *Britain, America and the Sinews of War, 1914–1918* (Boston, 1985).

Burnett, Philip Mason, *Reparation at the Paris Peace Conference from the Standpoint of the American Delegation*, vol. 1 (New York, 1965).

Butler, J.R.M., *Lord Lothian (Philip Kerr) 1882–1940* (London, 1960).

Butler, John, 'Select Documents XLV: Lord Oranmore's Journal, 1913–27', *Irish Historical Studies* 29:116 (November 1995), pp. 553–93.

Callwell, Major-General Sir Charles E., *Field-Marshall Sir Henry Wilson: His Life and Diaries*, 2 vols (London, 1927).

Campbell, Fergus, *Land and Revolution: Nationalist Politics in the West of Ireland, 1891–1921* (Oxford, 2005).

Campbell, John, *Lloyd George: The Goat in the Wilderness, 1922–1931* (London, 1977).

———, *If Love Were All ... The Story of Frances Stevenson and David Lloyd George*, paperback edn (London, 2007).

Cannadine, David, *The Decline and Fall of the British Aristocracy* (New Haven, 1990).

———, *Ornamentalism: How the British Saw Their Empire* (New York, 2001).

Canning, Paul, *British Policy Towards Ireland, 1921–1941* (Oxford, 1985).

Cassar, George H., *The Tragedy of Sir John French* (Cranbury, 1985).

———, *Kitchener's War: British Strategy from 1914 to 1916* (Washington, 2004).

———, *Lloyd George at War, 1916–1918* (London and New York, 2009).

Chamberlain, Sir Austen, *Down the Years* (London, 1935).

———, *Politics from Inside: An Epistolary Chronicle, 1906–1914* (New Haven, 1937).

Charmley, John, *Churchill: The End of Glory, A Political Biography* (London, 1993).

Charteris, Brigadier-General John, *At G.H.Q.* (London, 1931).

Checkland, Sydney, *British Public Policy, 1776–1939: An Economic, Social and Political Perspective* (Cambridge, 1983).

Chickering, Roger (ed.), *Imperial Germany: A Historiographical Companion* (Westport, 1996).

———, 'World War I and the Theory of Total War: Reflections on the British and German Cases, 1914–1915', in Roger Chickering and Stig Förster (eds), *Great War, Total War: Combat and Mobilization on the Western Front, 1914–1918* (Cambridge, 2000).

———, *Imperial Germany and the Great War, 1914–1918*, paperback edn (Cambridge, 2003).

Church, Roy, 'Edwardian Labour Unrest and Coalfield Militancy, 1890–1914', *Historical Journal* 30:4 (1987), pp. 841–57.

Churchill, Randolph S., *Lord Derby, 'King of Lancashire': The Official Life of Edward, Seventeenth Earl of Derby, 1865–1948* (London, 1959).

——, *Winston S. Churchill*, vol. 2, *1901–1914: Young Statesman* (Boston, 1967).

——, *Winston S. Churchill*, Companion vol. 2, *Part 2, 1907–1911* (Boston, 1969).

——, *Winston S. Churchill*, Companion vol. 2, *Part 3, 1911–1914* (Boston, 1969).

Churchill, Winston S., *The Aftermath* (New York, 1929).

Clark, Alan (ed.), *'A Good Innings': The Private Papers of Viscount Lee of Fareham* (London, 1974).

Clarke, P.F., *Lancashire and the New Liberalism* (Cambridge, 1971).

——, 'The Electoral Position of the Liberal and Labour Parties, 1910–1914, *English Historical Review* 90 (October 1975), pp. 828–36.

Clarke, Peter, 'Asquith and Lloyd George Revisited', in J.M.W. Bean (ed.), *The Political Culture of Modern Britain: Studies in Memory of Stephen Koss* (London, 1987).

Clegg, A., Fox, Alan and Thompson, A.F., *A History of British Trade Unions since 1889*, vol. 1: *1889–1910* (Oxford, 1964).

Clegg, Hugh Armstrong, *A History of British Trade Unions since 1889*, vol. 2, *1911–1933* (Oxford, 1985).

Clifford, Colin, *The Asquiths*, paperback edn (London, 2003).

Cline, Peter K., 'Eric Geddes and the 'Experiment' with Businessmen in Government, 1915–22', in Kenneth D. Brown (ed.), *Essays in Anti-Labour History: Responses to the Rise of Labour in Britain* (Hamden, 1974).

Coates, Tim (ed.), *The Amritsar Massacre: General Dyer in the Punjab, 1919* (London, 2000).

Coetzee, Frans, *For Party or Country: Nationalism and the Dilemmas of Popular Conservatism in Edwardian England* (New York, 1990).

Cohen, Eilot A. and Gooch, John, *Military Misfortunes: The Anatomy of Failure in War* (New York, 1990).

Cohrs, Patrick O., *The Unfinished Peace after World War I: America, Britain and the Stabilisation of Europe, 1919–1932* (Cambridge, 2006).

Colville, John, *The Fringes of Power: 10 Downing Street Diaries, 1939–1955* (New York, 1985).

Colvin, Ian, *The Life of Lord Carson*, vol. 3 (New York, 1937).

Connelly, Mark, 'J.P. Harris, *Douglas Haig and the First World War*', review, *Journal of Modern History* 82:3 (September 2010), pp. 694–95.

Coogan, Tim Pat, *The Man Who Made Ireland: The Life and Death of Michael Collins* (Niwot, 1992).

——, *De Valera: Long Fellow, Long Shadow*, paperback edn (London, 1995).

Cook, Chris, *The Age of Alignment: Electoral Politics in Britain 1922–1929* (London, 1975).

——, *A Short History of the Liberal Party, 1900–2001*, 6th edn (Houndmills, 2002).

Costello, Francis, *The Irish Revolution and its Aftermath, 1916–1923: Years of Revolt* (Dublin, 2003).

Cowling, Maurice, *The Impact of Labour, 1920–1924: The Beginning of Modern British Politics* (Cambridge, 1971).

——, *The Impact of Hitler: British Politics and British Policy 1933–1940* (Cambridge, 1975).

Cragoe, Matthew, *An Anglican Aristocracy: The Moral Economy of the Landed Estate in Carmarthenshire, 1832–1895* (Oxford, 1996).

——, *Culture, Politics, and National Identity in Wales, 1832–1886* (Oxford, 2004).

Craig, Gordon A. and Felix Gilbert (eds), *The Diplomats, 1919–1939* (Princeton, 1953).

Craton, Michael and McCready, H.W., *The Great Liberal Revival, 1903–6* (London, 1966).

Crawford, Elizabeth, *The Women's Suffrage Movement in Britain and Ireland: A Regional Survey* (London, 2006).

Cregier, Don M., *Bounder from Wales: Lloyd George's Career before the First World War* (Columbia, 1976).

Cronin, James E., *Industrial Conflict in Modern Britain* (London, 1979).

——, 'Coping with Labour, 1918–1926', in James E. Cronin and Jonathan Schneer (eds), *Social Conflict and the Political Order in Modern Britain* (New Brunswick, 1982).

——, 'Strikes, 1870–1914', in Chris Wrigley (ed.), *A History of British Industrial Relations, 1875–1914* (Amherst, 1982).

——, 'Strikes and Power in Britain, 1870–1920', in Leopold H. Haimson and Charles Tilly (eds), *Strikes, Wars, and Revolutions in an International Perspective: Strike Waves in the late Nineteenth and Early Twentieth Centuries* (Cambridge, 1989).

Crosby, Travis L., *Joseph Chamberlain: A Most Radical Imperialist* (London, 2011).

Crowson, N.J. (ed.), *Fleet Street, Press Barons and Politics: The Journals of Collin Brooks, 1931–1940* (London, 1998).

Daglish, Neil D., 'Lloyd George's Education Bill? Planning the 1906 Education Bill', *History of Education* 23:4 (1994), pp. 375–84.

Daly, M.W. (ed.), *The Cambridge History of Egypt*, vol. 2, *Modern Egypt, from 1517 to the End of the Twentieth Century* (Cambridge, 1998).

Darwin, John, 'Imperialism in Decline? Tendencies in British Policy between the Wars', *Historical Journal* 23:3 (1980), pp. 657–79.

——, *The Empire Project: The Rise and Fall of the British World System, 1830–1970* (Cambridge, 2009).

Daunton, Martin, *Just Taxes: The Politics of Taxation in Britain, 1914–1979* (Cambridge, 2002).

David, Edward (ed.), *Inside Asquith's Cabinet: From the Diaries of Charles Hobhouse* (New York, 1977).

Davidson, Roger, 'Llewellyn Smith, the Labour Department and Government Growth 1886–1909', in Cynthia Sutherland (ed.), *Studies in the Growth of Nineteenth-Century Government* (Totowa, 1972).

Davies, Norman, 'Lloyd George and Poland, 1919–20', *Journal of Contemporary History* 6:3 (1971), pp. 132–54.

——, 'Sir Maurice Hankey and the Inter-Allied Mission to Poland, July-August 1920', *Historical Journal* 15:3 (1972), pp. 553–61.

Davies, R.R., Griffiths, R.A., Jones, I.G. and Morgan, K.O. (eds), *Welsh Society and Nationhood: Historical Essays Presented to Glanmor Williams* (Cardiff, 1984).

Davis, Paul K., *Ends and Means: The British Mesopotamian Campaign and Commission* (Cranbury, 1994).

Davison, Roderic H., 'Turkish Diplomacy from Mudros to Lausanne', in Gordon A. Craig and Felix Gilbert (eds), *The Diplomats, 1919–1939* (Princeton, 1953).

Dawson, Michael, 'The Liberal Land Policy, 1924–1929: Electoral Strategy and Internal Division', *Twentieth Century British History* 2:3 (1991), pp. 272–90.

Dean, D.W., 'H.A.L. Fisher, Reconstruction and the Development of the 1918 Education Act', *British Journal of Educational Studies* 18 (1970), pp. 259–76.

Dean, Dennis, 'The Dilemmas of an Academic Liberal Historian in Lloyd George's Government: H.A.L. Fisher at the Board of Education, 1916–1922', *History* 79 (February 1994), pp. 57–81.

Debo, Richard K., 'Prelude to Negotiations: The Problem of British Prisoners in Soviet Russia, November 1918–July 1919', *Slavonic and East European Review* 58:1 (January 1980), pp. 58–75.

——, 'Lloyd George and the Copenhagen Conference of 1919–1920: The Initiation of Anglo-Soviet Negotiations', *Historical Journal* 24:2 (1981), pp. 429–41.

——, *Survival and Consolidation: The Foreign Policy of Soviet Russia, 1918–1921* (Montreal, 1992).

Desmarais, Ralph, 'Lloyd George and the Development of the British Government's Strikebreaking Organization', *International Review of Social History* 20, part 1 (1975), pp. 1–15.

Dockrill, M.L., 'David Lloyd George and Foreign Policy Before 1914', in A.J.P. Taylor (ed.), *Lloyd George: Twelve Essays* (New York, 1971).

——, 'British Policy during the Agadir Crisis', in F.H. Hinsley (ed.), *British Foreign Policy under Sir Edward Grey* (Cambridge, 1977).

—— and Goold, J. Douglas, *Peace Without Promise: Britain and the Peace Conferences, 1919–23* (Hamden, 1981).

Dodge, Tony, *Inventing Iraq: The Failure of Nation Building and a History Denied* (New York, 2003).

Donaldson, Frances, *The Marconi Scandal* (New York, 1962).

——, *Edward VIII* (Philadelphia, 1975).

Dunbabin, J.P.D., *Rural Discontent in Nineteenth-Century Britain* (New York, 1974).

Dutton, David, *Austen Chamberlain: Gentleman in Politics* (Bolton, 1985).

——, 'The "Robertson Dictatorship" and the Balkan Campaign in 1916', *Journal of Strategic Studies* 9:1 (March 1986), pp. 64–78.

——, 'His Majesty's Loyal Opposition': The Unionist Party in Opposition 1905–1915* (Liverpool, 1992).

—— (ed.), *Paris 1918: The War Diary of the British Ambassador, the 17th Earl of Derby* (Liverpool, 2001).

——, *A History of the Liberal Party in the Twentieth Century* (Houndmills, 2004).

Dwyer, T. Ryl, *Big Fellow, Long Fellow: A Joint Biography of Collins and De Valera* (New York, 1998).

Eaglesham, Eric, 'Planning the Education Bill of 1902', *British Journal of Educational Studies* 9:1 (November 1960), pp. 3–24.

Eckstein, Michael, 'Great Britain and the Triple Entente on the Eve of the Sarajevo Crisis', in F.H. Hinsley (ed.), *British Foreign Policy under Sir Edward Grey* (Cambridge, 1977).

Edwards, J. Hugh, *The Life of David Lloyd George* (London, n.d. [1913]).

Egerton, George W., *Great Britain and the Creation of the League of Nations: Strategy, Politics, and International Organization, 1914–1919* (Chapel Hill, NC, 1978).

——, 'The Lloyd George *War Memoirs*: A Study in the Politics of Memory', *Journal of Modern History* 60 (1988), pp. 55–90.

Egremont, Max, *Balfour: A Life of Arthur James Balfour*, paperback edn (London, 1998).

Elcock, Howard, 'Britain and the Russo-Polish Frontier, 1919–1921', *Historical Journal* 12:1 (1969), pp. 137–54.

——, *Portrait of a Decision: The Council of Four and the Treaty of Versailles* (London, 1972).

Eley, Geoff, *From Unification to Nazism: Reinterpreting the German Past* (Boston, 1986).

Emy, H.V., 'The Land Campaign: Lloyd George as a Social Reformer, 1909–14', in A.J.P. Taylor (ed.), *Lloyd George: Twelve Essays* (New York, 1971).

——, *Liberals, Radicals and Social Politics, 1892–1914* (Cambridge, 1973).

Erickson, Edward J., 'Strength Against Weakness: Ottoman Military Effectiveness at Gallipoli, 1915' *Journal of Military History* 65:4 (October 2001), pp. 981–1011.

——, *Ottoman Army Effectiveness in World War I: A Comparative Study* (London, 2007).

Evans, E.W. and Saville, John, 'Abraham, William (Mabon)', in Joyce M. Bellamy and John Saville (eds), *Dictionary of Labour Biography* (Clifton, NJ, 1972).

Evans, Olwen Carey, *Lloyd George was My Father* (Llandysul, Dyfed, 1985).

Evans, Richard J., *The Third Reich in Power*, paperback edn (London, 2006).

Fahey, David M., 'The Politics of Drink: Pressure Groups and the British Liberal Party, 1883-1908', *Social Science* 54:2 (Spring 1979), pp. 76–85.

Fair, John D., *British Interparty Conferences: A Study of the Procedure of Conciliation in British Politics, 1867–1921* (Oxford, 1980).

——, 'The Conservative Basis for the Formation of the National Government of 1931', *Journal of British Studies* 19 (1980), pp. 142–64.

——, 'The Second Labour Government and the Politics of Electoral Reform, 1929–1931', *Albion* 13 (1981), pp. 276–301.

Fanning, J.R., 'The Unionist Party and Ireland, 1906–10', *Irish Historical Studies* 15 (1966), pp. 147–71.

Ferguson, Niall, 'Germany and the Origins of the First World War: New Perspectives', *Historical Journal* 35:3 (1992), pp. 725–52.

——, 'Public Finance and National Security: The Domestic Origins of the First World War Revisited', *Past and Present* 142 (1994), pp. 141–68.

Ferris, John, '"Far Too Dangerous a Gamble?" British Intelligence and Policy during the Chanak Crisis, September–October 1922', *Diplomacy and Statecraft* 14 (2003), pp. 139–84.

Fink, Carole, *The Genoa Conference: European Diplomacy, 1921–1922* (Chapel Hill, 1984).

——, 'The NEP in Foreign Policy: The Genoa Conference and the Treaty of Rapallo', in Gabriel Gorodetsky (ed.), *Soviet Foreign Policy, 1917–1991: A Retrospective* (London, 1994).

——, 'The Minorities Question at the Paris Peace Conference: The Polish Minority Treaty, June 28, 1919', in Manfred R. Boemeke, Gerald D. Feldman and Elisabeth Glaser (eds), *The Treaty of Versailles: A Reassessment after 75 Years* (Cambridge, 1998).

——, Alex Frohn and Jurgen Heideking (eds), *Genoa, Rapallo, and European Reconstruction in 1922* (Cambridge, 1991).

——, Isabel V. Hull and MacGregor Knox (eds), *German Nationalism and the European Response, 1890–1945* (Norman, OK, 1985).

Fitzpatrick, David, *Politics and Irish Life 1913–21: Provincial Experiences of War and Revolution* (Cork, 1977).

——, 'The Geography of Irish Nationalism, 1910–1921', in C.H.E. Philpin (ed.), *Nationalism and Popular Protest in Ireland* (Cambridge, 1987).

——, 'The Irish in Britain, 1871–1921', in W.E. Vaughan (ed.), *A New History of Ireland*, vol. 6, *Ireland under the Union, II, 1870–1921* (Oxford, 1996).

Fitzroy, Sir Almeric William, *Memoirs*, vol. 2 (London, n.d.).

Florey, R.A., *The General Strike of 1926: The Economic, Political and Social Causes of that Class War* (London, 1980).

Foote, Geoffrey, *The Labour Party's Political Thought: A History* (New York, 1997).

Foster, John, 'Strike Acton and Working-Class Politics on Clydeside 1914–1919', *International Review of Social History* 35 (1990), pp. 33–70.

Foster, Roy, *Modern Ireland, 1600–1972* (London, 1988).

Fraser, Derek, *The Evolution of the British Welfare State: A History of Social Policy since the Industrial Revolution* (London, 1973).

Fraser, Peter, 'The Unionist Debacle of 1911 and Balfour's Retirement', *Journal of Modern History* 35:4 (December 1963), pp. 354–65.

——, 'British War Policy and the Crisis of Liberalism in May 1915', *Journal of Modern History* 54:1 (March 1982), pp. 1–26.

——, 'Lord Beaverbrook's Fabrications in *Politicians and the War, 1914–1916*', *Historical Journal* 25:1 (1982), pp. 147–66.

——, 'The British "Shells Scandal" of 1915', *Canadian Journal of History* 18:1 (1983), pp. 69–86.

Fraser, W. Hamish, *A History of British Trade Unionism 1700–1998* (London, 1999).

Freeden, Michael, *The New Liberalism: An Ideology of Social Reform* (Oxford, 1978).

French, David, 'The Military Background to the "Shell Crisis" of May 1915', *Journal of Strategic Studies* 2 (1979), pp. 192–205.

——, *British Economic and Strategic Planning, 1905–1915* (London, 1982).

——, 'The Origins of the Dardanelles Campaign Reconsidered', *History* 68 (June 1983), pp. 210–24.

——, 'The Meaning of Attrition, 1914–1916', *English Historical Review* 103 (April, 1988), pp. 385–405.

——, 'Who Knew What and When? The French Army Mutinies and the British Decision to Launch the Third Battle of Ypres', in Lawrence Freedman, Paul Hayes, and Robert O'Neill (eds), *War, Strategy, and International Politics* (Oxford, 1992).

——, *The Strategy of the Lloyd George Coalition, 1916–1918* (Oxford, 1995).

——, '"Had We Known How Bad Things Were in Germany, We Might Have Got Stiffer Terms": Great Britain and the German Armistice', in Manfred R. Boemeke, Gerald D. Feldman and Elisabeth Glaser (eds), *The Treaty of Versailles: A Reassessment after 75 Years* (Cambridge, 1998).

Friedman, Isaiah, 'The McMahon-Hussein Correspondence and the Question of Palestine', *Journal of Contemporary History* 5 (1970), pp. 83–122.

——, *The Question of Palestine: British-Jewish-Arab Relations: 1914–1918*, 2nd expanded edn (New Brunswick, NJ, 1992)

Fromkin, David, *A Peace to End All Peace: The Fall of the Ottoman Empire and the Creation of the Modern Middle East*, paperback edn (New York, 1989).

Fry, Michael G., *Lloyd George and Foreign Policy*, vol. 1, *The Education of a Statesman: 1890–1916* (Montreal, 1977).

——, 'British Revisionism', in Manfred R. Boemeke, Gerald D. Feldman and Elisabeth Glaser (eds), *The Treaty of Versailles: A Reassessment after 75 Years* (Cambridge, 1998).

Gannon, Franklin Reid, *The British Press and Germany, 1936–1939* (Oxford, 1971).

Garner, Les, 'Suffragism and Socialism: Sylvia Pankhurst 1903–1914', in Ian Bullock and Richard Pankhurst (eds), *Sylvia Pankhurst: From Artist to Anti-Fascist* (New York, 1992).

Garside, W.R., *British Unemployment, 1919–1939: A Study in Public Policy* (Cambridge, 1990).

Garvin, Tom, *Nationalist Revolutionaries in Ireland, 1858–1928* (Oxford, 1987).

Gawrych, George W., 'Kemal Ataturk's Politico-Military Strategy in the Turkish War of Independence, 1919–1922: From Guerrilla Warfare to the Decisive Battle', *Journal of Strategic Studies* 22:3 (September 1988), pp. 318–41.

George, William, *My Brother and I* (London, 1958).

——, *The Making of Lloyd George* (London, 1976).

——, *Backbencher* (Llandysul, 1983).

Gilbert, Bentley Brinkerhoff, *The Evolution of National Insurance in Great Britain: The Origins of the Welfare State* (London, 1966).

——, 'Winston Churchill versus the Webbs: The Origins of British Unemployment Insurance', *American Historical Review* 74 (April 1966), pp. 846–62.

——, *British Social Policy, 1914–1939* (Ithaca, 1970).

——, 'David Lloyd George: Land, the Budget, and Social Reform', *American Historical Review* 81:5 (December 1976), pp. 1058–66.

——, 'David Lloyd George: The Reform of British Landholding and the Budget of 1914', *Historical Journal* 21:1 (1978), pp. 117–41.

——, 'Pacifist to Interventionist: David Lloyd George in 1911 and 1914. Was Belgium an Issue?' *Historical Journal* 28:4 (December 1985), pp. 863–85.

——, *David Lloyd George: A Political Life*, vol. 1: *The Architect of Change, 1863–1912* (Columbus, Ohio, 1987).

——, 'David Lloyd George and the Great Marconi Scandal', *Historical Research* 62:149 (October 1989), pp. 295–317.

——, *David Lloyd George: A Political Life*, vol. 2: *Organizer of Victory* 1912–16 (Columbus, 1992).

Gilbert, Martin, *The Roots of Appeasement* (London, 1966).

——, *Winston S. Churchill*, vol. 6, *Finest Hour 1939–1941* (Boston, 1985).

——, *Churchill: A Life*, paperback edn (New York, 1991).

Gilmour, David, *Curzon: Imperial Statesman, 1859–1925* (London, 1994)

Glenny, M.V., 'The Anglo-Soviet Trade Agreement, March 1921', *Journal of Contemporary History* 5:2 (1970), pp. 63–82.

Goldstein, Erik, 'Great Britain and Greater Greece 1917–1920', *Historical Journal* 32:2 (1989), pp. 339–56.

——, *The First World War Peace Settlements, 1919–1925* (Harlow, 2002).

Gollin, Alfred M., *The Observer and J.L. Garvin, 1908–1914: A Study in a Great Editorship* (London, 1960).

——, *Proconsul in Politics* (London, 1964).

Gooch, John, 'The Maurice Debate 1918', *Journal of Contemporary History* 3:4 (October 1968), pp. 211–28.

Graham, Gerald S., *The Politics of Naval Supremacy: Studies in British Maritime Ascendancy* (Cambridge, 1965).

Graubard, Stephen Richards, *British Labour and the Russian Revolution, 1917–1924* (Cambridge, 1956).

Greaves, Rose, 'Iranian Relations with Great Britain and British India, 1798–1921', in Peter Avery, G.R.G. Hambly and C. Melville (eds), *The Cambridge History of Iran*, vol. 7, *From Nadir Sha to the Islamic Republic* (Cambridge, 1991).

Green, E.H.H., *The Crisis of Conservatism: The Politics, Economics and Ideology of the British Conservative Party, 1880–1914*, paperback edn (London, 1996).

Greenaway, John, *Drink and British Politics since 1830: A Study in Policy-making* (Basingstoke, 2003).

Greenhalgh, Elizabeth, 'Myth and Memory: Sir Douglas Haig and the Imposition of Allied Unified Command in March 1918', *Journal of Military History* 68:3 (July 2004), pp. 771–820.

——, *Victory through Coalition: Britain and France during the First World War* (Cambridge, 2005).

Gregory, Adrian, *The Last Great War: British Society and the First World War*, paperback edn (Cambridge, 2008).

Grey, Sir Edward, *Speeches on Foreign Affairs, 1904–1914*, selected by Paul Knaplund (London, 1931).

Grieves, Keith, 'Improvising the War Effort: Eric Geddes and Lloyd George, 1915–18', *War and Society* 7:2 (September 1989), pp. 40–55.

——, 'Sir Eric Geddes, Lloyd George and the Transport Problem, 1918–21', *Journal of Transport History* 13:1 (1991), pp. 26–27.

——, 'Haig and the Government, 1916–1918', in Brian Bond and Nigel Cave (eds), *Haig: A Reappraisal 80 Years On* (Barnsley, 2009).

Grigg, John, *The Young Lloyd George* (Berkeley CA, 1973).

——, 'Lloyd George and the Boer War', in A.J.A. Morris (ed.), *Edwardian Radicals 1900–1914: Some Aspects of British Radicalism* (London, 1974).

——, *Lloyd George: The People's Champion, 1902–1911* (Berkeley, 1978).

——, *Lloyd George: From Peace to War, 1912–1916* (London, 1985).

——, *Lloyd George: War Leader 1916–1918* (London, 2002).

de Groot, Gerard J., *Douglas Haig, 1861–1928* (London, 1988)

Guinn, Paul, *British Strategy and Politics, 1914–1918* (Oxford, 1965).

Gwynn, Denis, *The Life of John Redmond* (London, 1932).

Gwynn, Stephen (ed.), *The Letters and Friendships of Sir Cecil Spring-Rice: A Record* (London, 1929).

von Hagen, Mark, *Soldiers in the Proletarian Dictatorship: The Red Army and the Soviet Socialist State* (Ithaca, 1990).

Hague, Ffion, *The Pain and the Privilege: The Women in Lloyd George's Life* (London, 2008).

Hall III, Hines H., 'The Foreign Policy-Making Process in Britain, 1934–1935, and the Origins of the Anglo-German Naval Agreement', *Historical Journal* 19:2 (1976), pp. 477–99

——, 'Lloyd George, Briand and the Failure of the Anglo-French Entente', *Journal of Modern History* 50:2 (December 1978), D1121–38.

Hall, Richard C., '"The Enemy is Behind Us": The Morale Crisis in the Bulgarian Army during the Summer of 1918', *War in History* 11:2 (April 2002), pp. 209–19.

Hamer, D.A., *Liberal Politics in the Age of Gladstone and Rosebery: A Study in Leadership and Policy* (Oxford, 1972).

Hancock, W.K., *Smuts: The Fields of Force 1919–1950* (Cambridge, 1968).

Hankey, Baron Maurice Pascal Alers, *The Supreme Control at the Paris Peace Conference 1919: A Commentary* (London, 1963).

Harbaugh, William H., *Lawyer's Lawyer: The Life of John W. Davis* (New York, 1973).

Harkness, David, 'Britain and the Independence of the Dominions: the 1921 Crossroads', in T.W. Moody (ed.), *Nationality and the Pursuit of National Independence: Historical Studies XI* (Belfast, 1978).

Harris, J. Paul, 'Great Britain', in Richard F. Hamilton and Holger H. Herwig (eds), *The Origins of World War I* (Cambridge, 2003).

——, *Douglas Haig and the First World War* (Cambridge, 2008).

Harris, Jose F., 'Political Thought and the Welfare State 1870–1940: An Intellectual Framework for British Social Policy', *Past & Present* 135 (May 1992), pp. 116–41.

—— and Hazlehurst, Cameron, 'Campbell-Bannerman as Prime Minister', *History* 55:185 (October 1970), pp. 360–83.

Harrison, Brian, *Drink and the Victorians: The Temperance Question in England 1815–1872* (Pittsburg, 1971).

——, *Separate Spheres: The Opposition to Women's Suffrage in Britain* (New York, 1978).

——, *Peaceable Kingdom: Stability and Change in Modern Britain* (Oxford, 1982).

Hart, Jenifer, *Proportional Representation: Critics of the British Electoral System, 1820–1945* (Oxford, 1992).

Hart, Peter, *The IRA at War 1916–1923* (Oxford, 2003).

Hartcup, Guy, *The War of Invention: Scientific Developments, 1914–18* (London, 1988).

Hattersley, Roy, *David Lloyd George: The Great Outsider* (London, 2012).

Hawkins, Angus and Powell, John (eds), *The Journal of John Wodehouse, First Earl of Kimberley for 1862–1902*, Camden Fifth Series, vol. 9 (London, 1997).

Hawkins, Richard, 'Dublin Castle and the Royal Irish Constabulary (1916–1922)', in Desmond Williams (ed.), *The Irish Struggle, 1916–1926* (London, 1966).

Hazlehurst, Cameron, *Politicians at War: July 1914 to May 1915: A Prologue to the Triumph of Lloyd George* (New York, 1971).

——, 'The Baldwinite Conspiracy', *Historical Studies* 16/63 (1974–5), pp. 167–91.

—— and Christine Woodland (eds), *A Liberal Chronicle: Journals and Papers of J.A. Pease, 1st Lord Gainford, 1908–1910* (London, 1994).

Helmreich, Paul, *From Paris to Sèvres: The Partition of the Ottoman Empire at the Peace Conference of 1919–1920* (Columbus, Ohio, 1974).

Helmstadter, R.J., 'The Nonconformist Conscience', in Peter Marsh (ed.), *The Conscience of the Victorian State* (Hassocks, Sussex, 1979).

——, 'The Nonconformist Conscience' in Gerald Parsons (ed.), *Religion in Victorian Britain: Interpretations*, vol. 4 (Manchester, 1988).

Hennock, E.P., 'The Origins of British National Insurance and the German Precedent', in W.J. Mommsen and Wolgang Mock (eds), *The Emergence of the Welfare State in Britain and Germany, 1850–1950* (London, 1981).

Herwig, Holger H., *The First World War: Germany and Austria-Hungary, 1914–1918* (London, 1997).

Hewins, W.A.S., *The Apologia of an Imperialist: Forty Years of Empire Policy*, vol. 2 (London, 1929).

Hewitt, Nick, 'Writing about Jutland: Historiography and Hysteria', in Michael Howard (ed.), *A Part of History: Aspects of the British Experience of the First World War* (London, 2008).

Hill, Sir Norman, *War and Insurance* (London, 1927).

Himmer, Robert, 'Rathenau, Russia, and Rapallo', *Central European History* 9: 2 (June 1976), pp. 146–83.

Hinton, James, 'The Clyde Workers' Committee and the Dilution Struggle', in Asa Briggs and John Saville (eds), *Essays in Labour History, 1886–1923* (Hamden, 1971).

——, *Labour and Socialism: A History of the British Labour Movement, 1867–1974* (Amherst, 1983).

Hirshfield, Claire, 'Fractured Faith: Liberal Party Women and the Suffrage Issue in Britain, 1892–1914', *Gender and History* 2:2 (Summer 1990), pp. 172–97.

Hirst, F.W. and Allen, J.E., *British War Budgets* (London, 1926).

Hoerber, Thomas, 'Psychology and Reasoning in the Anglo-German Naval Agreement, 1935–1939', *Historical Journal* 52:1 (2009), pp. 153–74.

Holton, Bob, *British Syndicalism, 1900–1914: Myths and Realities*, paperback edn (London, 1976).

Holton, Sandra Stanley, *Feminism and Democracy: Women's Suffrage and Reform Politics in Britain, 1900–1918* (Cambridge, 1986).

——, 'The Making of Suffrage History', in Jane Purvis and Sandra Stanley Holton (eds), *Votes for Women* (London, 2000).

Hopkinson, Michael, *Green Against Green: The Irish Civil War* (New York, 1988).

——, 'The Craig-Collins Pacts of 1922: Two Attempted Reforms of the Northern Ireland Government', *Irish Historical Studies* 27:106 (November 1990), pp. 145–58.

—— (ed.), *The Last Days of Dublin Castle: The Mark Sturgis Diaries* (Dublin, 1999).

——, *Irish War of Independence* (Montreal, 2002).

——, 'Negotiation: The Anglo-Irish War and the Revolution', in Joost Augusteijn (ed.), *The Irish Revolution, 1913–23* (London, 2002).

Hoppen, Theodore, *Ireland since 1800:Conflict and Conformity* (London, 1999).

Horne, Alastair, *Harold MacMillan*, vol. 1, *1894–1956* (New York, 1988).

Howell, Chris, *Trade Unions and the State: The Construction of Industrial Institutions in Britain, 1890–2000* (Princeton, 2005).

Howkins, Alan, 'Edwardian Liberalism and Industrial Unrest: A Class View of the Decline of Liberalism', *History Workshop Journal* 4 (1977), pp. 143–61.

Hudson, W.J., *Billy Hughes in Paris: The Birth of Australian Diplomacy* (West Melbourne, 1978).

Hughes, Jackson, 'The Battle for the Hindenburg Line', *War and Society* 17:2 (October 1999), pp. 55–57.

Hughes, Matthew, *Allenby and British Strategy in the Middle East, 1917–1919* (London, 1999).

Hume, Leslie Parker, *The National Union of Women's Suffrage Societies, 1897–1914* (New York, 1982).

Hutcheson Jr, John Ambrose, 'Leopold Maxse and the *National Review*, 1893–1914: A Study in Unionist Journalism and Politics', PhD dissertation (Chapel Hill, 1974).

Hyde, H. Montgomery, *Carson: The Life of Sir Edward Carson, Lord Carson of Duncairn* (London, 1974).

Imlay, Talbot C., 'The Origins of the First World War', *Historical Journal* 49:4 (2006), pp. 1253–71.

Isaacs, Gerald Rufus, Marquess of Reading, *Rufus Isaacs: First Marquess of Reading* (New York, 1940).

Jack, Marian, 'The Purchase of the British Government's Shares in the British Petroleum Company 1912–1914', *Past and Present* 39 (1968), pp. 139–68.

Jackson, Alvin, *Ireland 1798–1998* (Oxford, 1999).

——, *Home Rule: An Irish History 1800–2000* (Oxford, 2003).

Jackson, D.M., *Popular Opposition to Irish Home Rule in Edwardian Britain* (Liverpool, 2009).

—— and MacRaild, D.M., 'The Conserving Crowd: Mass Unionist Demonstrations in Liverpool and Tyneside, 1912–13', in D. George Boyce and Alan O'Day (eds), *The Making of Modern Irish History* (London, 1996).

Jalland, Patricia, 'A Liberal Chief Secretary and the Irish Question: Augustine Birrell, 1907–1914', *Historical Journal* 19:2 (1976), pp. 421–51.

——, 'United Kingdom Devolution 1910–14: Political Panacea or Tactical Diversion?', *English Historical Review* 94:373 (October 1979), pp. 757–85.

——, *The Liberals and Ireland: The Ulster Question in British Politics to 1914* (Aldershot, 1993).

James, Robert Rhodes, *Gallipoli* (New York, 1965).

—— (ed.), *Chips: The Diaries of Sir Henry Channon*, paperback edn (London, 1970).

——, *Robert Boothby: A Portrait of Churchill's Ally* (New York, 1991).

Jarausch, Konrad H., 'Revising German History: Bethmann Hollweg Revisited', *Central European History* 21:3 (September, 1988), pp. 224–43.

Jarvis, David, 'British Conservatism and Class Politics in the 1920s', *English Historical Review* 111:440 (February 1996), pp. 59–84.

Jeffery, Keith, *Field Marshal Sir Henry Wilson: A Political Soldier* (Oxford, 2006).

—— and Peter Hennessy, *States of Emergency: British Governments and Strikebreaking since 1919* (London, 1983).

Jenkins, Roy, *Asquith* (London, 1964).

——, *Churchill: A Biography*, paperback edn (London, 2002).

Johnson, Franklyn Arthur, *Defence by Committee: The British Committee of Imperial Defence, 1885–1959* (New York, 1960).

Johnson, Gaynor, 'Curzon, Lloyd George and the Control of British Foreign Policy, 1919–22: A Reassessment', *Diplomacy and Statecraft* 11:3 (November 2000), pp. 49–71

Johnson, Paul Barton, *Land Fit for Heroes: The Planning of British Reconstruction, 1916–1919* (Chicago, 1968).

Jones, David S., 'The Cleavage between Graziers and Peasants in the Land Struggle, 1890–1910', in Samuel Clark and James S. Donnelly Jr (eds), *Irish Peasants: Violence and Political Unrest, 1780–1914* (Madison, 1983).

Jones, G. Gareth, 'The British Government and the Oil Companies 1912–1924: The Search for an Oil Policy', *Historical Journal* 20:3 (1977), pp. 647–72.

Jones, Gareth Elwyn, 'The "Welsh Revolt" Revisited: Merioneth and Montgomeryshire in Default', *Welsh History Review* 14:3 (June 1989), pp. 417–38.

Jones, J. Graham, 'The Real Lloyd George', *Journal of Liberal History* 51 (Summer 2006), pp. 4–12.

——, 'Life with Lloyd George', *Journal of Liberal History* 55 (Summer 2007), pp. 28–36.

——, *David Lloyd George and Welsh Liberalism* (Aberystwyth, 2010).

Jones, Margaret 'The 1908 Old Age Pensions Act: The Poor Law in New Disguise?', in Keith Laybourn (ed.), *Social Conditions, Status and Community 1860–c. 1920* (Stroud, 1997).

Jones, R. Merfyn, *The North Wales Quarrymen, 1874–1922* (Cardiff, 1982).

Jones, Raymond A., *Arthur Ponsonby: The Politics of Life* (London, 1989).

Jones, Thomas, *Lloyd George* (Cambridge, 1951).

——, *A Diary with Letters, 1931–1950*, reprint edn (London, 1969).

Jordan, Gerald H.S., 'Pensions not Dreadnoughts: The Radical and Naval Retrenchment', in A.J.A. Morris (ed.), *Edwardian Radicalism 1900–1914: Some Aspects of British Radicalism* (London, 1974).

Judd, Denis, *Lord Reading, Rufus Issacs, First Marquess of Reading, Lord Chief Justice and Viceroy of India, 1860–1935* (London, 1982).

Kaiser, David E., 'Germany and the Origins of the First World War', *Journal of Modern History* 55 (September 1983), pp. 442–74.

Katouzian, Homa, *Iranian History and Politics: The Dialectic of State and Society* (London, 2003).

Keddie, Nikki R., *Modern Iran: Roots and Results of Revolution*, updated edn (New Haven, 2006).

Keiger, John F.V., 'Raymond Poincare and the Ruhr Crisis', in Robert Boyce, *French Foreign and Defence Policy, 1918–1940: The Decline and Fall of a Great Power* (London, 1998), pp. 49–70.

Kelley, Matthew, 'The Irish Volunteers: A Machiavellian Moment?', in D. George Boyce and Alan O'Day (eds), *The Making of Modern Irish History* (London, 1996).

Kendall, Walter, *The Revolutionary Movement in Britain, 1900–21* (London, 1969).

Kendle, John, *Walter Long, Ireland, and the Union, 1905–1920* (Montreal, 1992).

Kennedy, Dennis, *The Widening Gulf: Northern Attitudes to the Independent Irish State, 1919–49* (Belfast, 1988).

Kennedy, Paul M., 'The Tradition of Appeasement in British Foreign Policy, 1865–1939', *British Journal of International Relations* 2 (1976), pp. 195–215.

——, *The Rise of the Anglo-German Antagonism, 1860–1914* (London, 1980).

——, *The Rise and Fall of British Naval Mastery* (Malabar, 1982).

Kent, Bruce, *The Spoils of War: The Politics, Economics, and Diplomacy of Reparations 1918–1932* (Oxford, 1989).

Kent, Marian, *Oil and Empire: British Policy and Mesopotamian Oil, 1900–1920* (London, 1976).

——, 'Asiatic Turkey, 1914–1916', in F.H. Hinsley (ed.), *British Foreign Policy under Sir Edward Grey* (Cambridge, 1977).

Kent, Susan Kingsley, *Sex and Suffrage in Britain, 1860–1914*, paperback edn (Princeton, 1990).

Kershaw, Ian, *The Nazi Dictatorship: Problems and Perspectives of Interpretation*, 4th paperback edn (London, 2000).

——, *Making Friends with Hitler: Lord Londonderry, the Nazis and the Road to World War II* (New York, 2004).

Keylor William R. (ed.), *The Legacy of the Great War: Peacemaking, 1919* (Boston, 1998).

Keynes, John Maynard, 'War and the Financial System, August, 1914', *Economic Journal* 24 (September 1914), pp. 460–86.

——, *The Economic Consequences of the Peace* (New York, 1920).

——, *Essays in Biography* (New York, 1951).

Kinnear, Michael, *The British Voter: An Atlas and Survey since 1885* (Ithaca, 1968).

——, *The Fall of Lloyd George: The Political Crisis of 1922* (Toronto, 1973).

Kinvig, Clifford, *Churchill's Crusade: The British Invasion of Russia, 1918–1920* (London, 2006).

Kirby, M.W., *The British Coalmining Industry, 1870–1946: A Political and Economic History* (London, 1977).

Kirkaldy, A.W., *British Finance During and After the War, 1914–21* (London, 1921).

Kissane, Bill, *The Politics of the Irish Civil War* (Oxford, 2005).

Kitchen, Martin, *The German Offensives of 1918*, paperback edn (Stroud, 2005).

Klieman, Aaron S., 'Britain's War Aims in the Middle East in 1915', *Journal of Contemporary History* 3 (July 1968), pp. 237–52.

Komarnicki, Titus, *Rebirth of the Polish Republic: A Study in the Diplomatic History of Europe 1914–1920* (London, 1957).

Koss, Stephen, 'Lloyd George and Nonconformity: the Last Rally', *English Historical Review* 89 (1974), pp. 77–108.

——, *Nonconformity in British Politics* (London, 1975).

——, 'Asquith versus Lloyd George: the Last Phase and Beyond', in Alan Sked and Chris Cook (eds), *Crisis and Controversy: Essays in Honour of A.J.P. Taylor* (New York, 1976).

——, *The Rise and Fall of the Political Press in Britain: The Twentieth Century*, 2 vols (London, 1984).

——, *Asquith*, paperback edn (New York, 1985).

Laffan, Michael, *The Partition of Ireland, 1911–25* (Dundalk, 1983).

——, *The Resurrection of Ireland: The Sinn Fein Party, 1916–1923* (Cambridge, 1999).

Lambert, W.R., *Drink and Sobriety in Victorian Wales c. 1820–c. 1895* (Cardiff, 1983).

Langhorne, Richard (ed.), *Diplomacy and Intelligence During the Second World War: Essays in Honor of F.H. Hinsley* (Cambridge, 1985).

Lawlor, Sheila, *Britain and Ireland, 1914–23* (Dublin, 1983).

Lawrence, Jon, *Speaking for the People: Party, Language and Popular Politics in England, 1867–1914* (Cambridge, 1998).

Laybourn, Keith, *The General Strike Day by Day* (Phoenix Mill, Gloucestershire, 1999).

Lee, J.J., *Ireland, 1912–1985: Politics and Society* (Cambridge, 1989).

Lentin, Antony, *Lloyd George, Woodrow Wilson and the Guilt of Germany: An Essay in the Pre-History of Appeasement* (Baton Rouge, 1985).

——, *Lloyd George and the Lost Peace: From Versailles to Hitler, 1919–1940* (Houndmills, Hants, 2001).

Lewis, Michael, *The History of the British Navy* (London, 1959).

Lloyd George, David, *War Memoirs*, new edn, 2 vols (London, n.d. [1939?]).

——, *Memoirs of the Peace Conference*, vol. 1 (New Haven, 1939).

——, *The Truth about Reparations and War-Debts* [1932] (New York, 1970).

Lloyd George, Frances, *The Years That Are Past* (London, 1967).

Lloyd George, Robert, *David and Winston: How a Friendship Changed History*, paperback edn (London, 2005).

Lockwood, P.A., 'Milner's Entry into the War Cabinet, December 1916', *Historical Journal* 7:1 (1964), pp. 120–34.

Long, Walter, Viscount Long of Wraxall, *Memories* (New York, n.d.).

Longford, Ruth, *Frances, Countess Lloyd-George: More than a Mistress* (Leominster, 1996).

Longrigg, Stephen Hemsley, *Oil in the Middle East: Its Discovery and Development*, 3rd edn (London, 1968).

Loughlin, James, *The British Monarchy and Ireland: 1800 to the Present* (Cambridge, 2007).

Lowe, C.J. and M.L. Dockrill, *The Mirage of Power*, vol. 2, *British Foreign Policy 1914–22* (London, 1972).

Lowe, Rodney, 'The Erosion of State Intervention in Britain, 1917–24', *Economic History Review*, 2nd Series, 31 (May 1978), pp. 270–86.

——, 'The Failure of Consensus in Britain: The National Industrial Conference, 1919–1921', *Historical Journal* 21:3 (1978), pp. 649–75.

Lukacs, John, *Five Days in London: May 1940* (New Haven, CT, 1999).

Lunn, Kenneth, 'Political Anti-semitism before 1914: Fascism's Heritage?', in Kenneth Lunn and Richard C. Thurlow (eds), *British Fascism: Essays on the Radical Right in Inter-War Britain* (New York, 1980).

Lyman, Richard W., *The First Labour Government, 1924* (London, [1957]).

Lynch, Patricia, *The Liberal Party in Rural England, 1885–1910: Radicalism and Community* (Oxford, 2003).

Lyons, F.S.L., *Ireland since the Famine*, paperback edn (London, 1989).

——, 'The War of Independence, 1919–21', in W.E. Vaughan (ed.), *A New History of Ireland*, vol. 6, *Ireland under the Union, II, 1870–1921* (Oxford, 1996).

Macfarlane, L.J., 'Hands Off Russia: British Labour and the Russo-Polish War, 1920', *Past & Present* 38 (December 1967), pp. 126–52.

Macfie, A.L., 'The British Decision Regarding the Future of Constantinople, November 1918–January 1920', *Historical Journal* 18:2 (1975), pp. 391–400.

——, 'The Chanak Affair (September–October 1922)', *Balkan Studies* 20:2 (1979), pp. 309–41.

MacKenzie, John M., *Propaganda and Empire: The Manipulation of British Public Opinion, 1880–1960* (Manchester, 1984).

MacKenzie, Norman and Jeanne (eds), *The Diary of Beatrice Webb*, vol. 1, *1873–1892* (Cambridge, 1982).

—— (eds), *The Diary of Beatrice Webb*, vol. 3, *'The Power to Alter Things'* (Cambridge, 1984).

—— (eds),*The Diary of Beatrice Webb*, vol. 4, *1924–1943: The Wheel of Life* (Cambridge, 1985).

Mackintosh, John P., 'The Role of the Committee of Imperial Defence before 1914', *English Historical Review* 77 (July 1962), pp. 490–503.

MacMillan, Margaret, *Peacemakers: The Paris Conference of 1919 and its Attempt to End War*, paperback edn (London, 2002).

Maiolo, Joseph A., *The Royal Navy and Nazi Germany, 1933–39: A Study in Appeasement and the Origins of the Second World War* (Houndmills, Hants, 1998).

Mallet, Sir Bernard and George, C. Oswald, *British Budgets: Second Series, 1913–14 to 1920–21* (London, 1929).

Manne, Robert, 'Some British Light on the Nazi-Soviet Pact', *European Studies Review* 11:1 (January 1981), pp. 83–102.

Mansergh, Nicholas, 'Ireland and the British Commonwealth of Nations: The Dominion Settlement', in Desmond Williams (ed.), *The Irish Struggle, 1916–1926* (London, 1966).

——, *The Unresolved Question. The Anglo-Irish Settlement and its Undoing, 1912–72* (New Haven/London, 1991).

Mantoux, Paul, *The Deliberations of the Council of Four (March 24–June 28, 1919) Notes of the Official Interpreter*, vol. 1, trans. and ed. Arthur S. Link (Princeton, 1992).

Marder, Arthur J., *From the* Dreadnought *to Scapa Flow: The Royal Navy in the Fisher Era, 1904–1919*, vol. 1, *The Road to War, 1904–1914* (London, 1961).

——, *From the* Dreadnought *to Scapa Flow*, vol. 3, *Jutland and After* (London, 1966).

——, *From the* Dreadnought *to Scapa Flow: The Royal Navy in the Fisher Era, 1904–1919*, vol. 5, *Victory and Aftermath* (London, 1970).

——, *From the Dardanelles to Oran: Studies of the Royal Navy in War and Peace, 1915–1940* (London, 1974).

Marks, Sally, 'Behind the Scenes at the Paris Peace Conference of 1919', *Journal of British Studies* 9:2 (1970), pp. 154–80.

Marquand, David, *Ramsay MacDonald* (London, 1977).

Marsh, Peter, *Joseph Chamberlain: Entrepreneur in Politics* (New Haven, 1994).

Martel, Gordon (ed.), *The Times and Appeasement: The Journals of A.L. Kennedy, 1931–1939* (London, 2000).

——, *The Origins of the First World War*, 3rd edn (Harlow, 2003).

Martin, Bernd, 'Churchill and Hitler, 1940: Peace or War?', in R.A.C. Parker (ed.), *Winston Churchill: Studies in Statesmanship* (London, 1995).

Mason, A., 'The Government and the General Strike, 1926', *International Review of Social History* 14 (1969), pp. 1–21.

Masterman, Lucy, *C.F.G. Masterman: A Biography* (London, 1939).

Mathias, Peter, 'The Brewing Industry, Temperance and Politics', *Historical Journal* 1:2 (1958), pp. 97–114.

Matthew, H.C.G. *The Liberal Imperialists: The Ideas and Politics of a post-Gladstonian Elite* (Oxford, 1973).

—— (ed.), *The Gladstone Diaries*, 14 vols (Oxford, 1994).

Matthews, Frank, 'The Building Guilds', in Asa Briggs and John Saville (eds), *Essays in Labour History, 1886–1923* (Hamden, 1971)

Maurer, John H., 'Churchill's Naval Holiday: Arms Control and the Anglo-German Naval Race, 1912–1914', *Journal of Strategic Studies* 15:1 (March 1992), pp. 102–27.

Mawdsley, Evan, *The Russian Civil War* (Boston, 1987).

Mayer, Arno J., *Politics and Diplomacy of Peacemaking: Containment and Counterrevolution at Versailles, 1918–1919*, paperback edn (New York, 1969).

Mayer, S.L., 'Anglo-German Rivalry at the Algeciras Conference', in Prosser Gifford and William Roger Louis (eds), *Britain and Germany in Africa: Imperial Rivalry and Colonial Rule* (New Haven, 1967).

Mayhall, Laura E. Nym, *The Militant Suffrage Movement: Citizenship and Resistance in Britain, 1860–1930* (Oxford, 2003).

McColgan, John, *British Policy and the Irish Administration, 1920–22* (London, 1983).

McCormick, Donald, *The Mask of Merlin: A Critical Biography of David Lloyd George* (New York, 1964).

McCready, H.W., 'Home Rule and the Liberal Party, 1899–1906', *Irish Historical Studies* 13 (1963), pp. 316–48.

McDonald, Andrew, 'The Geddes Committee and the Formulation of Public Expenditure Policy, 1921–1922', *Historical Journal* 32:2 (1989), pp. 643–74.

McDonald, Geoffrey, 'The Defeat of the General Strike', in Gillian Peele and Chris Cook (eds), *The Politics of Reappraisal, 1918–1939* (New York, 1975).

McDougall, Walter A., *France's Rhineland Diplomacy, 1914–1924: The Last Bid for a Balance of Power in Europe* (Princeton, 1978).

McDowell, R.B., *The Irish Convention, 1917–18* (London, 1970).

McEwen, John M., 'The Liberal Party and the Irish Question During the First World War', *Journal of British Studies* 12:1 (1972), pp. 114–15.

——, 'The Press and the Fall of Asquith', *Historical Journal* 21:4 (1978), pp. 863–83.

——, 'Lloyd George's Liberal Supporters in December 1916: A Note', *Bulletin of the Institute of Historical Research* 53 (1980), pp. 265–72.

——, 'Northcliffe and Lloyd George at War, 1914–1918', *Historical Journal* 24:3 (1981), pp. 651–72.

——, 'Lloyd George's Acquisition of the *Daily Chronicle* in 1918', *Journal of British Studies* 22:1 (Fall 1982), pp. 127–44.

——, *The Riddell Diaries, 1908–1923* (London, 1986).

McGill, Barry, 'Lloyd George's Timing of the 1918 Election', *Journal of British Studies* 14:1 (November 1974), pp. 109–24.

McIvor, Arthur J., 'Industrial Relations in Britain, 1900–1939', in Chris Wrigley (ed.), *A Companion to Early Twentieth Century Britain* (London, 2003).

McKercher, Brian 'Old Diplomacy and New: the Foreign Office and Foreign Policy, 1919–1939', in Michael Dockrill and Brian McKercher (eds), *Diplomacy and World Power: Studies in British Foreign Policy, 1890–1950* (Cambridge, 1996).

McKibbin, Ross, *Classes and Cultures: England 1918–1951* (Oxford, 1998).

McKinstry, Leo, *Rosebery: Statesman in Turmoil*, paperback edn (London, 2006).

McLean, David, 'Finance and "Informal Empire" before the First World War', *Economic History Review*, 30 (1976), pp. 291–305.

McLean, Iain, *Rational Choice and British Politics: An Analysis of Rhetoric and Manipulation from Peel to Blair* (Oxford, 2001).

Meacham, Standish, '"The Sense of an Impending Clash": English Working-Class Unrest before the First World War', *American Historical Review* 77 (1972), pp. 1343–64.

Mejcher, Helmut, *Imperial Quest for Oil: Iraq, 1910–1928* (London, 1976).

Middlemas, Keith (ed.), *Thomas Jones: Whitehall Diary*, vol. 1 (Oxford, 1969).

—— (ed.), *Thomas Jones: Whitehall Diary*, vol. 2, *1926–1930* (Oxford, 1969).

—— (ed.), *Thomas Jones: Whitehall Diary*, vol. 3, *Ireland 1918–1925* (London, 1971).

——, *Politics in Industrial Society: The Experience of the British System since 1911* (London, 1979).

—— and John Barnes, *Baldwin: A Biography* (New York, 1970), pp. 128–48.

Monroe, Elizabeth, *Britain's Moment in the Middle East, 1914–1971*, rev. edn (Baltimore, 1981).

Moorhouse, Roger, "'The Sore That Would Never Heal'": The Genesis of the Polish Corridor', in Conan Fischer and Alan Sharp (eds), *After the Versailles Treaty: Enforcement, Compliance, Contested Identities*, paperback edn (London, 2009).

Morgan, David, *Suffragists and Liberals: The Politics of Woman Suffrage in England* (Totowa, 1975).

Morgan, E. Victor, *Studies in British Financial Policy, 1914–25* (London, 1952).

Morgan, Kenneth O., *Lloyd George: Welsh Radical as World Statesman* (Cardiff, 1963).

—— (ed.), *Lloyd George: Family Letters, 1885–1936* (Cardiff and London, 1973).

——, *Lloyd George* (London, 1974).

——, *Wales in British Politics, 1868–1922* (Cardiff, 1980).

——, *Rebirth of a Nation: A History of Modern Wales*, paperback edn (Oxford, 1982).

——, *Consensus and Disunity: The Lloyd George Coalition Government 1918–1922*, paperback edn (Oxford, 1986).

——, *Labour People: Leaders and Lieutenants, Hardie to Kinnock* (Oxford, 1987).

——, 'Tom Ellis versus Lloyd George: the Fractured Consciousness of Fin-de-Siecle Wales', in Geraint H. Jenkins and J. Beverley Smith (eds), *Politics and Society in Wales, 1840–1922: Essays in Honour of Ieuan Gwynedd Jones* (Cardiff, 1988).

——, 'Lloyd George and Germany', *Historical Journal* 39:3 (September 1996), pp. 755–58.

—— and Morgan, Jane, *Portrait of a Progressive: The Political Career of Christopher, Viscount Addison* (Oxford, 1980).

Morley, John, Viscount, *Memorandum on Resignation, August 1914* (New York, 1928).

Morris, A.J. Anthony, *Radicalism Against War, 1906–1914: The Advocacy of Peace and Retrenchment* (Totowa, 1972).

Morris, Benny, *The Roots of Appeasement: The British Weekly Press and Nazi Germany during the 1930s* (London, 1991).

Mortimer, Joanne Stafford, 'Commercial Interests and German Diplomacy in the Agadir Crisis', *Historical Journal* 10:4 (1967), pp. 440–56.

Mulvey-Roberts, Marie, 'Militancy, Masochism or Martyrdom? The Public and Private Prisons of Constance Lytton', in Jane Purvis and Sandra Stanley Holton (eds), *Votes for Women* (London, 2000).

Munson, J.E.B., 'The Unionist Coalition and Education, 1895–1902', *Historical Journal* 20:3 (September 1977), pp. 607–45.

Murphy, Cliona, *The Women's Suffrage Movement and Irish Society in the Early Twentieth Century* (Philadelphia, 1989).

Murphy, Richard, 'Faction in the Conservative Party and the Home Rule Crisis, 1912–14', *History* 71:232 (1986), pp. 222–34.

——, 'Walter Long and the Making of the Government of Ireland Act, 1919–20', *Irish Historical Studies* 25 (1986–7), pp. 82–96.

Murray, Bruce K., 'The Politics of the "People's Budget"', *Historical Journal* 14:3 (1973), pp. 555–70.

——, *The People's Budget 1909/10: Lloyd George and Liberal Politics* (Oxford, 1980).

——, '"Battered and Shattered": Lloyd George and the 1914 Budget Fiasco', *Albion* 23:3 (Fall 1991), pp. 483–507.

Murphy, Richard, 'Walter Long, the Unionist Members, and the Formation of Lloyd George's Government in December 1916', *Historical Journal* 29:3 (1986), pp. 735–45.

Naylor, John F., 'The Establishment of the Cabinet Secretariat', *Historical Journal* 14:4 (December 1971), pp. 783–803.

——, *A Man and an Institution: Sir Maurice Hankey, the Cabinet Secretariat and the Custody of Cabinet Secrecy* (Cambridge, 1984).

Nevakivi, Jukka, *Britain, France and the Arab Middle East 1914–1920* (London, 1969).

Newton, Douglas, *British Policy and the Weimar Republic, 1918–1919* (Oxford, 1997).

Newton, Thomas Wodehouse Legh, 2nd Baron, *Lord Lansdowne: A Biography* (London, 1929).

Nicolson, Colin, 'Edwardian England and the Coming of the First World War', in Alan O'Day (ed.), *The Edwardian Age: Conflict and Stability 1900–1914* (Hamden, 1979).

Nicolson, Harold, *Sir Arthur Nicolson, Bart., First Lord Carnock: A Study in the Old Diplomacy* (London, 1930).

——, *Curzon: The Last Phase, 1919–1925. A Study in Post-War Diplomacy* (New York, 1939).

Nicolson, Nigel (ed.), *Harold Nicholson: Diaries and Letters 1930–1939*, vol. 1 (New York, 1966).

—— (ed.), *Harold Nicolson: Diaries and Letters, 1939–1945*, vol. 2 (London, 1967).

O'Brien, Conor Cruise (ed.), *The Shaping of Modern Ireland* (London, 1960).

O'Brien, Phillips Payson, *British and American Naval Power: Politics and Policy, 1900–1936* (Westport, 1998).

O'Connor, Raymond G., *Perilous Equilibrium: The United States and the London Naval Conference of 1930*, reprint edn (New York, 1969).

O'Day, Alan, 'Home Rule and the Historians', in D. George Boyce and Alan O'Day (eds), *The Making of Modern Irish History* (London, 1996).

——, *Irish Home Rule, 1867–1921* (Manchester, 1998).

Offer, Avner, *Property and Politics, 1870–1914: Landownership, Law, Ideology and Urban Development in England* (Cambridge, 1981).

——, *The First World War: An Agrarian Interpretation* (Oxford, 1989).

O'Halpin, Eunan, 'Historical Revision XX: H.E. Duke and the Irish Administration, 1916–18', *Irish Historical Studies* 22:88 (September 1981), pp. 362–76.

——, 'British Intelligence in Ireland, 1914–1921', in Christopher Andrew and David Dilks (eds), *The Missing Dimension: Governments and Intelligence Communities in the Twentieth Century* (Urbana, 1984).

——, *The Decline of the Union: British Government in Ireland, 1892–1920* (Dublin, 1987).

Olson, William J., 'The Genesis of the Anglo-Persian Agreement of 1919', in Elie Kedourie and Slvia G. Haim (eds), *Towards a Modern Iran: Studies in Thought, Politics and Society* (London, 1980).

Owen, Frank, *Tempestuous Journey: Lloyd George and his Times* (London, 1954).

Owens, Rosemary Cullen, *Smashing Times: A History of the Irish Women's Suffrage Movement, 1889–1922* (Dublin, 1984).

Packer, Ian, 'The Liberal Cave and the 1914 Budget', *English Historical Review* 111:442 (June, 1996), pp. 620–35.

——, *Lloyd George*, paperback edn (Houndmills, Hants, 1998).

——, *Lloyd George, Liberalism and the Land: The Land Issue and Party Politics in England 1906–1914* (Woodbridge, Suffolk, 2001).

Pankhurst, E. Sylvia, *The Suffragette Movement: An Intimate Account of Persons and Ideals* (London, 1931).

du Parcq, Herbert, *Life of David Lloyd George*, 4 vols (London, 1912).

Parker, R.A.C., 'British Rearmament 1936–39: Treasury, Trade Unions and Skilled Labour', *English Historical Review* 96 (1981), pp. 306–43.

——, *Chamberlain and Appeasement: British Policy and the Coming of the Second World War* (New York, 1993).

Paschall, Rod, *The Defeat of Imperial Germany, 1917–1918* (Chapel Hill, 1989).

Peden, G.C., *British Economic and Social Policy: Lloyd George to Margaret Thatcher* (Oxford, 1985).

——, 'The Road to and from Gairloch: Lloyd George, Unemployment, Inflation, and the "Treasury View" in 1921', *Twentieth Century British History* 4:3 (1993), pp. 224–49.

Pedersen, Susan, 'The Story of Frances Stevenson and David Lloyd George', in Wm Roger Louis (ed.), *Penultimate Adventures with Britannia: Personalities, Politics and Culture in Britain* (London, 2008).

Pelling, Henry, *Social Geography of British Elections, 1885–1910* (New York, 1967).

Phillips, G.A., *The General Strike: The Politics of Industrial Conflict* (London, 1976).

Phillips, Gregory D., 'The "Diehards" and the Myth of the "Backwoodsmen"', *Journal of British Studies* 16 (1977), pp. 107–20.

——, *The Diehards: Aristocratic Society and Politics in Edwardian England* (Cambridge, 1979).

——, 'Lord Willoughby de Broke and the Politics of Radical Toryism, 1909–1914', *Journal of British Studies* 20:1 (Fall 1980), pp. 205–24.

Philpott, William, 'Squaring the Circle: The Higher Co-ordination of the Entente in the Winter of 1915–16', *English Historical Review* 114:458 (September 1999), pp. 875–98.

Pottle, Mark, *Champion Redoubtable: The Diaries and Letters of Violet Bonham Carter, 1914–1945*, paperback edn (London, 1999).

Poulson, Stephen C., *Social Movements in Twentieth Century Iran: Culture, Ideology, and Mobilizing Frameworks* (Lanham, MD, 2005).

Pound, Reginald and Harmsworth, Geoffrey, *Northcliffe* (New York, 1960).

Powell, David, 'The New Liberalism and the Rise of Labour, 1886–1906', *Historical Journal* 29:2 (1986), pp. 369–93.

——, *The Edwardian Crisis: Britain 1901–14* (Houndmills, 1996).

Price, Emyr, *David Lloyd George* (Cardiff, 2006).

Prior, Robin and Wilson, Trevor, *Passchendaele: The Untold Story*, paperback edn (New Haven, 2002).

———, *Command on the Western Front: The Military Career of Sir Henry Rawlinson, 1914–18*, paperback edn (Barnsley, 2004).

———, *The Somme*, paperback edn (New Haven and London, 2006).

Pugh, Martin, 'Asquith, Bonar Law, and the First Coalition', *The Historical Journal* 17:4 (December 1974), pp. 813–36.

———, *Electoral Reform in War and Peace, 1906–18* (London, 1978).

———, 'Yorkshire and the New Liberalism?', *Journal of Modern History* 50:3 (September 1978), D1169.

———, 'Labour and Women's Suffrage', in K.D. Brown (ed.), *The First Labour Party, 1906–1914* (London, 1985).

———, *Lloyd George*, paperback edn (London, 1988).

———, *State and Society: British Political and Social History, 1870–1992* (London: 1994).

———, *State and Society: A Social and Political History of Britain, 1870–1997*, 2nd edn (London, 1999).

———, *The March of the Women: A Revisionist Analysis of the Campaign for Women's Suffrage, 1866–1914* (Oxford, 2000).

———, *The Making of Modern British Politics, 1867–1945*, 3rd paperback edn (Oxford, 2002).

———, *The Pankhursts*, paperback edn (London, 2002).

Purdue, A.W., 'The Liberal and Labour Parties in North-East Politics 1900–14: The Struggle for Supremacy', *International Review of Social History* 26 (1981), Part 1, pp. 1–24.

———, 'Jarrow Politics, 1885–1914: The Challenge to Liberal Hegemony', *Northern History* 18 (1982), pp. 182–98.

Quinault, Roland, 'Golf and Edwardian Politics', in Negley Harte and Roland Quinault (eds), *Land and Society in Britain, 1700–1914: Essays in Honour of F.M.L. Thompson* (Manchester, 1996).

Ramsden, John, *The Age of Balfour and Baldwin 1902–1940* (London, 1978).

——— (ed.), *Real Old Tory Politics: The Political Diaries of Sir Robert Sanders, Lord Bayford, 1910–35* (London, 1984).

———, *An Appetite for Power: A History of the Conservative Party since 1830*, paperback edn (London, 1999).

Ranft, Bryan, 'The Royal Navy and the War at Sea', in John Turner (ed.), *Britain and the First World War* (London, 1988).

Read, Donald (ed.), *Edwardian England* (New Brunswick, 1982).

Regan, John M., 'The Politics of Reaction: the Dynamics of Treatyite Government and Policy, 1922–33', *Irish Historical Studies* 30:120 (November 1997), pp. 542–63.

Reid, Alastair, 'Dilution, Trade Unionism and the State in Britain during the First World War' in Steven Tolliday and Jonathan Zeitlin (eds), *Shop Floor Bargaining and the State: Historical and Comparative Perspectives* (Cambridge, 1985).

Reinharz, Jehuda, *Chaim Weizmann: The Making of a Statesman* (New York, 1993).

Reinroth, Howard, 'Left-Wing Opposition to Naval Armaments in Britain before 1914', *Journal of Contemporary History* 6:4 (1971), pp. 93–120.

Renshaw, Patrick, *The General Strike* (London, 1975).

Renton, James Edward, 'The Historiography of the Balfour Declaration: Toward a Multicausal Framework, *Journal of Israeli History* 19:2 (Summer 1998), pp. 109–28.

——, 'Changing Languages of Empire and the Orient: Britain and the Invention of the Middle East, 1917–1918', *Historical Journal* 50:3 (2007), pp. 645–67.

——, *The Zionist Mandate: The Birth of the Anglo-Zionist Alliance, 1914–1918* (Houndmills, 2007).

Retallack, James, *Germany in the Age of Kaiser Wilhelm II* (London, 1996).

Rhodes James, Robert (ed.), *Memoirs of a Conservative: J.C.C. Davidson's Memoirs and Papers 1910–37* (London, 1969).

Richards, N.J., 'Religious Controversy and the School Boards 1870–1902', *British Journal of Educational Studies* 18:2 (1970), pp. 180–96.

——, 'The Education Bill of 1906 and the Decline of Political Nonconformity', *Journal of Ecclesiastical History* 23:1 (January 1972), pp. 49–63.

Richter, Donald, *Chemical Soldiers: British Gas Warfare in World War I* (Lawrence, 1992).

Riddell, George Allardice Riddell, Baron, *More Pages from My Diary, 1908–1914* (London, 1934).

Roberts, Andrew, *'The Holy Fox': A Biography of Lord Halifax* (London, 1991).

Robbins, Keith, *Sir Edward Grey: A Biography of Lord Grey of Fallodon* (London, 1971).

——, 'The Foreign Secretary, the Cabinet, Parliament and the Parties', in F.H. Hinsley (ed.), *British Foreign Policy under Sir Edward Grey* (Cambridge, 1977).

——, '"Experiencing the Foreign": British Foreign Policy Makers and the Delights of Travel', in Michael Dockrill and Brian McKercher (eds), *Diplomacy and World Power: Studies in British Foreign Policy, 1890–1950* (Cambridge, 1996).

Robbins, Simon, *British Generalship on the Western Front 1914–18* (London, 2005).

Rock, William R., *British Appeasement in the 1930s* (New York, 1977).

Rogers, Alan, 'Churches and Children – A Study in the Controversy over the 1902 Education Act', *British Journal of Educational Studies* 8:1 (November 1959), pp. 29–51.

Romero, Patricia W., *E. Sylvia Pankhurst: Portrait of a Radical* (New Haven, 1987).

Roskill, Stephen, 'The Dismissal of Admiral Jellicoe', *Journal of Contemporary History* 1 (1966), pp. 69–93.

——, *Hankey: Man of Secrets*, 3 vols (London, 1970).

Rose, Jonathan, *The Intellectual Life of the British Working Classes*, paperback edn (New Haven, 2002).

Rose, Michael E., 'The Success of Social Reform: The Central Control Board (Liquor Traffic) 1915–21', in M.F.D. Foot (ed.), *War and Society: Historical Essays in Honour and Memory of J. R. Western, 1928–1971* (London, 1973).

Rosen, Andrew, *Rise Up, Women! The Militant Campaign of the Women's Social and Political Union, 1903–1914* (London, 1974).

Rothwell, V.H., 'Mesopotamia in British War Aims, 1914–1918', *Historical Journal* 13:2 (1970), pp. 273–94.

Rover, Constance, *Women's Suffrage and Party Politics in Britain 1866–1914* (London, 1967).

Rowland, Peter, *The Last Liberal Governments: The Promised Land, 1905–1910* (New York, 1969).

——, *The Last Liberal Governments: Unfinished Business, 1911–1914* (London, 1971).

——, *David Lloyd George* (London, 1975).

Royle, Trevor, *The Kitchener Enigma* (London, 1985).

Rubinstein, William D., 'Henry Page Croft and the National Party 1917–22', *Journal of Contemporary History* 14 (1979), pp. 129–48.

Ruger, Jan, *The Great Naval Game: Britain and Germany in the Age of Empire* (Cambridge, 2007).

Ruotsila, Markku, 'The Churchill-Mannerheim Collaboration in the Russian Intervention, 1919–1920', *The Slavonic and East European Review* 80:1 (January 2002), pp. 1–20.

Russell, A.K., *Liberal Landslide: The General Election of 1906* (Newton Abbot, 1973).

Ryan, Meda, 'The Kilmichael Ambush, 1920: Exploring the "Provocative Chapters"', *History* 92:306 (April, 2007), pp. 235–49.

Sabahi, Houshang, *British Policy in Persia, 1918–1925* (London, 1990).

Sacks, Benjamin, *The Religious Issue in the State Schools of England and Wales: 1902–1914: A Nation's Quest for Human Dignity* (Albuquerque, 1960).

Salzmann, Stephanie, *Great Britain, Germany and the Soviet Union: Rapallo and After, 1922–1934* (Woodbridge, Suffolk, 2003).

Samuel, Rt Hon. Viscount (Herbert), *Memoirs* (London, 1945).

Savage, David W., 'The Attempted Home Rule Settlement of 1916', *Eire-Ireland* 2:3 (1967), pp. 132–45.

Sayer, Derek, 'British Reaction to the Amritsar Massacre 1919–1920', *Past and Present* 131 (May 1991), pp. 130–64.

Sayers, R.S., *The Bank of England, 1891–1944*, vol. 1 (Cambridge, 1976).

Scally, Robert J., *The Origins of the Lloyd George Coalition: The Politics of Social-Imperialism, 1900–1918* (Princeton, 1975).

Schneer, Jonathan, *The Balfour Declaration: The Origins of the Arab-Israeli Conflict* (New York, 2010).

Seabourne, Teresa, 'The Summer of 1914', in Forest Capie and Geoffrey E. Wood (eds), *Financial Crises and the World Banking System* (New York, 1986).

Searle, G.R., 'The 'Revolt from the Right' in Edwardian Britain', in Paul Kennedy and Anthony Nicholls (eds), *Nationalist and Racialist Movements in Britain and Germany before 1914* (London, 1981).

——, *Corruption in British Politics, 1895–1930* (Oxford, 1987).

——, *The Quest for National Efficiency: A Study in British Politics and Political Thought, 1899–1914*, paperback edn (London, 1990).

——, *The Liberal Party: Triumph and Disintegration, 1886–1929* (New York, 1992).

——, 'A.J. Balfour's Secret Coalition Talks Memorandum', *Historical Research* 66:160 (June 1993), pp. 222–29.

——, *A New England? Peace and War, 1886–1918* (Oxford, 2004).

Self, Robert (ed.), *The Austen Chamberlain Diary Letters: The Correspondence of Sir Austen Chamberlain with his Sisters Hilda and Ida, 1916–1937*, vol. 5 (Cambridge, 1995).

——, *The Evolution of the British Party System, 1885–1940* (Harlow, 2000).

—— (ed.), *The Neville Chamberlain Diary Letters*, 2 vols (Burlington, 2000).

——, *Neville Chamberlain: A Biography* (Aldershot, Hants, 2006).

Semmel, Bernard, *Liberalism and Naval Strategy: Ideology, Interest, and Sea Power during the Pax Britannica* (Boston, 1986).

Sharp, Alan, *The Versailles Settlement: Peacemaking After the First World War, 1919–1923* (Houndmills, 2008).

Sharp, Alan J., 'The Foreign Office in Eclipse, 1919–22', *History* 61 (1976), pp. 198–218.

Sheffield, Gary, *The Somme*, paperback edn (London, 2004).

—— and John Bourne (eds), *Douglas Haig War Diaries and Letters, 1914–1918* (London, 2005).

—— and Dan Todman (eds), *Command and Control on the Western Front: The British Army's Experience 1914–1918*, paperback edn (Stroud, 2007).

Sheffy, Yigal 'The Origins of the British Breakthrough into South Palestine: The ANZAC Raid on the Ottoman Railway, 1917', *Journal of Strategic Studies* 22:1 (March 1999), pp. 124–47.

Shepherd, John, 'Labour and Parliament: The Lib.–Labs. as the First Working-Class MPs, 1885–1906', in Eugenio F. Biagini and Alastair J. Reid (eds), *Currents of Radicalism: Popular Radicalism, Organised Labour and Party Politics in Britain, 1850–1914* (Cambridge, 1991).

——, *George Lansbury: At the Heart of Old Labour* (Oxford 2002).

Sherington, Geoffrey, *English Education, Social Change and War* (Manchester, 1981).

Simkins, Peter, *Kitchener's Army: The Raising of the New Armies, 1914–1916* (Manchester, 1988).

Skidelsky, Robert, *Politicians and the Slump: The Labour Government of 1929–1931* (London, 1967).

——, 'Keynes and the Treasury View: The Case for and Against an Active Unemployment Policy 1920–1939', in W.J. Mommsen (ed.), *The Emergence of the Welfare State in Britain and Germany, 1850–1950* (London, 1981).

——, *John Maynard Keynes*, vol. 1, *Hopes Betrayed, 1883–1920*, paperback edn (New York, 1994).

——, *John Maynard Keynes*, vol. 2, *The Economist as Saviour, 1920–1937* (New York, 1994).

Sluglett, Peter, *Britain in Iraq: Contriving King and Country*, 2nd edn (New York, 2007).

Smart, Nick, 'Debate: Baldwin's Blunder? The General Election of 1923', *Twentieth Century British History* 7:1 (1996), pp. 110–39.

Smith, Frederick Winston Furneaux, Earl of Birkenhead, *The Life of F.E. Smith, First Earl of Birkenhead* (London, 1960).

Smith, Harold L., *The British Women's Suffrage Campaign 1866–1928* (Harlow, 1998).

Smith, Jeremy, 'Bluff, Bluster and Brinksmanship: Andrew Bonar Law and the Third Home Rule Bill', *Historical Journal* 36:1 (March 1993), pp. 161–78.

Sonyel, Salahi Ramsdan, *Turkish Diplomacy, 1918–1923: Mustafa Kemal and the Turkish National Movement* (London, 1975).

Southern, David, 'Lord Newton, the Conservative Peers and the Parliament Act of 1911', *English Historical Review* 96 (October 1981), pp. 834–80.

Soutou, Georges-Henri, 'The French Peacemakers and Their Home Front', in Manfred R. Boemeke, Gerald D. Feldman and Elisabeth Glaser (eds), *The Treaty of Versailles: A Reassessment after 75 Years* (Cambridge, 1998).

Spender, J.A., *Life, Journalism and Politics*, vol. 1 (New York, n.d.).

——, *The State and Pensions in Old Age* (London, 1894).

Stamp, Sir Josiah, *Taxation During the War* (London, 1932).

Stannage, Tom, *Baldwin Thwarts the Opposition: The British General Election of 1935* (London, 1980).

Stansky, Peter, *Sassoon: The Worlds of Philip and Sybil* (New Haven, 2003).

Stein, Leonard, *The Balfour Declaration* (New York, 1961).

Steinberg, Jonathan, 'The German Background to Anglo-German Relations, 1905–1914', in F.H. Hinsley (ed.), *British Foreign Policy under Sir Edward Grey* (Cambridge, 1977).

Steiner, Zara S., *Britain and the Origins of the First World War* (New York, 1977).

——, 'Elitism and Foreign Policy: The Foreign Office before the Great War', in B.J.C. McKercher and D.J. Moss (eds), *Shadow and Substance in British Foreign Policy, 1895–1939: Memorial Essays Honouring C.J. Lowe* (Edmonton, Canada, 1984).

——, *The Lights that Failed: European International History, 1919–1933* (Oxford, 2005).

Stevenson, David, *French War Aims Against Germany, 1914–1919* (Oxford, 1982).

——, *Armaments and the Coming of War: Europe, 1904–1914* (Oxford, 1996).

——, 'French War Aims and Peace Planning', in Manfred R. Boemeke, Gerald D. Feldman and Elisabeth Glaser (eds), *The Treaty of Versailles: A Reassessment after 75 Years* (Cambridge, 1998).

——, *Cataclysm: The First World War as Political Tragedy* (New York, 2004).

Stevenson, John and Chris Cook, *The Slump: Society and Politics during the Depression* (London, 1977).

Stewart, A.T.Q., *The Ulster Crisis* (London, 1967).

Strachan, Hew, *Financing the First World War* (Oxford, 2004).

Strandmann, Hartmut Pogge von, 'Rapallo – Strategy in Preventive Diplomacy: New Sources and New Interpretations', in Volker Berghahn and Martin Kitchen (eds), *Germany in the Age of Total War* (London, 1981).

Stubbs, John O., 'Lord Milner and Patriotic Labour, 1914–1918', *English Historical Review* 87 (October 1972), pp. 717–54.

——, 'Beaverbrook as Historian: "Politicians and the War, 1914–1916" Reconsidered', *Albion* 14 (1982), pp. 235–53.

——, 'The Unionists and Ireland, 1914–18', *Historical Journal* 33:4 (1990), pp. 879–80.

Sumida, Tetsuro, *In Defence of Naval Supremacy: Finance, Technology and British Naval Policy, 1889–1914* (Boston, 1989).

Summers, Anne, 'Militarism in Britain before the Great War', *History Workshop* 2 (Autumn 1976), pp. 104–23.

——, 'The Character of Edwardian Nationalism: Three Popular Leagues', in Paul Kennedy and Anthony Nicholls (eds), *Nationalist and Racialist Movements in Britain and Germany before 1914* ((London, 1981).

Supple, Barry, '"No Bloody Revolutions but for Obstinate Reactions"? British Coalowners in their Context, 1919–20', in D.C. Coleman and Peter Mathias (eds), *Enterprise and History: Essays in Honour of Charles Wilson* (Cambridge, 1984).

——, *The History of the British Coal Industry*, vol. 4, *1913–1946: The Political Economy of Decline* (Oxford, 1987).

Sutherland, Cynthia (ed.), *Studies in the Growth of Nineteenth-Century Government* (Totowa, 1972).

Swanwick, H.M., *I Have Been Young* (London, 1935).

Swartz, Marvin, 'A Study in Futility: The British Radicals at the Outbreak of the First World War', in A.J.A. Morris (ed.), *Edwardian Radicalism, 1900–1914: Some Aspects of British Radicalism* (Manchester, 1974).

Sweet, D.W., 'Great Britain and Germany, 1905–1911', in F.H. Hinsley (ed.), *British Foreign Policy under Sir Edward Grey* (Cambridge, 1977).

Sykes, Alan, *Tariff Reform in British Politics, 1903–1013* (Oxford, 1979).

——, *The Rise and Fall of British Liberalism, 1776–1988* (London, 1997).

Sylvester, Albert James, *The Real Lloyd George* (London, 1947).

——, *Life with Lloyd George: The Diary of A.J. Sylvester*, ed. Colin Cross (London, 1975).

Tanner, Duncan, Thane, Pat and Tiratsoo, Nick (eds), *Labour's First Century* (Cambridge, 2000).

Taplin, Eric, *The Dockers' Union: A Study of the National Union of Dock Labourers, 1889–1922* (Leicester, 1986).

Taylor, A.J.P., *English History, 1914–1945* (New York, 1965).

——, *Lloyd George: A Diary by Frances Stevenson* (London, 1971).

——, *Beaverbrook* (London, 1972).

——, *My Darling Pussy: The Letters of Lloyd George and Frances* (London, 1975).

Terraine, John, *Douglas Haig: The Educated Soldier*, paperback edn (London, 2005).

Thane, Pat, 'Labour and Local Politics: Radicalism, Democracy and Social Reform, 1880–1914', in Eugenio F. Biagini and Alastair J. Reid (eds), *Currents of Radicalism: Popular Radicalism, Organised Labour and Party Politics in Britain, 1850–1914* (Cambridge, 1991).

Theakston, Kevin and Mark Gill, 'Rating 20th-Century British Prime Ministers', *British Journal of Politics and International Relations* 8:2 (May, 2006), pp. 193–213.

Thompson, Neville, *The Anti-Appeasers: Conservative Opposition to Appeasement in the 1930s* (Oxford, 1971).

Thompson, Paul, *The Edwardians: The Remaking of British Society* (Bloomington, 1975).

Thorpe, Andrew, *A History of the British Labour Party* (New York, 1997).

——, *The British Communist Party and Moscow, 1920–43* (Manchester, 2000).

Tichlear, Michael, 'Socialists, Labour and the Land: the Response of the Labour Party to the Land Campaign of Lloyd George before the First World War', *Twentieth Century British History* 8:2 (1997), pp. 127–44.

Tomes, Jason, *Balfour and Foreign Policy: The International Thought of a Conservative Statesman* (Cambridge, 1997).

Tomlinson, Jim, *Public Policy and the Economy since 1900* (Oxford, 1990).

Tooley, Hunt, *The Western Front: Battle Ground and Home Front in the First World War* (Houndmills, 2003).

Torrey, Glenn E., 'Rumania and the Belligerents, 1914–1916' *Journal of Contemporary History* 1:3 (July 1966), pp. 171–91.

Townshend, Charles, *The British Campaign in Ireland, 1919–1921: The Development of Political and Military Policies* (Oxford, 1975).

——, 'The Irish Republican Army and the Development of Guerrilla Warfare, 1916–1921', *English Historical Review* 94:371 (April 1979), pp. 318–45.

——, *Political Violence in Ireland: Government and Resistance since 1848* (Oxford, 1983).

——, *Ireland: The 20th Century* (London, 1999).

——, 'Historiography: Telling the Irish Revolution', in Joost Augusteijn (ed.), *The Irish Revolution, 1913–1923*, paperback edn (Houndmills, 2002).

——, *Easter 1916: The Irish Rebellion* (Chicago, 2006).

Toye, Richard, 'The Labour Party and the Economics of Rearmament, 1935–39', *Twentieth Century British History* 12:3 (2001), pp. 303–26.

——, *Lloyd George and Churchill: Rivals for Greatness*, paperback edn (London, 2007).

Trachtenberg, Marc, 'Reparation at the Paris Peace Conference', *Journal of Modern History* 51 (March 1979), pp. 24–55.

——, *Reparation in World Politics: France and European Economic Diplomacy, 1916–1923* (New York, 1980).

Travers, Pauric, 'The Priest in Politics: the Case of Conscription', in Oliver MacDonagh, W.F. Mandle and Pauric Travers (eds), *Irish Culture and Nationalism, 1750–1950* (New York, 1983).

Travers, Tim, 'A Particular Style of Command: Haig and GHQ, 1916–18', *Journal of Strategic Studies* 10:3 (September 1987), pp. 364–65.

——, 'The Evolution of British Strategy and Tactics on the Western Front in 1918: GHQ, Manpower, and Technology', *Journal of Military History* 54:2 (April 1990), pp. 173–200.

——, *How the War was Won: Command and Technology in the British Army on the Western Front, 1917–1918* (London, 1992).

——, *The Killing Ground: The British Army, the Western Front and the Emergence of Modern Warfare, 1900–1918*, paperback edn (Barnsley, 2003).

——, *Gallipoli 1915*, paperback edn (Stroud, 2004).

Trevelyan, G.M., *Grey of Fallodon* (London, 1948).

Tripp, Charles, *A History of Iraq*, 3rd edn (Cambridge, 2007).

Trumpener, Ulrich, 'The Road to Ypres: The Beginnings of Gas Warfare in World War I', *Journal of Modern History* 47:3 (September 1975), pp. 460–80.

Turner, J.A., 'The Formation of Lloyd George's "Garden Suburb": "Fabian-like Milnerite Penetration"?', *Historical Journal* 20:1 (March 1977), pp. 165–84.

——, *Lloyd George's Secretariat* (Cambridge, 1980).

Turner, John, 'State Purchase of the Liquor Trade in the First World War', *Historical Journal* 23:3 (September 1980), pp. 589–615.

——, 'Cabinets, Committees and Secretariats: The Higher Direction of War', in Kathleen Burk (ed.), *War and the State: The Transformation of British Government 1914–1919* (London, 1982).

——, *British Politics and the Great War: Conciliation and Conflict, 1915–1918* (New Haven, 1992).

Ullman, Richard H., *Anglo-Soviet Relations, 1917–1921*, vol. 2, *Britain and the Russian Civil War, November 1918–February 1920* (Princeton, 1968).

——, *Anglo-Soviet Relations, 1917–1921*, vol. 3, *The Anglo-Soviet Accord* (Princeton, 1972).

Valone, Stephen J., '"There Must Be Some Misunderstanding": Sir Edward Grey's Diplomacy of August 1, 1914', *Journal of British Studies* 27 (October 1988), pp. 405–24.

Vatikiotis, P.J., *The History of Egypt*, 3rd edn (Baltimore, 1985).

Vaughan, W.E. (ed.), *A New History of Ireland*, vol. 6, *Ireland under the Union, II, 1870–1921* (Oxford, 1996).

Vellacott, Jo, *From Liberal to Labour with Women's Suffrage: The Story of Catherine Marshall* (Montreal, 1993).

Verete, Mayir, 'The Balfour Declaration and Its Makers', in Elie Kedourie and Sylvia G. Haim (eds), *Palestine and Israel in the 19th and 20th Centuries* (London, 1982).

Villis, Tom, *Reaction and the Avant-Garde: The Revolt Against Liberal Democracy in Early Twentieth-Century Britain* (London, 2006).

Vincent, John (ed.), *The Crawford Papers: The Journals of David Lindsay, Twenty-Seventh Earl of Crawford and Tenth Earl of Balcarres during the years 1892 to 1940* (Manchester, 1984).

Waddington, G.T., '"An Idyllic and Unruffled Atmosphere of Complete Anglo-German Misunderstanding": Aspects of the Operations of the Dienststelle Ribbentrop in Great Britain, 1934–1938', *History* 82:265 (January 1997), pp. 44–72.

Walder, David, *The Chanak Affair* (London, 1969).

Walsh, Maurice, *The News from Ireland: Foreign Correspondents and the Irish Revolution* (London, 2008).

Wandycz, Piotr S., 'The Polish Question', in Manfred R. Boemeke, Gerald D. Feldman and Elisabeth Glaser (eds), *The Treaty of Versailles: A Reassessment after 75 Years* (Cambridge, 1998).

Ward, Alan J., 'Lloyd George and the 1918 Irish Conscription Crisis', *Historical Journal* 17:1 (March 1974), pp. 107–29.

Ward, Margaret, '"Suffrage First – Above all Else!" An Account of the Irish Suffrage Movement', *Feminist Review* 10 (February 1982), pp. 21–36.

——, *Unmanageable Revolutionaries: Women and Irish Nationalism*, paperback edn (London, 1989).

Warman, Roberta M., 'The Erosion of Foreign Office Influence in the Making of Foreign Policy, 1916–1918', *Historical Journal* 15:1 (March 1972), pp. 133–59.

Watkin Davies, W., *Lloyd George 1863–1914* (London, 1939).

Watt, Donald Cameron, 'The Anglo-German Naval Agreement of 1935: An Interim Judgment', *Journal of Modern History* 28:2 (June 1956), pp. 155–75.

——, *How War Came: The Immediate Origins of the Second World War, 1938–1939* (New York, 1989).

——, 'Churchill and Appeasement', in Robert Blake and Wm Roger Louis (eds), *Churchill* (New York, 1993).

Weiler, Peter, *The New Liberalism: Liberal Social Theory in Great Britain, 1889–1914* (New York, 1982).

Weinberg, Gerhard L., 'Hitler and England, 1933–1945: Pretense and Reality', *German Studies Review* 8 (1985), pp. 299–309.

Weinroth, Howard S., 'The British Radicals and the Balance of Power, 1902–1914', *Historical Journal* 13:4 (December 1970), pp. 653–82.

——, 'Left-Wing Opposition to Naval Armaments', *Journal of Contemporary History* 6:4 (October 1971), pp. 93–120.

Weston, Corinne Comstock, 'The Liberal Leadership and the Lords' Veto, 1907–1910', *Historical Journal* 11:3 (1968), pp. 508–37.

——, 'Salisbury and the Lords, 1868–1895', *Historical Journal* 25:1 (1982), pp. 103–29.

——, *The House of Lords and Ideological Politics: Lord Salisbury's Referendal Theory and the Conservative Party, 1846–1922* (Philadelphia, 1995).

—— and Kelvin, Patricia, 'The "Judas Group" and the Parliament Bill of 1911', *English Historical Review* 99 (July 1984), pp. 551–65.

Wheatley, Michael, *Nationalism and the Irish Party: Provincial Ireland, 1910–1916* (Oxford, 2005).

White, Joe, '1910–1914 Reconsidered', in James E. Cronin and Jonathan Schneer (eds), *Social Conflict and the Political Order in Modern Britain* (New Brunswick, 1982).

——, 'Syndicalism in a Mature Industrial Setting: the Case of Britain', in Marcel van der Linden and Wayne Thorpe (eds), *Revolutionary Syndicalism: An International Perspective* (Aldershot, Hants, 1990).

White, Stephen, 'Labour's Council of Action, 1920', *Journal of Contemporary History* 9 (1974), pp. 99–122.

——, *The Origins of Détente: The Genoa Conference and Soviet-Western Relations, 1921–1922* (Cambridge, 1985).

Wiest, Andrew A., 'Haig, Gough and Passcendaele', in G.D. Sheffield (ed.), *Leadership and Command: The Anglo-American Military Experience since 1861* (London, 1997).

Wigham, Eric, *Strikes and the Government, 1893–1974* (London, 1976).

Willequet, Jacques 'Anglo-German Rivalry in Belgian and Portuguese Africa?', in Prosser Gifford and William Roger Louis (eds), *Britain and Germany in Africa: Imperial Rivalry and Colonial Rule* (New Haven, 1967).

Williams, Andrew J., 'The Genoa Conference of 1922: Lloyd George and the Politics of Recognition', in Carole Fink, Alex Frohn and Jurgen Heideking (eds), *Genoa, Rapallo, and European Reconstruction in 1922* (Cambridge, 1991).

——, *Trading with the Bolsheviks: The Politics of East-West Trade, 1920–39* (Manchester, 1992).

Williamson, Philip, '"Safety First": Baldwin, the Conservative Party, and the 1929 General Election', *Historical Journal* 25:2 (1982), pp. 385–409.

_____ (ed.), *The Modernisation of Conservative Politics: The Diaries and Letters of William Bridgeman, 1904–1935* (London, 1988).

____, *Stanley Baldwin: Conservative Leadership and National Values* (Cambridge, 1999).

____ and Edward Baldwin (eds), *Baldwin Papers: A Conservative Statesman, 1908–1947* (Cambridge, 2004).

Williamson, Samuel R. Jr, *The Politics of Grand Strategy: Britain and France Prepare for War, 1904–1914* (Cambridge, 1969).

____, 'The Origins of World War I', *Journal of Interdisciplinary History* 18:4 (Spring 1988), pp. 795–818.

Wilson, John, *CB: A Life of Sir Henry Campbell-Bannerman* (London, 1973).

Wilson, Keith, 'The Agadir Crisis, the Mansion House Speech, and the Double-Edgedness of Agreements', *Historical Journal* 15:3 (1972), pp. 513–32.

____, 'The British Cabinet's Decision for War, 2 August 1914', *British Journal for International Studies* 1 (1975), pp. 148–59.

____, 'The Cabinet Diary of J.A. Pease, 24 July–5 August 1914', *Proceedings of the Leeds Philosophical and Literary Society, Literary and Historical Section* 19, part 3 (March 1983), pp. 39–51.

____, *The Policy of the Entente: Essays on the Determinants of British Foreign Policy, 1904–1914* (Cambridge, 1985).

____ (ed.), *British Foreign Secretaries and Foreign Policy: From Crimean War to First World War* (London, 1987).

____ (ed.), *The Rasp of War: The Letters of H.A. Gwynne to The Countess of Bathurst 1914–1918* (London, 1988).

____ (ed.), *Decisions for War 1914* (New York, 1995).

Wilson, Trevor, 'The Coupon and the British General Election of 1918', *Journal of Modern History* 36:1 (March 1964), pp. 28–42.

____, *The Downfall of the Liberal Party, 1914–1935* (London, 1966).

____ (ed.), *The Political Diaries of C.P. Scott, 1911–1928* (Ithaca, 1970).

____, *The Myriad Faces of War: Britain and the Great War 1914–1918* (London, 1986).

Wingerden, Sophia A. van, *The Women's Suffrage Movement in Britain, 1866–1928* (London, 1999).

Winter, Denis, *Haig's Command: A Reassessment*, paperback edn (London, 2001).

Winter, Jay and Prost, Antoine, *The Great War in History: Debates and Controversies, 1914 to the Present*, paperback edn (Cambridge, 2005).

Withers, Hartley, *War and Lombard Street* (London, 1916).

Woodward, David R., 'Britain in a Continental War: The Civil-Military Debate over the Strategic Direction of the Great War of 1914–1918', *Albion* 12:1 (Spring 1980), pp. 37–65.

____, *Lloyd George and the Generals* (Newark, 1983).

____, 'Did Lloyd George Starve the British Army of Men Prior to the German Offensive of 21 March 1918?', *Historical Journal* 27:1 (March 1984), pp. 241–52.

____, *Trial by Friendship: Anglo-American Relations, 1917–1918* (Lexington, 1993).

——, *Field Marshall Sir William Robertson: Chief of the Imperial General Staff in the Great War* (Westport, 1998).

——, *Hell in the Holy Land: World War I in the Middle East* (Lexington, 2006).

Wrench, John Evelyn, *Geoffrey Dawson and Our Times* (London, 1955).

Wrigley, Chris, *David Lloyd George and the British Labour Movement: Peace and War* (Hassocks, 1976).

——, 'The Ministry of Munitions: an Innovatory Department', in Kathleen Burk (ed.), *War and the State: The Transformation of British Government, 1914–1919* (London, 1982).

——, 'The Trade Unions between the Wars', in Chris Wrigley (ed.), *A History of British Industrial Relations*, vol. 2, *1914–1939* (Brighton, 1987).

——, *Lloyd George and the Challenge of Labour: The Post War Coalition, 1918–1922* (Hemel Hempstead, 1990).

——, 'Lloyd George and Gladstone', *The Historian* 85 (Spring, 2005), pp. 8–17.

Yapp, Malcolm, 'The Making of the Palestine Mandate', *Middle Eastern Lectures*, no. 1 (Tel Aviv, 1995).

Yearwood, Peter, '"On the Safe and Right Lines": The Lloyd George Government and the Origins of the League of Nations, 1916–1918', *Historical Journal* 32:1 (March 1989), pp. 131–55.

Zebel, Sydney H., *Balfour: A Political Biography* (Cambridge, 1973).

Ziegler, Philip, *King Edward VIII: A Biography* (New York, 1991).

INDEX